Mainstreams
of American Media History
A Narrative and Intellectual History

Hiley H. Ward
Temple University

Allyn and Bacon
Boston   London   Toronto   Sydney   Tokyo   Singapore

To the memory of my mentor in journalism history, Edwin Emery

Vice President, Humanities: Joseph Opiela
Editorial Assistant: Kate Tolini
Marketing Manager: Karon Bowers
Editorial-Production Administrator: Donna Simons
Editorial-Production Service: P. M. Gordon Associates, Inc.
Composition and Prepress Buyer: Linda Cox
Manufacturing Buyer: Suzanne Lareau
Cover Administrator: Suzanne Harbison
Text Designer: Glenna Collett

Copyright ©1997 by Allyn & Bacon
A Viacom Company
160 Gould Street
Needham Heights, MA 02194

Internet: www.abacon.com
America Online: keyword: College Online

Library of Congress Cataloging-in-Publication Data

Ward, Hiley H.
    Mainstreams of American media history : a narrative and intellectual
history / Hiley H. Ward.
        p.   cm.
    Includes bibliographical references and index.
    ISBN 0–205–14922–7
    1. Journalism—United States—History. I. Title.
PN4855.W37   1997
071'3—dc20   96–30900
                                                               CIP

Printed in the United States of America

10 9 8 7 6 5 4 3 2 1   01 00 99 98 97 96

Contents

Preface

Byron Dobell, when he was editor of *American Heritage,* was asked at a luncheon of editors if he missed his previous positions as an editor at *Time* and *Esquire.* He replied that being editor of *American Heritage* was much more exciting than being editor at the news magazine and the men's literary magazine. He felt there is always something new to be found in history. Thus it is more exciting than rehashing the events or topics of the day as the popular general circulation magazines do.

History is exciting, and so is journalism history. The aim of this introduction to media history is to capture the romance of ideas, events, and the people who made it all happen. Thus less emphasis is put on the development of equipment, although this is the first book to pay attention to the history of the computer in communication. Less attention is also given to the cost of newsprint and the business ledgers. While developments in the legal side of communication are very important, not much is said here about media legal matters, since in virtually all communication departments at the college level a separate, detailed course in communication law is required.

This is not a book that concentrates on lauding the media and their stars. The big events and developments are here, and so are the key players. But they are here with all of their warts, sins, and biases. They are treated as humans. Some of the books in the past have been regarded as progressive history; that is, there is a play of the good, namely the media pioneers and editors, versus the bad—the arbiters of government restrictions, regulations, censorship—with the good guys as winners. This book recognizes that good and evil are combined in human nature—a kind of theological emphasis that posits within humankind the harboring of evil as well as a divine spark of possibility, creativity, and goodwill. With humankind predisposed to both good and evil, an answer comes to the perennial question, Why do the media do the things that they do—from telling it straight to badgering and harassing individuals and, more often than one would like, getting it wrong? Editors are human, and their products are subject to human foibles.

Thus when a personality is presented here, the failings and the successes are both presented. When sensationalism is discussed, its link to entertainment, which has a positive possibility, is seen; when freedom is presented, the murky line between censorship and the preservation of values emerges; when government power is detected, media's own heavy hand in controlling events is perceived; when information is presented, it may conceal an effort to educate with sometimes a hidden agenda promoting a special cause; when reform or investigative reporting is undertaken, the end result might be a disservice or tragedy; when the media profess objectivity in covering political events, the bias often seems to persist, if only in the use of a loaded word; and when media are defining and enunciating values, often they are subtly or openly emitting their biases.

Attention is given to the context of American history as this media history book develops. Events and personalities are interpreted in context. That emphasis does not mean there is no application for today. To the contrary. The view of this book is that there is a consistency to human nature, and things that are peculiar today often have been done or occurred before, and sometimes more emphatically.

Selection of subjects is made on the basis of what is significant, interesting, and worth remembering. Ultimately, students, once they are away from a course, will remember very few of the names and facts and little of the interpretation. A guideline has been to present material that a student will recall or use later in life. Thus there is an emphasis on certain basic issues and ideas, as well as some documents of a lighter nature in the popular culture. The reader will find, among other selections, the "Yes, Virginia, There Is a Santa Claus" column; "Casey at the Bat," a poem by a columnist; and, in a tragic vein, William Allen White's tribute to his daughter Mary upon her death in a riding accident.

Also the "something extra" in each chapter includes informational sidebars—for example, how certain newspapers got their names, the most popular ads in television history, and background sidebars on the relevant context in American history.

The latest scholarship in books, dissertations, and academic journals is included. The author, as book review editor of *Editor & Publisher*, sees most of the new books on journalism and journalism history, and many of these are cited.

To make it more student-friendly, the book has three features: (1) The attempt has been made to maintain a chronology, but it is a loose chronology that allows for some chapters on special themes and personalities. (2) A basic grid of themes has been applied to the sections of most of the chapters. The structure of basic categories and ideas facilitates a student's study of selected areas. These categories and ideas include Media as Purveyors of Information/Education; Media as Fourth Estate: Adversaries of Government; Media as Political Organs; Media as Voices of Freedom; Media as Voices of Reform; Media as Businesses; Media as Vehicles of Sensationalism/Entertainment; and Media as Definers and Keepers of Values (and Biases). (3) Discussion and research questions appear at the end of each chapter.

Because students will likely remember the names of Pulitzer and Hearst among the five or six that will stick in their minds beyond the course, a little more attention is given to these two despite views of some critics that great men should be played down rather than up. Joseph Pulitzer and William Randolph Hearst may not be the Washington and Lincoln of the media, but they have a significance and a visability that have surpassed the auras of others.

The book reaches beyond the New York "Big Apple" complex. Even the treatment of New York media potentates Pulitzer and Hearst includes extended material on their initial days in St. Louis and San Francisco, respectively. This book also has material on the small-town papers across the United States.

In short, this book will seek to involve the reader in the story of media history by highlighting some of the exciting and challenging dimensions of that history. Emphasis will be on readability, human interest, intellectual stimulus, relevance, and learning primarily what is worth remembering.

The author wishes to thank Temple University for granting him a full leave for a semester to work on this project; the author's wife, Joan Bastel, for her unending patience; various students, some of whom are mentioned in the book; and a host of libraries and archives, including the following: in England: Bodleian Library at Oxford University, British Library, British Museum, Guildhall, and Museum of London; in Washington, D.C.: Smithsonian Institution, National Archives, and Library of Congress; in Philadelphia: Library Company, Historical Society of Pennsylvania, Paley Library at Temple University, and University of Pennsylvania Library; in New York City: New York Pubic Library, New-York Historical Society, Fordham University, New York University, *Editor & Publisher* magazine, American Society of Magazine Editors, Rare Book and Manuscript Library at Columbia University, and Museum of Television and Radio.

Also helpful were a series of university libraries, among them the libraries of University of California at San Diego, University of North Carolina at Chapel Hill, University of Washington, Aurora University, Winona State University, University of Pittsburgh, Pennsylvania State University, Yale University, Amherst College, Bloomsburg University, University of Nevada, Southern Illinois University, West Carolina University, University of Iowa, University of Rochester, University of Minnesota, State University of New York at Stony Brook, Cornell University, and University of Kansas.

Several colleagues also contributed to this book by offering their insight as they reviewed the manuscript at its various stages. Thank you to: Craig Allen, Arizona State University; Carolyn Crimmins, Georgia State University; George Everett, University of Tennessee; Owen Johnson, Indiana University; Sam Kuczun, University of Colorado at Boulder; Chris Lamb, Old Dominion University; Nick Mills, Boston University; Michael Murray, University of Missouri; Robert Ours, West Virginia University; Anna Paddon, Southern Illinois University at Carbondale; Donald Shaw, University of North Carolina at Chapel Hill; Jeff Smith, University of Iowa; and Patrick Washburn, Ohio University.

1

Introduction: Origins of Modern Media

Media history goes back to primitive times. There is even an early history of media sound, a kind of "broadcasting." Researchers of primitive cultures have been amazed how quickly news spread just by word of mouth or by human action. When a person died, for instance, the bereaved would exclaim the news from the rooftops. Evangelists and politicians still seek out live audiences to which they can proclaim the word.

In some societies messages were transmitted by drumbeat; in others, by smoke signals. Among Chinese and Peruvians, messages were sent by knots in a cord of rope. Intricate arranging of the knots and colors made a wide variety of messages possible.

From earliest times, people carved images and etched symbols in stone, and the messages of this "art" were carried wide and far. Archaeologists have noted the wide dissemination of messages by works in stone—among them, alleged Phoenician rock inscriptions in Brazil, Celtic temples in New England, and stone heads worshipped by Aztecs and Mayans in Central America.[1]

Early communities painted pictures on cave walls, including scenes of hunting of great animals, such as those found at Lascaux and Chauvet, France.[2] The *pictograph* was followed by an *ideograph* stage when the picture came to represent an idea or emotion. Most sophisticated of the picture writings that represented ideas were the *hieroglyphics*—etchings on walls of tombs, temples, and palaces. The symbols also kept track of transactions, such as taxes and sale of livestock and grain.

Camel caravans became like long, slow "telephone" connections, as merchants, traveling far and wide, carried news. The merchants, among them the Sumerians in Southern Iraq, kept records with wedgelike symbols—*cuneiform* writing—on clay

Ceramic tokens, 6200 B.C., from Iran are earliest known recording system in the Near East. Right, account clay tablets from Iraq, among earliest known records. Circles and vertical wedges represent numerals, the other signs are personal names. (University of Pennsylvania Museum, Philadelphia [neg. #S4-141943])

tablets and sometimes on little cone-shaped pillars or cylinders. The Chaldeans along the Persian Gulf developed a set of signs for numbers.

About 1900 B.C. the Egyptians cut their symbols to 25 and matched them to sounds. As written language developed, the ancients used baked clay, stones, and wood. The Egyptians made writing material from the papyrus plant; thus, the word *paper*. Later, parchment, made from the skin of animals, became popular for writing. The Chinese made paper from bark and rags.

THE ANCIENT ROMAN NEWS BOARD

People began to write long letters or epistles that informed individuals and groups. Journalism historian James Melvin Lee notes how the handwritten Roman epistles or newsletters, which educated slaves or paid scribes prepared for the elite of Rome in the first century B.C., were curiously modern in many respects. The writers were given credentials (press cards) to attend and report on Senate meetings; specialized reports were prepared by some of the elite's own special correspondents; as they do today, debates ensued over the use of trivia and sensationalism.[3]

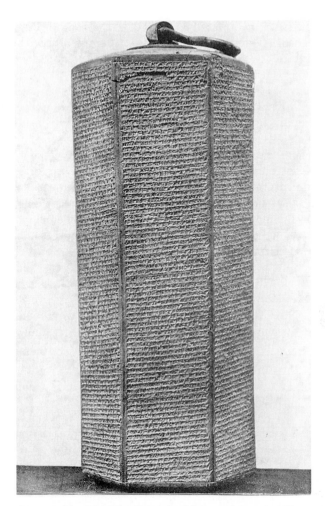

Account of Assyrian King Sennacherib's campaign against King Hezekiah of Judah in 701 B.C. (Smithsonian Institution, *Annual Report*, 1900)

Under Julius Caesar, in 59 B.C. "a prototype of the modern newspaper," as C. Anthony Giffard puts it, was inaugurated. The *acta diurna*, or "daily acts," was a kind of poster newspaper but had much the same news and features approach that modern papers have. The sheets of papyrus, posted at the edge of the forum, the government center of Rome, originally presented official news and decrees of the emperor and Senate but eventually included crime news and divorce news, especially regarding "celebrities."

Giffard suggests there was a development process to the *acta*. First came the *acta senatus*, which offered a daily record of senate actions; then came the *album*, a white tablet that listed the names of officials and provided information on festivals and dedications; next came the newsletters to private clients. One communication to Cicero was signed *Chresti compilationem*, "compilation by Chrestus," perhaps the first news byline.[4]

Yet it is possible to regard many of the early chroniclers and literary writers as journalists. The first writers were doing things not unlike those done by the writers and journalists of today. "They were writing of their own times and people," says Robert Desmond. "They were gathering and recording information and setting down their views on a variety of subjects, with or without an audience in prospect."[5] He cites Homer, Herodotus, Demosthenes, Pythagoras, Plato, Thucydides, even Confucius, as reflecting the happenings in their times.

Desmond also suggests that Scripture writers could be regarded as a kind of news reporters. He says the apostle Paul, considered the greatest missionary of the early church, and other apostles "conveyed 'news' of another sort to the peoples of the Mediterranean basin" in the first century A.D. He says that the apostles, like Jesus himself, "spoke to 'multitudes' gathered to listen. Their remarks were noted, it must be assumed, by some early 'reporters,' ultimately to become part of the New Testament, including Paul's 'epistles,' as well as the words of Matthew, Mark, Luke, and John." Desmond refers to a comment by Pope John XXIII made to a group of reporters covering a visit of President Dwight Eisenhower to the Vatican in 1959.

The opening of St. Paul's epistle to the Romans in Greek on papyrus.

The Pope said: "If St. Paul were alive now he probably would be a newspaperman. That would give him the means of spreading the doctrines of Christ."[6]

THE ERA OF PRINTING BEGINS

Printing—using carved wooden type and line etchings—emerged in China in the ninth century. The Chinese carved small blocks of wood for producing playing cards and small books. They created an ink from lampblack (carbon from the soot from burning oil), which proved useful in printing from wooden blocks. When Marco Polo went to the Far East in the thirteenth century, he brought back some of this elementary technology.

In Europe in the early fifteenth century printers used metal letters as dies, which they pressed onto a surface of clay. Hot lead was then spread across the surface, filling in the impressions to form a printing plate. The printing from these plates was often smudged and of poor quality.

It remained for Johann Gutenberg and others in Mainz, Germany, in the mid-fifteenth century to invent movable type, individual letters that could be kept and rearranged, instead of printing from one plate. Gutenberg also is credited with creating a frame with wedges to hold type in place, building a printing press adapted from a wine press, and making ink out of lampblack and oil. With Gutenberg and his contemporaries, a printing revolution was under way in Europe.

PICTORIAL PASSIONALS AND CALENDARS

The setting of type was laborious, and most of the populace, except for the elite, could not read. *Pictorials*, dramatizing subjects in a sensational way, appeared. They allowed the illiterate to be informed without reading.

Pictorials included *passionals* and *calendars*. These offered a panel sequence of pictures, much like the modern comic strip. They could be put on walls for a duration. A *passional* usually centered on the life of Christ and was meant for devotional use and meditation. Yet, as in polarized Germany with the rise of the Lutheran reformation in the early 1500s, it could take on political dimensions. One 1521 passional on display at the British Library in London, *Passional Christi und Antichristi*, depicted the pope as antichrist or demonic power.

A peasants' calendar (*Bauernkalendar*) in 1583, with color added, had symbols depicting phases of the moon; weather; best days for bleeding, bathing, and sowing; saints' days; three crowns for the Epiphany, the appearing of the wise men; and a fool's face for a carnival. "To be effective visually, issues had to be simplified, much as complex theology was reduced in the catechism responses," says the British Library documentation.

BALLADS AND BROADSIDES

Broadsides, early one-page news sheets printed on one side, often featured ballads and songs. Ballad singers were popular, and it was natural that some of the earliest

Another way to communicate: an English satirical playing card.
(The Library Company of Philadelphia, from J. R. Green, *A Short History of the English People,* 1895)

broadsides set down their ballads and songs, which could be occasioned by the death of a noble or a noted criminal. It would likely contain details and circumstances of the death and thus be informative and newsy. The ballad was not always put aside as easily as most news is. In the sixteenth century, an old story, perhaps having begun as news, would surface again years later in full bloom as tradition or folklore.[7] Since some ballads appeared to be a continuation of earlier ones, it can be argued they were the prototypes of the first newspaper (a definition of a newspaper usually requires that there be continuing publication).

Defining a Newspaper

"The most comprehensive effort ever made to frame a universally applicable definition of a newspaper is that of Dr. Otto Groth," who edited the German *Frankfurter Zeitung*, said Eric W. Allen, who taught at the University of Oregon. Allen noted that Groth gave a full 69 pages to defining a newspaper in his "monumental work," *Die Zeitung*. In short, Allen pointed out, Groth held that a true newspaper must be:

1. *Periodical* in publication, and, in practice, of a frequency not less than weekly. It must be regular.
2. *Mechanical* in its reduplication. This bars the handwritten newsletters, but admits the possible radio and screen newspapers.
3. *Available* to all comers who are willing to pay the price. Its circulation must not be exclusive or esoteric.

And its *contents* must be:

4. *Miscellaneous*, varied, catholic, universal, complete, including every occurrence that is publicly interesting, so long as this interest is
5. *General* in its appeal. The newspaper ideally should not include much matter that is interesting only to small groups. It should appeal to the public *as a public*.

And so long as the material is:

6. *Timely*. The German word for this quality is *actualität*, and it is, of course, fundamental.

Passing from content to organization, the newspaper should possess an

7. *Effective Organization*. It should be a going concern. Its continuity should be reasonably provided for. Organization and continuity become the seat of policy and influence—the power of the press.[8]

The broadsides were also used for civil announcements. For example, they would set forth fees and contributions expected from the people. In 1505 a broadside promised "graces" and "indulgences" to be granted by Pope Alexander VI: "Here foloweth Indulgens and full remissions for certein dayes in everi moneth in the yere."[9] One call for indulgences in a 1513 broadside has the double endorsement of the newly installed Pope Leo X and King Henry VIII, several decades before Henry's split with the Roman Church.[10] At the top of the broadside are woodcuts of the arms of the new pope, Leo X; a representation of Christ risen from the Holy Sepulchre, with the Roman soldiers asleep; and the royal arms of England, with the support of angels.

The broadsides were a means of education. A 1595 broadside informed the masses of the benefit of eating fish on designated fish days. It has the long title "A brief note of the benefits that grow to the Realme by the observation of Fish-daies, with a reason and a cause wherefore the lawe in that behalfe made is ordered. Very necessary to be placed in the house of all men especially common Victualers."[11]

Like the one-page passionals and calendars, the broadsides served as vehicles of propaganda for religious beliefs and causes. John Bunyan, author of *Pilgrim's Progress*, produced a broadside that had a series of rhyming stanzas, as "A Caution to Stir Up to Watch Against Sin."

During the plagues, broadsides cataloged names of victims, where they were from, and where they were buried. The plague hit London severely in 1602 and 1603, causing 47,000 deaths. In 1603 one broadside declared itself on a large sheet, 14 by 20 inches, to be "The True Copie of al the burials." A latter-day broadside from about 1714, the first year of the reign of King George I after the death of Queen Anne, sought to regulate traffic in London. It set forth an "Act for better Regulating Hackney-Coaches, Carts, Carrs, and Waggons, within the Cities of London and Westminster."[12]

Thus the broadsides conveyed news, educated the public on special issues, propagandized, and served as a means of record, functions which the modern newspaper does not ignore.

NEWS BOOKS

If continuity and regular publishing schedules are factors in determining a definition of a newspaper, then some notice should be made of sixteenth-century books and pamphlets. Journalism historians say a newspaper must be published regularly, must be printed on both sides of the paper, and must have a dateline and masthead. Frederic Farrar suggests the presence of news itself should be as important as production details in determining what is a newspaper.[13]

A German news periodical or book, printed in Latin twice a year at Cologne, then at Frankfurt, and known in England in 1594, was *Mercurius Gallobelgicus*, by a Dutch priest, M. Jansen.[14] Several single-issue pamphlets of foreign news called *relations* (referring to "relating" or "telling") were translated and appeared in London as early as 1545, but they were not published regularly.

Shaaber cites a sense of continuity in two separate complementary reports on a trial of witches in 1566. He also mentions two other books, one a continuation of the other, that report winter floods in 1607. These were, he says, "something like serial publications which are probably, however, not the genuine article."[15]

In London in 1625 the news book *The Continuation of Our Weekly Newes* appeared. It was published weekly, "relating" foreign news. (Sometimes such books were called "a true relation of.")

CORANTOS

Corantos (Italian from the Latin, meaning "to run," later a term for a lively dance) were one-page newsletters presenting foreign news much like the *relations* pamphlets. The name *coranto* itself suggests a continuation, a "running" of successive issues. The Dutch published *corantos*, also called *courants*, as early as 1607. In that year instructions from the Dutch East India Company "forbade anyone to remove any courant out of their office on penalty of a fine of three guilders."[16]

The oldest surviving Dutch *coranto* printed in English appeared December 2, 1620, having gone to press without getting all the news, for it starts off with "The new tydings out of Italie are not yet com." News historian Mitchell Stephens calls this the beginning of English newspaper journalism.[17]

The *coranto* news sheets were apparently being published with some regularity in England at the end of 1621, a Thomas Archer was punished "for making, or adding to, his corantos."[18]

The earliest existing *corantos* in England were published in London by "N.B."—Nathaniel Butter or, more likely, Nicholas Bourne—in the fall of 1621, with titles such as *Corante, or, newes from Italy, Germany, Hungarie, Spaine and France* (September 24, 1621). Shaaber suggests that six of the *corantos* in the series published by N.B. "have a very good claim to be called the first English newspaper."[19]

In 1622, the *coranto* format (foreign news) switched to news books or pamphlets of eight to 40 pages. Bleyer calls them news-book *corantos* and observes that from 1622 until 1665, with the establishment of the *Oxford Gazette*, all English news periodicals were pamphlets.[20]

DIURNALS

No domestic news was allowed to be printed in the news pamphlets until the House of Commons gave an imprimatur to a pamphlet by Samuel Pecke in 1641. This was the same year that the oppressive Star Chamber was abolished (see box). The pamphlet was titled *The Heads of Severall Procedings in this Present Parliament, from the 22 of November to the 29, 1641*. Over the beginning of the text appeared *Diurnall Occurences in Parliament*, the first use of the word *diurnal* in a title. This first English domestic news periodical soon changed its front-page title to the shorter *Diurnall Occurences or Heads*. A dozen or so other diurnals emerged. The competition became fierce. The word *perfect* was added by some, for example, *A Perfect Diurnall of the Passages in Parliament . . . More fully and exactly taken than by any other printed Copies*.[21] The news was not reported daily, but it was presented in daily reports for the weekly publications.

Parliament, through a Board of Licenses, restored some semblance of order by recognizing titles and making sure the diurnals were different and published on different days. Says one writer: " 'Anyone may write a news book, but he must not infringe another writer's title' seems to have been the rule. As a result at least one different news book appeared on each day of the week."[22]

These diurnals or diaries of Parliament were not necessarily like a *Congressional Record*, since they dealt with matters of politics and intrigue and the last steps in judicial appeal in Parliament. For instance, consider the discussion of the fate of Archbishop of Canterbury William Laud in January 1645. The conformist Church of England prelate whom some considered a secret Roman Catholic at heart supported King Charles I and opposed extreme reforms of the Presbyterian-minded Parliament (which abolished the ritualistic Prayer Book, bishops, etc.). Laud was sentenced to death on charges generally growing out of his high-handed ways. Even though the king (who himself was later to be executed) had given Laud a pardon, Parliament declined to exonerate him. Eventually the matter came down to how the

Monarchs and Censorship

Although printing had been brought to England in 1476 by William Caxton, it was a century and a half before it played a discernible role in disseminating news. Monarchs saw the adverse effect of agitation and rebellion that could be caused by the printed word and sought to curb all publications, including the Bible in English.

Controlling news printing, the Star Chamber had power to impose fines, imprisonment, even mutilation, but not death. It became a court without jury, but it was open to the public. Torture to get confessions was sometimes allowed. Publication of news invited more restraints than publication of books. Apart from licensing procedures, permission had to be obtained from the crown.

The Star Chamber, originally an apartment in the palace of Westminster where the King's Council or advisers met, gets its name from the blue ceiling speckled with gold-leaf stars. A first meeting of a council of advisers took place in 1453. In 1487 Henry VII named a commission of seven principal councillors and two judges to try offenders in the room. The chamber assumed special powers when Parliament was not in session.

Henry VIII (who ruled 1509–1547) in 1529 published a list of prohibited books. In 1534 he decreed that printers needed his permission before they could open a printing office. Another court, the Privy Council, which had responsibilities for supervising courts, also took on cases involving the press.

In 1557 Queen Mary, a harsh persecutor of non–Roman Catholic prelates (she burned them at the stake), renewed the Stationers Company. It had existed since 1357 as a group of court scribes. Now with membership extended to printers, its concern was with printers who published books, not with all printers. With unlimited power, the Stationers Company could smash open doors of those publishing without authority, mar type, and chop up the illegal presses or saw them into pieces. Printing was like the coining of money—strictly a privilege of government.

Under Elizabeth I (who reigned 1558–1603) a printer, William Carter, was tortured and hanged. Also hanged were Henry Barrowe and John Greenwood, originally jailed for holding separatist, anti–Church of England meetings. They had written religious treatises in prison and smuggled out the manuscripts to printers.

The Stationers continued, but with diminished effect. Denunciations of the Stationers could be heard in Parliament. In one debate the company was pictured as a corrupt monopoly, not only controlling and limiting the kinds of books, but also overcharging and substituting inferior paper for quality paper, even in publishing Bibles. Many books were printed overseas and brought secretly into the country. Elizabeth I tolerated a larger scope of books, with the exception of clearly Roman Catholic books and any that she thought called her reign into question.

In 1586 the Star Chamber Decree codified existing restrictions. This decree limited printing to London and the two universities, curtailed the number of printers, and decreed that all books prior to printing be examined by the Archbishop of Canterbury or the Bishop of London, or the Lord Chief Justice for law books.

In 1632 the Star Chamber extended its power over news books or pamphlets but continued to leave privately circulated newsletters untouched. In 1641, with the conflict between King Charles I and parliamentary factions accelerating, Parliament abolished the Star Chamber.

In 1643 another license system was

launched, with Charles I having power over the press. With Oliver Cromwell becoming dictator and Lord Protector of England, restrictions similar to the control of the press under the kings were reintroduced.

Licensing continued under Charles II and James II. Then in 1695, seven years after the "glorious" bloodless revolution and ascension of James II's daughter Mary and Dutch son-in-law William of Orange, the House of Commons failed to renew licensing. Government prosecution of the press after 1695 would center on seditious libel considered harmful to the government, charged after publication, with no prior restraints or conditions on publishing as such.

Front page of a parliamentary diurnal, 1649. Most diurnals were called "passages" after 1642. (Stanley Morrison, The English Newspaper, 1932) aging, distinguished archbishop would die. Because of a broken hamstring, he preferred not to have to climb to the gallows. One of the parliamentary diurnals carried details of the quibbling over the manner of executing Laud. He died the next day after the issue date, January 10, by the axe.[23]

MERCURIES

The diurnals, strongly biased against the king and monarchical system, were regarded as pro-Parliament in the ongoing conflict between Parliament and Charles I.[24] Thus the crown determined to launch a Saturday journal of its own, apparently to flout the Puritans' special reverence for Sunday. A strip of flowers was drawn across the top to contrast with Puritan severity. The crown picked up on the name "Mercury," the gods' messenger, and called it *Mercurius Aulicus, A Diurnal*

Media Background: The English Civil Wars

The political situation in England that triggered the proliferation of political publications (the diurnals, mercuries, etc.) in the mid-1600s grew out of a complex government situation, culminating in the English Civil Wars, 1642–1651. Although the conflicts seemed largely religious, there were underlying social and economic causes. The number of wealthy and influential merchants and members of the middle and upper classes had increased as the result of new markets and trade, and they wanted a greater say in the affairs of state. They also wanted greater say in religious life. It became a battle of Puritans versus King Charles I and his allegiance to the Church of England. The established church stood for formal Roman Catholic–like ritual, priests in clerical dress, making the sign of the cross, kneeling at the Lord's Supper (suggesting the adoration of the physical presence of Christ)—all abhorred by the Puritans. The Puritans also took issue with the system of bishops.

There were two groups of Puritans, the Separatists or early Congregationalists, who wanted to break with the Church of England, and the radical Puritans or Presbyterians, who sought major reforms in the Church of England. The Puritans believed in strict observance of the Sabbath, and when King James I in 1618 issued his "Declaration of Sports" decree that recommended popular games and dancing as proper observance of Sunday, the Puritan outrage was so great that it began to mold into political opposition.

"Puritanism was steadily growing as a political force all through James's reign," says church historian Williston Walker.[25] He also cites the King's high-handed treatment of Parliament and failure to become interested in the plight of Protestants on the continent. The attempt of the king to marry into Roman Catholic Spanish royalty further drove Parliament to the Puritan camp and the Anglicans (Church of England members) into the fold of the King. The Presbyterian agenda was legislated in Scotland over the objection of the king. "Scotland was seething with religious discontent when James died," says Walker.[26] James I was succeeded by his son Charles I (1625–1649).

In 1629, when Charles I clashed with Parliament over the royal prerogative to jail a person without cause and over matters of taxation and religion, the king dismissed Parliament. Parliament was not to meet again until 1640, when Scotland rebelled and invaded England. Charles, needing parliamentary help, reconvened Parliament, only to dissolve it again after less than a month. Charles was forced to make peace on Scottish terms. The Parliament that convened in 1640 later came to be known as the Long Parliament (it was to last off and on until dissolved in 1653).

When the king tried to arrest five members of the House of Commons on charges of trea-son in early 1642, a general civil war broke out, with the north and west siding with the king, the south and east with Parliament. Meanwhile, doctrines of Presbyterianism, in effect in Scotland, were adopted with some modifications by the English Parliament.

In the summer of 1644 the royal army was routed by a Puritan newcomer, Oliver Cromwell. A year later Cromwell wiped out the last vestige of royal opposition. However, Cromwell, more of an independent Congregationalist than a Presbyterian, found the new rigid Presbyterianism of Parliament not to his liking. There was now dissension in the ranks of the Puritan elite. Charles seized upon the situation and invited the Presbyterian-minded Scots to invade England. Facing Cromwell in battle in August 1648, the Scots were put to flight. Cromwell now reigned supreme. King Charles was beheaded on treason and other charges January 30, 1649.

Communicating the Intelligence and Affaires of the Court to the Rest of the Kingdom (aulicus, pertaining to the court of the king).[27]

The parliamentary faction answered the royal *Mercurius Aulicus* with the *Mercurius Britannicus*. Many mercuries followed, some printed with "authority" from the camps of the respective parliamentary and royal armies. Interregnum leader Oliver Cromwell sponsored an official news book, *Mercurius Politicus*. Other mercuries developed to serve the factions. But they were not a desirable lot, and their work was poor. According to Alexander Andrews, the mercury writers were "a shameless set of hireling scribblers; ignorant, unprincipled, and contemptible," who "sold their pens or extorted bribes, according to the temper of the party they attached, and lauded a man up to the skies for a meal, or flung him under the feet of the mob for refusing them one."[28]

The times were not as free as the mercuries seem to indicate. Freedom to print, a privilege at times heavily abused, did not last for long. News books were subjected to licensing, and many authors and printers were fined and imprisoned. "The mercuries or hawkers who sold them in the street," says Harold Herd, "were at times treated by authority as common rogues and whipped or sent to gaol."[29]

The whole period from 1641 to 1660 was a very dangerous time to be a journalist. But as Herd notes, "Suppression was not always complete, certain Royalist publications evading at one time the vigilance of Parliament—early examples of what we now call underground newspapers."[30]

Notorious among the women hawkers for royalist mercuries was the "double agent" known as Parliament Joan. Her real name was Elizabeth Alkin; she also had various aliases. Her husband had been a parliamentary spy behind royalist lines who was found out and hanged by the royalists. This big, "ill-kempt, rustic woman, or scullery-maid," as historian J. B. Williams called her, actually printed her own alleged royalist mercuries, only to fill them with parliamentary bias. She would pretend to be selling royalist mercuries and keep track of those who bought them so she could turn them in. The poor royalist would find not only that he was betrayed but also that in effect what he purchased was not the royalist mercury he thought it was.[31]

One royalist publication that came out of hiding in 1650, *The Man in the Moon*, remembered Parliament Joan. *The Man in the Moon* warned:

> Gentlemen, pray have a care of a fat woman aged about fifty—her name I know not—she is called by many "Parliament Joan"—and one Smith a printer a tall thin chapt' knave, if any such persons come pretending to search—look to yourselves and say Towzer gave you warning, there are some both male and female of the gang, that receive moneys to betray me, and then rob others by the same warrant.[32]

Parliament Joan, often referred to in both approved papers and royalist papers in 1649 and 1650, did publish in 1650, with editorial assistance, several briefly lived serious papers under her real name, Elizabeth Alkin. They included the *Modern Intelligencer* and a revival of *Mercurius Anglicus*, both, however, strongly denouncing the late King Charles I.[33]

After the royal mercuries ended for all practical purposes by 1649 with the death of the king and the establishment of England as a republic after Oliver Cromwell's defeat of the Scots and English royalists, publications became scarce. In 1655 there were only two English publications, *Mercurius Politicus* and *Publick Intelligence*, both 16-page news books published by Marchamont Nedham.[34] This man, despite having served on opposing sides during the Civil Wars, was the only editor to gain Cromwell's trust.

After Cromwell died in 1558 (he was succeeded briefly by his son, Richard), the monarchy was restored with Charles II. In 1660 the House of Commons decreed that no person could report any of its proceedings without its consent. The effect was to encourage the dissemination of newsletters rather than the development of the newspaper.[35]

Henry Muddiman was given exclusive right to publish news books. In 1662 Roger L'Estrange became official licenser of the press, and in 1663 he took over Muddiman's two official news books, the *Intelligencer* and the *Newes*. In his licensing capacity L'Estrange hounded unauthorized printers. Best known of L'Estrange's victims was printer John Twyn. Twyn printed some sheets that argued that justice was a concern of the people as well as of the magistrates. Apparently Twyn knew of a plot to kill the royal family in 1663 but refused to save his life by revealing the names of the perpetrators. Twyn's writings also helped to condemn him.[36] Twyn's house was raided, and "incriminating" material was found. He was hanged, disemboweled, and quartered.

THE FIRST NEWSPAPER

Henry Muddiman, who had been the crown's official news-books publisher, proceeded to conduct a personalized written newsletter service. When the royal court of Charles II fled to Oxford in the plague of 1665, Muddiman went along. He experimented with publishing a "paper," a single sheet on both sides. On November 16, 1665, the *Oxford Gazette*, the first full-fledged English newspaper, was born

---

What's in a Name?

Where do these popular newspaper names come from—the *News, Herald, Journal, Courier, Gazette, Intelligencer, Tribune, Post*? They go way back.

News (*Dallas Morning News, New York News, Philadelphia Daily News*). *Newes* meant "novelties" in Middle English; the word was in use from the twelfth through the fifteenth century. *News* can be traced back to the ancient Greek *neos*, which meant "new, young, fresh," and the Latin *novus* (*nova, novum*). News has always been associated with "novelty."

Herald (*Boston Herald, International Herald Tribune, Ottawa* [Kansas] *Herald*). A herald is a messenger, one who proclaims, from *heren*, "to proclaim," from the Old High German of the eighth through twelfth centuries.

Journal (*Milwaukee Journal, Wall Street Journal*). *Journal* comes from *acta diurna*, Latin for "daily acts." As we have seen, the latest news was posted in places such as the forum in Caesar's Rome for two centuries beginning in 59 B.C.

Diurnus comes from the Latin *dies*, "day"; from *diurnus* (*diurna, diurnum*) comes the Italian *giorna*, "day"; from *giorna, giornale*, a derivative is *journal*.

Courier (*Camden* [New Jersey] *Courier-Post, Forest City* [North Carolina] *Daily Courier, Louisville Courier-Journal*). A courier, coming from the Latin *currere*, "to run," is a messenger, one speeding along with important tidings. ("Mercury," referring to the swift messenger of the gods, also has been used in newspaper history.)

The word *courant* is also used, as in the *Hartford* (Connecticut) *Courant*. The *Daily Courant* in London in 1702 was the first English daily, and James Franklin's paper in 1721 was the *New England Courant*. *Courant* is the French present participle for the word "to run," *courir*. *Courante*, with an *e*, is a spirited French dance with running steps.

Gazette (*Billings* [Montana] *Gazette, Kalamazoo* [Michigan] *Gazette, Daily Hampshire* [Northhampton] *Gazette*). There

(Continued)

are several explanations for the origin of the word *gazette*. It could come from the Latin *gaza*, meaning a treasury or store; or from the Italian *gazza* or *gazzara*, a magpie or something that chatters. Most believe *gazette* comes from the name of a Venetian coin.

The price of the news sheet *Gazetta* in Venice was the coin *gazetta*, something like half a penny. Some, such as Alexander Andrews, believe the Venetian *Gazetta* news sheet, appearing about 1536, written in longhand and read aloud at designated places once a month, was the first modern newspaper.

Intelligencer (*Doylestown* [Pennsylvania] *Intelligencer, Seattle Post-Intelligencer, Washington Intelligencer*, now defunct). *Intelligencer* comes from the Latin *intelligentia*, referring to special insight or perception. Many of the first newspapers were called intelligencers because they sought to offer a close look into what was going on. When an "intelligence" community is thought of today, such as a surveillance agency like the Central Intelligence Agency (CIA), "information gathering" comes to mind. An intelligence report would be fresh news. The name occurs first in 1642 on a news pamphlet: *The Kingdomes Weekly Intelligencer: sent abroad to prevent mis-information*. Then in 1643 came the *Daily Intelligencer of Court, City and County* and also the *Compleate Intelligencer and Resolver*. Appearing in 1645 were the *Exchange Intelligencer* and the *Moderate Intelligencer*, and then in 1647 came the *Moderne Intelligencer*.

Tribune (*Chicago Tribune, South Bend* [Indiana] *Tribune, Tacoma* [Washington] *Morning News Tribune*). *Tribune* comes from the Latin *tribunus*. Originally meaning a tribal chief, the word in Rome came to mean a court official assigned to defend the rights of the common person against the favored patricians. It was also a rank in the Roman military. Newspapers called *tribune* like to see themselves as a defender of the people.

Post (*Birmingham* [Alabama] *Post-Herald, New York Post, Washington Post*). The word comes from its association with the mail and delivery. *Post* means to "announce" or display a notice. A poster is a sign with an announcement put up for all to see.

In the 1640s, *post* became a popular name for news pamphlets. John Hammond in 1643 published *The Kingdomes weekly Post, with his packet of Letters, publishing his message to the City and Country*. This *Post* had a 2$^{1}/_{2}$-by-3-inch cut showing a mounted postman blasting his horn. In 1644 Bernard Alsop issued a *Flying Post* which also had a woodcut of a mounted postman tooting his horn. The *London Post* pamphlet in 1645 showed a "post-boy" riding, with images of London and three other towns in the background. There was even one pamphlet called the *Post-Boy*.

(although the term *newspaper* did not come into general use until 1670). After 23 issues, the court returned to London and the *Gazette* became the *London Gazette*.

The first issue of the two-column paper led with a short announcement of the appointment of a new bishop of Oxford, followed by a list of sheriffs "pricked" for the next year. The rest of the two-page newspaper contained short reports identified by location of the news event and date. Most were reports of various wars. One two-line item at the end of the paper seems to have been the biggest news, giving the latest counts in death by the plague. A tag line said it was printed in Oxford, reprinted in London.

The days of informational calendars and passionals, ballads, broadsides, news books, relations, *corantos*, diurnals, and mercuries were over. The modern newspaper—printed regularly, dated, containing foreign and local news—had arrived.

QUESTIONS FOR DISCUSSION AND RESEARCH

1. Could an early "tangible" form of communicating information—from knots to hieroglyphics—be regarded as a newspaper? Why, or why not?
2. "The more modern and high-tech communication becomes—with emphasis on the visual (television, etc.) and design—the more primitive we seem to become." What might this statement mean?
3. If ancient cultures from the Egyptians to Native Americans, such as those "discovered" by Columbus—and the Incas and Mayans and Aztecs—had had radio and television, how might their response to the Western visitors have been different?
4. What's modern about the Roman *acta diurna*? What counterparts exist today?
5. How do today's calendars differ from the old pictorial passionals and calendars?
6. How might modern ballads or songs be like—and different from—broadside ballads of old?
7. Look up the meaning of *indulgence*. What kind of news reports could indulgences inspire?
8. Do newspapers or radio or television stations serve as propaganda organs for an administration or regime or ideology?
9. What do you think of "Parliament Joan"? Does she have any counterparts in society and even in the media today?
10. What would happen to John Twyn if he were an editor today?
11. Although many historians regard the *Oxford Gazette* as the first real newspaper, there is room for differences of opinion. What do you think was the first newspaper? What definition of a newspaper does your choice fit?
12. What are the names of three newspapers in your area? Where do their names come from?
13. Are there Star Chamber aspects about our judicial system today?
14. How would you define "news"?
15. Discuss: most newspapers and media are or are not puritanical.

ENDNOTES

1. Robert F. Marx, with Jenifer G. Marx, *In Quest of the Great White Gods: Contact Between the Old and New World from the Dawn of History* (New York: Crown, 1992).
2. Melissa Flower Jeangrand, "Lascaux: Communication in Caves," *Media History Digest*, Fall-Winter, 1992; Marlise Simons, "Newly Found Cave Paintings in France Are the Oldest, Scientist Estimates," *New York Times*, June 8, 1995, p. A18.
3. James Melvin Lee, *History of American Journalism* (New York and Boston: Houghton Mifflin, 1923), pp. 2–4.

4. C. Anthony Giffard, "Ancient Rome's Daily Gazette," *Journalism History*, vol. 2, no. 4, Winter 1975–76, pp. 106, 107.

5. Robert W. Desmond, *The Information Process: World News Reporting to the Twentieth Century* (Iowa City: University of Iowa Press, 1978), p. 14.

6. Ibid., p. 15.

7. Matthias A. Shaaber, *Some Forerunners of the Newspaper in England, 1476–1622* (New York: Octagon Books, 1966), p. 201.

8. Eric W. Allen, "International Origins of the Newspapers: The Establishment of Periodicity in Print," *Journalism Quarterly*, vol. 7, December 1930, p. 310; Otto Groth, *Die Zeitung—Ein System des Zeitungskunde (Journalistik)* (Mannheim: J. Bensheimer, 1928), vol. 1, p. 31 et seq.

9. *Bibliotheca Lindesiana Catalogue of English Broadsides, 1505–1897* (Privately printed, 1898; Aberdeen University Press).

10. *Catalogue of Collection of Printed Broadsides in the possession of the Society of Antiquaries of London*, compiled by Robert Lemon (London: Society of Antiquaries of London, 1866).

11. In Museum of London collection.

12. Ibid.

13. See Frederic Farrar, "Defining a Newspaper," *Editor & Publisher*, May 5, 1990, p. 29.

14. *Tercentenary Handlist of English and Welsh Newspapers, Magazines and Reviews, 1620–1920* (London: The Times, 1920), p. 5.

15. Shaaber, *Some Forerunners*, p. 302.

16. *Tercentenary Handlist*, p. 5; see also Folke Dahl, *Amsterdam—Earliest Newspaper Centre of Western Europe* (The Hague: 1939).

17. Mitchell Stephens, *A History of News* (New York: Viking, 1988), p. 157.

18. Willard Grosvenor Bleyer, *Main Currents in the History of American Journalism* (Boston: Houghton Mifflin, 1927), p. 6, quoting Thomas Birch's *The Court and Times of James the First*, vol. 2, p. 272.

19. Shaaber, *Some Forerunners*, p. 316.

20. Bleyer, *Main Currents*, p. 8.

21. Stanley Morrison, *The English Newspaper: Some Account of the Physical Development of Journals Printed in London Between 1622 and the Present Day* (Cambridge: Cambridge University Press, 1932), pp. 14, 15.

22. *Tercentary Handlist*, p. 11.

23. *A Diary, or an Exact journal, Faithfully communicating the most remarkable procedings in both Houses of Parliament*, Jan. 2–9, 1645.

24. J. B. Williams, *A History of English Journalism to the Foundation of the Gazette* (London: Longmans, Green, 1908), p. 40.

25. Williston Walker, *A History of the Christian Church* (New York: Charles Scribner's Sons, 1950), p. 466.

26. Ibid., p. 467.

27. Originally called the *Oxford Diurnal*, Jan. 1–7, 1643, but the next issue, number 1, Sunday the 8th, was called *Mercurius Aulicus*.

28. Alexander Andrews, *The History of British Journalism* (London: Richard Bentley, 1859; republished 1968 by Scholarly Press, Grosse Pointe, Mich.), p. 48.

29. Harold Herd, *The March of Journalism: The Story of the British Press from 1622 to the Present Day* (London: George Allen & Unwin, 1952), p. 24.

30. Ibid.

31. Williams, *History of English Journalism*, pp. 131, 132, 143; Parliament Joan was a survivor. Concludes Williams, p. 153: "Her last service as a spy was to testify in an international murder case—the brother of the Portuguese ambassador had killed an Englishman in London and was executed, despite international immunity. She was given a pension and spent her

final days nursing wounded sailors in the naval wars with the Dutch. Her influence was so great she petitioned for and secured the release of an ill Jesuit priest who had been imprisoned four years, possibly entrapped during her Mercury days."

32. *The Man in the Moon*, Feb. 13–20, 1650, quoted in Williams, *History of English Journalism*, p. 132.

33. Joseph Frank, *The Beginnings of the English Newspaper, 1620–1660* (Cambridge, Mass.: Harvard University Press, 1961), p. 216.

34. Williams, *History of English Journalism*, p. 157.

35. Frank, *Beginnings of the English Newspaper*, pp. 266, 362.

36. Williams, *History of English Journalism*, p. 186: "In his *Treatise of the Execution Justice*, Twyn encouraged the assassination of King Charles II, the Duke of York, and the royal family. . . . He wrote: 'God hath not forbid us to cut off the yoke of this present tyrant. . . . The execution of judgment is a duty incombent on the people. If a King hath shed innocent blood the law of God requireth the people to put him to death.' "

2

English Roots: Ideas That Persist

The American media, from the early colonial press to the present-day media, owe much to the English. The first American editors, the presses, and often much of the news came from England. Early printer-editor Benjamin Franklin went to England to learn more about the printing trade. Postrevolutionary-era editor William Cobbett started in England, came to the colonies, published a paper after the war, and returned. Most media histories, starting with an early history by Isaiah Thomas, who edited the *Worcester* (Massachusetts) *Spy* and pioneered in the book publishing industry, make a point of rooting American media history in England.

Consider some of the ideas, characteristics, and problems that persist from England and earlier even until today. The media have their inspiring, humanitarian ideas, and they also have been proving grounds for whims, biases, and business interests.

Browsing through old newspaper collections in and around London,[1] one is aware that what was of concern to editors then concerns them now.

Media as Purveyors of Information/Education

COVERING BATTLES AND DISASTERS

From the creators of primitive smoke signals to town criers to printers of ballads and news publications, communicators have been providers of information. Communicators have heralded news from the big overseas battle as well as the daily goings-on of Parliament.

This information was not always dramatic. For instance, in early news books the reader was likely to get informational lists. The news books were publications of record, much as the *New York Times* tries to be today. The *Times* publishes complete texts of important speeches and news conferences, plus its own lists of casualties of plane crashes and chronological lists explaining events and providing background.

A true publication of record was Thomas Archer's *Continuation of Our Weekly Newes in London*. The lead item in one issue is "A true Relation of the Defeat of 6000 men sent by the Duke of Feria to ayd Genoa, With the taking of the Towne and Castle of Ottagio. By his Hignes Charles Emanuel Duke of Savoy the 9 of April, 1625. Also, the name of those persons of note which were taken Prisoners, the Skirmish lasting from two of the clocke in the afternoone, untill Sun-set." And inside, beginning on page 5, is the list of the "Officers of the Spanish Army" captured. The list begins: "The Seigneur Thomas Caracciolo, Master of the Campe, Counceller of Warre to his Catholike Maiestie, and General of the Genouesi. The Seigneur Louis Guasco, Camp-master of three thousand foot," and so on.[2] Another issue includes the burning of a supply depot with a detailed list of "the quantitie and qualitie of the Victuals consumed," such as "6000 Sackes with Barley; 200 Barrells with Oyle, 200 Barrells with Butter," and so on.[3]

In the later part of the seventeenth century a reader could find local disaster coverage similar to standard modern fare, such as a fire story. Benjamin Harris, who was later considered a founder of perhaps the first newspaper in the colonies, once led off with the story of a major fire of the day. In London in 1679 he began an issue of the *Domestick Intelligence* with this:

> Yesterday about one a Clock in the Morning, there broke out a dreadful Fire in *Kent-Street* in *Southwark,* which burnt with great Violence for three or four hours, till it had consumed between sixteen and seventeen Houses; it happening in a place where it might have done abundance more mischief, there being several hundred Loads of Broom-staves, Birch and Heath just behind where it began, and which the Fire came very near to: it seems doubtfull whether it came Accidentally or by Design, but if it were done Treacherously, it could not have been contrived in a more dangerous place. We hear that it began first on the top of a stack of Heath, and the Woman of the House doth confidently affirm she had no fire in her house then, nor in three or four days before, but thanks be to God by the care and diligence of the People in playing the Water-Engines, and blowing up two Houses by Gunpowder it was happily quenched, and thereby prevented from doing any further mischief than that aforementioned, which has been to the great loss and damage of some particular Persons.[4]

Harris then followed with police news: an account of the trial of a young man accused of burning down a new prison and found not guilty. Then came the account of seven executions, among the condemned a child murderer and two guilty of treason for counterfeiting. Harris's idea of informing the public met one of the perennial criteria of news, news as conversation, conveying information that people would talk about.

Media as Voices of Freedom

LET TRUTH COMPETE, AND YOU HAVE A WINNER

What appears to be the first written document on press freedom—set down in 1484 on parliamentary scrolls—was an addendum to the first set of laws enacted in English (previously they had been recorded in Latin or Norman French). The act dealt primarily with restricting imports from Italy. The addition, apparently penned by Richard III, responding to entreaties from a handful of London booksellers and printers, exempted imports from bookmakers, writers, and printers.

The king's "amendment" to the act, paraphrased here in modern English, said, "Neither this nor any other act may hinder any craftsman or foreign merchant from importing or retailing manuscripts or printed books; nor may they prevent writers, illustrators, binders or printers from living here while offering for sale such things, or practicing such occupations."

Richard, the hunchbacked usurper protagonist in one of Shakespeare's plays, reigned only 25 months, but long enough to generate a measure of press freedom: the idea that the media should be excluded from commercial regulation. With only two print shops in operation in London, the monarch did not feel threatened as he apparently encouraged literacy and competition with the vast amount of printing that had developed on the continent.[5]

A series of seventeenth- and eighteenth-century English writers and philosophers made important statements on behalf of liberty of the press—ideas that found their way into the thinking of colonial editors.

Poet John Milton (*Paradise Lost*) prepared a powerful speech for Parliament, which he likely never delivered but which nevertheless "was and perhaps still is the most eloquent piece of English prose ever to attack the oppressive strictures of censorship."[6]

The *Areopagitica*[7] champions promulgating the truth at all costs. Milton attacked the Church of England and a new ruling by Charles I that said that no pamphlet could be published without a church license. Somehow Milton escaped the fate of other critics—death or having his ears cut off.

Milton's argument for freedom was known as "the self-righting principle."[8] Truth faced with untruth would eventually win the day. Arguing "that Truth is strong, next to the Almighty," he said: "And though all the winds of doctrine were let loose to play upon the earth, so Truth be in the field, we do injuriously, by licensing and prohibiting, to misdoubt her strength. Let her and Falsehood grapple; whoever knew Truth put to the worse, in a free and open encounter."[9]

Some would question Milton's sincerity because he took a job in the bureaucracy of Cromwell's dictatorship commonwealth with duties akin to that of a censor. As a Latin scholar he was useful in preparing formal state documents. Soon added to his duties, Fackler and Christians note, was the responsibility for licensing the official Cromwellian news publication, *Mercurius Politicus*. The Stationers' Register on March 17, 1651, has the notation "Entered . . . by order of Master Milton, 6 Pamphlets called Mercurius Politicus."[10] "It would seem that Milton, the great proponent of an unfettered press, had turned traitor to his own convictions,"

John Milton: Truth put to a test. (Free Library of Philadelphia)

say Fackler and Christians.[11] However, they go on to argue that the function of Milton, who was going blind, might have been more like that of an editor coupled with tasks comparable to the registering of copyrights today. Fackler and Christians say in a 10-month period as licenser Milton's contributions were primarily confined to "occasional paragraphs" added to "articles already written."[12]

The Influence of *Cato's Letters*

Popular in the new world were the writings of two English essayists, John Trenchard and Thomas Gordon. They called their writings *Cato's Letters.* (Marcus Porcius Cato was a second-century B.C. Roman historian, also a writer of verse and maxims.) Nearly every colonial editor, beginning with James Franklin in the *New England Courant* in Boston in 1721, quoted "Cato." Most popular of the volumes was *Of Freedom of Speech: That the same is inseparable from Public Liberty.* Cato believed that in a libel trial the truth itself can be a defense. The common practice allowed only that it be shown in court that the point at hand was said or published by the defendant. It did not help if the point in question was true. Truth as a defense became an issue in the trial of New York printer John Peter Zenger in 1735. Zenger, a harsh critic of the corrupt New York governor, published Cato's *Of Freedom of Speech* several times in his *New-York Weekly Journal.*

Media as Fourth Estate: Adversaries of Government

HELPING TO STEER THE SHIP OF STATE

The media appear to many to be a branch of government with their own authority and right to stand up to the other branches of government. Few would argue that the media do not indeed set the agendas that help to lead the nations. In most concepts of government there are three categories—the administrative executive (a monarch, president, dictator); a legislative body with various powers, depending on the nature of the system; and a judicial branch. Certainly the tripartite arrangement is the inspiration of the U.S. system, which balances the three branches. With these three estates, or categories, the extended role of the media has been interpreted as the fourth estate, the fourth branch of government.

The idea of the media as an arm of government emerged in the eighteenth cen-

The "Fourth Estate": Who Used the Term First?

Dominic F. Manno

The reference to the press as the "fourth estate" is by now a familiar one. (The first three estates were the traditional powers of medieval and early modern society: the nobility, the clergy, and the House of Commons.) But what is not familiar is who first used the phrase in that context.

As early as 1638 the phrase was used to refer to the British army. Henry Fielding, a principal justice of the peace and novelist (*Tom Jones*, etc.), used it to describe "the Mob" in his *Convent-Garden Journal* in 1752.

Although Thomas Carlyle in his *On Heroes and Hero-Worship* in 1841 quoted Edmund Burke (who died in 1797) as calling the Reporters' Gallery in Parliament "a Fourth Estate," most sources agree this is an error.

The earliest reference to the press as the "fourth estate" was by William Hazlitt, English literary critic and essayist, in 1821. Hazlitt, however, was referring to just one man,

Edmund Burke: The press is a fourth estate. (Portrait by Joshua Reynolds, Library of Congress)

William Cobbett, in *Table Talk* where he writes, none too admiringly, that Cobbett "is a kind of *fourth estate* in the politics of the country."

The Oxford English Dictionary cites a correspondent of *Notes & Queries* saying that he heard Lord Henry Peter Brougham, lord chancellor of England, use the phrase in the House of Commons in 1823 or 1824 to describe the press in general, and that at the time it was treated as original.

The first reliable citation is an essay by Thomas Babington Macaulay in 1828 in the *Edinburgh Review*. In his "On Hallam's Constitutional History," he wrote that "the gallery in which the reporters sit has become a fourth estate of the realm." Then comes Carlyle, who used the phrase several times, in his article on Boswell's *Life of Johnson* in 1832, in his history *The French Revolution* in 1837, and as quoted earlier.

tury in England as the call for greater freedom of expression was being heard. With the rapid growth of the number of newspapers, the departure of licensing, the development of the enlightenment movements in philosophy and religion, the diminished power of the monarchy, and the ascendancy of Parliament, published expression had a power of its own that played a role in influencing and directing the ship of state.

Among the first to offer his newspaper as an adversary of government in the eighteenth century was Henry Sampson Woodfall, who printed the *Public Advertiser*. He regularly published defiant essays by a writer believed to be Sir Philip Francis, under the pen name "Junius." King George III was the subject of fierce attacks from Woodfall's segment of the fourth estate. A typical letter of Junius in the *Public Advertiser*, addressed to King George III, began:

> Sir,
>
> It is the misfortune of your life, and originally the cause of every reproach and distress which has attended your government, that you should never have been acquainted with the language of truth, until you heard it in the complaints of your people. It is now, however, too late to correct the error of your education.[13]

Some risk was still attached to asserting the new authority of the press. Woodfall was arrested and prosecuted for running this letter. He was found guilty only of "printing and publishing" and was set free. However, two weeks earlier a monthly magazine publisher, John Almon, had been found guilty of reprinting the same letter in his *London Museum* magazine and fined.[14]

Wilkes' Poisoned Pen

One of the most vituperative of the gadflies was John Wilkes, so cantankerous that one historian wrote: "Wilkes himself began life not only with a grievance, but with a sense of desperation that dipped his maiden pen in gall, and gave him all mankind for his enemy."[15] In his *North Briton* newspaper, he wrote an essay, *No. 45*, which

John Wilkes, an "amiable rogue" with "political shrewdness," as
Paul Langford called him in The Oxford History of Britain
(*ed. Kenneth Morgan*).

mercilessly savaged King George III. (The number 45 was to become a symbol of
protest marked on doorposts.) Wilkes concluded that essay: "I wish as much as any
man in the kingdom to see the *honour of the crown* maintained in a manner truly
becoming *Royalty*. I lament to see it sunk even to prostitution."

The government regarded the article as a seditious libel inciting the people and
issued a general warrant for the arrest of Wilkes and others, including his *North
Briton* staff. Wilkes was locked up, but because he was a member of Parliament he
was released in a few days. Wilkes returned amid cheers, "Wilkes and Liberty!" He
promptly filed suit for wrongful arrest. All 48 who had been charged in the general
warrant were released and received damages, totaling 100,000 pounds.[16]

Wilkes' troubles were not over. He reprinted some back essays, including the
notorious *No. 45*, and on the initiative of Lord North in the House of Commons,
that body decided that indeed Wilkes' writings constituted a "false, scandalous and
seditious libel." And the House of Lords declared in a resolution that an essay by
Wilkes parodying Alexander Pope's *Essay on Man* with his own *Essay on Woman* was
obscene and an "impious libel."

Wilkes insisted he could not honor a summons from Commons because he was ill—he was suffering from wounds sustained in a duel. But he would not see the physician sent to examine him.[17] Rather than face sentencing, Wilkes fled to France. He was convicted in absentia of printing *No. 45* and the *Essay on Woman* and ousted from the House of Commons. He returned two years later, ran for Parliament in a different district, and won. His supporters brandished the symbol "No. 45." The law did catch up with him, and he was sentenced to 22 months in prison for reprinting *No. 45* and publishing the *Essay on Woman*. With others he launched a new newspaper in 1769, the *Middlesex Journal, or Chronicle of Liberty*. Among the contributors was the literary teenager Thomas Chatterton (he committed suicide at 17).[18]

In 1771 Wilkes, who became a city alderman and acting magistrate, opposed the arrest of two printers for violating the ban on printing reports of the debates in the House of Commons. After the legal process had run its course and riots erupted in the streets, Wilkes' position prevailed, and the House of Commons allowed publication of its reports directly in the newspapers.

Hancock's Editorial in England

Prior to the colonial Revolutionary War British government adversaries borrowed some help from the fourth estate in the colonies. Five months before the signing of the Declaration of Independence, the *London Packet or New Lloyd's Evening Post*, acting in its role of the fourth estate, carried a guest "editorial" by John Hancock, president of the Continental Congress and later the first signer of the Declaration of Independence. Hancock wrote of the abusive policies of ruin being followed by England and faulted the English leadership:

> The manner in which the last dutiful petition to his Majesty was received, and the subsequent proclamation, are considered by the Congress as further proofs of those malignant Councils which surround the Sovereign and distract the British empire. It is, however, happy for mankind that ministers can form destructive plans with much more facility than they can execute them. . . .
>
> As men and as descendants of Great Britain, the good people of these colonies will rely to the last on Heaven, and their own virtuous efforts, for security, against the abusive system pressed by administration for the ruin of America, and which, if pursued, must end in the destruction of a great empire.[19]

It is remarkable that these sentiments were reprinted in an English newspaper, an indication of the adversarial role now attained by the proliferating press in England—and the colonies—in the eighteenth century.

Media as Voices of Reform
INVESTIGATIVE REPORTING PLAYS A ROLE

Newspapers have a tradition of seeking reform. Although they exist primarily as purveyors of news—and opinion—newspapers have a history of aiming to make things better. Articles expose vice and corruption in business and government.

Today the Investigative Reporters and Editors organization keeps track of thousands of investigative articles written each year.

Even before formal newspapers, broadsides sometimes attacked corruption in government or in a system. Consider the English broadside that in 1620 had this long blurb as a title: "A brief collection of some part of the exactions, extortions, oppressions, tyrannies, and excesses toward the lives, bodies and goods of prisoners, done by Alexander Harris, Warden of the Fleete, in his foure years of misgovernment, ready to be proved by oath and other testimonies."

There follows a list of nineteen charges that have a modern investigative ring. The first point in the 1620 broadside details conditions in prison.

> 1. After knowne quarrels and fightings between two prisoners, lodging them in one chamber, where quarrelling and fighting againe, and notice to him thereof given, and of likely further mischief, this notwithstanding continueance of them together, untill the one murdered the other.[20]

The account charges bribery and other irregularities, and concludes that it would take "volumes" to tell all that three others named and others also did.

When the oppressive royal-appointed court, the Star Chamber, started compounding fees, charging for every motion and trivial matter, one broadside challenged the fearsome chamber by plainly stating the facts. It printed a list of all the areas of taxation and fees collected by the chamber. This story had the effect of investigative journalism.[21] Nearly 100 items were listed. There were fees "for every act passed in court," for each oath, for letters, for copies, and so on. At the end the writer called for indictments of any seeking even greater fees.

The English press tradition produced its share of hard-hitting reformers and investigative editors. Foremost was William Cobbett, a reformer who appeared on the American scene after the Revolutionary War and remained active over a long period.

Media as Vehicles of Sensationalism/Entertainment
PEOPLE IN EVERY AGE WHO BOIL PEOPLE

Sensationalism and entertainment are linked in that they involve the senses and evoke feelings of excitement and titillation. In eras gone by, without the benefit of television or film, both oral and printed stories reached out to imaginative and curious minds. Sensationalism, then as now, could rouse emotions. Satisfying curiosity and building suspense in crime and horror stories ensured an audience, as they in fact do today. But sensationalism could have its lighter side, ultimately eliciting responses of laughter instead of a settling into gloom.

Sensationalism, on the one hand, can be defined so widely that it refers to almost any kind of interesting news, the kind people talk about—a major world catastrophe, a local election, or some trivia, such as a cat in a tree. Conversational news—the kind you talk about—is sensational; you use the senses, you feel it, even smell, touch, taste, see, and hear it. It comes alive.

Sensationalism in a more narrow sense—and one in which it is more popularly used—includes a prurient angle or shock value. Sensationalism in the narrow frame gets the reader's attention by going against accepted mores and good taste. It is often negative. It makes the reader cringe and feel glad that something terrible is not happening to her or him. Thus one reads an account of an execution; a suicide, jumping from the Empire State building; charges of sexual improprieties, as in the Clarence Thomas nomination to the Supreme Court; or a scandal that topples a politician or affects a privileged business magnate, member of a prominent family, such as John DuPont, charged with murder in 1996, or sports figure, such as O. J. Simpson, tried on two counts of murder. There is the personal question, "What if it were me?" —perpetrator or victim, as if one tends to experience a sensational thrill, horror, or deprivation vicariously. Sensationalism goes beyond the surface level and instead touches the deepest wells of our psyches, fears, and desires.

Sensationalism is as old as the Bible and other Scripture records. Consider the cataclysmic drama of being cast out of the Garden of Eden; Cain murdering his brother; Lot's wife turning into a pillar of salt; an epic flood; Absalom murdering his brother Amon for sleeping with their sister, Tamar; David killing, of all things, a giant, Goliath; and so on.

Consider the sensational actions of the gods in Roman history—highly visible betrayal, immorality, even incest, patricide, regicide, orgies, human sacrifices, and death. Also consider the gods and avatars in Far Eastern writings, as they mix emotionally and sensually with humans.

The Christian era provided the terrifying sensational accounts of deaths of martyrs, first at the hand of the Romans, then at the hand of the church itself. Nothing is more terrifying than the sixteenth-century *Foxe's Book of Martyrs*.

The English news books, dealing with horror and personal sensationalism rather than politics, got past the censor. The mind was distracted, entertained. Mitchell Stephens in his *A History of News* maintains that anyone who holds to the idea that the sensationalism practiced by Rupert Murdoch and others today is unique "could be set straight by spending a few minutes with any of a number of sixteenth- or seventeenth-century newsbooks."[22]

Putting on the Pot

Stephens cites the example of a 1624 London news book printed for Nathaniel Butter called *The Crying Murther* (murder). With a half-page woodcut showing a quartet of people dismembering, decapitating, and disemboweling a person, the sensational blurb says: "Contayning the cruell and most horrible butcher of Mr. Trat, curate of olde Cleaue; who was first murthered as he trauailed upon the high way, then was brought home to his house and then quartered and imboweld: his quarters and bowels being afterwards perboyld and salted up, in a most strange and fearefull manner."[23]

That blurb went on to tell that the perpetrators—three men and a woman—died recently on the gallows. Such news books also dealt with the sighting of monsters and dragons. In 1616 in London one pamphlet, a "relation" titled *Miraculous Newes*, told of resurrections in Holdt, Germany: "There were plainly beheld three dead bodyes rise out of their graues."[24]

Benjamin Harris could hardly have been more sensational than he was with his *Domestick Intelligence*, published in England before he set sail for the colonies. The very first item in his newspaper of July 9, 1679, is a shocker:

> We have an Account from *Greenwich*, that a few days since there was found a Man hanging by the Arms in a Wood between that place and *Wotledge*, with his Head and Hands cut off, and his Bowels pulled out, who by a Paper found in his Pocket was known to be a Purser belonging to one of His Majesties New Built Frigats. It is thought it was done out of Malice or private Revenge, since there was 30 or 31 shillings found in his Pocket. All care is taken to Discover the Murtherers, which it is hoped may be effected.[25]

From the earliest records of happenings to the modern tabloid, the prurient, the unbelievable, and the shocking make news. And they do so not only in the tabloids and racy magazines. Regular, metropolitan and suburban newspapers—even conservative ones—highlight the sensational. Consider the source of the following story:

> John Vincent DiGregorio was found guilty Thursday of voluntary manslaughter and abuse of corpse in the Easter Sunday slaying and mutilation of his mentally ill daughter. . . .
>
> DiGregorio claimed he bludgeoned his 38-year-old paranoid-schizophrenic daughter, Carol, on April 15, Easter Sunday, in their Bensalem apartment with a two-pound car tool when she came at him with a knife after an argument.
>
> Carol then was dismembered and cooked during the next two days.[26]

This is from a regular daily newspaper, the *Intelligencer* from Doylestown, Pennsylvania, a quiet, proper, culturally oriented suburban community north of Philadelphia. Sensationalism is pervasive.

And, of course, dominating the news for weeks in 1991 was the Milwaukee case of Jeffrey Dahmer, who killed, mutilated, dismembered, and cannibalized seventeen victims. Four years earlier Gary Heidnik's "chamber of horrors" of torture and dismemberment, which left two women dead, dominated Philadelphia headlines.

Media as Definers and Keepers of Values (and Biases)
HOW IDEALISTIC CAN AN EDITOR BE?

High on the list of values of modern journalists is the idea of objectivity—treating everybody fairly, accurately, and as equally as possible and in an unbiased context. The concept of objectivity seems always to have existed in some form, if not as an attainable virtue, at least as a goal.

The motive for objectivity may not always be as "pure" as the concept of objectivity. In colonial America, Benjamin Franklin saw a kind of objectivity informed by good business. He tried to treat the business and political communities equally in a benign context. "I have avoided printing such Things as usually give Offence either to Church or State, more than any Printer that has followed the Business in this Province before," he said.[27]

First English Daily Pledges Objectivity

The first issue of the first daily newspaper in England, the *Daily Courant*, March 11, 1702, presented a ringing pledge of "objectivity" concerning its reports of foreign news (which constituted the paper's contents, along with some ads). One gets the impression that with the concentration on foreign news "objectivity" was a means to avoid offending the government and to stay out of trouble. In the *Daily Courant* there was no pledge of objectivity for domestic news. Editors were still capable of being mistreated, as the slaughter of the young editor Matthews seventeen years later attests (see box).

A Martyr for His Sources

The rain drove hard against the light sleigh that negotiated its way through the icy slush. The young editor, Matthews,[28] his breath vaporizing in the wind, sat, hands bound behind him, with his chaplain beside him.

Matthews was unusually composed, considering what was ahead for him. A grand jury of the city of London had found him guilty of high treason in November, 1719.

He mounted the gallows with its two upright beams and one crossbeam at the traditional execution site along the Tyburn, a tributary to the Thames near London. His death was not to be a simple one. The sentence decreed he was to be hanged, drawn, and quartered. Normal procedure was to hang the person for only a short time, take the victim down alive; then the victim was mutilated, drawn (disemboweled), his entrails burned so he could watch, decapitated, and the body quartered or divided into four parts.

And just what was Matthews' crime? He had printed *Vox Populi, Vox Dei*, "voice of the people, voice of God." Says one chronicler of the times: "This seems to have been a pamphlet first issued in 1709, and even attributed to Lord Somers in recent years. Nevertheless, Matthews would not disclose the name of the author so he was duly hanged, drawn and quartered, Nov. 6, 1719."[29]

An account some months later in a colonial paper said the pamphlet quarreled with the procedure of succession, asserting "the Chevalier's[30] right to the crown of these kingdoms." It told of a raid on Matthews' shop and incriminatory papers found on his press and papers in his pockets "he owned to be his."[31]

Just how did Matthews' fellow printers and editors treat his death? No doubt the others

(Continued)

were intimidated. Some papers, such as the *Weekly Journal or British Gazeteer* and the *Daily Courant* (first daily in England 17 years earlier) ignored the tragic event. The *Weekly Journal or Saturday's Post* on Saturday, November 7, 1719, included it among the social notes on page 5:

> We hear the Duke of Bolton, Lord Lt. of Ireland is preparing to return to Great Britain.
>
> Yesterday young Mr. Matthews, the Printer, was drawn in a Sledge from Newgate to Tyburn, and there executed according to the Terms of the Sentence for High Treason. He seemed mighty composed, and died without shewing any Terror or Dread at the Punishment. There was a very numerous appearance of all Sorts of People attending him, though the Weather was exceeding wet. His Brother was allowed his Body, which was taken away from the Place of Execution, and decently buried. He was assisted in this his private devotions by Mr. Skerres, the Reader of the Church of St. Martin, Ludgate.
>
> At the same Time Constable the Highwayman was hanged; as was Moor, alias Murray, the pretended blind man, who robbed the Landlord where he lodged, of Money and Watches, to the value of 150 £.

The curious thing about the Matthews execution is that it did not come in the peculiarly bloody centuries of English history. The year 1719 was nearly two centuries after the sixteenth century when Henry VIII butchered even his own wives and his successors had their streak of cruelty—Mary burning bishops at the stake and Elizabeth I hanging obstinate printers. And it was not the seventeenth century when a British king, Charles I, lost his head over a quarrel with Parliament.

People were more civilized or tentatively more pluralistic in the eighteenth century. Intellectually the famous *Cato Letters*, by John Trenchard and Thomas Gordon, began appearing in England in 1720, extolling freedom of discussion and principles of democracy. Yet George I allowed the barbaric execution of Matthews, apparently largely for failure to divulge a confidential source.

Protecting sources remains an issue in modern press and state relations. A number of states have passed shield laws which "shield" reporters from courts requesting to see notes and to identify sources. But such protection can be suspended in the consideration of a higher good, among them the guarantee of a fair trial. Myron Farber of the *New York Times* went to jail for 40 days on a contempt charge for not turning over his files for a story; William Farr, a *Los Angeles Herald-Examiner* reporter at the outset of the Charles Manson multiple-murder trial, refused to name one of his sources and was jailed.

The identity of the editor of the *Courant* has been the subject of discussion, since E. Mallet could be "Elizabeth" or "Edward." However, Mallet was editor for only a few weeks. In the first month the *Courant* carried the line, "London, sold by E. Mallet, next door to the King's Arm Tavern at Fleet Bridge." Five weeks later, in the April 22, 1702, issue, Mallet's name was no longer there. Instead, "London. Printed and sold by Sam Buckley at the Dolphin in Little-Britain" appeared.

Mallet's pledge to "objectivity," in an "editorial platform" in that first issue of March 11, 1702 (using incidentally the pronoun *he* for the editor) and is repeated in the second issue of the *Daily Courant*, states that the editor will not "take upon himself to give any Commente or Conjectures of his own, but will relate only Matter of Fact; supporting other People to have Sense enough to make Reflection for themselves."[32]

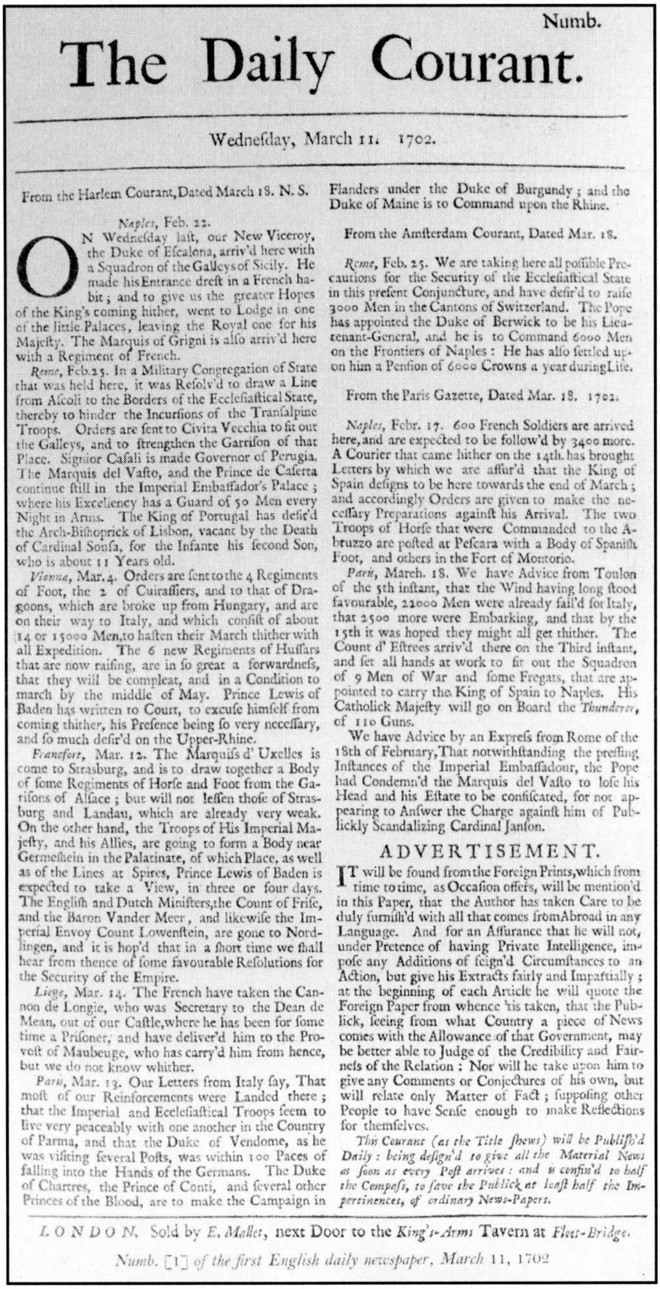

Numb.

The Daily Courant.

Wedneſday, March 11. 1702.

From the Harlem Courant, Dated March 18. N. S.

Naples, Feb. 22.

ON Wedneſday laſt, our New Viceroy, the Duke of Eſcalona, arriv'd here with a Squadron of the Galleys of Sicily. He made his Entrance dreſt in a French habit; and to give us the greater Hopes of the King's coming hither, went to Lodge in one of the little Palaces, leaving the Royal one for his Majeſty. The Marquis of Grigni is alſo arriv'd here with a Regiment of French.

Rome, Feb. 25. In a Military Congregation of State that was held here, it was Reſolv'd to draw a Line from Aſcoli to the Borders of the Eccleſiaſtical State, thereby to hinder the Incurſions of the Tranſalpine Troops. Orders are ſent to Civita Vecchia to fit out the Galleys, and to ſtrengthen the Garriſon of that Place. Signior Caſali is made Governor of Perugia. The Marquis del Vaſto, and the Prince de Caſerta continue ſtill in the Imperial Embaſſador's Palace; where his Excellency has a Guard of 50 Men every Night in Arms. The King of Portugal has deſir'd the Arch-Biſhoprick of Lisbon, vacant by the Death of Cardinal Souſa, for the Infante his ſecond Son, who is about 11 Years old.

Vienna, Mar. 4. Orders are ſent to the 4 Regiments of Foot, the 2 of Cuiraſſiers, and to that of Dragoons, which are broke up from Hungary, and are on their way to Italy, and which conſiſt of about 14 or 15000 Men, to haſten their March thither with all Expedition. The 6 new Regiments of Huſſars that are now raiſing, are in ſo great a forwardneſs, that they will be compleat, and in a Condition to march by the middle of May. Prince Lewis of Baden has written to Court, to excuſe himſelf from coming thither, his Preſence being ſo very neceſſary, and ſo much deſir'd on the Upper-Rhine.

Francfort, Mar. 12. The Marquiſs d' Uxelles is come to Straſburg, and is to draw together a Body of ſome Regiments of Horſe and Foot from the Gariſons of Alſace; but will not leſſen thoſe of Straſburg and Landau, which are already very weak. On the other hand, the Troops of His Imperial Majeſty, and his Allies, are going to form a Body near Germeſhein in the Palatinate, of which Place, as well as of the Lines at Spires, Prince Lewis of Baden is expected to take a View, in three or four days. The Engliſh and Dutch Miniſters, the Count of Friſe, and the Baron Vander Meer, and likewiſe the Imperial Envoy Count Lowenſtein, are gone to Nordlingen, and it is hop'd that in a ſhort time we ſhall hear from thence of ſome favourable Reſolutions for the Security of the Empire.

Liege, Mar. 14. The French have taken the Cannon de Longie, who was Secretary to the Dean de Mean, out of our Caſtle, where he has been for ſome time a Priſoner, and have deliver'd him to the Provoſt of Maubeuge, who has carry'd him from hence, but we do not know whither.

Paris, Mar. 13. Our Letters from Italy ſay, That moſt of our Reinforcements were Landed there; that the Imperial and Eccleſiaſtical Troops ſeem to live very peaceably with one another in the Country of Parma, and that the Duke of Vendome, as he was viſiting ſeveral Poſts, was within 100 Paces of falling into the Hands of the Germans. The Duke of Chartres, the Prince of Conti, and ſeveral other Princes of the Blood, are to make the Campaign in Flanders under the Duke of Burgundy; and the Duke of Maine is to Command upon the Rhine.

From the Amſterdam Courant, Dated Mar. 18.

Rome, Feb. 25. We are taking here all poſſible Precautions for the Security of the Eccleſiaſtical State in this preſent Conjuncture, and have deſir'd to raiſe 3000 Men in the Cantons of Switzerland. The Pope has appointed the Duke of Berwick to be his Lieutenant-General, and he is to Command 6000 Men on the Frontiers of Naples: He has alſo ſettled upon him a Penſion of 6000 Crowns a year during Life.

From the Paris Gazette, Dated Mar. 18. 1702.

Naples, Febr. 17. 600 French Soldiers are arrived here, and are expected to be follow'd by 3400 more. A Courier that came hither on the 14th. has brought Letters by which we are aſſur'd that the King of Spain deſigns to be here towards the end of March; and accordingly Orders are given to make the neceſſary Preparations againſt his Arrival. The two Troops of Horſe that were Commanded to the Abruzzo are poſted at Peſcara with a Body of Spaniſh Foot, and others in the Fort of Montorio.

Paris, March. 18. We have Advice from Toulon of the 5th inſtant, that the Wind having long ſtood favourable, 22000 Men were already ſail'd for Italy, that 2500 more were Embarking, and that by the 15th it was hoped they might all get thither. The Count d' Eſtrees arriv'd there on the Third inſtant, and ſet all hands at work to fit out the Squadron of 9 Men of War and ſome Fregats, that are appointed to carry the King of Spain to Naples. His Catholick Majeſty will go on Board the *Thunderer*, of 110 Guns.

We have Advice by an Expreſs from Rome of the 18th of February, That notwithſtanding the preſſing Inſtances of the Imperial Embaſſadour, the Pope had Condemn'd the Marquis del Vaſto to loſe his Head and his Eſtate to be confiſcated, for not appearing to Anſwer the Charge againſt him of Publickly Scandalizing Cardinal Janſon.

ADVERTISEMENT.

IT will be found from the Foreign Prints, which from time to time, as Occaſion offers, will be mention'd in this Paper, that the Author has taken Care to be duly furniſh'd with all that comes from Abroad in any Language. And for an Aſſurance that he will not, under Pretence of having Private Intelligence, impoſe any Additions of feign'd Circumſtances to an Action, but give his Extracts fairly and Impartially; at the beginning of each Article he will quote the Foreign Paper from whence 'tis taken, that the Publick, ſeeing from what Country a piece of News comes with the Allowance of that Government, may be better able to Judge of the Credibility and Fairneſs of the Relation: Nor will he take upon him to give any Comments or Conjectures of his own, but will relate only Matter of Fact; ſuppoſing other People to have Senſe enough to make Reflections for themſelves.

This Courant (as the Title ſhews) will be Publiſh'd Daily: being deſign'd to give all the Material News as ſoon as every Poſt arrives: and is confin'd to half the Compaſs, to ſave the Publick at leaſt half the Impertinences, of ordinary News-Papers.

LONDON, Sold by *E. Mallet*, next Door to the *King's-Arms* Tavern at *Fleet-Bridge*.

Numb. [1] of the first English daily newspaper, March 11, 1702

First issue of first English daily newspaper.

When J. Tonson launched *The Guardian* in London with its Latin motto, *ille quem requiris*—"that which you require or should know" and "to be continued Every Day"—he took on a gargantuan task perhaps better left to the gods. He was going to help make everybody better, lead them to achieve their best, and instill in them *all* the virtues. Here was lofty idealism at its highest. Tonson said in 1713:

> I shall publish in respective papers whatever I think may conduce to the Advancement of the Conversation of Gentlemen, the Improvement of Ladies, the Wealth of Traders, and the Encouragement of Artificers. . . .
>
> My Design upon the whole is no less, than to make the Pulpit, the Bar, and the Stage, all act in Concert in the care of Piety, Justice and Virtue. For I am past all the Regards of this Life, and have nothing to manage with any Person or Party, but to deliver myself as becomes an Old Man with one foot in the Grave, and one who thinks he is passing to Eternity. . . . Ambition, Lust, Envy, and Revenge, are Excrescencies of the Mind which I have cut off long ago.[33]

Normally when editors launch a new paper, they proclaim an inspiring manifesto of ideals. But it is questionable whether one can entirely live up to her or his ideals in print as terrible news of the day bids to be reported.

Applying the Ideal

One editor in later history tried to keep out all bad news. In March 1900 Charles Sheldon, a Congregational minister in Topeka, Kansas, and author of the popular book *In His Steps*, was given permission to edit the *Topeka Daily Capital* as Jesus would. A typical front page had uplifting items (such as a morning prayer), positive articles on such topics as the workability of Prohibition, a call for philanthropists to fight tuberculosis, and a plea to deal with the increase of unemployment due to saloons. And there was information on a famine in India, with an urgent plea for help. The Jesus approach lasted a week.[34] One competing editor responded that he was going to run his paper like the devil.

Nevertheless editors have tried to preserve a sense of values and humanitarian concerns in their ethics. Today editors and reporters and writers come together and publish codes that they would like all who work in their field to follow. Among these are the codes of the American Society of Newspaper Editors, Society of Professional Journalists, American Newspaper Publishers Association, Magazine Publishers Association, and American Society of Journalists and Authors.

Some feel codes of conduct for the media are difficult to follow, just as it would be for Tonson and Sheldon to realize their ideals. Yet, platforms and codes are evidence of a brighter glint in the countenance of editors.

Perpetuating Biases

Cultural biases probably appear in every news story. The upbringing of reporters and editors, as well as their education (life experience, type of university training), environment, and family background, shape their opinions. Today biases spelled out in well-reasoned opinions are formally allocated to editorial pages in editorials, letters, columns, and op-ed pieces.

The biases in early England were certainly heartfelt and often vicious, and they dominated many news publications. On one hand, the following from the *London Mercury* is a straight news account, but note the biased words in this 1688 report:

> Edinburgh, Dec. the 11th
>
> On Sunday most of the Apprentices of this City were assembled together, resolving to root out all papists, and to destroy the Chappel Royal, but that Night did not effect their Design, although not hindered by the Militia or Trained Bands.
>
> The next day they met together again, and went to the Abby of Holy-Road House, giving out, they would destroy all Idolatrous Worship, but they were opposed by one Captain Wallis a Papist, who kept the Place by order of the Chancellor that was Fled away. Captain Wallis upon their approach, fired upon them, Killing several, and wounding others. [The crowd regrouped and attacked again, but the captain escaped.] . . . So the next day not one Papist [was] to be found in and about the Town.[35]

A straightforward account, but there is little doubt where the writer's sympathies lay, as the writer used a derogatory term for one group, the "papists," but neutral terms for another, "apprentices assembled."

Benjamin Harris himself was a fiercely biased anti-Catholic, linking the Roman Catholic faith with "treason,"[36] publishing anti-Catholic children's books, and generally fomenting the spread of persecution of Roman Catholics. He even changed the name of his publication to *Protestant (Domestick) Intelligence.*

The expressed biases—literally in precise words or evident in selection of topics and treatment—were rooted in cultural consensus. The same is true today. For example, in U.S. war preparations and in actual conflicts, media are sufficiently patriotic, supporting the requisite general-consensus biases. Anyone not supporting or agreeing with the popular consensus is out of line and may pay a price. For instance, Joseph Reedy, an editorial writer at the *Kutztown* (Pennsylvania) *Patriot*, was fired for writing an editorial titled "How About a Little Peace?" at the height of the Persian Gulf War fever.

Media as Businesses

THE LITTLE SHOPS AROUND THE CORNER

Despite all their idealism, newspapers and their forerunners from the beginning were businesses. And there were many such businesses in England. Publications, from the one-page broadsides to the lengthy news books, were issued by commercial printers whose stores became the place to buy the paper. In some instances printers had other businesses, such as a pharmacy, book store, or coffee shop. At the end of a publication it was common to see a notation designating the printer and the address of the print shop where the publication was available.

For instance, the two-page *The Post Boy*, printed in London in March 1702, promoting its new updating plans (in competition likely with the new first English daily newspaper, the *Courant*, published in the same month), declared where the news "product" could be found:

> This is to give notice that the Post Boy, with a written postscript, containing all the Domestic Occurences with the translation of the Foreign Newes that arrives after the printing of the said Post Boy, is to be had only at Mr. John Shank, at Nandoe's Coffee house, between the two temple gates; and at Mr. Abel Roper's, at the end of Black Bay, over against St. Dunstan's Church in Fleet Street.[37]

Because money was the name of the game, it did not take long for advertising to appear. In the typical early English newspaper of two pages, half or a quarter of the second page would be given to advertising, predominantly classified-like ads for books and patent medicine. Three-fourths of the second page of *The Post Boy* was full of ads.

Front-Page Ads

In the American newspaper, from Benjamin Franklin Bache's *Aurora* in Philadelphia to the idealist Horace Greeley's *Tribune* in New York, advertisements filled the front page at times. Today ads are generally relegated to the inside, although some papers, even the *New York Times*, have small two- or three-line classified ads at the bottom of the front page as fillers or gimmicks. In 1993 *USA Today* began running ads on the front page of its business section.

Some magazines, particularly specialized trade or business magazines, sell their covers to advertising; a full-page cover ad, usually promoting a newspaper, appears on the front cover of each issue of the publication of the newspaper industry, *Editor & Publisher*. The editor of *Omni* magazine, Patrice Adcroft, quit in 1990 when the *Omni* cover space was sold to advertising. The editor of *Philadelphia Magazine*, Ron Javers, was fired in 1991 over what Javers considered the publisher's meddling in promoting products and services in editorial copy.

In newspapers today ads get the first claim of space, and every editor knows how a newly sold ad will replace a scheduled news story.

The English newspaper—from broadsides to lengthy news books to regular newspapers—offers insight into the modern American paper. The editors had their legal problems (subject even to charges of high treason, as in the cases of Twyn, Matthews, and others). They had courage, a sense of values, interest in reform, a love of freedom. The pristine goal of being objective also permeated early English print media.

Less idealistically, printers and editors also acquiesced in questionable government policies and ideologies; they conducted primarily a business, perpetuated biases, entertained with less than good taste, hyped the sensational.

In the pages that follow, the reader can see how these themes—the good and the bad, the ambivalent—play out and evolve and develop in the course of American journalism. How much insight into human nature emerges, and what human aspirations for the present and future are expressed in the English experiment with printed media?

QUESTIONS FOR DISCUSSION AND RESEARCH

1. Read a newspaper throughout (and/or listen to a television news program). List apparent values that the newspaper or telecast holds dear. What are the emphases? What gets good space, that is, high visibility in the layout of a page or position in the television news program lineup?
2. Is "reform" reporting (seeking to bring about reforms) the same as investigative reporting?
3. In how many ways can freedom of the press be curtailed (e.g., prior restraint, banning of access, etc.)?
4. Some forms of licensing seem always to be around. What forms does licensing take in the present, and what forms might it take in the future?
5. A newspaper is a business. How has this concept changed over the years? Is the newspaper business the same today in the United States as in England two or three centuries ago?
6. Can you find a news story that is without bias? Examine ten stories. Are our biases different from those of newspapers in "merrie olde England"?
7. Should editors respect the confidentiality of reporter sources at all times? (Minneapolis newspapers printed the name of a confidential source over the objections of the reporter who had promised the source anonymity.) At what cost? Any exceptions?
8. Bravery for an editor is to take some risk that might cost a publication its readers, or television its listeners. Look over the editorial page of your local newspaper for one or several weeks. Can any of the writings be called brave? Explain.
9. Would you have behaved like the martyr Matthews? What were his alternatives? What might be other variables or information that we don't know in the sparse account of the brave Matthews?
10. Debate the proposition: One should not try to be objective because it is impossible to be objective.
11. Were newspapers funnier in the olden days? What makes a paper funny? What is the place of humor in media today? In what ways can it be a gauge of our times?
12. If media constitute the fourth estate, what might be a fifth estate and sixth estate?
13. Whom do you consider the most important English philosophers/essayists/ journalists in their influence on today's media? Why?
14. Do you agree or disagree? (a) All good news is sensational. (b) Sensationalism is an acceptable means of entertainment.

15. Does sensationalism in the media today differ from printed sensationalism in the past?

ENDNOTES

1. British Library, British Museum, Museum of London, Guildhall, the Bodleian Library at Oxford University.
2. *The Continuation of Our Weekly Newes in London*, April 27–May, 1625. See Stanley Morrison, *The English Newspaper: Some Account of the Physical Development of Journals Printed in London Between 1622 and the Present Day* (Cambridge: Cambridge University Press, 1932), p. 14.
3. Ibid., April 14–April 21.
4. *Domestick Intelligence, Or News both from City and Country, published to prevent false reports*, Thursday, July 24, 1679.
5. Nicholas Russell, "Important Artifact in the Battle for a Free Press," in Media History section, *Editor & Publisher*, May 27, 1995, pp. 24, 25.
6. Mark Fackler and Clifford G. Christians, "John Milton's Place in Journalism History: Champion or Turncoat?" *Journalism Quarterly*, 1980, p. 563.
7. The word comes from the Greek *areiopagites*. An *areopagite* was a judge in a supreme court that met on a hill above the *agora*, or marketplace, beneath the larger Acropolis hill in Athens. The *Areios Pagos* was "Mars Hill" (*Areios* is an adjective for *Ares*, which is Greek for "Mars," the god's Latin name). In the New Testament, the philosophers and elite of Athens gathered to listen to the Apostle Paul and "brought him unto Areopagus. . . . Then Paul stood in the midst of Mars' hill, and said, Ye men of Athens, I perceive that in all things ye are too superstitious" (Acts 17: 19, 22—King James version).
8. *Cf.* J. Herbert Altschull, *From Milton to McLuhan: The Ideas Behind American Journalism* (New York: Longman, 1990), pp. 36ff.
9. John Milton, *Areopagitica*, in Frank Allen Patterson, ed., *The Works of John Milton*, vol. 4 (New York: Columbia University Press, 1931), p. 347.
10. G. E. B. Eyrie and Rivington, C. R. *A Transcript of the Stationers' Register: 1640–1708 A.D.*, 3 vols. (London: privately printed, 1913), I, p. 362. Quoted in Fackler and Christians, "John Milton's Place," p. 564.
11. Fackler and Christians, "John Milton's Place."
12. Ibid., p. 566, quoting the works of J. Milton French and others.
13. *Public Advertiser*, Dec. 19, 1769, Letter 35, quoted in Harold Herd, *The March of Journalism: The Story of the British Press from 1622 to the Present Day* (London: George Allen & Unwin, 1952), p. 70.
14. Herd, *March of Journalism*, p. 70.
15. T. H. S. Escott, *Masters of English Journalism* (London: T. Fisher Unwin, 1911), p. 99.
16. Herd, *March of Journalism*, p. 99.
17. Ibid., p. 100.
18. Ibid., p. 101.
19. John Hancock, Philadelphia, Nov. 25, 1775, in the *London Packet or New Lloyd's Evening Post*, Feb. 23–26, 1776.
20. *A brief collection of some part of the exactions, extortions, oppressions, tyrannies, and excesses towards the lives, bodies and goods of prisoners, done by Alexander Harris, Warden of the Fleete, in his foure years misgovernment, ready to be proved by oath and other testimonies*, a 1620 broadside, in Guildhall, London.
21. *A True Table of all such Fees as are Due, or can be claimed in any Bishops-Courts*, a 1681 broadside, in Guildhall, London.
22. Mitchell Stephens, *A History of News* (New York: Viking, 1988), p. 112.

23. Ibid., plate 6, between pages 178 and 179.
24. Research by Richard Streckfuss, University of Nebraska, Lincoln.
25. *Domestick Intelligence, Or News both from City and Country*, July 9, 1679.
26. Adam Bell, "DiGregorio Guilty in Kin's Killing," *Intelligencer*, Doylestown, Pa., Sept. 21, 1990, p. 1.
27. Benjamin Franklin, "An Apology for Printers," from the *Pennsylvania Gazette*, June 10, 1731, quoted in Albert Henry Smyth, *The Writings of Benjamin Franklin*, vol. 2 (New York: Macmillan, 1905), p. 178.
28. In accounts, only Matthews' last name is given, and it is spelled both Mathews and Matthews.
29. *Tercentary Handlist of English and Welsh Newspapers, Magazines and Reviews*, 1620–1920 (London: The Times, 1920), p. 5.
30. Perhaps a reference to the name of "Chevalier of St. George" given to James Stuart, son of James II. The son also became known as the Old Pretender to the throne, a figurehead of unrest and rebellion, 1708–1715.
31. *American Weekly Mercury*, Philadelphia, Jan. 12, 1719, p. 8.
32. *Daily Courant*, Wednesday, March 11, 1702, no. 1, p. 2.
33. *The Guardian*, London, March 12, 1713, no. 1.
34. *Topeka* (Kansas) *Daily Capital*, March 13, 1900, p. 1.
35. *London Mercury*, Tues., Dec. 18, to Sat., Dec., 22, 1688.
36. "We hear that the Pope out of his great zeal and tenderness for promoting the Catholic Cause, (that is to say Treason and Rebellion) has ordered Two hundred thousand Crowns to be sent for the Relief of the *English Roman Catholicks*." *Domestick Intelligence*, July 10, 1679.
37. *The Post Boy*, Tues., March 10, to Thurs., March 12, 1702, printed by B. Beadwell.

3

The First Hundred Years— Section One
Censorship and Trials: Beginnings and Early Years of American Media

Just as when there is smoke, there is fire, so it is that where there is printer's ink, especially in regard to newspapers, there is conflict. When an opinion is expressed or news is reported, inevitably authorities will find something disagreeable or offensive to them. The offending editor in the colonies, as in England, could expect to run afoul of authorities. Monarchs or their representatives could lord it over a pioneering, fledgeling newspaper. But as borders expanded and population increased in the colonies, so did a demand for information. Like any new product, the newspaper had to be tested, and the sought-after freedom of the press emerged from combat and the testing of rights. Persecuted and shut down at times in the colonies, newspapers nevertheless persisted. As the printing business expanded, the colonial press expanded and accepted a mantle of power of its own.

In the new world printing presses arrived on the heels of the explorers. A year before William Caxton set up the first press in England, presses had appeared in Spain in 1475, just several decades after Johannes Gutenberg's invention of movable type in Mainz, Germany. As the Spanish moved into the western hemisphere, they saw the need of printers to produce dictionaries and spiritual books. The first printer in the western hemisphere is believed to have been Esteban Martin, who set up a press in the City of Mexico in 1534. He was followed by Juan Pablos, who represented a publishing house in Seville. With a pressman and a black slave, Pablos produced the twelve-page *Brief and Most Concise Christian Doctrine in the Mexican and Spanish Tongues.*[1]

Within seven years news sheets appeared. Dealing mostly with news of foreign wars and disasters, these were called in Spain *hojas volantes, noticias, relaciones, suce-*

sos, or *relatos*; in Germany, *zeitung*, and in Italy, *avviso*. They were similar to the later corantos in Holland and England. In 1541 one of the *hojas volantes*, or "flying sheets," as some translate it, told of an earthquake and storm that leveled Guatemala City.

Its lead had a modern ring, noted Victoria Goff of the University of Wisconsin–Green Bay. The news sheet had all the details of the disaster, including printed lists of victims with identification of their families and jobs, plus religious editorial comment. Religion was important. The broadside said, "We have attributed it [the storm and earthquake] to our sins because we do not know how nor from where came such a great tempest." The clergy put a spin on the disaster. The *hoja* (titled *Relacion del espantable terremoto . . .*) reported: "In order to placate the wrath of God, the Bishop held a procession the next morning, and said many masses. . . . He told them that God had taken the good people to glory and that those remaining were left for testing."[2]

THE FIRST PRINTING PRESS IN THE COLONIES

A century later Jesse Glover, a dissenting English clergyman, set sail for the colonies in 1638, bringing with him a hired printer, Stephen Daye, a press, a supply of paper, and other materials.[3] However, Glover died en route. His widow opened a printing business in 1639 in Cambridge, Massachusetts, thus making her the "mother" of printing in America. She used the services of Daye. When Mrs. Glover married Henry Dunster, the president of Harvard College, in 1654, the printing business became closely associated with Harvard.[4] This first printing operation from its beginning in 1639 brought out the broadside *The Freeman's Oath*, the first in the New World.

Important forces were at work in the colonies that began shaping the new medium in the direction of a free and unshackled press. Nearly nine-tenths of the colonists were engaged in farming for their own needs or for export purposes.[5] The close large-scale network and class-feudal-system remnants in Europe did not apply. A libertarian influence from England was a factor. Also the colonists were diverse enough to shape inductively their own system and quest for freedom. From the beginning the colonies were a melting pot. There were sizable minorities of Dutch, French, Germans, Swedes, Spanish, and others.

In the eighteenth century Germans alone amounted to one-half of the population of Pennsylvania. Recognizing the political clout of the German community in Philadelphia and with political aspirations rooted in his ability to work with diverse groups, Benjamin Franklin, with Louis Timothy, a recent immigrant from Holland, prepared a prospectus of a first issue of the twice-monthly German-language *Philadelphische Zeitung* in 1732. But they did not follow with other issues. However, Christopher Sauer, a leader within the German community, had great success in the Philadelphia area a few years later with his *Hoch-Deutsch Pennsylvanische Geschicht-Schreiber* in Germantown. Franklin later tried several times with several partners to launch a German paper, even offering a bilingual German-English paper, the *Hoch Deutsche und Englische Zeitung* but failed to compete with Sauer's paper, which had reached a circulation of 9,000.[6] Philadelphia, which had the largest French population in the colonies, saw the birth of seven French-language newspapers between 1700 and 1800.

Unlike in England, where "the English political malcontents did not consider individual liberty safe under the tutelage of a sovereign Parliament," notes colonial historian Harry M. Ward, "the idea of popular sovereignty persisted." And Ward cites excerpts from colonial sermons that underscored the right of the populace to revolt against "arbitrary authority."[7] Far removed from the seat of empire, the colonists paid homage to ideas of independence and freedom from the start, eventually becoming defensive of their own emerging political tradition.[8]

Classless Communities

Colonial society was generally classless, although there was a subgroup of indentured (contracted) servants, apprentices, a system of tenancy, and various contractual service arrangements; and by the time of the Revolutionary War tax records showed a growing mercantile class, a middle class, and a working class.[9]

Despite times of intolerance with moments of atrocity—persecution of nonconformers and the extreme cases of killing witches—colonial America was marked by a growing spirit of assimilation and toleration. Out of a variety of religious bodies created by ethnic immigration and schisms within Protestant denominations came a semblance of tolerance. By the end of the Revolutionary War era there were twenty-eight denominations.[10]

The New Americanese Language

Changes were occurring in the language that encouraged assimilation into a new national identity different from the English. The ability to move around in America encouraged standardized expression. Different from England, the colonial experience fostered almost no linguistic distinction according to social status. Regional dialects were almost nonexistent.[11] Many different ethnic groups contributed to the new Americanese. Communities even kept their original Indian designations and accepted Indian words such as *squash, raccoon, persimmon, skunk*; from Spanish, *tomato, barbecue, savannah, chocolate*; from Dutch, *boss, sloop, cookie, sleigh*.

Despite the consciousness of a new developing culture and a new growing national identity, the colonial personality harbored a streak of discontent. Many were disillusioned from the beginning, sailing from a land in which they were oppressed or limited in opportunity—some even were convicts—to find the new dream arduous and often without rainbows. "American character traits posed a contrapuntal theme," says Ward. "On one hand were the ideals of morality, equality, and rule of law and on the other the realities of corruption, discrimination, violence, and savagery."[12] Into this duality—a continent promising opportunity and fulfillment but in reality marked with failed causes and still-distant unfulfilled dreams—came printers and editors who acknowledged an innate freedom and still pursued an elusive better tomorrow.

Quakers Harass a Printer

The English population in and around Phildelphia in the 1680s consisted largely of Quakers, the followers of George Fox. Known officially as members of the Society of Friends, they were at the far end of the spectrum from the liturgical, ritualistic Church of England. Fox felt that God chose who will serve him by imparting an inner light; thus ordinations were useless and professional ministers and clergy were unnecessary. The sacraments (imparting of grace) were also seen as happening internally. Fox rejected the formal use of titles. He opposed war, and many Friends today are pacifists. Oaths were seen as unnecessary. Hounded in England, Fox's followers often met persecution in the colonies as well; for example, in Massachusetts four were hanged for their beliefs.[13]

One of the Friends' principal converts was William Penn, son of a British admiral. The younger Penn decided to aid his new brothers and sisters of the faith and secured from King Charles II the grant of Pennsylvania ("Penn's Woods"). Involved in the transaction was the cancellation of a debt owed by the king to Penn's father. Philadelphia ("City of Brotherly Love") was founded in 1682.

Anxious for his new colony to have a printer, Penn brought with him from England a 19-year-old, William Bradford. (This is not the same as an earlier William Bradford who came over on the Mayflower, became governor of Plymouth Colony, and died in 1657.) Although William Bradford, the printer, was the son of another William Bradford in England, the printer brought from England by Penn is regarded in America as William Bradford I; there followed him a long line of a family that continued repeatedly to use the same name.

William Bradford stayed only briefly, then returned to England. A few years later, in 1685, he returned to the colonies, bringing with him letters from George Fox. Fox described Bradford as "a civil young man convinced of Truth." On Fox's recommendation, Bradford became printer for the gentle-minded Quakers in Philadelphia.[14]

But the Quakers were not always so gentle-minded, and Bradford had his own idea of truth. Bradford's first publication, an almanac printed in 1685, inadvertently plunged him into trouble with the Quakers. In it was a reference to "the begining of Government here by the Lord Penn." Since the Quakers did not like exalted titles, they were offended at this reference to Penn as "Lord." Bradford was cautioned "not to print any thing but what shall have lycence from ye council."[15]

When the people quarreled with the governor over their rights in 1689, Bradford published the charter for Pennsylvania to set the record straight on rights. Perhaps suspecting trouble, Bradford left his name off the document. The Pennsylvania governor, John Blackwell, and the provincial council summoned him and sought to have him admit that he had published the document. Bradford pleaded his friendship with Penn, and indeed it was understood that Penn expected him to print such documents. But Bradford did not admit the printing: "If I had printed them, I do not know that I had done amiss," and he caustically suggests that he did not know of any imprimatur appointed authority over printing. The governor exclaimed: "Sir, I am 'Imprimatur'; and that you shall know."[16] The governor told Bradford that he would be bound by a $500 bond "that you shall print nothing but what I do allow."[17]

While still official printer for the Quakers in Philadelphia, in 1692 Bradford printed several pamphlets for Quaker schismatic George Keith. The main group of loyal Fox Quakers took legal measures to silence Keith. Bradford was seized not only on the grounds that he had printed seditious matter but that he had printed the pamphlets without the printer's name, a requirement outlined in an obscure law.[18] English common law said that in a charge of seditious libel the authorities had to show only that the accused printed the item and that the truth or falsity of the document was of no concern. In fact, the common interpretation of the law was that the greater the truth, the greater the seditious libel because of its threat to the established order. At his trial Bradford was ahead of his time in suggesting that this narrow confine of the law was wrong.

The trial then took a comical twist. The prosecuting attorney introduced the metal type locked in a frame from which he alleged Bradford had printed the pamphlets. Someone apparently loosened the "quoins," or screws of the frame, as it was passed around. The metal type fell out and scattered. The type was so thoroughly mixed up it could prove nothing. Charges were dismissed and Bradford's equipment returned.[19]

Bradford had planned to return to England, but he received a bid to become the royal printer for New York in 1693. He proceeded to print the acts of the New York assembly and proclamations and official documents. But Bradford ran afoul of a new New York governor, the Earl of Bellomont. Like a modern politician, the governor wanted to exploit his discussion with savage Indians, with whom he had conversed in close quarters for eight days. The governor reported the Indians were doused with bear grease, smoked tobacco, and reeked of rum. He thought an account would be impressive reading back home in England. Bradford, however, ignored the matter, feigning sickness. The peeved governor cited him for his neglect, failing to publish the diaries in four months, and ordered the printer replaced.[20]

The governor died four months after the decree of replacement. The new governor, Lord Cornbury—a weird sort who wore women's clothes on public occasions to show himself resembling his cousin, Queen Anne—had Bradford reinstated.[21] In 1725 Bradford, at age 52, launched the first newspaper in New York, the *New York Gazette*.

From Witchcraft to a Libel Trial

A Quaker was also the subject of the first criminal libel trial in Massachusetts, in 1695. Thomas Maule came from Salem—the infamous town that executed fourteen women and six men for alleged witchcraft in 1692. He had been in trouble with the authorities as far back as 1669. He had received ten stripes for saying that a certain Mr. Higginson "preached lies, and that his instruction was the doctrine of devils." By Maule's own account he had been whipped three times, deprived of his goods three times, and jailed five times.

In 1695 Maule announced plans to print a book setting forth his own brand of

The new governor, Lord Cornbury, who wore women's clothes, reinstated William Bradford as printer. (The Library Company of Philadelphia, from J. G. Wilson, *A Memorial History of the City of New York,* 1892)

theology and sent the manuscript off to New York, where it was published. But when the book was brought into Massachusetts he was immediately prosecuted. The Council said the book, *Truth Held Forth & Maintained,* contained "many Notorious, and Wicked Lies, and Slanders not only on private persons, but upon Government, and also divers Corrupt, and pernicious Doctrines, utterly, Subversive of the *True Christian,* and professed Faith."[22] In two days the House of Representatives concurred.

The trial seems to have turned out to be a farce. Maule showed up with a Bible under his arm and pleaded that the Good Book could not always be interpreted literally.[23] Maule was charged with publishing the biblically offensive book and with denying the accuracy of Scripture. He won an acquittal.[24] It seems that the attempt to silence the Salem printer was just too much like the witch hunts of old. After all, the Bible does say, "Thou shalt not suffer a witch to live" (Exodus 22:18). Who, after the horror in Salem had been repudiated, was to quarrel with Maule when he argued that the Bible could not always be taken literally?

With freedom, a new cultural gauntlet, and a promise of creating a new promised land before them,[25] editors in this less than utopian new world were sure to encounter conflict with established and emerging forces. Almost from the beginning of newspaper publishing in America, tension existed between the media and authorities and between media themselves.

THE "FIRST" PAPERS IN THE COLONIES

Three publications contend for the honor of being the first newspaper—a real newspaper—in the colonies:

- *The Present State of the New-English Affairs*, published in 1689 by Samuel Green, Jr.
- *Publick Occurrences, Both Forreign and Domestick*, published in 1690 by Benjamin Harris.
- *Boston News-Letter*, published in 1704 by John Campbell, with Bartholomew Green, one of the nineteen children of the senior Samuel Green. The senior Green had been the successor to printer Stephen Daye at Cambridge and had printed an Indian Bible.

The senior Green's namesake son, Samuel, Jr., brought out a one-sheet publication in the fall of 1689, *The Present State of the New-English Affairs*, with the approval of Massachusetts authorities. "This is published to prevent false reports," said a motto just under the logo. Green, Jr., had been a writer of newsletters that he distributed in manuscript form. The broadside was an experiment in printing one of them. He died less than a year after publishing, putting an end to any plans he might have had for developing a continuing publication. The 8-by-14^1/$_2$-inch Green broadside appeared only once, leaving some question whether it was intended to be a newspaper. Featured was an extract of a letter of the Reverend Increase Mather to Simon Baldwin, Massachusetts colony governor. Mather had interceded with the British king concerning grievances in the colony.

William Shillaber, who reproduced old newspapers, argued in 1902 that Green's broadside was "the first attempt at newspaper publication on this side of the Atlantic Ocean."[26] Other writers, beginning with Joel Munsell in 1874, have also regarded it as a newspaper, while a half-dozen other scholars have insisted that the sheet was just a one-shot broadside.[27]

In 1690 the energetic, sometimes irascible Benjamin Harris launched a version of his London *Domestick Intelligence*. On September 25, 1690, he produced *Publick Occurrences, Both Forreign and Domestick*. It had four pages, three of them filled with print and one blank, possibly for the reader to add his or her own news before passing the publication along. The first issue was "Number 1." (Numbering issues is a sign of continuity.) It promised to be published once a month or more, "if any glut of occurrences happen." Like Harris's spicy London publication, Harris's Boston effort was largely sensational.

In issue number one,[28] *Publick Occurrences* announced that "the Christianized Indians in some parts of Plimouth, have newly appointed a day of Thanksgiving to

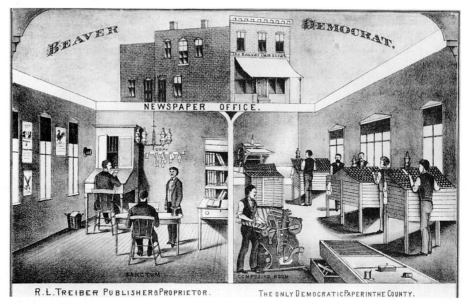

An early newspaper office and composing room. (Library of Congress)

God." There was also an item that said, "While the barbarous Indians were lurking about Chemsford, there were missing about the beginning of this month a couple of Children . . . both of them supposed to be fallen into the hands of the Indians." Reported also were the suicide of a despondent old man, the spread of "epidemical Fevers and Agues," the outbreak of smallpox in Boston, and the latest expeditions into Canada. Indian wars between pro-French and Pro-English tribes with various atrocities received attention: "When Capt. Mason was at Fort Real, he cut the faces, and ript the bellies of two Indians, and threw a third Over board in the sight of the French, who informing the other Indians of it, they have in revenge barbarously Butcher'd forty Captives of ours that were in their hands."

Then there was the juicy tidbit from France about the French king and his son: "France is in much trouble (and fear) not only with us but also with his Son, who has revolted against him lately and has great reason if reports be true, that the Father used to lie with the Sons Wife." The authorities, fearing repercussions from the coverage of the Indians whom they were courting and evoking a Puritan sensitivity over the item about the French king's dalliance, suspended publication of the paper. Some insist that although it published only once, this paper had the philosophy of a modern paper, because it published without an official license and, with intentions of continuing, it indeed met the marks of a true paper, no matter that it was not allowed to proceed.

It remained for John Campbell, with one of the sons of Samuel Green, Sr., Bartholomew Green, as printer, to start the first colonial news publication that met literally the requirement of a newspaper—that it be published regularly, among other things. Campbell, like Samuel Green, Jr., was engaged in sending out hand-written newsletters. These proved so popular that Campbell decided to put them into print instead of continuing to copy them over and over. As postmaster in Boston he had a ready distribution system. Campbell embraced little of the prurient and sensational side of news, as Harris had done. In the first issue of Campbell's *Boston News-Letter*[29] most items were brief and vague. For example, "Mr. Nathaniel Oliver a principal Merchant of this place died April 15 & was decently inter'd April 18," and, "His Excellency Dissolved the Gen. Assembly."

With Boston as a major shipping port, Campbell gave space to seafaring matters. In the first issue he spent about half a page telling about privateers' seizures of ships and various encounters using hastily conscripted militia. Issue number two told of a military expedition "last winter against the Spaniards and Spanish Indians."[30]

The Bostonians did not have to worry about crime in the streets, but did worry about violence attributed to Indians. In the second issue, Campbell has several scalping stories: "There was a man found Dead and Scalpt near Dover, but whither kill'd by English or Indians, not yet known," and, "On Tuesday the 25 Nathanael Meader of Dover in Oyster River, being at work in his Field, and burning Brush, was waylaid by a Company of Indians, as he returned home about Sunset, who shot him through the thigh & leggs, then took, Scalpt, kill'd, and stript him Naked." After a few issues, Campbell was publishing ads for items for sale from "spurn yarn" to a "lusty Negro Man-Slave to be Sold by Thomas Palmer Esq. and to be seen at his House in Boston."[31]

Enter the Franklins

Campbell seems to have fallen into disfavor with the authorities—perhaps he was dragging his feet with postal duties; maybe the authorities were just tired of his rather lackluster newspaper. William Brooker was named to succeed Campbell, but Campbell declined to relinquish his *News-Letter* to a new publisher. Brooker, now the postmaster, started his own Boston paper, the *Gazette*, in 1719. It was the second ongoing successful paper in the colonies. Campbell hung onto the *News-Letter* until 1722, when he passed it on to his printer, Bartholomew Green. John Tebbel makes an interesting observation that is as modern as today: "Momentarily there was little news at home, and eager mouths spread it faster than Campbell could print it."[32] The "sound bite" of conversation in small communities had the effect of modern radio and television, audibly and instantly scooping the print media.

The third ongoing newspaper in the colonies (after Campbell's *News-Letter* and Brooker's *Gazette* in Boston) was the *American Weekly Mercury* of Andrew Bradford, William Bradford's son. The *Mercury* appeared in Philadelphia on December 22, 1719, one day after the launching of Brooker's *Gazette*.

Then in 1721 in Boston came the *New England Courant*, which some, such as Tebbel, consider to be "the first American newspaper worthy of the name," and its editor, James Franklin, older half brother of Benjamin, to be "the first real newspaper editor in America."[33] That view, shared by a number of media historians, is strongly contested by some later writers, such as William David Sloan of the University of Alabama.

James Franklin had been a printer for Brooker's *Gazette*, but when the *Gazette* changed hands in less than a year to another editor and publisher, Franklin was angered and was recruited by a group of Church of England malcontents to edit and print the *Courant*, the fourth ongoing paper in America.

Dispelling the myth that James Franklin was a great pursuer of freedom as he challenged authorities, Sloan makes him out as a religious bigot who was mean-tempered and even indifferent to the plight of those suffering from a plague of smallpox.

The Smallpox Controversy

In the fall of 1721, panic had gripped Boston over the spread of smallpox. Before the outbreak finally ebbed, 6,000 of Boston's residents had contracted the disease, 800 dying. Cotton Mather, a leader of the Puritans, had come to believe that inoculation—injecting the disease into the healthy—would be a way to build up a defense against the disease.

Inoculation was no mere pricking or scraping of the skin, but in those crude times involved a sizable slit in the arm. English physicians developed a complicated process for smallpox inoculations that began with purging the patient (with enemas) and then bleeding the patient. The inoculation itself was performed with a double-edged, pointed surgical blade, and the infective agent was bound into the wound. "The cure could be worse than the disease," says medical historian Roderick E. McGrew. He points out that because live virus was used, sometimes infections and cases of smallpox resulted. Causing an epidemic was a risk. In the nineteenth century, the procedure of vaccination (using killed virus) developed by English physician Edward Jenner proved safer and won wide acceptance.[34]

The *Courant* at the outset attacked the idea of inoculation, mostly on the ground that the Puritan leadership favored it, according to Sloan.[35] Arguments against inoculation said that it was sacrilege to tamper with a scourge believed sent from God. Also there were racist insinuations that what was said to be practiced in some primitive nations, as in Africa, was probably an inferior treatment for the more cultured nations. And would not giving the disease to prevent it actually spread it? Gradually Mather was exonerated as statistics showed that those who were inoculated experienced lower death rates than those who contracted the disease without inoculation.

James Franklin Banned

When the *Courant* criticized the government for dragging its feet in hunting down pirates, the authorities forbade James Franklin from continuing to print the paper. He circumscribed the ban by listing his half brother Benjamin's name instead of his own. As the new publisher, Benjamin promised in the February 4, 1723, issue that he would be a "man of good temper," "courteous," and of "sound judgment." Benjamin, who has alluded to "harsh and tyrannical treatment" from his half brother in his autobiography,[36] did not stay long, but slipped out one night onto a boat for New York. The *Courant*, with James returning, now without overriding topics such as the inoculation controversy and with dwindling advertising, folded June 25, 1726.

In New York Benjamin Franklin called on William Bradford, who had left Philadelphia and had been publishing the *Gazette* in New York since 1725. Bradford did not have any work for the young Franklin but referred him to Philadelphia to his son Andrew Bradford, who was publishing the *American Weekly Mercury*. Franklin was treated kindly by Andrew Bradford and the elder Bradford, who also visited Philadelphia. The younger Bradford did not have an immediate opening but fed Franklin and offered him lodging and some part-time work if he did not find regular work.

There was another printer in town, and the elder Bradford accompanied Franklin to introduce him to Samuel Keimer. Franklin hired on, but was unimpressed with Keimer, as he had been with Andrew Bradford. "These two printers," he wrote in his *Autobiography*, "I found poorly qualified for their business. Bradford had not been bred to it, and was very illiterate; and Keimer tho' something of a scholar, was a mere compositor, knowing nothing of presswork."[37]

Ben Franklin Befriended

Then one day the governor of Pennsylvania, William Keith, came with an aide seeking Franklin at Keimer's shop. Keimer was excited, thinking the visitor had come to see him. Keimer ran out to meet the governor. "But the governor enquir'd for me. . . . Keimer star'd like a pig poison'd," wrote Franklin.[38] The governor offered Franklin the possibility of taking on the government printing provided he got some assistance from his father. Franklin's father declined to provide financial backing for a startup in Philadelphia, so Keith said he would do it. The governor asked Franklin for an inventory of what he would need. He had decided to send Franklin to England to purchase the necessary equipment and materials. In England, Franklin, running short of money, worked for several printers before returning to America.

Back in Philadelphia, Franklin went to Keimer's shop. They soon quarreled, and Franklin was fired. However, another employee of Keimer, Hugh Meredith, quit and joined Franklin to set up a print shop using money from Meredith's father.

Franklin decided to launch a newspaper. But plans for the paper were leaked. Keimer, deciding to jump the gun with his own paper, on Christmas eve, December 24, 1728, brought out a rather curious four-page paper, *The Universal Instructor in all Arts and Sciences: and Pennsylvania Gazette*. The first page or so indeed was dedicated to instruction. Keimer even began publishing what would be called today an annotated dictionary or encyclopedia—bit by bit, starting with defining words beginning with *A*.

Martha Careful and Caelia Shortface

Franklin, not yet prepared to launch his own paper, cleverly decided to try to run Keimer out of the newspaper business. He wrote entertaining pieces aimed at Keimer for Bradford's *American Weekly Mercury*. He began "The Busy-Body" essays (he apparently wrote the first five and the eighth; the two others were by a Joseph Brienthal). In the week before "The Busy-Body" started, the *Mercury* led off with a group of satirical "Letters from the Female Sex, complaining of S. K." One letter signed by Martha Careful (several other letters were signed by Caelia Shortface) declared:[39]

> Mr. Andrew Bradford,
>
> In behalf of my Self and many good modest Women in this City (who are almost out of Countenance) I Beg you will Publish this in your next Mercury, as a Warning to Samuel Keimer: That if he proceed further to Explore the Secrets of our Sex, in That audacious manner, as he hath done in his Gazette, No. 5. under the Letters, A.B.O. To be read in all Taverns and Coffee-Houses, and by the Vulgar: I say if he Publish any more of that kind, which ought only to be in the Repository of the Learned; my Sister Molly and my Self, with some others, are Resolved to run the Hazard of taking him by the Beard, at the next Place we meet him, and make an Example of him for his Immodesty and subscribe on the behalf of the rest of my agravated Sex.
>
> Yours,
>
> 24 Jan. 1728 Martha Careful

What was it in Keimer's paper that disturbed this fictitious woman, probably the creation of Franklin? Keimer's ongoing dictionary in his paper had "abortion" and its definition under "ABO."[40]

> ### ABO
>
> ABORTION, in Medicine, an immature Exclusion of the Foetus. . . . This may happen at any Time of Pregnancy. . . .
>
> We have Instance of Abortions by the Way of the Mouth, the Anus, the Navel, etc.
>
> The usual Cause of Abortion are immoderate Evacuations, violent Motions, sudden Passions, Frights, etc.

With such fare in the *Mercury*, Franklin and Bradford could count on Keimer's paper losing women readers.

Andrew Bradford's *American Mercury* was one of the earliest to print the Cato Letters of John Trenchard and Thomas Gordon from England. Defending the right of liberty for all, the letters ran in the *Mercury* from 1722 to 1724. Among them was "The Right and Capacity of the People to Judge of Government." Bradford indicated the wide favorable response by including a column signed Americo-Britanus. It said: "You have obliged these Western Parts of the World with several valuable Letters from Cato, and we have found them worthy of that Name, since they give us the true Notions of Liberty, and the Policy of a free Government. . . ."[41]

Bradford was only one of many using the Cato Letters. The colonists constantly initiated discussions of liberty, as editors printed the Cato writings of Trenchard and Gordon. The Cato Letters appeared in most papers in the colonies, creating a rallying point and a measure of political unity by 1760.[42]

When Bradford wrote about the "dying credit of the Province," he was hauled in by the Council and censured by the governor. He was told not to publish anything about the affairs of the government without permission in the future. When he printed a summary of Cato's Letters, September 18, 1729, in a Busy-Body essay dealing with liberty as compared to government by inherited power, he was arrested. The charges, however, were quickly dropped. One of his adversaries, a member of the Council, was Andrew Hamilton. Bradford made a point to ignore Hamilton, failing for instance to report Hamilton's election to the Assembly as representative from Bucks County.[43] (Andrew Hamilton turns up defending, instead of restricting, liberty in the Zenger trial in 1735.)

First Published American Cartoon

Andrew Bradford may have published the first American political cartoon, although first honors have usually gone to Benjamin Franklin's wagoner appealing to Hercules for help in Franklin's 1747 pamphlet *Plain Truth* or his segmented snake "Join or Die" in the May 9, 1754, issue of the *Pennsylvania Gazette*. Philip Lapansky, research librarian at the Library Company of Philadelphia, argues that a small, nearly square woodcut used for an initial leading into a *Mercury* article showing Liberty handing a pen to a writer, who in turn hands the paper to a traveler, is the first political cartoon in the colonies. Published in the *Mercury* April 18–25, 1734, the cartoon has the words "Liberty" and "Property" above and below the figures.

Andrew Bradford was not always a paragon of personal liberty, it seems. Apparently he dealt in the slave trade. In 1722, he carried this ad with his address, same as that of his paper:[44]

> A very likely Negro Woman, fit for all Sorts of House-Business, to be sold by Andrew Bradford in the Second-Street, Philadelphia.

Benjamin Franklin bought out Keimer and shortened *The Universal Instructor in all Arts and Science: and Pennsylvania Gazette* to *Pennsylvania Gazette*. Beginning with the issue of Sept. 25–Oct. 2, 1729, he became a fierce rival of Andrew Bradford.

Franklin resorted to making fun of Bradford. But Bradford got the last laugh. On February 13, 1741, he beat Franklin by three days to become the publisher of the first magazine in the colonies. Bradford's *The American Magazine, or a Monthly View of the Political State of the British Colonies* lasted only three months; Franklin's magazine, *General Magazine, and Historical Chronicle, for all the British Plantations in North America*, held on for six months.

Bradford died the next year, and his widow Cornelia ran black borders in the two subsequent issues. She was the sole publisher for several months and then in February 1743 added Isaiah Warner, whom she called a "young beginner" as a part-

Is "Liberty" first political cartoon in America? (The Library Company of Philadelphia)

ner. The move perhaps angered the Bradfords' adopted son, a nephew, William Bradford III. William proceeded to launch his own paper, the *Pennsylvania Journal*, which under William's editorship and that of his son Thomas became an important patriot organ during the Revolutionary War.

"The Delight of All That Knew Him"

When Franklin took over the *Gazette* in 1729 he promised the people of Pennsylvania a "good News-Paper" in contrast to the boring and somewhat irrelevant approach of Keimer with his printing of annotated dictionary definitions. He also believed that a paper should be "as agreeable and useful an Entertainment as the Nature of the Thing will allow."[45] In that issue he printed a message by the governor, reports from overseas, datelined reports from around the colonies, and local people news (from society goings-on to death sentences). The whole back page was dedicated to advertisements, ranging from calls for return of runaway slaves to sales pitches for "hard soap" and Bibles.

The Lighter Side

Ben Franklin Always Had the Right Word(s) for It

Benjamin Franklin, intrigued by the large number of "distant, round-about phrases" used to indicate that someone was inebriated, compiled the following collection of such phrases in his "Drinker's Dictionary" for Poor Richard's Almanac. Here, much abridged, are some of the words and phrases in use in the mid-1700s indicating that someone was smashed, swizzled, looped or just plain drunk. (This writing of Franklin's was selected by Roy Goodman, research librarian of the American Philosophical Society.)

He is addled.
He's in his airs.
He's biggy.
Bewitch'd.
Buzzey.
His head is full of bees.
He sees the bears.
He's kiss'd Black Betty.
He's cat.
Cherry merry.
Crack'd.
Half way to Concord.
Got corns in his head.
He's crocus.
He cuts his capers.
Cock'd.
Chipper.
Loaded his cart.
Kill'd his dog.
Took his drops.
Has dipp'd his bill.
He's dagg'd.
Cockeyed.

Got a brass eye.
He's eat a toad and a half for breakfast.
Fox'd.
Fuddled.
Frozen.
Fears no man.
Been to France.
Froze his mouth.
His flag is out.
Gold-headed.
Glaiz'd.
As dizzy as a goose.
Got the glanders.
Top heavy.
Got by the head.
Loose in the hilts.
Jolly.
Been to Jerico.
He's a king.
Seen the French king.
Got kib'd heels.
Het his kettle.
He's in liquor.
Lappy.
Limber.
He sees two moons.
Seen a flock of moons.
Maudlin.
Mellow.
He's eat the cocoa nut.
Nimptopsical.
Got the night mare.
He's oil'd.
Smelt of an onion.
Overset.
Pidgeon ey'd.
Pungey.
Priddy.

As good conditioned as a puppy.
Has scalt his head pan.
Been among the Philistines.
He's contending with Pharaoh.
He's rocky.
Raddled.
Lost his rudder.
Ragged.
Been too free with Sir Richard.
Like a rat in trouble.
He's stitch'd.
Seafaring.
In the suds.
Been in the sun.
As drunk as David's sow.
Swampt.
He's got his top gallant sails out.
As stiff as a ring-bolt.
Half seas over.
Staggerish.
He carries too much sail.
Stew'd.
Soak'd.

Been too free with Sir John Strawberry.
He's right before the wind with all his studding
    sails out.
He's topp'd.
Tongue-ty'd.
Tann'd.
Topsy-turvy.
Tipsy.
Has swallow'd a tavern token.
He's thaw'd.
He's in a trance.
Valiant.
Got the Indian vapours.
The malt is above the water.
He's wet.
He's been to the salt water.
He's water-soaken.
He's very weary, out of the way.
He's drunk as a wheelbarrow.

Source: Philadelphia Inquirer, Aug. 29, 1990.
Reprinted by permission.

One of the more touching stories in the *Gazette* over the years was Franklin's report of the death from smallpox of his four-year-old son, Francis Folger Franklin. On the gravestone Franklin and his wife, Deborah, put the words, "The delight of all that knew him." It would be a sorrow that the couple would carry with them the rest of their lives. In the *Gazette* Franklin urged the public to benefit from a lesson he learned—to be inoculated, shades of the earlier controversy in which his half brother, James, opposed inoculation. But Benjamin Franklin said he really did favor it but had failed to inoculate the boy.[46]

Franklin formed a partnership with David Hall, and after January 1748 the *Gazette* printers were listed as B. Franklin and D. Hall. The paper gave entire pages over to reports on lotteries, and ads filled half the paper. Caught up in the unrest of the times and growing defiance concerning England, the *Gazette* in January 1761 printed the entire text of King George III's speech to Parliament taken from the *London Gazette*. When in 1765 Parliament passed the Stamp Act to tax printed matter and legal documents in the colonies, the *Gazette* suspended publication; in its place for two weeks was a broadside entitled "No Stamped Paper to be had," which was circulated with a four-page leaflet, *Remarkable Occurences*.

In 1766 the partnership of Hall and Franklin was dissolved and only Hall's name now appeared. Hall formed a new partnership with William Sellers. In 1778 the title became *The Pennsylvania Gazette and Weekly Advertiser*, only to be shortened again in 1782 to *The Pennsylvania Gazette*. Hall's sons continued the paper in other partnerships until the paper ceased publication in 1815, with promises to re-sume at a later time. But no other copies of the *Pennsylvania Gazette* are known to exist. Half of the last issue was still devoted to advertising.

Media as Purveyors of Information/Education
NUGGETS OF NEWS AMONG TRIVIA

The colonial and early American papers following the British format often led off with a page or more of foreign news, especially in the spring, summer, and fall, when ships arrived from Europe more frequently. Much of the news in the earliest colonial papers was invariably European. Also, more and more often the front pages and parts of inside pages were given to ads. Inside were datelined reports from other areas and regions.

A kind of explosion in the amount and variety of information in the papers occurred about 1730 and continued until 1765 when matters affecting the colonies were given greater emphasis as news topics. In that period, according to David Copeland, of Emory & Henry College, Emory, Virginia, "Colonial news-papers were very similar to newspapers of twentieth-century America, that is, a multitude of topics are discussed." But he says the colonial papers were also sim-ilar to the present because when an important issue emerged, the papers focused on it.[47]

The papers sought to be vehicles of record. Thus important documents such as the Declaration of Independence and the draft of the Constitution were printed in full. Attention was given to the workings of colonial legislatures and later to day-by-day proceedings of Congress. The papers included debate over urgent domestic matters such as the countering of the Whiskey Rebellion when western Pennsylvania farmers defied federal excise tax on corn whiskey in 1794.

Sometimes the real news would get lost in faithfulness to recording proceedings in detail. The *Pennsylvania Gazette* on June 21, 1775, led off with a series of reports from the colonies. The report from Philadelphia came later, and buried in it was perhaps the most important news, the appointment of a supreme commander of rebel forces:

> Yesterday Morning the Three Battalions of this City and Liberties, to-gether with the Artillery Company, a Troop of Light Horse, several Companies of Light Infantry, Rangers and Rifle-men, in the Whole about 2000, marched out to the Commons, and having joined in Brigade, were re-viewed by General WASHINGTON, who is appointed Commander in Chief of all the North-American Forces by the Honourable Continental CONGRESS, when they went through the Manual Exercise, Firings, and Manoeuvres, with great Dexterity and Exactness.
> On Thursday, the 15th Instant, was married the Rev. Mr. GEORGE CRAIG, of Chester, to Mrs. MARGARET CURRIE, of the same Place.[48]

Breaking Police, Fire Stories

While given to considerable trivia, from reporting travels and the arrival of visitors to reporting minutes of sessions, the breaking police and fire story did find its way into the paper. The news writer could pack in the "5 Ws"—the who, what, where, when, and why, and how—much as modern reporters are trained to do, but the most important information did not always appear first. Consider this "thorough" capsule report of a fire in Philadelphia in the *Gazette of the United States*. The time of day is not really the most important information. Yet the story is reasonably complete, and told as one long running sentence:

> A fire broke out this morning, about 11 o'clock A.M. in a Mr. Dawson's White Smith's Shop, back of Fourth street, near Cherry street—the shop was burnt down, but by the timely exertions of the citizens, no other material damage ensued; altho' at one time much was to be apprehended, as the fire took affect upon the roof of the German Church, which has been lately rebuilt, after having been destroyed by that terrible element.[49]

The news writers often were intent on setting the scene, giving the reader a picture of the situation before getting at the heart of the story, in this case, the stabbing of three men. From the *Aurora*:

> Yesterday several French sailors belonging to the privateers in this part, after having paraded the streets for sometime with colours flying and music playing, went on board of the Ship Apollo, lying at Champney's wharf, and asked for a loan of her colours, which the crew refused to give up. A French man then presented a national cockade [probably a ribbon of national colors] to one of the Apollo's crew, and desired him to kiss it which he objected to; upon which an affray ensued, in which three of the seamen were stabbed with daggers.[50]

And the report concluded with the jailing of the Frenchmen. The human-interest angle, at least to the extent of creating a narrative effect, dominated the ordering of the facts in eighteenth-century news reporting.

Franklin, the Educator

Articles aiming to educate, uplift, and generally improve the social and moral character of the reader found their way into the paper. Franklin, for instance, with his broad interests and scientific bent, felt it was part of his calling to try to educate his readers on some matters. Consider his celebrated essay on drunkenness in the *Pennsylvania Gazette*. In the form of a letter from an anonymous writer, the article starts off with noticing the "Occasion of a Woman whose sudden Death the Coroner's Inquest ascrib'd to the violent Effect of strong Drink"; he discusses the "Family of Poisons, to wit, *Vinous Spirits and distilled intoxicating Liquors*" and exclaims, "O happy Temperance! never too much to be praised."[51]

Franklin's *Gazette* and other papers carried announcements on the developments in medicine, including reports by Dr. John Morgan, founder of a medical college in Philadelphia. Morgan campaigned through the papers for greater regulation of the medical profession and for specialization with designated surgeons doing surgery, pharmacists dispensing drugs, and so on. Because the advanced idea of specialization would lead to a loss of revenue from practitioners who delved into all aspects of the medical profession, Morgan endured considerable criticism and even felt compelled to apologize in print for his views.

Media as Fourth Estate: Adversaries of Government

THEY CAME OUT SWINGING: THE POOR PRINTER VERSUS THE GOVERNOR

The most famous media trial in American history was the John Peter Zenger trial of 1735. Zenger, a poor printer, was recruited by a popular party faction to publish a new paper, the *New-York Weekly Journal*, to criticize the flamboyant, corrupt newly arrived governor of New York, William Cosby. Complaints against Cosby mounted from the beginning. Zenger historian Livingston Rutherfurd itemizes some of these. For instance, shortly after he arrived from England as governor, Cosby voided an agreement with the Mohawk Indians so he could collect new fees under a new

William Cosby: Corrupt governor. (Collection of The New-York Historical Society)

grant; there were reports that Cosby had refused to give land grants to settlers unless he received a third of the amount for himself;[52] Quaker voters were disfranchised for refusing to take an oath; and there were reports that the clerk of common pleas court bought his job from Cosby.[53]

Long before the American two-party system of today, two highly charged groups opposed each other in the 1730s, the court or Cosby's party and the popular party, the followers of Chief Justice Lewis Morris. The popular party gained a majority of the seats in the Assembly. Among the party leaders besides Morris were lawyers James Alexander and William Smith, both of whom had represented an interim governor who had argued that newcomer Cosby had cheated him out of fees or a partial salary.

Cosby was served by the fact that New York had only one newspaper, the *New York Gazette*, which was subsidized by the government and edited by the same William Bradford who had run into trouble with authorities in Philadelphia. He received 50 pounds a year from the Cosby government and maintained the title of the king's printer for the province of New York.[54]

Bradford's *Gazette*, eight years old in 1733, served a city of about 10,000, of which almost one-fifth (1,700) were black slaves. Quail could be shot on what is now Broadway.[55] The *Gazette* largely ignored domestic events and used primarily foreign news and ads. Bradford had working for him a German-born printer, John Peter Zenger. Some regarded Zenger as uneducated, even illiterate, even though he was a printer working with letters and words. It is known that most, if not all, of what was to appear in Zenger's own newspaper was written by others. Yet journalism historian Frederic Hudson says Zenger "was a good printer . . . something of a scholar."[56]

Zenger came to the colonies at the age of 13 in 1710, his father having died on board ship in the crossing. The next year at 14 he was apprenticed to William Bradford for eight years. Zenger later settled in Kent County in Maryland as a printer and in 1720 won a contract from the Maryland Assembly to print the session laws.

The agreement called for him to be paid 700 pounds of tobacco. In 1723 he went to New York, where he married for the second time (he was a widower). His wife, Anna, was a pioneer in Protestant Sunday school work. She was to become active in helping him put out his New York paper, and indeed some say she was the behind-the-scenes editor.

Zenger joined Bradford in a partnership in 1725, but, as Rutherfurd points out, it did not last. Apparently, only one book exists that had the imprint of both Bradford and Zenger. Zenger went into business for himself, producing mostly Dutch-language theological books and some political tracts. In 1730 he published the first arithmetic book in the colony.

A Faction Signs Up Zenger

The popular party, Morris and his allies, needed a newspaper to counter Cosby's influence in Bradford's *Gazette*. They enlisted Zenger, who proceeded to bring out the

New-York Weekly Journal, promising "the freshest Advices, Foreign and Domestic," on November 5, 1733. The mainstay power behind the *Journal* continued to be lawyer James Alexander. Much of the paper reprinted English essayists, such as Addison and Steele and "Cato," the work of Trenchard and Gordon. In the *Journal* on occasion Morris and other members of the popular party authored anti-Cosby letters anonymously.

Even the ads included bogus entries that attacked Cosby or his close advisers, such as Francis Harison, whose writings in the *Gazette* praised Cosby. Note this *Journal* ad concerning F. H.:

> A Large Spaneil, of about Five Foot Five Inches High, has lately stray'd from his Kennel with his Mouth full of fulsom Panegericks and in his Ramble dropt them in the NEW-YORK-GAZETTE; when a Puppy he was mark'd thus ⊣⊏, and a Cross in his Forehead, but the Mark being worn out, he has taken upon him in a heathenish Manner to abuse Mankind, by imposing a great many gross Falsehoods upon them. Whoever will strip the said Panegericks of all their Fulsomness and send the Beast back to his Kennel, shall have the Thanks of all honest Men, and all reasonable Charges.[57]

Such ads as these had the effect of political cartoons. Cosby was once linked to a description of a monkey.[58]

Cosby lost his patience. After two months of ingesting the *Journal*, he asked the Assembly and the Council to rein in Zenger. The Assembly declined to act on four issues of the paper which the governor had determined were particularly obnoxious, but the Council joined with the governor in the crusade against Zenger. The governor himself offered awards of 50 pounds for the conviction of the author of articles in the *Journal* and 12 pounds for the conviction of the writer of several opposition ballads that were circulating.[59]

Zenger Arrested

On a warrant from the Council, Zenger was arrested on November 17, 1734. The *Journal* skipped but a beat, missing the next issue, then reappearing. Zenger told of his arrest in the *Journal* and promised to continue to "entertain" the reader "thro' the Hole of the Door of the Prison" with the aid of his wife and "servants."[60]

At first Zenger's defenders, James Alexander and William Smith, aimed to confuse the court by challenging the commissioning of two of the new Supreme Court justices, James De Lancey, the young lawyer whom Cosby named to replace Morris, and Frederick Philipse. The new Chief Justice De Lancey reacted by promptly disbarring Alexander and Smith. Actually, Alexander himself may have been the main target of Cosby. The governor had complained vehemently to London about the "factious, disaffected and illegal behavior of Mr. Alexander," referring to Alexander's pivotal role in setting up Zenger as printer of the new paper.[61]

Zenger was charged with seditious libel, which is publishing words that incite people to resist or rebel against a government (sedition is not as clear-cut as the overt act of treason). As in the earlier trial of William Bradford as a printer for the Quakers in Philadelphia, the truth of a statement was not a defense against

A visitor studies a diorama of the burning of John Peter Zenger's New-York Weekly Journal — *an exhibit at the Sub-Treasury Building, New York.* (UPI; Temple University Libraries Photojournalism Collection)

the charge of seditious libel. It had only to be shown that the person charged made the scandalous statement. A printed viewpoint was libelous if it incited unrest and anarchy. Theoretically any statement critical of an authority could be so judged. Also the jury did not have the authority to blaze new paths in law. Its only task was to decide simply if the accused published the offensive words. English common law allowed for the freedom to publish; that is, there could be no prior restraint. But upon publication anything critical of a government was potentially seditious libel.

The Morris popular faction engaged an aged, prominent lawyer, Andrew Hamilton, from Philadelphia to take on the Zenger defense after the disbarment of Alexander and Smith. Hamilton was noted for his brilliant oratorical style and dedication to a cause. But he did not enter without some personal grudge motives of his own. He had taken part in the past in prosecuting William Bradford's son, Andrew, in Philadelphia, when Andrew criticized the Pennsylvania Assembly (Hamilton was the speaker of the Assembly). And Andrew Bradford had attacked Hamilton personally. Now was the chance for Hamilton to defend Zenger, a competitor of William Bradford, the father of Hamilton's old nemesis, Andrew Bradford.[62]

Bradford Criticizes Zenger

William Bradford responded to the Cato essays in the *Journal* by reprinting English documents that supported the regime. He apparently thought the status quo represented the people's interest, as well as his. Bradford's *Gazette* picked at Zenger's use of Cato, charging that Zenger by splicing together pieces of Cato's documents misrepresented Cato. The *Gazette* argued that Zenger put the emphasis in the wrong place by use of large type in the *Journal*. And, of course, Zenger's scurrilous ads constituted low blows "as secret arrows that fly in the dark, and wound the reputation of men much better than others."[63]

Bradford's *Gazette* filled itself with foreign news—mostly European, reports from key colonial cities, some philosophical essays, even entertainment. For example, a headline in 1733, the year that Zenger started the *Journal*, said, "For the entertainment of our readers we shall incert the following Account of the Greenland Bear, lately brought into Boston by Capt. Atkins as reported by him." The article noted the bear "is very fierce and roars" and indicated where in the city he was being exhibited.[64] Occasionally there was a report on Cosby's coming and going, such as a trip by Cosby to meet with leaders of six Indian nations in Albany, or a report to a law body in New Jersey, also under Cosby's control.

In the *Gazette*, Zenger's *Journal* gets limited attention but does elicit a few volleys—for example, the *Journal* is rapped for its silence on a "real grievance" of the Morrisites taking over the city and running it like what today would be called a party machine and for the "stupidity and barroness" of "Zenger's Correspondence" involved in the usurping of the power of mayor by a new city "Corporation."[65] Bradford was likely showing that he was generally unimpressed with what some regarded as the shrillness, lack of sincerity, and "quaisi-theater" of the "Zenger Affair."[66]

In Zenger's defense, Hamilton argued that the falsehood of a statement should exist in order to gain a conviction on seditious libel. He said the prosecution was living in the past, relying on law as defined by England's Star Chamber, which had ceased to exist in 1641. He argued that libel cases should be regarded in the same vein as other cases, including murder, where the evidence is heard and a "general" verdict of innocent or guilty is returned. Hamilton further maintained the real issues of the case were subtle. He argued that the law of seditious libel was meant to protect a king and not governors; that what is acceptable law in England does not mean it is the best law elsewhere; that a right to criticize a government is inherent in the guarantees of liberty. He said free speech was especially important in the colonies where there were no means to make the appointed governors accountable or to bring them to justice.

Interpreting the Media Trial of the Century

Some regarded the Zenger case as an extension of growing unrest in England and noted the *Journal* was modeled after the English *Craftsman*, which challenged Robert Walpole, long-term English prime minister.[67] In fact, to some the trial looked more English than American. More editions of the trial transcript were to be published in England than in the colonies before the Revolutionary War.[68]

Copeland points out that papers outside New York did not mention Zenger at the time of the trial.[69]

Some believe that the trial had more to do with religion than anything. David Paul Nord says the joining of the idea of political liberty with religious dissent was the foundation on which many of the key arguments and the trial were built. "The fundamental question was: What is truth, and how is it revealed to man?" Nord says.[70]

The Zenger trial fostered a sense of individualism, individual competency. For it was left to the individual, or a group of individuals, to decide what truth is, a concept that certainly has its roots in the Protestant Reformation, with its emphasis on the self-sufficiency of the Scriptures and the right of the individual in faith to interpret them.

Nord links the themes of Zenger and his defense with the message of the Protestant revivals that were sweeping the nation. In fact, he notes that several revival sermons dealing with the ascertaining of truth were published in Zenger's print shop. "Like the ministers of 'awakened' congregations, who were willing to reject the authority of creeds and hierarchies," says Nord, "the Zenger jurors were willing to reject the instructions of the chief justice of New York." Like the converts at revivals who insisted on their right to interpret the laws of God, the Zenger jury upheld what the jurors perceived as the right of the common person to interpret the laws of mankind. Yet "in both cases, the operative principle was not freedom, but truth. Andrew Hamilton, like a revival preacher, told the jurors that authority lay, not in them, but in truth. He did not ask them to condone individualism or to approve individual diversity of expression—only truth."[71]

A Cheering Courtroom

Zenger was acquitted in the one-day trial in August 1735, having languished in prison since November of the previous year. His acquittal set off a round of cheers.

His victory had been one reflecting politics, the power of the popular party. Nothing would change the common law as perceived until the aftermath of a similar case in 1802–1804, the attempt of a Thomas Jefferson faction to silence the cantankerous Harry Croswell. Cosby died the year after the Zenger verdict in 1736. Yet it has been said that the Zenger trial actually helped neutralize libel as a tool to restrict speech and represented an early awareness of the developing popular basis of American politics. Although there was no real legal victory (the trial had been decided contrary to existing law, and the jury had no right to make new law), the Zenger trial did provide an inspiration to later fourth estate adversaries of government and planted psychologically the seeds of a two-party system.[72]

Zenger himself was named public printer for New York two years later and continued to print a fairly dull *Journal* until his death in 1746.

XCIII.

THE
New-York Weekly JOURNAL

Containing the freſheſt Adwices, Foreign, and Domeſtick.

MUNDAY Auguſt 18th, 1735.

To my Subſcribers and Benefactors.

Gentlemen ;

I Think my ſelf in Duty bound to to make publick Acknowledgment for the many Favours received at your Hands, which I do in this Manner return you my hearty Thanks for. I very ſoon intend to print my Tryal at Length, that the World may ſee how unjuſt my Sufferings have been, ſo will only at this Time give this ſhort Account of it.

On *Munday* the *4th* Inſtant my Tryal for Printing Parts of my Journal *No.* 13. and 23. came on, in the Supreme Court of this Province, before the moſt numerous Auditory of People, I may with Juſtice ſay, that ever were ſeen in that Place at once ; my Jury ſworn were,

1 *Harmanus Rutgers,*
2 *Stanley Holms,*
3 *Edward Man,*
4 *John Bell,*
5 *Samuel Weaver,*
6 *Andrew Marſchalk,*
7 *Egbert Van Borſen,*
8 *Thomas Hunt,*
9 *Benjamin Hildrith,*
10 *Abraham Kiteltas,*
11 *John Goelet,*
12 *Hercules Wendover,*

John Chambers, Eſq; had been appointed the Term before by the Court as my Council, in the Place of *James Alexander* and *William Smith,* who were then ſilenced on my Account, and to Mr. *Chambers's* Aſſiſtance came *Andrew Hamilton,* Eſq; of *Philadelphia* Barreſter at Law ; when Mr Attorney offered the Information and the Proofs, Mr. *Hamilton* told him, he would acknowledge my Printing and Publiſhing the Papers in the Information, and ſave him the Trouble of that Proof, and offered to prove the Facts of thoſe Papers true, and had Witneſſes ready to prove every Fact ; he long inſiſted on the Liberty of Making Proof thereof, but was over-ruled therein. Mr. Attorney offered no Proofs of my Papers being *falſe, malicious* and *ſeditious,* as they were charged to be, but inſiſted that they were Lybels tho' true. There were many Arguments and Authorities on this point, and the Court were of Opinion with Mr. Attorney on that Head : But the Jury having taken the Information out with them, they returned in about Ten Minutes, and found me *Not Guilty* ; upon which there were immediately three Hurra's of many Hundreds of People in the preſence of the Court, before the Verdict was returned. The next Morning my Diſcharge was moved for and granted, and ſufficient was ſub.

John Peter Zenger's New-York Weekly Journal *No. 93 (August 18, 1735)*
The issue published after the celebrated trial, which announced the vindication of a free press.
Lent by the Library of Congress.

*Zenger announces trial verdict and plans. (Philadelphia Bulletin;
Temple University Libraries Photojournalism Collection)*

QUESTIONS FOR DISCUSSION AND RESEARCH

1. What are some of the reasons—economic, religious, political—for the early arrival of printing in the Americas?
2. In what ways did English culture, law, and practice leave their mark on colonial newspapers?
3. What facets of the colonial paper that reflect the English experience continue to this day?
4. Compare the colonial reading audience and today's.

5. Today's newcomers in journalism are expected to serve a kind of trial period or apprenticeship, but how is the idea of "apprenticeship" today different from the colonial idea of apprenticeship?

6. How has language, including spellings, changed, and why? Discuss some examples.

7. Consider some of the religions and denominations prominent in your community. What role did they play in developing the role of the press and its ideas?

8. Were there some "witch-hunts" involving early editors? Define and explain. (We will see the term *witch-hunts* as a popular phrase in the 1950s as Congress, members of Congress, and committees reacted to the fear of communism.)

9. Whose claim to having launched the first newspaper in the colonies do you support? Why?

10. What do you like and dislike about the Franklins—James and Benjamin?

11. Was Samuel Keimer as dumb as Benjamin Franklin and some accounts make him sound?

12. Think of ways the reader could rely on the colonial newspaper for information and education.

13. How would you rewrite the two news items on page 57 (fire and French sailors stories) for use in a newspaper today?

14. Assess the results of the Zenger trial. How important was it? What did it help change and what did it not change?

15. What are several ways in which newspaper advertising was different in colonial times?

ENDNOTES

1. In Spanish, *Breve y Mas Compendiosa Doctrina Cristiana en Lengua Mexicana y Castellana*. See Al Hester, "Newspapers and Newspaper Prototypes in Spanish America, 1541–1750," in *Journalism History*, vol. 6, no. 3, Autumn 1979, pp. 73, 74.

2. Victoria Goff, *Hojas Volantes: The Beginning of Print Journalism in the Americas*. A paper presented to a meeting of the American Journalism Historians Association, Oct. 3–7, 1990, in Coeur d'Alene, Idaho. The original copy of the 1541 *Relacion del espantable terremoto* is in the Hemeroteca Nacional de Mexico.

3. John W. Moore, *Historical Notes on Printers and Printing 1420 to 1886* (first published, 1886; reprinted, New York: Burt Franklin, 1968), p. 145. Journalism historians differ on Glover's first name: Willard Grosvenor Bleyer in *Main Currents in the History of American Journalism* (Boston: Houghton Mifflin, 1927) says Joseph, p. 43; John Clyde Oswald in *Printing in the Americas* (New York: Gregg, 1937; Hacker Art Books, 1968), says Jose, p. 41.

4. Bleyer, *Main Currents*, p. 43.

5. Harry M. Ward, *Colonial America, 1607–1763* (Englewood Cliffs, N.J.: Prentice Hall, 1991), p. 7.

6. Ralph Frasca, " 'To Prepare the Minds of the Publick': Benjamin Franklin's German-Language Printing Partnerships," a paper presented at the Association for Education in Journalism and Mass Communication convention, Atlanta, Aug. 10, 1994.

7. Ward, *Colonial America*, p. 192.

8. Ibid.

9. Maurice R. Cullen, Jr., "Middle-Class Democracy and the Press in Colonial America," *Journalism Quarterly*, Autumn 1969, vol. 46, no. 3, p. 532.

10. Ward, *Colonial America*, p. 267.

11. Ibid., p. 368.

12. Ibid., p. 370.

13. Williston Walker, *A History of the Christian Church* (New York: Charles Scribner's Sons, 1950), pp. 479, 480.

14. John William Wallace, "An Address Delivered at the Celebration by the New-York Historical Society, May 20, 1863, of the Two Hundreth Birthday of Mr. William Bradford" (Albany, N.Y.: J. Munsell, 1863), p. 25.

15. Wallace, "An Address," p. 27, quoting "Minutes of Provincial Council," pp. i, 115.

16. Ibid., pp. 49, 50. Examination was Feb. 9, 1689.

17. Ibid., pp. 51, 52.

18. Anna Janney DeArmond, *Andrew Bradford: Colonial Journalist* (Newark: University of Delaware Press, 1949), p. 5.

19. Wallace, "An Address," p. 57.

20. Ibid., p. 75, quoting "Minutes of the Council," Oct. 31, 1700.

21. Ward, *Colonial America*, p. 195.

22. "General Court Records" (Mss.), vi, 283; quoted in Clyde Augustus Duniway, *The Development of Freedom of the Press in Massachusetts* (Cambridge, Mass.: Harvard University Press, 1906), p. 71.

23. Duniway, *Development of Freedom*, p. 73.

24. Ibid., 73. Duniway quotes from the account of the trial in the "Records of Superior Court of Judicature, 1695–1700, Ipswich."

25. Bernard Bailyn, *The Ideological Origins of the American Revolution* (Cambridge, Mass.: Belknap Press of Harvard University Press, 1967), p. 33.

26. *The Club of Odd Volumes*, printed for William G. Shillaber by the University Press, Cambridge, U.S.A., Boston, 1902.

27. Lyman Horace Weeks and Edwin M. Bacon, *An Historical Digest of the Provincial Press* (Boston: Society for Americana, 1911), p. 21.

28. *Publick Occurrences*, Sept. 25, 1690.

29. *Boston News-Letter*, April 24, 1704.

30. Ibid., May 1, 1704.

31. Ibid., Aug. 28, 1704.

32. John Tebbel, *The Compact History of the American Newspaper* (New York: Hawthorn Books, 1963), p. 16.

33. Ibid., p. 17.

34. Roderick E. McGrew, in *The Encyclopedia of Medical History* (New York: McGraw-Hill, 1985), pp. 155, 156.

35. William David Sloan, The *New-England Courant: Voice of Anglicism*, a paper presented to a meeting of the American Journalism Historians Association, Oct. 3–7, 1990, in Coeur d'Alene, Idaho.

36. Benjamin Franklin, *The Autobiography*, part 1, in J. A. Leo Lemay, compiler, *Franklin Writings* (New York: Library of America, 1987, by Literary Classics of the United States, New York), p. 1324.

37. Franklin, *Autobiography*, p. 1331.

38. Ibid., pp. 1332, 1333.

39. *American Weekly Mercury*, Jan. 21–Jan. 28, 1728–1729.

40. *Pennsylvania Gazette*, Nov. 21, 1728.

41. *American Weekly Mercury*, May 31, 1722.
42. Gary Huxford, "The English Libertarian Tradition in the Colonial Newspaper," *Journalism Quarterly*, vol. 45, no. 4, Winter 1968, p. 679.
43. DeArmond, *Andrew Bradford*, p. 90.
44. *American Weekly Mercury*, Feb. 19–26, 1722.
45. *Pennsylvania Gazette*, Sept. 25–Oct. 2, 1729.
46. *Pennsylvania Gazette*, Dec. 30, 1736.
47. David A. Copeland, "It Was Really a Feast: Correcting Misconceptions about Colonial Newspaper Content," paper presented at the American Journalism Historians Association meeting in Roanoke, Va., October 1994.
48. *Pennsylvania Gazette*, June 21, 1775.
49. *Gazette of the United States*, Jan. 11, 1798.
50. *Aurora*, May 14, 1794.
51. *Pennsylvania Gazette*, Feb. 1, 1732–1733.
52. Livingston Rutherfurd, *John Peter Zenger: His Press, His Trial and a Bibliography of Zenger Imprints* (Gloucester, Mass.: Peter Smith, 1933; Dodd, Mead & Co., 1941), p. 38.
53. Ibid., pp. 20–23.
54. Rutherfurd, *John Peter Zenger*, p. 8; William Smith, *History of the Colony of New York from Its Founding to 1762*, vol. 2, p. 15.
55. Rutherfurd, *John Peter Zenger*, p. 25.
56. Frederic Hudson, *Journalism in the United States, from 1690 to 1872* (New York: Harper & Row, 1969), p. 81.
57. *New-York Weekly Journal*, Nov. 26, 1733.
58. Ibid., Dec. 10, 1733.
59. Rutherfurd, *John Peter Zenger*, p. 43.
60. *New-York Weekly Journal*, Nov. 25, 1734.
61. Cathy Covert, " 'Passion Is Ye Prevailing Motive': The Feud Behind the Zenger Case," *Journalism Quarterly*, vol. 50, Spring 1973, p. 3.
62. DeArmond, *Andrew Bradford*, pp. 84–113.
63. *New-York Weekly Journal*, March 25–April 1, 1734.
64. *New York Gazette*, April 9–16, 1733.
65. *Gazette*, Oct. 27–Nov. 3, 1735.
66. Stephen Botein, "Introduction," in American Antiquarian Society Facsimiles, No. 3, *Mr. Zenger's Malice and Falsehood—Six Issues of the New-York Weekly Journal, 1733–34*, a publication of the American Antiquarian Society's Program in the History of the Book in American Culture (Worcester, Mass.: AAS, 1985), p. 6.
67. Ibid.
68. Ibid., p. 5.
69. Copeland, "It Was Really a Feast."
70. David Paul Nord, "The Authority of Truth: Religion and the John Peter Zenger Case," *Journalism Quarterly*, vol. 62, Summer 1985, p. 231.
71. Ibid., p. 235.
72. Paul Finkelman, "The Zenger Case: Prototype of a Political Trial," in Michal R. Belknap, *American Political Trials* (Westport, Conn.: 1981), pp. 21–42. Cited by Botein, "Introduction," p. 5.

4

The First Hundred Years—
Section Two
Revolution and Restrictions:
Rounding Out the Century

The Zenger trial offered some hint of the passion for revolution. Although it took nearly seventy years for the cause of Zenger to take legal root, at least a psychological note for greater freedom was sounded in the Zenger trial. Historian Bernard Bailyn pointed out in *Faces of Revolution* that a contributory factor to the Revolutionary War was a strong distaste in colonial America for corruption, inspired perhaps by the religious bearings of the colonies. The spirited hurrahs that rang through the courtroom following the decision that vindicated Zenger were a celebration of the people over the corrupt activities of a governor. Symbolically, it could be noted, the acclaim was an expression of the power of the people, a power that could challenge existing laws. Citizens were particularly aroused by the movement of Parliament in the years that followed from a policy of benign neglect to one of imposing regulations and taxation that the colonists saw as tantamount to slavery.[1]

The French and Indian War—an extended skirmish between the French and British, with Indian allies, beginning in 1754 then catapulting into the Seven Years' War, which raged on a broad scale in Europe—was an occasion for discussion of solidification. The British needed a united front or at least a cooperative effort on the part of colonial militia to ward off the threat of the French and their hostile Indian allies. And there was growing awareness of a need for unity in order to work toward home rule.

A famous "revolutionary" symbol was born in this early period—the drawing (political cartoon?) of a divided snake, which has power if its parts are joined, with the words "Join, or Die," which appeared in Franklin's *Pennsylvania Gazette* in 1754. Later becoming a symbol for uniting against Britain, the fragmented snake symbol, printed twenty-two years before the Declaration of Independence, originally called

The symbol of a divided snake, used to rouse the patriots against the British, was originally drawn to encourage unity under Britain against the French in the French and Indian War. It appeared in the Pennsylvania Gazette *in 1754.*

for a uniting of political and military strength for the greater good of the colonies and the crown.

At the end of the Seven Years' War in 1763, Britain, being 130 million pounds in debt, turned to the burgeoning American colonies. First there was the Revenue Act of 1764, known as the Sugar Act, the first law passed by Parliament with the explicit purpose of raising funds for the crown in the colonies. It raised the duties on refined sugar, thus striking at the profitable colonial trade in rum. Then came the first internal tax imposed on the colonies by Parliament, the Stamp Act of 1765. It called for buying stamps to be put on all newspapers, licenses, bonds, advertisements, and legal documents. In so doing, Parliament stirred up perhaps the two most influential groups in colonial society, the newspaper editors-printers and the lawyers.

The multifaceted opposition to the crown was coming to a head, as violence rippled across the colonies. The day the Stamp Act took effect, a screeching mob in New York broke into the governor's property, destroyed his carriage, and then stormed uptown to the dwelling of a particularly avid enforcer of the Stamp Act, ransacked the house, burned the books, pulled up the garden, and made good use of the agent's liquor supply. Mobs destroyed houses and furniture of tax agents in Boston and terrified another agent in Charleston.

The media reacted almost uniformly in opposition to the Stamp Act. They protested by editorials, brief cessation of publication, or even making the point in layout. William Bradford III (nephew of Andrew Bradford) printed his paper, the *Pennsylvania Journal and Weekly Advertiser*, with a heavy border shaped like a tombstone. The response was pivotal in shaping the press and its power, says Julie Hedgepeth Williams, of the University of Alabama. "The press did print a consistent, unvarying picture to all colonists at the time of the Stamp Act," she says. "In that way, the Stamp Act press became young America's first true mass medium, for it communicated the same ideas and the same stories to everyone, regardless of locality."[2]

In England, Parliament followed with the Declaratory Act, which affirmed the right of Parliament to "bind" the colonies in any way, in effect stating the right to extend taxation. Then came the controversial Townshend Acts, one of which ordered suspension of the New York Assembly until it complied with the Quartering Act, which called for providing housing and food for British troops. A second act levied taxes on lead, glass, paper, painters' products, and tea. A third act gave agents of the crown the right to search for contraband products in warehouses and private homes. A final act in the series created new courts to try without a jury those who violated the law.

Media as Voices of Freedom

BEATING THE DRUMS OF REVOLUTION

A conservative Philadelphia lawyer, John Dickinson, tried to play the role of mediator, and he was influential with a series of twelve "Farmer's Letters," which he wrote for colonial papers. Advising calm, he called for pursuing liberty within the royal framework. Contrary to his intentions, his writings probably had more influence on the coming schism than the author had expected. Typically he wrote:

> The cause of liberty is a "cause of too much dignity, to be sullied by turbulence and tumults." . . .
> I hope, my dear countrymen, that you will in every colony be upon your guard against those who may at any time endeavour to stir you up under pretences of patriotism, to any measures disrespectful to our sovereign and our mother-country. Hot, rash, disorderly proceedings injure the reputation of a people.[3]

Yet Dickinson, despite his conservatism in his "Letters" series, wrote stirring freedom ballads. In "The Liberty Song," in 1768, he rang out with "Come, join Hand in Hand, brave AMERICANS all, And rouse your bold Hearts at fair LIBERTY'S Call; No tyrannous Acts shall suppress your just Claim, Or stain with Dishonour AMERICA'S Name. In FREEDOM we're BORN, and in FREEDOM we'll LIVE."[4]

Catalyst of Dissent

But a fiery brand—a hot, rash, disorderly sort—emerged to stir the cauldron of revolution. Such inspiration came from an unknown trained, nonpracticing lawyer and failed businessman, who, it was discovered, had a flair for leadership and organization. Raised in a strict religious home—he could say the Lord's Prayer at age two—and shaped in his academic years by English philosopher John Locke, Samuel Adams gave the growing discontent a sense of mission and the urgency of a holy war. He gave fury to John Locke's beliefs that no government was absolute, that the people retain rights of their own, and that a government that is not acting for the public good loses its mandate from the people. People have a right to overthrow such governments, Locke maintained. Further he held that government functions

Samuel Adams: Stirring the cauldron of revolution. (Portrait by John Singleton Copley)

should be separate, with distinct executive, legislative, and judicial branches. Adams' notebooks contained many quotations from Locke.[5]

When Samuel Adams failed as a businessman (his actual business is not known) after graduating from Harvard, he was taken into the family brewery business by his father. ("Samuel Adams" beer is still a brand today.) Adams perhaps acquired his interest in politics from his father, who was a member of the Massachusetts Bay General Assembly.

When the 25-year-old Adams was banned from membership in the exclusive Caucus Club because of his youth, he and others formed their own club for political debate, first without a name, then dubbed the Whipping-Post Club. They published a weekly newspaper, the *Public Advertiser*, and circulars. The paper, offering little news, contained mostly opinion. Adams produced an essay, "Loyalty and Sedition," which portended his eventual role as a first-rate propagandist. He presented his themes in simple, direct terms, reducing even the most complicated issues to fundamentals. He used exaggerated images and generously interspersed his writing with exciting adverbs and adjectives that would win the day with his readers. "There were few grays in the written world of Sam Adams," says his biographer, Paul Lewis. "His convictions were presented as unalterable truths, and to oppose them he set up straw men he then demolished."[6]

Adams, a cousin of future President John Adams, was like a tornado when the Stamp Act was passed in 1765. Sam Adams, in the forefront of organizing meetings of opposition, published a series of essays in the *Boston Gazette*. Blamed for helping to incite the rioting in Boston, Adams, nevertheless, penned a forceful article in the *Gazette* condemning the mob actions.

Adams wrote letters to radical leaders in the colonies and kept the correspondence going even if they did not reply. He included news from Boston and tidbits and gossip that he picked up from other papers and sources. Others sent him items. Out of those who exchanged news and various items came the focal Committee of Correspondence, eventually a base for forming the First Continental Congress. Adams and his radical colleagues, the Sons of Liberty, launched an intercolonial propaganda publication, the *Journal of Occurences*. Its fare ranged from complaints of lack of representation to alleged crimes of assault and rape by British troops quartered in Boston.

Wordsmith of the Revolution

Arriving on the troubled colonial scene from England at the end of 1774 was perhaps the person who was to become the best known of the radical writers who stirred the emotions that fomented and defended the revolution. A former corset maker and tax man in England, Tom Paine came to the colonies with letters of recommendation from Benjamin Franklin, who was in England lobbying on behalf of the colonies. Paine, given a chance to contribute to the first issue of Robert Aitken's *Pennsylvania Magazine*, so impressed Aitken that Paine was made editor. He wrote informational pieces and some crusading articles, such as his antislavery essay "African Slavery in America." He also attacked the practice of dueling, the inhumane treatment of animals, and the use of excessive titles.

Paine's pamphlet *Common Sense*, appearing in January 1776, helped ignite the fire of revolution. Starting off modestly with a printing of 6,000, by March it had sold 120,000 copies, becoming perhaps the continent's first best-seller. Already the first shots of the Revolutionary War had been fired April 19, 1775, at Lexington, Massachusetts, as the British marched to Concord to destroy a munitions dump. They were met by a small force of minutemen. Rallying at Concord's North Bridge, the colonial contingent turned back three companies of British infantry.

Common Sense, coming on the threshhold of the Declaration of Independence, outlined the purpose of government—to serve the people. It attacked the British system as "imperfect, subject to convulsions, and incapable of producing what it seems to promise." Paine argued that all people are created equal and invoked the Almighty on the side of the patriots. He proceeded at length to reason with "simple facts, plain arguments, and common sense,"[7] refuting that a British connection is necessary, that Britain is a protector of the colonies, and that Britain acts like a

Tom Paine: Not a paragon of common sense. (Painting by Romney, National Archives)

good parent. He outlined disadvantages of continuing union with Britain—it would only involve the colonies in Britain's ongoing European wars, for instance. He then called for creating a continental conference to draw up a constitution or "Charter of the United Colonies." He reaffirmed America's natural right to form a government. The last cord between crown and colonies "is now broken," he declared.[8] He signed off with a call for a first step, a Declaration of Independence.

Paine's *Common Sense*, despite its influence and power, along with Paine himself are not fully appreciated by some historians. Harvard's Bernard Bailyn called Paine "an ignoramus, both in ideas and in the practice of politics, next to Adams, Wilson, Jefferson and Madison. He could not discipline his thoughts. . . . Paine's writing was not meant to probe unknown realities of a future way of life, or to convince or to explain; it was meant to overwhelm and destroy."[9]

After the Declaration of Independence, Paine enlisted in a volunteer militia, then served as an aide-de-camp to General Nathanael Greene. With the defeat of George Washington on Long Island and the flight of Washington and his ragtag army to the Delaware in a bitter winter, Paine wrote the first of his *Crisis* papers, acknowledging, "These are the times that try men's souls."

Paine in Danger in Europe

Paine later went back to Europe and became involved in both British and French affairs. In England, this contentious man who created the best-seller in America, *Common Sense*, produced *The Rights of Man*, which he estimated sold nearly a half million copies in a decade, becoming perhaps the most widely read book in England up to that time. It called for dethroning of mad King George III ("His Madjesty," Paine called him) and empowering the common man. Paine had to stay one step ahead of the law, hounded by government agents and the endless propaganda the British government unleashed on this most controversial man in Britain. Labeled "a wicked, malicious, seditious, and ill-disposed person," he was charged with propagating "seditious libel."[10]

In addition, in Britain, it was a tug-of-war between Paine with no-nonsense language versus the flowery and formal utterings of statesman Edmund Burke. Paine's tactic was to pay "attention to techniques such as the choice of idiom, the rhythm of the prose, and the pattern of sentence construction, all of which aimed to subvert the conventionally pompous prose of Burke's tract," says Paine's biographer, John Keane.[11]

In France, given honorary citizenship and elected a representative from Calais to the revolutionary National Convention, Paine was given special status and often addressed the revolutionary body. Siding apparently with the Girondin faction against the more hotheaded Jacobins, Paine dared to argue for sparing the life of the deposed king, Louis XVI, suggesting that he be exiled to the United States. Blind to the dark side of the revolution at first, Paine continued to take unpopular views even in the rebel assembly. Finally he got a message that he would appear on a future death list, and though he wanted to leave France, he did not dare try. Taken away at last in the dark hours of an early morning, Paine languished for months in the notorious Luxembourg prison. He was released at last at the ebbing of the revolution and by the intervention of the U.S. minister to France, James Monroe.

When Paine returned to America in 1802, he was at first warmly received, but then denounced even by his old friend Samuel Adams as an infidel. Paine, who was also a bridge designer peddling his ideas overseas, over the years alienated himself with an American audience. He attacked Washington, and, because his *Age of Reason* described a godless world, he loomed as a threat to the status quo. He was even allegedly implicated, perhaps unjustly, in developing a plan for revolutionary France's takeover of the new nation, the United States.[12]

Back in America after the turn of the century, he wrote pieces for the *New York Public Advertiser*. He had few friends. Innkeepers refused him lodging. Drinking even more heavily and without friends, he died in 1809. It is said only six persons attended his funeral.

Traitor or Double Agent?

During the Revolutionary War there were, of course, loyalist or Tory editors who affirmed their allegiance to the king. James Rivington, owner of the first book chain in the Americas—with outlets in Boston, New York, and Philadelphia—was also publisher of a newspaper, *Rivington's New York Gazetteer or the Connecticut, New Jersey, Judson's River and Quebec Weekly Advertiser*. He at first was noted for his objectivity, but after hostilities started, he renamed his paper the *Royal Gazette*. For all practical purposes, it seemed to be the flagship paper for the royal cause. Rivington was so despised as he continued his *Gazette* in New York under British occupation that Governor William Livingston of New Jersey declared: "If Rivington is taken, I must have one of his ears; Governor Clinton [of New York] is entitled to the other; and General Washington, if he pleases, may take his head."[13]

But when patriot troops entered New York, Rivington was allowed to stay. The fact he got off scot-free has suggested to some writers and historians that perhaps he played a double role, actually working for General Washington while appearing to side with the British and publishing a Tory paper behind British lines. There are references to him in a code dictionary designed for the use of spies in 1779, and there are several letters from Washington's spies that quote Rivington. But such evidence is not enough to keep alive the myth that Rivington was a spy for Washington, according to John L. Lawson, who researched Rivington in his studies at the University of California. Believing that any information that allegedly came from Rivington was of little military value and noting that George Washington showed hostility against the publisher in satirical comments long after the war, Lawson argues that Rivington and other "Tory" editors were left unmolested after the war because of a respect for freedom of the press.[14]

Media as Voices of Reform

A PIONEER OF MODERN INVESTIGATIVE REPORTING

One of the strong-willed editors of the era after the war for independence was a chunky, keen-eyed Tory, William Cobbett. Having come to America in 1792 in flight from the law in England, he curiously throughout his life retained a loyalty to his native country. Besides being a firebrand, denouncing fellow editors in Philadelphia where he settled (returning to England in 1800), he had a passion for reform and justice. "In his liberal use and analysis of documentary evidence," says one of his biographers, Daniel Green, "he may well be thought of as a pioneer of what is now called investigative journalism."[15]

His investigative work began with his attempt to reform the British army where he served for seven years. In the barracks, joined by another concerned soldier as a witness, he stayed up late at night copying records that showed that officers reported false musters to gain new rations, took work money from privates for favors, sold off clothing, cheated on food and fuel supplies, and so on. He later wrote: "To work we went, and during a long winter, while the rest were boozing and snoring, we gutted no small part of the regimental books, rolls and other documents. Our way was this: to take a copy, sign it with our names, and clap the regimental seal to it, so that we might be able to swear to it, when produced in court."[16] Cobbett

William Cobbett: A probing editor always in trouble. (Portrait by J. R. Smith, Library of Congress)

waited until he was out of the army to press charges. But the army countered to protect its own. Cobbett learned that members of his former regiment were about to swear that he had made an unpatriotic toast at a party. Since he was still in the military at the time, this raised the possibility of his being arrested for treason. When the men were acquitted of corruption charges, he also learned that they were about to sue, and so he fled to America.

In Philadelphia in his writings—poems, articles, pamphlets—Cobbett took up the cause of England against France, savaged the pro-French Tom Paine, and hurled his "venom" toward Thomas Jefferson and the Republicans. His remarks were so barbed that a critic compared him to a porcupine. In March 1797 he launched a newspaper, and because he liked being thought of as a porcupine, he called it *Porcupine's Gazette and Daily Advertiser.*

Beyond attacking foes of George Washington and John Adams and the foes of the Federalists in general, Cobbett embarked on reforming crusades. He exposed the scheme of two businessmen who sought to enlist the help of congressmen to buy 20 million acres of Indian Territory; the two would then offer shares to all congressmen who voted to permit the sale. Cobbett took to covering special issues and let his wrath fall on all parties. He gathered examples of how slaves and blacks were treated by Republicans and Federalists and showed how such treatment belied the axiom that all are created equal. He crusaded for "family values," showing how ads in newspapers led to breaking of family ties. In *Porcupine's Gazette*, June 1797, he cited as an example an ad from a John Bolton who was cautioning the public to avoid his wife who had eloped from home and was behaving in an "indecent manner."

Bloodletting Cure Exposed

But one celebrated crusade of Cobbett's investigative reporting was to prove the cause for his return to England in 1800. Philadelphia was in the throes of yet another yellow fever epidemic in 1797. One of the theories for combating it, practiced by the noted Dr. Benjamin Rush, was to relieve the "pressure" in the body in order to curb hemorrhages and vomiting associated with the disease. This the good doctor would do by inducing excessive bleeding, purging, and restricting the patient to a starvation diet until the "pressures" abated.

Good investigative reporter as he was, Cobbett followed "the paper trail." He compared the death statistics with those of the doctors who had treated the deceased. He found that more of Dr. Rush's patients succumbed to yellow fever than patients of other doctors. He attacked Rush in the *Gazette* and his pamphlets, nicknaming him "Dr. Sangrado," after the barber-surgeon in Alain René Le Sage's popular novel of the day, *Gil Blas of Santillane.* Cobbett put it simply, satirically: "Every farmer's son is, in some degree, a practical phlebotomist. I have cut the throats of scores of geese and little pigs, and I have always perceived that the moment the blood was out of the body the poor creature died."[17]

Other doctors backed Cobbett, and Federalist editor John Fenno of the *Gazette of the United States* sided with him. But it was Cobbett whom the irate Rush cited in a libel action. Cobbett moved to New York to be out of the Pennsylvania court's jurisdiction, but was convicted in absentia. He was assessed $5,000 for damages and $2,000 for costs. With very little cash at hand, with his capital invested in his business, Cobbett faced disaster. Appeals failed. His Philadelphia property was seized and sold at a pittance. Persisting with his vendetta against Rush and the justice system, he published a monthly, *The American Rush-Light.* This quickly opened the possibility of new libel actions. Cobbett's lawyers begged him to get out of the country fast. At last getting the message, Cobbett sailed in June 1800 back to England. Except for a return period in 1817–1818, he remained in England until his death in

1835. In England he edited the *Political Register* and began the publication of proceedings of Parliament—*Parliamentary Debates*—and his *Parliamentary History of England*, which would run 36 volumes between 1806 and 1820, both of which were "of the greatest historical importance."[18]

Always the reformer, he campaigned for what Americans would call separation of church and state in funding matters. He objected to new laws passed by Parliament supplementing the salaries of poor clergy and providing 1 million pounds for new church buildings in urban areas in 1818, all at public expense. In both instances, Cobbett thought the church itself should pay the expenses and not expect a heavily taxed population to shoulder further burdens.[19]

He attacked the excessive pensions of government officials in his *Register*. His challenge of the horror of flogging as a military discipline resulted in his being hauled to court on a seditious libel charge—it was said he undermined morale and encouraged mutiny. Convicted, he spent two years in prison. In his last days he was a member of the House of Commons, where he proved to be the ever-ready gadfly, giving more speeches than most and crusading for relief for the poor and shorter working hours for children in factories. "There was," says Green, "in short, something of the bulldog as well as of the Porcupine in the man who would always inimitably remain William Cobbett."[20]

Media as Vehicles of Sensationalism/Entertainment

DEATH OF A QUEEN MAKES A FRONT PAGE

From Benjamin Harris's 1690 attempt at a newspaper with its stories about Indian barbarity and the French king's dalliance with his daughter-in-law to the vituperative, name-calling rivalries in the politicized press at the end of the century, sensationalism in terms of content was alive and well. The masses were titillated and provided with human interest and entertainment. With all the horrible details that would make modern tabloids envious, the distinguished Isaiah Thomas in his *Massachusetts Spy* surely caught the attention of prurient and serious readers alike with his front-page account of the death of French queen Marie Antoinette:[21]

> When she heard her sentence read, she did not shew the smallest alteration in her countenance, and left the Hall without saying a single word to the judges or to the people. It was then half past four in the morning, Oct. 16. The Queen was conducted to the condemned hold in the prison of the Conciergerie.
>
> At five o'clock the Generale was beat.—At seven, the whole armed force was on foot; cannon were planted on the squares, and at the extremities of the bridges, from the Palace to the Square de la Revolution. At ten o'clock numerous patroles passed through the streets.
>
> At half past eleven in the morning, Marie Antoniette was brought out of the prison, dressed in a white dishabille. Like other malefactors, she was conducted upon a common cart to the place of execution.
>
> Her beautiful hair from behind was entirely cut off, and her hands were tied behind her back. Besides her dishabille, she wore a very small white cap. Her back was turned to the horse's tail.

During her trial she wore a dress of a white and black mixture.

On her right, upon the cart, was seated the executioner; upon the left a constitutional priest, belonging to the Metropolitan Church of Notre Dame, dressed in a grey coat, and wearing what is commonly called a bob wig. The cart was escorted by numerous detachments of horse and foot. Henriot, Roussin, and Boulanger, Generals of the Revolutionary army, preceded by the rest of the staff officers, rode before the cart.

An immense mob, especially women, crowded the streets, insulting the Queen, and vociferating "Long live the Republick!" She seldom cast her eyes upon the populace, and beheld with a cold indifference the great armed force of 30,000 men, which lined the streets in double ranks.

The sufferings which she sustained during her captivity had much altered her appearance, and the hair on her forehead appeared as white as snow.

The Queen, without anguish or bigotry, was speaking to the priest seated by her side. Her spirits were neither elevated nor depressed; she seemed quite insensible to the shouts of "Vive la Republique!" She even shewed a kind of satisfaction in looking for the moment which might rid her of her miserable existence.

When she passed through the street called Rue St. Honore, she sometimes attentively looked at the inscriptions of the words LIBERTY AND EQUALITY, affixed to the outside of the houses.

She ascended the scaffold with seeming haste and impatience, and then turned her eyes with great emotion towards the garden of the Tuilleries, the former abode of her greatness.

At half past twelve o'clock the guillotine severed her head from her body. She died in the 38th year of her age.

The executioner lifted and shewed the bloodstreaming head from the four different corners of the scaffold, which is shewn only from one side in all other common executions. The mob instantly vociferated, "Long live the Republick!"

A young man who dipped his pocket handkerchief in the Queen's blood, and pressed it with veneration to his breast, was instantly apprehended. Upon him were found the portraits of Louis XVI. and Marie Antoniette.

The corpse of the ill fated Queen was immediately after buried in a grave filled with quick lime, in the church yard called de la Madelaine, where Louis XVI. was buried in the same manner.

Entertainment Reviews

The papers carried extensive announcements of formal entertainment, namely news of the most recent theater offerings. A night in the theater offered double and triple headers of plays, music, and dance. For instance, the *General Advertiser* in Philadelphia promised theatergoers March 3, 1794, this complete fare of entertainment: "A comedy called The School for Scandal . . . at the end of the Comedy a new comic Dance, composed by Mr. Francis, called The Scheming Clown, or, The Sportsman Deceived by Mr. Francis, Mr. Darling, jun., and Mrs. de Marque. To which will be added a comic opera, called The Poor Soldier, with the original overture and accompaniments."[22]

Rather sophisticated full reviews sometimes followed the theater announcements. In the *Gazette of the United States* a play review began with this sarcasm:

> The new Comedy of the Will, which was brought forward at the New-Theatre last evening, wanted in nothing but a more perfect acquaintance with the characters on the part of the performers. . . . It is an evil which admits of no extenuation, that Mr. Prompter is the most conspicuous actor in every original representation. This is not only an injustice to the author but a disgrace to the performer—for 'tis a sin in a man to neglect the prime duty of his vocation.[23]

Media as Definers and Keepers of Values (and Biases)

TRADITIONS UPHELD BY WOMEN PRINTERS

Family values emphasizing the close-knit family and the work ethic certainly were high in the ranking of practical values, standards, and goals. Families carried on family businesses, much like small businesses today, with the wife and offspring involved and carrying on when the male head of the household died. They worked together. Printers were no exception.

Newspaper mastheads are full of names of widows who replaced their husbands. The first woman editor of a newspaper in America, some believe, was Elizabeth Timothy, who took the helm of the *South Carolina Gazette* when her husband was killed in an accident in 1738.[24] Among other widows who became editors were Dinah Nuthead and Anne Catharine Green in Maryland, Clementina Rind in Virginia, Elizabeth Oswald in Philadelphia, and Ann Franklin and Sarah Updike Goddard in Rhode Island. Goddard's daughter and son, Mary Katherine and William, worked together on the *Maryland Journal* (after working with their mother in Rhode Island); Katherine was manager for 10 years as William devoted his time to developing a postal system. And, of course, the widows of the famous John Peter Zenger and Andrew Bradford carried on the family tradition and continued their work after their husbands' deaths. In many cases these women did not just fall into the job, but were well educated and trained, with high motivation.[25]

A number of women distinguished themselves as printers of books and other materials. Lydia Bailey was a printer for 53 years (1808 to 1861) in Philadelphia, taking over for her deceased husband. For more than 30 of those years she was the official printer for Philadelphia.[26] Other women printers in Philadelphia included Ann Cochran and Jane Aitken, both of whom also served as official printers for Philadelphia.[27]

Among women receiving literary attention was Phyllis Wheatley, who was born in West Africa and came to the colonies as a slave, bought by a Boston merchant, John Wheatley. She wrote odes, eulogies, and various poems that received attention. She went to London for treatment of an illness. She published a book of poetry in London and became a favorite at the royal court. She had admirers in high places in the emerging new nation. George Washington wrote her that he would "be happy to see a person so favored by the Muses" and signed the letter, "your obedient humble servant."[28] She died at age 29.

Male-Oriented Values and Biases

Children could be expected at an early age to work long hours at the type case and other chores. Some became a part of the apprenticeship system, as did Benjamin Franklin, who quit school at 10 to work in his father's candle shop, and two years later was contracted to work at the *New England Courant* for his half brother James until age 21. John Peter Zenger was bound in servitude to William Bradford for eight years between the ages of 13 and 21. Hours were long, usually the entire duration of daylight.[29]

A certain machismo seemed to reign as a value for men, who felt women's place was basically still in the home, keeping house and bearing children when not helping with the business. Effeminacy on the part of certain men was disparaged. Isaiah Thomas underscores the male-oriented values and biases included in the value system of his times. In his description of his one-time partner Daniel Fowle, Thomas faults him for being "effeminate, and better skilled in the domestic work of females, than in the business of a printing house." But Thomas cited what he regarded as Fowle's positive traits. "Yet, in justice to his character, it ought to be mentioned, that he did business enough to give himself and family a decent maintenance. Although he did not acquire property, he took care not to be involved in debt. He was honest in his dealings, and punctual to his engagements."[30]

Benjamin Franklin espoused the value of thrift. Many a struggling printer could agree with Franklin's "A Penny sav'd is Twopence clear."[31] Thrift was already a virtue of the stern Puritans, but it received a new theological base with the advent of John Wesley, not so much from his rather uneventful trips to America in the mid-1700s but rather from the return from England of full-blown Methodism, the result of Wesley's work. Wesley believed in living at a mere subsistance level and in giving the rest of one's means away. "Having gained, in a right sense, all you can and saved all you can: in spite of nature, and custom and world prudence, give all you can."[32]

Methodism brought a new brand of religion, a pietism that had an active, positive, social-action side. Further, Methodism contributed to the pluralism by its decentralization of a hierarchy of bishops without a single unifying prelate over all. In Protestantism there was a mix of Congregationalists and Baptists with rights retained in the local group, the levels of representative hierarchy of the Presbyterians (who had presbyteries and synods), and the Methodist divisions by districts, areas, and jurisdictions.

Pluralism as a value was in evidence, from a new freedom in architecture and the arts to the pluralist form of government, with its branches balancing power. But pluralism created its own social compacts and groups sanctioning majority rule, which also in turn spawned a downside consensus of legitimizing social ills, not the least of which was a prevailing toleration of slavery.

At the end of the century, positive family and personal values still were etched in the social fabric, as exemplified by this tribute to the Rev. Jacob Duck, upon his death:

> He was a good man, and a good Christian; exemplary in his morals, mild and
> affectionate in his dispositions, and of universal benevolence. While disease and

extreme infirmity clouded the latter years of a life, in its commencement
unusually brilliant, they did not disturb that cheerfulness, resignation and
equanimity, founded on the basis of unaffected religion.[33]

Media as Businesses

MAKING MONEY ON "THROWAWAY MATERIAL"

Newspapers were often a new business proposition for an established printer, especially if the incentive was sweetened with a government contract for printing and
postmaster responsibilities, as in the case of John Campbell and William Brooker.
But the work to put out a disposable product as compared to more lasting items
such as ballads, pamphlets, and even books did not prove overwhelmingly profitable. At the threshold of the Revolutionary War, for a population of 2.8 million,
only thirty-seven newspapers were being published. Total circulation came to about
23,000.[34]

The colonial editor was generally in the business out of some kind of love and
devotion, not just for profit. S. N. D. North notes that as businesses, newspapers
were "uncertain and unattractive," and the reasons and circumstances that brought
many into the business and resulted in the multiplying of the number of newspapers did not foster adequate income.[35]

North traces the rise of demand for newspapers to the new era following the
Revolutionary War. People were "divided quickly into groups upon issues which
concerned altogether their own internal affairs," he says, and this division involved
the public in controversies, "soon to become warm, which everywhere demanded
methods of public expression and intercommunication." The political impetus, he
says, may be attributed to "the immediate multiplication of newspapers, and the fact
that they rapidly attained a degree of influence hitherto unknown in America, and
probably not previously paralleled in the world."[36]

A number of printers/editors went on to amass fortunes in their newspaper
businesses. One was John Dunlap, who had a number of historical scoops as
publisher of the *Pennsylvania Packet or The General Advertiser*; he was the first to
publish the Constitution in 1787 and George Washington's Farewell Address in
1796. Although Benjamin Towne had the honor in 1783 in Philadelphia of
publishing the first daily in America, the *Pennsylvania Evening Post*, lasting only 17
months, Dunlap's *The Pennsylvania Packet or The General Advertiser*, started a year
later, became the first successful daily in the country. He invested in land tracts in
Philadelphia and in Kentucky (131,000 acres). When he died in 1812 his estate was
estimated at $300,000.[37]

Slaves Included in Press Sale

To buy a newspaper in colonial times could be a complex venture, as the distinguished Isaiah Thomas, who became one of America's premier publishers at the
turn of the century, found out in his early days. He had worked at the *Halifax*

Gazette in Nova Scotia, in New Hampshire, and in Boston. Following a tip, he went to Wilmington, North Carolina, where a printer had a press for sale. In the negotiations, the printer raised the ante and said Thomas would also have to purchase a black woman and child. After considerable argument, Thomas accepted the terms, thinking he could sell the woman and child off at cost. Then the printer said Thomas must also buy "a quantity of common household furntiture." At that, Thomas by his own account backed off, bewildered by just what was involved in getting a press.[38] Eventually Thomas joined a partnership in Boston with Zechariah Fowle and launched the *Massachusetts Spy*.

With the Revolutionary War clouds beginning to appear, Thomas found with the polarization of viewpoints his business could not serve the whole populace. He settled on serving the Whigs—"the animated advocates for American liberty"—over against the Tories.[39] During the war, he fled with his printing business to Worcester, thus creating the first inland printing operation in Massachusetts. Later, he took up book publishing and opened a bookstore in Worcester. He then added a bookstore in Boston and another in Walpole, New Hampshire, where he launched *The Farmer's Museum* newspaper. He continued opening bookstores in other cities, including Baltimore and Albany. By the turn of the century, with sixteen presses, Thomas was profitably publishing Bibles, geography and other books, and a monthly magazine, *The Massachusetts Magazine*.[40]

While the newspapers after the Revolutionary War were caught up in intense political debates that encouraged readership, they were no less engrossed in a commercial war to print announcements of products and services through advertising. The reader could count as many as thirty-three ads on the front page of Benjamin Franklin Bache's *General Advertiser (Aurora)*, with additional advertising inside the four-page paper. On the front pages were ads for florists, paperhanging, mahogany logs, rentals, cutlery, sailings, liquor, bank stock, a plantation, teaching of Latin and French, books, "a man servant" wanted, the "time of a most active boy" who "can wait on tables, etc.," copies of the Constitution, and a position-wanted ad—"wants employment" as "a compleat book-keeper."[41] A regular advertiser was a "Doctor Smith" who could cure venereal diseases and other awful maladies with promised privacy and a guarantee that "the utmost secrecy may be depended on."[42]

A half-page ad from time to time dealt with upcoming tax delinquent property sales—150 such properties could be listed on the front page.[43] Compared to earlier colonial periods and the English press where ads tended to run to books and patent medicines, the press in new America at the end of the eighteenth century offered a growing variety of services and goods.

Media as Political Organs
A WAR WAGED AMONG PARTY PAPERS

With editors relishing the new-found freedom, a newspaper war, on political grounds, such as never seen since, marked the first decade of the new nation. And the divisions along political lines continued into the next century. Isaiah Thomas found that out of the 362 newspapers he said were being published in 1810, all but 17 were identified with the Republican or Federalist parties.

With the new country and new form of government came political parties, marked by an exciting exchange of political points of view. Now a Federal government, with a new Constitution ratified by all thirteen states between December 7, 1787, and May 29, 1790, coalesced a wide variety of immigrant cultures. In 1791 a Bill of Rights—the First through the Tenth amendments—was added to the Constitution. Among the basic rights guaranteed were assurances in the First Amendment that "Congress shall make no law respecting an establishment of religion, or prohibiting the free exercise thereof; or abridging the freedom of speech, or of the press; or the right of the people peaceably to assemble, and to petition the Government for a redress of grievances."

Women played a role in new Republican publications. According to Karen List, of the University of Massachusetts, "the tension between republican rhetoric and women's reality [their confinement to the home] was resolved by new republican periodicals through promulgation of the idea of 'republican motherhood.' " Many of the publications had special sections or departments for women, with names such as "women's post," "women's sphere," and "women's station." Whatever the special women's part of the publication was called, says List, "women were to exercise their role as citizens in the new republic at home by influencing their husbands and sons, who then would move into the public arena. In this way, domesticity was endowed with significance: the personal was made political."[44]

Background on Party Differences

To understand the fierce political rivalry that developed and the media's role in it, it is necessary to look to what was happening in Europe. When the British and French began hostilities in 1793 after the guillotining of French King Louis XVI, the American populace was divided. The country had sympathies for England (from where most of the early settlers had come) and yet held affection for France, which had sent troops with the Marquis de Lafayette to support the patriots in the American Revolution. Further, there was a pregovernment alliance in 1778 by which America would enter on the side of France in case of war. President Washington recognized the new French revolutionary government but otherwise elected to stay neutral. The next year, 1794, Congress passed the Neutrality Act, making it illegal for Americans to take part in the British-French war, including banning the use of American soil for any war preparations by either side.

A series of events followed in relation to Britain and France that polarized American politics: the Genet Affair, Jay's Treaty, and the XYZ Affair.

First, the French, ignoring U.S. official neutrality, believed they had more to expect in the way of support from America. A young representative of the French government, Edmond Genet, came to the United States, bypassed President Washington in Philadelphia, and went to Charleston where he connived to outfit

George Washington and the Press

Harry M. Ward

Every president has come to rue the power of the press—even George Washington was not an exception. Yet Washington, commander-in-chief of an improbable military force that at least kept an edge over the British and that was ultimately victorious, enjoyed a reputation almost without a blemish.

Unanimously elected twice to the presidency, Washington could expect and receive the respect of his countrymen as he laid the foundations of the new republic. Nevertheless, the early years of the republic saw the proliferation of newspapers, all bent, so it seems, on discovering and extolling the virtues of the new nation, while serving as watchdogs against corruption of power and deviance from virtuous ideals.

Washington's first term was a period of grace—at worst his subordinates were attacked. Where Washington erred in maintaining his nonpartisan rule was in his decision to serve a second term. Inevitably, his image became more that of a politician and less that of a national savior.

About the only participation (in the press) by Washington himself, before and after the war, was advertising horses for stud and, during the 1780s, promoting the breeding of Royal Gift, a jackass presented by the Spanish minister.

During the war, Washington could expect, as have American commanders during the big wars since, a moratorium on personal criticism. After all, during the Revolution it was the Continental Congress—legislature and executive rolled into one—that was fair game for anything that went wrong.

With no electioneering required of Washington in 1788 or 1792 and with the formation of party rivalry only in the embryo stages, political criticism of Washington was delayed. It developed cautiously, only to burst out during the last two lame-duck years as the struggle for the presidency in 1796 neared.

French vessels in American ports. He lined up shipowners to provide ships for privateers and issued commissions to Americans to serve in an expedition against Spain, which was an ally of Britain.

When Genet at last went to the capital, pro-French crowds cheered him, but an icy reception awaited him from President Washington. Washington ordered Genet home, but suddenly the balance of power shifted in France. Genet's party, the Girondins, was ousted, and the more brutal Jacobins ascended to power. Washington granted Genet asylum. Genet retired to a Long Island farm, but not without having added to the schism in American politics.

Then for a time the nation's wrath turned toward England. The British began seizing American ships that were trading with the French in the French West Indies. Americans were also wary because of word from the northwestern territories that a Canadian official was stirring up Indians for an attack. Worried about the deteriorating relations with Britain, the American government sent Chief Justice John

Jay to England to negotiate reparations for seized ships and withdrawal of British troops from the northwest. Jay came away, however, with a treaty that gave to the British more than Americans expected. The treaty said that the British could still search American ships and unload enemy (French) property in British ports. Means of setting reparations by the British concerning past American ships and cargoes seized were vague, with payment to be determined by arbitration.

The French, angered by the treaty, started seizing American ships themselves and, when a new minister to France from America, Charles C. Pinckney, was sent to replace the popular minister, future U.S. president James Monroe, the French refused to accept him. Deciding to pursue peace with France, three emissaries from the United States went to France to meet with three representatives from the French government (designated X, Y, and Z in a report on these events). The French representatives, however, set a condition of a bribe for each French participant and a loan for France before they would negotiate. Pinckney, one of the members of the U.S. team, blurted out: "No! No! Not a sixpence!"[45]

The Lighter Side

Was Washington a Woman?

Deane and Peggy Robertson

On the 25th of January 1783, the portly, prosperous readers of London's *Whitehall Evening Post* must have choked on their port as they read that "General Washington is actually discovered to be of the female sex."

Confiding that it was quoting from the *Dublin Register*, which got it from the *Pennsylvania Gazette* of November 11, 1782, the *Whitehall Evening Post* told its fascinated readers:

> This important secret was revealed by the Lady who lived with the General as a wife these 30 years, and died the 6th inst. at the General's seat in Virginia, to the Clergyman who attended her.
>
> What is extraordinary, the Lady knew this circumstance previous to the ceremony of marriage, and both agreed to live together from motives of the most refined friendship.

There followed a roundup of reminiscences about women who had distinguished themselves in the manly art of warfare, from Joan of Arc in the fifteenth century to Hannah Snell, who had served as a private in the British Army in the Revolutionary War.

The story, which appeared alongside news of the end of the war with the former American colonies, concluded, "and now the rights of America have been asserted, and her Independence established, through the amazing fortitude of a woman. Perhaps it is fortunate that this circumstance was not known at a more early period of the contest."

The news of the "lady General" apparently swept London; an illustrator for *Rambler's Magazine* in the April 1, 1783 issue depicted Washington in female attire, topped off with sword and military hat.

Yet library research shows that readers of the *Whitehall Evening Post* would have been wise to take its George Washington "scoop" with a whole bag of salt.

The *Pennsylvania Gazette*, from which the *Dublin Register* supposedly had "extracted" the story, did not print an issue on Nov. 11,

1782, as cited. Its regular weekly issues fell on Nov. 6 and Nov. 13, 1782, and George Washington's gender was not mentioned in either those or subsequent issues. Nor did any such story appear in the five other Pennsylvania papers of the day.

The *Dublin Register*, if it ever existed, apparently sank without a trace. Neither the British Library's Newspaper Library nor the National Library of Ireland has any record of the *Register*'s existence, nor did any other Dublin paper have such a story.

The *Whitehall Evening Post* did have the grace to call what it supposedly had copied from the Dublin paper "an improbable article," and it avoided mention of the General's gender in later issues.

No doubt Martha Dandridge Curtis Washington would have been surprised to read of her touching death-bed scene with "the Clergyman who attended her" for she was very much alive on Jan. 25, 1783, and she would have noted that in 1783 she and George had been married only 24 years, not 30 as the story said. They were wed on Jan. 6, 1759. Not only was she alive and well when the story was written, she lived for another 19 years, dying on May 22, 1802, three years after George.

If Martha ever heard of the *Evening Post*'s scoop, she must have had some satisfaction from the fact that she survived not only George but also the *Whitehall Evening Post*, which went under in 1801.

Undoubtedly the *Whitehall Evening Post* faked the whole thing, tossing in the names of a respectable-sounding Dublin newspaper and the *Pennsylvania Gazette*, which was well-known in London, just to give an air of credibility to the story. Most out-of-town news was copied from other newspapers in the eighteenth century, before the telegraph and the wire service were invented, so the *Post*'s reader would have seen nothing odd about the story having been filtered through two other newspapers before it reached them. . . .

The *True Briton* charged that reporters particularly specialized in "Entertaining us with Lyes from Abroad" because the reader had no way of checking on such stories. So perhaps the great George Washington scoop was merely a fiction published to entertain.

George Washington in woman's attire swings at Britannia as Holland, France, and Spain look on, from April 1, 1783, issue of Rambler's Magazine. (The Trustees of the British Museum)

Source: Media History Digest, Fall–Winter, 1987. Reprinted by permission.

Congress, pressed by President John Adams, passed laws severing all trade with France, voided the treaty of 1778, and approved seizure of French vessels by U.S. ships. For all practical purposes, with the pro-British Adams and the Federalists in power, an undeclared war existed between the United States and France from 1798 to 1800.

"Lightning Rod, Junior"

The editors, buffeted by the vitriolic political style of the day, took sides. Among the anti-Federalists, or Republicans, was the sharp-tongued Benjamin Franklin Bache, Ben's grandson, sometimes called "Lightning Rod, Junior," a reference to his grandfather's electricity experiments. Bache's *General Advertiser* (*Aurora*), in Philadelphia, assailed Washington and Adams in nearly every issue. He had even called earlier for the impeachment of Washington: "Let us make our appeal to that body which has the power of impeachment."[46]

Hammering away, Bache portrayed the president as "a great admirer and warm panegyrist of that political monster, the British form of government."[47] With the election looming that would put Adams in office, Bache declared: "Let the People choose between the existence of the Constitution in its purity; or Mr. Adams as their President, the avowed enemy of its principles."[48] In the same vein, six days before the election, Bache issued "an alarm": "John Adams, the advocate of a kingly government, and of a titled nobility to form an upper house, and to keep down the swinish multitude . . . is to be your president unless you will turn out on Friday the fourth day of November, and by your votes call forth Thomas Jefferson, the friend of the people, a republican in principle and manners." (Signed by "one of the people.")[49] Jefferson lost, but took the helm in 1801.

Jefferson's Editor Freneau

Also on the Republican side was the sometime poet-editor Philip Freneau. A war hero who had been imprisoned on a British ship for weeks in the New York harbor, his poems during the Revolutionary War—including one dealing with the naval officer John Paul Jones—inspired the patriots. Freneau was given to writing satire, especially aimed at the new nation's "monarchists." Working for Jefferson, when Jefferson was secretary of state, 1791–1793, Freneau edited the *National Gazette*. Without continued financial support from Jefferson, Freneau let the paper die after two years. His writings further accented the religious differences between the Federalists and the Republicans, the Federalists leaning toward strong-dogma religions, namely that of the Church of England; Freneau, an admirer of Paine, promoted "enlightenment" and deism—anti-ecclesiastical religion based on humanism and reason rather than theism (theism emphasizes revelation and a participating active deity or God-figure). Deism and enlightenment were among the themes of the French Revolution.

From his first issue, Freneau's *National Gazette* seemed overtly pro-French at times. He would carry speeches of French visitors, such as a reprint in translation of an "address from two French Physicians of New-York to the Citizens of the Capital" on the front page.[50] Sometimes he would have an item in French, untranslated, for example, a notice for "Les Français amis de la liberté."[51]

On the Federalists' editors' team were William Cobbett, that feisty "investigative," argumentive reporter/editor who came from and returned to England, and John Fenno, who edited the *Gazette of the United States*. Fenno's paper at times purported to be the very voice of President Adams himself. The paper would show Adams patting himself on the back, taking a position of humility, and launching a few disguised barbs for the likes of Freneau and particularly Bache.[52]

Riding on the fear of the possible spreading of the French wave of terror and anarchy, the American government mobilized troops and prepared coastal defenses. The Federalist-controlled Congress sought to pass laws to control the movements and influence of aliens and their sympathizers, such as Republican editors. Adams could see a twofold thrust of laws restricting aliens. They could lessen threats to the security of the nation, and they could stifle criticism from the Republicans, many of whom were French- or Irish-born (thus also anti-English).

CURBING POLITICAL EXPRESSION— THE ABOMINABLE ACTS

Even with the guarantee in the First Amendment that Congress would not legislate laws "abridging the freedom of speech," Congress did just that in 1798 by passing the highly controversial and subjective Alien and Sedition Acts, which favored the party in power—the Federalists. The four acts were clearly aimed at silencing the party out of power—the Anti-Federalists or Republicans.

The first of the 1798 Alien and Sedition Acts, the Naturalization Act, said no one who was a citizen of or lived in a country at war with the United States could become a citizen; the Alien Act gave the president power to have deported any person he thought was dangerous to the country; the Alien Enemies Act authorized the roundup and detention of all males, 14 or over, who were subjects of the hostile nation; the Sedition Act said any one considered to be conspiring "with intent to oppose any measure or measures of the government of the United States" would be fined $5,000 and imprisoned up to five years. Further it said that any person who spoke or published "any false, scandalous and malicious writing or writings" against the Congress or the president could be fined up to $2,000 and jailed up to two years.

The Alien Act did not result in conviction of any editors, although Federalists used it to take aim at John Daly Burk, Irish-born editor of the New York *Time Piece*. Burk was a successor of *Time Piece* editor Freneau, who had gone to the *Time Piece* after the folding of the *National Gazette*. Burk was arrested and his *Time Piece* paper folded. Out on bail, Burk went into hiding until after the expiration of the Alien and Sedition Acts in 1801.[53]

The "Lyon" That Roared

Scholars document 24 or 25 arrests under the Sedition Act. Fifteen were indicted with only 10 or 11 cases going to trial. Of the 10 found guilty, seven were newspaper editors.[54] Application of the acts was complex, but colorful. First convicted under the Sedition Act was Vermont Congressman Matthew Lyon. He is best known in history as the congressman who cast the vote which at last made Thomas Jefferson president in the deadlocked 1800 election. An owner of a sawmill and other businesses in Fair Haven, Vermont, Lyon was the first in America to use wood pulp to make paper, and he invented a process by which paper was made from bark. When he failed to win his first bid for the House, he launched the weekly newspaper *Farmer's Library* in 1793. The feisty Irishman won his bid to Congress in the next election and took his seat in 1797 in the midst of the scare of possible war with France. He founded a political publication, *The Scourge of Aristocracy and Repository of Important Political Truths.* When his Federalist opponent in the 1798 elections, Stanley Williams, called Lyon the "Vermont beast" in Williams' journal, the *Rutland Herald*, and would not let Lyon reply,[55] Lyon published the reply himself in the *Scourge*. He charged Adams with "unbounded thirst for ridiculous pomp, foolish adulation, or selfish avarice."[56] Lyon said he would take aim at "every aristocratic hireling . . . down to the dirty Hedge-hogs and groveling animals" who were "vomiting forth columns of lies, malignant abuse and deception."[57]

Lyon became a prime target of the Federalists when he spit in the face of Roger Griswold, a Federalist leader from Connecticut who mocked Lyon's war record. Griswold alluded to the cashiering ("dishonorable" discharge) of Lyon for cowardice, namely, for not leading his men forward under fire. Lyon, however, had reentered the army and seen distinguished service. A day after Lyon spit in his eye, Griswold took a cane to Lyon in the House. Lyon responded to the attack by beating Griswold with a pair of nearby fire tongs.

For his remarks concerning Adams and perhaps more for his general attitude, Lyon was taken into court, where a Federalist judge sent him to jail for four months and fined him $1,000. Confined to a 12-by-16-foot cell, "the Lyon had hardly been caged before he began to roar," says James Morton Smith.[58] Lyon wrote letters for newspapers across the country denouncing his "savage" treatment, as he conducted his campaign for re-election. Friends raised funds for the fine, and when Lyon was freed, a procession, longer than for presidents, accompanied him back to the capital of Philadelphia.

An obvious prime target for application of the Federalist-inspired Alien and Sedition Acts was Benjamin Franklin Bache. So anxious were the Federalists to silence Bache that three weeks before the signing of the Alien and Sedition Acts he was arrested and faced a federal common law indictment for seditious libel against the president. Bache's *Aurora*, the leading opposition paper in the nation, drew fire from Federalists of all quarters. The prominent William Cobbett in his *Porcupine's Gazette* tagged Bache as "a dull-edged, dull-eyed, haggard-looking hireling of

Congress free-for-all, 1798. Federalist Roger Griswold canes Matthew Lyon, who responds with pair of tongs. (The Library Company of Philadelphia)

France."[59] Because of Bache's prominence and his volumes of criticism against the administration, the Federalists were relishing the event of his trial. But Bache, out on bail and two surety bonds, died of yellow fever during an epidemic in September 1798, a month before his scheduled trial.

Bache's successor, William Duane (who married Bache's widow), was no less audacious in his opposition to the Alien and Sedition Acts, the presidency of John Adams, and Federalists in general. Duane was indicted on several counts for alleging British influence on the U.S. government and for some disparaging remarks about the behavior of American troops.[60] Since Duane had a copy of a letter from Adams purportedly acknowledging some British interest in one of his appointments, the Federalists, fearing a repercussion should Duane circulate the letter, put off the trial. He was again indicted for libel and sedition several more times, and the secretary of state recommended his deportation.

Curiously, Thomas Jefferson, a Republican, as vice president and presider over the Senate signed a Senate warrant for Duane to be taken into custody for contempt of the Senate when Duane did not honor a Senate summons. Yet it was with

Jefferson that Duane's fate ultimately rested. When the Alien and Sedition Acts were left to expire and were not renewed at the installation of Jefferson, the new president discontinued prosecutions under the Alien and Sedition Acts, and both court and Senate proceedings against Duane were dropped. For with the opprobrious acts now dead, criticism of Congress and the president was no longer actionable offenses.

Among others arrested and convicted in the two-year reign of the Alien and Sedition Acts was Luther Baldwin, who, a bit tipsy while watching a presidential parade on a hot night in July in Philadelphia, remarked that the cannons should be firing at the president's rear end.

The last trial involved James Callender, a Scottish immigrant, who had worked on the *Aurora* with Bache and Duane before going to Petersburg, Virginia, where he joined the staff of the *Richmond Examiner*. Although known to the authorities for earlier political writing, his pamphlet *The Prospect Before Us*, promoting the election of Jefferson as president, put him in deep trouble. "The reign of Mr. Adams has been one continued tempest of malignant passions," Callender wrote.[61] Callender was found guilty, fined, and sentenced to jail for nine months, and he remained in jail until the Alien and Sedition Acts expired and a pardon came from Jefferson.

One woman, Ann Greenleaf, a widow who published the *New York Argus* and the *Patriotic Register*, was indicted for sedition during the reign of the Alien and Sedition Acts. Facing incessant harassment, she sold both papers before the trial date in April 1800. The Federalist authorities, fearing repercussions during the election year 1800 for prosecuting a poor widow, especially after the mounting bad publicity from other prosecutions, decided, with support from President Adams, to drop the charges against Mrs. Greenleaf.[62]

The Legacy of the Alien and Sedition Acts

The Sedition Act, the fourth of the Alien and Sedition Acts, brought up positive points in the quest for freedom of the press, at least in principle. It allowed truth as a defense and the right of juries to decide the law. The Sedition Act said: "It shall be lawful for the defendant, upon the trial of the cause, to give evidence in his defence, the truth of the matter contained in the publication charged with libel. And the jury who shall try the cause, shall have a right to determine the law and the fact, under the direction of the court, as in other cases."

Leonard Levy put a positive spin on the Sedition Act. He said it did not dilute the emphasis of truth as a defense in the Zenger trial and "better protected the freedom of the press than did the test that emerged from the Croswell case." He explained that "the Sedition Act made truth a defense without requiring the defendant to prove, additionally, good motives or justifiable ends, and it placed upon the prosecution the burden of proving malice."[63]

Although the principle was there, it was subject to interpretation and adjustment to a particular bias, that of the Federalists. One scholar avowed that allowing the truth of the alleged libel to be used as a valid defense "depended, of course, upon the construction put upon it by the courts. By refusing to distinguish between fact and opinion and by requiring that every item in every allegation should be fully proved the courts would deprive the provision of all value as a protection for the accused. This is exactly what was done."[64]

The negative impact of the experience with the Alien and Sedition Acts was so strong on the American psyche that nothing similar appeared again until the wartime measures of World War I—the Trading with the Enemy Act of 1917 and the Sabotage Act and the Sedition Act of 1918. The first peacetime sedition act since the Alien and Sedition Acts did not appear until 1940, when Congress passed the Alien Registration Act (known as the Smith Act after its sponsor, Representative Howard Smith of Virginia). That act sought to oppress "subversive" political groups, required aliens to register, made alien subversives subject to deportation, and made advocating the violent overthrow of the government a crime. An antiterrorism act passed in 1996 had provisions that would permit deportation of alleged alien terrorists without disclosure of classified evidence against them.

Efforts were made to extend the Sedition Act for a year, but in the final resolve it yielded to political pressure and was extended only until March 3, 1801, when President Adams' term expired. In Kentucky and Virginia, where the Republicans dominated the legislatures, two resolutions (Thomas Jefferson wrote the one for Kentucky, James Madison the one for Virginia) were passed saying that the Sedition Act was unconstitutional and null and void in those two states. The moves were affirmations of states rights, with implication for the Civil War era and throughout the course of American political life. When the Alien and Sedition Acts did expire, one statute passed at the time of the acts remained and is still on the books today: the Logan Act of 1798, which says private citizens cannot take part in negotiation with an enemy during wartime.

Despite the fact that the incoming president, Jefferson, was an anti-Federalist and a Republican (in the premodern sense of the word in the United States) and might have turned the Alien and Sedition Acts against the Federalists if the laws had remained on the books, many of the Federalists favored continuing the acts. By a final vote of 53 to 49, the laws were left to expire, with no Republican voting for the extension. So why did the Federalists want their repressive laws continued when they could have been turned against them? John D. Stevens, writing in *Journalism Quarterly*, wondered why the Federalists would want the extension when they were to be out of power. Stevens suggested that "many Federalists in the House of Representatives probably believed that the procedural safeguards in the sedition law offered more protection to a critic of the government than did the common law, and that therefore they would be in less danger if the law were continued." He suggested further that some Federalists might have been wanting to show their good intentions "since they had been roundly painted as blackguards intent on persecuting political opponents." They would have little to fear from their bravado. Stevens says they may have had their courage shored up by the fact that Jefferson had pledged not to use such a law "and by the comforting thought that the federal court trial judges were certain to be Federalists (with life tenure) for many years to come. Still others may have been trying to hand Jefferson a tempting weapon with hopes of daring him to use it."

The effect of the Alien and Sedition Acts, says Stevens, is that they left such a bad taste that not only were such laws not passed again until 116 years later in World War I, but "perhaps most important, the debate on the sedition law opened a dialogue on the role of free expression within a democracy (particularly at a time of crisis) which has continued to this day."[65]

With the start of the new nineteenth century with freedom on political matters affirmed in general, criticism of incumbent politicians from the president on down became common. Many journals were started as political organs for candidates. Yet, with human nature as it is, legal means were still found to bring to trial outspoken members of the opposition party. Thomas Jefferson was now in power, beginning in 1801. The freethinking leader, who as a Republican opposed the Alien and Sedition Acts, curiously now looked for a way to prosecute the most offending Federalists during his administration. And he did.

DOCTRINE OF LIMITED PROSECUTION/PERSECUTION OF THE PRESS

A libertarian, Jefferson nevertheless apparently saw some advantage in an occasional prosecution under state law. He said that people "have learnt that nothing in a newspaper is to be believed," and if "a few prosecutions of the most prominent offenders" would occur in the states, then the press would have a better chance to be restored to "its credibility." He believed such actions would raise press standards while avoiding "a general prosecution for that would look like persecution. But a selected one . . . would have a wholesome effect in restoring the integrity of the presses."[66]

Croswell "Stings" Jefferson

Jefferson soon had a perfect target for a selective prosecution: an angry 22-year-old, Harry Croswell, working as a junior publisher on *The Balance and Columbian Repository* in the lively port town of Hudson, New York. Croswell received the permission of his senior partner, Ezra Sampson, to put out an aggressive, vituperative four-page paper, *The Wasp*. It was not to be a parlor publication on politics as usual. *The Wasp* would STING. Croswell promised in his preamble to the first issue that he would go after the *Balance*'s rival, the *Bee*, published by Charles Holt, who had been convicted under the Alien and Sedition Acts and spent several months in jail in 1800:

> The editor will make but few promises.—Wasps produce but little honey: They are chiefly known for the stings; and the one here proposed will not materially

differ from others.—The Wasp is declared to be at enmity with the Bee.—
Wherever the Bee ranges, the Wasp will follow—over the same fields, and on the
same flowers.—Without attempting to please his friends, the Wasp will only
strive to displease, vex and torment his enemies—with his sting always sharped
for ever, he will never accept of peace.—He will never accede to the philosophical
doctrine, that "We are all Wasps—We are all Bees."[67]

Croswell tweaked the nose of the Jeffersonian Democrat Republicans with his
ditties, such as

Democratic Ding-Dong

THE Democrats—(I know them well)
Their heads are like a crier's bell—
A hollow sconce—a noisy thing
Hangs in the middle, pealing—ding—
   Ding-dong—a pealing bell,
   A Demo's head will do as well.[68]

This was all being said in Columbia County, New York, from which the
Jeffersonian attorney general of New York hailed, thus assuring that Croswell would
not go unnoticed. But then Croswell reached out of state to rein in a Richmond
editor, James Callender. Callender had been a supporter of Jefferson until the president
denied Callender's request to be postmaster of Richmond. Callender had expected
the appointment in return for having written an anti-Federalist pamphlet,
The Prospect Before Us, which had attacked Jefferson's political enemies, Washington
and John Adams. Disgruntled, Callender now said in print that when he was working
on the pamphlet Jefferson had even sent him a $100 encouragement to say that
George Washington was a robber and traitor. The charge was potentially politically
damaging, but Jefferson explained it away by saying that the $100 was just an act of
charity. Croswell's *Wasp* exclaimed: "They declare that the one hundred dollars
were charity to Callender. Good heavens!"[69] Croswell also scored Jefferson's relation
with his purported slave mistress and Jefferson's alleged efforts to seduce the
wife of a good friend.

Croswell Arrested

Croswell was indicted on two counts of libel and ordered to stand trial at the Court
of General Sessions in Claverack, the Columbia County seat. (In Philadelphia
another rabid Federalist editor, Joseph Dennie, also was indicted for seditious libel.
Dennie did not attack personalities but the concept of democracy as unworkable.
He was acquitted.)

The *Balance* proceeded to give a full account of the arrest of Croswell:

On the 11th day of January 1803 Harry Croswell, the junior editor of the
Balance, was taken by an officer on a bench warrant, and carried before the
Court. . . . Two indictments were read to him. One of the indictments with the

usual epithets and inuendoes charged Mr. Croswell with having published a paper called the "Wasp" in which "Jefferson" was charged with having paid Callender for calling Washington a traitor, a robber and a perjurer; for calling Adams a hoary headed incendiary; and for libelling almost all the worth and virtue in the country.[70]

The second indictment stated in effect that Harry Croswell in the same edition published a piece entitled "a few squally facts"—which set forth five administrative acts of Jefferson that Croswell said violated the Constitution. He said Jefferson misused treasury funds, "displaced honest patriots" with foreigners and flatterers on jobs, destroyed the judiciary, remitted a fine of a criminal, and released on his own authority William Duane, among others, imprisoned under the Alien and Sedition Acts.

Croswell's attorneys sought to have the truth considered as a defense and the right of the jury to make law or set a new course. But unlike the Zenger trial, where a popular party influenced the system, Croswell was found guilty. Croswell's attorneys moved for a new trial on grounds that the jury had not been properly instructed and truth should be introduced as evidence as in other trials. The New York Supreme Court agreed to hear the case. Croswell's Federalist contingency trotted out their chief gun for his defense, Alexander Hamilton, chief intellect of the Washington administration and former secretary of the treasury. He argued that so-called seditious libel did not preclude a foreign threat:

> If the doctrine for which we contend is true, in regard to treason and murder, it is equally true in respect to libel. For there is the great danger. Never can tyranny be introduced into this country by arms; these can never get rid of a popular spirit of enquiry; the only way to crush it down is by a servile tribunal.[71]

Hamilton did not come through as an absolutist on freedom of the press. He said, "In speaking thus for the Freedom of the Press, I do not say there ought to be an unbridled licence; or that the characters of men who are good, will naturally tend eternally to support themselves. I do not stand here to say that no shackles are to be laid on this license." He believed truth with some qualification should reign: "I contend for the liberty of publishing truth, with good motives and for justifiable ends, even though it reflect on government, magistrates, or private persons."[72]

The New York Supreme Court upheld the Croswell conviction, but the New York state Assembly in 1805 took note of Hamilton's eloquent pleas and developed a truth-in-libel bill. There was division on whether to begin a new Croswell trial. A sentence could have been entered at this point against Croswell, but the matter was dropped in the light of the new legislation. At least nineteen states have in their constitutions a clause permitting truth as a defense in libel cases.[73]

The Six-Cent Libel Case

Croswell was to have one more brush with a libel suit in what was to become one of the more curious, if not comical, cases in libel history. In his farewell edition of

The Wasp, Croswell did not let well enough alone. He laid on heavy satire and said he was repenting of his ways. He would designate as lies some of the most outrageous statements, but the tone indicates that he believed the opposite. He wrote at the end of his last edition in 1803 (before the outcome of his appeal in 1804):

> I am resolved, for once to turn my rusty-coat, and to occupy some part of this number of the Wasp with DEMOCRACY and LIES.
> See here I begin:—I believe that Thomas Paine and Thomas Jefferson are the two greatest men that ever were or ever will be upon earth. . . .
> I do not believe that [Ambrose] Spencer's Foote [Sen. Ebenezer Foote] was ever a cobler, because I do not believe he has ingenuity sufficient for that profession. I do not think that if the said Foote possessed a tail, he would precisely resemble a monkey.
> I do not believe that Foote has sufficient ingenuity for a swindler. In short, and to waste no more paper, I do not believe that Foote is a consummate blockhead.[74]

Spencer and Foote both sued for libel. Spencer won $126, but the luckless Foote—who a witness said was known to cheat at cards—was awarded damages of only six cents.[75]

As for Croswell, he bowed out of publishing and became an Episcopal priest. He started with a parish in Hudson, then moved to a church in New Haven where he served for 43 years. He washed his hands of politics, never even voting again.[76]

Occupying Jefferson's attention on a grander scale were matters of security—the French were still considered a threat, and, with growing pains in the populace, frontiers provided new opportunities. In April 1803, three months after Croswell's indictment, the United States bought from France a 828,000-square-mile tract, from New Orleans up the Mississippi Valley to the Rockies (known as the Louisiana Purchase), instantly doubling the size of the United States. The national attention was suddenly directed toward expansion.

QUESTIONS FOR DISCUSSION AND RESEARCH

1. Suggest ten causes for the Revolutionary War.
2. History has a way of revising in the long run ideas and reputations that were popular. For example, views of presidents are sometimes changed long after the time in which they lived. Discuss persons and ideas that existed at the time of the Revolutionary War. Has history changed public perception so that attitudes are different from what they were at the time?
3. Were there any similarities between radical patriot Samuel Adams and his cousin, President John Adams?
4. Did Tom Paine deserve to become an outcast—a *persona non grata*?
5. Consider the investigations William Cobbett conducted. What would be a parallel topic in each case for a modern investigative reporter?

6. True or false: Sensationalism in the colonial and early American newspaper was a way to entertain. Explain.

7. Compare the values of one or several colonial editors to editors' values today and to your values.

8. Dan Fowle, criticized by his associate, Isaiah Thomas, as lackadaisical, is rather likable, with his good and bad traits. Actually such characters with obvious strengths and weaknesses make good characters in plays and novels. From among the people you met in Chapters 3 and 4, who would you include as a model for an interesting character in a play or novel, and why?

9. If you were a young person in colonial times and wanted to go into the newspaper business, how would you proceed?

10. Compare the use of the terms *Democrat* and *Republican* in early America to the use of the terms today.

11. Has the role of women in the media changed since colonial times?

12. Do vestiges of a slave-master mentality of some colonial editors remain today? Explain.

13. Assess the effect, good and bad, of the Alien and Sedition Acts of 1798 on American life.

14. Compare the lives of William Cobbett and Harry Croswell.

15. How would you define libel in colonial times and today? How have attitudes and the law changed on libel? Compare the terms *sedition* and *malice* in libel history.

ENDNOTES

1. Bernard Bailyn, *Faces of Revolution: Personalities and Themes in the Struggle for American Independence* (New York: Alfred A. Knopf, 1990).

2. Julie Hedgepeth Williams, "The Stamp Act Press: The First True Mass Medium," from a paper presented to the American Journalism Historians Association, Lawrence, Kans., 1992, p. 13.

3. John Dickinson, *Letters from a Farmer in Pennsylvania*, "Letter III," in Harry R. Warfel et al., *The American Mind*, vol. 1 (New York: American Book Company, 1937), pp. 142, 143. Quoted in Calder M. Pickett, *Voices of the Past: Key Documents in the History of American Journalism* (Columbus, Ohio: Grid, Inc., 1977), pp. 43, 44.

4. Warfel, *The American Mind*, p. 45.

5. Paul Lewis, *The Grand Incendiary: A Biography of Samuel Adams* (New York: Dial Press, 1973), p. 7.

6. Ibid., p. 16.

7. Thomas Paine, *Common Sense: Addressed to the Inhabitants of America* . . . (Danbury, Conn.: Medallic Art Company, facsimile of first edition, first issue of 1776), I, p. 29.

8. Ibid., p. 59.

9. Bernard Bailyn, "Thomas Paine," *American Heritage*, vol. 25, no. 1, December 1973, pp. 92, 93.

10. John Keane, *Tom Paine: A Political Life* (New York: Little, Brown, 1995), p. 346, quoting a prosecutor, Spencer Percival, later prime minister of England.

11. Ibid., p. 294.

12. Mariam Touba, "Tom Paine's Plan for Revolutionizing America: Diplomacy, Politics, and the Evolution of a Newspaper Rumor," *Journalism History*, vol. 20, nos. 3 and 4, Autumn–Winter 1994.
13. Theodore Sedgwick, *A Memoir of the Life of William Livingston* (New York: 1833), p. 247.
14. John L. Lawson, "The 'Remarkable Mystery' of James Rivington, 'Spy,' " *Journalism Quarterly*, vol. 35, Summer 1958, p. 394.
15. Daniel Green, *Great Cobbett: The Noblest Agitator* (London: Hodder and Stoughton, 1983), p. 158.
16. *Political Register*, June 17, 1809.
17. *The Democratic Judge*, 1798, quoted in Green, *Great Cobbett*, p. 170.
18. E. L. Carlyle, *William Cobbett: A Study of His Life as Shown in His Writings* (London: Archibald Constable and Co., 1904), p. 114.
19. William Osborne, *William Cobbett: His Thought and His Times* (New Brunswick, N.J.: Rutgers University Presss, 1966), p. 203.
20. Green, *Great Cobbett*, p. 142.
21. "Last Moments of the Late Queen of France, From a London Paper," *Thomas's Massachusetts Spy: Or, The Worcester Gazette*, Feb. 13, 1794.
22. *General Advertiser and Political, Commercial, Agricultural, and Literary Journal* (after Nov. 3, 1794, it was called *Aurora*), March 3, 1794.
23. *Gazette of the United States, and Philadelphia Daily Advertiser*, Jan. 3, 1798.
24. Ira L. Baker, "Elizabeth Timothy: America's First Woman Editor," *Journalism Quarterly*, vol. 54, Summer 1977, p. 280.
25. Susan Henry, "Sarah Goddard, Gentlewoman Printer," *Journalism Quarterly*, vol. 57, Spring 1980, pp. 23–30.
26. Karen Nipps, curator of printed books for The Library Company in Philadelphia, has created a partial list of more than 700 books published by Lydia Bailey.
27. Research by Adrienne L. Petrisko, assistant reference librarian, The Library Company, in Philadelphia.
28. Donald F. Mitchell, *American Lands and Letters* (1897), p. 152.
29. Lawrence Wroth, *The Colonial Printer* (Charlottesville: Dominion Books, University Press of Virginia, 1964; 1931 edition by the Grollier Club of the City of New York; 1938 edition by the Southworth-Anthoensen Press).
30. Isaiah Thomas, *The History of Printing in America* (New York: Burt Franklin, 1874, reprint, 1972; the book first appeared in 1810), vol. 1, pp. 135, 136.
31. J. A. Leo Lemay, compiler, *Benjamin Franklin: Writings* (New York: The Library of America; New York: Library Classics of the United States, 1987), p. 1204.
32. John Wesley, "The Danger of Riches," *Arminian Magazine*, 1781, quoted in Hiley Ward, *Creative Giving* (New York: Macmillan, 1958), p. 157.
33. *Gazette of the United States*, Jan. 8, 1798.
34. S. N. D. North, *History and Present Condition of the Newspaper and Periodical Press of the United States* (Washington, D.C.: 1884), p. 27.
35. Ibid., p. 31.
36. Ibid.
37. Malone Jonson, ed., *Dictionary of American Biography*, vol. 3, "John Dunlap" (New York: Scribner's, 1959).
38. Thomas, *History of Printing*, p. 163.
39. Ibid., p. 165.
40. Ibid., p. 183.
41. *General Advertiser*, Jan. 1, 1794.
42. Ibid., Oct. 26, 1796.

43. Ibid., May 13, 1794.

44. Karen K. List, "Realities and Possibilities: The Lives of Women in Periodicals of the New Republic," *American Journalism*, vol. 11, no. 1, Winter 1994, pp. 22, 23. See also Karen K. List, "The Post-Revolutionary Woman Idealized: Philadelphia Media's 'Republican Mother,'" *Journalism Quarterly*, vol. 66, Spring 1989, pp. 66–75.

45. Richard N. Current, T. Harry Williams, and Frank Freidel, *American History: A Survey* (New York: Alfred A. Knopf, 1961), p. 147.

46. *General Advertiser*, Sept. 17, 1793.

47. *Aurora*, Oct. 20, 1796; item signed "Sidney."

48. *Aurora*, Oct. 20, 1796.

49. *Aurora*, Oct. 29, 1796.

50. *National Gazette*, Oct. 6, 1793.

51. Ibid., July 7, 1792.

52. *Gazette of the United States*, April 14, 1798.

53. Alfred McClung Lee, *The Daily Newspaper in America* (New York: Macmillan, 1937), p. 413; James Morton Smith, *Freedom's Fetters: The Alien and Sedition Laws and American Civil Liberties* (Ithaca, N.Y.: Cornell University Press, 1956), p. 218.

54. William Grosvenor Bleyer, *Main Currents in the History of American Journalism* (Boston: Houghton Mifflin, 1927), p. 121; Lee, *Daily Newspaper*, p. 48; Smith, *Freedom's Fetters*, pp. 185, 186: "Federalist enforcement machinery ground out at least seventeen verifiable indictments. Fourteen were found under the Sedition Act, and three were returned under the common law, two before and one after the passage of the statute. Although most of the prosecutions were initiated in 1798 and 1799, the majority of the cases did not come to trial until April, May, and June, 1800. Indeed, the chief enforcement effort was tied directly to the presidential campaign of 1800."

55. Smith, *Freedom's Fetters*, p. 227.

56. Ibid., p. 230.

57. *The Scourge of Aristocracy*, Oct. 1, 1798, quoted in Smith, *Freedom's Fetters*, p. 227, and in J. Fairfax McLaughlin, *Matthew Lyon: The Hampden of Congress* (New York: 1900), p. 327. The Hampden in the title is English statesman John Hampden, who fought for the rights of Parliament against Charles I.

58. Smith, *Freedom's Fetters*, p. 237.

59. *Porcupine's Gazette*, July 1797.

60. Smith, *Freedom's Fetters*, p. 285.

61. Ibid., p. 339.

62. Ibid., p. 415.

63. Leonard Levy, *Emergence of a Free Press* (New York: Oxford University Press, 1985), p. 130.

64. Frank M. Anderson, "The Enforcement of the Alien and Sedition Laws," in *Annual Reports of the American Historical Association for the Year 1912* (Washington, D.C.: 1914), p. 126.

65. John D. Stevens, "Congressional History of the 1798 Sedition Law," *Journalism Quarterly*, Summer 1966, p. 256.

66. "Jefferson to Pennsylvania Governor Thomas McKean," Feb. 19, 1803, in Andrew Lipscomb, ed.-in-chief, *The Writings of Thomas Jefferson* (Washington, D.C.: 1904–1905), 9:449, 452.

67. *The Wasp*, July 7, 1802.

68. Ibid.

69. *The Wasp*, Aug. 23, 1802.

70. *The Balance and Columbia Repository*, Jan. 25, 1803.

71. *The Speeches at Full Length of Mr. Van Ness, Mr. Caines, the Attorney-General, Mr. Harrison, and General Hamilton in the Great Cause of the People against Harry Croswell, on an indictment for a*

libel on Thomas Jefferson, President of the United States (New York: G. & R. Waite, 1804; reprint, New York: Arno Press, 1970), p. 77.

72. Ibid., pp. 63, 64.

73. Kyu Ho Youm, "The Impact of *People v. Croswell* on Libel Law," *Journalism Monographs*, no. 113, June 1989, pp. 12, 13.

74. *The Wasp*, Jan. 26, 1803.

75. Thomas J. Fleming, "Verdicts of History 4: 'A Scandalous, Malicious and Seditious Libel,' " *American Heritage*, December 1967, p. 106.

76. Ibid.

5

Rendezvous with Destiny (1800–1850)

T he energetic, whiskered Horace Greeley of the *New York Tribune* summed up the mood of the country in the middle of the nineteenth century when he said in 1850, "Go west, young man, and grow up with the country." Expansionism became a dominating theme of the new nation and its media. As land, minerals, and products beckoned, rivers became crowded with newcomers, trappers, and lumberjacks transporting their products. Expansionism was a part of the American way of life.

THE CALL OF THE FRONTIER

The pulling force of the frontier was a way of understanding American history, argued historian Frederick Jackson Turner in a paper, "The Significance of the Frontier in American History," which he delivered at the Columbia Exposition in Chicago in 1893. While he recognized the influence of Central Europe and England on the American mentality, he saw the beckoning of the frontier and its opportunities as an explanation for much of the direction of the nation.

With the frontier emphasis, there came a loosening of the bonds with Europe and by inference a loosening of control of the Old East in the United States. In the essay "Why Did Not the United States Become Another Europe?" Turner explained the importance of growing geographically: "Each annexation meant not only more American territory, but the exclusion of dangerous parts of the European state system, fragments which aroused the cupidity and intrigues of rival European states, germs of the European malady."[1]

Turner, however, had his critics over the years, some of whom thought that his premise was too limited and that it slighted the influence of other factors shaping America, such as urbanization, the influence of the southern plantation system, the

"Hey, Mac! Which way is west?" *Greeley advised young people hundreds of times to go west. One young man who had tuberculosis and was in love wanted to know what to do. Greeley told him to marry her and go west. He did so, according to William Hale in* Horace Greeley: Voice of the People. *The young man with his bride settled in Illinois and he lived to be 97.* (Drawing by George Price; © 1952, 1980. The New Yorker Magazine, Inc.)

looseness of the Constitution, and conflicts between capital and labor groups, among other factors.[2]

Also embedded in the popular concept of expansionism was a converse theme of isolation. The nation embraced a philosophy of separatism to protect the country from the wiles of older powers. Despite the Neutrality Proclamation by George Washington in 1793 in response to the French declaration of war on England, the new country found it was still entangled in the affairs of European nations. As the

French and British sought to involve the United States in their war, and with war between the United States and Britain from 1812 to 1815, the new nation was reminded that it would have difficulty in extricating itself from European matters.

Not only was the matter a problem of relating to traditional governments. In an incident that sounds strangely modern, U.S. citizens—sailors—were taken hostage by pirates in Tunisia in 1813, and President James Madison had to send a negotiator, Mordecai Noah, an editor (*Charleston* [South Carolina] *Gazette*) and playwright, to ransom their freedom.[3] The United States was forced to be involved on the world stage.

The nation soon discovered an ideology that served its new mood and emerging responsibilities, Manifest Destiny, as it came to be known. It meant, as Harvard historian Frederick Merk, noted, "expansion, prearranged by Heaven."[4] The country simply had a calling—from God or the motivating force in the universe.

As a country without a past and desperately in search of a "usable past," the young nation needed a national purpose. It turned to symbols it knew and understood, taking as a beacon the call of the wilderness, drawing strength from the Puritans' dependence on God in their exodus from England. Historians Charles M. Segal and David C. Stineback observed, "The overriding objective of the Puritan errand into the wilderness of New England was to establish a 'city upon the hill,' a new Jerusalem that would be a beacon unto the world, complete the Protestant Reformation, and usher in the millennium."[5] The Puritans saw themselves as a chosen people, just as the Israelites of the Old Testament were. In addition, Manifest Destiny gave the members of the new nation self-reliance. Julius W. Pratt suggests "believers in 'Manifest Destiny' derived their faith . . . in part from a conviction of the superiority of American talents and political institutions over those of neighboring countries."[6]

The Country as "Temple of Freedom"

Geographical arguments entered the debate on the nation's destiny and definition. North and South America were set off to be one by the oceans on each side, with the western hemisphere meant to be made one by the blessings of leadership of the specially anointed United States. Many politicians and writers throughout the rest of the nineteenth century assumed that it was merely a matter of time—years or centuries—before all of North America and—some even believed—the South American continent joined "the temple of freedom,"[7] as Merk refers to the United States experiment. Outsiders who passed up opportunities to join the "temple" were considered badly misinformed, illiterate, and, in the boosterism style of much of the editorial journalism of the day, less than human.

But the "temple"—the beneficent, anointed nation—had to be protected. The Atlantic Ocean was not enough to keep out the colonizing nations. In 1823, in his annual message, President James Monroe enunciated a policy of hands off the Americas. Known as the Monroe Doctrine, the new foreign-policy principles said the American continents were free and independent and no longer open to colonization by European nations. Any attempt to extend the European influence in the western hemisphere would endanger peace. Although the doctrine drew a line against further intrusions by France, England, and Spain—a line not always observed—the Monroe Doctrine did have an inverse effect. It put the western hemisphere under the protection of the United States, and, in the name of protection and extending the benefits of the "temple," the nation made some land grabs itself. The nation had its eyes on the British northwest and Texas and even on extending its protection into the Pacific to the Sandwich Islands (later the Hawaiian Islands).

Editor Creates "Manifest Destiny"

A New York editor prepared the way for the new terminology of Manifest Destiny in 1845. John L. O'Sullivan, founder of the *Democratic Review* in 1837 and founder with future presidential candidate Samuel Tilden of the *New York Morning News* in

John O'Sullivan: He gave Manifest Destiny its name. (Harper's Weekly, Nov. 14, 1874; Collection of The New-York Historical Society)

1844, included in the *Review* an unsigned editorial that apparently used the term for the first time. The editorial "Annexation" in the *Review* of July–August 1845 (published by O'Sullivan with O. C. Gardiner) declared: "It is time now for opposition to the Annexaton of Texas to cease, all further agitation of the waters of bitterness and strife. . . . It is time for the common duty of Patriotism to the Country to succeed. . . . Texas is now ours. . . . She is no longer to us a mere geographical space. . . . She comes within the dear and sacred designation of Our Country." The editorial went on to insist that annexation was "the fulfilment of our manifest destiny to overspread the continent allotted by Providence for the free development of our yearly multiplying millions."[8]

In similar language in December the *Review* defended "the right of our manifest destiny to overspread and to possess the whole of the continent which Providence has given us for the development of the great experiment of liberty and federative self government entrusted to us."[9] The concept assumed the continent was an empty land and not belonging to those already living there.

Newspapers had much to do with developing the theory of Manifest Destiny. From the *Ohio Statesman* in Columbus and the *Illinois State Register* in Springfield to the New York papers came calls for expansion and annexation. The *New York Herald* also called for the annexation of all of Mexico. Noting coverage, Merk observes, "nothing was more sensational or exhilarating than the soul-stirring doctrine of Manifest Destiny."[10]

The Racist Side of Manifest Destiny

Many of the editorials supporting Manifest Destiny were outright racist. During the Mexican War the *California Star* talked about "that civil liberty which our race has created for men . . . that liberty is a sacred deposit which Heaven has entrusted to the keeping of their superior intelligence and courage." It argued that as "the East Indian bows to Britain, it is thus that this continent opens its vales to our flag."[11]

The papers had their epithets for the Mexicans. The *California Star* noted the "excitable nature of Mexicans," prone to brawls. The *New Orleans Weekly Bulletin*, referring to Mexico, warned of "provocations from inferior powers." Thomas Hart Benton, a senator from Missouri, spoke in the *Bangor* (Maine) *Daily Mercury* of the "bigoted priests and savage army" of Mexico. The *Little Rock* (Arkansas) *Gazette* talked of Americans' duty to the "down-trodden," such as Mexicans.[12]

By 1844 the Manifest Destiny theme was prevalent enough to decide the presidential election. Democrat Martin Van Buren opposed annexation of Texas, and the Whigs' Henry Clay ignored the issue; both lost (Van Buren failing even to get his party's nomination). "Dark horse" Democrat James Polk, totally devoted to annexing Texas and taking back the rest of Oregon (the northwest corner) from the British, won. With Polk came the Mexican War, and with its conclusion, the Rio Grande boundary with Texas.

Media as Purveyors of Information/Education
WIDENING COVERAGE ON THE DOMESTIC SCENE

The preoccupation with Manifest Destiny in the nineteenth century, as the nation's eye turned in on itself, occurred along with increasing interest in domestic news. Donald Ray Avery and other journalism historians put the War of 1812 as the point where the predominant concern with matters British and European began to give way to a new interest in matters at the national, state, and local levels in the United States. A study of 1,395 editions in the period 1808–1812 revealed that space given to foreign news ebbed significantly as domestic news increased. Regional coverage also increased, reflecting the growing sectionalism in U.S. politics.[13] Advertising called attention to new opportunities in newly acquired Indian lands to the west and the opening of state or territorial "land agencies" to regulate sales and taxation on parcels.

Timeliness was still not a major factor in news. Not until the invention of the telegraph in 1844 by Samuel F. B. Morse and the coming of instantaneous transmission of news—and the competitiveness of the mass-circulation New York papers—did an emphasis on the time element and the scoop mentality emerge. In the first part of the nineteenth century it still could take several weeks to close the gap between the event and the reporting of it. (The War of 1812 had been officially over for fifteen days when General Andrew Jackson, unaware of the news, fought and won the Battle of New Orleans against the British on January 8, 1815.)

Susan R. Brooker-Gross's study of "timeliness" in the early papers suggests that the lag in reporting an event was more than the effect of geographical limitations and slow transportation. The editors were just content to publish news when they received it.[14] In some ways that is true today in one-newspaper towns, where the sole newspaper can use a story any time without worrying about competition. However, with the presence of broadcasting, which can sometimes, but not always, report the story first, the newspaper became more competitive. In fact today the newspaper scooped by radio and television is forced to give more attention to the future—the second-day lead and update and the analysis and backgrounding of the breaking story.

Surprisingly even in the politically charged media milieu of the first half of the nineteenth century, such urgent matters as life-threatening health problems of the president could be taken in stride. Francis Blair seems to have taken his time in reporting the health lapse of lame-duck president Andrew Jackson after the November 1836 election. The *Washington Globe* carried a report, "The President's Health," dated a day earlier at the top of its front page: "Two nights ago the President was taken with a cough, which was succeeded by a considerable bleeding from the lungs. He had suffered for sometime previously with severe pain in his side."[15] A one-line sentence treated as a separate story, set off by rules, announced: "The Vice President reached this city a few days since." Very important news, but not reported with undue speed.

Cultivating Celebrities

Celebrity reporting, which seems so modern, was in full bloom. Hardly any celebrity reporting in history can match the effusive coverage given the Revolutionary War hero from abroad, the Marquis de Lafayette (Marie-Joseph-Paul-Yves-Roch-Gilbert du Motier). The *National Intelligencer*, generally the more reasoned and neutral of Washington papers, detailed every move of the marquis during his extended tour, even giving Latin inscriptions on ceremonial rings given him. The *Intelligencer* flipped over the people's hero when he finally arrived in the capital:

> Let this day, on which we are to receive in the Capitol the Guest of the American People, be sacred to harmony, gratitude, and unmixed pleasure! Never was there, on any occasion, a more emphatically spontaneous popular movement than that which the visit of the General Lafayette has produced. There is nothing in history which can compare with it. All hearts are moved by the same impulse; there is but one mind among a People of Ten Millions.[16]

The newspaper proceeded to print a ten-stanza ballad glorifying Lafayette, beginning, "Chief of the mighty heart! All hail!"

The attention to the celebrity general Lafayette just a few weeks before the U.S. presidential elections in 1824 did not hurt the prospects of America's own famous feisty general, a newcomer on the presidential scene, General Andrew Jackson (who almost made it to the presidency that year and did so the next time around in 1828). In all the Lafayette hoopla, Amos Kendall at the *Argus of Western America*, in Frankfort, Kentucky, was comparing his hero, Jackson, to George Washington . . . and Lafayette.[17]

Reporting Straw Polls

The popularity factor brought on political polls. The election of 1824 with its many candidates (Secretary of State John Quincy Adams; Secretary of the Treasury William Crawford, of Georgia; Henry Clay, Speaker of the House of Representatives; General and U.S. Senator Andrew Jackson; and for a time, John C. Calhoun, of South Carolina) saw the introduction of political polls and their results reported in the newspapers. Until 1824 presidential candidates were nominated by a congressional caucus. The system came under attack, particularly by Calhoun, who regarded the caucuses as instruments of deception. When Crawford jumped the gun by receiving endorsement from a small group of congressmen, Crawford was criticized for pre-empting the usual general caucus. Newspapers began to report some local straw polls at militia meetings and the consensus toasts offered candidates at Fourth of July gatherings.

The *Raleigh Star* reported these local straw polls and editorialized:

> As elections for members of the General Assembly are about to be holden in all counties of the State, would it not be advisable that polls be opened at the several election grounds at the same time, to test the strength of the different candidates for the Presidency?[18]

James W. Tankard, Jr., in his study of polling and the 1824 election, noted that on August 6, 1824, the *Star* gave a table with the aggregate votes of 49 meetings. The polls showed that Jackson had 3,423 votes, Adams 470, and Crawford 358.[19] These early polls were something to reckon with, as they sought to better inform readers about political developments and trends.

Media as Fourth Estate: Adversaries of Government
MEDIA APPLY MANIFEST DESTINY TO THE WEST

The newspapers, already recognized as a fourth estate or "branch" of government that exerted pressure and stood up to other branches of government, also had the effect of creating community and, more ambitiously, national policy. That may seem a bold claim for the humble pages of the daily journals. But consider Daniel Boorstin's belief that newspapers could define a community, if not create one. This former librarian of Congress noted, for example, that the first issue of the *Green Bay* (Wisconsin) *Intelligencer* announced that "its one principal object in view" was "the advancement of the country west of Lake Michigan." Boorstin also noted that Milwaukee's first newspaper, the *Advertiser*, was "not merely a pioneer newspaper, it was itself a pioneering enterprise, committed to the task of creating the city it hoped to 'advertise.' "[20]

The fourth estate likely had its influence on Jackson's policies. Andrew Jackson is remembered for a Manifest Destiny–inspired oppressive Indian policy, namely, the enactment of the Indian Removal Act in 1830 during his administration, contributing eventually to the tragic forced long march of the Cherokees from the Southeast to Indian Territory (now Oklahoma) in which 4,000 of 15,000 died and were buried along the way. Editors apparently played a hand in the developing policy, a combination of racial containment and land-grabbing Manifest Destiny mentality. One such supportive editor was Amos Kendall, editor of the *Argus of Western America*, in Frankfort, Kentucky. Kendall, who became the influential member of Jackson's powerful informal "Kitchen Cabinet," editorialized on Indian containment.

In the *Argus* (before it was renamed the *Argus of Western America*) Kendall appeared on the one hand to be supporting the welfare of the Indians, noting that Indian policy often had ignored the welfare of the Indians, and on the other hand to be giving reasons for containment. He expounded on a rationale for the reservation because otherwise "tribes could be so surrounded with white settlements as to cut off their game and make agriculture necessary to their subsistence,"[21] thus making the savage hunting ways passé.

The newspapers shaped their own versions of internal Manifest Destiny and "civilizing" efforts to bring the savage into the honored temple of the nation. Newspapers, reflecting a general pursuit of expansionism with a philosophy of containment and educating the "savage," were catalysts of federal policies on internal Indian and other matters.

The *Washington Gazette* had once noted: "We every day witness the extensive and almost absolute influence of the power of the press over the minds of people. . . . Even the government of our union is so much swayed by the press, that it has not been inappropriately styled a government of newspapers."[22]

Amos Kendall: Kentucky editor joins Jackson. (National Portrait
Gallery; The Free Library of Philadelphia)

Media as Political Organs
BOOSTING THE OUTSIDER AND UNDERDOG

In the close election of 1824, curiously all the challengers were Republicans (or
"Democratic-Republicans," in the old sense of the words). Yet the candidates in
this one-party system had their special interests, if not overriding differences:
John Quincy Adams, a shaper of foreign policy and the Monroe Doctrine as
Monroe's secretary of state; William Crawford, of Georgia, backed by the states-
rights wing of the Republican party; Henry Clay, a promoter of the "American
System" of internal improvements and supporter of higher tariffs to generate
greater home markets for home-produced goods; and Andrew Jackson, who had
taken few positions on the issues of the day. The election came down to a battle of personalities.

American politics had seen personal invective before, as the Federalists and the
anti-Federalists battled with one another. Washington, in his second term, and John
Adams had offended the sensitivities of Jefferson and proponents of broader represen-

tation and affirmation of states rights. This all played out against the backdrop of pro-British monarchical tendencies (the inclination of the Federalists) and pro-French representative government (the inclination of the Republicans). But the new politics of the 1820s was ushered in with an "era of good feelings," a term coined by the *Columbian Centinel* in Boston to reflect the peaceful hue of James Monroe's administration. The era followed the settling of the European wars that so stirred American politics. Monroe, the last Revolutionary War veteran to serve in the White House, had swept the electoral vote in the 1820 election (231 to 1). The stage was set for new beginnings. The cults of personalities (going beyond mere hero worship as with Washington) were about to emerge. By 1840 the forces were whipped into shape and symbols developed to create specially controlled images and serviceable personality cults.

Suddenly, New Personalities

Social and economic factors, reflected in the coverage and interests of the media, contributed to the interest in personalities. (1) There was a whole new generation and the opportunity to create new leaders. (2) The rise of sections, namely the West and the South, guaranteed a more varied cast of participants in the political life of the nation. (3) The issues were complex, for example, setting acceptable tariffs on goods (the North wanted high tariffs in order to protect its manufacturing interests from foreign competition, while the South favored lower tariffs so it could get goods from lower cost manufacturers in England). Then there was the growing tension over slavery as new states were being added: should the states be free or slave? The Missouri Compromise of 1820 saw Maine enter as a free state, Missouri as slave, and slavery barred from the rest of the Louisiana Purchase territory. With issues so far from definitive solutions, the voters looked beyond the issues to the man. (4) A growing interest in satire and deflating those in power developed. The writings of Seba Smith and Charles Augustus Davis under the pen name "Major Jack Downing" poked fun at politicians, opening up an interest in the foibles of those in power. (5) Printing images of personalities gained momentum in 1829 after lithography (the process of printing from stone or other flat surfaces, using the principle that grease repels water—with ink absorbed on the nonwet parts) joined line engraving as a means of reproducing art. Nathaniel Currier and James Ives employed the process, and their works included reproductions of political cartoons. The coming of photography, and particularly the development in the 1840s of photography and daguerreotype portraits, made images of personalities more accessible.

With the advent of Andrew Jackson in politics, personal lives became issues. He fought off innuendoes about the legitimacy of his marriage—the divorce decree of his wife, Rachel Donelson Robards, had not been final when they married, and eventually the Jacksons went through a second marriage rite.

Jackson had been wounded several times in duels, and in 1806 he shot a lawyer to death. In the election of 1828, opponents circulated a campaign poster published in Philadelphia called "The Coffin Handbill." It showed eighteen coffins, implying that Jackson had caused the death of eighteen men, including the execution some believed unnecessarily, of two British seamen in the War of 1812.

The Lighter Side

"Major Jack Downing" and Manifest Destiny

Critical voices of Manifest Destiny were not easy to detect in much of the news coverage of politics and events of the day, particularly in Democratic papers, but criticism certainly could be found in the writings of a noted newspaper humorist of the early and middle nineteenth century. He was Seba Smith (1792–1868), who wrote as "Major Jack Downing" in the *Portland* (Maine) *Courier*. His dedication to the use of dialect contributed to the linguistic break with England, a longer process than the political break, according to one commentator on Smith.[23]

Smith collected his Downing writings into several books; one of them, *My Thirty Years Out of the Senate*, published in 1859, contained most of the Downing series. Seba Smith researchers Patricia and Milton Rickels include three excerpts from Smith (Downing) on Manifest Destiny, along with their comments:

On Manifest Destiny

After the personality of [President] Polk, Smith's second target is ideological—Manifest Destiny. His thematic work is "annexing," and his method is exaggeration to show the concept of Manifest Destiny as a rationalization of lust for power. As Polk's confidential representative, Jack writes from Mexico:

I hope there ain't no truth in the story that was buzz'd about here in the army, a day or two ago, that Mr. Polk had an idea, when we get through annexin' down this way, of trying his hand at it over in Europe and Africa, and round there. And to prevent any quarreling beforehand about it on this side of the water, he's agoing to agree to run the Missouri Compromise line over there, and cut Europe up into Free States and Africa into Slave States. Now, I think he had better keep still about that till we get this South America business all done, and well tied up. It isn't well for a body to have too much business on his hands at once.

In addition to Jack's direct statement, Smith also attacks the fanaticism and danger of Manifest Destiny in a dream-allegory:

I dreamt t'other night that we had got through annexin' all North and South America; and then I thought our whole country was turned into a monstrous great ship of war, and Cape Horn was the bowsprit, and Mr. Polk the captain. And the captain was walking the deck with his mouth shet, and everybody was looking at him and wondering what he was goin' to do next. At last he sung out, "Put her about; we'll sail across now and take Europe, and Asha, and Africa in tow—don't stop for bird's-egging round among the West India Islands; we can pick them up as we come back along—crowd all sail now and let her have it."

Smith expresses both the danger of the adventure in Mexico and the essential evil of war in a story that Jack tells of Bill Johnson. Polk is mistaken, Jack writes, in his conviction that peace can be conquered:

"It's a good deal as 'twas with Bill Johnson, when he and I was boys, and he undertook to conquer a hornet's nest, expectin' to get lots of honey. He took a club, and marched bravely up to it, and hit it an awful dig, and knocked into a thousand flinders.

" 'There, blast ye,' says Bill, 'I guess you're done to now,' as he begun to look around for the honey. But he soon found 'twasn't conquered—'twas only scattered. And presently they begun to fly at him, and sting him on all sides. . . . At last Bill found he should soon be done to, himself, if he stayed there, so he cut and run.

" 'Hullo,' says I, 'Bill, where's your honey?'

" 'Darn it all,' says he, 'if I hain't got no honey, I knocked their house to pieces; I've got that to comfort me.' "

Source: Patricia and Milton Rickels, *Seba Smith* (Boston: Twayne Publishers, 1977), pp. 125–127; excerpts from Major Jack Downing, *My Thirty Years Out of the Senate* (New York: Oaksmith & Co., 1859), pp. 273, 280, 281.

The personal lives of Jackson's cabinet members even became talk of the town. When Jackson's secretary of war, John Eaton, married an innkeeper's daughter whose husband had committed suicide, the "proper" wives of Jackson's cabinet members and others in government decided to snub the woman, Margaret (Peggy) O'Neale Eaton. Jackson, remembering how his own wife, Rachel, had been snubbed, was incensed and set about reorganizing his cabinet. Eaton resigned from the cabinet, but so did Secretary of State Martin Van Buren, thus encouraging Jackson to call for other resignations. Eaton himself challenged several of his ex-colleagues to duel, but they declined.

The pro-Jackson *Globe* denounced the *United States Telegraph* for publishing the "slanders" against Peggy Eaton. Van Buren was rewarded by being appointed minister to Britain for his action in resigning the cabinet so Jackson could clean house. However, the Senate with Vice President John Calhoun, at odds with Jackson over states rights, cast the deciding vote that rejected Van Buren's appointment. The *Globe* proceeded to treat Van Buren as a martyr and paved the way for him to be Jackson's next vice president, replacing Calhoun. The *Globe* editor, Francis Preston Blair, denounced detractors who voted against Van Buren's appointments as traitors, and then as an added thought, because of the tension of the times, he started carrying a pistol in his umbrella for protection.[24]

Blair had been brought by Jackson to Washington to start a new Jackson newspaper after the defection of Duff Green at the *United States Telegraph*. Green's *Telegraph* had been the main organ in Washington supporting the Jackson candidacy in 1828. But Green was ostracized by the president when he sided with Calhoun, who favored nullification rights, that is, the rights of states to secede. With Jackson saying that traitors—nullifiers, presumably including his vice president Calhoun—should be hanged from the highest pole, Jackson could count no longer on editorial support from the *Telegraph*.

Blair became the most important man in Jackson's advisory "Kitchen Cabinet." "Give it to Bla'ar," the old general-president could often be heard saying. Blair had been associated with Amos Kendall, becoming editor of the *Argus of Western America* briefly after Kendall sold the *Argus* to G. E. Russell in 1829.

Amos Kendall and Mrs. Clay

Jackson owed a lot to Kendall and his dedicated support in the *Argus* in the election of 1828. In an election that saw a war of personalities rather than issues conducted by editors, Kendall's own personal life became embroiled in the political coverage in the newspapers. Kendall had been a supporter of Henry Clay earlier in Clay's political career.

In fact, Kendall had every reason to be in the camp of Clay, as he was a special friend of Mrs. Clay, and, when Clay was away in Europe for a year, Kendall was the tutor of the Clay children. Mrs. Clay nursed Kendall back from a serious illness during Clay's absence. Kendall described his devotion to the Clays in one of several open letters to Clay in the *Argus of Western America*, after Kendall broke with Clay to support Jackson instead of Adams. Adams had named Clay secretary of state in 1825 after Clay threw his votes to Adams in the 1824 election at the expense of Jackson. In the *Argus*, Kendall responded to charges by the *National Daily Journal* (pro-Adams) that he had betrayed the trust of the Clays and was no better than a beggar. Kendall laid out an extensive personal history in his published letter to Clay, insisting, "I did not go to your house as a *beggar*, as those who accuse me of ingratitude have represented. I went as a hired teacher."[25]

Kendall went on after the Jackson victory in 1828 not only to be one of Jackson's closest advisers (with Blair) but also to serve as an administrator of the Treasury Department and as postmaster general. He returned to publishing in 1840 with his *Kendall's Expositor,* and, after Samuel F. B. Morse launched the telegraph in 1844, Kendall served as Morse's agent and contributed to development and proliferation of the telegraph.

Media as Voices of Reform

EDITORS SEE "SPOILS SYSTEM" AS REFORM

The Jackson administration is remembered in part by its haste to give jobs to those who supported the president in the election of 1828. The "spoils system" had been around, especially at the state level, but Jackson's enthusiastic embrace and defense of the system, which some thought to be actually a form of corruption, were unique. "The common man, too long thwarted by official indifference, had to be given a sense that the government was in truth the people's government," says Arthur M. Schlesinger, Jr., in *The Age of Jackson*. "Jackson's answer was shrewd and swift: a redistribution of federal offices."[26]

Contrary to being a manifestation of corruption, with jobs as payoffs to political supporters, the system was touted by Jackson and his aides, among them newspaper editors, as a basic reform measure. Jackson rationalized that the spoils-system reform turned out of office unrepresentative groups and also prevented the development of an office-holding class. The president explained in his first annual address: "The duties of all public officers are, or at least admit of being made, so plain and simple that men of intelligence may readily qualify themselves for their performance; and I cannot but believe that more is lost by the long continuance of men in office than is generally to be gained by their experience. . . . He who is removed has the same means of obtaining a living that are enjoyed by the millions who never held office."[27] He discharged 252 out of 612 presidential appointees—about 40 percent,[28] and 919 civil servants out of 10,000 overall.[29]

"Reform-minded" editors, favoring the spoils or "rotation system," took some of the jobs themselves. Newspaper editors were named to major positions. All four of the editors of the *Boston Statesman* received federal jobs, for instance. One of them became collector of customs at Boston, one of the best-paid federal jobs in the nation. Duff Green of the *United States Telegraph* became official printer for both houses of Congress, and three of his editors received jobs. Kendall at the *Argus* was named fourth auditor of the Treasury Department. Herbert Ershkowitz estimated that in all some 60 editors were named to patronage jobs by Jackson.[30]

This kind of "reform" did not go unchallenged by some editors. Thomas Ritchie of the *Richmond Enquirer* warned: "Invade the freedom of the Press and the freedom of elections by showering patronage too much on editors of newspapers and on members of Congress, and the rights of the people themselves are exposed to imminent danger."[31]

The "reform rotation" system became known as the "spoils" system after a New York Democratic senator, William Marcy, who supported Van Buren, remarked that he saw "nothing wrong in the rule that to the victor belong the spoils of the enemy."[32] The system still exists, although curtailed by the passing of the Pendleton Act in 1883, which set up the Civil Service Commission to test and screen applicants for federal jobs.

Anne Royall's Independent Voice

One editor's voice that remained independent and declined to be a mouthpiece for a party was that of Anne Royall, who initially wrote acclaimed travel books (ten in all), then late in life, at age 62, launched two newspapers in succession, *Paul Pry* and *The Huntress*. Her crusades ranged from calling for reform in the justice system in order to improve the treatment of immigrants and Native Americans, to better accountability in Congress, to free public education; and foremost on her list was an avid belief in the separation of church and state. She saved most of her attack for evangelical Christians (those who believe a prime duty is to convert others) and the anti-Masons (those who opposed secret lodges such as the Masons). Having accepted her late husband's rationalist ideas based on deist ideas (God is absent from a direct role in the world) of François Voltaire and Thomas Paine, she had no use for organized religions that pressured people to believe in a God actively participating in the world through the Trinity—Father, Son, and Holy Spirit.

She fought back against physical and psychological means to convert her. "When bands of children, prompted either by mischief or adults in the congregation, broke the windows of her home," says Maurine Beasley, of the University of Maryland, "church members gathered beneath the shattered panes and prayed for her soul. But Mrs. Royall declined meek submission to their ministrations. She became vociferous, she yelled names, she staged scenes and she spewed venom."[33] She was charged with being a "common scold," drawing upon an obscure law, and ordered to stand trial in a Washington courtroom. Ten witnesses for the prosecution told how she had spilled out a flood of vulgarities and obscenities. James Gordon Bennett, a young Washington reporter later famous for founding the *New York Herald*, who would have his own run-in with religious leaders, sat at her side as an adviser.

The trial in the summer of 1829 received maximum attention. Royall had lined up her own impressive list of defense witnesses. She even had the audacity to ask the new president, Andrew Jackson, to testify on her behalf, but he sent Secretary of War John Eaton. He testified she had always been a lady when she came to his office for interviews.[34]

Royall was convicted on the "common scold" charge and ordered to pay a $10 fine and post a $100 bond to keep the peace for a year. Her newspaper friends chipped in to pay the fine and bond. Always hard-strapped for cash (she lost her inheritance from her husband in a court challenge by other relatives), she died near penniless at age 85 and was buried in a pauper's grave.

Media as Voices of Freedom

MINORITY MEDIA PIONEERS: THEIR CAUSE WAS CLEAR

Although ethnic papers—French, German, and others—had been in vogue since early colonial days, the voices of oppressed nonwhite minorities in America began to be heard in media of their own in the 1820s. In March 1827 the first black newspaper in America, *Freedom's Journal*, appeared, and in February of the next year the first Native American newspaper, the *Cherokee Phoenix*, came out. But the new newspapers serving nonwhites, coming 137 years and 138 years after the first paper in the colonies, had a formidable task in seeking to penetrate the system of economic and cultural imperialism that institutionalized subordination.

Freedom's Journal appeared at a time of hope for African Americans in New York state, which had passed a law in 1817 that said slaves in New York state were to begin to be freed on July 4, 1827—"males at 28, and females at 25 years old, and all slaves born after the 31st of March, 1817, shall be free at 21 years old, and also all slaves born before the 4th day of July, 1799, shall be free on the 4th day of July, 1827."[35] Although, largely as a result of the law, the number of slaves in New York state went from 10,088 in the 1820 census to 75 in the 1830 census,[36] "the state was still a happy hunting ground for kidnappers" under the 1793 Fugitive Slave Law.[37] Slaves were still held across the river in New Jersey. Although blacks had the right to vote in New York state from 1824, the New York state constitution required blacks to have at least $250 to vote, while whites did not have to meet this requirement. And as black historian Frederick Detweiler points out, the local press in New York at the time made "the vilest attacks on the Afro-American."[38] And the abolitionist press was not to get off the ground until 1830.

The Founding of *Freedom's Journal*

In this atmosphere two African-American men who had never been slaves, joined by a dozen freedmen, launched their own voice of freedom in New York City,

Samuel Cornish (left) and John Russwurm (right): Cofounders of Freedom's Journal. (The Free Library of Philadelphia)

Freedom's Journal, March 16, 1827. The cofounders were Samuel E. Cornish, pastor of the first black Presbyterian church in America, and John Brown Russwurm, a native of Jamaica. Cornish had attended Princeton, and Russwurm, Bowdoin College in Brunswick, Maine. "We wish to plead our own cause," they said in a statement of purpose in the first issue. "Too long has the publick been deceived by misrepresentations, in things which concern us dearly." They said that their paper, whose motto was "Righteousness exalteth a nation," would call into question the views of good and respected people as well. "From the press and the pulpit we have suffered much by being incorrectly represented. Men, whom we equally love and admire have not hesitated to represent us disadvantageously." And while seeking to inform and educate, the paper "would not be unmindful of our brethren who are still in the iron fetters of bondage."[39]

In its two years, *Freedom's Journal* dedicated a number of columns to the discussion of the colonization movement that sought to resettle American blacks in Africa. At first, both editors objected to colonization, believing in the eventual emergence of equal opportunity in America. But after six months Russwurm began to support colonization, with Cornish still opposed. Cornish resigned, citing his health among the reasons, and returned to church work. His presence, however, continued in

Freedom's Journal; he was listed as general agent, and *Freedom's Journal* ran ads for Cornish and printed notices of weddings at which he officiated.[40] Eventually Russwurm began printing minutes of the colonization society. Russwurm despaired of hope for the black person in America, saying that being "united will avail him little; after all, he is considered a being of inferior order."[41]

Russwurm quit his post as editor, and the paper was discontinued for a brief time. Some say he was forced to resign because of his new support for colonization.[42] Within a few months Russwurm himself sailed for Africa. He edited the *Liberia Herald* and became Liberian superintendent of education and governor of the Maryland Colony. Cornish returned as editor and changed the name to *Rights for All*. He continued to promote education and causes such as equal voting rights. But with inadequate financial backing, the renewed paper failed in six months.

Some, such as Roland Wolseley, suggest that *Freedom's Journal* (*Rights for All*) was aimed mostly at whites because of a low literacy rate among blacks at the time.[43] Barrow notes, however, that 71,047 of the 105,891 free blacks in the North, according to the 1850 census, were classified as "literate." He concludes: "Even if the percentage had been considerably lower in 1827 than it was in 1850, there still should have been enough to support the paper's circulation of 800–1000 subscribers."[44] Nevertheless, he says, it served as a medium to give "blacks a voice of their own and an opportunity not only to answer the attacks printed in the white press but to read articles on black accomplishments, marriages, deaths, that the white press of its day ignored."[45]

The *Cherokee Phoenix* Appears

The *Cherokee Phoenix*, the first Native American newspaper, appearing in New Echota, Georgia, on February 21, 1828, lasted six years, until May 31, 1834. Founder and editor for the first four and a half years was Elias Boudinott, a young Cherokee schoolteacher. He was aided by a missionary to the Cherokees, Samuel A. Worcester, who had experience in a print shop in New England. Worcester encouraged a national mission board to help finance a Cherokee newspaper. Boudinott, who was educated at Andover Theological Seminary, Newton Centre, Massachusetts, and was a tutor of Worcester in the Cherokee language, set off for a speaking tour to New England to help raise funds.[46]

The paper, according to a prospectus written by Worcester, would print the laws and documents of the Cherokee nation, matters of education and religion, news of the day, and articles to promote the Cherokee culture. The paper would also take up Cherokee causes.[47]

Early issues of the *Phoenix* discussed the development of the rather recently devised Cherokee written language. The paper was published in English and Cherokee. Lifestyle articles on dress costumes and housing appeared. A symbol of the bird phoenix rising from ashes was at the center of the logo, but later it was

Elias Boudinott: Editor, Cherokee Phoenix
(Georgia Department of Natural
Resources, Historic Preservation Section)

replaced and the words "and Indian Advocate" inserted. The symbol was, however, revived later.

Curiously, the wealthy members of the tribe kept black slaves, and the Cherokees, like their white counterparts, had laws discriminating against blacks. One Cherokee law forbade intermarriage between black slaves and Indians. Another Cherokee law made it illegal for slaves to own livestock and called for confiscation of any such property owned by slaves.[48] The *Phoenix* engaged in some racist humor, such as printing black-dialect anecdotes.[49]

A group of 300 Cherokees, Boudinott among them, signed the Treaty of New Echota, which called for the Cherokees to move to territory in the west, today's Oklahoma, with a $5 million payment for their Georgia lands. The bulk of the tribe resisted passively until the government evicted them and put them in camps, leading to the 1838–1839 forced march, the "Trail of Tears."

For their role in signing the settlement document, Boudinott and several other participants were slain with knives and hatchets by Cherokees.

Boudinott's legacy, however, is more than being the editor of the first Native American newspaper. Barbara F. Luebke, in a tribute to Boudinott, notes that he was influential as an editor and saw his articles reprinted widely in other papers. He was the father of a "dynasty" of Indian journalists. Two of his sons were associated with later Cherokee papers. Luebke says, "Above all else was Boudinott's integrity as an editor. He worked hard to live up to the principles he set forth."[50]

Mexican War Restrictions

The Mexican War, 1846–1848, saw military suppression of ten newspapers by military commanders, namely, by generals Winfield Scott and Zachary Taylor. A Spanish-language paper, *El Liberal*, started in Matamoros in northern Mexico behind the American lines, was especially vicious in denouncing "the barbarians from the North," and Taylor closed it after only one issue.[51] Next suppressed, also in Matamoros, was the American-owned *Republic of the Rio Grande*, which was critical of President Polk's policies. In all, five American-operated and five Mexican-operated newspapers were shut down. Yet, as Tom Reilly noted, war correspondents generally were not involved, only newspapers threatening the peace in military-occupied zones.[52]

Media as Businesses
EDITORS NEEDED EXTRA INCOME

Patronage—support for an editor—from a candidate or candidate backer was a way for papers to survive. "Financial subsidies to the partisan press were common and vital," says Gerald J. Baldasty in his book on the commercialization of the news in the nineteenth century. "For editors, the subsidies often provided financial stability in a notoriously unstable business."[53] Two-thirds of all newspapers started in North Carolina from 1815 to 1836 failed within several years. In one period of twelve months, one paper folded every other month.[54] Many editors were paid in produce and other goods, if they were paid by subscribers at all. More likely than not editors experienced a shortage of cash—unless they were in on the subsidies. Baldasty also cites the studies of Wisconsin newspapers by Carolyn Stewart Dyer, who found that most papers depended on patronage.

Subsidies as a form of patronage came to the papers in many ways. Editors who were in favor of reigning politicians could count on printing contracts from the government and politicians. By signing their names to newspapers, politicians could send newspapers free through the mails, and many editors allowed politicians to mail the bulk of their papers. And, of course, politicians rewarded their favorites with extra jobs. In 1830 twenty-two editors alone were serving as postmasters in New York state.[55] State politicians also rewarded cooperating editors with legal printing contracts and jobs such as clerks.[56]

Actually, the government had contracted with private printers—many of them publishers and editors—from the earliest colonial times. But by 1819, says William

E. Ames, several developments called this practice into question. First, the bid system did not really produce much money for the printer, as the competitive bids kept the profits down. Editors found that they were actually losing money. The lack of quality of government printing—produced in understaffed shops—caught the attention of the government. A government committee investigating alternatives opted for creating a government printing office. But since the government was not ready to move in that direction, the committee then suggested a system of set fees, "quite generous in nature, which enabled the printer to carry out the work expeditiously" and with quality workmanship.[57] Henry Clay had been behind the plan, hoping to inaugurate a system that would help the *National Intelligencer* in Washington in turn for the paper's support. The *Intelligencer* was a distinguished paper, remembered for its courage in assailing the British in the War of 1812 (the British in the city of Washington made a point to destroy the paper in 1814). Clay's "contract system" had the effect of enabling "each house [of Congress] to select a newspaper spokesman so that the country now had congressional as well as presidential quasi-official journals," says Ames. This system was important in the period 1819 to 1846, he says, "for frequently the congressional printing contracts enabled newspapers opposing the administration to remain alive and to provide a voice for various factions."[58]

In Debt to the Bank of the United States

Some editors found themselves in a quandary over their financial allegiances. Jackson's close aide Francis Blair had borrowed from the Second Bank of the United States before he departed the *Argus of Western America* to edit the *Washington Globe* for Jackson. Favoring a decentralized banking system and greater circulation of money, Jackson fiercely opposed the Second Bank.

The First Bank of the United States, launched in 1791 as a central bank to issue currency and to serve as a depository for federal funds, also took part in commercial banking. It was nevertheless a private corporation with virtually no government control over its transactions. Competing with state-chartered banks, it also held the notes of the state banks. The First Bank could threaten to call in the notes for redemption in hard cash, which had the effect of curtailing the amount of paper money a state or local bank could issue. Farmers and those in debt who favored policies of plentiful or "cheap" money were vehemently opposed to the First Bank's "hard money" policies.

When the Second Bank of the United States was created, after the charter of the First Bank expired, opposition by the "common man" in the South and West to the bank had materialized. They saw the bank as dominated by Philadelphia financier Nicholas Biddle and the eastern establishment.

The pro-Jackson editors who took loans from the Second Bank may not have been generally compromised. Yet there appeared to be exceptions, such as James Watson Webb of the *Morning Courier and New York Enquirer*. After dealing with the bank, he changed from opposing the recharter of the bank to favoring it. One writer on the bank says the charge that Webb and some others were bribed "was a natural one."[59]

Media as Definers and Keepers of Values (and Biases)
TURNING AN INSULT INTO A CAMPAIGN SLOGAN

The media found two important themes that they could apply in judging news "value": (1) the preoccupation with the humble-origin theme, the *underdog*, and (2) the *outsider*, in conflict with the rich and privileged. The emphasis worked for Jackson, who came from outside the eastern establishment and as an underdog challenged an entrenched incumbent. The approach also worked later for William Henry Harrison, with the log cabin and hard cider slogans that placed him in the public image as a common man.[60]

To get elected in 1840 a candidate had to be larger than life. He still had to run in the image of the great hero, Andrew Jackson, the victor of the War of 1812 and a man identified with the rigor and strength of the frontier. The new candidate had to be an astute politician with a knack for knowing when to lunge forth or when to lay back and let the people come to him. He would ride in on a wave of discontent, just as Jackson capitalized on the discontent with the unpopular John Quincy Adams, who held the press at bay and was virtually unconcerned with image making.

The new president elected in 1840 would also likely be one who countered the aristocratic, high-handed image of Jackson's handpicked successor, Democrat Martin Van Buren, who had won in 1836. Van Buren's administration was cursed largely by an economic panic started in 1837. Yet the successful candidate in 1840 would be a frontier hero, a "pseudo-Crockett," as Bernard A. Weisberger put it, filling in for the logical missing frontier candidate (Davy Crockett had failed in a bid for Congress in 1834 and perished at the Alamo in 1836).[61]

The "Log Cabin" Candidate

The man to fit the bill was General William Henry Harrison, largely retired at his farm in North Bend, Ohio, 16 miles west of Cincinnati. Although he had spent much of his life on the frontier, he came from a rich Virginia family. He was a war hero, made friends easily, was identified with the fresh new party, the Whigs, and was free of the accumulated baggage of Jackson and Van Buren. Harrison had led troops victoriously against Indians at Tippecanoe Creek near Lafayette, Indiana, in 1811. During the War of 1812 he crushed Tecumseh's Indian confederacy at the Battle of the Thames (October 5, 1813) in Ontario—a victory over a sizable force of British troops and Indians.

After a career in government, first as administrator of the Northwest Territory and then as governor of the newly created Indiana Territory for more than ten years, and terms in the Ohio Senate and the U.S. Senate, in 1840 Harrison waited, like the

Roman Cincinnatus at his plow, ready to be summoned to lead his nation from suppression. He was now merely a clerk of the Court of Common Pleas in Hamilton County, as he enjoyed the good life in the magnificent mansion built around a four-room cabin he had bought from his father-in-law after leaving the military in 1796.[62] He fit the Whig perennial stance of an underdog. "Whig candidates were often underdogs, usually running against Democratic incumbents," said campaign

Beginnings of Photography

Although some of the principles for the development of photography had been known since nearly the beginning of time, it was not until almost the middle of the nineteenth century that photography became a reality.

The chemical action of light was observed by prehistoric humans as the sun's rays dried skins and tanned human skin. The creating of images mechanically, in contrast to cave art and the classical sculptures and tapestries of later times, goes back about 1,000 years.

A forerunner of photography as known today was the *camera obscura*, literally a "dark room." It was a big closed box or small room with a tiny hole in the wall through which light came and left an inverted image of the scene that was outside the "peephole." These shadow images could not be literally fixed, but they could be traced, and therefore formed a reasonably true picture.

It was up to Frenchman Joseph Nicephore Niepce in the early 1800s to find a way to fix an image, "making light draw for him."[63] He coated a sheet of glass, pewter, or copper with varnish made up of bitumen of Judaea, a kind of tar or asphalt, and exposed it to light for a lengthy time. When the picture emerged and the varnish hardened, Niepce submitted the plate to an acid bath that removed the varnish. He would then give the plate to an artist/engraver who cut in lines and inked it for printing.

Niepce, historians believe, made the first permanent impression from a *camera obscura* in 1822. However, the first photograph that exists today is a picture by Niepce on pewter, from an exposure of eight hours of a rooftop outside Niepce's room. He continued to improve his "heliographs" by exposure of the plate to iodine fumes.

A Showman's Daguerreotype

Meanwhile Louis-Jacques-Mandé Daguerre, a showman who created large diorama scenes for exhibits, was doing his own experiments in Paris. He proposed that he and Niepce work together, and a ten-year pact was signed. Niepce, the older of the two, died in 1833. Continuing experimenting, Daguerre discovered in 1837 that the fumes from the heating of mercury would allow the developing of a more perfect image. The "daguerreotype," as it was called, however, was susceptible to the change in light. It would disappear in direct rays of the sun and would have to be held at certain angles away from the direct sun.

Daguerre is credited with the first picture of a human being. Shot from a window or roof of a five- or six-story building in 1839, the picture shows a Paris boulevard. A figure—almost a stick-figure image—can be

(Continued)

seen with a left leg raised on a flower-container, or is it a vertical water pump? Perhaps it is a man tying his shoes or cleaning them.

The daguerreotype image was considered superior to the rough image that another inventor, Henry Fox Talbot, working in England at the same time as Daguerre, was able to achieve on paper. However, Talbot improved on the process and invented the paper negative from which multiple positive prints could be made. In 1844 he produced *The Pencil of Nature*, the first book with "photography," as his process was called.

A picture of a distant fire raging through Hamburg, Germany, in 1842 is considered the world's first news photograph. The first war photographer under fire was Englishman Roger Fenton, who took his "photographic van" darkroom to the front as he recorded the Crimean War of 1854–1856 in which England, France, and Turkey defeated Russia for domination of southeastern Europe. Also by midcentury tourists were carrying cameras with them.

It was left to George Eastman in 1886 to produce a small, handheld box camera that contained a roll of forty-eight negative frames. "Two years later," says photo historian Peter Pollack, "he developed the perfect amateur camera of its day and coined a word which has been synonymous with 'camera'

George Eastman with a Kodak camera in 1890. (Fred Church; George Eastman House)

Frances Benjamin Johnston: First woman to gain a reputation for news and documentary photography. A noted photographer of presidents, she got the last pictures of President William McKinley before the fatal shooting by an assassin.

ever since, 'Kodak.' . . . It was George Eastman's slogan, 'You press the button, we do the rest.' "[64]

The use of photographs in publications was slow in coming. The practice was to have artists convert the photograph to lines so that it could be reproduced as a woodcut or zinc etching—an acid bath would eliminate material between lines, thus making the lines stand out for impressions when printing. Thousands of artists were employed doing the photo conversions for newspapers and magazines.

First Use of Halftones

Frederic Ives, head of the photo laboratory at Cornell, succeeded in 1878 in the student newspaper in producing a halftone—a photo broken up through a screen into small dots so the dots would pick up the ink on the presses. Stephen Horgan is credited with achieving quality production of halftones with a print called "Shantytown," which appeared in 1880 in the *The New York Graphic*, where Horgan was art editor. Halftones were not used on the big rotary presses, where they had to be adapted to curved plates, until 1897.

chronicler Keith Melder. "And Whigs tended to nominate leaders not closely identified with partisanship, such as old generals."[65]

Being an underdog and outsider forced Harrison into an aggressive mode despite his moderate countenance. He became the first presidential candidate "to go out on the stump in his own behalf," making twenty-three speeches (all in Ohio).[66]

Harrison had Thurlow Weed and his Whig-bent organ the *Albany* (New York) *Journal*. But Harrison also had a youthful, ambitious newcomer, Horace Greeley. Fresh out of the print shop, Greeley, the future founder of the *New York Tribune*, listened to Weed and Weed's ally, Governor William H. Seward of New York, and launched *The Log Cabin*, a full-size weekly paper devoted to the presidential bid of General Harrison in 1840.

"Tippecanoe and Tyler, Too"

Greeley carried woodcuts of the general and detailed narratives of his crusades against the Indians. And curiously Greeley included songs—words with music—praising the general and his running mate, John Tyler. Some fifteen songs were printed during the campaign by *The Log Cabin*. Most notable perhaps is the one dedicated to the familiar political slogan about the general and his running mate, "Tippecanoe and Tyler, Too," sixteen stanzas in all:[67]

> What has caused this great
> commotion, motion, motion,
> Our Country through!
> It is the Ball a rolling on,
> For Tippecanoe and Tyler too—
> Tippecanoe and Tyler too,
> And with them we'll beat little Van,
> Van, Van is a used up man,
> And with them we'll beat little Van. . . .

Harrison got some help from a little-known plainsman, Abraham Lincoln. At 31, Lincoln, himself running for the Illinois House of Representatives, stumped the state for the "log cabin" candidate. In one encounter, Lincoln, suspecting the Democratic opponent in his debate of being as vain and pompous as Van Buren, reached over and tore open the Democrat's coat, showing beneath it a ruffled silk and velvet vest and a gold watch and chain. Lincoln went on to joke about his own days growing up in buckskin.[68]

"A Barrel of Hard Cider"

Harrison's supporters knew not only how to capitalize on the foibles of an opponent, but also how to turn around a nasty comment into a cheerful slogan on the general's behalf. When Harrison began to emerge as a possibility for the nomination over perennial Whig candidate Henry Clay, Clay's followers wondered aloud how they could get rid of Harrison. Jokingly, a reporter, John de Ziska of the *Baltimore Republican*, in December 1839, suggested that the way was to "give him a barrel of hard cider, and settle a pension of two thousand a year on him, and my word for it, he will sit the remainder of his days in his log cabin by the side of a 'sea coal' fire, and study moral philosophy."[69]

A month later the article was remembered when two Harrison men, a banker and a Harrisburg, Pennsylvania, editor, met to create some symbols for the Harrison campaign. One of them suggested that "passion and prejudice, properly aroused and directed, would do about as well as principle and reason in a party contest."[70] They decided that the aristocratic-born Harrison would be a "log cabin" candidate. They drew up a campaign picture of a log cabin that had a coonskin nailed to the wall with a woodpile and a cider barrel nearby. Pro-Harrison newspapers alternated different log cabin drawings on their front pages. The *Sangamo Journal* ran one with a big flag waving over the log cabin; another depicted a free-standing flagpole and a gentleman sitting by a barrel marked "hard cider"; another showed an officer (general) welcoming a distinguished visitor in long coattails to a cabin with the "hard cider" barrel by the door.

Log cabins were raised across the country as Harrison headquarters; hard cider flowed at picnics and other occasions, courtesy of the followers of "Old Tip," or "Old Tipler," as some critics now began to call him. When Old Tip showed up at Fort Meigs, Ohio, for a rally in a six-city Ohio swing, he faced a tidal wave of 40,000 persons.[71]

The Whig strategy was to avoid taking stands on any issue, for to do so would have fractionalized the party. They would rely strictly on image, the compound values of (1) the underdog, the people's choice, and (2) the outsider. And the two-pronged campaign worked for Harrison, as it still works for others. Recent presidents, such as Jimmy Carter and Bill Clinton, came to the fore from outside the eastern establishment to win against incumbents.

In 1992 the *New York Times* still could not forget William Henry Harrison, the president who served only a month before his death from pleurisy. A discussion headlined "Tips Not Needed if Born in Log Cabin," besides offering strategies for insiders, made points, such as "Because they have been out, women are in."[72] The media are quick to note the roles of the humble, the outsider, and the underdog and to engage in image creating of such otherwise nondescript candidates as William Henry Harrison. The guiding, or rather workable, principles of that 1840 campaign offer a ranking of values for determining news that are hard for media to resist today.

Media as Vehicles of Sensationalism/Entertainment

THE NEW ANTI-INTELLECTUALISM: LOVE LETTERS, FUNERAL PARADES

Sensationalism in the early part of the nineteenth century appeared as "items" of one or several paragraphs and not generally as the full-blown epic scandal or horror story that would fill some front pages of the cheap penny press era starting in the 1830s. News was relegated to categories, such as "foreign" and "domestic." So on page 3 of the *New Hampshire Sentinel* in 1820 there is a report (six paragraphs), a "lamentable occurence" in New York, concerning the stabbing death of the son of the Spanish consul by a knife concealed in a stick; also reports of "a large building" fire (one paragraph) and a "melancholy shipwreck" (one paragraph) in which eleven of the crew lashed themselves to a split-off section of the deck, which then floated ashore.[73]

The "gee whiz" news among items on a front page of *The Microcosm* (Providence, Rhode Island) in May 1826 could be as varied as "Three sheep, owned by Mr. James Philbrick of Rye, have brought him eighteen lambs within one year!" or a report that the funeral of the Russian ambassador who died aboard a ship was "celebrated with great parade."[74]

The offbeat, humorous story got attention, such as a one-paragraph story on the front page of the *Connecticut Courant* in November 1819: "Curious Love Letter." It tells of a young couple who parted when the rustic young man's employment took him to a distant port. "They were now, of course, obliged to have resort to correspondence; but, alas! how was this to be carried on? for poor Mary could not write." When the young man proposed to her in a letter read to her by a friend, poor illiterate Mary, not wanting her friend to know the answer, composed her own reply. She wrote the letter "i" and included a chunk of sheep wool, thus "I wool." The item continued: "It was well understood, and received with much real pleasure . . . and they were married with as little delay as possible."[75]

With the end of the "era of good feelings" and the approaching influence of frontier America with the election of Jackson in 1828, there emerged a new anti-intellectualism dominated by cults of personality. In terms of sensationalism in the news, this new attitude of anti-intellectualism (less concern with rhetoric and substantial issues) and the preference for personalities led to full-scale coverage of trials and disasters in terms of people involved. Comparing the election of 1828 with the Adlai Stevenson versus Dwight Eisenhower election of 1952, George S. Hage made the point that the anti-intellectual attitude continues. He said: "The resources of a continent to be settled and developed, the emergence of the businessman as a dominant figure in the culture, the democratic stress on equalitarianism—all are factors which have contributed to the attitude's [anti-intellectualism] continued prevalence."[76] News coverage in an age of the new sensationalism was about to give way to full-scale treatment of personalities, crimes, and disasters in a growing anti-intellectual climate.

The Manifest Destiny doctrine had played its role in shaping media. Anti-intellectualism, sloganeering, and stereotyping—by a blind, even irrational faith in Manifest Destiny—would come to characterize media seeking mass circulation. The lofty Manifest Destiny theme, with an appeal to the will of the Deity, had shown the power of an orchestrated theme and the power of focusing and concentration in a new sensationalism.

QUESTIONS FOR DISCUSSION AND RESEARCH

1. How far back in the history can media be found orchestrating the concept of Manifest Destiny?
2. Was the concept extolled in colonial papers? In what terms?
3. Could the Revolutionary War be seen through the eyes of Manifest Destiny terminology? By whom, the rebels or the British, or both?
4. Would Manifest Destiny be as viable today if it weren't for the media? What role have modern media played in setting the Manifest Destiny agenda?
5. What are some of the terms political writers and others use today that have a ring of Manifest Destiny?
6. Look at today's newspaper reports. What shades of Manifest Destiny emerge?
7. Is Manifest Destiny a good or bad concept? Consider the alternative, such as subscribing to a nonpurposeful society. Or are there better rallying themes? For instance?

8. Should media have any editorial guidelines concerning acquiescing in Manifest Destiny rhetoric?

9. Certainly the breakup of the "communist" block and democratization of Eastern Europe encouraged a presence or supervisory role for the United States. What other factors, including cultural factors, encourage keeping the U.S. Manifest Destiny alive? What role might the socialist and Marxist media of these countries themselves have contributed to the emboldening or shattering of the Marxist dream?

10. What three presidents in the early to mid-nineteenth century did the most to promote the idea of Manifest Destiny? What three editors?

11. What will become of Manifest Destiny once (and if) a world order, a political global village, or a planetary federation is in place? How will such an evolution affect media?

12. What would editor John O'Sullivan, who's credited with coining the term Manifest Destiny in the 1840s, say about Manifest Destiny today? Would he phrase the concept the same way or differently?

13. Read an editorial on foreign affairs. Do you detect the interplay of religious concepts in the opinion of the editorial?

14. Look at a contemporary religious magazine. Do you detect any ring of Manifest Destiny?

15. Which president discussed in this chapter would work best with modern media? Why?

ENDNOTES

1. Frederick Jackson Turner, *Frederick Jackson Turner's Legacy: Unpublished Writings in American History*, ed. Wilbur R. Jacobs (Lincoln: University of Nebraska Press, 1965), p. 122.

2. Charles A. Beard, "The Frontier in American History," *New Republic*, Feb. 16, 1921, pp. 349, 350.

3. Sidney Kobre, "The Editor Who Freed Hostages," *Media History Digest*, vol. 1, no. 2, Spring 1981, p. 55.

4. Frederick Merk, *Manifest Destiny and Mission* (New York: Vintage Books, Random House, 1966), p. 24; cf. also Julius Pratt, "John L. O'Sullivan and Manifest Destiny," in *New York History*, vol. 14 (1933), p. 213.

5. Charles Segal and David Stineback, *Puritans, Indians, and Manifest Destiny* (New York: G. P. Putnam's Sons, 1977), p. 105.

6. Julius Pratt, "Manifest Destiny," in *Dictionary of American History*, vol. 4 (New York: Scribner's, 1940, 1976), p. 239; cf. also Julius Pratt, "The Origin of Manifest Destiny," *American Historical Review*, vol. 32.

7. Merk, *Manifest Destiny*, p. 26.

8. *Democratic Review*, July–August 1845, p. 5.

9. *Democratic Review*, December 1845.

10. Merk, *Manifest Destiny*, p. 56.

11. *California Star*, vol. 1, no. 25, June 26, 1847.

12. *California Star*, June 10, 1848; *New Orleans Weekly Bulletin*, July 8, 1844; *Bangor Daily Mercury*, May 30, 1844; *Little Rock Gazette*, March 16, 1845.

13. Donald Ray Avery, "The Newspaper on the Eve of the War of 1812: Changes in Content Patterns, 1808–1812," Ph.D. dissertation, Southern Illinois University at Carbondale, 1982.
14. Susan R. Brooker-Gross, "Timeliness: Interpretations from a Sample of 19th Century Newspapers," *Journalism Quarterly*, vol. 58, no. 4, Winter 1981, p. 594.
15. *Washington Globe*, Nov. 23, 1836.
16. *National Intelligencer*, Oct. 21, 1824.
17. *Argus of Western America*, Oct. 20, 1824.
18. *Raleigh Star*, quoted in James W. Tankard, Jr., "Public Opinion Polling by Newspapers in the Presidential Election Campaign of 1824," *Journalism Quarterly*, vol. 49, Summer 1972, p. 363.
19. Ibid.
20. Daniel Boorstin, *The Americans—The National Experience* (New York: Vintage, 1965), p. 128.
21. "The Indians," *The Argus*, March 5, 1823.
22. *Washington Gazette*, March 20, 1822, as quoted in William E. Ames and S. Dean Olson, "Washington's Political Press and the Election of 1824," *Journalism Quarterly*, vol. 40, Summer 1963, p. 350.
23. Karl E. Meyer, *Pundits, Poets, & Wits: An Omnibus of American Newspaper Columns* (New York: Oxford University Press, 1990), p. 34.
24. Elbert B. Smith, *Francis Preston Blair* (New York: Free Press, 1980), p. 61.
25. *Argus of Western America*, Feb. 27, 1828.
26. Arthur M. Schlesinger, Jr., *The Age of Jackson* (New York: Book Find Club, 1946), p. 445.
27. James D. Richardson, *A Compilation of the Messages and Papers of the Presidents* (New York: 1899), vol. 2, p. 448.
28. Samuel Eliot Morison and Henry Steele Commager, *The Growth of the American Republic*, vol. 1 (New York: Oxford University Press, 1962), p. 472.
29. Richard Hofstadter, William Miller, and Daniel Aaron, *The United States: The History of a Republic* (Englewood Cliffs, N.J.: Prentice-Hall, 1963), p. 219.
30. Herbert Ershkowitz, "Andrew Jackson: Seventh President and the Press," *Media History Digest*, vol. 5, no. 2, Spring 1985, p. 13.
31. John Spencer Bassett, *Correspondence of Andrew Jackson* (Washington, D.C.: 1929), vol. 4, p. 17, quoted by Ershkowitz in *MHD*, p. 14.
32. *Family Encyclopedia of American History* (Pleasantville, N.Y.: Reader's Digest Association, 1975), p. 1056.
33. Maurine Beasley, "The Curious Career of Anne Royall," *Journalism History*, vol. 3, no. 4, Winter 1976–1977, p. 99.
34. *Morning Courier and New York Enquirer*, July 17, 1829, quoted in Bessie Rowland James, *Anne Royall's U.S.A.* (New Brunswick, N.J.: Rutgers University Press, 1972), p. 259.
35. *Freedom's Journal*, April 27, 1827, cited by Lionel C. Barrow, Jr., " 'Our Own Cause': *Freedom's Journal* and the Beginnings of the Black Press," *Journalism History*, vol. 4, no. 4, Winter 1977–1978, p. 122.
36. Barrow, "Our Own Cause," p. 118, quoting U.S. Department of Commerce, *Negro Population in the United States, 1790–1915* (New York: Arno Press, 1968), p. 57.
37. Barrow, "Our Own Cause," p. 118, quoting Martin E. Dann, ed., *The Black Press, 1827–1890* (New York: Capricorn Books, 1972), p. 15.
38. Barrow, "Our Own Cause," p. 119, quoting Frederick G. Detweiler, *The Negro Press in the United States* (Chicago: Chicago University Press, 1922), p. 56.
39. *Freedom's Journal*, March 16, 1827.
40. Bernell Tripp, *Origins of the Black Press: New York, 1827–1847* (Northport, Ala.: Vision Press, 1992), p. 20.

41. *Freedom's Journal*, March 7, 1829.
42. Tripp, p. 22.
43. Roland Wolseley, *The Black Press, U.S.A.* (Ames: Iowa State University Press, 1971), p. 18, as quoted by Barrow, "Our Own Cause," p. 122. A later edition of Wolseley's book appeared in 1991.
44. Barrow, "Our Own Cause," p. 122.
45. Ibid.
46. Sam G. Riley, "*The Cherokee Phoenix*: The Short, Unhappy Life of the First American Indian Newspaper," *Journalism Quarterly*, vol. 53, Winter 1976, p. 667.
47. Ibid.
48. Sam G. Riley, "A Note of Caution—The Indian's Own Prejudice, as Mirrored in the First Native American Newspaper," *Journalism History*, vol. 6, no. 2, Summer 1979, p. 45.
49. *Cherokee Phoenix*, Feb. 18, 1829, quoted in Riley, "A Note of Caution," p. 45.
50. Barbara F. Luebke, "Elias Boudinott, Indian Editor: Editorial Columns from the *Cherokee Phoenix*," *Journalism History*, vol. 6, no. 2, Summer 1979, p. 53.
51. Tom Reilly, "Newspaper Suppression During the Mexican War, 1846–1848," *Journalism Quarterly*, vol. 54, no. 4, Winter 1977, pp. 263, 264.
52. Ibid., p. 270.
53. Gerald J. Baldasty, *The Commercialization of News in the Nineteenth Century* (Madison: University of Wisconsin Press, 1992), p. 19.
54. Ibid. Baldasty cites Daniel J. McFarland, "North Carolina Newspapers, Editors and Journalistic Politics, 1815–1836," *North Carolina Historical Review*, vol. 30, no. 3, July 1953, pp. 376, 277.
55. Baldasty, *Commercialization of News*, p. 20. He cites Milton W. Hamilton, *The Country Printer: New York State, 1785–1830* (New York: Columbia University Press, 1936), p. 120.
56. Baldasty, *Commercialization of News*, p. 21.
57. William E. Ames, "Federal Patronage and the Washington D.C. Press," *Journalism Quarterly*, vol. 49, Spring 1972, p. 24.
58. Ibid., p. 25.
59. James L. Crouthamel, "Did the Second Bank of the United States Bribe the Press?" *Journalism Quarterly*, vol. 36, Winter 1959, p. 35.
60. Hiley H. Ward, "The Media and Political Values," in William David Sloan, *The Significance of the Media* (Northport, Ala.: Vision Press, 1993).
61. Bernard A. Weisberger, "Whangdoodling," *American Heritage*, February 1989, p. 24.
62. For Harrison's life story, see Dorothy Goebel, *William Henry Harrison: A Political Biography* (Indianapolis: Historical Bureau of the Indiana Library and Historical Department, 1926), vol. 14; Freeman Cleaves, *Old Tippecanoe* (New York: Charles Scribner's Sons, 1939).
63. Peter Pollack, *The Picture History of Photography: From the Earliest Beginnings to the Present Day* (New York: H. N. Abrams, 1969), p. 59.
64. Ibid., p. 236.
65. Keith Melder, *Hail to the Candidate: Presidential Campaigns from Banners to Broadcasts* (Washington, D.C.: Smithsonian Institution Press, 1991), p. 69.
66. Ibid., p. 88.
67. "Tippecanoe and Tyler, Too—The New Whig Song, and Chorus Arranged for The Log Cabin," in *The Log Cabin*, Sept. 23, 1840.
68. Carl Sandburg, *Abraham Lincoln—The Prairie Years* (New York: Dell, 1958), vol. 1, p. 236.
69. *Baltimore Republican*, Dec. 11, 1839, quoted in Robert Gray Gunderson, *The Log Cabin Campaign* (Lexington: University of Kentucky Press, 1957), p. 74.
70. Gunderson, *Log Cabin Campaign*, p. 76.

71. "Harrison's Great Speech at the Wonderful 'Log Cabin' Campaign Meeting at Ft. Meigs, in 1840," from the *Toledo Blade*, in the *Ohio Archaeological and Historical Quarterly*, vol. 17, no. 2, April 1908, p. 206.

72. Sam Roberts, Metro Matters column, "Tips Not Needed if Born in Log Cabin," *New York Times*, April 20, 1992, p. B3.

73. *New Hampshire Sentinel*, Jan. 1, 1820.

74. *The Microcosm*, May 19, 1826.

75. *Connecticut Courant*, Nov. 23, 1819.

76. George S. Hage, "Anti-intellectualism in Press Comment: 1828 and 1952," *Journalism Quarterly*, vol. 36, Fall 1959, p. 439.

6

The Wave of Cheap Penny Papers (1833–1851)

Journalism historians have generally placed the birth of the penny papers—those selling for one cent instead of six cents—in the era largely following the Jackson administration up to the decade before the Civil War. They see it as a beginning of an era that does not end with the twentieth century. Almost without exception, journalism history books have singled out and given a special section to the penny press as a milestone in the development of the press.

To some, such as John Nerone, such attention to the penny press is tantamount to labeling its emergence as a kind of revolution, as if everything changed with the coming of the cheap papers to be sold to a mass audience, an obvious necessity if the reduction from six cents to one cent a copy were to cover costs. He, however, believes, with the new approach to selling aside, that the new cheap papers were merely following the conservative tradition set by early printer-editors and even keeping the same basic content that had been in vogue in the era of party papers. The new papers were moral in tone (despite the urge to play up police news and disasters); they were business oriented, as papers had been before; and they reached large broad audiences, but so had the partisan papers. They were not primarily for the working class, Nerone maintains, and the New York experience that he sees as tending to emphasize their working-class appeal was not typical of the mass of penny papers that developed across the country. There was also no real difference in news content between the penny papers and the standard six-cent dailies, says Nerone.[1]

A DAWNING LIBERATION

Yet something was happening in this period, which Nerone prefers to see as an "evolution," not a revolution. Walter Lippmann saw a continuing evolving from

133

the throes of political parties, a kind of dawning "liberation" of the press. He said the penny press represented the third "epoch" in media development. In the first period, the monopoly of government controlled the press; in a second phase, the government monopoly was breached, and political parties held sway over the press; then, third, newspapers became "politically independent of government and party by enlisting the commercially profitable support of a large body of readers."[2]

Writing in 1931, Lippmann envisioned a fourth stage, a professionally trained journalism that would be more independent and active, with less homage to commercialism and free of political parties and government. Actually all four stages would still have some role in the modern media: government-manipulated sources and news, the political stands of newspapers, the continued reign of the bottom line in business-oriented media, and the presence of standards among trained journalists.

Arthur Kaul and Joseph McKerns saw the emergence of the penny press not only as a part of an evolution but also as a process of dialeticism in which a new opposing trend confronts the current scene and a consensus results with a new challenge replacing the previous status quo. But they have forgone the older progressive, optimistic view of journalism historians, replacing it with a prediction that it is all coming to naught, at least for the printed page. "The conflicts, contradictions and crises inherent in the newspaper's evolution have generated a species of information organization that has reached the end of its life cycle," they say. "The newspaper has evolved into a media 'dinosaur,' incapable of adapting to a rapidly changing environment."[3] In this evolutionary pattern, the penny press follows "a prevariation phase," where newspapers were small unorganized businesses. The next stage, 1825 to 1845, encompassing the first part of the penny press era, as defined by others, is a relatively short, disruptive "variation stage." Then Kaul and McKerns say, came "a longer period of selection, 1845–1900," ending in a brief crisis period, 1890–1900, "generated by a crowded field of newspaper organizations. Survivors of the selection stages evolved through the retention stage, 1900–1980, only to face a crisis period in the post-1960s when survival is constrained by the 'dinosaur effect' and displacement by newly evolving communication technologies."[4]

REASONS FOR THE PENNY PRESS

As a stage in an ongoing or doomed evolution, or as a revolution that interrupted the process of development, the penny press did represent a change in publishing because it produced an affordable variety of papers for the masses. Among factors contributing to the change are the following.

Concentration of Large, Growing Populations in Cities.   Although the nation was still primarily rural, more people settled in principal cities. The *Public Ledger* in Philadelphia noted early in the penny press era that New York and Brooklyn had reached a third of a million population, and the new penny papers could claim a daily circulation of 70,000 in 1836. "This is nearly sufficient to place a newspaper in the hands of every man in the two cities, and even of every boy old enough to read," said the *Public Ledger*. The papers could be found "in every street, lane, and alley; in every hotel, tavern, counting house, shop."[5] Workers going to and from work and in breaks such as lunchtime could be seen with a newspaper in hand. The concentration of large populations made the mass-audience penny press possible. News became something people talked about in the shared circumstances. The appearance of newsboy hawkers on streets made the distribution more complete.

A Broad Appeal. In colonial days everyone knew the news by word of mouth before it appeared in print, but in big cities such as New York, where population increased 40 percent from 1828 to 1849, those who came in from rural areas or as immigrants found themselves in unfamiliar surroundings and isolated from personal news sources. Old familiarities, where a citizen knew everyone else in the community, did not and could not exist in the massive concentrations of the big city. The penny press, reaching out to a mass of people rather than to one ideology, ethnic group, or class, pursued common-interest themes with enough variety to embrace many interests and to give a sense of participation in community.

Yet some scholars argue against an amalgamation theory and believe the penny papers were serving primarily one class over another. Michael Schudson touted the idea of a "market economy," with the new availability of goods as a creative force and an equalizer, resulting in an expanded middle class. "In the market there were no special categories and privileges," says Schudson. "Land could be bought and sold, and even human labor had a price set by supply and demand, not by custom. In the market, one individual was as good as the next."[6]

The view that readers were an upwardly mobile, purchasing class is supported by content studies of the penny papers by Donald Shaw of the University of North Carolina. Applying the readability formulas of Rudolf Flesch, Shaw and his researchers found that, despite serving a new massive audience, the new papers were not particularly readable, thus creating a middle- and upper-class appeal. The study found that from 1820 to 1860 the pattern of four of ten stories judged "difficult" or "average" in the earlier period remained constant for the later period, suggesting that an educated class, a middle class, prevailed.[7]

However, Dan Schiller contends that "commercial interests and attitudes do not of themselves make one 'middle class.' "[8] Schiller sees the audience for the new mass papers as consisting more of the working class than of a unified middle class. Although workers had warring factions among themselves, by the 1830s "one may indeed argue that an American working class—not a classic industrial proletariat, but a working class just the same—had traveled a good distance along the road to self-definition."[9]

Serving the Common Person. Many of the penny papers were consistently prolabor and against monopolies, at least in their public utterings if not in practice, as they supported equal rights and sought the public good. The papers' attention to local government news, with a lookout for corruption, bore out the support of the cause of the common citizen. In New York the *Sun* embraced the right of workers to organize unions;[10] the *Herald* said it was "always in favor of the right of journeymen";[11] the *Tribune* backed labor on many issues. The upscale *Journal of Commerce* complained, as Schiller notes, about "the subserviency which, from the nature of their circulation," the penny publications "are compelled to exercise towards Trade Unions and such like humbug affairs."[12]

Role of Education.   The working person was becoming more educated. In the 1830s an interest in state-supported basic education developed. The demand came not only from reformers—such as Horace Mann in Massachusetts, Henry Barnard in Connecticut and Rhode Island, and Thaddeus Stevens in Pennsylvania—but also from working persons who believed that "book learning" might lead their children to an improved status. In the 1830s school districts were organized in New York to educate all children, as they had already been organized in other states. By the 1850s all states accepted the idea of tax-supported elementary schools.[13] Private academies also proliferated, and the possibility of adult education was extended by the founding of libraries and self-improvement clubs. The readers attracted by the penny press were members of both the working and middle classes.

The penny papers themselves contributed to education. They met demands for information, described in their pages phenomena from the working of machines and the human heart (one paper carried a diagram of the heart on the front page), and reported on amusements and business developments. A source of information to the consumer was the volume of ads on a variety of services.

Better-Trained Journalists.   A more educated and professionally committed journalist began to appear, in contrast to the many stodgy printers and politicians who ran the papers of a previous day. "Journalists with brains and boldness were making their appearance," says Frederic Hudson, who was a part of the penny press era. "Young writers and reporters, with active minds, educated as newspaper politicians and statesmen, began to get restive on the old party papers and under selfish dictation. They were seeking a change and a chance for expansion."[14]

Role of Ideas.   Exciting ideas cut across party lines. Among them were transcendentalism and its belief that truth is illuminated by an inner light, the women's rights movement, the abolition of slavery movement, a temperance—an antialcohol—movement, and new developments in science. Newspapers took radically different positions on the new issues, but the discussion crossed over party lines and enlisted a general audience.

Shared Entertainment.   A common denominator that linked the diverse ethnic groups within the masses was a thirst for entertainment. The world of music, once curtailed by Puritan leaders, broadened, as evidenced by the increase in sale of pianos and the presence of traveling artists, such as Swedish soprano Jenny Lind, who received $1,000 for each of 150 concerts managed by showman P. T. Barnum at the beginning of the 1850s.[15]

Law and Order.   The interest in security and safety in cities—law and order—had become a concern, as it is today. The *Sun* became largely a police blotter, and its competitors also gave considerable space to police news. Eventually a separate journal on crime, the *National Police Gazette*, was launched in 1845.

Effect of Magazines.   The attention to magazines—there were 700 American magazines by 1865—likely influenced the content of the cheap papers, which also carried poems, short stories, and novel serializations, in addition to in-depth analyses of the topics of the day. The emphasis was on variety and comprehensive coverage; much of this philosophy was shared with magazines.

Religion.   The penny papers represented a kind of civil religion if not a spirit of ecumenism. The *New York Herald* carried religion stories regularly, but the reports sometimes had a skeptical edge, perhaps resulting from a reaction of founder James Gordon Bennett to his training for the priesthood. Horace Greeley's *Tribune* offered a generalized outlook on religion couched in an interest in transcendentalism and social concerns. "Greeley's romantic Christian socialism saw God as a divine mix of deistic and romantic principles, the universe running by natural law but needing reform," says Gary Whitby. "His beliefs led him to become an advocate of social good, brotherly love and cooperation, and the reconstruction of society in these terms."[16] Henry Raymond's *Times*' interest in religion was reflected in its interfaith religion section. The first of the successful penny papers, the *Sun*, actually became a religious paper for a brief period before the Civil War, after founder Benjamin Day left. Religious coverage was extended, and daily prayer meetings were held in the editorial rooms. Mott suggests that such emphasis on religion as developed in the penny press was the result of revival movements such as the Great Revival of 1858.[17]

Foreign Coverage.   Despite the concentration on local news, the penny press editors embraced the world, as they used specialized firsthand reports by foreign correspondents or reports from editors who were themselves traveling. Greeley, for instance, used the expertise of Karl Marx in northern Europe and England to write economics and revolution columns, as well as Margaret Fuller to cover the conflicts in Italy; he also reported from overseas himself, as did his editors. Bennett and Raymond, living abroad with their families much of the time, also reported from overseas.

For the *Herald*, toward the end of Bennett's days, Henry Morton Stanley trekked in 1871 into the heart of Africa to find the elusive medical missionary–explorer David Livingstone. Stanley found Livingstone ill, discouraged, and just about out of supplies on the shores of Lake Tanganyika. Stanley greeted the old doctor with words that have become immortal: "Dr. Livingstone, I presume?"[18]

New Techniques.   Improved printing technology encouraged the mass production of newspapers. In 1822 Dan Treadwell's horsepower press used a real horse to
drive the press. "Horsepower" was replaced the next year with steam power. In
1825 Robert Hoe presented a cylinder press that could put out in rotation many
more copies per minute than a simple flatbed press. Stereotype copies of a set page
of metal type were made (created by pressing wet papier-mâché onto the type and
letting it dry, resulting in a reverse matrix which when dried was bent to fit the
cylinder; then molten metal was poured over the matrix to form a cylinder plate for
the press). The first really high-speed cylinder press made its debut in 1847 when
the *Philadelphia Public Ledger* installed a four-cylinder press requiring four persons
to feed in paper. Capacity was 8,000 sheets an hour on one side, and, as John
Tebbel put it, "It revolutionized the newspaper business."[19]

Cheaper Paper.   The decline in the cost of paper was a seminal factor in the development of the penny newspaper. Up to the middle of the nineteenth century
most paper was created from rags (ground or chopped, watered, turned into pulp,
and spread out to dry in sheets). The expensive process discouraged excess use of
paper. In midcentury a cheaper way to produce paper was found by combining
wood pulp from the ample forests in the nation with the rag product. George Henry
Payne noted, "Reduction in the cost of materials made possible the penny paper
which led many editors and journalists to appreciate more quickly the democratic
movement that was going on around them."[20]

ORIGINS OF THE PENNY PRESS

The idea of cheap or penny papers was not entirely new when they appeared in the
United States in the 1830s. In England a cheap paper existed as early as 1706, with
the appearance of the *Orange Postman*, which sold for half a penny. Frederic
Hudson labels that paper "the father of the penny press."[21] Selling newspapers on
the street by newsboy hawkers—important in the distribution of the penny press in
America—was in vogue in England in the eighteenth century.

In America *The Cent*, published in Philadelphia in 1830, is believed to be the
first American paper to sell for a penny an issue. Little is known of the short history
of this paper. In New York in 1833 Horace Greeley, who was to become an important Whig party editor and then founder of the *New York Tribune* in 1841, made an
abortive attempt to launch a penny paper. Actually, when Greeley and a partner
brought out the *Post*, it sold for two pennies. Unfortunately the first issue debuted
during a horrendous snowstorm. Newsboys could not find anyone on the streets to
buy the papers. Greeley and associates continued for two weeks and reduced the
price to one cent, but still could not get the paper off the ground.

The first successful American penny paper was Benjamin Day's *New York Sun* in
1833. Others quickly followed. In Philadelphia the *Veto*, a Jacksonian campaign
paper, appeared in 1834; the *Public Ledger* came out in 1836, followed by the short-
lived *Orb* and the *Focus*, which was "hidden among the many other penny papers
which attempted to dispute the supremacy of *The Public Ledger* for a time and then

Benjamin Day: Founder of the Sun. (The Bettmann Archive)

disappeared,"[22] according to James Melvin Lee. The *Baltimore Sun* was first published in 1837. By 1848 more than thirty penny newspapers had been started in Cincinnati.[23]

The Penny Papers in New York

In New York, following the *Sun*, penny papers included the *Transcript* and *The Man*, 1834; the *Herald*, 1835; the *Ladies' Morning Star* (a penny paper for women); and the *New Era*, 1836. Horace Greeley's *Tribune* debuted in 1841 and Henry Raymond's *New York Times* in 1851. Among the largest and most influential of the New York penny papers were the *Sun, Herald, Tribune*, and *Times*. They were very different from each other, at least at their inception. Yet they all reached out for a more general audience and appealed to more than just the members of one political party or class.

The four penny papers that reached instant success with large circulations in New York were widely imitated in communities across the country. Especially copied were the devotion to and coverage of local news and war news at the outbreak of the conflict between North and South.[24] The four editors were enterprising, hardworking, creative men with vision.

New York Sun.   Launched on September 3, 1833, by Massachusetts-born printer Benjamin Henry Day, the *Sun* sported a feisty eagle amid a banner of stars on its first issue. But the logo was soon changed to a drawing of a rising sun over a bay of ships and the inscription "It shines for all." Later, in the same vein, the symbol was a printing press shedding light upon the earth. Day's aim was to be as universal as the rays of the sun and to stretch across the terrain to reach even the humblest reader. Filled with humorous and ridiculous reports from the police court, Day's paper was one of the first in America, and one of the few in history, to rely so heavily on humor. But this emphasis paid off. Within two months Day was boasting a circulation of 2,000,[25] and in one more month it doubled to 4,000.[26] By the end of its second year the *Sun* could announce that it had the largest circulation of any daily in the world,[27] with 19,360 copies sold. It outclassed even the London *Times*, which had a circulation of 17,000.

Day owed much of his success to his police news. Some believe that Day was determined to concentrate on police news, "for he saw, from the first day of the paper, that that was the kind of stuff that his readers devoured."[28] Day knew of the success of police news in British papers. James Stanford Bradshaw, of Central Michigan University, notes that Day originally hired an editor who did not work out.[29] Day then decided he needed a writer and settled on an unemployed printer, George Wisner, at $4 a week if he would cover the 4 A.M. police court sessions.

Wisner became half owner of the *Sun* in early 1834, but failing health forced him to give up the paper. He settled in Pontiac, Michigan, where he worked for the Pontiac *Courier*, earned a law degree, and successfully ran for the state legislature. However, his health failed, and he died at age thirty-seven in 1849. His younger brother Moses was elected governor of Michigan in 1859.[30]

When the *Sun* was sued for libel in May 1837, Day responded by taking his name off the masthead. The verdict in 1838 was against the *Sun*, and the paper was fined $3,000 for saying that a lawyer had once been indicted for conspiracy to defraud but neglecting to say that he had been cleared. Day's name never again appeared on the paper. In 1838, following the libel judgment, Day sold the paper to his bookkeeper and brother-in-law, Moses Yale Beach.

Day later launched another penny paper, the *True Sun*, but sold it after several months. He tried his hand at another penny paper, the *Evening Tatler*, but this quickly failed. He then helped found a literary magazine, *Brother Jonathan*, which he edited for twenty years. He died in 1889 at age seventy-nine. His biographer, Frank O'Brien, summed up his life: "There were better newspapermen than Day . . . but they did not know the people. . . . Day started something that went rolling on, increasing in size and weight until it controlled the thought of the continent. . . . Anybody could do the trick—after Day showed how simple it was."[31]

New York Herald. James Gordon Bennett also demonstrated how simple it was to start a great paper. With $500 and some boards laid across fruit crates in a damp cellar in lower New York City, Bennett opened the office for his *Herald*. The ease with which he proceeded and the immediate success he experienced do not tell the whole story.

It was a long route from his native Scotland, where he had trained for the priesthood. In the new world he first taught school in Halifax, Nova Scotia, then in Addison, Maine. He then came to Boston, where he worked as a proofreader for three years. He packed up again and went to New York, where the owner of the *Charleston* (South Carolina) *Courier* was looking to hire a buyer of printing supplies. Bennett got the job and so impressed the owner that Bennett was hired to report and write for the South Carolina paper, an experience that made Bennett more amenable to views of the South later in his life.

Bennett edited the *National Advocate* in New York and briefly took over the *New York Courier*, the first Sunday paper in the country, but the paper soon failed. In 1827 he was writing for the *New York Enquirer*, where he pioneered in producing humorous essays. In "Shaking Hands" he told of the many ways people greet each other around the world, and he followed with a satire on intemperance. Circulation of the *Enquirer* jumped. He reported from a number of cities for the *Enquirer*, including Washington, where he became the first Washington correspondent for an out-of-town newspaper. He wrote much like a modern columnist, "injecting something of himself into the context,"[32] says one of his biographers.

As a roving reporter for the *Courier and Enquirer* in 1830, Bennett gained fame by covering a celebrated murder trial in Salem, Massachusetts. The Massachusetts attorney general slapped tight restrictions on the dozen reporters on the scene. Bennett responded by infuriating the attorney general and judges with reports that argued, "The honesty, the purity, the integrity of legal practice and decisions throughout this country, are more indebted to the American Press, than to the whole tribe of lawyers and judges, who issue their decrees. The Press is the living Jury of the Nation."[33] In response the court forbade Bennett and the other reporters to take notes. But Bennett kept up his demand for recognition of the people's right to know, and eventually he won, as Massachusetts and other states proceeded to open their courtrooms to the press.[34]

In 1832 Bennett launched the *Globe*, "resolved to aid the great cause of Jackson and Democracy," but once the election was over, the paper failed, perhaps convincing Bennett that the wave of the future would not be in party papers. He bought an interest in the *Pennsylvanian* in Philadelphia and became editor. His expectation that Jacksonians, such as Martin Van Buren, would sustain him did not materialize. Nicholas Biddle and the United States Bank, which Jacksonians and Bennett opposed, were headquartered in Philadelphia, "and the Biddles left no stone unturned to wreck Bennett's new venture."[35]

Thus when Bennett introduced his *Herald* in May 1835, he had had enough of politics. He declared: "We shall support no party—be the organ of no faction or COTERIE, and care nothing for any election or any candidate from president down

James Gordon Bennett: He pursued a story. (The Bettmann Archive)

to a constable. We shall endeavor to record facts on every public and proper subject, stripped of verbage and coloring, with comments when suitable, just, independent, fearless and good-tempered."[36] In the course of Bennett's nearly thirty-seven years as editor, the *Herald* supported a variety of candidates—Whigs, Democrats, Republicans.[37]

Ever a reporter, Bennett would cover some of the stories personally. He tweaked the noses of politicians, church divines, and theater celebrities. In 1840 clergy and financiers alike combined to denounce him as a bad influence in the community. In 1855 he lost a libel judgment of $6,000 to a theatrical manager. The *Herald* had called the man's opera house a den of prostitutes and gamblers.[38] Bennett's wife and children stayed out of the fray by spending most of their time in Europe. He died in 1872 at the age of seventy-eight.

New York Tribune.   While Day's *Sun* sought to entertain and Bennett's *Herald* sought to give a variety of information, even sensationalizing the news with his passion for significant details and in-depth approach to trials and disasters, Horace

Horace Greeley: Eager editor, politician. (UPI/The Bettmann Archive)

Greeley, arriving on the scene with his penny paper the *Tribune* in 1841, had other ideas. The largely self-educated New Hampshire farm boy who at 15 was an apprentice at the *Northern Spectator*, East Poulney, Vermont, sought to educate and lead the reader through a field of causes. These included women's suffrage, vegetarianism, temperance and abstinence in alcohol, and the philosophies of communalism and socialism. "Many of such activities were news, but most newspapers mentioned them only to ridicule," says Henry Luther Stoddard. Yet he never backed down, as he became the "burden-bearer for all the causes urged by agitators."[39]

But somehow this whiskery man with his large round face, who almost got fired from an early printing job because he was so strange looking, thought that a way to start his paper was to be ponderous and boring. Still dedicated to the memory of the U.S. president, William Henry Harrison, who had died in the previous week, Greeley's first issue carried as its motto beneath the logo the last words of the dying president: "I desire you to understand the true principles of government. I wish them carried out— I ask nothing more.—Harrison." True to his fallen leader, Greeley proceeded to deal with matters of government. In his first issue he gave the entire front page and part of the second to the "Case of Recorder Morris." Subhead: "Opinion of William Hall, attorney general, on the legality of the conduct of Robert H. Morris, Recorder of the City of New-York." In legal language, the reader was told how the recorder allegedly had seized some private papers in violation of the Bill of Rights in "a manifest usurpation of a power" and also engaged in a "conspiracy to carry an election by Fraud."[40]

It was a precarious beginning that did not lend itself to generating enthusiasm and leading the masses to want the paper. Greeley wised up almost immediately. Two days later he promised to get off of his political high horse: "We have been obliged thus far, and shall be to-morrow, to devote a large share of our columns to Political matter. After Tuesday, we shall be better able to please our non-political readers." Two days later he was appealing to the fantasy readers, as the *Sun* did. Greeley's front-page lead story now was "The Dyaks in the Island of Borneo."[41]

Yet by the end of the first month, Greeley, the political animal, the idealist, had thought through his philosophy and was not ready to change. He wrote in an editorial that he had usually been on the side of a minority and saw no reason to cater to a crowd or popular opinion: "No man ever suffered permanently for advocating unpopular truth with good motives and in a right spirit."[42]

In the 1840s some idealists looked to "association" movements, among them the utopian communities of Charles Fourier, a Frenchman. Fourier's communal groups, called phalanxes, drew their symbolism from a Roman army formation that put the soldiers with their shields side by side to make one indivisible charging or defensive unit. After a Greeley editorial, March 1, 1842, in the *Tribune* titled "Association; or, principles of a true Organization of Society," *Tribune* readers between 1841 and 1859 organized forty sharing communities, or phalanxes. Greeley even printed a new magazine, *The Future Devoted to the Cause of Association and a Reorganization of Society*. For a decade he ran the columns of the godfather of communism, Karl Marx, who wrote on economic ills and unrest in Europe and who complained like a capitalist of not being paid enough by Greeley. He took a four-month trip to Europe himself, analyzing train service, newspapers, and culture.[43]

In 1848 Greeley was elected to Congress as a Whig to fill the seat left vacant by the death of a congressman. He entered the fray with all the idealism and enthusiasm he had in his paper. He introduced a land reform bill in settling new lands, exposed in the *Tribune* excesses in congressional mileage expenses, spoke out against slavery, attacked absenteeism in the House, and publicized other matters that made him unpopular. "An honest man in the House of Representatives of the United States seemed to be a foreign element, a fly in the cup," he wrote in his journal during the session.[44] Greeley was passed over for reelection. His biographer, James Parton, said: "No man ever served his country more faithfully. No man ever received less reward."[45]

Greeley hired Margaret Fuller to do a range of writing from book reviews to investigative reporting. Among her stories was an exposé of prison conditions on Blackwell Island. She also spent one Christmas with convicts at Sing Sing.

The Greeley-Fuller friendship deepened, and Fuller moved into the Greeley home in the Turtle Bay section of lower middle Manhattan. Generally, Greeley's wife, Mary, liked Fuller, and Fuller was devoted to the Greeley children. While Greeley sang her praises—"the most remarkable, and in some respects, the greatest woman

Margaret Fuller: Foreign correspondent, close to Greeley. (Free Library of Philadelphia)

who America has yet known,"[46] she had her detractors. Edgar Allan Poe grumbled: "Humanity can be divided into three classes—Men, Women, and Margaret Fuller."[47]

Experiencing a need for adventure, Fuller took off for Europe where, as the first American woman foreign correspondent, she continued to write for the *Tribune*. In Rome she had a child, then married. Returning to the United States, the three—Fuller, husband, and child—perished in a shipwreck off the coast of New York City.

Greeley's career lasted until 1872. In that year, a somewhat rattled sixty-one-year-old, he received the nomination for president on both the Democratic and Liberal Republican tickets. Opposition was great. And he gave his opponents plenty of stones to throw. He had personal eccentricities—such as his special diet requirements and his donning of a long white coat, white bell-crowned hat, and boots, all of which were grist for cartoonists. Moreover, Bernard Weisberger notes, "The spectacle of Greeley embracing the Democratic Party, which he himself had long equated with Tammany Hall [New York City political organization], corruption and copperhead [northerners opposed to the North's policies in the Civil War] sentiments, made an all too easy target."[48] Incumbent president Ulysses S. Grant won by a landslide. Greeley mused after his defeat that he hardly knew whether he had been "running for the Presidency or the penitentiary."[49] Greeley died shortly after the election, November 29, 1872, at age sixty-one.

New York Times.   In the first half of the nineteenth century, beginning in 1813, some seven publishers launched a newspaper in New York called the *Times*. "Most of these ventures had gasped only briefly before they died," said Meyer Berger,[50] a historian of the *New York Times*. It was left to another farm boy, Henry Jarvis Raymond, to launch a successful *Times*, the one that still exists as a major New York City and national newspaper. Raymond, who gained attention as a boy orator at farm and university junior programs, first worked as a teacher in Wheatland, New York, at age sixteen. When he graduated from the University of Vermont at age twenty in 1840, he did freelance writing in New York. While weighing whether to be a minister or schoolteacher, Raymond took a job at $8 a week on Greeley's magazine, *The New Yorker*. When it folded, he joined Greeley on the *Tribune*. But when Raymond fell seriously ill, Greeley, exhibiting a darker side, cut off Raymond's salary. Recovered and angry at the treatment he had been given by Greeley, Raymond demanded $20 a week to stay. Greeley obliged.

Berger attributes much of the early success of the *Tribune* to Raymond's writing. Raymond was so aggressive that in covering one story—a crucial speech by Daniel Webster in Boston—he took a printer with him. As Raymond wrote the story aboard ship returning from Boston, the printer set the story in type before they docked. With type ready for the press, they handily scooped other reporters on board. For $5 more a week, Raymond left the *Tribune* to go to work at the *Courier and Enquirer* for General James Watson Webb, a conservative editor who had a reputation for irascibility, gained in part by assaulting Bennett and other editors with a cane.

Raymond won a seat as a Whig assemblyman from the Ninth Ward in New York in 1849 and went to the state capital, Albany. With his oratorical skills, he became speaker of the House and won reelection in 1850. In Albany, Raymond renewed acquaintance with George Jones, a banker. The two had met when both were working for Greeley. Raymond and Jones, impressed with Greeley's continued success, decided to launch their own newspaper. They appealed to a growing audience who were interested in a paper that printed the news objectively and with balance, without the social "isms" of the *Tribune* or the sensationalism of the *Herald*. Elmer Davis notes in his history of the *Times*: "In his views on public questions Raymond was if anything too well balanced. He often lamented a habit of mind which inclined him to see both sides in any dispute. This may have hampered him as a politician, but on the whole it probably did *The Times* more good than harm."[51]

Nevertheless, the *Times* could not help but be preachy as it added "moral" messages and lessons to the stories of the day. A case in point is the running accounts of the execution of Aaron Stookey for murder. One front-page article on the day of execution contained an interview with Stookey in which he gave his life story. That article concluded with a word about the construction of the gallows. "Aaron B. Stookey to Be Executed—A Sketch of His Life" was followed by a shorter article, "The Execution To-Day," which told of the crunch to get tickets. Deploring the activity, the *Times* said: "The applications for admission to witness the execution have been very large—about eighteen hundred—but most of the applicants were refused. This desire to obtain admission to the gallows yard, is, we think, highly reprehensible, and we are glad to know that the Sheriff has decided not to gratify it."[52] The next day a long article on the front page described the execution in detail, and, of course, there was an attempt to suggest a lesson: "Thus ends the existence of another human being for the murder of his fellow man, and we trust his awful fate will always be remembered by those, who in the heat of passion, or otherwise, may be tempted to strike a deadly blow." And finally there is a word of appreciation to the Sheriff and others "for the facilities rendered us in the discharge of our duty."[53]

On Saturdays the *Times* carried a column of "Items in Morals and Religion," primarily a report on what religious groups were doing. One such column in October 1851 had several dozen reports of Presbyterians, Baptists, Mormons, Unitarians, Lutherans, Roman Catholics, Episcopalians, and Methodists, among others.[54] While Bennett and others carried religious items, it seems the *Times* was a pioneer in establishing a full-fledged religion section.

Raymond's life paralleled Bennett's in that his family settled for a time in Europe. In 1859 Raymond—partly as an excuse to see his family in Paris—reported on the decisive battle of the Franco-Austrian war at Soferino, Italy. Like the Greeleys, the Raymonds were faced with tragedy with their children, losing three of them to death.

Raymond could not shake off his personal interest in politics. He was elected lieutenant governor of New York in 1854. In 1856 he gave the keynote speech at a convention of Whigs and new Republicans in Pittsburgh that planned the first national Republican Party convention in Philadelphia. The party had been launched in Ripon, Wisconsin, in 1854 by various opponents of the spread of slavery into the territories. The speech, seeking the repeal of the Kansas-Nebraska Act, which allowed those in the Kansas and Nebraska territories to decide whether to have slavery and calling for the admission of Kansas as a free state, was adopted as the platform for the new party at the convention in Philadelphia. In the election of 1864, Raymond, running on the same Republican ticket as Lincoln, was elected to Congress. A moderate, favoring civil rather than military control of the South after the war, he was outmaneuvered by the Radical Republicans and fell out of favor with the party. He voted against the move to impeach President Andrew Johnson. Johnson nominated him to be minister to Austria, but the nomination was tabled by the Senate. Raymond plunged back into his work at the *Times*. In June 1869, following a stroke, he died at the age of forty-nine.

Media as Definers and Keepers of Values (and Biases)
NUGGETS OF HUMOR IN POLICE STORIES

Besides lofty intrinsic and universal values there are workaday pragmatic values, as illustrated in the effective William Henry Harrison campaign of 1840. Used sometimes in the news-planning enclaves of the media is the term *news value*. "Does this item have any news value?" News values, of course, are myriad. Information; instruction; insight; intrusions into celebrity lives; reports on riots, crime, terrorism, invasions, incompetence, the incredible—and the list goes on—have news value.

Overlooked over the years are the use and value of humor. The lack of humor in modern newspapers is all too evident. The old "gray ladies," as many major metropolitan newspapers used to be called, have been spruced up lately with the introduction of color and some modular design, but they still do not emit much life or humor—or conversational value.

Some press critics have suggested that what modern newspapers need is a strong infusion of humor. One such critic was the ombudsman and media critic for the *Washington Post*, Howard Kurtz. In his 1993 book *Media Circus: The Trouble with America's Newspapers,* he lists some things "newspapers need to do more of." They range from "make people mad" to "connect with the community." In his list also is "Make us laugh." He says: "Newspapers take themselves much too seriously. Let's pay less attention to the public-policy nerds and explore the lighter side of the human condition. . . . Surely we can find more comic relief amid the depressing headlines."[55]

This is what Benjamin Day did in 1833. He found humor in the mundane. Generally ignoring political news, or merely mentioning an important political happening in a line or two, he gave long paragraphs and columns to police and courtroom news, usually with a humorous twist. Borrowing a leaf from popular English papers that were filled with police and court trivia—much of it humorous, all of it of human interest—Day, relying on George Wisner, kept an eye out for the funny little items that somehow filled the police blotter and court files every day. Even on items with a tragic note, he put on a humorous slant. As it is at a funeral where tense mourners suddenly start laughing, some of his items were so depressing—they were funny. After all, much of humor—ranging from the put-down to the slapstick—is vicarious. A disaster is funny, even if depressing, when it is happening to others, but "not to me." Day went fishing in a wide ocean of everyday life seen through the spectrum of people in trouble and served up his quarry with relish, embellished.

No domestic quarrel was too common or trivial for the *Sun* to print, with a little bit of colorful prose and spin added. Consider these examples:

> [In court, he stated] she was more ill-natured than usual last night, and took occasion to give him something of a flogging . . . but finding himself unable to cope with her in the matrimonial combat, he howled "murder," which brought a watchman to his assistance. The injured husband, with the assistance of the watchman, succeeded in capturing his tyrannical rib, and brought her, a prisoner, to the watch-house. On their promising to live together peaceably for the future, they were discharged.

> John McMan, brought up for whipping Juda McMan, his darling wife—his excuse was that his head was rather thick, in consequence of taking a wee drop of whiskey. Not being able to find bail he was accommodated with a room in Bridewell.

> William Scott, from Centre Market brought up for assaulting Charlotte Gray, a young woman with whom he lived. The magistrate, learning that they were never

married, offered the prisoner a discharge, on condition that he would marry the injured girl who was . . . willing to withdraw the complaint on such terms. Mr. Scott cast a sheep's eye toward the girl, and then looking out of the window, gave the Bridewell a melancholy survey; he then gave the girl another look, and was hesitating as to which he should choose—a wife or a prison. The Justice insisted on an immediate answer. At length he concluded he "might as well marry the critter," and they left the office apparently satisfied.[56]

Day also found humor in the antics at the ports and wharves. Consider the report on two sailors brought into the police "for disorderly conduct and collecting a mob at half past 10 o'clock at night." One of the two drunks had donned a sheet and pretended to be a ghost; the other wielded a dagger and "sallied forth to Quixote for adventure." They scared women and children, but eventually "were carried captive to the watch-house, whence in the morning, having been transmogrified again into gross flesh and blood, they were both sent to prison, to club their wits for new adventures."[57]

A Bull Battles a Train

Even such unglamorous incidents as a bull being hit by a train did not escape the appetite for humor of the *Sun*. Consider an item in the *Sun* attributed to the *U.S. Gazette* in Philadelphia, tagged "A Bull Fight with Steam":

> A few days since, as the locomotive steam engine was passing along the Columbia Railroad, the engineer espied a noble bull driving aross the field, apparently to give battle to the machine. He was coming at the top of his speed, his tail stuck right into the air, and his head down, as if for immediate attack. As the bull errant rushed onward, the director checked the car, and received the blow upon the front wheel. The animal recoiled several steps—the puffing of the steam pipe seemed to challenge him to a second onset, and on he came, bellowing and tearing up the earth, while his eyes seemed to shoot forth baneful fire. The engineer thought that his safety consisted in moving—he therefore put on the whole head of the accumulated steam, and the car started like the wind. The enraged beast struck short of his aim, he missed his footing, and rolled down a high embankment, to the infinite gratification of those who had watched his behaviour, and to the glory of the engineer.[58]

Today while police blotter humor goes largely untapped, media do include on occasion the cute story, involving children and animals. A close-up picture of a child singing or playing in the water at a fire hydrant in summer can make a front page. Concerning animals, a Philadelphia television channel covered the rescue of baby ducks that had fallen into a runoff pit; in the Philadelphia suburbs, the *Doylestown Intelligencer* carried front-page stories of "Postal Pooch," the post office mutt who likes to put his nose to the mail slot from the inside to greet startled mailers; the story of a woman giving CPR to her neighbor's dog, successfully; then in another front-page story, a report on the birth of a king-size litter of Dalmatian puppies. Day would have found such stories interesting and humorous, and he would have been proud.

Media as Purveyors of Information/Education
THE RACE TO BE FIRST

As the nineteenth century developed, just to publish was not enough. There was an emphasis on speed and on being first. The competition and the passion for being first were not entirely new, but the scoop mentality became a part of the penny paper scene. In the late 1820s the New York morning papers pitched in together to hire a boat to meet ships arriving from Europe. But James Watson Webb's *Courier and Enquirer*, where Bennett was working, backed out of the arrangement and used its own boat. In reaction the *Journal of Commerce* designed a faster boat. "At last there had developed a spirited rivalry between the newspapers as each sought to be first with the foreign news," says Carlson.[59] In 1831 six news boats were in use. The rivalry accounted for "flash news" briefs on the front pages of the papers. "Extras" also appeared with the latest overseas news, sometimes nearly a month old.

Webb and Bennett began to suspect that some of the very fast news in other papers was in fact stolen from the *Courier and Enquirer*. So one day the *Courier and Enquirer* printed the latest news arriving by the ship *Ajax*. Only there was no such ship. Only a limited number of the *Courier and Enquirer* papers contained the fake news column, and these few papers were distributed at places near the offices of the other newspapers. The *Journal of Commerce* took the bait and printed the exclusive news from the *Ajax*, obviously stolen from the *Courier and Enquirer*. "The rejoicing at the *Journal of Commerce* for its scoop soon turned to mortification as word spread about the city that there was no 'Ajax' arriving from Europe. The paper with the high moral tone had been caught red-handed stealing its news from the *Courier and Enquirer*."[60]

The telegraph, which became operational in 1844, linked cities and outposts. Ingenious reporters would vie to be the first one at the telegraph office. Once a reporter sent a story, he or she would tie up the line by having a part of a book or Bible transmitted in order to keep competitors from also using the line in time for a deadline.

Genesis of the Associated Press

This cutthroat competition was counterproductive for all. Representatives of a half dozen newspapers—among them, the *Herald, Sun*, and *Tribune*—met in 1848 in the office of the *Sun* and decided more could be accomplished by working together. The group launched both the cooperative Harbour Association, which would use one fleet of boats to serve all the participating papers equally, and the New York Associated Press, which would relay by telegraph news for all from the main centers of the nation.[61] Day's biographer says: "Thus in the office where some of the bitterest invective against newspaper rivals had been penned, there began an era of good feeling. So busy had the world become, and so full of news," and with the speed provided by the telegraph, "the invention of opprobrious names for Mr. Bennett ceased to be a great journalistic industry."[62] O'Brien says that the *Sun*, now under Moses Y. Beach, was no longer the same. The steamship, the railroad, and the telegraph had their effect on American journalism. "The police-court items, the little local scandals, the animal stories—all the trifles upon which Day had made his way to prosperity—were now being shoved aside to make room for the quick, hot news that came in from many quarters."[63]

The First Interview Article

The way information was presented took some new turns in the penny press era: (1) the use of the interview as a technique and (2) the creation of the in-depth story, coupled with the follow-up technique to keep the story alive.

Differences in opinion exist as to when the first published interview appeared in the American press.[64] The standard interview involves questioning and answering and the use of quotes. With that definition, Bennett's interview with royalty, under the headline "Interview with the King of Sandwich Islands," September 7, 1835, is excluded because it used indirect quotes. Nils Gunnar Nilsson mentioned a report on Bennett's visit with President Martin Van Buren in 1839, but was it more of a conversation than an interview? Nilsson also mentioned Bennett's use of verbatim quotes from a man complaining in his office interspersed with Bennett's comments, but that does not involve the usual question-and-answer, give-and-take techniques. *Frank Leslie's Illustrated Newspaper* published an interview in 1857 with Dred Scott, who was at the center of a Supreme Court ruling that denied blacks the right to sue for freedom in federal court.

Gerrit Smith, who financially backed John Brown's raid on Harper's Ferry, was interviewed by the *Herald* in 1859. That interview article is regarded as a forerunner of the interview article as we know it today.[65]

Usually the most-cited candidates for initiating the full-fledged interview are James Gordon Bennett's investigative interview with the brothel madam a few days after the murder of Ellen Jewett, a young woman of the night, in 1836, and Horace Greeley's interview in Utah with Mormon leader Brigham Young in 1859.

Some might discount Bennett's interview for its police-routine line of questioning and a Q-and-A format. Yet it does have description of setting and moods. Whether in question-and-answer form or not, it is an interview. The Q-and-A format is popular in published interviews today, from *Playboy* magazine to *Ms.* magazine.

The Ellen Jewett Murder Mystery.   Ellen Jewett, a beautiful and cultured twenty-three-year-old, was found killed by blows of an ax in a burning bed in a brothel. A cape belonging to nineteen-year-old Richard Robinson was at the scene. Robinson was arrested and tried for the murder. He was acquitted. At first Bennett treated Robinson as the murderer, but following several visits with the madam of the house he had doubts, which likely played a role in Robinson's acquittal (see box).

The Brigham Young Interview. In his celebrated interview with Brigham Young, Greeley describes the Mormon leader in detail before he gets to questions and answers: "He [Brigham Young] spoke rapidly, not always with grammatical accuracy, but with no appearance of hesitation or reserve. . . . He was very plainly dressed in thin summer clothing. . . . He is a portly, frank, good-natured, rather thick-set man of fifty-five, seeming to enjoy life." In the course of the questions and answers, the talk got personal:

> *Greeley:* What is the largest number of wives belonging to any one man?
> *Brigham:* I have fifteen. I know no one who has more; but some of those sealed to me are old ladies whom I regard rather as mothers than as wives.[66]

The Big Story

The penny papers probed every detail of the big stories and followed up the initial report by other stories that would appear day after day. Although the other papers gave continuing coverage to the great Wall Street fire of 1836 that destroyed twenty blocks of prime buildings, Bennett's *Herald* spared no effort in reporting the details of the fire with numerous background stories or "sidebars." In addition to the main story, one issue carried these articles: "A Visit to the Scene," in which he reports first-hand his own observations of the ruins; "List of Sufferers"; "Estimated Loss"; "Origin of the Fire"; and "Anecdote," little stories ranging from a store owner who could not get fire insurance locally because he was an abolitionist to the account of a hatter giving free hats to those who helped in the disaster, only to have one complain the hat did not fit.[67] The next day Bennett continued with "Additional Particulars of the Late Conflagation." On page 2 Bennett quipped: "We have abundance of dull news from Washington, but who cares for that?" The day of the big story had arrived.

Bennett Plays Detective in Early Interview

In his interview with the madam of the brothel where the young Ellen Jewett was murdered, Bennett began descriptively:

> I knocked at the door—a young man acquainted with the lady mistress, was with me—we entered. The back sitting parlor is composed of two large rooms opening into each other by large sliding doors. Rosina Townsend, the keeper of the house, is a tolerable good looking woman, with a dark devil of an eye, and a slight emaciation in the contour of her visage. She sat on the sofa, talking—talking—talking, of Ellen—

Ellen—Ellen. After a few words of immaterial import, she launched out on the incidents preceding the horrible night in question. She said she had never seen young Robinson to notice him, until a few nights before the fatal one in question.

She goes on to recount Ellen saying how handsome he was. Then Bennett began to editorialize:

> On the night in question, Mrs. Townsend says he came in about nine o'clock—did not

come into the parlor, but went up stairs and entered Ellen's room.

All the particulars related by Mrs. Townsend are of an extraordinary nature. There are several facts, however, we have heard, which are even more so. Mrs. Townsend, I understand, had borrowed money of Ellen.

Bennett told of a strange picture on a wall of two savages lifting tomahawks to give a young woman a blow. He asked:

If a woman who had borrowed money or jewells of Ellen—if a rival in the same line of life, wanted to make away with such a troublesome competitor, could not that picture . . . suggest to female vengeance or design—the very act perpetrated? Why are all of these women in that house now at large and out of custody? Why is Rosina Townsend out of custody? Why should her solemn assertion be taken rather than Robinson's?[68]

Bennett wrote a few days later:

Knowing that the only evidence on the identification of Robinson was that of Rosina Townsend [the madam], we made on Tuesday afternoon last a visit to 41 Thomas street, in company with a gentleman who was present during the conversation. We were met at the door by Rosina Townsend, the keeper of the house, who on our entering, asked us into the parlor. She there stated to us the following particulars, every one of which the gentleman and ourself was ready to be sworn to.

Mrs. Townsend told Bennett that she took a bottle of champagne to the room of Ellen (she called her Helen) and knocked. Bennett continued:

Q. What was he doing?
A. He was lying on his left side, with his head resting on his arm in the bed, the sheet thrown over him and something in his other hand.
Q. What was that?
A. I can't say.
Q. Was it a book?
A. I think it was—either a book or a paper—I saw his face.
Q. What did he say?
A. Nothing—Helen said to me, "Rosina, as you have not been well today, will you take a glass of champagne with us?—I replied, "No, . . ." I then left the room. . . .
Q. How did you know that this person you let in was Frank [Robinson used the name of Frank Rivers]?
A. He gave his name.
Q. Did you see his face?
A. No—his cloak was held up over his face. I saw nothing but his eyes as he passed me— he had a hat and cloak.
Q. Who first discovered the fire?
A. I did as I got up.
Q. On the morning of the transaction did you see Frank? . . .
A. I did; he was in the back parlor, standing by an officer.

And Bennett worked in some observations: "Is it not extraordinary that she should know a man so easily without seeing his face? . . . They [her eyes] are the eyes of the devil. . . . She wanted, the very day after her death, to take possession of Ellen's property and valuables."[69]

Media as Vehicles of Sensationalism/Entertainment

TELLING A GOOD STORY

For many, James Gordon Bennett's excessive coverage of the Ellen Jewett murder and ensuing trial is a pinnacle of sensationalism in the nineteenth century. It was, as John Stevens noted, "the first time newspapers really exploited a crime story."[70] That the story was sensational is evident because of the prurient nature of the subject—a gruesome murder of a young woman—and the vicarious nature of

the subject—"Thank God it didn't happen to me." It was made particularly sensational by the full front-page treatment and continued coverage. Here was a story
sensational in subject and made more so by the "exploitation" (as Stevens calls it) of
space. Yet it can be argued that the attention to crime, justice, and injustice delineated a moral concern.

But there is something inherent in the style of the coverage that makes the
Jewett murder story more sensational. It is the narrative approach, with narrative
techniques, namely, the use of significant detail that fires the imagination, essential
in all storytelling. Listen to the details that feed the imagination as Bennett goes to
the murder scene with haste:

> We mounted the elegant staircase—dark and gloomy. . . .
> "Here," said the Police officer, "here is the poor creature."
> He half uncovered the ghostly corpse. I could scarcely look at it for a second
> or two. Slowly I began to discover the lineaments of the corpse as one would the
> beauties of a statue of marble. . . .
> The countenance was calm and passionless. Not the slightest appearance of
> emotion was there. One arm lay over her bosom—the other was inverted and
> hanging over her head. The left side down to the waist, where the fire had
> touched, was bronzed like an antique statue. For a few moments I was lost in
> admiration of this extraordinary sight—a beautiful female corpse—that surpassed
> the finest statue of antiquity. I was recalled to her bloody destiny by seeing the
> dreadful bloody gashes on the right temple, which must have caused instanta-
> neous dissolution.[71]

Narrative technique requires setting the scene—description of location—plus a
slowing down of the happenings in moments of intense drama. In his sensational
account Bennett brings alive the mood of the hour and takes his time in giving significant details.

Some scholars who have studied style in writing see a link between short sentences and words and sensational reporting. Percy Tannenbaum and Mervin Lynch
have found that the use of short sentences and often-used short words creates a sensational tone.[72] Donald Shaw and John Slater argue also, "Sensationalism is, to be
sure, in the topic, but it also is in the style of presentation."[73]

Not only did narrative fiction have its place in such publications as *The New-
York Mirror: A Weekly Journal, Devoted to Literature and the Fine Arts*, but the mass
circulation dailies of the period also found room for fiction—sometimes at great
length. In the spring and summer of the first year of the *New York Tribune*, 1841,
Greeley ran more than fifty chapters or installments (sometimes two in an issue) of
Charles Dickens' *Barnaby Rudge*. The violent saga of crime and public unrest was
Dickens' first effort in historical fiction.

The Great Moon Hoax

In August 1835 on the front page of the *Sun*, a lengthy tale of scientists discovering
life—and not only life, but bat people—on the moon began. It was an elaborate
hoax cooked up by reporter Richard Locke (a Cambridge-educated relative of John

Locke). The use of significant detail and its "gee whiz" attitude gave it a life of its own, and the *Sun* soared in circulation.

Locke took care to make the entertaining, sensational series sound authentic. The discovery was first announced in the *Sun* on August 21, 1835:

> We have just learnt from an eminent publisher in this city that Sir John Herschel, at the Cape of Good Hope, has made some astronomical discoveries of the most wonderful description, by means of an immense telescope of an entirely new principle.

The series actually began at the top of the front page four days later. Notice the precise details, as essential in a practical joke or hoax as they are in fiction narrative:

> We this morning commence the publication of a series of extracts from the new supplement to the Edinburgh Journal of Science, which have been very politely furnished us by a medical gentleman immediately from Scotland, in consequence of a paragraph which appeared on Friday last from the Edinburgh Courant. The portion which we publish to-day is introductory to celestial discoveries of higher and more universal interest than any, in any science yet known to the human race. We are necessarily compelled to omit the more abstruse and mathematical parts of the extracts however important they may be as a demonstration of those which we have marked for publication; but even the latter cannot fail to excite more ardent curiosity and afford more sublime gratification than could be created and supplied by any thing short of a direct revelation from heaven.[74]

In the 18,000-word series, soon published as a book, the reader met all kinds of creatures, some bearing resemblance to earth creatures, although they might be blue (see box).

Some of the newspapers in the area reprinted the series in part and even praised the *Sun*. Day was quick to lift out the laudatory items and take note. But he could expect no support from Bennett, who was silent at first. Then tongue in cheek, Bennett observed: "The town has been agape two or three days at the very ingenious astronomical hoax, prepared and written for the Sun newspaper, by Mr. Locke, formerly the police reporter of the Courier and Enquirer. Mr. Locke is an Englishman by birth, is a graduate of Oxford or Cambridge—was intended for the Church, but in consequence of some youthful love affair, getting a chambermaid in some aukward plight, abandoned religion for astronomy." Locke wrote a protest to Bennett, which Bennett carried. Bennett chuckled in his own reply: "As to the 'indecorous liberties' we took with his 'biography,' 'the chamber maid. etc.' we take that back."[75]

Bennett Counters with "Hi" and "Ho"

The next day Bennett got into the fun himself with "A Better Story—Most Wonderful and Astounding Discoveries, by Herschell, the Grandson, L.L.D., F.R.S., R.F.L., P.Q.R., etc. etc. etc." Bennett told how it has been learned that "Ho, and Hi, the celebrated Chinese astronomers penetrated into the solitudes of immensity" in the universe. What did they see?

They Knew of "Batman" in the 1830s

Following are excerpts from Richard Locke's great moon hoax, *New York Sun*, August 25–31, 1835:

Having continued this close inspection nearly two hours, during which we passed over a wide tract of country, chiefly of a rugged and apparently volcanic character; and having seen few additional varieties of vegetation, except some species of lichen, which grew everywhere in great abundance, Dr. Herschel proposed that we should take out all our lenses, give a rapid speed to the panorama, and search for some of the principal valleys known to astronomers, as the most likely method to reward our first night's observation with the discovery of animated beings. . . .

Presently a train of scenery met our eye, of features so entirely novel, that Dr. Herschel signalled for the lowest convenient gradation of movement. It was a lofty chain of obelisk-shaped, or very slender pyramids, standing in irregular groups, each composed of about thirty or forty spires, every one of which was perfectly square, and as accurately truncated as the finest specimens of Cornish crystal. They were of a faint lilac hue, and very resplendent. I now thought that we had assuredly fallen on productions of art.

In the shade of the woods on the south-eastern side, we beheld continuous herds of brown quadrupeds, having all the external characteristics of the bison, but more diminutive than any species of the bos genus in our natural history. . . .

The next animal perceived would be classed on earth as a monster. It was of a bluish lead color, about the size of a goat, with a head and beard like him, and a *single horn*, slightly inclined forward from the perpendicular. . . .

On examining the centre of this delightful valley, we found a large branching river, abounding with lovely islands, and water-birds of numerous kinds. A species of grey pelican was the most numerous; but a black and white crane, with unreasonably long legs and bill, were also quite common. We watched their pisciverous experiments a long time, in hopes of catching sight of a lunar fish; but although we were not gratified in this respect, we could easily guess the purpose with which they plunged their long necks so deeply beneath the water. Near the upper extremity of one of these islands we obtained a glimpse of a strange amphibious creature, of a spherical form, which rolled with great velocity across the pebbly beach, and was lost sight of in the strong current which set off from this angle of the island. . . .

We were thrilled with astonishment to perceive four successive flocks of large winged creatures, wholly unlike any kind of birds, descend with a slow even motion from the cliffs on the western side, and alight upon the plain. They were first noticed by Dr. Herschel, who exclaimed, "Now, gentlemen, my theories against your proofs, which you have often found a pretty even bet, we have here something worth looking at: I was confident that if ever we found beings in human shape, it would be in this longitude, and that they would be provided by their Creator with some extraordinary powers of locomotion: first exchange for my number D." This lens being soon introduced, gave us a fine half-mile distance, and we counted three parties of these creatures, of twelve, nine, and fifteen in each, walking erect towards a small wood near the base of the eastern precipices. Certainly they *were* like human beings, for their wings had now disappeared, and their attitude in walking was both erect and dignified. . . . They averaged four feet in height, were covered, except on the face, with short and glossy copper-colored hair, and had wings composed of a thin membrane, without hair, lying snugly upon their backs, from the top of the shoulders to the calves of the legs. The face, which was of a yellowish flesh color, was a slight improvement upon that of the large orang outang, being more open and intelligent in its expression, and having a much greater expansion of forehead. The mouth, however, was very prominent, though somewhat relieved by a thick beard upon the lower jaw, and by lips far more human than those of any species of the simia genus. In general symmetry of body and limbs they were infinitely superior to the orang outang; so much so, that, but for their long wings, Lieut. Drummond said they would look as well on a parade ground as some of the old cockney militia! The hair on the head was a darker color than that of the body, closely curled, but apparently not woolly, and arranged in two curious semicircles over the temples of the forehead. Their feet could only be seen as they were alternately lifted in walking; but, from what we could see of them in so transient a view, they appeared thin, and very protuberant at the heel.

Whilst passing across the canvass, and whenever we afterwards saw them, these creatures were evidently engaged in conversation; their gesticulation, more particularly the varied action of their hands and arms, appeared impassioned and emphatic. We hence inferred that they were rational beings, and although not perhaps of so high an order as others which we discovered the next month on the shores of the Bay of Rainbows, that they were capable of producing works of art and contrivance. The next view we obtained of them was still more favorable. It was on the borders of a little lake, or expanded stream, which we then for the first time perceived running down the valley to a large lake, and having on its eastern margin a small wood.

Some of these creatures had crossed this water and were lying like spread eagles on the skirts of the wood. We could then perceive that they possessed wings of great expansion, and were similar in structure to those of the bat, being a semi-transparent membrane expanded in curvilineal divisions by means of straight radii, united at the back by the dorsal integuments. But what astonished us very much was the circumstance of this membrane being continued, from the shoulders to the legs, united all the way down, though gradually decreasing in width. The wings seemed completely under the command of volition, for those of the creatures whom we saw bathing in the water, spread them instantly to their full width, waved them as ducks do theirs to shake off the water, and then as instantly closed them again in a compact form. Our further observation of the habits of these creatures, who were of both sexes, led to results so very remarkable, that I prefer they should first be laid before the public in Dr. Herschel's own work, where I have reason to know they are fully and faithfully stated, however incredulously they may be received. . . . The three families then almost simultaneously spread their wings, and were lost in the dark confines of the canvass before we had time to breathe from our paralyzing astonishment. We scientifically denominated them the Vespertiliohomo, or man-bat; and they are doubtless innocent and happy creatures, notwithstanding that some of their amusements would but ill comport with our terrestrial notions of decorum.

The first object that met his sight was the Editor of the New York Sun, seated on a three legged stool, with a great sledge hammer in his hand forging "truths," in the same manner that Jove forged thunderbolts. The District Attorney of that place was serving him with notice of trial at the next sessions, for a libel on the inhabitants. He was distinctly, heard to say "that he should plead guilty, but wished to be recommended to mercy."

The next view was, twelve live lions, stuffed with straw, casting type. Two or three were at work at the press, which was something in the shape of a lobster. The paper was composed of rotten eggs, and was of a yellow color, and stiff as pasteboard.[76]

As to the *Sun*'s series about the moon and its creatures, Locke eventually spilled the beans, when a friend of his, reporting for the *Journal of Commerce*, told him in a

Bat people of the moon seem happy in Richard Locke's hoax. (The Bettmann Archive)

social encounter—perhaps in a barroom—that the *Journal of Commerce* had decided it must get copies of the series to reprint it. Locke told his friend to hold off, that he had indeed created the discovery himself.

Day sought to have the last word two weeks later when he said in an editorial: "Certain correspondents have been urging us to come out and confess the whole to be a hoax; but this we can by no means do until we have the testimony of the English or Scotch papers to corroborate such a declaration."[77] Circulation jumped, and the success of the *Sun* was secured. Day had found the value of sensationalism and entertainment, for readership at least, even if the compelling narrative was not true.

Media as Voices of Freedom
THE IRREVERENT MR. BENNETT

The so-called Moral War, waged by other newspapers and important powers of the community against James Gordon Bennett's *Herald* in 1840, was a testing of the freedom of the press. Bennett, publishing all kinds of news, from business to religion, at times inserted opinions or slants that sometimes ran counter to the image that the leaders and divines wanted to create. Isaac Pray, Bennett's biographer, sums up the issue: "These leaders were desperate to overthrow a newspaper that was testing the freedom of unshackled opinions."[78] Mostly the critical comments and boycotts instigated by the other papers, historians generally agree, resulted from the editors' jealousies over Bennett's success. "They were chagrined and maddened to see jocose, quizzing, and lampooning paragraphs maintaining favor in the public mind, while their own carefully written, and sometimes brilliant essays, were wholly neglected," said Pray.[79]

Mott lists some of the "most insulting epithets" applied to Bennett, "this ink-smeared Satan of the press." Mott notes that "the *Signal* called him an 'obscene vagabond,' a 'polluted wretch,' and a 'venomous reptile'; to the *Evening Star* he was a 'common bandit' and a 'turkey buzzard'; while the *Courier and Enquirer* said that its former associate editor was an 'unprincipled adventurer' whose 'reckless depravity' made the *Herald* a 'ribald vehicle' of 'moral leprosy.' "[80]

Clergy Boycott the *Herald*

Clergy called for a boycott of the paper; advertisers pulled ads. And during the year of the Moral War, 1840, the *Herald* lost one-third of its circulation.[81]

While economic and competitive factors played a role, Judith M. Buddenbaum, in writing on the religion journalism of Bennett, insists that the name itself, the "Moral War," suggests that "there was more to it than the desire to remove a dangerous competitor from the scene. For unlike other press wars, this one was fought on ostensibly moral grounds. And certainly the perpetrators had ample grounds for complaint."[82]

Bennett attacked the wealth of the churches and what he regarded as lack of concern for the poor. He wrote satirically about the Episcopalians' purchasing of expensive Christmas trees:

> The property of the Episcopal Church in this city is immense. . . . It is utterly impossible to get rid of the property, or to bring the revenue within the limits of law, unless we expend it in every way that can be devised.
>
> The purchase of beautiful evergreens at the very highest prices not only helps to get rid of this surplus revenue of the Church, but it also circulates money during the present pressure and furnishes, besides, a very fine relief to the eye when you enter church. . . . It is true, the poor might be much aided by a few hundred dollars, as suggested by kindly Harriette Smith [a letter writer], but Eliza, her sister, says that the poor are so much accustomed to hunger and want, that pinching is necessary for their health and spirits at this season of the year.[83]

Although most of Bennett's religion coverage was positive, he couldn't resist mocking the stuffiness as well as the finances of churches on occasion:

> The Doxology (long metre) was then sung; the Rev. Dr. Milnor delivered an effective prayer; and the crowds in the house all moved in masses as swiftly as decorum would allow, into the open air; all delighted; though the ladies looked excessively fatigued, excited, and pale.[84]

Bennett did not help himself by his own statement of faith:

Religion—true religion—consists not in eating or drinking—not in high salaries—not in hanging round the apron strings of rich old women—not in presuming to judge the opinions of others beyond what their acts will justify. Neither does true religion—or real Christianity consist in believing the dogmas of any church—or the *ipse dixit* of any set of men. The Bible is before me. Have I not a right to read the book—to draw out from it religious opinions—and to create a belief and a church of my own?[85]

Bennett, Mott believes, was not a winner in the Moral War. He was forced to promise that he would try in the future not to offend people over sensitive matters, "and never in his own lifetime did he entirely emerge from the cloud of obloquy that the moral warriors of 1840 threw over him."[86] While it is possible to argue that the Moral War showed the strength of institutional boycotts to curb the freedom of expression, nevertheless Bennett extended the parameters of topics—even sacred topics—that could be addressed critically by the press.

THE SLAVERY QUESTION LOOMS

The slavery question in antebellum times, of course, tested the freedom of the press. Could antislavery and abolitionist positions be expressed where there was a proslavery faction among readers? James Gillespie Birney, who ran for president on the Liberty Party ticket in 1840 and 1844, was challenged and threatened as editor of the *Philanthropist*, a paper he launched in 1836 in Cincinnati. Three of the papers in Cincinnati, "which represented the Whig and Democratic parties, abused him unmercifully, and one of them even suggested lynching."[87] Birney countered by asserting the right of freedom of the press and his right to set up a paper to discuss slavery. A mob broke into his office and destroyed most of his equipment.

Cassius Clay, who published the antislavery *True American* in Lexington, Kentucky, armed his office with rifles and two cannons. However, a group succeeded in seizing the premises and boxed up his press and sent it north to Cincinnati. He then printed the paper in Cincinnati, but edited it in Lexington.[88] Clay had a feisty reputation. He fought a number of duels, disemboweled one person with a knife, and destroyed an ear and an eye of another. Despite being an abolitionist, he served in the Kentucky legislature, served as minister to Russia under Lincoln, and was named a Union general. He declined the appointment unless the slaves were freed. Later in life a court ruled him insane.[89]

Elijah Lovejoy Martyred

In St. Louis Elijah Lovejoy edited a Presbyterian weekly, the *St. Louis Observer*, which attacked slavery. In 1835 he moved across the Mississippi to Alton in the free state of Illinois. Upon his arrival a mob broke up his press. Friends helped him get a new press. This too was destroyed, and so was a third press. Proslavery readers were incensed at his call for the founding of a state antislavery society. He raised money for a fourth press, and when it arrived Lovejoy stood before it at the warehouse and faced off a mob. He was shot five times as he attempted to push a ladder being used by charging thugs who were seeking to torch the roof of his office. He died almost instantly, becoming perhaps the country's first martyr for freedom of the press.[90]

Media as Political Organs
PARTISAN VIEWS ABOUND

The penny papers did not fill a vacuum. In fact, they did not really dominate the American scene. Mott says: "Whatever may be said of the enterprise and success of the penny press, and however important its part may have been in the news revolution, the fact remains that up to the time of the Civil War it was not the independent penny press but the partisan political press that dominated American journalism."[91] The legacy of the early American papers working hand in hand with the government—even accepting subsidies—and the legacy of Federalist and anti-Federalist papers and the control by political parties, among them the Whigs and Democrats, were in evidence even as mass-circulation independent papers developed. An editorial writer in the *Democratic Review* complained as late as 1852: "Every shade of political persuasion has its organ. . . . Each of these organs is a propagandist after its own fashion."[92]

A leading Democratic paper in New York, the *Post*, opposed slavery and monopolies and supported the abolitionists and free speech. As the Democrats leaned more to proslavery, the *Post* under William Cullen Bryant switched to supporting the newly formed Republican Party in 1854. There were prominent Democratic papers in other cities: in Boston, the *Post*; in Philadelphia, the *Pennsylvanian*, the paper once edited briefly by Bennett. Whig papers were prominent into the 1850s, but most of them, like the *North American* in Philadelphia, turned to the new Republican standard.

The vituperative rhetoric could match that of an earlier day. The *Weekly Oregonian*, in Salem, hissed against the Democrats: "The next legislative assembly are pre-eminently democratic. They were elected . . . under the *lash* of party drivers—under the cry of *dimocracy*." Furthermore, the paper referred to "the nests of the democratic vultures, who are laboring hard to hatch out a swarm of scorpions." But other papers were independent and recommended split tickets. The *Pacific News* of San Francisco urged: "Vote the ticket which, upon due examination, you most approve. If you wholly approve no ticket offered, scratch it, and put on other names which you like better."[93]

Lincoln Attracts Media

Although they were not organized and funded as party papers, the new mass circulation papers invariably did support candidates. The cults of personalities, evident from the Andrew Jackson and William Henry Harrison days, attracted editors. In fact, editors often played a role in creating these personalities. When Abraham Lincoln gave his famous Cooper Union speech in New York, on February 27, 1860, on the dais were Bryant, Horace Greeley, and other editors. Both Bryant and Greeley went back and tolled the bells for Lincoln. Bryant: "When we have such a speech as that of Abraham Lincoln of Illinois . . . we are tempted to wish that our columns were indefinitely elastic. . . . It is wonderful how much a truth gains by a certain mastery of clear and impressive statement."[94] Greeley took flight with his unequivocal praise of Lincoln: "No man ever before made such an impression on his first appeal to a New York audience."[95] Back in Illinois, the *Chicago Tribune*'s Joseph Medill reportedly was so caught up in the personality and electricity of the moment that a Lincoln speech could create that Medill "joined the clapping and cheering and stamping."[96]

The small parties and groups organized around special issues, such as antislavery and universal suffrage, had their organs to influence the political debate.

Abolitionist Editors

Among the most famous of the abolitionist editors was William Lloyd Garrison, who founded the *Liberator* in Boston in 1831. He regarded the Constitution as "a covenant with death and an agreement with Hell" (for not condemning slavery) and once publicly burned the Constitution in protest of the Kansas-Nebraska Act of 1854.

In 1847 the *National Era*, edited by Gamaliel Bailey, a former Methodist magazine editor, became the organ of the Abolition Party. The Anti-Masonic Party and later the Anti-Monopolist Party had their publications.

Solomon Southwick's *National Monitor* backed the Anti-Masons. Thurlow Weed, before he edited the influential *Albany Evening Journal* (which absorbed the *Monitor*), edited the *Anti-Masonic Inquirer* at Rochester. Weed lost a libel suit and had to pay $400 for saying that a member of an Anti-Mason committee was actually in the pay of the Masons—this following a famous trial in 1828 involving the murder of an alleged Mason informer.[97] Ignatius Donnelly, a Philadelphia lawyer transplanted to Minnesota, edited the *Anti-Monopolist* for the Anti-Monopoly Party.

Suffrage Publications

Among suffrage publications was the *Lily*, begun by Amelia Bloomer in 1849 as a temperance, anti-alcohol newspaper. The name *Lily* was deceiving, "a rather inappropriate name for so aggressive a paper," said women's suffrage pioneer Elizabeth Cady Stanton, "advocating as it did all phases of the women's rights question."[98] Among Bloomer's crusades was the right for women to dress more freely and comfortably. The properly dressed genteel woman "had voluminous trailing skirts that picked up dirt and unsanitary matter from the streets, a minimum of six full petticoats, and tightly laced whalebone corsets." The outfit, weighing up to 15 pounds, "made housework difficult, and frequently left the wearer short of breath. A few women regarded such clothes as a masculine conspiracy to hamper women's activ-

Amelia Bloomer: Founder of anti-alcohol, suffrage paper, Lily.
(Portrait by J. C. Buttré; Collection of The New-York Historical
Society)

ities. Some felt they were unhealthy. Most looked on them as perhaps inconvenient
but fashionable."[99]

When a cousin of Stanton took to wearing full Turkish pantaloons, Stanton and
Bloomer followed. Bloomer included patterns and pictures of herself and Stanton in
Turkish garb in the *Lily*. The national press, largely hostile, dubbed the new protest
fashion "bloomers." Bloomer eventually "gave up the attire because of ridicule that
deflected attention from other feminist issues,"[100] note Maurine Beasley and Sheila
Gibbons. Other suffrage publications included Paulina Wright Davis's *Una*,
launched in 1853.

An offbeat suffrage publication, too radical for many feminists, was *Woodhull
and Claflin's Weekly*, published by a spiritualist and stock speculator, Victoria
Claflin Woodhull, and her sister, Tennessee Claflin. Promoting women's political
rights and free love as well, Victoria Woodhull was a presidential candidate on the
Equal Rights Party ticket in 1872, the same year that Greeley went down in defeat
as a candidate. Receiving only a scattering of votes, on election day Woodhull was
in jail with her sister on "obscenity" charges in connection with her published re-

Victoria Woodhull: Suffrage editor, presidential candidate.
(Portrait by Mathew Brady; Collection of The
New-York Historical Society)

port on the Rev. Henry Ward Beecher's alleged involvement with the wife of
Theodore Tilton, editor of the religious *Independent*, once edited by Beecher.

A wide range of political voices, political endorsements, outright political organs, and specialized one-issue organs affected the political scene before the Civil
War and immediately afterward.

Media as Fourth Estate: Adversaries of Government

A NEW POWER BASE

The nonparty penny papers were obviously freer to take aim at whatever and whoever displeased them, from the president and the political scene to one another.
They supported the men of their choosing for the highest office and helped carry
the day for the victor. The editors even created enough of a power base to enable
them to serve in the inner sanctums of power themselves. Raymond of the *Times*, for
instance, a founder of the Republican Party, was floor leader for President Andrew

Johnson in Congress; Horace Greeley served briefly as a congressman before he secured the nomination for the presidency on two tickets.

While the penny papers were watchdogs of government and adversaries of corrupt government (for example, Greeley exposing city election rigging in 1841[101] and the *Times*, the *Herald*, and others exposing the graft of New York political boss William Tweed, in 1871), the accumulated power of the penny press gave further credibility to the claim of the media as a fourth estate or branch of government.

The *Herald*'s influence extended to Europe, where it developed an audience. A Paris edition continues to this day in the form of the *International Herald Tribune*. Not only was Bennett regularly "consulted by presidents and cabinet members, by governors, senators, mayors," but also "foreign dignitaries always made it a point to call on him, for the *Herald* was the only well-known American newspaper in Europe and South America."[102]

Pray made Bennett's *Herald* itself sound more important than other branches of government by insisting it was the very pulse of America. "The *New York Herald* is now the representative of American manners, of American thought," he said. "It is the daily daguerreotype of the heart and soul of the model republic. It delineates with faithfulness the American character. . . . The *New York Herald* is the face of the Western half of the earth."[103]

Media as Businesses
MAKING ADS FRESH AND PROFITABLE

The inexpensive price of the papers at one cent and later at two necessitated the development of advertising. Formerly many ads contained small woodcut illustrations. As the volume of ads increased, an equalization process set in. Bennett wanted to eliminate favoritism caused by illustrating some ads but not others, and he also wanted to make ad sections more attractive by giving them an orderly, uniform look. He introduced categories set off by subheads. He even made the ads more consumer-friendly by publishing a directory of categories, indicating the page and column on which the ads appeared. Multiple-column display ads were not popular in the early days of the penny press, but the "Bonner" effect was. Robert Bonner, publisher of the *New York Ledger*, began repeating a small two- or three-line ad from the top of a column over and over down the column. In May 1858 Bonner purchased seven whole pages in the *Herald* for this kind of advertising to promote a new fiction serial. It was the largest ad that had appeared in a newspaper.[104]

Bennett came to see ads as news, important not just for producing revenues but also for spreading the information of the day. Frederic Hudson said: "The advertisements of the *Herald* are a feature. They are fresh every day. . . . They are the hopes, the thoughts, the joys, the plans, the shames, the losses, the mishaps, the fortunes, the pleasures, the miseries, the politics, and the religion of the people. Each advertiser is therefore a reporter."[105]

Bennett's newly created category of advertising "personals" became a way for people to communicate with each other, even across international or North and South borders. While ads conveyed considerable trivia—for example, telling a friend to buy tickets for a minstrel or theater production—they also served as a way to inform people of one's welfare or to request help to locate a missing person. "Friends and separated families living at the North and South during the rebellion of 1861–65 communicated their welfare, sickness, and movements to each other through this medium in the *New York Herald*," says Hudson. Then the ads were copied in the southern papers.[106] He also notes that French exiles in London in 1865 could get word to their families in France through the *Herald*.

To keep ads fresh, in 1847 Bennett set a policy that no ads would run more than two weeks. The large circulation of the penny papers allowed advertising rates to be set high, encouraging turnover of ads. Also the papers were now in a position to demand cash before running the ads. These were among the "radical innovations" in advertising at the time, according to Alfred McClung Lee.[107]

From London to New York there seemed to be an increase in the amount of space given to advertising. Hudson noted that in one issue in 1861 the *London Times* included 4,000 ads. In an April 1869 issue of the *New York Herald* more than half the paper was ads—50 columns out of 96.[108] Even Greeley's sophisticated, issue-oriented *Tribune* gave way to the stampede of ads. On December 27, 1859, for instance, the first 3½ pages and one-third of pages 7 and 8 of the eight-page paper were ads. The front page was given over to the repetitive Bonner approach. Advertising indeed was the new principal means of newspaper support. Yet subscriptions, in addition to street sales, were not overlooked.

Media as Voices of Reform
SOUNDING OFF FOR JUSTICE

Were the penny paper editors reformers? With some exceptions, such as the exposure of the corruption of Tammany Hall and the Boss Tweed ring in New York, their mission was to entertain and seek out sensational police and offbeat stories, particularly Day's *Sun* and Bennett's *Herald*. But it can be argued that in their early and formative days the efforts of the penny papers prepared the way for in-depth treatment in magazines and the later-century muckraking, or investigative reporting. The penny papers at least called attention to the plight of laborers and later the middle class. The emphasis on the police blotter by Day and Bennett, along with Bennett's opening up his columns to greater specialized coverage of financial institutions, education, religion, the arts, and other areas, put more of the life and interests of society under scrutiny.

While the *Times* moralized at the end of its city news, Greeley, with all of his self-righteousness and idealistic causes, brought the judgment of a reform-minded editor to bear on even the prurient items of the day. Greeley did not just publish an item on seduction of a minor; he called for reform:

Rev. Mr. Van Zandt of Rochester is accused of the seduction of a member of his own church only sixteen years of age. The seduction is most evident; but Mr. Van Zandt firmly denies that he is the seducer, and accuses the girl of conspiring to ruin him. He has been suspended from his clerical office, held to bail on a civil suit for $3,000, and the Bishop has directed an investigation. The accused is a wealthy married man, and the father of three or four children.

And now we ask the journals which are so eager to trumpet this case in all its revolting details, to unite with us in demanding *the passage of a law to punish such atrocious villany*. Will they do it? Of course, we do not judge this man—we await the evidence which shall establish his guilt or proclaim his innocence—but if guilty, he is an infamous traitor to Society, to Humanity, to God, and ought to be severely punished. Say, gentlemen of the Press, shall the starving thief be sentenced to toil, privation and the lash, in our State Prison, and the deliberate, treacherous seducer go utterly untouched by our criminal laws? The devil laughs at such justice![109]

Without strict political party allegiances, the penny papers transcended the interests of regions. In particular, Bennett's *Herald* regularly gave columns to news and views from the South.[110] However, as objective as most of these reports were, Bennett remained a racist. Crouthamel sums up his views of blacks: "His basic premise was white racial superiority and black inferiority. . . . The word *Negro* was seldom used in the *Herald; nigger* was the word of choice."[111]

Reforming the slavery system was on the mind of Raymond, whose *Times* urged an end of slavery but wanted it to be achieved by a go-slow approach.[112] Republicanism was not to be equated with abolitionism. The issue at hand was not slavery itself but the extension of slave territory. As lieutenant governor of New York he declared in a speech: "The Republican Party has no sectional aim: it claims only the reaffirmation of a principle of compromise."[113] Direct reform of the institution of slavery was a more urgent aim of Greeley's *Tribune*, which published at length the writings of the abolitionists.[114]

WHAT HAPPENED TO THE BIG PENNY PAPERS?

The *Sun, Herald, Tribune*, and *Times* all survived into the twentieth century, but only the *Times* remains intact today. The *International Herald Tribune* maintains two of the names, but among its owners are the publishers of the *New York Times* and *Washington Post*.

The *Sun* passed from the hands of Benjamin Day in 1838 to Day's brother-in-law, Moses Y. Beach, who published it for ten years. In 1868 Charles Dana, who had lived at the Brook Farm commune in West Roxbury, Massachusetts, in the 1840s and had worked for Greeley at the *Tribune* for fourteen years, became an owner of the *Sun* and edited it until his death in 1897.

Two endearing editorials are remembered from the Dana era. By Dana himself, "Our Office Cat," January 12, 1885, put the blame on a fictitious cat when an important message of President Grover Cleveland blew off the editor's desk into the

Santa's girl, Virginia O'Hanlon, age unknown.
(Associated Press)

street. Another editorial in the *Sun* by Francis P. Church, appearing September 21, 1897, less than a month before Dana died, is a response to a letter from an eight-year-old girl who had been told there was no Santa Claus. Church replied with an editorial that declared, "Yes, Virginia, there is a Santa Claus."

A specialist in newspaper consolidations, Frank Munsey, merged the *Sun* with the *Globe* in 1923. Still alive in 1950, the *Sun* was merged by Roy Howard with the *Telegram* and *World* to form the *World-Telegram & Sun*. This then merged with the *Herald-Tribune* and *Journal-American* in 1966 to form the *World Journal Tribune*, which folded in 1967.[115]

When James Gordon Bennett of the *Herald* died in 1872, he was succeeded by his playboy son, James Gordon Bennett, Jr., who spent much of his time at sea captaining a yacht. His *Henrietta*, with himself at the helm, won the first trans-Atlantic yacht race from New Jersey to the Isle of Wight, England. A humorous article on the outrageous sportsman in the *Smithsonian* magazine told how while stark naked, the Commodore, as he was called, would drive his horse-drawn coach at night through the countryside and shriek at the top of his lungs, startling farmers and other bystanders.[116]

A Regrettable Incident

The best-remembered anecdote on Bennett, Jr., is the incident that broke up his engagement. The *Smithsonian* presents one version:

On New Year's Day 1877, after paying a number of holiday calls, Bennett arrived for a party at his fiancée's house. What occurred in the Mays' drawing room is obscured by Victorian sensibilities, but the most reliable story is that Bennett urinated into the grand piano.

That regrettable incident not only ended the engagement, but two days later Miss May's brother Frederick accosted Bennett outside the Union Club and vigorously applied the traditional horsewhip. The publisher challenged May to a duel. They met on a cold January afternoon at Slaughter's Gap, Delaware, near the Maryland border. May fired into the air. Bennett, an excellent shot, apparently fired at his opponent but missed.[117]

Is There a Santa Claus?

For all of the doubting Virginias of today, here is Francis P. Church's editorial in the *Sun* on September 21, 1897, as appropriate today as it was then:

We take pleasure in answering at once and thus prominently the communication below, expressing at the same time our gratification that its faithful author is numbered among the friends of the *Sun*.

"Dear Editor: I am eight years old.
"Some of my little friends say there is no Santa Claus.
"Papa says, if you see it in the *Sun* it's so.
"Please tell me the truth, is there a Santa Claus?"

Virginia O'Hanlon
115 West Ninety-Fifth Street

Virginia, your little friends are wrong. They have been affected by the skepticism of a skeptical age. They do not believe except they see. They think that nothing can be which is not comprehended by their little minds. All minds, Virginia, whether they be men's or children's, are little. In this great universe of ours man is a mere insect, an ant, in his intellect, as compared with the boundless world about him, as measured by the intelligence capable of grasping the whole truth and knowledge.

Yes, Virginia, there is a Santa Claus. He exists as certainly as love and generosity and devotion exist, and you know that they abound and give to our life its highest beauty and joy. Alas! how dreary would be the world if there were no Santa Claus. It would be as dreary as if there were no Virginias. There would be no childish faith then, no poetry, no romance, to make tolerable this existence. The eternal light with which childhood fills the world would be extinguished.

Not believe in Santa Claus! You might as well not believe in fairies! You might get your papa to hire men to watch in all the chimneys on Christmas Eve to catch Santa Claus, but even if they did not see Santa Claus coming down, what would that prove? Nobody sees Santa Claus, but that is no sign that there is no Santa Claus. The most real things in the world are those that neither children nor men can see. Did you ever see fairies dancing on the lawn? Of course not, but that's not proof that they are not there. Nobody can conceive or imagine all the wonders there are, unseen and unseeable in the world.

You may tear apart the baby's rattle and see what makes the noise inside, but there is a veil covering the unseen world which not the strongest men that ever lived could tear apart. Only fancy, poetry, love, romance can push aside that curtain and view and picture the supernatural beauty and glory behind. Is it all real? Ah, Virginia, in all this world there is nothing else real and abiding.

No Santa Claus! Thank God! he lives and he lives forever. A thousand years from now, Virginia, nay, ten times ten thousand years from now, he will continue to make glad the heart of childhood.

The *Herald* suffered from his long absences "and his frequently capricious behavior when he was heard from," observes the *Smithsonian*. His best staffers deserted for other papers. However, at age seventy-three the old bachelor married Baroness de Reuter, a widow of a member of the Reuter's news service family. He suddenly became serious and tried to reverse the direction of his failing newspaper. On his seventy-seventh birthday in 1918 he died, nearly bankrupt (he had used up a $40 million fortune).[118]

The *Herald* and the *Tribune*

Frank Munsey bought the *Herald* in 1920, then sold it in 1924 to the widow of Whitelaw Reid, who owned the *Tribune*. John Hay Whitney bought the *Herald-Tribune* in 1958.

Whitelaw Reid, a thirty-six-year-old associate editor at the *Tribune*, had succeeded Horace Greeley at the *Tribune* on Greeley's death in 1872. While catering to the sensationalism reigning in the media at the end of the century, Reid still managed to keep the paper at a higher moral level than most papers.[119] When he died in 1912, his wife, Elizabeth Mills Reid, became owner. When Munsey tried to buy the *Tribune*, she turned the tables and purchased the *Herald* from Munsey. The *Herald-Tribune* passed into the hands of her son Ogden and his wife, Helen Rogers Reid, before it was absorbed in the multiple merger of 1966 and died with the others in 1967.

The *Times*

When Henry Raymond of the *Times* died in 1869, the business manager and co-founder of the *Times*, George Jones, took over and ran the paper until his death in 1891. A group of staff members, headed by Charles Miller, bought the *Times* in 1893 but could not pull it out of the cellar where it had fallen, having the lowest circulation (9,000) of New York's eight morning dailies. More than $300,000 in debt, the *Times* was on the verge of bankruptcy.[120]

A successful Chattanooga editor, Adolph Ochs, was looking to expand in the newspaper business and negotiated a refinancing plan that would put him in charge of the *Times* if he could put the paper back on its feet in four years. Ochs took a non-sensational approach. The *Times* increased financial coverage and became a paper of record, reported real estate sales, listed court cases, developed its book review section, and refused to run comics. Then Ochs reduced the price to a penny. Circulation and advertising went up.[121]

Ochs hired a scholarly mannered journalist, Carr Van Anda, who, the legend goes, persisted and found an error in an Einstein equation. When the *Titanic* hit an iceberg in 1912, Van Anda got the jump on other newspapers by assuming the silence of the telegraph aboard the *Titanic* meant the ship had sunk. He had illustrations and a passenger list in the *Times* while other papers were waiting for confirmation of the story. The *Times* under Van Anda earned the first Pulitzer Prize gold medal in 1918 for "meritorious service."

From 1896 to the present day the slogan of the *Times* has been "All the news

Henry Raymond: Times *founder, politician.* (Harper's Weekly, July 3, 1869)

that's fit to print." Ochs and his staff chose the slogan but offered $100 to anyone who could come up with a better slogan not exceeding ten words. For weeks the paper printed alternative slogans but settled finally on the first one. Ochs continued as publisher until his death in 1935. He was succeeded by Arthur Hays Sulzberger, husband of the Ochs' only daughter, Iphigene Bertha.

Today the *Times* is still a paper of record and maintains a somewhat old-fashioned front page, vertically designed with stacked heads and subheads, while using some of the most exciting layouts in sections within the paper. Although true to the vision of Raymond, the *Times* today owes something to the tradition of Day as it mixes in features and even humor here and there, but unlike Day covers crime only selectively. With a strong editorial page, op-ed page and transcripts, the *Times* reflects the seriousness of Greeley and reflects both the internationalism of Greeley and Bennett as well as the specialized coverage of Bennett. The spirit and ideas of the penny press era live on in the lone survivor of the initial New York penny dailies.

QUESTIONS FOR DISCUSSION AND RESEARCH

1. Name ten reasons for the rise of the penny press.
2. Identify the initial policies of the *Sun, Herald, Tribune,* and *Times* in New York.

3. Which editor would you most liked to have worked for: Day, Bennett, Greeley, or Raymond? Why?
4. On occasion the penny papers used fiction—for instance, the *Sun*, the moon hoax story; the *Tribune*, serialization of Dickens. Where can you find "fiction" in today's newspapers?
5. What are some story or narrative elements important in developing an exciting "sensational" article?
6. How could the moon hoax have been handled to make its use ethical?
7. How were the large penny papers different from earlier party-aligned publications?
8. Did celebrity journalism thrive or fade during the penny press era?
9. What do you think of the humor approach of the *Sun*? Was some of it sexist? Suggest (1) ways more humor could be used in modern papers and (2) some guidelines for doing so.
10. Assume Day, Bennett, Greeley, and Raymond were somehow equal partners and copublishers of a newspaper. Design a front page that reflects the concerns of all four.
11. Was the penny press hostile to religion? Explain. (You may want to define religion.)
12. What contribution did the penny press make to nineteenth-century literature and vice versa?
13. What contribution did the penny press make to the freedom of the press?
14. How did the penny press further refine the idea of the press as the fourth estate?
15. Were the penny press editors reform minded?

ENDNOTES

1. John C. Nerone, "The Mythology of the Penny Press," *Critical Studies in Mass Communication*, vol. 4, 1987.
2. Walter Lippmann, "Two Revolutions in the American Press," *Yale Review*, vol. 20, no. 3, March 1931, p. 435.
3. Arthur J. Kaul and Joseph P. McKerns, "The Dialectic Ecology of the Newspaper," *Critical Studies in Mass Communication*, vol. 2, 1985, p. 217.
4. Ibid., p. 222.
5. *Philadelphia Public Ledger*, March 25, 1836, quoted in Frank Luther Mott, *American Journalism* (New York: Macmillan, 1947), p. 241.
6. Michael Schudson, *Discovering the News* (New York: Basic Books, 1978), p. 58.
7. Donald Lewis Shaw, "At the Crossroads: Change and Continuity in American Press News, 1820–1860," *Journalism History*, vol. 8, no. 2, Summer 1981, p. 49.
8. Dan Schiller, *Objectivity and the News: The Public and the Rise of Commercial Journalism* (Philadelphia: University of Pennsylvania Press, 1981), p. 10.
9. Ibid.
10. Ibid., p. 50.
11. *New York Herald*, June 7, 1836, quoted in Schiller, *Objectivity and the News*.
12. *Journal of Commerce*, June 29, 1835; quoted in Schiller, *Objectivity and the News*; also

Frederic Hudson, *Journalism in the United States* (New York: Harper & Row, 1873, 1969), p. 425.

13. Richard N. Current et al., *American History: A Survey* (New York: Alfred Knopf, 1961), p. 307.

14. Hudson, *Journalism in the United States*, p. 427.

15. Thomas A. Bailey, *The American Pageant: A History of the Republic* (Boston: D. C. Heath, 1956), p. 348.

16. Gary Whitby, "The Oversoul of Reform: Horace Greeley and New England Transcendentalism," paper presented at the meeting of the Association for Education in Journalism and Mass Communication, San Antonio, Aug. 1–4, 1987.

17. Mott, *American Journalism*, p. 373.

18. See John Bierman, *Dark Safari: The Life Behind the Legend of Henry Morton Stanley* (New York: Knopf, 1990). Also Frank McLynn, *Stanley: The Making of an African Explorer* (Lanham, Md.: Scarborough House, 1990).

19. John Tebbel, *The Compact History of the American Newspaper* (New York: Hawthorn Books, 1963), p. 94.

20. George Henry Payne, *History of Journalism in the United States* (Westport, Conn.: Greenwood Press, 1970; originally published by Appleton in 1920), p. 240.

21. Hudson, *Journalism in the United States*, p. 416.

22. James Melvin Lee, *History of American Journalism* (Boston: Houghton Mifflin, 1923), p. 193.

23. Nerone, "The Mythology of the Penny Press," p. 386.

24. David J. Russo, "The Origins of Local News in the U.S. Country Press, 1840s–1870s," *Journalism Monographs*, no. 65, February 1980, p. 5.

25. *New York Sun*, Nov. 9, 1833.

26. Ibid., Dec. 17, 1833.

27. Ibid., Aug. 28, 1835.

28. Frank M. O'Brien, *The Story of The Sun* (New York: George H. Doran, 1918), p. 38.

29. James Stanford Bradshaw, "George W. Wisner and the New York *Sun*," *Journalism History*, vol. 6, no. 4, Winter 1979–80, p. 117.

30. William David Sloan, "George W. Wisner: Michigan Editor and Politician," *Journalism History*, vol. 6, no. 4, Winter 1979–80, p. 115.

31. O'Brien, *The Story of the Sun*, pp. 129, 131.

32. Oliver Carlson, *The Man Who Made News: James Gordon Bennett* (New York: Duell, Sloan and Pearce, 1942), p. 87.

33. Ibid., p. 106.

34. Ibid., p. 107.

35. Ibid., p. 112.

36. *New York Herald*, May 6, 1835.

37. James L. Crouthamel, *Bennett's New York Herald and the Rise of the Popular Press* (Syracuse, N.Y.: Syracuse University Press, 1989), p. 69.

38. Ibid., p. 41.

39. Henry Luther Stoddard, *Horace Greeley: Printer, Editor, Crusader* (New York: G. P. Putnam's Sons, 1946), p. 80.

40. *New York Tribune*, April 10, 1841.

41. Ibid., April 12, 1841.

42. Ibid., April 26, 1841.

43. William Harlan Hale, *Horace Greeley: Voice of the People* (New York: Harper & Brothers, 1950), p. 155.

44. Entry of Jan. 3, 1848, in James Parton, *The Life of Horace Greeley* (New York: Mason Brothers, 1855), p. 306.

45. Ibid., p. 318.

46. Hale, *Horace Greeley*, p. 115.

47. Quoted in Laurie James, *Why Margaret Fuller Ossoli Is Forgotten* (Dix Hills, N.Y.: Golden Heritage Press, 1988), p. 26.

48. Bernard Weisberger, chief consultant, *Family Encyclopedia of American History*, "Horace Greeley" (Pleasantville, N.Y.: Reader's Digest Association, 1975), p. 474. See Glyndon G. Van Deusen, *Horace Greeley: Nineteenth Century Crusader* (Philadelphia, 1953).

49. Hale, *Horace Greeley*, p. 347.

50. Meyer Berger, *The Story of* The New York Times: *1851–1951* (New York: Simon and Schuster, 1951), p. 3.

51. Elmer Davis, *History of* The New York Times, *1851–1921* (New York: Greenwood Press, 1921), p. 14.

52. *New York Times*, Sept. 19, 1851.

53. Ibid., Sept. 20, 1851.

54. "Items in Morals and Religion," *New York Times*, Oct. 23, 1851.

55. Howard Kurtz, *Media Circus: The Trouble with America's Newspapers* (New York: Times Books, 1993), p. 370.

56. *New York Sun*, Sept. 3, 1833.

57. Ibid., May 11, 1835.

58. Ibid.

59. Carlson, *The Man Who Made News*, p. 103.

60. Ibid., p. 104.

61. O'Brien, *The Story of the Sun*, p. 167.

62. Ibid.

63. Ibid., p. 168.

64. Nils Gunnar Nilsson, "The Origin of the Interview," *Journalism Quarterly*, vol. 48, Winter 1971, p. 707.

65. Ibid.

66. "Brigham Young's Religion, Wealth, Wives, Etc.," *Harper's Weekly*, Sept. 3, 1859.

67. *New York Herald*, Dec. 18, 1836.

68. *New York Herald*, April 14, 1836.

69. Ibid., April 16, 1836.

70. John D. Stevens, *Sensationalism and the New York Press* (New York: Columbia University Press, 1991), p. 42.

71. *New York Herald*, Sept. 12, 1836.

72. Cited in Donald L. Shaw and John W. Slater, "In the Eye of the Beholder? Sensationalism in American Press News, 1820–1860," *Journalism History*, vol. 12, Autumn–Winter 1985, p. 87.

73. Ibid.

74. *New York Sun*, Aug. 25, 1835.

75. *New York Herald*, Sept. 1, 1835.

76. Ibid., Sept. 2, 1835.

77. *New York Sun*, Sept. 16, 1835.

78. Isaac C. Pray, *Memoirs of James Gordon Bennett and His Times* (New York: Stringer & Townsend, 1855; reprint, New York: Arno Press, 1970), p. 265.

79. Ibid., p. 264.

80. Mott, *American Journalism*, pp. 236, 237.

81. Ibid., p. 237.

82. Judith M. Buddenbaum, " 'Judge . . . What Their Acts Will Justify': The Religion Journalism of James Gordon Bennett," *Journalism History*, vol. 14, no. 2–3, Summer–Autumn 1987, p. 55.

83. "Holy Evergreens," *New York Herald*, quoted in Buddenbaum, "Judge . . . What Their Acts," p. 59.

84. Ibid., May 15, 1840, in Buddenbaum, "Judge . . . What Their Acts," p. 61.
85. "Religion and Salvation," *New York Herald*, Dec. 14, 1838, in Buddenbaum, "Judge . . . What Their Acts," p. 60.
86. Mott, *American Journalism*, p. 237.
87. George Henry Payne, *History of Journalism in the United States* (Appleton, 1920; reprint, Westport, Conn.: Greenwood Press, 1970), p. 227.
88. Mott, *American Journalism*, p. 263.
89. Weisberger, *Family Encyclopedia of American History*, pp. 229, 230.
90. Paul Simon, *Freedom's Champion: Elijah Lovejoy* (Carbondale: Southern Illinois University Press, 1995).
91. Mott, *American Journalism*, p. 253.
92. Ibid.
93. *Weekly Oregonian*, Salem, July 21, 1855; *Pacific News*, vol. 1, no. 29, Oct. 30, 1849.
94. *New York Post*, Feb. 28, 1860.
95. *New York Tribune*, Feb. 28, 1860.
96. Mott, *American Journalism*, p. 285.
97. Hudson, *Journalism in the United States*, p. 746.
98. "Mrs. Stanton on Mrs. Bloomer," in Appendix, D. C. Bloomer, *Life and Writings of Amelia Bloomer* (Arena Press, 1895; reprint, New York: Shocken Books, 1975), p. 375.
99. Ibid., p. xi.
100. Maurine H. Beasley and Sheila J. Gibbons, *Taking Their Place: A Documentary History of Women and Journalism* (Washington, D.C.: American University Press, 1993), p. 68.
101. *New York Tribune*, June 21, 1841.
102. Carlson, *The Man Who Made News*, p. 382.
103. Pray, *Memoirs of Bennett*, p. 412.
104. Mott, *American Journalism*, pp. 299, 300.
105. Hudson, *Journalism in the United States*, p. 470.
106. Ibid., p. 473.
107. Alfred McClung Lee, *The Daily Newspaper in America: The Evolution of a Social Instrument* (New York: Macmillan, 1937), p. 317.
108. Hudson, *Journalism in the United States*, p. 469.
109. *New York Tribune*, July 23, 1841.
110. See, for example, *New York Herald*, Oct. 16, 1856.
111. Crouthamel, *Bennett's New York Herald*, p. 70.
112. *New York Times*, Sept. 27, 1851.
113. Francis Brown, *Raymond of the Times* (Westport, Conn.: Greenwood Press, 1951), p. 146.
114. See, for example, "A Letter from Theodore Parker to a Friend in Boston," *New York Tribune*, Dec. 27, 1859.
115. See Joseph Sage, *Three to Zero: The Story of the Birth and Death of the World Journal Tribune* (American Newspaper Publishers Association, 1967).
116. Julia Lamb, " 'The Commodore' Enjoyed Life—but N.Y. Society Winced," *Smithsonian*, November 1978, p. 132.
117. Ibid., p. 137.
118. Ibid., p. 140.
119. Mott, *American Journalism*, p. 425.
120. Berger, *The Story of* The New York Times, pp. 99, 100.
121. Michael and Edwin Emery, *The Press and America: An Interpretative History of the Mass Media* (Englewood Cliffs, N.J.: Prentice-Hall, 1954, 1988), p. 274.

7

A Divided Nation and Media

What should the role of the media be in times of national conflict and war? The Revolutionary War and the War of 1812 were small wars in an undeveloped country where the newspapers were small and isolated. The Mexican War (1846–1848), occurring far away from the East, also did not attract a significant press corps. But when the Civil War broke out, great armies were pitted against each other throughout the nation, and most families were involved in some way (there were three-quarters of a million casualties). With a sizable press corps scattered throughout the war zones and with the aid of the telegraph, news could be reported almost immediately, not allowing for review. Some principles and guidelines for the press, at least in terms of the security of forces, were needed—and tested—as the nation entered the inevitable conflict.

ROOTS OF THE CONFLICT

The roots of the conflict were deep. From the earliest colonial days and the beginnings of the new republic, cultural and political differences drove wedges between North and South. The North developed urban centers and industry; the South was more sparsely settled, and predominantly rural. The nurturing of states rights by Jefferson and Madison (through the Kentucky and Virginia Resolutions aimed at voiding the national Alien and Sedition Acts) gave John C. Calhoun a basis for presenting his nullification doctrine in response to the federal tariff act of 1828, which restricted southern commerce with British industry markets. The slavery debate—exacerbated by the Missouri Compromise of 1820, the gag rule in Congress in 1835–1836 tabling antislavery bills, the Texas annexation in 1845, the Compromise of 1850, and the Kansas-Nebraska Act of 1854—increasingly dominated the news.[1] Donald Shaw, in a study of slavery coverage in newspapers from 1820 to

1860, saw an increase in coverage over the decades, with the largest percentage of slavery-related stories (41 percent) occurring during the 1850s.[2]

Yet the causes of the war between the states remain complex. Shaw asks: "Was blame to be laid upon differences in economic systems, upon states versus national rights, or upon competing social systems—one based upon free labor and the other resting upon the sweated brows of slaves?" Or, he wonders, "was there something even more fundamentally different; was it a clash of regional cultures? . . . Was the Southern version of emerging national life unable to fit into the national pattern, without force?"[3]

Editorial Voices in the Confederacy

A key event that drove the South to dissolve the union by secession was the election of Abraham Lincoln in 1860. So hostile were southerners to Lincoln that editors announced that there would be no hope for the union with the infidel Lincoln in office. The stormy Rhetts (Robert Barnwell Rhett and Robert Barnwell Rhett, Jr.) of the *Charleston* (South Carolina) *Mercury* "were looking to an immediate convention to carry the state out of the Union while the resentment over the election was still at its height," says the senior Rhett's biographer, Laura White.[4]

A Richmond editor, predicting that the inauguration day of March 4, 1861, would become as memorable as Caesar's death day, the Roman Ides of March, reminded the reader of Lincoln's "imbecility, buffoonery, and vulgar malignity." The consequences, said John M. Daniel, of the *Richmond Examiner*:

> The new President has climbed to his place on the fragments of a shattered Confederacy, and the mere necessity of things will force him to deluge them in blood long before the Ides of another March has come again. . . . He is inaugurated to-day as John Brown was hung, under the mouths of cannon leveled at the citizens whom he swears to protect; and with the bayonets of mercenary battalions commanding every road to the fountain of mercy and justice. What can come of all this but civil war and public ruin?[5]

Both Daniel and Rhett later became strong critics of the Confederate administration as the war developed. (Daniel was wounded in a duel with the treasurer of the Confederacy in 1864; he had also been wounded in the arm as a major at Mechanicsville.) Yet their antipathy to Lincoln preceded all their complaints about the Confederacy.

Lincoln's Objectives

Lincoln himself did not make the slavery issue primary but cast the matter in the inviolability of the union and the need to preserve the union under the federal government at all costs. *New York Tribune* editor Horace Greeley had goaded Lincoln in a famous editorial, "The Prayer of Twenty Millions," to take a more definitive position against slavery, namely, by creating an emancipation policy. Greeley, expressing pain and disappointment, scored Lincoln's advisers: "We think you are unduly

Four Lincoln cartoons: 1, "President Lincoln's Inaugural," Thomas Nast in Frank Leslie's Illustrated Newspaper, *March 9, 1861. 2, Lincoln as warmonger. 3, "A President-elect's Uncomfortable Seat,"* Frank Leslie's Illustrated Newspaper, *March 2, 1861. 4, "Prof. Lincoln in His Great Feat of Balancing,"* Vanity Fair, *March 23, 1861.* (Reproduced in *Media History Digest*, vol. 6, no. 2, Fall/Winter 1986)

influenced by the counsels, the representations, the menaces, of certain fossil politicians hailing from the Border Slave States."[6]

Lincoln, who was to issue the Proclamation of Emancipation of the slaves a month later, on September 20, responded to Greeley with a letter:

> My paramount object in this struggle is to save the Union, and is *not* either to save or to destroy slavery. If I could save the Union without freeing *any* slave I would do it; and if I could save it by freeing *all* the slaves I would do it; and if I could save it by freeing some and leaving others alone I would also do that. What I do about slavery, and the colored race, I do because I believe it helps to save the Union; and what I forbear, I forbear because I do *not* believe it would help to save the Union. I shall do *less* whenever I shall believe what I am doing hurts the cause, and I shall do *more* whenever I shall believe doing more will help the cause. . . . I have here stated my purpose according to my view of *official* duty; and I intend no modification of my oft-expressed *personal* wish that all men every where could be free.[7]

Yet the editors settled to a large degree on the symbolic status of slavery, writing editorials for or against slavery. At one extreme, Daniel at the *Richmond Examiner* saw a morality in slavery: "The presence of an inferior race influences and *helps* to mould the manners and the character of the white man in the South. It inspires every citizen with the feeling of pride and decent self-respect; renders him dignified in deportment and more circumspect in conduct."[8]

At the other extreme, in the North Frederick Douglass wrote in *Douglass' Monthly* of "effectively putting down the whole class of pestiferous slaveholders, so that the nation shall know them no more, except in history, to be execrated and loathed, with all other robbers and tyrants which have cursed and ruined human society."[9]

Media as Purveyors of Information/Education
SATURATION ON-THE-SPOT JOURNALISM

The Civil War was war as Americans—and American journalists—had never seen it before. "In the two things which most impress the imagination," said E. L. Godkin (who edited the *New York Evening Post* and the *Nation* magazine) of the war, "the size of the forces engaged, and the desperation of the fighting, there has been nothing like it since Napoleon's campaign."[10] Never before had so many reporters been assigned to one story. The *New York Herald* had forty reporters or special correspondents—or "specials," as they were called—in the field. One monument on a mountain between Burkitsville and Boonsboro, Maryland, pays tribute to 135 writers and artists who covered the war.[11] One female Civil War reporter, Mary Leader, has a monument at a cemetery in Hanover, Pennsylvania, paying tribute to her as a "pioneer newspaper woman. . . . Her first-hand report of Lincoln's Gettysburg address bore witness to its greatness. In her account for the *Hanover Spectator* she garnered Lincoln's words from his own lips," and tradition has it that she was one of the first to realize the speech's greatness. She is said

Frederick Douglass: Abolitionist, editor, orator. (The National Archives)

to have walked 15 miles in wintry weather to get to the Gettysburg ceremony.[12] *New York Tribune* reporter A. D. Richardson estimated that the North had 500 reporters in the field, and the South, 200.[13]

Saturation coverage had been growing since Bennett told every facet of the Ellen Jewett murder. Correspondents had been sent to Kansas to cover the bloody upheavals—"genuine clashes of a small civil war"[14]—in the 1850s, and they trailed and dogged Lincoln and Stephen A. Douglas in their tilt for the Senate in 1858. "It was one of the first major American political campaigns to be covered in a modern style," says Tom Reilly, of California State University–Northridge. "Breaking new ground, reporters traveled extensively with the candidates, made intensive use of shorthand to record campaign speeches and fought for the recognition of the press's right to cover the events."[15]

The war coverage was as deeply personal as it was comprehensive. Correspondents often became part of the story, each one vying to be first in presenting the news of the day. During battles they hid in trees, or put on army uniforms; one dressed as a bum and wandered behind Confederate lines; one even got a job as a guard and gained access to John Brown's cell.

Civil War Pictorials

Two names stand out in the Civil War era in the visual arts as the most productive and influential—Mathew Brady, photographer, and Thomas Nast, cartoonist.

When war broke out in 1861 Brady had two studios, in New York and Washington. He was on hand from the very beginning, having rushed out to the first battle of Bull Run with two wagons of equipment. However, in the ensuing Union retreat his photo plates were destroyed.

A budding artist, Brady had been encouraged by telegraph inventor Samuel F. B. Morse, whose specialty in preparing daguerreotypes intrigued Brady. In 1844 Brady opened his own gallery in lower Manhattan. He created a collection of photos of famous persons, *Gallery of Illustrious Americans*, which included Andrew Jackson, James Fenimore Cooper, and Edgar Allan Poe.

Posing Lincoln

In 1860, when Lincoln was in town for the Cooper Union speech, he wandered into Brady's New York studio. Brady fussed with him, raising his low collar and strengthening his stringy tie. With Lincoln's instant fame from the Cooper Union speech, Brady had his hands full printing pictures of the promising politician. On more than one occasion Lincoln remarked, "Brady and the Cooper Union speech made me president."

Lincoln posed again for Brady shortly after he arrived in Washington for the inauguration. George Story, whom Brady had brought in to help pose Lincoln, recalled, "He did not utter a word, and he seemed absolutely indifferent to all that was going on about him; he gave the impression that he was a man who was overwhelmed with anxiety and fatigue and care."

Story rejected Brady's request that he pose Lincoln, exclaiming instead, "Pose him? No! Bring the camera at once!" And while Lincoln was deep in thought, a very natural portrait was taken, which was a far departure from the "Napoleonic" pose common in those days.[16]

One day Lincoln arrived unexpectedly at Brady's Washington studio with his son "Tad." Eight portraits resulted, one of them being the one on the five dollar bill.

During the Civil War Lincoln gave Brady a "press card," a note that said, "Pass Brady." Brady sent his aides as teams into different theaters of battle. By the end of the war he had put twenty teams into the field. Each team carted a wagon of photographic supplies.[17]

Dragging Bodies into Picture

Some of Brady's aides also achieved fame with their war pictures—among them, Alexander Gardner, Timothy O'Sullivan, and George Barnard. Gardner's picture of the dead "rebel" in a trench at Gettysburg is one of the most famous of the war and, indeed, was selected by *Time* magazine as one of the ten "greatest images of photojournalism" in its commemorative issue on the 150th anniversary of photography in the fall of 1989. *Time* added a postscript to Gardner's picture of the rebel sharpshooter fallen at his post. "In fact," says *Time*, "Gardner dragged the body there from a nearby field. He had earlier photographed the same corpse from a different angle and identified it in his caption as that of a Union sharpshooter."[18] *Time* also showed how the Gardner picture was reprinted as a woodcut in *Harper's Weekly*: "For eyes still accustomed to the compositional formality

(Continued)

Mathew Brady's photographic outfit in the field near Petersburg, Virginia, 1864.
(The National Archives)

and noble sentiment of war paintings, a photograph could seem too stark. *Harper's* adjusted the scene, and the mood, by adding bodies, a broken cart and a fallen horse borrowed from other photos."[19]

Brady capped his Civil War pictures with a distinguished picture of Robert E. Lee after the Confederate general surrendered. Brady had expected to get rich from selling copies of his Civil War pictures. However, since there was no direct printing of pictures in newspapers—only laborious renderings by artists copying the pictures—there was no real market for his photos. He died nearly penniless.

The Enduring Symbols of Thomas Nast

An artist-chronicler of the Civil War and the turbulent days of politics that followed the war, Thomas Nast gave the country some of its best-known symbols. He is credited with popularizing the version of Santa Claus known today[20] and the symbols of the donkey for the Democratic Party and the elephant for the Republican Party.

Nast began when as a fifteen-year-old he applied for a job with *Leslie's Illustrated Newspaper*. To test the youthful artist, the publisher, Frank Leslie, told Nast to draw people scurrying aboard the boat bound for the Elysian Fields, a resort beyond Hoboken, New Jersey, at the last call of "All aboard." No one was more surprised than Leslie when Nast aptly completed the assignment. He was hired for four dollars a week. (Leslie died in 1880 and was succeeded by his wife Miriam who changed her name legally to Frank Leslie.)

Nast was soon drawing political-reform cartoons—for example, one of ill-fed and sick cows held up by pulleys in barns as Nast and *Leslie's* exposed the contaminated, diluted "swill milk" industry. He drew illustrations of police scandals for *Harper's Weekly*, then went to London for the *New York Illustrated News* to cover a prizefight. Before returning, he went

Thomas Nast: He drew Santa Claus and political satire.
(*Philadelphia Bulletin;* Temple University Libraries
Photojournalism Collection)

to southern Italy to cover the revolutionary
Giuseppe Garibaldi. Nast's sketches of ruined
palaces, whole areas in ashes, crowds armed
with pickaxes, and surrendering generals were
printed widely in Europe as well as America.
Returning, he began to send Civil War drawings to *Harper's Weekly*. In the summer of 1862
he was hired as a regular staff member.

Opposes "Peace at Any Price"

It was the presidential campaign of 1864 that
pushed Nast to produce his most effective
politically oriented war cartoons. At the
Democratic convention in Chicago, the party

had declared the war a failure and called for
"peace at any price." The cartoonist was
angered that, for the sake of peace, the
Democrats were apparently willing to allow
the Confederate government to continue.

Nast's drawing depicted a downcast,
unarmed, one-legged Union soldier with
crutches shaking hands with a southerner who
is fully armed, smiling, standing tall. Between
them is a grave. The southerner has one foot
on the grave and has broken in two a knife
lying there. One-half of the knife reads

(Continued)

Nast cartoon: Compromise with the South.

"Northern," and the other "Power." Columbia, a female personification of the United States, is weeping beside the grave. The tombstone reads, "In memory of our Union-heroes who fell in a useless war."

Under this, originally, was a Union army hospital scene, a slave in chains, and an "Auction of federal soldiers and their families," but this part was suppressed by the editors at *Harper's*. Nevertheless, the picture's success was startling. An increased edition of *Harper's Weekly* had to be issued, and the page was used as a campaign poster. Lincoln called Nast "our best recruiting sergeant. His . . . cartoons have never failed to arouse enthusiasm and patriotism and have always seemed to come just when those articles were getting scarce."

After the war Nast turned to highly charged political commentary. He caricatured President Andrew Johnson. In 1869 Nast did his best cartooning when he began attacking New York City Democratic Party "Boss" William Tweed and the Tweed Ring at Tammany Hall, the influential political club named after a Delaware Indian chief.

The Carnage of a Tiger

Fletcher Harper at *Harper's Weekly* made up his mind that the publication should join efforts with New York newspapers and do what it could to rid New York of Tweed and his cronies. This decision, combined with Nast's moral sense and social concern, gave rise to his "war" against the Tweed Ring. In 1871, when Tweed ascended to the top of Tammany Hall, Nast's cartoons became more direct if not more vicious.

The famous Tammany tiger appeared in Nast's cartoons on the eve of the New York municipal elections of 1871. Nast got the idea for the tiger from the emblem of Tweed's Big Six fire company, which was a tiger head. The first tiger cartoon was of

Frank Leslie: Pioneer in illustrated journalism. (New York Public Library)

the beast unleashed in a coliseum, mauling Columbia, with Tweed and his cohorts looking on placidly. "What are you going to do about it?" reads the caption.

Harper's circulation tripled during the onslaught, and the drawings continued to pique the anger of New York's average citizen. The Tweed Ring was voted out of power in 1871, marking the end of Nast's most creative period of cartooning.

Nast published 3,000 cartoons in *Harper's Weekly* during the twenty-five years he worked there, until 1887 when he quit over creative differences. An unsuccessful investment in a mining effort in Colorado, along with other investment failures, led to his financial disaster.

In 1892 he allied himself with the *New York Gazette* and soon became the chief editor.

(Continued)

"The Tammany Tiger Loose: What are you going to do about it?" by Thomas Nast in Harper's Weekly, *November 11, 1871. New York boss William Tweed and gang look on as Republic is devoured.* (All rights reserved. The Metropolitan Museum of Art, Harris Brisbane Dick Fund, 1928)

A year later he changed the name to *Nast's Weekly*. However, no one involved with the paper knew anything about the business side of publishing, and that lack, combined with waning political support, killed the paper.

When he was offered the post of consul general in Guayaquil, Ecuador, in 1902, he sent to Secretary of State John Hay a drawing of himself on the beach with a suitcase in one hand and a golf bag in the other. "Say the word," read a note on the edge. Nast readily took the post, embarking for Ecuador in June, but he soon became ill and died there of yellow fever in 1902 at age 62.[21]

Reporter Finds His Own Dead Son

On-the-spot journalism was sometimes poignant. *New York Times* correspondent Samuel Wilkeson wrote his report on the battle at Gettysburg crouched next to the body of his dead son. He began his description of the battle:

> Who can write the history of a battle whose eyes are immovably fastened upon a central figure of transcendingly absorbing interest—the dead body of an oldest born, crushed by a shell in a position where a battery should never have been sent, and abandoned to death in a building where surgeons dared not to stay?

> The battle of Gettysburgh! I am told that it commenced on the 1st of
> July, a mile north of the town, between two weak brigades of infantry and
> some doomed artillery and the whole force of the rebel army.

He concluded his main report (there were also some "sidebars" on anecdotes and casualty lists):

> Oh, you dead, who at Gettysburgh have baptized with your blood the sec-
> ond birth of Freedom in America, how you are to be envied! I rise from a
> grave whose wet clay I have passionately kissed, and I look up and see
> Christ spanning this battle-field with his feet and reaching fraternal and lov-
> ingly up to heaven. His right hand opens the gates of Paradise—with his left
> he beckons to these mutilated, bloody, swollen forms to ascend.[22]

In the Speaker's Chair

On-the-spot journalism reached a certain nadir in the symbolic act of Thomas
Morris Chester, the only black Civil War correspondent. Working for the
Philadelphia Press, in the ebbing moments of the war, Chester entered the
Confederate capital of Richmond with General A. G. Draper's brigade, the first
Union unit to enter the city. Chester decided that he would write his first report
from no lesser a place than the desk of the speaker of the Confederate House,
"aware of the irony and eager to thumb his nose at the Confederacy, that ultimate expression of oppression, exploitation, and human misery," as his biographer R. M. J. Blackett put it.[23] A paroled Confederate officer was enraged and
ordered Chester out. "Chester looked up briefly, then continued writing. The
irate officer rushed Chester but was greeted by a well-placed punch that sent
him tumbling. Chester adjusted his sleeves and returned to the desk. . . .
Looking around for a moment and obviously savoring the situation Chester
commented cryptically, 'I thought I would exercise my rights as a belligerent,'
before returning to his writing."[24] Chester began his article, datelined
Richmond, April 4, 1865: "Seated in the Speaker's chair, so long dedicated to
treason, but in the future to be consecrated to loyalty, I hasten to give a rapid
sketch of the incidents which have occurred since my last despatch."[25]

Sing Sing Alumni and Scholars

The reporters were a motley bunch. They were young, two-thirds in their twenties.[26] They ranged in background from Augustus Cazaran, a Boston reporter
who had spent time in Sing Sing prison, to Henry Norman Hudson of the *New
York Evening Post*, a noted Shakespearean scholar.[27] Half were college educated
and, in a country that was still predominantly rural, half came from cities.[28]

Despite the craving to get "scoops" on their competitors, a "herd" mentality
developed much like the groupings in later wars. In the Vietnam War, for example, where it was difficult to get accurate, verifiable information, reporters
would gather in groups in bars and other locations, often swapping information

with their friends. The herd mentality gets a boost when military authorities limit travel and access. Other factors sometimes get mixed up in the bonding. Andrews tells of a group of Bohemians who settled on lodging in the home of a widow "who also had a pretty daughter to whom the Bohemians were properly attentive."[29] Group thinking was also encouraged when Lincoln spoke to gatherings of reporters at the White House, inaugurating, John Tebbel suggests, "the modern presidential press conference."[30]

Bylines were used on some stories, largely with the encouragement of the military, in order to pin the responsibility of a story on a particular writer should it develop later that incorrect information or national security secrets had been transmitted. But a perusal of Civil War newspapers shows that bylines were not universally printed with the stories, and even when a byline was used, it was likely a pen name. "Agate," for instance, was the pen name of Whitelaw Reid, a star reporter for Cincinnati, Chicago, and New York newspapers. "Shadow" was the pen name for a Confederate columnist who wrote first for the *Memphis Daily Appeal* and then for the *Mobile Register and Advertiser*.[31]

New Era of Reporters

The Civil War shifted attention from editors as personalities to reporters and facts. "The Civil War signaled the end of the kind of journalism associated with the penny press era, in which an editor's personality dominated and people read the newspaper for his views," says Hazel Dicken-Garcia of the University of Minnesota. The report of the correspondent became more important than an editor's editorial.[32] Readers whose lives were touched by the war wanted news; they wanted the facts as quickly as possible. Horace Greeley, backtracking after repercussions from the failed Union effort at Bull Run after the *Tribune*'s raucous "On to Richmond" editorial, set a future "just the facts" policy for his reporters. He wrote: "Henceforth I bar all criticism in these columns on Army movements, past or future. . . . Correspondents and reporters may state fact, but must forebear comments."[33] Louis Starr noted that the editor "was jostled, suddenly, by a man in his late twenties, in mud-spattered mufti or Federal blue, astride the inevitable sway-backed nag—saddlebags bulging with mackintosh, notebooks, Faber No. 2's, field glasses, pipe, sometimes potables—riding among the troops with half an eye out for the provost marshal's men: the American newspaperman, at last come into his own."[34]

Specialized bureaus or departments emerged, such as the southern bureau at the *Herald*. Its staff collected and filed clippings and any information that came from the South.[35]

Dependence on Sources

Cultivating sources to ensure access to information was important. And there were no better sources than the high brass themselves. A technique was to praise a particular general or cabinet member and then expect help in getting information from that person. The flamboyant "chevalier," Henry Wikoff, an unofficial writer for Bennett's *Herald*, is believed to have purloined an early copy of Lincoln's first annual address to Congress from a special friend, Mrs. Lincoln herself. Efforts also were made to use multiple sources, to play one source against another in order to get a true picture of events.

Newspapers began to be redesigned. Instead of the one-column, one-line announcement of a topic, multideck headlines in large bold type began to be used, and after the Civil War, the bold headlines spread to multiple columns. Sidebars isolating an event or idea appeared. Large maps were regularly used on the front pages, heralding the day of the illustrated newspaper. Magazines in particular made wide use of photographs converted to fine line drawings by artists.

A Changed Style

The style of newspaper writing changed, but not as much as some commentators maintain. Perhaps the summary lead—the inverted pyramid, with the important facts first—did make its debut with the Civil War. Perhaps because of the high costs of transmission and the unpredictability of the telegraph message getting through in its entirety, some correspondents summarized the story at the outset, putting forth the who, what, when, where, why, and how of a story. Tebbel may have a point that this is the beginning of the standard "get-right-to-the-facts" lead of modern journalism.[36] Yet much of the reporting was evidence to the contrary. For one thing, the telegraph seemed quite capable of sending great tomes. Andrews notes that in one day alone in 1864 some 58,000 words were relayed to newspapers from the Washington telegraph office. Also, the summary lead was not unknown in other eras, with examples appearing as far back as the early English newspapers.

Ironically, the development of the inverted-lead news format might owe something to the use of press statements and briefings by authorities in the Civil War—in other words, to "public relations" copy. David Mindich credits Secretary of War Edwin Stanton with writing announcements with fact-heavy leads and distributing the items widely. "Because Stanton's terse, impersonal dispatches appeared unedited on the front pages of newspapers across the Union," says Mindich, "he was widely read throughout the war." Mindich seeks to show that Stanton was a writer of inverted pyramids and proceeded "to reconcile this form with his tight rein on discourse—journalistic and otherwise—during the Civil War period." Yet Mindich admits that four years of reporting the war before the assassination of Lincoln were basically "chronological and self-conscious."

Mindich considers the Lincoln assassination as a possible turning point in newspaper style, toward the inverted pyramid. "At the earliest," he says, "it seems, the inverted pyramid was born with the coverage of Lincoln's death." Mindich mentions the dispatch by Associated Press reporter Lawrence Gobright at the first word of the shooting: "THE PRESIDENT WAS SHOT IN A THEATRE TONIGHT AND PERHAPS

MORTALLY WOUNDED."[37] This indeed was a right-to-the-point summary lead of key facts. But detractors point out that this is all that Gobright wrote in his first dispatch—and a mere bulletin or alert it was at that. Later, when he had additional information, he produced a chronological account for newspapers. And one dispatch does not make a trend.

Mott prefers to see very little or no real innovation in development in news style, although he saw signs of a new directness. The lead of the modern news story had not yet been perfected, says Mott, but he notes that news writing was more direct than before the Civil War. Official information from the war area appeared in full, instead of being summarized in the main story. Articles were likely to be printed chronologically, with the oldest dispatch at the top of the column.[38] Lists of casualties printed in small type followed the main account. Andrews also discounts the development of the summary standard lead. "Although the news writing of the sixties was more direct than that of the previous decade," he says, "the stilted rhetoric which even the best army reporters commonly employed contrasts sharply with the simpler journalistic style of the present day." He goes on to list examples of flowery writing, for instance, purple prose containing such phrases as "the grim blood-dripping visage of war" and "the proud, towering rebel edifice of folly, fraud and reckless passions."[39] Weisberger observed: "Type was small and columns were long, so that there was little need for writers to be herded into terseness. Wherever foursquare statements could be replaced by euphemism, the substitution was made, apparently on the theory that a naked fact was an indecent affront to sensitive subscribers."[40]

Yet "conciseness" was in the air. Lincoln's Gettysburg Address in 1863, with its emphasis on *le mot just*, "the right word," was to have its influence on American culture and letters. Garry Wills makes the point that "Lincoln forged a new lean language to humanize and redeem the first modern war."[41] Wills insists Lincoln's Gettysburg speech (in contrast to the two-hour opening rhetorical address by orator Edward Everett, a former secretary of state and senator) "worked several revolutions, beginning with one in literary style.... Lincoln's remarks anticipated the shift to vernacular rhythms that Mark Twain would complete twenty years later."[42]

Newspapers, especially small ones without a war staffing budget and with cutbacks in their staffs by enlistments, made use of some of the hometown boys off to war to supply them with copy. In using "letters" sent home, papers achieved some of the "vernacular rhythms" of a Lincoln in contrast to some of the more pompous, even though direct, writing of the professional "special correspondents" in the field. The *Baraboo* (Wisconsin) *Republic* started carrying firsthand war reports from the "Sauk Co. boys" on its front page. Wrote soldier D. K. Noyes early in the war: "This was a sad day for many of us. In the morning our first dead was buried, and in the afternoon necessity required that we send our ladies, who had accompanied us so far, home."[43] The letters of the participants, in the growing doom, assumed their own "Gettysburg Address" kind of cadence and rhythm.

Media as Vehicles of Sensationalism/Entertainment
"IMPORTANT, IF TRUE . . ."

With the demand for information in the context of the excitement of war, sensationalism played a role, especially in the North, where the penny press had paved the way with its emphasis on the entertainment value of news. At the start of the war the southern press was two or three decades behind the North in the use of sensationalism. Havilah Babcock suggests that the unilateral "autocracy of the slaveholders" and the "general benightedness of the section" did little to encourage extravagance in coverage.[44] In the Civil War the tightly monitored southern press had little motive for creative and inventive coverage, and certainly less manpower for such endeavor.

The war was sensational enough, with its repetitious bouts of slaughter and mayhem. Thomas Morris Chester found it natural to begin one report by stating, "The latest sensation in this army is the explosion which happened at City Point on the 9th inst."[45] The reporters, beginning with the coverage of violence before the war in Kansas, knew the power of a pure, unembellished atrocity story.[46]

The northern press in particular traded in rumor and exaggeration in the rush to get reports back to their offices. Often these reports were written by newly appointed, untrained reporters. "To some extent, the entire corps, made up preponderantly of legitimate and accredited representatives of the leading newspapers," says Andrews, "was brought into disrepute by the misconduct of a little band of 'newspaper guerrillas,' " which could be found in Washington soon after the start of the war. "Many of these 'guerrillas' were fakers who paid little attention to facts in their pursuit of news items and over whom the chiefs of the Washington offices had comparatively little control."[47]

But the news—true, rumor, fake—would likely be used anyway. Mott notes that the heading "Important, If True" placed above war stories was commonplace. He cites a *Baltimore Sun* discussion of the problem. That paper under the heading "Rumors and Speculations," said:

> Rumors of every kind multiply. Every hour gives rise to the most extravagant reports. . . . The press North and South seems to have entered upon a war of crimination and recrimination, and instead of calming the excitement and allaying unfounded prejudices, to rejoice in adding to the excitement of the moment.[48]

A Fabricated Battle

Some of the grossest examples of outright fabricated reporting in the war were inspired by the battle at Shiloh in southwestern Tennessee in 1862. "Probably no battle fought during the Civil War excited a greater amount of controversy than did the Battle of Shiloh," says Andrews, "and for this the army correspondents were in no small degree responsible." Working without adequate information, they nevertheless wrote long accounts, sprinkled with incidents cut from whole cloth, such as accounts of hand-to-hand fighting that did not happen. They made up a story of Sherman's men being bayoneted in their tents. "Shiloh was the first battle of the war in which the faking of eyewitness accounts of the fighting took place on a large scale." Some of the correspondents never got closer to the battle than Cairo in southern Illinois. So there developed a new term for those who faked their stories, the "Cairo war correspondent."[49]

One fake story that had serious repercussions was a carefully conceived hoax that made its way into the *New York World* and the *Journal of Commerce*. In 1864 the papers printed an untrue story stating that Lincoln had issued a proclamation calling for the draft of 400,000 men. The forgery was created by Joseph Howard, Jr., city editor of the *Brooklyn Eagle*. His aim was to use the hoax to cash in on the reaction in the stock market. He sent the announcement to many newspapers. All except the *World*, the *Journal*, and the *Picayune* in New Orleans, which copied the account, declined to publish the story without verification. The *World* and *Journal* were ordered shut down for two days by the provost marshal in New York, and the *Picayune* was ordered suspended for two weeks. Howard was jailed for three months in a military prison, but went on to a successful newspaper career, including being elected in 1897 as president of the International League of Press Clubs.[50]

A post–Civil War readership accustomed to day-by-day doses of excitement in the news—real or imagined—during the war continued to have special appetites that needed to be satiated. The expectation of sensational accounts, says Babcock, "led to melodrama in the news, to flaring headlines, coloring and all the seductive accompaniments of the modern sensationalized press."[51]

Media as Businesses

NEW SHARED WAYS TO COVER NEWS

Newspapers became big businesses during the Civil War. Circulation skyrocketed, nearly doubling. The *New York Times*, for instance, saw circulation jump from 45,000 to 75,000 right after the start of the war.[52] (New York City's population was to reach one million in 1870, compared to 60,000 in 1860.) Gross income and profits soared.

So did costs. The *Herald* spent nearly a million dollars on its correspondents. And to keep up with the demand to print large quantities and also in response to staffing shortages during the war, papers had to invest heavily in improved equipment.

The pressure for wider news coverage daily and the demand for more advertising space led to the inauguration of Sunday editions. At first the *Times* Sunday edition sold for two cents, then in a year, three cents, with the cost of use of the telegraph and the rising cost of paper contributing to the increase. In 1864 the *Times*, daily and Sunday, sold for four cents—a price maintained for nineteen years.[53]

Financial considerations brought cooperative efforts. In addition to the Associated Press, which served a number of papers in the North, a cooperative news agency developed in the South. Unable to keep pace with cost demands, southern editors decided they would be better served by a mutual news service. Editors of six southern newspapers met in Atlanta, Georgia, in 1862 and discussed the possibility of launching a press service. A year later, with more than a dozen editors from Georgia, Alabama, North Carolina, and Mississippi present in Macon, Georgia, the Press Association of the Confederate States of America was born.[54]

Birth of Syndication

The wire services, the Associated Press (AP) in the North and the Press Association (PA) in the South, primarily moved the news stories of the day along one at a time. An editor in the small southwest Wisconsin town of Baraboo developed formal, regular, preprinted features and became a pioneer of syndication in America. A bronze sign on an eating place on the square of Baraboo—the former winter home for the Ringling Brothers circus—sums it up:

> ### Historic Site in Journalism
>
> When the printer quit to fight in the Civil War, editor Ansel N. Kellogg kept the *Baraboo Republic* in publication by ordering two pages of preprinted war news each week from a Madison newspaper and printing Baraboo news on the blank sides in his shop on this site. Other newspapers joined in buying the readyprints, and Kellogg developed his idea into the first newspaper syndicate.

As the plaque in Baraboo states, Kellogg found himself suddenly shorthanded when his one-man printing staff, Joseph Weirich, joined the Union Army. An experienced replacement in wartime was next to impossible to find.

There was an easy answer to this dilemma, Kellogg thought. He went to a smaller, half-sheet size, and ordered a preprinted insert of war news from publishers of the *Wisconsin State Journal* in Madison, 30 miles to the southeast. Kellogg came out with a four-page, full-size paper, with two pages printed by the Madison paper, and two by himself.

Four other Wisconsin papers, also faced with shortages of help during the war, began using preprinted pages. Thus by 1861 a full-fledged preprinted syndication, initiated by Kellogg, was in full operation. During the next year fifteen papers signed up.

It was the first continuous syndication, but it was not the first effort. Moses Yale Beach, publisher of the *New York Sun*, in 1841 printed extra editions of one sheet containing a speech of President John Tyler and sold the sheets to more than a dozen other newspapers. These newspapers merely substituted their own logo when they included the speech in their publications. However, the project seems to have been a one-time affair. A directory of business names was also distributed to newspapers in 1846 by Volney Palmer, regarded as the nation's first advertising agent.

And Andrew Jackson Aikens in 1847 ordered preprinted pages of a speech of President James Polk from a Boston paper and filled the blank side of the *Woodstock (Vermont) Spirit of the Age* with local news. He did not continue the project.

When Kellogg began using preprinted pages on a regular basis, some papers feared the new procedure and warned of state control. The *Portage* (Wisconsin) *State Register* said, "The plan, if universally adopted, would give almost absolute control of state affairs to the editors who would be employed do all the thinking for the papers in the state."[55]

On the other side of the debate, the *Berlin* (Wisconsin) *Courant* countered that the fear that a "couple of editors will, in fact, edit all the country papers in the state" is groundless. "There is no more ground for fear than there is that the telegraphic reporter for the Associated Press will control all the papers that print the reports."[56]

When the Civil War was over, Kellogg sold his Baraboo paper and headed for Chicago to try his hand in the big city. He now offered his own preprinted sheets to country weeklies. The orders came in rapidly. Soon Kellogg was also producing the *Publishers' Auxiliary*. It was intended primarily to be a means of promoting the Ansel N. Kellogg newspaper syndicate. Two of the four pages were from his syndicated service; the other two pages carried trade news and advertising of interest to publishers.

By 1886, when Kellogg died in Thomasville, Georgia, his corporation did a $200,000-a-year business, serving 1,400 newspapers with printed pages and stereotyped plates. Twenty years after his death, in 1906, the Kellogg Newspaper Company had nine offices and 1,827 customers when it was taken over by a competing syndicate, the Western Newspaper Union.[57] The National Editorial Association (now called the National Newspaper Association), representing primarily weeklies and smaller papers, bought the *Publishers' Auxiliary* from the FWP Corporation (formerly Western Newspaper Union), owned by Farwell W. Perry, of New York City, in 1962.

The *Auxiliary* continued to be published, although in 1962 the NEA had its own 42-year-old *National Publisher*, in Washington. In 1968 the two were combined, keeping the name of the nation's oldest newspaper trade journal, the *Publishers' Auxiliary* of Ansel Nash Kellogg.

Media as Fourth Estate: Adversaries of Government

THE PRESS SETS THE AGENDA

During the Civil War the media acted as a fourth branch of government by playing a strong role in setting the agenda that molded attitudes, often along sectional and regional lines. Newspapers saw to it that readers got their views through tinted glasses of the region. When the North ran accounts from the South, it did so selectively to reaffirm certain biases against positions of the South. And southern newspapers generally did not bother to include a northern viewpoint on issues. Donald Reynolds quotes one Virginia paper which declared: "Newspapers and Telegraphs have ruined the country. Suppress both and the country could be saved now."[58] Reynolds adds, "Without the press, the task of those who divided the nation would have been infinitely more difficult."[59] But, alas, the power of the press as it took up regional stances made itself a factor in "government."

On one level the Civil War was a war of personalities. The media, with their correspondents attached to a particular general and army, set the stage for what the public would know about the general and other high officials. Personalities vacated the scene after intense press criticism. The *New York Times* was incessantly critical of Major General John C. Frémont's Missouri campaign. The general was removed from that command, with perhaps some thanks to the *Times*. The power of the press as the Fourth Estate nearly forced the demise of General Ulysses Grant. James G. Randall observed: "So desperate did Grant become at one time because of the use of the press against him by his rivals that he planned to return home, and his purpose was only altered by Sherman's strenuous persuasion."[60] The Civil War press had certain power—if not veto power—over the *dramatis personae* of the war.

In some areas of the South the importance of the editor and reporters was considered so great that they were exempt from military service. A bill passed by the Virginia legislature in 1862 exempted from military service one editor and one assistant editor from each daily newspaper, as well as any employees that the editor might certify on her or his honor to be indispensable for producing a daily newspaper.[61]

The Copperheads

The Civil War had its adversaries in the media, with editors doing their best to wield the power of the word against the official policies of the government. Most extreme in the North were the Copperheads, northern opponents to Union war

---

The Lighter Side

How the Press Made Fun of Ol' Abe

Alan Metcalf

Lincoln humor was plentiful on both sides in the Civil War. On the Confederate side, Charles Henry Smith, using the alias Bill Arp, lightened southern spirits. Writing for the *Southern Confederacy* in Rome, Ga., he addressed four jocular letters during 1861–1862 to "Mr. Linkhorn, Sur." Written in the style of a

hillbilly cracker, one of the letters' trademarks was misspelling. Arp posed as a Union sympathizer pretending to advise the president on such matters as military maneuvers and the Emancipation Proclamation. He professed his letters to be "pertinent to the occasion that provoked it, and very impertinent to those

(Continued)

they held up to the public eye." (Charles Henry-Smith, *Bill Arp, So Called*)

Responding to Lincoln's April 1861 order for dispersal of rebel troops, he wrote:

> The fact is, we are most obleeged to have a few more days, for the way things are happening, it is utterly onpossible for us to disperse in twenty days . . . Old Virginy, and Tennessee, and North Callina are continually aggravatin us into tumults and carousements, and a body can't disperse until you put a stop to sich onruly conduct on their part. . . .

Amused by the story that Lincoln donned a disguise on his first trip to Washington as president-elect, Arp wrote to the president:

> I would like to have your Skotch cap and kloak that you travelled in to Washington. I suppose you wouldn't be likely to use the same disgize again when you left, and therefore I would propose to swap.

A second letter to Lincoln included:

> Mr. Abe Linkhorn, sur, the 8teenth is the annyversary of the day when Georgy tore herself frantically loose from the aberlition dienasty. . . . We kalkerlate to celebrate that day, and I am authorized to invite you and Bill Seward over to purtake of our hospitalities. Where is Hamlin? I allow that he's ded, or I would ax him too.

Among Lincoln's bitterest partisan adversaries in the press was Marcus Mills (Brick) Pomeroy, who published the *La Crosse* (Wis.) *Tri-Weekly Union and Democrat*. Pomeroy's satire showed little respect for Lincoln, the candidate or president.

On page one, under a heading, "Punish Enemies and Reward Friends," Pomeroy frequently printed one-liners. One, referring to a picture which made Lincoln look blind, suggested the picture be captioned, "Old blind Abe." (June 13, 1860)

Pomeroy spared no abuse when commenting on the president's physical appearance:

> The Madison papers compliment Hon. Tim O. Howe, by saying that he resembled Lincoln! We think Howe would be justified in calling those Madison chaps out!
>
> We hereby give notice that under no considerations will we be held responsible for any damage arising from an exhibition of this picture [of Lincoln] in the family, so people will be on their guard!
>
> The Republicans who are circulating Old Abe's pictures would have better success if they would have a rear instead of a front view of their candidate. It would not look half as hard. . . .

Lincoln anecdotes were satirized by a more benign Robert Henry Newell, writing under the name of Orpheus C. Kerr, a pun on "office-seeker." In the *New York Sunday Mercury* and other New York papers, Newell's major target for ribbing was the Army of the Potomac, referred to as the Mackerel Brigade. The Orpheus C. Kerr Papers were eventually published in three volumes in 1862, 1863 and 1865. Newell spoofed Lincoln in fictional visits with the president, portraying him as the consummate storyteller. He often referred to Lincoln as "the Honest Abe," a man who confronted grave national crisis with one anecdote after another.

Newell's humor also displayed warmth toward Lincoln, as Orpheus C. Kerr talked about ". . . our Honest Abe, who still goes about smiling, like a long and amiable sexton, and continues to save our distracted country in the manner of an honest man." One Orpheus C. Kerr story told a Lincoln anecdote about a dissenter against the Emancipation Proclamation who was in the state of permanent confusion after listening to the president.

In one contrived interview Kerr observed, "The Honest Abe is a well-meaning executive enough, but I wish he'd do something to save his country, instead of telling small tales all the time." Another White House visitor who insisted on a more vigorous prosecution of the war, met with yet another Lincoln anecdote.

Orpheus C. Kerr remarked, "Our President, my boy, has a tale for every emergency, as a rat-trap has an emergency for every tail."

Poking fun at the young Lincoln, Kerr said, ". . . he split so many rails that his whole county looked like a wholesale lumberyard for a week." On the president's appearance, Kerr remarked, "that when he took to flat-boating, he was so tall and straight, that a fellow once took him for a smoke-stack on a steamboat, and didn't find out his mistake until he tried to kindle a fire under him." On young Lincoln's eloquent defense of an accused horse-thief, Kerr recounted that the defendant "made him a present of the horse as soon as he was acquitted."

Of all the Civil War humorists, David Ross Locke ranked as one of Lincoln's staunchest supporters. A young radical journalist he founded two early newspapers. In 1861, he edited the Findlay, Ohio, *Jeffersonian*, publishing letters under the name of Petroleum V. Nasby. The Nasby letters so entertained Lincoln that the president insisted on reading one at a cabinet meeting before discussing slave emancipation.

Locke portrayed Nasby as an ignorant, bigoted Copperhead (a Northern supporter of the South), writing from "Confederit X Roads, Kentucky." Similar to Arp's letters, Nasby trademarks were gross misspellings, twisted grammar, warped ideas and exaggerations. The Nasby letters intended to rail the Copperhead who in turn reviled Lincoln.

In pretending to interview Lincoln, Nasby wrote:

> . . . knowin also that you er a goriller, a feendish ape, a thirster after blud, I speek . . . Restore to us our habis corpusses, as good ez new. Arrest no more men, wimmen, and children for opinyun's saik. Repele the ojus confisticashen bill, wich irritaits the Suthern mind and fires the Suthern hart. Do away with drafts and conskripshens. Revoke the Emancipashen Proclamashen, and give bonds that you's never ishoo another . . . Disarm yoor nigger soljers,

and send back the niggers to their owners, to conciliate them.

On the surrender of Robert E. Lee, Nasby said:

> I survived the defeat uv Micklellan . . . becoz I felt ashoored that the rane uv the goriller Linkin wood be a short wun; that in a few months, at furthest, Ginral Lee wood capcher Washington, despose the ape, and set up there a constooshnal guverment, based upon the great and immutable trooth that a white man is better than a nigger. . . .
> Linkin rides into Richmond! A Illinois rail-splitter, a buffoon, a ape, a goriller, a smutty joker, sets hisself down in President Davis's cheer, and rites despatches!

Expressing great admiration for Locke's creation of Nasby, the president reportedly said, "I am going to write to Petroleum to come down here and I intend to tell him if he will communicate his talent to me, I will swap places with him."

Humor about Lincoln's frontier background emerged from the pen of Charles Ferrar Browne, writing under the name of Artemus Ward. Unlike the non-partisans Twain and Newell, Ward adhered to the pro-Democratic, pro-Douglas policy of the *Cleveland Plain Dealer* for whom he wrote until he took over the editorship of *Vanity Fair* in 1861.

A piece entitled "A Political Sermon by the Rev. Hardshell Pike" read:

> What did Lincoln ever do besides splittin rails and bossing a flat boat? . . . No doubt he kin split a fair rail . . . But my Brethering, he can't keep a hotel.

Ending nearly every paragraph was a reference to Lincoln who "split some rails in Illinoy and bossed a roarin' flatboat."

After Lincoln's election, Ward treated him more sympathetically in a piece entitled, "Artemus Ward on His Visit to Abe Lincoln,"

(Continued)

where the president is overwhelmed by applicants for office. Ward fictitiously recounted:

> I found the old feller in his parler, surrounded by a perfeck swarm of orfice seekers. Knowin he had been capting of a flat boat on the roarin Mississippy, I thought I'd address him in sailor lingo, so sez I, "Old Abe ahoy! . . .
>
> Sum (office-seekers) wanted post orfices, sum wanted collectorships, sum wanted furrin missions, and all wanted sumthin. I thought Old Abe would go crazy. (*Vanity Fair*, December 8, 1860).

Ward's editorship of *Vanity Fair* continued the magazine's self-professed mission of creating satire to preserve the Union against rebels, copperheads, abolitionists and others that it thought were destroying it.

Vanity Fair spoofed Lincoln's evasiveness by mocking his speeches: "As to my policy, or policies—for I have several—I will have my two life policies in two good companies for $5,000, each in favor of Mrs. Abe." (January 12, 1861)

Lincoln's humor was treated as unoriginal and silly, by *Vanity Fair*'s Charles Augustus who ridiculed him in a fabrication of his Springfield address on his departure for Washington: "My friends, I haven't time to make a speech, so I will tell you a gag."

Overseas, the British comic periodical *London Punch* was aiming its share of potshots at the president. Its cartoons often portrayed him as patronizing and exploitative of blacks.

In one caricature, Lincoln was shown as saying, "What a nice White House this would be, if it were not for the blacks!" (William Walsh, *Abraham Lincoln and the London Punch*) In "One Good Turn Deserves Another," Lincoln is seen warmly extending a weapon

and knapsack to a former slave, saying, "Why I du declare it's my old friend, Sambo! Course you'll fight for us Sambo, Lend us a hand, old hoss, du!"

Another cartoon showed Lincoln in a card game playing his last card with a spade-shaped blackface. The end of an accompanying poem accused Lincoln of hypocrisy by freeing the slaves of Rebels but allowing loyal Unionists to keep theirs:

> There! If that 'ere Proclamation
> Does its holy work,
> Rebeldom's annihilation
> It oughter work;
> Back to Union, and you're welcome
> Each to wop his nigger:
> If not, at White let slip darky
> Guess I call that vigour!

For his 1864 reelection a *Punch* cartoon showed an evil caricature of Lincoln's head atop a huge bird, sitting upon burning wood. It was labeled "Free Press," "Habeas Corpus" and "United States Constitution." *Punch* then printed a mock-Lincoln inaugural speech, depicting the president as a teller of base, coarse and racist anecdotes, and as a man giving mindless pep talks to easily swayed, ignorant masses.

His contemporaries' humor ran the gamut from mild ribbing and drollery to broad derision, with only a fine line between harsh satire and outright abuse. As one whose sense of humor persisted in spite of the barbs, Lincoln kept his good will, even toward those who lacked a perspective for the national good. Much of the lighter humor perhaps helped the nation to survive its recent tragedy.

Source: Media History Digest, Fall/Winter 1976.

policies. The Copperheads got their name from an 1861 *Detroit Free Press* editorial that said:

> These neutral papers are always deceptive. In some parts of the country they go by the name of rattlesnake papers; but a friend suggests to us that they ought to be called Copperheads—because the first named reptile always gives notice before he bites, whereas the neutral papers never show their colors before they apply their fangs.[62]

Indeed their rhetoric was vicious, charging the government with base and sinister motives. Yet they had solid reasons to be against government war policies. Some opposed a war which in some instances was a war against their blood relatives in the South; some were opposed because of a commitment to states' rights; others denounced the war for economic and political reasons. Some of the Copperhead editors wanted to preserve economic investments in the South.[63]

Some southern newspapers were hostile to the Confederate administration but not to the war effort, as in the case of the Rhetts, and the government for all practical purposes ignored them. Some Confederate correspondents, such as Peter Alexander, writing for Savannah, Atlanta, and Mobile newspapers, extolled the bravery of the soldiers and glorified the cause but also presented the "seamy" side of the war with all its horror.[64] But the North could hardly put off entirely its Copperheads who hissed and struck at the heart of the enterprise.

Media as Voices of Freedom

CONTROLS AND A COURT-MARTIAL

With the conflict between the states raging on such a broad perimeter and with hundreds of reporters in the field, some of them unprincipled, there was legitimate concern that information useful to the enemy would be sent on by reporters. In fact, General Robert E. Lee's staff regularly monitored daily papers from the North to glean information on the effects of battles and the movement of troops and new fortifications.

However, nobody knew just how to go about controlling the day's news. Constitutional questions had loomed over slavery and the secession threat for so long that talk of controls immediately hailed the Constitution into the fray. Politicians did not want to be seen as prohibiting free speech. Not only would such action make the authorities seem tyrannical, but also controls and suppression would inevitably involve specific newspapers. Such actions would make the suppressed publication, and others sympathetic to it, adversaries of the politician. Lincoln, always practical, knew this result would occur. He believed "that the Constitution remained in effect during war, and its extraordinary powers allowed the government to carry on the war effectively," notes John Marszalek. "Lincoln's position won out over the other views and the war was fought with the Constitution stretched but unimpaired. . . . The Civil War's First Amendment debate was part of these more general constitutional questions."[65]

No Formal Legal Censorship

There were no systematized, legally enacted measures of censorship in the Civil War, but there were controls on means of transmission. As could be expected, congressional records and the *Official Records* of the war do not contain the word *censorship* in their indexes. Also, the Civil War laws prohibiting disloyalty, the Conscription Act and the Treason Act, said nothing about newspapers.[66]

Lacking a specific, unified policy, the government did seek in various ways to control the access of the correspondents and their reports. It was left largely to cabinet members or generals in the field to apply methods of control, only to be reversed at times by the president when the furor escalated.

Military Closes Papers

The military shut down a few newspapers, but in most cases the measures backfired and the papers were soon printing again. In addition to the suppression of the *New York World*, the *Journal of Commerce*, and a New Orleans paper for publishing a hoax about a new draft call for troops, the *Chicago Times* under its editor, Wilbur F. Storey, was accused of discouraging enlistments, even encouraging desertions in the Union army. The *Times* carried alleged letters from Union soldiers telling their disgust for the war and their disillusionment with "abolitionist" goals for the war.[67] Storey wrote that Union soldiers were "indignant at the imbecility that has devoted them to slaughter for purposes with which they have no sympathy."[68] As Craig D. Tenney put it, "It was hardly writing calculated to encourage a rush on enlistment offices."[69]

Major General Ambrose E. Burnside ordered the newspaper closed. When Storey defied the order and continued publishing, troops were sent into the building to seize all available copies. Crowds in the street reacted critically, and at a meeting that evening it was asserted that if the *Times* could not print, its supporters would shut down the rival, progovernment *Tribune*. A group of businessmen, including a stockholder of the *Tribune* and Congressman I. N. Arnold, convened. At the recommendation of former Chicago mayor William Ogden the group passed a resolution calling on Lincoln to revoke the suppression order. Lincoln asked Secretary of War Edwin Stanton, if he agreed, to tell Burnside to revoke the order. But a committee of party faithful, supporting Burnside, put pressure on Congressman Arnold to change the original group's request. Arnold contacted the president again with the explanation that they did not really mean the order should be revoked. Lincoln then vacillated. He sent another message to Stanton to advise Burnside that he did not need to act with haste and could let the matter of suppression rest until he received a letter from the president. Again it is a case of the political winds blowing on the subject of censorship.[70]

Burnside pursued another northern "Copperhead," Clement Vallandigham, a former editor and congressman from Ohio who was a leader of Copperhead "peace Democrats." At Burnside's orders, Vallandigham was arrested for treason. Convicted by a military court, he was sentenced to prison. Lincoln, however, intervened and ordered him into exile in the South. Vallandigham returned during the war in 1864 and at the Democratic convention in Chicago offered an antiwar resolution that passed. One editor who supported Vallandigham, Samuel Medary, of the *Crisis* and the *Ohio Statesman* in Columbus, was indicted. A sympathetic editor at the *Cincinnati Enquirer*, who saw Medary's arrest as a challenge to press freedom, put up the bond for his release. Medary, however, died before the case came to trial.[71]

Censorship efforts in the Civil War centered largely on attempts to control telegraph transmissions. Congress passed a bill giving the president the right to control the telegraph lines and the railroads in a wartime emergency. Lincoln signed it into law and ordered all telegraph lines to come under military control. The law said that any telegraph communication on military topics not authorized by the commanding general or the secretary of war would be banned. As a consequence, any such offending newspaper would forfeit use of telegraph lines and the railroads.

Bypassing Telegraph Censors

Telegraph and rail censorship was far from effective. The government did not have enough people to act as censors at the transmission levels, and many who were given the assignment did not understand what they were doing. Reporter Albert Richardson in his memoirs tells the story of a Chicago reporter who, standing on a wharf at Cairo, Illinois, noticed two gunboats load and slip up the Ohio River. He wired a story about what looked like the making of a new offensive. The censor had the idea that if the story looked untrue, he could let it pass in order to confound the enemy. He approved the story, which correctly alerted readers to Grant's intended secret maneuver to attack Fort Henry in Kentucky.[72]

Reporters ingeniously found ways to get around the telegraph censors. Reporters sometimes took night trains to personally deliver their copy, if the paper was not too far away. They engaged messengers to deliver the stories personally, and they relied on the mails. Sometimes they sent their stories in code.[73] They were clever in concealing stories on themselves or their messengers. Hudson tells of the story of a Union soldier who had been imprisoned in the Confederacy along with several *Herald* correspondents. Hudson noted: "This soldier, on his arrival in New York, called at the *Herald*, cut off one of his hollow military buttons, and presented it to the editor. 'You will find a letter in that,' said he." Indeed, a letter was found, written on tissue paper, describing affairs in Richmond, which made three quarters of a column in the *Herald*. No one knew how that intelligence reached that office.[74]

At the outset the post office started withholding mail headed toward enemy territory. Then the government targeted certain newspapers for publishing allegedly treasonable articles. A grand jury failed to get indictments, but the postmaster general, Montgomery Blair, went ahead on his own initiative and denied these papers use of mail services. In March 1862 he extended his ban, or threat of banning, to any newspaper publishing anything that had been censored on the telegraph. The Judiciary Committee of the House of Representatives challenged Blair's authority on the matter, but later acquiesced in his action as a necessary wartime special-power move. But like efforts to curb certain material on the telegraph, it was difficult to fully control the mails because of the extensiveness of the mail system.

General George McClellan made an agreement with reporters in his sphere of war. The reporters promised not to send any secret or revealing information, and the government promised access to communication channels. The agreement did not work overall. Some individual reporters also had their personal agreements with specific generals, as they puffed up the generals in their copy in return for laxer controls.

A military code of laws enacted by Congress in 1806 was revived. The 57th article of war in the code said that anyone "convicted of holding corespondence with or giving intelligence to the enemy either directly or indirectly shall suffer death or such other punishment as shall be ordered by the sentence of a court martial." Secretary of War Simon Cameron issued an order in 1861 with Lincoln's concurrence which said that all communication by correspondents about military matters without approval of the commanding general would be a violation of the 57th article of war and reporters could be subject to the death penalty for violations.

The Only Reporter Ever Court-Martialed in the United States

The only court-martial of a correspondent under the 57th article (and the only court-martial of a reporter in American military history) was ordered by General William Sherman, who nursed a fierce hatred of the press. He was offended by what he regarded as a practice of reporters—describing generals who aided them glowingly, while putting down those who did not. Sherman also believed that the press regularly supplied sensitive information to the Confederate armies. He wrote his brother, a Republican senator from Ohio, that he would not be "abused by a set of dirty newspaper scribblers who have the impudence of Satan. . . . They are a pest and shall not approach me and I will treat them as spies which in truth they are."[75]

Sherman indeed treated Thomas Knox of the *New York Herald* as a spy and gave Knox the scare of his life in life-and-death court-martial proceedings. When Sherman was ordered to Memphis to prepare for an assault on Vicksburg, a pivotal Confederate stronghold on the Mississippi, he made it clear through a special order that his maneuver would be off bounds, and "any person whatever . . . found making reports for publication which might reach the enemy . . . will be arrested and treated as a spy."[76] Knox and several others ignored the order and followed Sherman's troops. Sherman's attack on Vicksburg failed, and Knox was on hand to record it all. Knox sneaked his story out, along with two maps of the battlefield, in an envelope deposited with an army mail clerk. It was addressed to a decoy in Cairo, Illinois, where it would find its way onto the telegraph for the *New York Herald*.

Knox's article said, among other things, that if Sherman had proceeded "as earnestly and persistently against the rebels as against the representatives of the press" he would have succeeded at Vicksburg. Knox also charged Sherman with managing the battle poorly, overlooking the wounded, and wasting equipment.[77] Knox praised some other officers involved, but added concerning Sherman:

"Insanity and inefficiency have brought their result; let us have them no more. With another brain than that of General Sherman's, we will drop the disappointment at our reverse, and feel certain of victory in the future."[78]

Sherman exploded. Knox, who had returned to the Sherman camp, was hailed before the general and quizzed concerning the article, line by line. Knox said he tried to write the truth, but if he didn't have the whole truth, he had to write something. And to Sherman's face, Knox declared: "Of course, General Sherman, I had no feelings against you personally, but you are regarded as the enemy of our set, and we must in self-defence write you down."[79]

Knox was arrested on charges of spying and brought before a military tribunal of one brigadier general, four colonels, and two majors. Thoroughly frightened, Knox wrote a letter of "recantation," saying that he had been ignorant of orders. He now praised the general's plans and apologized for some of his comments. Weisberger says: "Knox had yielded unnecessarily to panic. Even to please the commanding general, the court-martial could hardly have hanged him for conveying information to the enemy in a letter printed nearly three weeks after the engagement."[80] Knox was convicted merely of flouting orders without criminal intent and banished from the area. Reporters appealed to Lincoln on Knox's behalf to have the ban lifted. Lincoln, dodging the matter, said it would be up to Grant, Sherman's superior. Meanwhile, Sherman had his own view, saying that if Knox showed up again he would go "down the Mississippi floating on a log."[81]

One soldier was court-martialed for his writings in a newspaper. Private Newton B. Spencer had written a critical letter to his hometown newspaper, the *Pen Yan Democrat*, in upstate New York concerning the Battle of the Crater near Petersburg, Virginia, in July 1864. The offenses committed in his letter to the editor, according to the charges, included "conduct to the prejudice of good order and military discipline, contempt and disrespect to his commanding officer, giving aid and comfort to the enemy, and . . . violating the 57th Article of War."[82] He was convicted on only two of the minor charges—conduct prejudicial to good order and military discipline, and showing contempt and disrespect to Major General George Meade—and acquitted of the other charges. Spencer was returned to duty, fined $8 per month for six months, and reprimanded.

On Word of Honor

Attempts were made to inaugurate a "parole" procedure, "parole" meaning "on word of honor" or promise to follow set guidelines. The parole system allowed reporters to be their own censors provided they followed a lengthy list of rules. The two-page parole document, attached to a necessary War Department press pass, proved too cumbersome. "Guards generally passed anyone who presented the parole rather than take the trouble of reading through it,"[83] said Andrews. Applicable primarily to the Peninsula campaign in Virginia, the parole system did not result in any reporters being called in for alleged violations.

All in all, the interest in censorship in the Civil War, in the North and South, was in controlling sensitive military information primarily on the telegraph, and the censorship was done largely by generals in command on their own initiative. There was an occasional suppression of a newspaper and an arrest of an erring reporter or editor, but usually the matter was quickly settled after protests by other reporters and editors. Generally freedom of the press, with the First Amendment guarantees intact, prevailed. (After the war, in the South, occupying forces under Union district commanders suspended various newspapers that were critical of the troops and the state of affairs.)[84] It would be up to future generations to prepare applicable, firmer regulations for media during wartime and periods of war scares.

Media as Political Organs

IF THE PARTISAN LABEL FITS, WEAR IT

Although the day of strong party papers, founded and favored if not funded by a party, was largely over, the newspapers endorsed candidates. It was possible to tag certain newspapers, or at least their editors, with a political label. Most clear-cut were, on the one hand, the "peace Democrats," anti-Lincoln and antiwar, and, on the other hand, the ultraloyal Republican papers, such as Henry Raymond's *New York Times*, "the leading popular advocate of the administration before the country," as Mott called it. Actually, in 1864 Raymond, as chairman of the national Republican committee, was in charge of the campaign to reelect the president and was himself running successfully as a Republican for Congress. Samuel Bowles' *Springfield* (Massachusetts) *Republican* and the Springfield (Illinois) *Daily State Journal* were consistently Republican. And the *Washington Chronicle*, founded in 1861 by John W. Forney, editor of the *Philadelphia Press* (a Democratic paper turned Republican), became recognized as a quasi-mouthpiece, if not actual mouthpiece, of the Lincoln administration.[85]

Yet Lincoln could not depend on any of the other big city newspapers for consistent support. "Greeley was unpredictable," says Tebbel. "Bryant (at the *Post*) was offensively moral. Bennett could never be counted on."[86] Greeley, always edging the president to action, had views of the president that ranged from the lowest to the most exalted published.[87] Bryant was a radical Republican, often more "steadfast" and "far-seeing" than Greeley.[88]

Bennett's *Herald* was generally Democratic at the start of the war but did not cast in with the "peace Democrats." Throughout the war Bennett was consistently mean-spirited in his attacks on the president, but he supported the war in principle. Curiously, late in the 1864 campaign, Bennett switched to supporting the Republicans, possibly, says Mott, in the hope that Lincoln would give him a significant diplomatic post for his support.[89]

The Two-Faced Image of Chicago's Medill

The *Chicago Tribune* under Joseph Medill, whom some considered the most powerful publisher outside New York,[90] was instrumental in helping Lincoln receive the nomination in 1860. A very close confidant of Lincoln in his earlier years, Medill is believed to have once told Lincoln during a visit, "Dammit, Abe, git yore feet off my desk."[91] In 1864, however, Medill warned that he might withdraw the *Tribune*'s support if Lincoln did not clean nonradicals out of his Cabinet. In a letter to Congressman Elihu Washburne in 1864, Medill spoke of Lincoln's "very weak and foolish traits of character."[92] Publicly Medill was antislavery, but he could be very racist in his correspondence, such as in a letter to his brother, a general who died at Gettysburg. Editor Medill wrote, "In future wars black and yellow men will be freely used to fight. We will not be so careful about spilling the blood of niggers."[93]

Some believe that Medill, without the president's knowledge, actually helped organize a "stop-Lincoln" movement in 1864.[94] *Tribune* editorials in 1864, while on the surface supportive, criticized Lincoln for having put in and kept such an incapable general as McClellan,[95] and in one editorial, "Lincoln Weaknesses," seemed to defend Lincoln for his independence, or was the paper actually being critical indirectly?[96] Joseph McKerns points out that after the war Medill "stood solidly on the side of the white, Anglo-Saxon, Protestant, native business class of Chicago and against the immigrant, mostly Catholic and Jewish laboring class."[97]

First Black-Owned Daily

Beleaguered in the South, the *New Orleans Tribune*, the first black-owned daily in the United States, became the Louisiana Republican Party's organ in the South in October 1864. Lasting until 1870, the *Tribune* was founded by Louis Charles Roudanez. He had been an owner of *L'Union*, a French-English newspaper, the first black-owned newspaper in the South. Roudanez "provided the rationale for the political thrust of the two papers," notes Laura Velina Rouzan, *L'Union* crusading for emancipation, fair treatment of black troops, and suffrage, and the *Tribune* also supporting suffrage and the Freedmen's Aid Association, which provided material and legal aid to freed blacks.[98]

Influence of Frederick Douglass

Black newspapers existed, among other reasons, to affect the political agenda. Back in 1847 when escaped and later freed slave Frederick Douglass launched his *North Star*, he said in an ad carried in the black paper *The Ram's Horn* that "the object of the NORTH STAR will be to attack Slavery in all its forms and aspects; Advocate Universal Emancipation; exalt the standard Public Morality; promote the Moral and Intellectual improvement of the COLORED PEOPLE; and hasten the day of FREEDOM to the Three Millions of our Enslaved Fellow Countrymen."[99] Douglass proceeded with the new paper despite the discouragement of abolitionist leader William Lloyd Garrison, who felt the paper was impractical and that Douglass's real talent was with his "powers of oratory."[100]

In 1851, Douglass merged the *North Star* with the *Liberty Party Paper* to form *Frederick Douglass' Paper*, with the motto "All Rights for All." The abolitionist Liberty Party itself had by this time merged with the new Free Soil Party, which was opposed to the extension of slavery in new territories. In 1858 Douglass also started publishing *Douglass' Monthly*, aimed at a British audience to develop support against

William Lloyd Garrison: Editor of militant abolitionist paper, the Liberator. (The National Archives)

slavery. In 1860, facing a money crisis, he stopped publishing *Frederick Douglass' Paper*. During the war he helped recruit black troops for the Union. He was unhappy with Lincoln for dragging his feet on slavery and personally for not following through with a promised military commission. After the war, Douglass was associated with the Washington weekly *New National Era*, which crusaded for full rights for blacks. He continued to be involved in politics and served as U.S. minister to Haiti.

Printing Patronage in the South

A system of political patronage to newspapers emerged for a time analogous to the old party press arrangements of early America. In 1867 Congress authorized federal printing contracts to be issued to two newspapers in each southern state. These grants went largely to support Republican newspapers. Usually facing a boycott of advertisers, these pro-Union Republican papers needed the government subsidies to survive. If the paper proved not to be Republican enough, the contract would be withdrawn and given to a more surefooted Republican paper, as happened with a Savannah paper's contract withdrawn to be given to a more orthodox Republican paper in Atlanta.[101]

"While federal printing patronage supported many of the South's moderate Republican newspapers," says Donna L. Dickerson, "city and state printing contracts and advertising subsidized Democratic newspapers. Throughout the South, political sponsorship ensured a lively exchange of political viewpoints."[102]

Media as Voices of Reform

SOME IN-DEPTH REPORTING SURFACES

Editor, writer, and orator Frederick Douglass was foremost a reformer,[103] as were Garrison and other abolitionists, including a number of black writers who wrote for Garrison's *Liberator*, such as poet-writer Sarah Louise Forten and her father, James.[104] For Douglass, the spirit of reform was never ending, not to be concluded with the end of the war. "Calling on northern reformers to 'ameliorate the condition' of the former slaves," says David Blight, "he repeatedly cautioned his audiences that abolitionists' work would not cease when the war ended. . . . No 'do nothing' doctrine. . . . The freedmen's needs, Douglass believed, would require the work of 'all the elevating and civilizing institutions of the country.' "[105]

Radical reformer editors took on President Andrew Johnson for turning soft on the South. The *Rutland* (Vermont) *Daily Journal* moaned: "Once he [Johnson] professed great regard for the welfare of the negro, promising to become his 'Moses'; now he brings the whole power of his administration to crush any measure for the amelioration of his condition. Once he violently denounced the copperheads of the North; now he bestows upon them all the patronage of the Federal government."[106]

Douglass, who interviewed President Johnson in 1866, concluded that the president's Reconstruction policies were anything but "just, fair, or wise." Douglass was particularly offended when the president boasted of owning and buying slaves, but never selling one.[107] Douglass declined to support the Fourteenth Amendment, which was passed in 1866, on the grounds that it did not make provisions for blacks to vote as it guaranteed citizenship and due process for all persons born or naturalized in the United States.

Cincinnati Papers Expose Army Abuses

Besides seeking reforms that included the abolition of the system of slavery and reforms in Reconstruction policies after the war, newspapers did engage in seeking reforms to relieve the plight of citizens and soldiers on a more localized level. Whitelaw Reid reported for the *Cincinnati Gazette* on conditions of Union troops at Grafton, southeast of Wheeling in what today is West Virginia. According to Andrews, Reid "took special note of how little was being done to promote the comfort and well-being of the common soldier." In his first letter to the editor of the

Gazette, Reid sent a sample of the shoddy cloth, made of factory clippings and sweepings, used for uniforms.[108] Reid had occasion to notice the shabbiness of the shoes on Confederate prisoners. The soles were made of wood and glued to an upper part covered with stained paper. Then, Andrews said, Reid "realized, with something of a shock, how little difference there was between army contractors on either side."[109] Newspaper reports on inferior clothing in the military triggered a governor's proclamation in Ohio for a drive for heavy clothing for the troops.

Abuses in army administration proved to be fair game for correspondents, especially when there was a lull in battlefield action. William G. Crippe, under the pen name "Invisible Green," wrote for the *Cincinnati Times* about ripoffs by the quartermaster (an officer who assigns provisions and clothing) and commissary personnel. He exposed one western Virginia quartermaster who he said stole $1,000 and the failure of anyone to take action.

A Vicksburg, Mississippi, paper was concerned about the lack of discipline in military ranks. *The Daily Citizen* chronicled cases of soldiers and others attached to the army stealing chickens, fruit, and vegetables. "Several cases have come to our knowledge, wherein the offenders have, in open daylight, entered premises, seized cattle and other things, and defied the owners to their teeth." The paper defended the vigilante action of a citizen who wounded two prowling soldiers. "We make this public exposure, mortifying as it is to us, with the hope that a salutary improvement in matters will be made by our military authorities."[110]

All in all, the Civil War reporters, covering the big scenes of movement and encounter, missed opportunities for digging into issues and topics for the big in-depth, investigative piece. Weisberger says the reporters, for instance, missed "the story of a century in the freedman and his bewildering position." The reporters' reform consciousness generally did not go beyond a day's observation.[111]

Media as Definers and Keepers of Values (and Biases)

MEANING IN THE VALLEY OF THE SHADOW OF DEATH

Perhaps the intensity and length of the Civil War owe something to the conviction on both sides of the presence of the Lord, God's own strong arms uplifting and sustaining the participants. Lincoln invoked the Deity on occasion, as he did in his Gettysburg Address: "We here highly resolve . . . that this nation, under God, shall have a new birth." From the first Union troops were urged on with the spirit of righteousness. Bursting with enthusiasm, troops went off to battle with the words of militant feminist and abolitionist Julia Ward Howe, words written after Howe watched Union troops retreating to the capital in 1861: "Mine eyes have seen the glory of the coming of the Lord; He is trampling out the vintage where the grapes of wrath are stored; He hath loosed the fateful lightning of His terrible, swift sword; His truth is marching on." The final refrain ends with "Our God is marching on!"[112]

The Role of the Deity

The *Chicago Tribune* expressed the northern thought:

> Now, at the end of three years the nation has passed through the valley of the shadow of death. She has put on the angelic robe of purity from all unrighteousness. The crown of redemption rests upon her brows. . . . Henceforth she is irresistably dedicated to perfect freedom by a vow which she has registered with the God of Nations.[113]

Southern editorials at the beginning of the conflict also purported to have the hand of God on the South's side. At the prospect of Lincoln's election and secession, the *Charleston Mercury* rationalized: "God has so constituted the human heart that we *can* love only *what is lovely*—and we must hate what is morally *wrong and detestable.* We do not wish to judge others harshly, but it does appear to us that no one in the South can *love* or *reverence* the Union *as it exists.*"[114] Also looking to God, the *Daily Nashville Patriot* intoned: "If we can but pass this crisis safely, the Republican party will be scattered. It cannot prolong its existence after another defeat. It will dissolve like the mists of the morning before the rays of the God of day; and the South may secure peace and repose."[115]

Idealism, shored up with unflagging hope, permeated the journalism of the time as it did the political and social strata. As Sherman was at the gates, editorialized the *Atlanta Daily Intelligencer*: "Our hopes are not too sanguine, for the prospect to us, has never been without the beautiful sunlight of prospective victory lighting our hearts through the gloom and the dark shade of defeat."[116] And: "So long as the feeling that all will end well, enthuses us, we are unconquerable and we will be successful."[117]

A Matter of Principle

Idealism and the longer view could reign in everyday ethics in pursuit of the story. While numerous incidents abound concerning freebies and slanting of stories to achieve certain ends, including favoritism to the reporter, incidents exist where the reporter did not give in to pressures to compromise his work. When Franc B. Wilkie of the *New York Times* was broke and needed cash right away, a colleague, Albert Richardson of the *New York Tribune*, offered him $125 in gold if he would give a story to the *Tribune*. Wilkie was not actually under an exclusive contract with the *Times*, and it would take two weeks for any money to come for his article from the *Times*. The *Tribune* amount would also likely be three times the pay from the *Times*. Still, Wilkie stood on his principles. His honor and reputation had a certain value, and he declined the offer. Things worked out to the good anyway. Thomas Knox loaned Wilkie money to see him over for a few weeks. When *Times* editor Henry Raymond learned of the situation, he gave Wilkie a substantial payment and a weekly wage, "an amount that I had never even dreamed of in my wildest aspiration for journalistic earnings," said Wilkie. He had gotten his story of the battle at Lexington in the Missouri campaign, when, unable to join the Union camp, he joined the prisoners being taken by the Confederate army and solicited successfully the protection of the Confederate general. Raymond editorialized rhapsodically that probably no other example could be found of "similar courage and devotion on the part of a newspaper correspondent."[118]

JOURNALISM COMING OF AGE

Much was left to the enterprise and values of the reporter in the Civil War. Free access, censorship and its carefree application, and the failure to install pervasive, formal effective controls would survive as topics on an agenda for the media and government in other wars.

In sum, the Civil War saw all kinds of practitioners of the trade. There were golden moments of enterprise—getting the story at all costs and great risks—and there were moments of herd journalism, sticking together and watching from the sidelines. There were golden moments where reporters respected the collective good and security arrangements, while there were some who broke the rules and used sensitive information. Some used information for their own good, including one who used privileged information to trade in the stock market. Wilkie used his intelligence and daring to the utmost to get the story, while adhering to his principles of keeping a commitment and playing fair. During the Civil War not only was journalism a growing industry, but it was coming of age in terms of responsibility, in some quarters roughly hewing out some parameters for the trade or profession in the future.

QUESTIONS FOR DISCUSSION AND RESEARCH

1. If you were a reporter in the Civil War, what code of ethics would you follow? Write a short one.
2. Was the cult of personalities in operation? If so, explain the nature of it and how it affected Civil War reporting.
3. Was there pervasive and overall censorship of the press in the Civil War? Explain.
4. Newspapers caused the Civil War. True or false? Explain.
5. Compare the approach to reporting the war in the South and in the North.
6. The Civil War brought on objective reporting. True or false? Explain.
7. What was the "Copperhead" press? Are there any opprobrious labels used for segments of the media today?
8. Can a case be made that the newspapers, in many instances, were political organs, despite the general demise of the party press?
9. What are the best ways for a government to control news and adverse opinion in wartime?
10. What are the main contributions of the Civil War to the development of journalism?
11. Was sensational reporting in the 1860s during the Civil War different from sensational reporting of the 1830s and 1840s, the early days of the penny press?

12. How did the editor's role change during the Civil War?
13. How did the Gettysburg Address affect literary and newspaper style, according to Garry Wills?
14. What role did women journalists play in the Civil War?
15. Simulate a Lincoln press conference on today's current issues, if Lincoln were president today.

ENDNOTES

1. The Missouri Compromise admitted Maine as a free state and Missouri as a slaveholding state and forbade slavery in the rest of the Louisiana Purchase; the Compromise of 1850 admitted California as a free state, but created a stronger Fugitive Slave Act that favored the South; the Kansas-Nebraska Act of 1854 permitted residents of Kansas and Nebraska to vote on whether to allow slavery in their states. See William W. Freehling, *The Road to Disunion,* vol. 1, *Secessionists at Bay, 1779–1854* (New York: Oxford University Press, 1993).
2. Donald Lewis Shaw, "News About Slavery from 1820–1860 in Newspapers of South, North and West," *Journalism Quarterly*, vol. 61, Autumn 1984, p. 388.
3. Ibid., p. 483.
4. Laura A. White, *Robert Barnwell Rhett: Father of Secession* (The American Historical Association, 1931; reprint, Gloucester, Mass.: Peter Smith, 1965), p. 173.
5. John M. Daniel, *The Richmond Examiner During the War* (New York, 1868; reprint, Arno Press, 1970), pp. 7, 8.
6. *New York Tribune*, Aug. 20, 1862.
7. Ibid., Aug. 22, 1862.
8. Daniel, *The Richmond Examiner*, July 8, 1861, article, p. 17.
9. David W. Blight, *Frederick Douglass' Civil War: Keeping Faith in Jubilee* (Baton Rouge: Louisiana State University Press, 1989), p. 85.
10. Rollo Ogden, *Life and Letters of Edwin Lawrence Godkin* (New York, 1907), vol. 1, pp. 204, 205. Quoted in J. Cutler Andrews, *The North Reports the Civil War* (Pittsburgh: University of Pittsburgh Press, 1955), p. 638.
11. Bernard A. Weisberger, *Reporters for the Union* (Boston: Little, Brown, 1953), pp. ix, x.
12. "Magazine Calls Attention to Mary Leader Monument," *Evening Sun*, Hanover, Pa., Feb. 12, 1952. Research by Heidi Hormel, Temple University.
13. Louis M. Starr, *Bohemian Brigade: Civil War Newsmen in Action* (Madison: University of Wisconsin Press, 1987), p. 61.
14. Weisberger, *Reporters for the Union*, p. 24.
15. Tom Reilly, "Lincoln-Douglas Debates of 1858 Forced New Role on the Press," *Journalism Quarterly*, vol. 56, no. 4, Winter 1979, p. 734.
16. Concetta Garistina, "Lincoln's Lensman: Mathew Brady," *Media History Digest*, vol. 6, no. 2, Fall–Winter 1986, p. 20.
17. Peter Pollack, *The Picture History of Photography* (New York: Abrams, 1969), pp. 188, 189.
18. *Time*, Special Collector's Edition, "150 Years of Photo Journalism," Fall 1989, "The Sharpshooter," p. 6.
19. Ibid., "Putting a Picture on Paper, with a Little Rearranging," p. 15.
20. William Cullen Bryant II, writing in the *New York Times*, suggests that Nast did not create the familiar image of Santa, but rather the honor belongs to Robert Walter Weir, who exhibited his "striking portrait" of Santa at the National Academy of Design in 1837, three years before Nast was born. "Santa Before Nast," in "Letters" column, *New York Times Book Review*, Dec. 26, 1993, p. 23.

21. Mark Brakeman, "Thomas Nast: Pen with Power," *Media History Digest*, vol. 5, no. 4, Fall 1985, pp. 25–27, 48, 49.
22. *New York Times*, July 6, 1863.
23. R. J. M. Blackett, *Thomas Morris Chester, Black Civil War Correspondent: His Dispatches from the Virginia Front* (Baton Rouge: Louisiana State University Press, 1989), p. 42.
24. Ibid.
25. Ibid., p. 288.
26. Starr, *Bohemian Brigade*, p. 61.
27. Ibid.
28. Ibid.
29. Andrews, *The North Reports*, p. 130.
30. John Tebbel, *The Compact History of the American Newspaper* (New York: Hawthorn Books, 1963), p. 118.
31. Barbara Ellis and Steven Dick, "Who Was 'Shadow'? The Computer Knows: Using Grammar-Program Statistics in Content Analyses Finally May Solve This Civil War Riddle and Other Writing Mysteries," paper presented to the Association for Education in Journalism and Mass Communication meeting in Washington, D.C., August 1995.
32. Hazel Dicken-Garcia, *Journalistic Standards in Nineteenth-Century America* (Madison: University of Wisconsin Press, 1989), p. 53.
33. Editorial "Just Once," *New York Tribune*, quoted in Starr, *Bohemian Brigade*, p. 53.
34. Starr, *Bohemian Brigade*, p. 57.
35. Frederic Hudson, *Journalism in the United States, from 1690 to 1872* (New York: J. & J. Harper Editions, 1873; reprint, New York: Harper & Row, 1969), p. 483.
36. Tebbel, *Compact History*, pp. 121, 122.
37. David T. Z. Mindich, "Edwin M. Stanton, the Inverted Pyramid, and Information Control," *Journalism Monographs*, no. 140, August 1993.
38. Frank Luther Mott, *American Journalism* (New York: Macmillan, 1947), p. 330.
39. Examples from *New York Times*, May 21, 1864, and *Cincinnati Daily Commercial*, April 25, 1862, respectively, quoted in Andrews, *The North Reports*, p. 646.
40. Weisberger, *Reporters for the Union*, p. 293.
41. Garry Wills, *Lincoln at Gettysburg* (New York: Simon & Schuster, 1992), p. 174.
42. Ibid., p. 148.
43. *Baraboo* (Wisconsin) *Republic*, Aug. 14, 1861.
44. Havilah Babcock, "The Press and the Civil War," *Journalism Quarterly*, vol. 6, no. 1, March 1929, p. 3.
45. Blackett, *Thomas Morris Chester*, p. 95.
46. See Weisberger, *Reporters for the Union*, pp. 32–34.
47. Andrews, *The North Reports*, p. 59; see also "Arms and the Press: 1. The First News Blackout," *American Heritage*, vol. 36, no. 4, June/July 1985, p. 25.
48. Mott, *American Journalism*, p. 330.
49. Andrews, *The North Reports*, p. 179
50. Mott, *American Journalism*, pp. 351, 352.
51. Babcock, "The Press and the Civil War."
52. Andrews, *The North Reports*, p. 32.
53. Elmer Davis, *History of The New York Times, 1851–1921* (New York: Greenwood Press, 1921), p. 63.
54. Quintus C. Wilson, "Confederate Press Association: A Pioneer News Agency," *Journalism Quarterly*, vol. 26, no. 2, June 1949, p. 160.
55. Quoted in Elmo Scott Watson, *A History of Newspaper Syndicates in the United States, 1865–1935* (Chicago, 1936), a master's thesis at Northwestern University, p. 8.

56. Ibid., pp. 8, 9.

57. *Baraboo* (Wisconsin) *News Republic*, "Ceremony Will Honor Ansel N. Kellogg," vol. 118, no. 229, Sept. 29, 1973, p. 1.

58. *Fredericksburg Herald*, quoted in *Alexandria* (Virginia) *Gazette*, Jan. 3, 1860, quoted in Donald E. Reynolds, *Editors Make War: Southern Newspapers in the Secession Crisis* (Nashville: Vanderbilt University Press, 1970), p. 217.

59. Reynolds, *Editors Make War.*

60. M. A. De Wolfe Howe, ed., *Home Letters of General Sherman* (New York, 1909), pp. 227, 228, quoted in James G. Randall, "The Newspaper Problem in Its Bearing Upon Military Secrecy During the Civil War," *American Historical Review*, vol. 23, no. 2, June 1918, p. 308.

61. Rabun Lee Brantley, "A Southern Paper and the Civil War," *Journalism Bulletin*, vol. 22, p. 23.

62. *Detroit Free Press*, May 5, 1861, quoted in Joe Skidmore, "The Copperhead Press and the Civil War," *Journalism Quarterly*, vol. 16, no. 4, December 1939, p. 345.

63. Skidmore, ibid., p. 346.

64. Ford Risley, "Peter W. Alexander: Confederate Chronicler and Conscience," paper presented at the Association for Education in Journalism and Mass Communication meeting in Washington, D.C., August 1995.

65. John F. Marszalek, *Sherman's Other War* (Memphis: Memphis State University Press, 1981), p. 9.

66. Ibid., p. 10.

67. Craig D. Tenney, "To Suppress or Not to Suppress: Abraham Lincoln and the Chicago *Times*," *Civil War History*, vol. 27, no. 3, September 1981, p. 251.

68. Ibid., quoting *Chicago Times*, April 13, 1862.

69. Ibid.

70. Ibid., pp. 255–257.

71. Michael Emery and Edwin Emery, *The Press and America*, 6th ed. (Englewood Cliffs, N.J.: Prentice-Hall, 1988), p. 163.

72. Albert D. Richardson, *Personal History of U. S. Grant* (Boston: 1868; reprint, 1885), p. 209, in Starr, *Bohemian Brigade*, pp. 84, 85.

73. Randall, "The Newspaper Problem," p. 305.

74. Hudson, *Journalism in the United States*, p. 484.

75. Quoted in Weisberger, *Reporters for the Union*, p. 108.

76. Thomas H. Guback, "General Sherman's War on the Press," *Journalism Quarterly*, vol. 36, 1959, p. 172.

77. Ibid.

78. Ibid., p. 173.

79. Ibid.

80. Weisberger, *Reporters for the Union*, p. 113.

81. Ibid., p. 114.

82. "The Court-Martial of Private Spencer: From the Records of the U.S. Army," *Civil War Times Illustrated*, vol. 27, February 1989, p. 35.

83. Andrews, *The North Reports*, p. 196.

84. See Donna L. Dickerson, "From Suspension to Subvention: The Southern Press During Reconstruction, 1863–1870," *American Journalism*, Fall 1991.

85. Mott, *American Journalism*, p. 346.

86. Tebbel, *Compact History*, p. 117.

87. Mott, *American Journalism*, p. 343.

88. Ibid., p. 344.

89. Ibid., p. 350.

90. Tebbel, *Compact History*, p. 118.

91. Emery and Emery, *The Press and America*, p. 156.

92. Joseph McKerns, "Joseph Medill," in *Dictionary of Literary Biography*," vol. 43, "American Newspaper Journalists, 1690–1872" (Detroit: Gale Research Co., 1985), pp. 321, 323.

93. Ibid., p. 321.

94. Tebbel, *Compact History*, p. 118.

95. *Chicago Tribune*, June 19, 1864.

96. *Chicago Tribune*, July 1, 1864.

97. McKerns, "Joseph Medill," p. 323.

98. *Dissertation Abstracts*, Laura Velina Rouzan, "A Rhetorical Analysis of Editorials in 'L'Union' and the 'New Orleans Tribune' (Louisiana, Civil War, Reconstruction)," Ph.D., Florida State University.

99. *The Ram's Horn*, Nov. 5, 1847.

100. *The Liberator*, July 23, 1847, quoted in Bernell Tripp, *Origins of the Black Press* (Northport, Ala.: Vision Press, 1992), p. 58.

101. Dickerson, "From Suspension to Subvention," pp. 238, 239.

102. Ibid., p. 239.

103. Blight, *Frederick Douglass' Civil War*, p. 172.

104. Bernell E. Tripp, "Alternative Voice of the Abolitionist Movement: The Rhyme and Reason of Sarah Louise Forten," a paper presented at the Association for Education in Journalism and Mass Comunication meeting in Washington, D.C., August 1995.

105. Douglass in *The Liberator*, Sept. 16, 1864, quoted in Blight, *Frederick Douglass' Civil War*, pp. 180, 181.

106. *Rutland* (Vermont) *Daily Journal*, Nov. 9, 1866.

107. Blight, *Frederick Douglass' Civil War*, p. 191.

108. Andrews, *The North Reports*, p. 103.

109. Ibid.

110. *The Daily Citizen*, July 2, 1863.

111. Weisberger, *Reporters for the Union*, p. 168.

112. Julia Ward Howe, "Battle-Hymn of the Republic," in James Dalton Morrison, ed., *Masterpieces of Religious Verse* (New York: Harper & Brothers, 1948), pp. 519, 520.

113. "Our Peace Platform," *Chicago Tribune*, July 23, 1864.

114. *Charleston Mercury*, July 25, 1860, "The Union," in Dwight Lowell Dumond, ed., *Southern Editorials on Secession* (Gloucester, Mass.: Peter Smith, 1964), p. 153.

115. *Daily Nashville Patriot*, "To the Friends of the Constitution and the Union," in Dumond, *Southern Editorials*, p. 191.

116. Alan Bussel, "The Atlanta *Daily Intelligencer* Covers Sherman's March," *Journalism Quarterly*, vol. 51, no. 3, Autumn 1974, p. 409.

117. Ibid., pp. 409, 410.

118. *New York Times*, Oct. 3, 1861, quoted in Andrews, *The North Reports*, p. 128.

8

Grassroots Voices:
The Spawning of Populism

After the Civil War the lot of farmers was essentially the same. Although new luxuries and opportunities came to the cities, farm life remained one of hard toil with few extra benefits. Everything seemed to add to the farmers' debt—tight money and high interest, high tariffs on necessary goods, the cost of new machinery, fertilizers, and failed crops—and, even in the time of a successful harvest, exorbitant rail transportation rates ate up profits. Anger was aimed especially at the rail bosses who controlled the transportation networks, as they also controlled state legislatures. "Put simply," said D. Sven Nordin, a chronicler of farm unrest, "the farmer found himself in a new, cold world, and he was not gladdened by the prospects facing him."[1]

Few expected the farmer to react effectively. His work was too demanding, and he was too isolated. A prevailing opinion that the farmer could not cope intellectually was offered by the *St. Louis Globe-Democrat*:

> The farmer has no time to study general financial laws or the effects of tariffs, or to familiarize himself with the phenomena of political economy. He must pick up information on these as best he can, and is too often misled by the ingenious demagogue, who cunningly leads him astray by stating only half truths.[2]

With such opinions of them being voiced, it is no wonder that some farmers and their groups looked suspiciously at large newspapers and national magazines. "The newspapers are largely subsidized or muzzled; public opinion is silenced," the contentious Minnesota maverick politician Ignatius Donnelly said in 1892 at the organizing convention for the National People's Party.[3]

THE RISE OF THE GRANGE MOVEMENT

The development of the farm protest began to take form in the late 1860s with the organization of the Patrons of Husbandry, or the Grange movement, which brought farmers together on a social basis and for the exchange of political concerns.

The Grange idea was born after Oliver Hudson Kelley of Itasca, Minnesota, was invited in 1867 by the commissioner of agriculture to make a study of the economic conditions of farmers in the South. Kelley found considerable hospitality, largely because of the fraternal bonds that he shared as a member of the Masons. It occurred to him that a similar fraternity would help unite farmers. Aided by his niece, a Boston schoolteacher, he launched such a movement in November 1867. The purpose was to bring comfort to farmers' homes, develop better character, produce more, buy less, and buy and sell together.[4]

When the depression or panic of 1873 brought failures of banks, mills, and 18,000 businesses, farmers were ripe for coming together for mutual interest. Grange newspapers began to appear in Minnesota and across the country. A Grange paper was published in St. Paul, Minnesota. Another was the *Grange Advance*, published by a young lawyer, businessman, and former farm boy, B. B. Herbert, in Red Wing, Minnesota, on the Mississippi River border with Wisconsin. Herbert was to become the founder and first president of the National Editorial Association, later

A local meeting of the Grange in Edwardsville, Illinois, drawn for Frank Leslie's Illustrated Newspaper, *January 31, 1874.* (Joseph Beale, artist; Collection of The New-York Historical Society)

renamed the National Newspaper Association and representing today 8,000 newspapers, mostly weeklies. A box in Herbert's paper said that the *Grange Advance* "deals with the living, vital issues of the day. It is the sworn enemy of Monopolies and Humbugs." His motto was "In Union Strength—in Knowledge Power."

Herbert's Volume 1, Number 1 issue of the *Advance* had almost a proletariat Marxist manifesto ring to it:

> Farmers, Mechanics, and Laborers of Minnesota, to the front! is the universal order of the hour, and the firm, determined tramp, tramp, tramp of the toiling masses, who have hitherto lagged in the rear, is heard all over the world in the great onward march. Shall the 75,000 farmers, mechanics and laborers of Minnesota fail to obey the order, or obeying in part still fail to take their stand in the very front ranks? There is no place on the world's mighty battlefield where the hosts of the Monopolists are attacking the people with greater zeal, determination and ferocity than in our own state. There is no place on the mighty line where it is more important that the enemy should be repulsed, crushed and routed, foot and dragoon, than right where we stand. Are we ready for the work?[5]

Herbert's *Advance* called for "cheap transportation" and regarded the railroads as "public corporations" that "must and shall be made to subserve the public interests."[6]

Leftist Label Rejected

Although the Grange movement and the later populist[7] amalgamations such as the National People's Party of 1892 (platform written by Ignatius Donnelly) seem to smack of socialism and perhaps communism, some would argue there was always a distinction. As George McKenna points out, the populist movement lacked a "class consciousness" and believed "fancy dialectics [of class strife] are unnecessary . . . because the 'plain people' of America, which . . . includes almost everyone, are in basic agreement."[8]

Nevertheless, some editorialists in the East, such as E. L. Godkin in *The Nation*, insisted on discussing the new farmer movement in terms of Marxism. Noting that the farmers were not clear in calling for distinctions between old existing rail corporations and the new ones, thus implying they should all be treated alike, Godkin declared "the application of any such rule now to roads already in operation would be spoliation pure and simple—spoliation as flagrant as any ever proposed by Karl Marx."[9]

A farm movement more militant than the Grange, called the Farmers' Alliance, emerged primarily out of the discontent of Kansas, Nebraska, South Carolina, and Texas farmers. With economic distress compounded by the drought in 1887 and early frost and invasions of insects, such as chinch bugs, half the population of western Kansas headed back east. Their wagons bore such signs as "In God we trusted, in Kansas we busted." The Kansas farmers, Nordin says, were "caught in a three-way squeeze by mortgages, tight money, and high transportation rates. . . . It seemed to spring up by some spontaneous combustion, and these diverse brush fires immediately fused a number of ideologically diverse people and ignited hundreds of schoolhouse meetings."[10]

In the central states, where farmers had greater commitments and were less speculative in their investments, they gritted their teeth and faced the adversity. Most of the farmers who remained and suffered became a group prepared for the doctrines of political and economic revolt, which some were ready to stir up.[11]

Chicago Editor Creates Alliance

The first successful Farmers' Alliance was founded by a Chicago newspaper editor, Milton George. He had been a farmer in Fulton County in west central Illinois and knew the hardships of a farming life. He stumbled into journalism when an editor of the Chicago farm journal *Western Rural* failed to repay money he owed George. To recover some of his losses, George took over the *Western Rural*. He attacked the railroads, denouncing discrimination against the farmer and the bribery of high-level politicians by free rail passes. George called for government rail regulation and for clubs and alliances to come to the defense of the farmer. On his own, he organized a Farmers' Alliance for Cook County, Illinois, in the Chicago area, in April 1880. Using it as a central base, he sought through his editorials to encourage the launching of alliances nationwide.

Bringing together several hundred delegates from Alliance chapters, the Grange, and various rural clubs, George launched the national Alliance movement through a Farmers' Transportation Convention in Chicago in October 1880. Rival farm journals criticized George as an opportunist seeking to increase his publication's circulation. But George prevailed. By the time a third convention was held in St. Louis in October 1882, 2,000 Alliance chapters across the country sent delegates.[12]

While uniting rural dissatisfaction, the new Alliances ran into conflict where they least expected it. In addition to the expected thunder from the eastern establishment and trusts, local businesspersons complained that the farmers' organizations were scaring away eastern investment capital that many believed accounted for much of the growth in rural areas. Also, hometown business owners worried about the farmer agitators coming into government and pushing for tough interest laws that would curtail high interest rates.

Local business people and the elite were concerned that the role of a town or village as a supplier would be replaced by cooperatives and ordering by catalogs, such as the Montgomery Ward catalog. Indeed, Alliance stores opened up all over. In addition, the message of economic cooperation was spread through a network of traveling lecturers, giving farmers "a new sense of their own capability and a new political culture that led them to form the People's (Populist) Party."[13] As populist historian Lawrence Goodwyn points out, "The cooperatives recruited farmers to the Alliance, and the Alliance made people Populists."[14]

Media as Definers and Keepers of Values (and Biases)
SCRIPTURE FUELS POPULIST ZEAL

The populist movement was intertwined with religious values and causes, and the enthusiasm of crowds for the populist message certainly made participants feel they were doing holy work. They took their cues and symbols from scripture, largely ignoring the therapeutic value of suffering and the atonement, focusing more on the realized kingdom itself, here as well as in an afterlife. Fueling dreams of a kind of socialistic utopia was a best-selling book, *Looking Backward* by Edward Bellamy. Found in the hands of most populist leaders, and distributed by populist newspapers as a bonus for subscriptions, the 1888 book told of the world of the year 2000 where there would be no money, just a common credit card that gave everyone the same amount of credit for a year. Wealth would be shared and equal. Stores would have only samples. Orders would be relayed to a central warehouse from which the item would be delivered to the home of the buyer. Curiously the predictions anticipated today's credit card use and television home shopping by display samples.

Populist leaders in the 1880s and 1890s were seen as messianic, apocalyptic, and prophetic. One populist announced that "Christ himself was the author and President of the first Farmers' Alliance."[15] The populist governor of Kansas, Lorenzo Lewelling, cited biblical personalities in his rhetoric. A front-page *Emporia Gazette* article about the progress of the march of a quarry owner, Jacob Coxey, and his improvised army of the unemployed heading for Washington began under the words, "A Holy Movement":

> TOPEKA, KAN.—Governor Lewelling said this morning of the Coxey movement: "The Coxey movement is an uprising of the people, a result of preceding causes which Populists think they understand. It is the John the Baptist of the present time which precedes the overthrow of the Republican party which is the mouthpiece of corporate power and greed."[16]

Many Alliance and populist leaders were clergy, even high in denominational ranks.[17] Alliance meetings progressed like a church service, noted Keith Lynn King in his doctoral research at the University of Illinois. "They began with a prayer and included hymns," he says. "Members exhorted each other by recounting their experiences as farmers. . . . The Gillespie County [Texas] Alliance even forced one member to acknowledge his faults and receive a 'pardon for his sins.' "[18]

Women's Farm Paper Launched

One-fourth of all members of the Alliance were women. In Kansas women even had their own newspaper, the *Farmer's Wife.* Co-owners were Emma Pack and her husband, Ira, both of whom had edited other Kansan publications—Ira, a paper that dealt with real estate and land sales, and Emma, a fiction and fashion journal in Topeka. Contributors to the *Farmer's Wife*, which was published in Topeka from 1891 to 1894, were Bina Otis, wife of populist congressman John Otis; Fannie McCormick, foreman of the Kansas Knights of Labor and the first president of the National Women's Alliance; Women's Christian Temperance Union officers Mary Livermore and Frances Willard; and the orators Annie Diggs and Mary Elizabeth Lease. These women writers for the *Farmer's Wife* were part of the more radical faction of the Kansas Alliance movement. "Like some of their male counterparts, they were more interested in cooperative ventures than in winning political elections or organizing a party," says Kansan historian Marilyn Dell Brady. "Their commitment to urban workers and their advocacy of prohibition and woman suffrage set them off from those in their party who were ready and willing to accept fusion with the Democrats."[19]

The farm-labor movement reached across ethnic groups—German, Dutch, Bohemian, and so on—and George Hosmer, one-time Kansan editor, carried the new farmer radicalism to the Spanish speaking in his *Springer* (New Mexico) *Banner*. The fourth page of his newspaper reprinted the first page in Spanish. His mottos were "The People's Paper" and "Democratic in Politics." Hosmer's front page regularly had a reprint from the *Farmers' Alliance Herald* and similar journals. In one article, "A Solid Front," readers were urged to remember "the people who founded this government. . . . Good government depends upon the action and efforts of the people."[20]

A Dark Side of Populism

Never fully as "ecumenical" as it appeared, the populist movement was in fact fraught with divisive currents while working for shared economic and social goals. The South found it difficult to depart from the Democratic Party, and blacks stuck by the Republican Party of Lincoln. Support for ideas crossed lines for a time, but neither rural nor urban America was a true melting pot.

Biases of one ethnic racial or social group against another prevailed. Populists were caught up in other grassroots memberships, sometimes with less than lofty goals, as they worked for a better life through the Alliances. Stanley Parsons quotes an anti-Semitic item from the populist *Hamilton* (Nebraska) *County Register* in 1891 as an example of the oppressive feelings that some of the populists had:

> Dear Uncle Sam:
>   Your dream, I fear, is to be verified very shortly. The English Jew bankers own the earth. They have mortgaged mankind. . . . You may not know it, but those same English Jew bankers supplied certain persons in this country whom we know as monopolists with the money with which to buy the stocks and bonds of the corporations of this country for them.[21]

In the West, farm-labor groups were strongly hostile to the continued immigration of Chinese and other Asians. Platforms in labor (Knights of Labor) and Alliance coalitions in the northwestern states called for banning Chinese immigration. In September 1885 Knights of Labor massacred Chinese miners in Wyoming; two months later Knights organizer Daniel Cronin led a mob forcing most of the Chinese of Tacoma to flee.[22]

Some populists could be found in the American (Know-Nothing) Party, formerly a secret society (the Order of the Star-Spangled Banner), organized in 1854. Members were opposed to aliens, particularly Roman Catholics, as a threat to American life. The American Party and other groups, such as the American

Protective Association, which took over the American Party, reached combined membership of 21 million in 1893. Such groups favored the native, or current, citizens (thus such groups were tagged as *nativist*), as they backed curbs on immigrants who might take away their jobs. The American Party called for a twenty-one-year waiting period before one could become a citizen. When asked about their beliefs, they often replied, "I know nothing." Thus came the epithet, the Know-Nothing Party. It nominated former president Millard Fillmore as its candidate for president in 1856.

Some of the populists, who were heavily involved in the prohibition movement, opposed new immigrants from predominantly Roman Catholic countries, where there was a laxer attitude toward alcohol.

The populist movement that ebbed at the close of the century was a harbinger of grassroots movements of the twentieth century and new parties and party organs. Eugene Debs, who led the extensive Pullman strike as president of the American Railway Union in 1893, which received favorable coverage in the farm belt, went on to help form the Socialist Party in 1901 and edit its publication, *Appeal to Reason*.[23]

Noticeable since World War II has been a decided flip in populism from the left to the right, creating such demagogues as Senator Joseph McCarthy and his "witch-hunt" for communists, and segregationist Governor George Wallace of Alabama, who sought the presidency. Much of the new left, becoming secure in its middle-class status, has largely passed on the torch to the right, according to populist historian Michael Kazin.[24]

Media as Purveyors of Information/Education
SOCKLESS JERRY, MARY YELLIN', AND LITTLE ANNIE

The closing decades of the nineteenth century preceded the advent of radio, movies, and television, and much of the communication absorbed by farmers and so-called mechanics (urban factory workers) was transmitted orally. Roving orators—often sponsored by populist and other papers—informed the populace and spread the gospel of populism.

They were a colorful bunch in the 1880s and 1890s. Among the "full-throated" populists (to use a term coined by the *New York Times* a century later)[25] was the flamboyant Ignatius Donnelly, who in the 1860s had served as a Republican in the House of Representatives before taking up reform politics. In the 1870s he helped organize the Anti-Monopoly Party and was one of five Grangers elected to the Minnesota state senate. Donnelly launched his own newspaper, the *Anti-Monopolist*. Back in his law days in Philadelphia, before he headed west and tried to organize a farm utopia in Minnesota, he had been editor of the *Emigrant Aid Journal*. Donnelly dabbled in writing fantasy science fiction, including a book on the lost city of Atlantis. A Chicago paper placed him in a category of those "with a wheel loose."[26]

Nativist Journalism Still Abounds

Nativism, fueled by rampant change and the ascendancy of multi-ethnic ideals, exists today in a smattering of political parties and their journals. Founded in 1984, the Iowa-based Populist Party brings together elements of dissident groups, such as the Constitution Party, the American Party of Indiana, the American Independent Party of California, and Christian Identity groups from Indiana and Florida, according to Donald M. Kimball, the party's national secretary from Fayette, Iowa. A chief backer is Willis Carto, founder of the Liberty Lobby. The most influential undertaking of the Populist Party is the Liberty Lobby's *Spotlight*, the weekly newspaper claiming a circulation of 150,000 and offering a "wacko view of a world run by Zionist bankers, Mossad agents, and scheming socialists," reported the *Village Voice*.[27]

In 1988 the Populist Party of America, with its national committee in Washington, supported David Duke, former grand wizard of the Ku Klux Klan and Louisiana State representative, for president. The party was served by *The Populist Observer*. One of its platforms (1984) pledged to "reduce foreign aid, repeal income tax, prohibit foreign ownership of land, revitalize the family farm . . . , reject ERA [Equal Rights Amendment] and gay rights . . . , [support] anti-busing and repulse immigration."[28]

Other contemporary "populist" publications include the non-Nativist *Grass Roots*, put out by the People's Party, which was founded in Dallas in 1971. A liberal group, it offered controversial baby doctor Benjamin Spock as a presidential candidate.[29]

Then there is the National States Rights Party, which beat the bushes for an unknown, "Vote for the White People's Candidate. . . . Stop race mixing insanity. . . . Restore respect for Jesus Christ by returning prayer and Bible reading to the public schools,"[30] and so on.

The *Kansas City Star* summed up the characteristics of modern-day populism on the right:

> There are no identifying marks, no hidden symbols and no secret language linking members of groups of right-wing extremists that populate the Midwest. . . .
>
> What they share is white skin and a belief that non-whites are genetically inferior.
>
> They also share a vision that the world is skidding toward calamity and that Caucasians—excluding Jews—have been chosen by God to prevail after the second coming of Jesus Christ.
>
> For some the lure is patriotism, for others it's machismo. Some see it as divine direction and others are drawn by the community of the combat ready.[31]

Such is the ongoing lure of the darker side of political and social populism, some with militias, that continues to make the front pages and airwaves.

Another "loose wheel" was Jerry Simpson, dubbed Sockless Jerry because this rough, crude, generally ignorant man, as the *Topeka Capital* regarded him, once did not wear socks when debating an opponent who wore silk socks. The Kansan was swept into office in a populist "hurricane," as a paper called it in 1890.[32] The influential *Kansas Farmer* extolled his political virtues. It said Jerry Simpson "will probably perform more work and receive less credit for it than any of our new members. He is a plain, blunt man, affable, friendly, accommodating, generous, and yet does not need a moment's training to reduce him to his fighting weight. He is well read in history and politics."[33] Simpson served eight years in Congress in the 1890s. He then published a newspaper, *Jerry Simpson's Bayonet*, which he wielded to cut up those who fiercely attacked him when he was in Congress.[34]

Women—teachers, writers, editors—also extended the message, turning orators. Most popular was Mary Elizabeth Lease, who wrote on special assignment for Joseph Pulitzer's *New York World*. She gained the nickname of "Mary Ellen" because Ellen rhymed with "yellin'." Some historians today still list her as Mary Ellen Lease.

Born in Pennsylvania (like Donnelly), although she sometimes claimed to be from Ireland, Lease migrated west and taught in a parochial school at Orange Mission, Kansas. She married the local druggist, and they took up farming in Texas and Kansas. Together they were confronted with the many woes of the farmer. She studied law on the side while raising four children and was admitted to the bar in Kansas in 1885. After she gave a speech to the convention of the new Union-Labor Party, word of her talent as an orator spread.

Elizabeth Lease: Populist orator who advised Kansas farmers to "raise less corn and more hell." (The Bettmann Archive)

A Chauvinistic William Allen White

Even Lease's detractors praised the voice of this dynamo. The noted editor of the *Emporia* (Kansas) *Gazette*, William Allen White, grumbled: "She put into her oratory something which the printed copies did not reveal. They were dull enough often, but she could recite the multiplication table and set a crowd hooting or hurrahing at her will."[35] But editor White, who cavorted with presidents and was known for his reasonableness, could by description betray his dislike politically for a person. A chunky bulk of a man, who more nearly resembled a sedentary Santa Claus than a dashing Romeo in appearance himself, he savaged Mrs. Lease with this description: "She stood nearly six feet tall, with no figure, a thick torso, and long legs. To me, she often looked like a kangaroo pyramided up from the hips to a comparatively small head. . . . She wore her hair in a Psyche knot, always neatly combed and topped by the most ungodly hats I ever saw a woman wear. She had no sex appeal—none!"[36]

William Allen White (right), with Wichita (*Kansas*) Eagle *friend.*

William Allen White: Great Editorials

William Allen White, editor of the *Emporia* (Kansas), *Gazette* from 1895 until his death in 1944, won two Pulitzer prizes—one for an editorial, "To an Anxious Friend," explaining White's support of railroad workers' right to strike, in 1922, and another for his *Autobiography of William Allen White*, published posthumously in 1946. Yet White is best known for two other editorials—"What's the Matter with Kansas?" in which he criticizes the overzealous populists, August 15, 1896, and an editorial, May 17, 1921, in memory of his daughter, "Mary White," who died following a riding accident. Here are the beginning and ending of White's soulful tribute to his daughter:

May 17, 1921

The Associated Press reports carrying the news of Mary White's death declared that it came as the result of a fall from a horse. How she would have hooted at that! She never fell from a horse in her life. Horses have fallen on her and with her—"I'm always trying to hold 'em in my lap," she used to say. . . . Her death resulted not from a fall but from a blow on the head which fractured her skull, and the blow came from the limb of an overhanging tree on the parking.

The last hour of her life was typical of its happiness. She came home from a day's work at school, topped off by a hard grind with the copy on the High School Annual, and felt that a ride would refresh her. She climbed into her khakis, chattering to her mother about the work she was doing, and hurried to get her horse and be out on the dirt roads for the country air and the radiant green fields of the spring. As she rode through the town on an easy gallop, she kept waving at passers-by. She knew everyone in town. For a decade the little figure in the long pigtail and the red hair ribbon has been familiar on the streets of Emporia, and she got in the way of speaking to those who nodded at her. She passed the Kerrs, walking the horse in front of the Normal Library, and waved at them; passed another friend a few hundred feet farther on, and waved at her.

The horse was walking, and as she turned into North Merchant Street she took off her cowboy hat, and the horse swung into a lope. She passed the Tripletts and waved her cowboy hat at them, still moving gayly north on Merchant Street. A Gazette carrier passed—a High School boy friend—and she waved at him, but with her bridle hand; the horse veered quickly, plunged into the parking where the low-hanging limb faced her and, while she still looked back waving, the blow came. But she did not fall from the horse; she slipped off, dazed a bit, staggered, and fell in a faint. She never quite recovered consciousness.

But she did not fall from the horse neither was she riding fast. A year or so ago she used to go like the wind. But that habit was broken, and she used the horse to get into the open, to get fresh, hard exercise, and to work off a certain surplus energy, that welled up in her and needed a physical outlet. . . .

Her funeral yesterday at the Congregational Church was as she would have wished it; no singing, no flowers except the big bunch of red roses from her brother Bill's Harvard classmen—heavens, how proud that would have made her!—and the red roses from the Gazette forces in vases, at her head and feet. . . .

It would have made her smile to know that her friend, Charley O'Brien, the traffic cop, had been transferred from Sixth and Commercial to the corner near the church to direct her friends who came to bid her good-by.

A rift in the clouds in a gray day threw a shaft of sunlight upon her coffin as her nervous, energetic little body sank to its last sleep. But the soul of her, the glowing, gorgeous, fervent soul of her, surely was flaming in eager joy upon some other dawn.

However, to others less jaundiced than White on the subject of populism, Lease did not seem so ridiculous. The *Kansas City Star* wrote:

> Mrs. Lease is a tall woman—fully five feet ten inches, and rather slender. Her face is strong, good, not pretty, and very feminine. There is no mark of masculinity about her. She is woman all over. Her hair is a dark brown and evenly parted in the center and smoothed down at the sides with neat care. Her nose, chin and cheek bones announce themselves strongly. However, they give no sense of harshness to her face.[37]

Another fiery orator spreading the populist message was Annie L. ("Little Annie") Diggs, a Kansas writer and editor who expounded on "doctrines of socialism."[38] She had worked on a publication in Washington before heading west to take a job in a music store in Lawrence, Kansas, where she married a postman. They raised three children. She picked up later on her journalistic interests by going to Boston as a representative of Kansas newspapers and continued speaking on reform matters. She returned to Lawrence and signed on as a columnist for the *Lawrence Journal*. Later she became an associate editor of *The Advocate* in Topeka and helped spur the paper to reach 80,000 circulation in the 1890s.

The *Kansas City Journal* contrasted the two great populist women communicators:

> Mrs. Lease is the Irish woman . . . and the chief charm of her oratory (and it has a charm even if one does not believe a word of it) is her graphic Irish way of putting things. . . . Mrs. Lease is a woman of rhetoric, Mrs. Diggs is a woman of much feeling. Mrs. Lease thinks she is a logician; Mrs. Diggs never practices self-deception of any kind. Mrs. Lease is a politician; Mrs. Diggs is a woman; where Mrs. Lease would be tempted to go on and wrangle to the bitter end, Mrs. Diggs would be tempted to have a good cry about it first. When one sees Mrs. Diggs on the platform he is inclined to regret that a woman should be there; when Mrs. Lease follows he is sorry she is not a man.[39]

Where the Setting Sun Makes News

The "heartland" newspapers, with limited scope and staffs in news gathering, dwelt on farm and small-town matters, from trivia and reporting on the "nonnews" of the day to offering market listings and analysis and self-help features for farmers. The *Iowa State Reporter*, Waterloo, edited by Matt Parrott (a future governor of Iowa and an arch critic of abuses by railroads), gave considerable space to farm and "horticultural" news and self-help articles, for example, articles on "the varieties of apples" and understanding "the language among animals."[40]

In Kansas, the *Leavenworth Daily Times*, flanked by a column of advertising on one side and a column detailing a jail assault and a local drowning on the other, a column labeled "city news" found nothing amiss in reporting "nonnews" or merely undeveloped ideas:

The sun went down nearly clear last evening.

The Continental hotel is being repainted and generally cleaned up.

About $200 was received into the country [sic] treasury yesterday.

Do not forget Prof. McCarty's lecture tonight, at the Presbyterian church.

The boys at the fire department were busy cleaning up their engines yesterday.

Weddings are more plentiful this summer than heretofore during the hot weather.

The old fire engine, No. 2, did good service at the late fire, under the management of Pat Burns.

The air last night was cool and fresh, and those who could afford it enjoyed a comfortable sleep.

The levee is now nearly covered again with drift wood which has been gathered during the last rise.

A handsome little ornament, representing a dove with an olive branch in its mouth, is one of the attractions at M. P. Cranston's store.[41]

These items, too trivial or vague to be real news, had a homespun quality nevertheless. They were things that the populist orators—the vocal communicators—especially Mrs. Lease, if William Allen White was right about her power as a speaker, could, if she had had a chance, have put life into.

Media as Voices of Reform and as Political Organs

THE PEOPLE'S PARTY AND A CROSS OF GOLD

Reform during the populist ascendancy of the 1880s and 1890s meant politics. While the main newspapers of the cities and regions debated the issues, often in terms of the two-party system, myriad small populist-oriented newspapers sprang up to carry the battle for the populist causes. Kansas alone had 150 newspapers linked to the Farmers' Alliance. About a thousand Alliance papers, representing hundreds of thousands in circulation, formed the National Reform Press Association, creating a network that helped pave the way for a national political party.[42] The NRPA, along with several of the larger reform papers, prepared and distributed "lessons" on populist principles to be read in the papers and used at the Alliances' political clubs. One set of lessons, linking ancient Greek history with America, was prepared by Charles Macune's *National Economist*, the official organ of the National Farmers' Alliance and Industrial Union (NFA&IU).[43] The *Kansas Farmer* prepared a pamphlet-length teaching document, *The Way Out*, which it ran in five installments.[44]

Editors could become members of the NRPA by having their papers reviewed for political correctness and by promising to endorse the political agenda of the NFA&IU and other sanctioned groups such as the Farmers' Mutual Benefit Association and the Knights of Labor, plus paying an initiation fee. This participation entitled the editors to receive ready-to-use printing plates of populist articles and cartoons.[45]

One of the most influential and aggressive populist papers was Tom Watson's *People's Party Paper*, published in Atlanta every Friday with the motto "Equal Rights

The Metal Currency Debate

For the last third of the nineteenth century the money question loomed large in elections. There were basically three groups—the Greenbackers, who favored the inflationary paper-money greenbacks of the Civil War years, and two groups of hard-metalists who felt the currency should be backed by hard money, either silver or gold. Silver, especially after major discoveries of the metal in the West, came to represent a cheaper metal that could be more plentiful. Yet most of the world was on a gold standard and, with silver somewhat scarce before the new discoveries, the U.S. Congress adopted a demonetizing of silver in favor of a gold standard in 1873.

Populists were in later years to call this "the crime of '73."

A compromise allowing a bimetal standard was reached by means of the Bland-Allison Act in 1878. This kept gold as the primary standard so the nation could deal in foreign markets and allowed a limited coinage of silver to appease the average workers. "The amount to be coined was too low, however," said Margaret Canovan in her study of populism. It did not "create the inflation hoped for by debtors and dreaded by creditors. Meanwhile the silver grievance rumbled on, to contribute a plank to the Populist platform and eventually, in 1896, to swamp the rest of it."[46]

to All—Special Privileges to None." It reported on oppression in the big city as well as in the small northern and southern towns, as it also dealt with such issues as the money standard debate. The Georgia readers learned on the front page about "Crime, Death and Tenements—Frightful Vice on the East Side the Result of Overcrowding and Attendant Evils" in New York from an article attributed to "the New York Press."[47]

Another article on the front page of the same issue of the *People's Party Paper* in 1893—a text of "an address to the people of the United States"—was headlined "The Evils of a Gold Standard—Populists and Silverites Join in a Free-Coinage Address." The text of the address was signed by the "Populist senators and members and by the Nevada senators."

In Omaha in July 1892 the new national party, the National People's Party, popularly known as the Populist Party, was launched. Nominated for president was a former union general, James B. Weaver, and for vice president, James G. Field, a former Confederate general. The party pulled more than a million votes for 9 percent of the total cast and picked up twenty-two electoral votes.

William Jennings Bryan Nominated

In 1896 western farmers won control of the Democratic convention and helped to nominate William Jennings Bryan, who enthralled the convention with his "cross of gold" speech, one of the most famous in U.S politics. He thundered, "Destroy our farms and the grass will grow in the streets of every city in the country." And he ended with a powerful salvo crashing against the opponents of silver: "You shall not press down upon the brow of labor this crown of thorns; you shall not crucify mankind upon a cross of gold."[48]

The Populist Party, except for the southern wing, found Bryan's planks close to their own principles and endorsed Bryan, but not his running mate, Maine banker Arthur Sewall. Instead, the populists' choice for vice president was editor Tom Watson of the *People's Party Paper* in Atlanta.

Republican William McKinley won over Bryan in that 1896 election, 7.1 million to 6.5 million, which translated into 271 electoral votes for McKinley, 176 for Bryan. The vice presidential nominee, editor Watson, went on to win the Populist Party's nomination for president in 1904 as the party was dying out. In 1920 he was elected to the Senate, where he became an ardent foe of the League of Nations. History remembers him in his later years as a "hatemonger," publishing tirades against minorities.

Media as Voices of Freedom

ONE WOMAN NOT POLITICALLY CORRECT

Pressure from the mainline parties made life difficult at times for the farm and populist editors. The *Kansas Farmer* said, "Several months ago we were informed by partisan politicians that unless this paper refrained from championing the objects of organized farmers they would ruin the paper." The paper did not flinch, but courageously declared, "We have no apologies for making a good all-around farm journal that in times of sore need could strike a few blows for the cause of the 'Farmers' Movement.' . . . The *Kansas Farmer* will always be a watch guard of farmers' interests and industries."[49]

But once populism gained power, it too could be oppressive, and it took courage for some rebel editors to oppose the farm and populist movement and hold out for the freedom of the press. One fiercely independent editor who bucked the tide was Ellen Dortch, who took over the *Carnesville* (Georgia) *Tribune* from her father in 1890. She supported many of the aims of the Georgia Alliance, such as the encouragement of farmers to diversify crops and launch cooperatives. But to her many of the Alliance concerns were impractical and visionary. She said, for instance, that promoting government ownership of railroads would lead to greater debt and higher taxes. She denounced Alliance leaders, such as Leonidas Livingston, president of the Georgia Alliance, as demagogues who were no better than political bosses. She supported an effort to investigate the Alliance on corruption charges. When Mary Elizabeth Lease addressed the Georgia legislature and called for a new political party, Dortch denounced Lease and urged women to avoid Alliance membership. In return some sub-Alliance chapters in the county began to boycott the *Tribune*.[50]

Her editorial war with the Alliance heated up with the death of her father, who had been school commissioner. He had suffered a stroke that left him partly paralyzed. Soon afterward, the county school board (most of whose members were Alliance men) fired him, alleging drunkenness, neglect of duty, and malfeasance of office. Ellen Dortch maintained that he was ill. The elder Dortch died during an appeal process, and Dortch felt the Alliance was responsible for her father's death. When the Alliance asked that school board members receive extra pay for their deliberations on the elder Dortch case, Dortch was incensed, charging "absolute monarchism" and demagoguery.[51]

Dortch won her case, and board members were not paid. She faced a new battle, which threatened publication. When a group of Alliance men bought the *Carnesville Enterprise*, they called for a boycott of "unfriendly" papers and asked county officials to switch the official legal ads from the *Tribune* to the *Enterprise*. "At this time in her battle with the Alliance," says William F. Holmes, "Dortch presented herself as standing against a secret organization dedicated to undermining freedom of the press. She predicted that the Alliance would not achieve its sinister goals."[52] She roared:

> The boycotters who seek to kill the *Tribune* have a hopeless task before them. The *Tribune* is strong and brave and fearless. The men who are boycotting us are weak and cowardly and would go around and burn up men's houses while they are asleep. We are not afraid of cowards. You can not kill the *Tribune* unless you burn our office and you are afraid to do that.[53]

Dortch prevailed and went on to attack the organization of the People's Party. She left the paper after the 1892 elections and became assistant state librarian in Atlanta; she was the first woman to hold a state office in Georgia. In 1897, at age 34, she married the former Gettysburg Confederate general, James Longstreet, who was 42 years older than she (he died in 1904). During World War II she was a riveter in a bomber plant and crusaded for civil rights. She died at age 99 in 1962.[54]

Media as Fourth Estate: Adversaries of Government

EDITOR GROUPS WIELD POWER

While the National Reform Press Association sought political clout as it supported populist causes, rural and small-town newspapers had banded together in a national organization that could serve as a concerted voice and wield a measure of power.

The National Newspaper Association, born as the National Editorial Association in 1885, with its name changed to the National Newspaper Association (NNA) in 1965, was on the one hand simply a fellowship of editors who escaped their isolation once a year for a good time. They took free rail passes and went to a convention where many of them drank too much and on one occasion some were arrested for too much hell-raising. The serious side of the organization included its role as the fourth estate. The records of the national conventions are packed with resolutions aimed at affecting decisions of Congress. The NNA every year held its own legislative conference, made appointments with the president, and kept a lobbyist in Washington.

In its early days NNA members made common cause with the populists on railroads, seeking cuts in costs of travel and transportation of produce. The NNA has sounded populist if not nativistic in its calls for patriotism. From its beginning in New Orleans in 1885 in an organizing resolution it asserted that it accepted that the press is "the bulwark of society, and the protector of the people, and the educator of the masses."[55]

Over the years the NNA has fought government attempts to control or restrict media through adverse postal regulations. It challenged high tariffs on newsprint that kept more resourceful Canadian competitors out of the U.S. market and the cost of newsprint high; it bristled loudly under the regulation of the media through the press code of the National Recovery Act of 1933.

In 1938 the NNA denounced a bill proposed by Sherman Minton of Indiana calling for "Making it a felony to publish as a fact anything known to be false." The measure was withdrawn.[56] In 1951 the NNA in a Chicago convention viewed with apprehension a security order restricting the public's right to know, and urged President Truman to rescind it.[57] The executive order gave federal authorities broad authority to classify and restrict information without giving a basis or reason for such classification. The NNA continued to fight the order into the Eisenhower administration. In 1958 the association rapped an Internal Revenue Service proposal to tax public utilities advertising as "an obvious effort to employ a tax penalty to circumvent the freedom of speech and of the press . . . by taxing the expression of opinion."[58] In 1975 the NNA challenged President Gerald Ford's veto of amendments to the 1966 Freedom of Information Act and continued to oppose tampering with it by following administrations.

A number of NNA presidents stood up to the powers that be. George Hosmer, who developed newspapers in many places and who at his paper in Trinidad, Colorado, broke in Damon Runyon of *Guys and Dolls* fame as a writer, regularly took on the authorities. A 1912 "Extra" edition of Hosmer's *Morgan Co. Herald*, Fort Morgan, Colorado, carried three front-page articles about a former deputy district attorney accused of taking a bribe in letting a sex offender go free.[59]

In his book *Ink on My Hands*, the NNA (NEA) president in 1936, Clayton Rand, tells of his staunch stand against the Ku Klux Klan and how "the controversy became the bitterest in which my papers ever participated."[60] He assailed the Klan for its "fanaticism and racial hatred" and declared: "Intimidation, duress and coercion go with the Inquisition and the Dark Ages. They have no place in this Republic." Rand ridiculed the "clown suits" of the Klan. Politicians and preachers alike denounced Rand for opposing the Klan. Rand recalls, "I was forced to collar one preacher, threatening that if he preached another dirty sermon about me I'd kick him in the pants."[61]

Another NNA president had summed up the fourth estate responsibility of the media in 1913. John Oswald, of the *American Printer*, New York, said:

> I look forward to a time when to hold a private post as guiding spirit of a great
> newspaper will be a greater responsibility and honor than to sit in the chair of

some great public office. . . . He will be greater than the public official, because the official will merely transmit into action the will of the people as the newspaper creates and directs it.[62]

Media as Businesses

PAYING ATTENTION TO ADVERTISING

The press associations that have developed over the years have as one of their aims "financial advantage" as well as "mutual protection" and "social enjoyment," as B. B. Herbert put it in his keynote speech as the first president of the National Newspaper Association meeting in New Orleans in 1885. A financial concern was and still is that of advertising. At the outset Herbert urged "compacts" (agreements) and "legislation" to protect isolated editors against advertising brokers who bought space and sold off chunks of advertising space at higher rates.[63]

But some delegates wanted a tighter fist and a more practical approach to advertising. One such delegate was W. H. Brearley, an energetic advertising man of the

With a sense for business, young Tom Edison hawked newspapers aboard trains. (Department of the Interior, National Park Service)

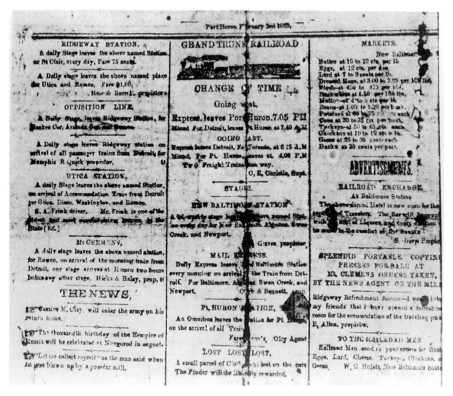

Edison's newspaper, The Weekly Herald, *published on the Grand Trunk Railway.*

Detroit Evening News with a passionate interest in the business side of newspapers. He took that interest to Cincinnati in 1886 for the second meeting of the NNA (NEA). Brearley's Detroit, an industrial center, was in the throes of growth, and Detroit's *Journal, Free Press, News,* and *Tribune* competed for the same advertising dollar and faced new business problems and labor organizing. Brearley was put off by what he perceived as too much interest in social events and good times at the conventions. He was all business.

In the 1886 meeting Brearley presented a paper on "The Advertising Department." His speech by today's standards would seem a little insulting to editors. He began: "I presume it will be conceded, at the outset, that the only truly interesting portion of a newspaper is the advertising it contains. There, if anywhere, can rest be found from editorial partisanship and exaggeration."[64]

The fledgling NNA (NEA) formed a committee on advertising. The committee, with Brearley a member, asked that newspapers set a minimum rate scale per inch, per issue, per 1,000 circulation and that advertising become a topic of the state associations. But Brearley had clearly hoped to do more. Despite his work on the committee, Brearley returned bitter. He wanted more than a report; he wanted action.[65]

Brearley went on to bring a half dozen big city editors and business managers together at a Western Associated Press meeting in Detroit in the fall of 1886. He held proxies from twenty-two other publishers and business managers.[66] Out of the efforts came the American Newspaper Publishers Association, representing big city dailies. On Brearley's mind those several years: sorting out respectable advertising agencies from the glut of new agencies, stepping up ad income, standardizing rates and commissions.

A Look at Advertising Ethics

The country editors in the NNA (NEA) were also discussing the ethics of advertising. Walter Williams, the future president of the NNA, in his *Columbia* (Missouri) *Herald* argued that advertising is a part of a whole moral fabric and "advertising in papers without moral standing does not pay. People like honesty and reliability in a newspaper as in an individual."[67]

In the 1890s advertising became so paramount that some publishers came to "view their own newspapers as marketing devices," say media business researchers Gerald Baldasty and Jeffrey Rutenbeck. Advertisers wielded their influence as they preferred to see more positive news and less concern with politics in the media. Papers reached out to women, whom department stores and other stores wanted to attract.[68] In the late nineteenth century papers continued to diversify, seeking new audiences and new areas of interest as they worked to achieve increased circulation, which in turn provided a better base for advertising rates.

The NNA organized an office and rule-setting agency for advertising, the National Advertising Service, Inc. (NAS). The NAS eventually split with the NNA, bought out the competing American Press Association (APA), and formed the Weekly Newspaper Representatives, which in 1961 was renamed the American Newspaper Representatives (ANR). Before television increasingly attracted the national accounts, ANR handled $9 million in advertising, with three-fourths of it from the auto companies.

In 1992 the ANPA merged with the Newspaper Advertising Bureau and six other marketing associations to form the Newspaper Association of America (NAA). The new merged group pledged "to advance the cause of a free press and to ensure that newspapers have the economic strength essential to serve the American people." Cathie Black, first NAA president and CEO, promised the NAA would keep newspapers "as vibrant and compelling tomorrow as they are today."[69]

Media as Vehicles of Sensationalism/Entertainment
HE TANGLED WITH A CIRCULAR SAW

The gory news continued to find its way onto the front pages, with such stories as "Beheaded—A Man's Head and Right Arm Cut Off," which appeared in the *Leavenworth* (Kansas) *Times* in 1877. Working in a factory with a circular saw, a

The Lighter Side

Twain's "Petrified Man"

With the Civil War under way in 1861, Samuel Clemens gave up his piloting job on the Mississippi and headed west to try his hand at mining gold and silver. Things were rough, and he joined the staff of the *Territorial Enterprise* in Virginia City in western Nevada. The future author and humorist, who penned many books, among them *The Adventures of Huckleberry Finn* and *Innocents Abroad*, under the pen name Mark Twain, mined a vein of humor if not gold at the *Enterprise*. He occasionally published stories that were made up from whole cloth. One of his most popular hoaxes was "The Petrified Man," which appeared in the *Enterprise*, October 4, 1862. The article was reprinted throughout the country and the world, even ending up in a London scientific journal.

> A petrified man was found some time ago in the mountains south of Gravelly Ford. Every limb and feature of the stony mummy was perfect, not even excepting the left leg, which has evidently been a wooden one during the lifetime of the owner—which lifetime, by the way, came to a close about a century ago, in the opinion of a savan who has examined the defunct. The body was in a sitting posture, and leaning against a huge mass of croppings; the attitude was pensive, the right thumb resting against the side of the nose; the left thumb partially supported the chin, the fore-finger pressing the inner corner of the left eye and drawing it partly open; the right eye was closed, and the fingers of the right hand spread apart. This strange freak of nature created a profound sensation in the vicinity, and our informant states that by request, Justice Sewell or Sowell, of Humboldt City, at once proceeded to the spot and held an inquest on the body. The verdict of the jury was that "deceased came to his death from protracted exposure," etc. The people of the neighborhood volunteered to bury the poor unfortunate, and were even anxious to do so; but it was discovered, when they attempted to remove him, that the water which had dripped upon him for ages from the crag above, had coursed down his back and deposited a limestone sediment under him which had glued him to the bed rock upon which he sat, as with a cement of adamant, and Judge S. refused to allow the charitable citizens to blast him from his position. The opinion expressed by his Honor that such a course would be little less than sacrilege, was eminently just and proper. Everybody goes to see the stone man, as many as three hundred having visited the hardened creature during the past five or six weeks.

man slipped—his left arm was shredded, and when he reached with his right arm, it was severed; then, falling further into the saw, he lost his head.[70] But the same front page also told of exciting news about a growing national rail strike, and the coverage of it in this issue and subsequent issues enunciated another dimension of sensationalism: anticipatory sensationalism.

Since people like to read about what they fear, with the comfort of knowing that some terrible thing described has not happened and is not happening to them—maybe the worst is to come—headlines on stories could be sensational by their anticipatory nature. In a front-page story about the developing Baltimore and Ohio railroad strike the main headline said, "The Stubborn Strikers." The drop-heads that followed were sensational in their anticipation: "Fears That the Strike May Extend to the Pan Handle Road—The General Situation." Also: "The Strikers

Ready for Anything"; "Another Strike Feared"; "No Bloodshed Yet."[71] The next day the main headline said, "Red Riot" and the dropheads included "The City Running Wild With Excitement and More Serious Trouble Feared."[72] The next day: "The American Commune," a reference to the short-lived revolutionary government in Paris in 1871. This news report told of the militia firing upon the mob, killing eight or ten persons. And the story became more sensational with the anticipatory dimension: "A General Massacre Feared at Pittsburg[h], the City Being in the Hands of the Rioters"; "Several Gun Stores Gutted to Procure Arms for the Enraged Communists"; "Twenty Dead at Pittsburg, and Bloody Work Expected to-Day." And the next day: Under "A Sad Sabbath," these dropheads: "Red Riot Holds High Carnival at Pittsburg"; "Every Available Soldier in the U.S. to be Brought Forward—Sheridan Ordered to Pittsburg."[73] Apparently ideology and fear of communism and socialism compounded with physical and other fears to heighten the sensationalism by anticipation.

The fear of epidemics seized the imagination in 1892. News stories in the *Savannah* (Georgia) *Tribune* told of "A Ship Load of Cholera" that arrived in New York from Germany. There was indeed reason for concern. Thirty-two of the ship's passengers were already dead from cholera, and the remaining passengers were quarantined. Auxiliary articles told of the "rage" of the cholera epidemic in Hamburg, Germany, and how there "the death list is growing appallingly larger and larger." Two days later the *Tribune* invoked the dreaded historic image of a plague. It declared: "The Plague at Our Doors"; "A Ship Arrives in New York Loaded With Cholera Infected Passengers"; "The Country Is Becoming Alarmed at the Proximity of the Scourge." The ship did not just contain cholera cases but was "loaded" with victims who were in the "proximity."[74] Anticipation, the possibility of the worst to come, a general plague, fueled the sensationalism.

An In-Depth Sensationalism

Another kind of sensationalism—in-depth sensationalism—appeared. In 1881 radical populist Henry Demarest Lloyd published an in-depth but incendiary article against the monopolies established by the late railroad kingpin Cornelius Vanderbilt and Standard Oil's John D. Rockefeller, anticipating the 1901–1904 work of Ida Tarbel on Standard Oil and Rockefeller. Lloyd's 12,000-word article, "Story of a Great Monopoly," appeared in the *Atlantic Monthly* in March 1881. Lloyd, who also wrote for the *Chicago Tribune* and was a lawyer assisting anarchists tried for murder in the Chicago Haymarket labor riot of 1886, told of the abuses, price fixing, and tax breaks of the monopolies in his *Atlantic Monthly* article. He charged that the Standard Oil monopoly developed and was sustained because of "conspiracy with the railroads. . . . The Standard killed its rivals, in brief, by getting the great trunk lines to refuse to give them transportation."[75]

Lloyd detailed facts gleaned from government records and congressional hearings. He left no doubt where his sympathies lay as he told of the "outrages," including stories of the oppressed common man. He offered correctives, such as

An Uncommon Man: Chain Builder E. W. Scripps

"**H**is interest was, naturally, a peoples' party for the blue collar class, imagining himself the potential leader," says a biographer of the indomitable press lord E. W. Scripps.[76] If Scripps did not fancy himself as a populist, he did at least see himself as a self-styled servant of the underclass. He satisfied this itch to serve and preach by founding dozens of newspapers that sold for a mere penny or two cents, compared to the five cents of competitors. He kept articles short and simply written to appeal to the blue-collar urban reader.

A Simple Editing Formula

The simple news editing and writing formula was inspired by a small book, *The Peter Parley Tales*, brought from England by the Scripps brothers' father. The book contained short stories about romance, crime, and travel. "The new format was starkly basic," says Scripps biographer Jack Casserly. "Condense stories into simple language that even a child would understand. The format for quick, easy reading would literally sweep across American newspapers like a prairie fire." E. W. extended the Peter Parley formula by "championing the masses and accenting human, reader-interest stories."[77]

Despite lofty ideals and innovations, Edward Wyllis Scripps' personal image is tainted. He was downright cantankerous. In fact, one book drawn from his extensive writings and notes was called *Damned Old Crank*. A tall monstrous man in boots, he drank up to a gallon of whiskey a day, chased women, built a magnificent estate on 2,100 acres in southern California, quarreled with his family and most who knew him, lived apart from his wife much of the time, and, in his later years, like Pulitzer, retreated to a yacht.

Scripps was born on a farm near Rushville, Illinois, in 1854; he dropped out of school at age fifteen in order to help his ailing father on the farm. He maintained a dislike for formal schooling throughout his life. At eighteen he followed his half brothers James, who had gained some newspaper experience in Chicago, and George to Detroit, where the pair were putting out a fledging newspaper, the *Detroit Tribune and Advertiser*. James and George declined to take in the young Scripps at first, making him prove himself at a pharmacy job. The *Tribune* building burned

E. W. Scripps at original home of Washington *(D.C.)* Daily News.

(Continued)

down. Paid $30,000 by an insurance company, the Scripps brothers sought to launch a better newspaper, the *Detroit Evening News*, this time with E. W. aboard to help with building circulation. It was the beginning of the Scripps empire.

When James became ill, E. W. took over. But soon E. W. wanted his own newspaper. Borrowing $10,000 from his sister Ellen, who remained his closest friend and adviser throughout his life, and his half brothers, he launched the *Penny Press* in Cleveland in 1878 (later called the *Cleveland Press*). He became involved in all kinds of controversies. One was a premature announcement of President James Garfield's death. Having only enough paper for an extra 2,000 issues when Garfield was shot July 2, 1881, he allowed his telegraph editor to say that the president was dead. But the next day the president was still alive, and indeed lasted until September 19. Two days after the shooting, the *Press*, with no apology, had it both ways:

> The President, dead or dying, is creating a tremendous impact on the political scene.
> The Associated Press report of the President's death at 7:10 p.m. Saturday was so much in accordance with the probabilities that it found universal credibility all over the country.[78]

Scripps Wins in Racy Libel Case

In 1881 Scripps was sued for libel in Cleveland by Edwin Cowles of the competing *Cleveland Leader* for saying of Cowles: "To start with, the old man who lost the roof of his mouth by youthful indiscretions and who now edits the *Leader*, uttered a witless, thoroughly transparent falsehood. All the papers are a sorry lot and the *Press* takes no pride in their company." Scripps also said without proof that Cowles "lost his horse and his watch at lewd and disreputable places."[79] The closely watched trial was billed as the

case of a poor man's defender (Scripps) against the rich (Cowles). It took a jury twenty-seven hours to find Scripps not guilty.

Buoyed by success in Cleveland, with the help of his brothers Scripps bought the *St. Louis Chronicle*; and in Cincinnati they acquired the *Penny Paper* and changed its name to the *Cleveland Press*. When James went to Europe, E. W. moved to expand the *Detroit News*. This action only angered James, who promptly fired E. W. from his post as president of the Scripps Publishing Company. E. W. kept control of the *Cincinnati Post*, which he turned into a firebrand crusader against corruption in city hall. He brought in Milton McRae as business manager and with half brother George formed a partnership, the Scripps-McRae League. Although they often argued, McRae and Scripps worked together for twenty-five years.

Scripps had started a wire service, the United Press, which later merged with William Randolph Hearst's International News Service to form the United Press International (UPI). When McRae retired, Scripps brought in the hard-driving Roy Howard, the chief at UP, as executive editor of the papers, with son Robert Scripps. In 1922 the Scripps operation took the name of Scripps-Howard. Today it operates more than twenty newspapers, ten television stations, five radio stations, and cable TV in ten states.

When E. W. and his eldest son, Jim, split up and went their separate ways in 1920, Jim took several small papers with him. Jim bequeathed those papers to his widow, Josephine, when he died at age thirty-four. Eventually, Josephine Scripps, with her sons Ed and Jim (named after his father), founded what became known as the Scripps League Newspapers, now comprising forty-six newspapers.

E. W. died on his yacht *Ohio* off the coast of Liberia in 1926 and was buried at sea.

making railroad records public and prices equal, stable, and reasonable. He said a national board should be established "to hear the complaints of citizens and railroads, with power to take testimony, to investigate abuses, to publish the results, and to call upon the legal officers of the government to prosecute."[80] Lloyd represented populism and sensationalism at their most constructive levels.

QUESTIONS FOR DISCUSSION AND RESEARCH

1. What's the definition of a populist? What gave rise to the term in U.S. history?
2. Which is more of a populist medium: radio, television, films, magazines, newspapers? Why?
3. Identify populist strands and catchwords on editorial pages of three different newspapers.
4. What did the rural and big city populists have in common, and not in common?
5. Report on an evening of television programs—news broadcasts, sitcoms. Identify populist themes and chords. Also identify the elitist, favor-the-rich elements.
6. What other catchwords besides *populist* do the media use regularly for themes of articles around election time?
7. How can labeling a candidate *populist* help or hurt her or him?
8. Who were several of the "populist" presidents in a general sense? What role did the press play in creating a people-candidate image?
9. *Fourth estate* is usually thought of as a term for the press as an adversary of government. How might the role of fourth estate be broadened in concept in light of this chapter?
10. Does editor Herbert's platform in the *Grange Advance* apply to populists today? Are today's populists different? Why, or why not?
11. Why do grassroots movements that bid for and rise to power change and proliferate? What role do the media have to play in the diversification and disassembling of such movements?
12. There are newspapers in the world that have *people* or a derivation of *populus* in their titles. For instance, *Il Popolo*, a Christian Democrat paper in Rome, and the socialist paper, *Le Populaire*, in Paris. Is the *People's Paper* or *The Populist* a good name for a newspaper? Why, or why not?

ENDNOTES

1. D. Sven Nordin, *Rich Harvest: A History of the Grange, 1867–1900* (Jackson: University of Mississippi, 1974), pp. 1, 2.
2. *St. Louis Globe-Democrat*, Aug. 28, 1880.

3. Cited in Scott G. McNall, *The Road to Rebellion: Class Formation and Kansas Populism, 1865–1900* (Chicago: University of Chicago Press, 1988), p. 4.

4. Thomas Clark Atkeson, *Outlines of Grange History* (Washington, D.C.: National Farm News, 1928), pp. 17, 18.

5. *Grange Advance*, vol. 1, no. 1, Oct. 15, 1873.

6. Ibid.

7. "Populist" comes from the Latin word for "people," *populus*.

8. George McKenna, *American Populism* (New York: Putnam, 1974), p. xiv.

9. E. L. Godkin, publisher, "The Latest Device for Fixing Rates of Transportation," *The Nation*, vol. 17, no. 420, July 17, 1873, p. 36.

10. Nordin, *Rich Harvest*, p. 171.

11. John D. Hicks, *The Populist Revolt: A History of the Farmers' Alliance and the People's Party* (Minneapolis: University of Minnesota Press, 1931; reprint, University of Nebraska Press, 1961), p. 33.

12. Ibid., pp. 98–100.

13. Robert C. McMath, Jr., *American Populism: A Social History, 1877–1898* (New York: Hill and Wang, 1993), p. 15.

14. Lawrence Goodwyn, *Democratic Promise: The Populist Moment in America* (New York: Oxford University Press, 1976), quoted in McMath, *American Populism*, p. 15.

15. McMath, *American Populism*, p. 153.

16. *Emporia Gazette*, April 21, 1894.

17. Robert C. McMath, Jr., "Populist Base Communities: The Evangelical Roots of Farm Protest in Texas," *Locus*, vol. 1, no. 1, 1988, p. 55.

18. Keith Lynn King, "Religious Dimensions of the Agrarian Protest in Texas, 1870–1908," Ph.D. dissertation, Graduate College of the University of Illinois at Urbana-Champaign, 1985, p. 114.

19. Marilyn Dell Brady, "Populism and Feminism in a Newspaper by and for Women of the Kansas Farmers' Alliance, 1891–1894," *Kansas History*, vol. 7, no. 4, Winter 1984/1985, pp. 280–283.

20. "A Solid Front," *Springer* (N.M.) *Banner*, June 11, 1891.

21. Stanley B. Parsons, *The Populist Context: Rural Versus Urban Power on a Great Plains Frontier* (Westport, Conn.: Greenwood, 1973), p. 101.

22. McMath, *American Populism*, p. 121.

23. *Sioux City Journal*, Nov. 23, 25, 1895.

24. Michael Kazin, *The Populist Persuasion: An American History* (New York: Basic Books, 1994).

25. Robin Toner, "Arkansas Chief Seeks to Lead Democrats to Middle Ground," *New York Times*, Aug. 14, 1991, p. 1.

26. Hicks, *The Populist Revolt*, p. 291.

27. James Ridgeway, "Populist Party of the People," *Village Voice*, Oct. 29, 1985.

28. Flier filed in the "populist" clipping collection of the Kenneth Spencer Research Library, University of Kansas, Lawrence, Kansas.

29. Art Seidenbaum, "A Dose of Dr. Spock," *Los Angeles Times*, reprinted in *Grass Roots*, May 19, 1972, Kenneth Spencer Research Library collection, University of Kansas.

30. Flier, Kenneth Spencer Research Library collection, University of Kansas.

31. Editorial, *Kansas City Star*, July 25, 1982.

32. "Election Outside of Kansas," *Kansas Farmer*, Nov. 12, 1890.

33. "Our New Congressmen," ibid.

34. O. Gene Clanton, *Kansas Populism: Ideas and Men* (Lawrence: University Press of Kansas, 1969), p. 235.

35. Ibid., p. 75.

36. Ibid., quoting the unabridged William Allen White, *Autobiography* (New York: Macmillan, 1946), pp. 218, 219. The second edition, revised and abridged (Lawrence: University Press of Kansas, 1990), excises the unkind material about Mrs. Lease.
37. Ibid., p. 265.
38. Ibid., p. 78.
39. *Kansas State Ledger*, Aug. 5, 1892, quoting a column from the *Kansas City Journal*.
40. *Iowa State Reporter*, Waterloo, April 2, 1873.
41. *Leavenworth (Kansas) Daily Times*, "City News," July 20, 1977.
42. Hicks, *The Populist Revolt*, p. 131.
43. McMath, *American Populism*, p. 150
44. "The Way Out," *Kansas Farmer*, Dec. 18, 1889–Feb. 12, 1890.
45. McMath, *American Populism*.
46. "Crime, Death and Tenements," *People's Party Paper*, Atlanta, Dec. 1, 1893.
47. Margaret Canovan, *Populism* (New York: Harcourt Brace Jovanovich, 1981), pp. 24, 25.
48. Donald A. Ritchie, "1896," in Arthur M. Schlesinger, Jr., ed., *Running for President: The Candidates and Their Images*, vol. 1 (New York: Simon & Schuster, 1994), p. 428.
49. *Kansas Farmer*, Dec. 10, 1890.
50. William F. Holmes, "Ellen Dortch and the Farmers' Alliance," *Georgia Historical Quarterly*, vol. 69, no. 2, Summer 1985, p. 158.
51. *Carnesville (Ga.) Tribune*, Sept. 30, 1891, in Holmes, "Ellen Dortch."
52. Holmes, "Ellen Dortch," p. 161.
53. *Carnesville Tribune*, Sept. 30, 1891, in Holmes, "Ellen Dortch," p. 162.
54. Holmes, "Ellen Dortch," p. 172.
55. *New Orleans Times-Democrat*, Feb. 21, 1885.
56. Resolutions committee report, on "Censorship," from the manuscript, 1938.
57. NEA "Resolutions," 1951.
58. Resolutions committee report, no title, from the manuscript, 1958.
59. *Morgan County Herald*, Nov. 4, 1912.
60. Clayton Rand, *Ink on My Hands* (Gulfport, Miss.: Dixie Press, 1940), p. 316.
61. Ibid., p. 324.
62. National Editorial Association, *Proceedings*, 194, p. 13.
63. B. B. Herbert, *The First Decennium of the National Editorial Association, 1885–1895—Ten Conventions, Convention Cities and Excursions*, vol. 1 (Chicago: B. B. Herbert, 1896), p. 74.
64. Ibid., p. 84.
65. Edwin Emery, *History of the American Newspaper Publishers Association* (Minneapolis: University of Minnesota, 1950), p. 19.
66. Ibid., p. 20.
67. Sara Lockwood Williams, *A Study of the Columbia Missouri Herald from 1889 to 1908*, master's thesis, University of Missouri, 1931, p. 241.
68. Gerald J. Baldasty and Jeffrey B. Rutenbeck, "Money, Politics and Newspapers: The Business Environment of Press Partisanship in the Late 19th Century," *Journalism History*, vol. 15, nos. 2, 3, Summer/Autumn 1988, p. 66.
69. "NAA Celebrates First Day," *Editor & Publisher*, June 20, 1992, p. 17.
70. *Leavenworth (Kan.) Times*, July 20, 1877.
71. Ibid.
72. Ibid., July 21, 1877.
73. Ibid., July 23, 1877.
74. *Savannah (Ga.) Tribune*, Sept. 5, 1892.
75. Harry Demarest Lloyd, "Story of a Great Monopoly," *Atlantic Monthly*, vol. 47, March 1881, p. 322.

76. Vance Trimble, *The Astonishing Mr. Scripps: The Turbulent Life of America's Penny Press Lord* (Ames: Iowa State University Press, 1992), p. 114.

77. Jack Casserly, *Scripps: The Divided Dynasty* (New York: Donald I. Fine, 1993), p. 9.

78. Trimble, *The Astonishing Mr. Scripps*, p. 83.

79. Ibid., p. 81.

80. Lloyd, p. 333.

9

Pulitzer and Hearst: The Roar of the Crowd

Perhaps the best known of American newspaper publishers were Joseph Pulitzer and William Randolph Hearst, whose careers overlapped for a time at the turn of the century. Their legacies are still with us. Pulitzer lent his name to journalism's most prestigious award, the Pulitzer Prize, engraved on media a passion for accuracy, and prized human-interest, entertainment, and investigative values. Hearst, with a less firm grip on accuracy, underscored these other values and pursued them to the limit, often with what seemed to be unfathomable funding from family sources. Both Pulitzer and Hearst gave priority to "conversational" news, the news that one would be most apt to talk about with others. Hearst, however, also liked people to see the exclamation point in a story and say, "Gee whiz!"

Pulitzer was a pioneer in creating journalism for the masses and energizing readers to action, whether corralling schoolchildren to give their coins to help pay for a base for the Statue of Liberty or calling attention to the plight of tenement dwellers. Hearst, who admired Pulitzer and worked briefly for Pulitzer's *New York World*, had his own crusades and investigations of civic corruption. With a newspaper and publication-chain management career that spanned eight decades in two centuries, Hearst forged a link between eras of American history and corresponding periods in media history. He lived through key eras, influencing them as they influenced him.

I. THE WIDE WORLD OF JOSEPH PULITZER

Just as penny press editor James Gordon Bennett and others had done before him, Joseph Pulitzer embraced diversity. For the educated, Pulitzer offered more sophisticated coverage in politics and financial matters than other papers. For others, he captured their attention with stories of crime and scandal, features, comics, art-rendered pictures, and cartoons.

Media as Purveyors of Information/Education
CREATING MASS COMMUNICATION

Pulitzer provided more than an amalgamation of diverse readers for his *New York World*. He unified and molded his crowd of readers. Pulitzer, who had at times been in politics, was adept at crowd control. Speaking at national political conventions and out on the stump, he could hold the crowd in the palm of his hand. He treated his readers as a crowd he could shape and cajole. Pulitzer did not deal with small entities of society as such but with the masses, which he saw as having a collective mind of their own.

One researcher says Pulitzer introduced "a new variant, the decisive crowd." According to James Feast, "Certainly, Pulitzer aspired to mold his readers and thus the relation of his paper to them" and this effort "involved the presence of a director. Let us say, though, that the first step was to endow the crowd with reason."[1]

Pulitzer, the Teacher

It was time for the newspaper to be a kind of teacher. In the 1870s the average American received only a fourth-grade education. The Chautauqua movement, a type of continuing-education lecture program, had caught on. The Chautauqua meetings also provided entertainment, such as musicians and humorists. The enrichment formula was one that would work with newspapers.

Pulitzer's daily, the *World*, a kind of correspondence school, "would serve the masses by helping them to read and understand the news through an understanding of politics, psychology, and economics." Feast believes, "Such ideas nourished the first truly mass media. Pulitzer's perception of what was to be done entailed a new depiction of the crowd. . . . This crowd had horse sense. It was not ready to be governed but to be taught."[2]

Pulitzer would offer one lesson a day in his mass classroom. He wrote:

> What is the one distinctive feature, fight, crusade, public service or big exclusive? No paper can be great, in my opinion, if it depends simply upon the hand-to-mouth idea, news coming in anyhow. One big distinctive feature every day at least. One striking feature each issue should contain, prepared before, not left to chance.[3]

Frank Luther Mott saw the Pulitzer approach to news as a "new journalism" (the term is not to be confused with the so-called "new journalism" of the 1960s and 1970s that embraced a subjective literary style in journalism). Mott says Pulitzer's formula for a new journalism had six points, none of which is entirely unique with Pulitzer, but in concert they helped forge a new dynamism to move ahead in competitive journalism. Pulitzer's *World* offered (1) a news policy that had reporters combing the city "for incidents, events, and situations which could be made inter-esting" and "presented as colorfully as possible"; (2) crusades and stunts—crusades such as the fund drive for the Statue of Liberty pedestal and his many efforts at reform—stunts, ranging from trying to rescue a white girl allegedly taken by Indians (the girl turned out to be an Indian girl) and the sending of a reporter around the world in a race against time (as we shall see); (3) an editorial page of "high charac-ter," with editorials that would elucidate and back a crusade or cause put forth else-where in the paper; (4) a big paper, the only two-cent eight-page paper, the *World* liked to remind readers, later going to sixteen pages without changing price; (5) illustrations, with portraits of people in the news, display art for ads, diagrams of crime scenes, and eventually cartoons; and (6) vigorous self-promotion, rashly offering coupons and contests as the paper sang praises to itself.[4] Pulitzer aimed to entertain, interest all people, make money, shape lives, and uniquely mold minds and destinies.

The Early Pulitzer

Joseph Pulitzer was born in Mako, Hungary, about 130 miles southeast of Budapest on April 10, 1847. His mother, Louise, a Roman Catholic, was Austro-German; his father, of Jewish background, was Hungarian. Pulitzer's father, Fulop (Philip) Politzer, a grain merchant, became the most prominent businessman in Mako.[5] Joseph was the oldest of the four Pulitzer children. Second was Louis; third, Albert; and fourth, a sister, Irma. Both Louis and Irma died young. The careers of Joseph and Albert overlapped, both going to the United States and both ending up as reporters, then editors, of major newspapers in New York City.

When Pulitzer's father died the family moved to Budapest. There his mother re-married, and Joseph decided he wanted to get away from home. He set his sights on becoming an officer in the Austrian army, but the seventeen-year-old, with a weak body and poor eyesight, did not make much of an impression. Rejected, he set out to join the romanticized French Foreign Legion, hoping for service in Mexico. These officers too felt he was physically unfit for service. However, freelance recruiters for the Union Army during the American Civil War found him, and the awkward, stumbling, red-haired Pulitzer signed up.

Arriving in the port of Boston, he learned that the recruiting agents were going to collect a fee for delivery of each recruit. The independent Pulitzer dived overboard under the protection of night and swam to shore, where he collected the bounty himself. Saying he was eighteen instead of seventeen to meet the legal requirements, he joined a Union cavalry unit made up largely of German recruits. The regiment had been organized by Carl Schurz, whom Pulitzer met again later in St. Louis.

The Brunt of Jokes

In the cavalry the awkward and homely young German-speaking teenager became the brunt of jokes and hazing. Pulitzer was immensely unhappy with his career. His temper flared. He punched a noncommissioned officer who picked on him, an offense for which he could have been court-martialed. However, a captain who enjoyed playing chess with Pulitzer intervened, and the young immigrant was spared.

After the war the eighteen-year-old Pulitzer looked for work in New York. Always conscious of his appearance, he tried to keep his shoes shined. Once when he went in for a shine at French's Hotel he was asked to leave. He was told guests did not like to have ex-soldiers loitering around. Pulitzer was later in life to buy the hotel.

Everywhere he turned—including applying for a job on a whaler—he was rejected. He set out across the country. Hitching rides on freight cars, he arrived in East St. Louis, on the Illinois bank of the Mississippi. He shoveled coal aboard a ferry to pay his way across the river to St. Louis.

Mule Driver, Gravedigger

He found an advertisement in a St. Louis German paper, *Westliche Post*, for a caretaker of mules. He got the job, but finding the stubborn animals too much to handle and the food inedible, he quit in two days. He went through a series of short-lived jobs, from construction work to waiting on tables at a posh restaurant—a job that ended when he dropped a steak on a diner's head. Once he headed for what he thought was a top-paying job on a Louisiana plantation. He paid $5 to a fast-talking promoter and boarded a steamboat headed south. However, the boat let Pulitzer and the other plantation recruits off 30 miles downstream and took off without them. The men walked the 30 miles back to St. Louis. Pulitzer was so incensed he wrote an article for the *Westliche Post*. This is believed to be his first published article.[6]

Thirsting for knowledge, he hung around the local library and law offices. Some of the lawyers, among them William Patrick, took a liking to him and gave him work serving papers and running errands. During the cholera plague of 1866 he worked as warden of Arsenal Island, where unburied corpses were stacked. He kept the records—some 3,500 persons from St. Louis died—and he personally helped with the burials.

At the library he joined in chess games with Carl Schurz and Emil Preetorius, owners and editors of the leading German daily, the *Westliche Post*. The position of a reporter opened up, and Pulitzer got the job. But it was not to be smooth sailing. "His eagerness in the search of news, his imperfect English, and his gaunt figure topped by a bulbous head with its small pointed chin, tufted with a few strands of red," says Seitz, "made him a figure to be laughed at by his rivals on the local press other than German."[7] Sometimes other reporters supplied him with false information, causing the ever eager Pulitzer to set off to find the story. But the pranksters ceased to laugh, as even on a wild goose chase Pulitzer always seemed to find a real story of significance before he returned.

Soon after Joseph Pulitzer joined the *Westliche Post* he became the paper's legislative correspondent at the state capital, Jefferson City, Missouri. In the 1869 session he found himself doubling as a reporter and serving on the side as secretary of the senate committee on banks and banking. To his surprise, when a special Republican convention was held to decide on a candidate to take the seat of a legislator who had resigned, Pulitzer was nominated. He was endorsed by the Republican organ, the *Missouri Democrat*, and was elected to represent a St. Louis district. Actually his candidacy should have been declared void because at age twenty-three he was a year short of the minimum age of twenty-four. He continued to be a *Westliche Post* reporter while he served in the Missouri house.

Pulitzer Shoots a Critic

Pulitzer fought for court reforms, favoring elections instead of appointments to the bench. He attacked those who received favoritism from the courts. One such man was Captain Edward Augustine.

Augustine ran into Pulitzer at a hotel office and called the tense young reporter a liar for his articles on court reform. Pulitzer demanded a retraction from the captain. The thin, frail Pulitzer was not about to swing at the chunky captain, who was built like a modern professional football lineman. Yet Pulitzer could not control his anger. He rushed back to his rooming house, took a pistol from a drawer, and returned to the hotel. Encountering Augustine, Pulitzer called him a liar. The big Augustine retorted that Pulitzer was just a "puppy."[8] Pulitzer drew his pistol and fired twice, hitting Augustine in the knee. The big man threw himself at Pulitzer and wrestled him to the floor. Pulitzer paid a $5 fine in police court for disturbing the peace. He was indicted on a charge of assault with intent to kill, and was fined only $100, plus $300 in court costs.[9]

Pulitzer in Politics

Pulitzer launched headlong into national politics after his boss, editor Schurz, was elected by the state legislature in 1869 to the U.S. Senate. A Republican, Schurz decided to join the new Liberal Republican movement created in reaction to the corruption in the administration of President Ulysses Grant. Pulitzer was tapped by Schurz to be his chief lieutenant in the 1870 election that swept Liberal Republican B. Gratz Brown in as Missouri governor. Brown appointed Pulitzer as one of the three members of the St. Louis police board. Here Pulitzer's personality dominated as he waged war against gamblers and vice establishments.[10]

Pulitzer was elected by a Jefferson City convention to be a delegate to the national convention of Liberal Republicans in Cincinnati in 1872. With Pulitzer as secretary of the convention, the Liberal Republicans chose Horace Greeley as their nominee for president and Brown as their candidate for vice president. Brown went down with Greeley in ignominious defeat that year. Schurz stayed on in Republican circles and was named secretary of the interior by President Rutherford B. Hayes in 1876. But Pulitzer had had enough of Republican politics and became a Democrat. He made speeches against Grant, and when the Democrats carried Missouri in 1874 he was elected a member of the Missouri constitutional convention that met in 1875. In 1876 he stumped the state for the Democratic presidential nominee, Samuel Tilden. Pulitzer was so popular that the Tilden camp enlisted him for speeches in Indiana, Michigan, and New York.

In 1876 he went to New York to try to talk Charles Dana of the *Sun* into issuing a German edition of the paper. Instead Pulitzer signed on as special correspondent for the *Sun* in Washington. He filed stories on the electoral controversy involving three southern states and the eventual decision of Congress to rule that Hayes was elected over Tilden.

Pulitzer practiced law briefly in Washington and was admitted to the bar of the District of Columbia. He married a young Washington woman, Kate Davis, and they honeymooned in Europe. Pulitzer used the occasion to write a number of stories on Europe for the *Sun*. In one of the bylined reports he dealt forthrightly with fears of German militarization and attacked poverty and oppression in Germany. "One thing is certain—there can be no remedy except revolution," he said. "Prosperity and liberty go together. The very spirit of this age forbids a prosperous despotism."[11]

Returning from Europe, Pulitzer looked for a newspaper to buy. He found a bargain on December 9, 1878, in St. Louis at the public auction of the bankrupt *St. Louis Dispatch*. For $2,500 Pulitzer picked up a paper that had a much-desired Western Associated Press franchise. When he bought the *Dispatch*, Pulitzer had an eye on the eleven-month-old *St. Louis Post* published by John A. Dillon. The two papers were merged, forming the *Post and Dispatch* (later changed to *Post-Dispatch*). Pulitzer shared the helm with Dillon as coproprietor.

Was the Young Candidate Corrupt?

Even as he developed his own news formula of entertainment, education, sensationalism, and political action and reform, the excitable Pulitzer kept his hands in politics. Pulitzer, apparently paying money up front to St. Louis Democratic machine boss Ed Butler, was assured, so he thought, of the nomination for Congress on the Democratic ticket. The actual nominee was to be selected at a primary election. Laughed the *St. Louis Globe Democrat*: "Motto for Democratic conventions—'You pay your money, and sometimes you don't get your nomination.' "[12] Pulitzer apparently was so unpopular, and the reaction against him—seen as a hothead immigrant and lackey of the corrupt Butler—was so great, that even Ed Butler dumped his protégé at the last minute to support a new candidate, Thomas Allen. The independent Democrat organ, the *Missouri Republican*, warned that if Pulitzer were the party's prime nominee "the likelihood is all will go down together" with him.[13] The *Republican* said this of Pulitzer:

> Mr. Pulitzer at all times came to the front as the apologist for, and defender of all the work of this organization [the "Dark Lantern," Butler's machine], from the levy of heavy assessments upon the friends of candidates for judicial and other positions to the stuffing of ballot-boxes. He had even declared the parties charged

and proved to have been guilty of these practices, to be honorable gentlemen and good citizens.[14]

The *Republican* attacked Butler and Pulitzer in another editorial, "A Corrupt Bargain," in which Pulitzer was accused of a mudslinging campaign: "The violence and bitter malignity of the *Post-Dispatch's* attacks on Mr. Thomas Allen are wholly without a parallel in the history of politics."[15] The only way to stop the conspiracy of the Dark Lantern, the paper said, "is to bury Pulitzer out of sight at the Democratic primary election today."[16]

Much of the righteous indignation of the *Repubican* can no doubt be attributed to the bias of a competitor of Pulitzer. But nevertheless Pulitzer was overwhelmed in the primary. Allen went on to win the election, as did Democrats in the first and third districts as well. In the primary Allen had more than 4,000 votes to 700 for Pulitzer, and in one ward Pulitzer did not get a single vote. The *St. Louis Republic* (formerly the *Republican*) in a 1910 election recalled the alleged scandal of 1880 in which Butler supposedly received $6,000 from Pulitzer to "buy" a key place on the Democratic ticket. It called on Pulitzer and Butler, who were both still living in 1910, to speak out about the "veracity" of this episode in history,[17] but there appears to be no record of a response.

When Joseph Pulitzer took over the *St. Louis Post* to merge it with the *Dispatch*, he promised former *Post* readers that he would not let them down.[18] Not only were *Post* readers used to having two editions a day with the latest news right up to press time, but they also had been promised before the Pulitzer takeover that "theatrical, musical and literary items will receive proper recognition, and the departments of fashion and society will be in the hands of competent specialists."[19] Pulitzer included the entertainment aspect along with ideas he had for service and reform in the community. Eventually he had a racing column and a miscellaneous "amusements" column, flanked by ads promoting trotting clubs and races, places to eat, and carriage rentals for the fair.[20]

THE BROTHERS PULITZER

Meanwhile younger brother Albert, impressed by how Joseph got his feet on firm ground in the new world, decided to come to the United States and also settled in St. Louis. Albert was a bright young man who liked to write plays, his first being completed at age thirteen. In St. Louis, through Joseph's contacts, Albert took a job teaching German at a local high school. The two brothers were as different in their personalities as they were in their appearances. Unlike the gaunt, serious Joseph, Albert was "plump, cheery, an enormous eater who often topped off a heavy lunch with a whole apple pie and then sent out for sandwiches and wine in the afternoon."[21] The two brothers in St. Louis quarreled over Albert's passion for great quantities of ice cream. Joseph "loved luxury but detested all forms of gluttony."[22] After a year, Albert was in Leavenworth, Kansas, teaching German to a high school class of young women.[23]

Brother Albert (right) beat brother Joseph to the New York scene by launching the New York Journal. *(St. Louis Post-Dispatch)*

In 1870 Albert became a reporter for the Illinois *Staats-Zeitung* in Chicago. He covered music and drama and served as telegraph editor and as city editor.[24] Moving to New York during the next year, Albert worked briefly at Charles Dana's *New York Sun* before going over to the *New York Herald* as a Washington correspondent. He became internationally known as a reporter covering the Russo-Turkish war, and European newspapers reprinted his interviews with leading personalities.[25] Back in New York, Albert, with help from earnings from a corporation he had founded, scraped together $25,000 to start the *New York Morning Journal* in 1882. Albert sought to borrow something of the St. Louis entertainment formula. His *Journal* was notably without a social or serious conscience, yet it did not suffer in the entertainment category. Albert printed gossip unsparingly along with the latest in theater and sporting news. Perhaps Albert saw himself appealing also to the tradition of readers of Ben Day's and now Charles Dana's *Sun*, as the *Sun* used news with humor and mirth. Albert's formula, which proved an immediate success, was, he said, as follows: "The Morning Journal will appeal to those who love to look at this world from its humorous side, to laugh rather than to weep, to enjoy the quaint sayings and doings of the hour, the jests of the passing moment,—all that variety of personality and fun that floats, as it were, on the crest wave of New York life."[26]

Nothing in the society whirl was overlooked in Albert's paper. "The *Morning Journal* was hell-bent for society news, and would get it if it had to make it," says Henry Kellett Chambers in his memoir of Joseph Pulitzer. Thus Albert's *Journal* gave about five times as much space as others to the preparations for socialite Anne Gould's marriage to Count Boni de Castellane. For weeks before the wedding, its star reporter watched the shop windows and pounded out two or three columns daily about the underwear and other garments that he thought Miss Gould might be buying for her trousseau. "And the paper's 'art department' illustrated his clairvoyant flights with sketches of chemises, stockings, and ball gowns. It became a marvel of research and endurance."[27]

Sibling Rivalry

But Albert was soon to have company in the competitive journalism field in New York in his brother Joseph, four years his senior. Financier Jay Gould was casting about for a person—or a sucker, as Seitz puts it[28]—to buy Gould's lagging *New York World*. Joseph came calling and eventually struck a deal with Gould to buy the *World* at $346,000, a price which Seitz says was greatly inflated. The night before the contracts were drawn up, Joseph visited Albert, who argued that two Pulitzers cannot occupy the same space and succeed. But the older brother was determined to proceed.

Tale of Two Cities

Joseph Pulitzer ran two newspapers from New York, the *New York World* and the *St. Louis Post-Dispatch*. Each week he received long letters from a handful of trusted St. Louis editors and friends. Principal among them were John Dillon, co-owner with Pulitzer of the *Post-Dispatch*, who sold his interest to Pulitzer only to be named the paper's editor in 1882 before Pulitzer took off for New York; Henry W. Moore, managing editor; Ignaz Kappner, business manager; and his close lawyer friend, Charles Gibson.

The letter writers, each different in tone, kept him informed of the ups and downs of the editorial and business sides of the *Post-Dispatch*. Dillon, reaffirming his loyalty by following every bidding of Pulitzer, could be chatty—"Spick, poor fellow, had a paralytic attack last night and is not expected to live. The last new reporter is Miss Downs [handwriting not clear here] who broke a window to get into jail."[29] One very short letter started, "Mr. Moore's message to the effect that you did not wish to be bothered with details from this office leave me little or nothing to report."[30]

Editor Kills Lawyer

Dillon differed with Pulitzer on the aftermath of a tragic incident in St. Louis involving the *Post-Dispatch*'s managing editor, Colonel John A. Cockerill. The

Beginnings of Journalism Education

Joseph Pulitzer was a firm believer in journalism education. In 1904 he offered to help start a school of journalism at Columbia University and pledged $2 million. He gave the first million at once but put off the second installment until the actual agreement was firmed. Disagreements over the membership of an advisory board of professionals and academics (the Columbia president did not want a Harvard or Cornell member on the board) and other matters held up the opening of the school for years. The second million became available upon Pulitzer's death in 1911, and in July 1912 Mrs. Pulitzer laid the cornerstone for Columbia's new school of journalism at 116th Street and Broadway in New York City.

The idea of education for journalism had been talked about as far back as 1799, when John Ward Fenno, son of the founder of the *Gazette of the United States*, called for some training and standards, "requiring some qualifications and pledges from men on whom the nation depends for all the information . . . it receives."[31]

After the Civil War, defeated Confederate General Robert E. Lee became interested in the training of future journalists to contribute to the renewal of the South. At Washington College (later renamed Washington and Lee University) in Lexington, Virginia, where he became president, Lee encouraged his students to become editors. Five future journalists were given scholarships in 1870. Lee died in that year, and the program of scholarships was last offered in the school's catalog in 1878. Many editors opposed the program, as they themselves had come up the hard way, laboring for years in print shops before becoming editors. They did not want half-prepared, ready-made young editors.[32]

In 1869 Norman J. Colman, a Missouri editor who became the first secretary of agriculture, called for a course of study to prepare young men for newspaper work. Possibly the first course in journalism, "The History of Journalism," was given by professor David McAnnaly, Jr., in 1877 at the University of Missouri.

In 1896 the Missouri Press Association appointed a nine-editor committee to map out a journalism course of study. In 1908 the University of Missouri opened the first school of journalism in the nation. First dean of the school was Walter Williams, member of the board of curators of the University of Missouri. Williams, who had only a high school education, had been editor of the *Herald* in Columbia, Missouri, and had served as one of the youngest presidents of the National Editorial Association (later renamed National Newspaper Association).

Essential to the new school, he told NEA delegates in convention in St. Paul, Minnesota, in 1908, would be a hands-on approach. "The distinctive feature of the university's school of journalism," he said, "aside from its recognition of journalism as a profession, is this employment of the laboratory plan. There will be issued each school day a newspaper—not a college publication, but a general newspaper, small but well balanced, upon which the work—other than the mechanical—will be done by the students under the supervision, direction and instruction of the instructors."[33] Williams was a successful short-story writer, and among his many interests was religion—he wrote sermons and taught the largest Bible class (Presbyterian) in the nation. Despite his limited education, he went on to become president of the University of Missouri, a feat that would not be likely today.

hot-tempered Cockerill had criticized a lawyer who was a candidate for Congress. One of the candidate's law partners, A. W. Slayback, charged into the *Post-Dispatch* offices and screamed at Cockerill. The managing editor pulled a gun from his desk and shot Slayback dead. The incident (Cockerill was not convicted) caused quite a furor in St. Louis, and the *Post-Dispatch* suffered a considerable setback in community support. When Pulitzer threw the *Post-Dispatch*'s endorsement behind a candidate whom Dillon regarded as a scoundrel, John Glover, who had been a rival of Slayback's law partner, Dillon objected and warned about further defection of readers.[34]

Charities and a Special Friend

Moore wrote to complain of colleagues and nepotism (Gibson trying to get a job for his son on the staff), to thank Pulitzer for the Christmas turkeys, and at least once to borrow money, to which Pulitzer agreed. Kappner was all business, with financial reports and budgets detailed. Gibson often led off his letters with reports on a special friend, Mrs. Patrick. Her husband, William, who had earlier befriended the young Pulitzer, was now confined to a mental institution.

These letters illustrate Pulitzer's charitable nature, if not a special fondness for a woman friend. Wrote Gibson in 1883: "Mrs. Patrick finally decided not to accept the check and return it. I stated to her . . . that I had not at any time known a more generous offer and that I knew it was proffered as an act of friendship only. She appreciated all this—said she knew you well—and what a good friend you were—and was very grateful—but I think she feels her situation and fears its acceptance might be misconstrued by others altho she did not say so in words. She is living at her father's comfortably. . . . Poor Patrick is, I fear, clean gone. Mrs. Patrick goes to the asylum everyday, but is only allowed to see him at a distance unknown to him."[35] At the start of 1885 Gibson wrote: "I delivered your message about educating one of her sons—She broke down during the conversation—She is really and deeply grateful for your goodness."[36] Pulitzer, in fact, educated two of her sons.[37]

Kappner, also keeping Pulitzer informed on Mrs. Patrick, wrote in September: "She inquired about you and the family's health and wished to be kindly remembered. On leaving I handed her the envelop as desired and she, guessing its meaning, wished me to express her thanks."[38]

Suddenly Darkness

Concern developed over Pulitzer's health. Problems in his mental state and physical health, not the least of which was deteriorating eyesight, increased. "The patient was troubled with asthma, weak lungs, a protesting stomach, insomnia, exhaustion and fits of depression" in 1888, notes Swanberg. On top of all this he was suffering from a "serious, if undiagnosed, psychosis. . . . there seems no doubt that Pulitzer was what would now be called a manic-depressive."[39]

While traveling around the world, hoping to regain his health and peace of mind and most of all to heal his troubled eyes, Pulitzer stopped off in Constantinople. Standing at the rail of the ship as it was about to leave, Pulitzer turned to an aide and noted, "How suddenly it has gotten dark." The aide said it was still daylight. "Well, it's dark to me," Pulitzer said, and dark it would be the rest of his life as he lived in near total blindness.[40]

Joseph Pulitzer kept an active hand in the affairs of the *World*, often communicating from his yacht in a distant port. In 1907 he officially retired at age sixty.

Albert's Suicide

Albert's death came in October 1909, two years before Joseph's. Hypersensitive to the slightest changes in temperature and light, and suffering from incurable neurasthenia, "passing restless nights which caused despondency,"[41] Albert was living as a virtual recluse in Vienna. He sought to buy lethal prussic acid from a pharmacist, but the druggist was suspicious of Albert's intent and gave him a harmless almond extract instead.[42] Indeed Albert was trying to kill himself, and he swallowed the harmless contents of the vial. When the extract did not do the job, he pulled out a pistol and shot himself. The *New York Times* obituary read: "Mr. Pulitzer was found on the floor. A revolver in his right hand, and a wound in the right temple removed all doubt as to the cause of his death. Also, it seems, he had taken a dose of poison, as a partly emptied bottle was found near him."[43]

Joseph, in Europe at the time of Albert's death, was ill and unable to travel, but he did arrange burial in a Jewish cemetery in Vienna and sent an aide to the sparsely attended funeral. Albert's son Walter became a journalist, and even wrote for the *World*, but was generally ignored by Joseph Pulitzer and his family. Perhaps not intending it so, Joseph was estranged from Albert at death as in life.

Media as Vehicles of Sensationalism/Entertainment
A SPICY FORMULA: TELLING IT LIKE IT IS

There had been indications of Pulitzer's bent toward sensationalism from the outset of his career at the *Westliche Post*. After he took charge of the paper, sordid tales appeared with greater frequency. A new column, "In the Courtroom," appeared, "reporting trials of milkmen who watered down their wares, of men accused of murder, and of girls found guilty of theft. Fires, burglaries, white slavery, assaults, mysterious murders, embezzlings, inheritance feuds—these became the main diet for *Westliche Post* readers."[44]

Pulitzer brought the sensationalism formula to the *Post-Dispatch*. Swanberg says: "The *Post-Dispatch* developed an inordinate interest in the sins of the respectable and prosperous, with spicy headlines: 'AN ADULTEROUS PAIR,' 'DUPED AND DESERTED,' 'KISSING IN CHURCH,' 'LOVED THE COOK,' 'A WILY WIDOW.' " Swanberg called it "sensational creativity . . . the ability to find human drama in events overlooked by others."[45]

On May 10, 1883, the day before Pulitzer took over from Jay Gould as owner of the *World*, the front page contained dull and trivial articles on new commissioners and dog show prizes. In contrast, Pulitzer's first issue of the *World* the next day, May 11, led off with "The Deadly Lightning—Six Lives and One Million Dollars Lost—One Hundred Thousand Barrels of Oil Ignited by an Explosion"; also a pending execution: "Cornetti's Last Night—Shaking His Cell-Door and Demanding Release—He Refuses to Listen to Priest or Minister—The Death Warrant Hand[ed] to Him"; a Wall Street tycoon mortgaging his estate; "Ward McConkey Hanged—Shouting from Under the Black Cap That His Executioners Are Murderers"; "Dynamite in Hayti—The Rebels Use It to Kill and Wound 400 People." Such were the headlines at the top of the "new" *World* under Pulitzer. Pulitzer kept up the "gee whiz" if not prurient pace. The next day his front page offered two full columns of congratulations: "A Flattering Welcome—How 'the World's' New Departure Was Received—Interviews With Prominent Politicians and Journalists and What They Think of the Pleasant Surprise." Other featured front-page stories ranged from "10,000 Damages Wanted—Mr. Flaherty Not Satisfied With a Divorce" to "Screaming for Mercy—How the Craven Cornetti Mounted the Scaffold—Gagged and Pinioned by the Guards and Dragged Resisting to a Prayerless Doom."

Pulitzer began to react to critics of his brand of sensationalism, but generally stuck by his guns. A year later, bristling before his critics, Pulitzer thought it was important to note, "The World certainly does not seek to make a specialty of crime." He nevertheless defended his choice of topics, noting that there was much evil in the world to reflect.[46]

He had also responded: "The complaint of the 'low moral tone of the press' is common but very unjust. A newspaper relates the events of the day. It does not manufacture its record of corruptions and crimes, but tells of them as they occur. If it failed to do so it would be an unfaithful chronicler. . . . Let those who are startled by it blame the people who are before the mirror, and not the mirror, which only reflects their features and actions."[47]

Enter "The Yellow Kid"

Using art, Pulitzer could produce a fun story or campaign sensationally for social justice. In the Sunday edition that he developed he was able to use more feature material, including comics. Artist Richard F. Outcault created a comic panel, called "Hogan's Alley," that was about life in tenement slums. A vigorous bald toothless kid in a yellow "nightshirt" was the main character.

One person who wrote a book about the "kid" suggests that the gown was yellow because the pressroom supervisor, Charles W. Saalburgh, had difficulty finding a nonsmear yellow ink and was testing his latest formula. As to why Outcault made the kid bald, the researcher says, he gave the character "vaguely Asian features, no doubt intending to lampoon the yellow peril hysteria that had erupted the previous year in the wake of the Sino-Japanese war." People "loved the Kid for the manic gleam in his eye and the sense that wherever he appeared, mayhem could be expected to erupt at any moment."[48]

The Yellow Kid became so popular that the new journalism, encompassing entertainment and sensationalism, became known as "yellow journalism."

"The Yellow Kid" orginally was one big frame drawing with a lot going on; then it evolved into a panel format, anticipating the arrival of the comic strip. "The Yellow Kid" also appeared in ads, such as cigar ads in which the brat would be puffing away.

Around the World in Seventy-two Days

One of Pulitzer's great entertainment features was the sending of the feisty young reform-minded journalist Elizabeth Cochrane, pen-named Nellie Bly, on a jaunt around the world. She was to try to beat the time of Jules Verne's fictitious Phileas Fogg who went around the world in eighty days. Nellie did it in seventy-two days, six hours, eleven minutes.

What is little known, and was unknown to Bly on most of her trip, was that she was being pursued in time by another woman journalist, Elizabeth Bisland, representing *Cosmopolitan* magazine. Bly headed for Europe; Bisland headed for the Orient. The year was 1889, and the race would go into January 1890.

The female journalists told of the missed boats, the terror of the storms at sea, the men they met, and tourist-like views of sites and scenes in the countries visited.[49]

Nellie Bly yearned for the assignment from the *World* and traveled light. Bisland did not want to go and dragged a trunk of clothes with her. While Bly's trip was front-page news across the country, Bisland was largely ignored in the media. Bisland filed monthly for a magazine and Bly for a daily newspaper. When Bisland ultimately made it—in seventy-six days—her arrival was only briefly noted on the inside of several newspapers.

Bly in her stories seems to have been more interested in the cultures and countries she visited, even in digging out some hard news; Bisland seems to have been more interested in the men and offered more than one description of the good looks and solid bodies of the men she met.

Bisland supported the U.S. bias against Oriental immigrants and argued that "the pigtails" could overrun the country. On the other hand, Bly went out of her way to meet and understand the Chinese people.

Bly's curiosity took her to the killing grounds of China, where mass torture and executions took place. She describes graphically the blood-soaked soil and is taken aback as a guide starts pulling heads out of a barrel. She describes the tortures—from the fast-growing bamboo shoot that slowly impales to covering a person with lime so that, when he at last drinks water, he perspires and activates the lime.

Pulitzer supported Bly's sensational trip with dramatic graphics. One full page of the *World* on January 26, 1890, upon her return, was a game titled "Round the World With Nellie Bly." Much like a modern "Monopoly" board game, the Nellie Bly game in the newspaper had place designations that players could land on— seventy-two in all. The readers were urged to "cut out this game" and "place it on a table or paste it to cardboard." Fine print at the bottom of the page told how to use pennies or checkers as "voyagers" and how to move them along with the throw of a die or by other devices to determine moves.

Bly proved so popular that once she reached San Francisco, ready for the last leg of the trip by train to New York, mobs awaited her. Cheering wildly, they crammed in as close to the train as possible to try to touch her.

From covering stories that mirrored life to horror stories and executions to manufacturing a fun story such as the Nellie Bly around-the-world escapade, Pulitzer knew how to stir the senses and emotions as well as the mind.

Media as Voices of Reform

"BAKED BABIES" AND "LINES OF LITTLE HEARSES"

"It is one of the axioms of journalism that a new editor always begins his career by undertaking to reform somebody or something," observed an editorial in Pulitzer and Dillon's *Post-Dispatch* in 1879, commenting on an editorial change in another newspaper.[50]

The axiom was certainly true for Pulitzer. From the beginning he wanted to reform. Not only did he espouse pursuing the shocking, sometimes unsavory story that people would talk about, but he also saw blowing the whistle on corruption and misdeeds as prime stories that would interest and educate people and indeed be talked about also.

At the outset at the *Westliche Post* he did not rely on handouts from politicians but edged his way into party caucuses and reported firsthand. At the *Westliche Post* he named lobbyists paid by the railroad barons, gas companies, and banks, and he named those who tried to bribe him.

Nellie Bly, ready to travel—far.

Exposing Gambling Dens

In 1881 the *Post-Dispatch* sent its reporters into all of the gambling houses they could find, documented the operations, and named the locations of the numerous illegal dens. "Where's the Police?" the paper wanted to know.[51] The paper also printed locations of illegal houses of prostitution.

The paper documented insurance swindles and the misrepresentation concerning benefits allegedly paid but not forthcoming. It hit hard at monopolies, among them the St. Louis Gas-Light Company, which fixed high rates and paid two other newspapers not to criticize the company.

In New York at the *World*, Pulitzer pursued some of the same issues he had in St. Louis. Together the two papers slashed at the railroad monopoly and how the lines were hedging on paying taxes and were delivering poor services and were unsafe. The headlines were punchy: "Our Railroad Cancer"[52] and "The Scurvy Railroad."[53]

Lack of ways to cope with overbearing heat waves were scored in July 1883. "How Babies Are Baked," "Lines of Little Hearses," and "Dead and Dying Infants" were *World* headlines during one summer heat wave. Articles told of parasites attacking infants in the baked tenements and described how occupants scrambled onto rooftops for gasps of fresh air.

The *World* carried stories of tenement-house squalor and deaths and asked why conditions were so pitiful across the city. It investigated the death of young Kate Sweeney, who died when a sewer flooded the tenement-house basement where she slept. The paper put the blame for clogged pipes and toilets on the city board of health. "Misery and Disease Among the East Side Dwellers—Foul Odors Which the Poor Have to Breathe," said one headline.[54]

The *World* crusaded against the use of contaminated milk. "Our Maggoty Milk Supply" told of "Poisonous Refuse From Breweries Used to Feed Cows."[55] Reporters also visited various food and bakery shops to find and record sanitary violations.

The *World* sounded out for the underdog, namely, underpaid laborers. One article told how one woman survived on 30 cents a day.[56] The *World* reporters followed workers home to report on the boxlike squalid conditions maintained on substandard wages. One story told of one girl who worked from 7:30 A.M. to 11:00 P.M. for five dollars a week and had to support her dying father. Nellie Bly checked out the horrors incognito. At a box factory, she endured substandard conditions and wages.

The "Crazy" Reporter

In 1887 Nellie Bly feigned insanity in order to be admitted to the notorious Blackwell's Island Lunatic Asylum. She practiced making grimaces and screaming wildly before she staged going berserk in a home for women. Four doctors checked her and certified that she was demented. At Blackwell's she ate spoiled food and experienced forced labor, icy baths, and the general cruelty of the staff. She had difficulty getting back out, but the intervention of the *World* got her released after ten days. Bly also posed as an unskilled worker seeking a job and exposed fraudulent employment agencies. As a "lobbyist" she was able to prove that one man was bribing New York State assemblymen, and the article resulted in his indictment. She also acted as a patient in the free city dispensaries for the poor to show how badly the poor were treated. In collusion with a friend, she made up a story of stealing some money from her friend's purse and got herself arrested, which gave her a chance to report on the inadequate and filthy conditions of the prison.

Pulitzer's *World* was a true pioneer in exposé/investigative journalism but also probably did more than any paper before or since in participatory journalism, that is, allowing on occasion reporters to work incognito to become part of a story, thus putting a finger on the pulse of social ills.

Media as Fourth Estate: Adversaries of Government
Media as Voices of Freedom

"INDEGODDAMPENDENT" EDITORIALS

Pulitzer looked far and wide to get just the right editorial writers. One of the most famous was Frank Irving Cobb, who had been an editorial writer at the *Detroit News* and the *Detroit Free Press*. Joining the *World* in 1904, Cobb stayed until his death in 1923, twelve years after Pulitzer's own death. Pulitzer appreciated Cobb's independent nature, once referring to Cobb as his "indegoddampendent" editor. They could not always agree, and once Pulitzer, miffed but perhaps as much in jest, put the unrelenting Cobb off his yacht in the middle of nowhere in the Jersey coast highlands in the middle of the night. When the skipper protested on behalf of Cobb, who no doubt would be stranded for some time, Pulitzer quipped: "I don't care how much trouble he has getting back to New York. The more trouble he has the better I'll be pleased." Several days later Cobb got a conciliatory note from Pulitzer: "What would you think of a trip to Japan during July and August at my expense?"[57]

The *World*'s editorials shaped national policies and destroyed and created politicians. In 1905 *World* reporters showed how officers of the Equitable Life Assurance Society and other insurance companies had channeled funds to their own private use. News reports and editorials resulted in resignations and legislation to regulate the insurance industry. The *World* even suggested the counsel for the investigative committee. He was Charles Evans Hughes, who would become the Republican candidate for president in 1916 and later secretary of state (under President Warren Harding) and chief justice of the Supreme Court.

One of the greatest challenges the *World* faced—which also provided Pulitzer with one of his greatest scares—came when the *World* two-fistedly took on President Theodore Roosevelt. In the ebbing days of 1908 the editorial staff of the *World* took notice when an *Indianapolis News* editorial, voicing suspicions of corruption on the part of the government in Panama Canal property negotiations, aroused the ire of the feisty President Roosevelt. The *News* under editor Delavan Smith had written:

> It has been charged that the United States bought from American citizens for $40,000,000 property that cost those citizens only $12,000,000. There is no doubt that the Government paid $40,000,000 for the property. But who got the money?[58]

Also it appeared unnecessary to pay the $40 million. A French company had had plans to build a canal in Panama but had given up. The rights were for sale through the French government. There was every possibility that a future canal could take another route, such as through Nicaragua. The French company was not in a position to barter, and the rights could be had for $12 million. A figurehead company was set up in the United States to handle the purchase. Suspicion was that much of the $40 million had been returned to a special group or syndicate set up by William Nelson Cromwell and other Americans involved in the New Panama Canal Company.

The president declared that the *Indianapolis News* had been in error and insisted that he did not know of an American syndicate set up to handle the Panama Canal transaction. A *World* editorial responded, calling Roosevelt a liar. The editorial went on to document its statements, including pointing out that Cromwell had testified before a Senate committee that there was an American syndicate that had given him authority to deal with the French canal organization.

The editorial concluded that it was incidental whether the present or future president's relatives were in on the take, as some charged:

> Whether they did or not, whether all the profits went into William Nelson Cromwell's hands, or whatever became of them, the fact that Theodore Roosevelt as President of the United States issues a public statement about such an important matter full of flagrant untruths, reeking with misstatements, challenging line by line the testimony of his associate Cromwell and the official record, makes it imperative that full publicity come at once through the authority and by the action of Congress.[59]

Roosevelt, incensed, called on the U.S. attorney for New York, Henry Stimson, to bring criminal libel action against Pulitzer. The president addressed Congress, charging Pulitzer with "blackening the good name of the American people."[60] Hearing a report on the tirade read to him, Pulitzer sat quietly at first, then rose from a couch and with clenched fist declared, "The *World* cannot be muzzled! The *World* cannot be muzzled! That's the headline," and he began to spew out words and ideas for the editorial.[61]

The editorial the next day said:

> Mr. Roosevelt is mistaken. He cannot muzzle The World.
> . . . If The World has libeled anybody we hope it will be punished, but we do not intend to be intimidated by Mr. Roosevelt's threats, or by Mr. Roosevelt's denunciation, or by Mr. Roosevelt's power. . . .
> So far as The World is concerned, its proprietor may go to jail . . . but even in jail The World will not cease to be a fearless champion of free speech, a free press and a free people.
> It cannot be muzzled.[62]

On Feb. 17, 1909, a District of Columbia grand jury indicted Pulitzer, two of his editors, and the publishing company of the *World* on five counts of criminal libel. Delavan Smith and another editor at the *Indianapolis News* were indicted on seven counts, the first such actions since the prosecutions under the Alien and Sedition Acts of 1798.

Cobb brushed the development off sardonically. He intoned:

> Mr. Roosevelt is an episode. The World is an institution. Long after Mr. Roosevelt is dead, long after Mr. Pulitzer is dead, long after all the present editors of this paper are dead, The World will still go on as a great independent newspaper, unmuzzzled, undaunted and unterrorized.[63]

A federal court hearing the case against the *Indianapolis News* dismissed it, causing Roosevelt at a later time to call the judge "a jackass and a crook."[64] When the charges against Pulitzer were aired in January, the judge quashed the indictment.

Pulitzer expressed his views on the power of the fourth estate in a signed article, "The Power of Public Opinion," in *Encyclopedia Americana* in 1904. He said that as the press does its work, "so shall the power of public opinion make for justice in Government, for purity in politics and for a higher morality in the business and social life of the nation."[65]

Media as Political Organs
PULITZER'S ROLE IN ELECTING A PRESIDENT

The fact that newspapers were largely not funded as political organs in the late nineteenth century, as they had been in the early eras, does not mean that some of them did not function as quasi-political organs. A case in point is Joseph Pulitzer and his *World*. The Democrats could not have created a more perfect tool for their cause in the 1884 presidential election than the *World*. Regarded as an independent journal, the *World* selected its causes, and when the old educator/sensationalist took hold of a cause—even a political cause—there was not much left undone.

Pulitzer, having been a Democrat since 1874, found a candidate to his liking in the person of Grover Cleveland, governor of New York. With coaxing from Pulitzer, Cleveland was challenging Republican candidate James G. Blaine, former representative and senator from Maine. "The man who would play the most powerful single part in the campaign was Joseph Pulitzer of the *World*," says Pulitzer biographer James Wyman Barrett.[66]

The Mulligan Letters

Blaine, who had been a leading newspaper editor in Maine, was largely regarded as corrupt—a reputation that cost him dearly in his bid for the Republican nomination for president in 1876 and 1880. In 1876 he was accused of having done favors when he was speaker of the House for a rail company in return for a loan of $64,000. The House had decided to investigate the charges. A bookkeeper, James Mulligan, announced that he had incriminating letters from Blaine to the railroad's president.

Pulitzer not only resurrected and trumpeted the existence of the Mulligan letters, but also came up with other embarassing letters written by Blaine. One set of letters proved that Blaine was a liar and that he had holdings in a shady investment operation. Filling almost the entire front page of the *World* on October 8, 1884, were copies of handwritten letters outlining "Blaine's Hocking Valley Investment." The letters showed that despite Blaine's denials of owning even a dollar's worth in the Hocking Valley coal lands or other Ohio mines, "the true facts of the case" show "that he was and still is a stockholder in the companies that mine coal in the

Hocking Valley where the laborers were compelled to work at starvation wages, and to-day are in need and almost dying from hunger and neglect." The letters are records of payments and receipts involved in Ohio coalfield projects. The headline across six of the seven columns of letters said of Blaine, "Twenty Years in Congress—on the Make."[67]

Mercilessly, day after day in the 1884 campaign, the *World* ran giant front-page four- to seven-column cartoons mocking Blaine, along with countless short items throughout the paper denouncing his candidacy. The cartoon for September 27 showed Blaine sinking in a boat in a storm-tossed sea, and over the clouds and lightning were the words "Popular Opinion." The next day a giant-size cartoon showed "Castle Blaine" crumbling from a force of lightning labeled "Mulligan Letters." On October 10 appeared "The Blaine Circus in Ohio," replete with clowns and silly animals. A montage of dignified speakers and platforms with a huge well-mannered crowd, extolling Cleveland, "Scenes at the Great Cleveland Demonstration in Brooklyn Yesterday," appeared October 17.

Most famous of the cartoons is the full-page-width "The Royal Feast of Belshazzar Blaine and the Money Kings," published after Blaine showed up at a banquet with financial kingpins. Belshazzar is a reference to the last king of Babylon, who was warned of defeat through handwriting on a wall. In the cartoon the gluttons with Blaine are feasting on "lobby pudding, Navy contract, patronage, monopoly soup, Gould pie."[68]

"Rum, Romanism, and Rebellion"

Various factors entered in to sway votes both ways. Cleveland was accused of having an illegitimate child and owned up to it; Blaine let go unchallenged a remark of a clergyman in his presence that the Democratic Party was one of "Rum, Romanism, and Rebellion," an insult to Roman Catholic voters and the Irish in particular.

New York became the deciding state in the extremely close election. Cleveland won New York by a mere 1,200 votes, and in fact his margin in the overall popular vote was only 24,000 out of 10 million. The relentless and sensational support of Cleveland by Pulitzer's "independent!" *World* must certainly have made a difference. Pulitzer had helped elect a president. Although the *World* did not beat the drums for him, Pulitzer himself scooted into a seat in Congress in that election, only to resign early in the year because of the demands of political office.[69]

Media as Businesses
POLITICS FOR PROFIT

Pulitzer's politics was good business. By embracing the Democratic Party in general while remaining independent, he could appeal to the needs and expectations in the city's melting pot. The immigrant population in New York, representing many nationalities, was growing rapidly, with four out of five in the 1.4 million population by 1890 being foreign born. The Democratic Party in New York itself was factious, with no clear leadership coming from the media. At the outset Pulitzer joined New York's Democratic-leaning Manhattan Club, where he mixed with the Democrat bigwigs. And he called for Democratic harmony hinged on basic premises. His own Democratic platform called for taxing luxuries, inheritances, large incomes, monopolies, and privileged corporations. He also urged a tariff for revenue and reform of the Civil Service. In addition, he would "punish corrupt officers, punish vote buying, punish employers who coerce their employees in elections."[70]

The "good politics/good business" path was obvious in congratulatory messages concerning the advent of the *World*. "Mr. Pulitzer announces that he will serve no faction, but merely the whole Democratic party," said the *New York Graphic* in welcoming Pulitzer as owner of the *World*. "It is a difficult role for a New York Democratic organ, but it is the only course that The World can take and become the great Democratic organ of the country that it aims to be. Mr. Pulitzer has an easy task. All he has to do is to make a good newspaper, and at the same time a good Democratic journal."[71]

By the end of September 1884, in the heat of the presidential campaign, the *World* could boast a fourfold increase. A promoter par excellence, Pulitzer marked the occasion of reaching 100,000 circulation with a 100-gun salute in City Hall Park.[72]

The Newsboys Strike

Although Pulitzer, true to his Democratic principles, was courageously pro-labor, as in his support of the workers in the 1892 Homestead, Pennsylvania, steel strike that turned violent, he had his share of labor troubles, ranging from printers going on strike for soap and ice in 1884 to a massive strike by newsboys later in his career in 1899.

The newsboys' strike, organized by a hastily formed newsboy union, was at first brushed off by Pulitzer aides, but its full force was later realized. The "newsies," as the boys were called, objected to the raising of the cost of the papers to them from five to six cents for ten papers, and they objected to being stuck with paying for papers they could not sell. When the *World*—and Hearst's *Journal*—sought to hire "scabs," namely, men off the street, the boys pursued the new "homeless" recruits and persuaded them of the rightness of their cause; the hapless men then also balked at distributing the paper. With strong community support, the boys' boycott of the *World*—and *Journal*—was awesome. The *World*'s press run was reduced from 360,000 to 125,000 before the *World* compromised with the children's crusade.[73]

Ads in Bad Taste

Pulitzer had learned early the importance of advertising. In his first year as head of the *St. Louis Post-Dispatch* he promised that ads would be interesting to readers as well as profitable.[74] In an issue where the whole front page except for several paragraphs was given to ads, Pulitzer explained in a series of pithy editorial statements his regard for ads:

> A large amount of editorial and other matter is unavoidably crowded out of this issue by the rush of advertisements.
>
> In the conflict between the editor and the advertiser, the latter becomes the former.
>
> The pen may be mightier than the sword, but the advertiser is mightier than the editor.
>
> Even eight pages are to-day not sufficient to meet the problem of equally gratifying both our readers and our advertising patrons.
>
> We cannot express our opinion about the President's message, the meeting of Congress, and many other important events until our advertising friends will give us leave and space.[75]

Some critics found Pulitzer's ads in bad taste. There was no stronger critic on the matter than Pulitzer's own, often docile son, Joseph Pulitzer II. "When I see you, please be ready to receive a strong kick on the disgraceful medical ads that we print," wrote the son. He cited ads for nose surgery, hemorrhoid cures, and the elimination of wind from the stomach as well as ads telling how men could get new vitality. The ads, he said, "are not only disgusting but are a mean deception of an ignorant public that can in no way be justified."[76]

Joseph senior fired back: "You were sent out to learn your profession—not to kill the medical ads. You have plenty to do with that study. Leave disagreeable problems of management alone. You are not a competent judge."[77]

Joseph II made the charge again, attacking entrepreneurs who "suck the very life out of the ignorant poor. We should kill these ads before we are exposed."[78] The younger Pulitzer saw the ads as not only fraudulent but also disgusting "because they tend to undermine whatever elevating influence the paper derives from the tone of its undoubtedly high-class editorial page."[79] The letter brought a harsh response from the ailing senior Pulitzer.

The *World* became a complex organization as it moved into the vanguard of emerging giant news corporations. With a $10 million valuation and an annual profit of $1 million in the middle 1890s, the *World*, like other papers, was now hiring specialists—advertising, business, circulation, and sales executives. As the Emerys point out, the frantic rush for advertising, circulation goals, new costs in improved equipment and newsprint, and bigger payroll problems, coupled with more complex relations with labor, made necessary the rise of "a managerial corps" in newspaper operations.[80]

Media as Definers and Keepers of Values (and Biases)
RIGHT OUT OF A HORATIO ALGER BOOK

Newspapers were no longer running short stories or novel excerpts on their front pages as some of the papers in the penny press era had done, but the sense of nar-

History of the Pulitzer Prizes

In addition to funding education and a school of journalism at Columbia University, Joseph Pulitzer provided $550,000 to launch a set of annual prizes "for the encouragement of public service, public morals, American literature and the advancement of education."

Although Pulitzer died in 1911, his will, caught in a tangle of disputes among family, trustees, and various beneficiaries, was not settled until January 1916.

The following year the first Pulitzer Prizes were awarded. Administered by the Columbia University School of Journalism, the prizes are awarded following the recommendations of a board consisting of noted newspaper persons and the president of Columbia University.

Originally Pulitzer's will provided $16,500 in prizes, four prizes in journalism in addition to four for literature and drama and one for education, according to John Hohenberg's history, *The Pulitzer Prizes*.[81] The original journalism categories were meritorious public service by a newspaper; best editorial; "the best example of a reporter's work . . . the test being strict accuracy, terseness, the accomplishment of some public good commanding public attention"; and the best history of services rendered to the public (awarded only once).

Over the years the categories have evolved and expanded. Today the journalism awards are for public service, general news reporting, investigative reporting, explanatory journalism, specialized reporting, national reporting, international reporting, feature writing, commentary, criticism, editorial writing, editorial cartooning, spot news photography, and feature photography.

The first winner in the original "news reporting" category in 1917 was Herbert Bayard Swope of the *New York World* for a series of reports from Germany just before the United States entered World War I. Among the Pulitzer Prize winners over the years were Alvin Goldstein and James Mulroy's 1924 *Chicago Daily News* stories that turned up clues in the Loeb-Leopold murder case, in which two young university students eventually were convicted for the "thrill" killing of a fourteen-year-old boy, and William Burke Miller's 1925 *Louisville Courier-Journal* report on a young man, Floyd Collins, hopelessly trapped in a Kentucky cave.

Winning subjects have ranged from a parade in Detroit to Hiroshima after the atomic bomb, an air crash, riots, a school bus disaster, a building collapse, and general police reporting. Most significant in recent times have been Seymour Hersh's 1969 Dispatch News Service expose of the My Lai massacre in Vietnam, which helped turn public opinion against the Vietnam War, and Bob Woodward and Carl Bernstein's *Washington Post* stories on the 1972 Watergate break-in and cover-up that eventually helped topple President Richard Nixon in 1974.

The awarding of the Pulitzer Prizes has stirred various controversies. Among the fiascos: various controversies in which the originality of material in prize-winning entries was later questioned, the bumping by the board of screening juries' selections and putting in other names, the awarding of the prize to the wrong photographer, and—the most celebrated scandal—Janet Cooke of the *Washington Post* having to return her prize in 1981 after the discovery that she had fabricated her story of an eight-year-old drug addict.

rative or "a story to tell" prevailed in news coverage. No basic plot motif received more attention than the poor outcasts of society—an underprivileged child, a wronged woman, a laborer—overcoming odds and triumphing, becoming rich themselves.

It was the era of Horatio Alger's youthful novels of newsboys and others going from rags to riches. A teacher and journalist turned Unitarian preacher, Alger (1834–1899) penned 135 books, mostly for juveniles. A number of popular juvenile magazines took up the "rags to riches" theme, among them *The Youth's Companion, Our Young Folks, Harper's Young People*, and *St. Nicholas*. Religious denominational youth papers pursued the theme of eternal values superseding those of the material realm.

Nobody took to heart the reigning values delineated by Alger more than Joseph Pulitzer. His very life embodied the protagonists that Alger was writing about. Once a frail lad who spoke a foreign language and was reduced to doing menial jobs when he first arrived in the United States, Pulitzer had pulled himself up by hard work and by pursuing unwaveringly lofty ideals. His life had the contradictions of some of Alger's characters. He knew money was bad in the hands of the selfish tycoons, but on the other hand he accepted the idea that money and riches were just rewards for the poor boy who made good and who would use the newly achieved wealth responsibly.

"A dominant motif of the success archetype focused on the biblical injunction against seeking earthly rather than heavenly treasures," says Paulette D. Kilmer of Northern Michigan University. "Treatment of monarchs in narratives and the news during the Gilded Age (1870–1910) reinforced the common notion that through Divine Providence, the New World had escaped the decadence of the class-ridden Old World. Both reporters and popular authors celebrated the aristocrats created by nature rather than by heredity."[82]

Of true aristocracy, Pulitzer said:

> The *World*'s aristocracy is the aristocracy of labor. The man who by honest, earnest toil supports his family in respectability, who . . . fights his way through life courageously . . . is the proudest aristocrat in the American republic.[83]

A QUIET END ON A YACHT

In his last hours, aboard his yacht *Liberty*, the certifiably blind Pulitzer nourished his desire for someone to read to him, a task performed daily by several readers. A German reader was with Pulitzer at the end aboard the yacht in the harbor of Charleston, North Carolina. It was the custom when Pulitzer became drowsy for the reader to taper off. Pulitzer would give the command for winding down, "Leise, ganz leise, ganz leise," "softly, quite softly, quite softly." These were his last words on October 29, 1911.[84]

Pulitzer listening to his secretary read at Villa Lisert, Nice, France, in 1908, three years before Pulitzer's death. (St. Louis Post-Dispatch)

II. WILLIAM RANDOLPH HEARST—"GEE WHIZ" JOURNALISM

William Randolph Hearst began his career in the Gilded Age, a period of shining prosperity and pretenses that hid cheapness and corruption beneath the surface. Life looked brilliant, gilded with gold, but in fact the glitter merely covered the cheap and corrupt. Like Pulitzer, Hearst was committed to exposing graft and corruption in high places.

He embraced major party politics as well as the percolating ideologies on the fringe during the eras in which he lived. Agreeing with much of the populist agenda, except the plank calling for silver as a money base, Hearst and his *New York Journal* supported the People's Party and Democratic candidate William Jennings Bryan in 1896. The *Journal* was the only major paper in the East endorsing Bryan.

Following the eclipse of the populist party, Hearst pursued his reform goals and antimonopoly causes as an ardent progressive in the Progressive Era, 1900–1920. He sought through government programs and legislation to solve social and systemic ills as the nation was propelled toward an idealistic new and better society.

When World War I shattered the dreams of progress and a heaven on earth, and as international communism raised its threatening head, Hearst retreated into an America-first brand of anticommunism. His stance anticipated the repressive era of McCarthyism of the 1950s (the "witch-hunts" of allegedly communist-leaning celebrities by Wisconsin Senator Joseph McCarthy), in which anticommunist zeal supplanted other issues in the national agenda. Hearst would go full cycle, from a beneficent populism railing against the conspiracies of the railroad and industrial trusts to party politics to an aggressive progressive agenda, only to retreat into patriot populism with its new conspiratorial theories on an international level.

It was in 1887, four years after Joseph Pulitzer went from St. Louis to take over the *New York World*, that a twenty-three-year-old William Randolph Hearst persuaded his politician father to give him the neglected *San Francisco Examiner* to run. It was the beginning of the Hearst media empire that continues today.

As Hearst became one of the richest men in America and one of the most powerful, he even made a run for the presidency, gaining a respectable 263 votes toward the nomination at the Democratic convention in 1904. Some years later he positioned himself to help broker the nomination of Franklin Roosevelt by influencing a section of the convention voting to go the way of Roosevelt in the continuing balloting.

As he entered the New York journalism fray against Pulitzer and fifteen other English-language dailies in the city,[85] Hearst had already tested in San Francisco his "gee whiz" slant that outpaced Pulitzer's formula that news was what people would talk about. Hearst wanted readers to say, "Oh, my God!" on nearly every story.

Hearst demonstrated early not only that crime, sex, and misfortune could get top play, but also that items normally worth only a paragraph or two, with the right approach and space, could be expanded on and made very important indeed. He elevated the importance of features over news items. His feature articles were often centered on a theme or idea rather than a news event, and they unfolded with the elements of plot, conflict, and character development, as in fiction.

He aggressively sought out the best talent that money could buy and elevated promotional campaigns to a fine art. Within three months after he took over the *Journal*, Hearst had hired the whole Sunday staff of Pulitzer's *World*. Circulation of the *Journal* soared from 20,000 to 150,000 in those three months (Pulitzer's *World* had 185,000).[86]

Hearst "cultivated the masses with a style of schoolboy simplicity and with his characteristic orgy of promotion," says Hearst biographer W. A. Swanberg.[87] Hearst mailed pennies to registered voters along with reasons why the best buy for a penny was the *Journal*. He distributed free coffee and sweaters to the jobless. Billboards and brass bands heralded the message that the reader got more for a penny with the *Journal* than for two cents with the *World*.[88]

At the peak of his power in 1935,[89] Hearst owned or controlled twenty-six daily newspapers (mostly in big cities), thirteen magazines, two movie companies, eight radio stations, International News Service, Universal Service, International News Photo Service, 240,000 acres in California with a 100-room, $30 million "castle" on the hills of San Simeon, one of the great art collections of the world, and real estate in New York City, Mexico, and Wales. He trumpeted his views, influencing millions, through a long life, dying in 1951 at age eighty-eight.

A HELL-RAISER YOUTH

Hearst entered the world almost literally with a silver spoon in his mouth. His father, George Hearst, had gone west from a Missouri farm in the middle of the nineteenth century to search for gold. He bought a gold mine near Nevada City, but the mine proved worthless for gold. Yet a curious blue-black ore was in abundance, getting in the way of the would-be gold miners. The seller thought he had put one over on George Hearst, but the elder Hearst realized the blue-black ore contained silver. The mine became a part of the famous Comstock Lode, "the richest silver deposit in the world," Oliver Carlson and Ernest Bates point out. The seller of the mine went on to run a peanut stand; George Hearst became rich and went to the Senate from California.[90]

William Randolph Hearst was born April 29, 1863, in San Francisco. An only child, he grew up pampered by riches and doted on by his mother. Bright and mischievous, always looking to play a joke on others, he gained a bad boy reputation in every school he entered. At an elementary school in San Francisco, "bad deportment was his chief distinction," says Ferdinand Lundberg. The Hearsts put the boy in a private school in Concord, New Hampshire, but he was immediately expelled "for the good of the school."[91]

Next on his tortuous route to an education, young Willie studied at home under a tutor whose instructions were to prepare the boy for Harvard. At Harvard the mischievous Hearst was constant trouble. He and his friends threw rotten fruit and pies at performers in a Boston theater. "It was apparently necessary for Hearst to assert himself in a robust fashion," Lundberg explains. "His voice had turned out to be high-pitched—in an era that preferred the basso profundo in a man. Indispensable to most of Hearst's Harvard parties were young ladies not from Boston's Back Bay, and plentiful supplies of liquor."[92]

His one legitimate or career interest was journalism. He served as business editor of the Harvard humor publication, the *Lampoon*, and dropped in as often as he could at the newsroom and offices of the *Boston Globe*. Everything interested him, from the presses to the business office and the circulation department. He studied Joseph Pulitzer's *New York World* each day and would sing the *World*'s praises in his rounds of the *Globe* operation.

Hearst clearly had something on his mind. It was the *San Francisco Examiner* owned by his father, a lackluster publication with which the elder Hearst was losing money. The young Hearst told his friends he was going to use Pulitzer's methods to run his father's paper and would provide jobs for his Harvard buddies.

Alligators and Roosters

At Harvard, Hearst continued to be an oddity. He kept a live alligator in his room for a while, and he turned roosters loose on campus so their crowing would wake up faculty and some of the students very early in the morning. As business editor of the *Lampoon*, he put its finances into shape when he increased the advertising base by pursuing advertisers who had placed ads in other campus publications.

Using caricature cartoons of faculty in the *Lampoon* was forbidden, but Hearst let some cartoons of faculty appear in its pages anyway. He was sharply reprimanded. Hearst responded by sending beautifully wrapped Christmas gifts to selected faculty members, some of whom were the best known academics in the nation, such as philosophers William James and Josiah Royce. Each gift was a chamber pot, a portable bucketlike container used in bedrooms as a toilet. Scholars disagree as to what was at the bottom of the chamber pots. W. A. Swanberg says each chamber pot had the name of the faculty member receiving it "ornamentally lettered";[93] Hearst biographer John Winkler says the pots were "adorned with the recipient's name and photograph";[94] John Tebbel says the pots had cartoons of faculty members.[95] Simply, and coarsely, Hearst was saying, "Let the people urinate on you."

A Dream Come True

His academic life aborted, the young Hearst stopped off in New York, where he signed on at Pulitzer's *World*. He worked two months under one of the sharper newsmen of the day, Ballard Smith. A tug of will developed between William Randolph Hearst and his good-natured father, George Hearst. The rough-edged senior Hearst wanted Willie eventually to direct his properties, including a million-acre ranch in Chihuahua, Mexico, and the rich Anaconda silver and copper mine and a successful gold mine in South Dakota. But bemoaning the fact that what his son, Willie, wanted in life he usually got, the senior Hearst, who was spending his time across the country as a senator in Washington, relented. Willie could try his hand at running the *San Francisco Examiner*.

The younger Hearst was ebullient. He knew with his energy, his ideas—wild, wild ideas—and hard, hard work, he could make the paper sing and overtake the competition, which he did in shorter time than he had planned.

On March 4, 1887, Hearst saw his name on the masthead of the *Examiner*. He added staff, including some of his chums from Harvard, and he worked night and day, at a frenzied pace, espousing his "gee whiz" journalism. Circulation in the city of 300,000 quadrupled, going to 80,000 quickly. In two years the *Examiner* "had been transformed into the foremost feature newspaper in the West—and within five or six years the paper had become by far the biggest money-maker on the Coast."[96]

His father, the senator, died in 1891, but the old man had understood his son with his carefree playboy notions. The entire estate, worth $17 million, went to his widow, Phoebe. Willie applauded the action and pledged his love and support to his mother. She in turn proved generous; she handed out much of the fortune to support her son's endeavors as he moved on like a consuming fire to engulf other papers.

Hearst's mother, Phoebe: She inherited $17 million.
(International News Photo)

Media as Purveyors of Information/Education

GETTING THE MOST OUT OF A NEWS EVENT

Despite harboring innovative and exciting ideas on how a newspaper should be run, William Randolph Hearst gave little hint at first where he was headed when he took over the *San Francisco Examiner*. Within a week, however, the younger Hearst had expanded the paper and promised comprehensive no-strings-attached coverage of domestic and community news as well as foreign news.

Yet, at first, as he let foreign news dominate, Hearst indulged his long fascination with Germany. In his school days, traveling with his mother in Germany, the two of them had taken German lessons and spoke only German at meals. He had studied German at Harvard. The *Examiner* led off on March 21, 1887, with the report "The Kaiser, Preparations for the Celebration of His Ninetieth Birthday." A change in headline style was in evidence the next day as the *Examiner* led off again with the kaiser at the top left of the front page with what today is called a hammer head—one large word, followed by read-out dropheads. The one word in bold, "NINETY," was followed by lighter type, "Germany's Beloved Emperor Reaches the Age of Four Score and Ten."

On March 23, leading off with the kaiser in the number one spot for the third day in a row, Hearst showed off some of his revolutionary ideas: a humorous, light-hearted approach to headlines and giving the whole front page over to one story. The leadoff bold type was "HOCH! HOCH!" (variously translated "great, great," or "cheers, cheers," as in a toast). This flippant streamer head was followed by ten decks of headlines: "The Celebration of Kaiser Wilhelm's Ninetieth Birthday," "The Great Holiday Throughout the Fatherland," "Berlin Blazing with Brilliant Decorations," and so on. The rest of the front page was filled with articles on the kaiser: congratulatory messages for the kaiser, a description of the reception and celebrations in Berlin, decorations in Berlin, the main procession, a student parade, an article on how students celebrate with songs and beer, and the obligatory biography of the kaiser. Hearst indeed signaled that in the future the *Examiner* would be a very different kind of newspaper.

A good story needed space to develop scenes and settings, characters and dramatic moments. Hearst was the master of the installment once he latched onto a subject. When he took an interest in the plight of the lovely Evangelina Cosio y Cisneros, daughter of a rebel leader in the Cuban revolt before the Spanish-American War of 1898, he carried installments every day. They told of her exile to an island prison, her transfer to another prison, and her escape at last disguised as a boy in a plan engineered by a Hearst reporter who took lodging next to the prison and helped cut the bars. The installments ended with her triumphant reception and parade in New York. Normally she would have been no more than a footnote, but Hearst, who liked women in distress in his news formulas, made her a cause célèbre, enlisting the support of famous American women, among them Clara Barton, President McKinley's mother, and Julia Ward Howe.

"Mistress of the Castle"

Hearst's passion for continuity and installments carried over into his ventures into the fledgling movie business. In 1913 he began producing newsreels and fiction serials for theaters—each week there would be a new episode in the ongoing story. One of them, the trials and tribulations of a young woman, *The Perils of Pauline*, became a classic. One of his company's new movie stars caught his eye one day in 1917. She was Marion Cecilia Douras, who used the stage name Marion Davies. "She had taffy-blond hair, eyes of pastel blue, and an excited little stammer. She bubbled with fun and animal spirits,"[97] says Winkler. Hearst's wife, Millicent, refused to give him a divorce.

Hearst (left), his mistress, actress Marion Davies, and a friend (center).
(Wide World)

Davies became Hearst's constant companion and "chatelaine" (mistress of a castle) at his home at San Simeon. Successful in movies, not without a little help from Hearst, Davies gave a million dollars in 1937 to help bail Hearst out of a severe cash-flow problem when he was on the verge of bankruptcy. It was repaid.[98]

Seeking Women Readers

At the *Examiner*, in his attempt to appeal to women, Hearst featured fashion articles and employed Pulitzer's technique of collages or composite articles of people (Pulitzer had a collage of vignettes and sketches of Wall Street barons). There was a full page on "The Merry Drummer—Pictures by Pen and Pencil of California's Sample Men";[99] another page of thirty-four vignettes and sketches of exemplary young soldiers from California with their handsome mustaches and uniforms.[100] In the *New York Journal*, just after he bought it in 1895, there was a portrait gallery of "A Bouquet of Millionaires," including head and shoulder drawings of a Vanderbilt, a Rockefeller, and even Joseph Pulitzer.[101] Then there was the drawing of handsome men in tuxedos holding hands on a dance floor: "The Men Who Will Lead the Cotillions This Winter." His series of vignettes and collages would also deal with children. One composite featured millionaires' children; another featured sketches of the children of the condemned Chicago Haymarket labor "anarchists" in 1887.

At times Hearst filled up his front pages with overblown accounts of important weddings. The coverage would continue on inside pages. Such was the treatment of the marriage of the Duke of Marlborough and a Vanderbilt.[102]

Puffing Billy Graham

Hearst also took an interest in religion. In fact, late in his life, in 1949, Hearst gets some credit, in addition to God, for the launching of the career of popular, distinguished evangelist Billy Graham. Hearst directed his chain of newspapers prior to a Los Angeles crusade meeting led by the then largely unknown Graham to "PUFF GRAHAM." Hearst papers played up Graham, and the evangelist was on his way to success. Graham himself preferred to credit the "hand of God" instead of Hearst.[103] Hearst had from the beginning played up selected evangelists, for example, D. L. Chubbuck: "A Revivalist—A Sketch of One Who Sings as Well as Preaches the Gospel. Evangelist Chubbuck. An Early Vicious Career Turned to One of Gentleness and Christian Charity."[104]

The scandalous religious story Hearst saved for the front page, as most newspapers would do today. One was a report of protests of Episcopalian clergy refuting charges made by an Episcopalian priest in a letter in an Episcopalian journal, *The Churchman*. The clergyman said that immorality was rampant and unchecked "among those who wear the Episcopal cloth" in New York.[105]

But then Hearst had another approach to the news, beyond straightforward reporting and highlighting the conflict story. He had his own twist on sensationalism, even in regard to religion stories. His strident kind of sensationalism became a precursor for tabloid journalism today.

Media as Vehicles of Sensationalism/Entertainment

EXPLOSIVE DESIGN AND THE RIDICULOUS

Sensationalism may have some or all of these features: (1) an appeal to the lurid and the prurient; (2) a conflict (crime, corruption, war, etc.); (3) an intimate, exciting story or narrative approach; (4) an identification with the underdog, outsider, or common person as he or she is wronged by pompous and corrupt characters or forces; (5) simplicity, with the story unfolding as melodrama, as evil challenges innocence and purity; and (6) an appeal to traditional, standard values. These were among the facets of Hearst's formula for sensationalism.

But Hearst's sensationalism, or "yellow journalism" (the term that originated with Pulitzer's "yellow kid" comic), had at least five other facets that went beyond the basic sensationalism often found in news reports. Hearst's sensationalism was not ordinary. The Hearst formula for sensationalism as it developed included the following attributes:

1. *Explosive design.* Headlines were blown up out of proportion, with some type as large as a fist. In some respects the type and design had a magazine look—the headline could be breezy and titillating like a title in a magazine article announcing a theme or a slant to a story. Hearst's *New York Journal* layouts often were horizontal and modular, with large multicolumn type flowing across the page rather than in narrow vertical columns.

Magazine techniques encouraged concentration and exaggeration that were inviting to the reader. The entire front page could be devoted to one story. Hearst, in fact, early on regarded at least the Sunday edition as a magazine. "The daily newspaper has now reached a point in its development," he said, "where one of its issues each week is nothing less than a 'magazine,' fully equal in point of literary quality to any—the best—of the monthlies."[106] And: "To-day's issue, which is no better than those furnished every week, contains more than a first-class magazine, and much of it is equal to the magazine in finish and superior in virility."[107]

2. *Catering to the ridiculous.* Hearst and his editors looked for the offbeat, unusual aspect in a story about an event or personality. If the fact looked ridiculous, so much the better. An example is the Hearst treatment of the pious entrepreneur James L. Kraft, who founded the Kraft cheese empire. Holding a copy of the Hearst *Chicago American*, the elderly Kraft once pointed out with amusement an article about himself to a Chicago college freshman who was visiting his posh office in the Chicago loop.[108] (The charitable Kraft, who gave much of his wealth away, was providing lodging in his lake-shore mansion for the youth, who was studying journalism at Northwestern that summer.) It seems that Kraft, a devout Baptist, had started off as a poor cheese peddler with a cart and donkey. One day the donkey, as Kraft told it, turned and spoke to him and told him to get right with God (much like the biblical Balaam listening to his donkey—Numbers 22). Kraft heeded his vision, mended his ways, and went on to develop a cheese-processing method that made him a household name—through the product and through advertising on television shows, including one bearing the Kraft name. How did Hearst editors illustrate the Kraft article? Emphasizing the "ridiculous." Across two pages, a donkey was depicted turning and speaking to Kraft in his wagon.

3. *Implying more than there is.* The Hearst approach could take an item of history, archaeology, or science and present it as if it had just happened or give it more meaning and significance than it deserved. For instance, the headline across two pages with oversized illustrations in the *New York Journal* in February 1898 said, "Picture of the Saviour's Crucifixion by a Roman Soldier Who Was Present." The wide drophead said: "From Photograph Taken Specially for the *Sunday Journal.* . . . Found on the Walls of the Palace of Emperor Tiberius." The layout includes a statement by a professor, Orazio Marucchi, who "discovered" an etching on a wall in the palace of Tiberius on Palatine Hill in Rome. "To the Editor of the Journal: Directly I saw the picture . . . ," he wrote. "I formed the idea that it represented the Crucifixion of Jesus Christ. I have never renounced it, and all my studies have strengthened it."[109] Of course, it was not a picture in any photographic sense—1,800 years before the advent of photography. And the reader doesn't really know who the professor is or how important he is or even whether the "picture" is something that tourists have normally been looking at all along.

In the same vein there was an announcement of a "Massacre of a Village" in large type in the *Journal,* December 22, 1895. One has to look carefully in the small-type dropheads to see just how old the story is: "Entire Population of an Arizona Settlement Slaughtered." "Entrapped by Their Enemies and Burned Alive Like Rats in a Hole." "The Government Has Only Just Learned of It, Though It Happened in 1700." "History of the Mound of Death." "Ethnologist Fewkes Unearthed the Multitudinous Bones of the Victims and Thus Amply Confirmed an Old Moqui Legend." And a large drawing showed "The Underground Golgotha, Containing the Bones of Two Hundred Massacred Christians."

Brontosaurus in the Window. In a science article it seemed that dinosaurs were up and about. "Most Colossal Animal Ever on Earth Just Found Out West."[110] Of course, what was really found were some bone fragments believed to belong to an ancient brontosaurus. An illustration of the animal as if it were in New York was captioned: "How the Brontosaurus Giganteus Would Look If It Were Alive and Should Try to Peep into the Eleventh Story of the New York Life Building."

In reporting hard news, even if he was scooped and got onto the story a day or so late, Hearst could relive the story and make it more vivid and fresh than ever. Less than a month after taking over the *Examiner,* he was shocked to learn that he had been scooped by the *San Francisco Chronicle* and *Call* on a fire that destroyed the popular Del Monte Hotel in Monterey.[111] Hearst promptly chartered a train, put aboard dozens of writers and artists, and rushed to the fire scene. They returned to put out a big special edition. Although a day late, the report of the fire had all the urgency of an event that had just happened. The headlines on the "old" news: "HUNGRY, FRANTIC FLAMES . . . They Leap Madly Upon the Splendid Pleasure Palace by the Bay of Monterey . . . Encircling Del Monte in Their Ravenous Embrace From Pinnacle to Foundation . . . 'Leaping Higher, Higher, Higher, With Desperate Desire' . . . Running Madly Riotous Through Cornice, Archway and Facade . . . Rushing in Upon the Trembling Guests with Savage Fury . . . Appalled and Panic-Stricken the Breathless Fugitives Gaze Upon the Scene of Terror . . . The Magnificent Hotel and Its Rich Adornments Now a Smoldering Heap of Ashes . . . The 'Examiner' Sends a Special Train to Monterey to Gather Full Details of the Terrible Disaster." And a blurb told of other articles in the paper about the fire: how it started, history of the hotel, rebuilding plans, and so on.[112]

4. *Overkill in use of pictures and art.* In the story on the Duke of Marlborough–Vanderbilt wedding, gigantic drawings showed guests arriving for the wedding, police restraining onlookers, the exchange of vows, even a reproduction of the French menu at the reception. In another vein, the coverage of the arrest of two members of a crime ring featured large sketches of the accused, with the caption "They were taken from their cells yesterday afternoon and sketched by a *Journal* artist." There is also on the front page a "portrait" of one of the guns used; inside there is a large sketch of one of the accused climbing stairs with a guard.[113] Never too many pictures and never too big seemed to be a Hearst motto, a key ingredient of his overplaying sensationalism.

5. *Entertain, entertain, entertain.* Always interested in the theater and the arts, Hearst saw his newspapers as theater stages, with the curtain going up anew each day with an expanding audience to win over. "In the strict sense, the Hearst papers were not newspapers at all," argues Swanberg. "They were printed entertainment and excitement—the equivalent of bombs exploding, bands blaring, firecrackers popping, victims screaming, flags waving, cannons roaring, houris dancing, and smoke rising from the singed flesh of executed criminals. . . . He had a juvenile worship of size, noise and display."[114]

Fascination with Fireworks

To Hearst a newspaper had to be like a fireworks display that captured the utmost attention and awe. He wanted to hear the sighs, the exclamations, the bang. A fireworks buff in his youth, Hearst never lost the awe of explosions. Fireworks, says Swanberg, "remained almost an obsession with him—an item interesting to analysts who suspect some sexual motivation in an inordinate love for fire and fireworks. He also thought them unexcelled for attracting crowds,"[115]

Hearst, wondering whether there were any grizzly bears left in California, persuaded one of his staffers, Allen Kelly, an outdoorsman, to find out. Kelly went to the mountains of southern California and set up a dozen bear traps. It took three months, but he caught a bear, giving every detail in his paper. He chained and boxed it for shipment to San Francisco, where it was paraded in a beer wagon before great crowds. The beast was named Monarch, from the *Examiner*'s slogan, "Monarch of the Dailies." It ended up caged at the city's Golden Gate Park.

Hearst had fun, and he was not the only one who did. Take this story, for instance: "Miss Victoria Rhino Under an Operation." "And Is Now Feeling Better, Says Her Keeper." "A Zoo Two-Horned Wonder." "Was Troubled with Necrosis of Her Powerful Jaw, So the Surgeons Were Called in." That fluffy but fun story about Miss Victoria appeared not in the *Journal* but in the *New York Times*.[116]

Hearst did not have a monopoly on sensational, yellow, fun, entertainment journalism.[117] But he did bring it all together in a new package, put in the fireworks, and lit the fuse. A curious side note: When he put on an actual fireworks display in 1902 at Madison Square Garden for some 40,000 persons to celebrate his election to Congress, the display went awry. Eighteen people died in the explosion, and a hundred were injured.

Media as Fourth Estate: Adversaries of Government

STAY PUT: "I'LL FURNISH THE WAR"

It was a popular conception that William Randolph Hearst caused the Spanish-American War in 1898. He and his publishing empire functioned with a sense of power, reaching the ears of a considerable constituency and doing so more rapidly than government executive and deliberative bodies. The empire was capable, if not literally of creating the war, at least of creating the frenzy for war.

Perhaps the remark of Hearst that is most often regarded as contributing to the outbreak of war appears in a cablegram he allegedly sent to Frederic Remington, the noted artist whom Hearst had sent to Cuba before the war, along with star reporters Richard Harding Davis and James Creelman. Remington was restless. Nothing was happening. He wired Hearst, according to Creelman, who could have been present when his colleague had the exchange with Hearst:

> W. R. Hearst, New York Journal, N.Y.:
> Everything is quiet. There is no trouble here. There will be no war. I wish to
> return.   Remington

Hearst is said to have replied:

> Remington, Havana:
> Please remain. You furnish the pictures, and I'll furnish the war.
> W. R. Hearst[118]

Although most biographies of Hearst present this exchange as fact, with attribution to Creelman, some question its authenticity. Winkler says that Hearst later denied sending a telegram with such wording but allows that a different but similar message might have been sent. Hearst's son and namesake, William Randolph Hearst, Jr., writing in his eighties just before his own death, good-

Richard Harding Davis: For him and others, the war was provided.
(Free Library of Philadelphia)

naturedly tried to set the record straight. Noting that those who recorded the story never consulted his father as to its accuracy, WRH, Jr., said in his book on his life with his father: "It's a wonderful story, of course, and has gotten many a wry chuckle. The only trouble is, it's not true. Pop told me he never sent any such cable. And there has never been any proof that he did. But with headline salvos against Spain, he did in fact help to furnish the war."[119] Remington stayed, and his drawings were used in the *Journal*.

Many factors other than Hearst were pushing the United States toward war. (1) The United States had not been involved in a war for a generation, and the immediate horrors of war were lost in easy excitement. (2) The gospel of Manifest Destiny remained alive, especially as the United States was developing strength and industrial muscle, and Spain loomed as an easily defeatable small country. (3) The navy had been built to new strength and had not had a chance to test its new vessels in battle. (4) American businessmen were worried about their $100 million investments in Cuba and wanted their investments under the control of the United States instead of Spain. (5) Farmers saw improved markets; "the war would probably benefit our farmers," said J. E. Junkin's *Bulletin and Gazette* in Sterling, Kansas.[120] (6) The struggle for freedom in Cuba wasn't going well and had dragged on for four years.

Hearst was not alone among publishers as he fanned war fever. Pulitzer and others also stirred up the masses. Hearst and Pulitzer, engaged in a circulation war, saw in the plight of Cuba a superb story that had conflict, sex, and other ingredients. One page in Pulitzer's *World*, for example, showed "Spanish brutality" with drawings of a woman and a child facing a Spanish firing squad, torture by the Spanish, a Spanish soldier slashing a woman, and two severed heads hanging from a large door key.[121]

Shipboard Strip Search

In addition to offering the reader bloody tales, Hearst created a sensation with a report by Richard Harding Davis that young women suspected of carrying secret letters were being strip-searched by Spanish police who pursued them even aboard foreign vessels. One such incident was depicted in a Remington drawing of a young nude lady among Spanish officers aboard the USS *Olivette*. The drawing spanned five columns. The combative Pulitzer, suspecting the story was not true, tracked down the woman and found that she had been searched only in the presence of a woman officer. Hearst publicized the death of a U.S. dentist, Dr. Ricardo Ruiz, in a Cuban jail, and published an intercepted letter by a Spanish diplomat criticizing President William McKinley (in fact, Hearst had been critical of the president). All this fueled American anger.

But not to be forgotten was the heartland press in America—with its home-grown racism and religious bias. At first the smaller papers and religious journals were not in favor of war. As time went on they were influenced by Hearst and Pulitzer. Yet the fact is that the smaller papers and journals played a role as well, exercising a collective power as a fourth estate concerning the prosecution of the war.

Smaller Heartland Papers Delay War Cry

In the heartland the cry for war was not pronounced at first, perhaps as a reaction to the sensationalist eastern papers. A Kansas editor, George W. Marble, tweaked the nose of the *Journal* with humor over the war in his *Fort Scott* (Kansas) *Tribune*: "The *New York Journal*'s war with Spain goes bravely on. Each day one blast of a reporter's breath puts a thousand Spaniards to flight."[122]

Reacting also to the eastern dailies, Guy U. Hardy wrote in his *Canon City* (Colorado) *Record*, in a town of 2,500 in the 1890s, "There will be no war with

Spain, the declaration of all the sensational daily papers to the contrary not with-standing."[123]

Similarly, William Allen White's *Gazette* in Emporia, Kansas, initially de-nounced war in beautifully written editorials, particularly in "The Gaiety of War," which describes the flapping of flags and "little children on fences," and the waving of handkerchiefs which "tomorrow . . . will be heavy with tears."[124]

Manifest Destiny Again, and Racism

But there were factors at play in the heartland papers other than the desire for peace. From the beginning, White's *Gazette*, although opposing war, was caught up in the ethnic prejudice and racism of the time, the blindness of Manifest Destiny, and it was not long before the paper moved from its biases to all-out support of the war as "punishment." At first opposing the war, the *Gazette* had added:

> A war with Spain over anything would be beneath the dignity of the United States. A gentleman cannot strike a sore-eyed, mangy leprous beggar, no matter what provocation he may have. As between Cuba and Spain there is little choice. Both crowds are yellow-legged, garlic-eating, dagger-sticking, treacherous crowds—a mixture of Guinea, Indian and Dago. One crowd is as bad as the other. It is folly to spill good Saxon blood for that kind of vermin . . .[125]

By May White's *Gazette* had lost its restraining inclination and caved in to the pervasive jingoism. War—now on racist, ethnic, and religious grounds—was right-eous: "As long as there is evil on the earth, as long as unrighteousness triumphs in diverse places, as long as right is trodden under foot, there will be war, and it will be of God."[126]

As national sentiment came around to favoring war, the Midwest papers continued to fire at Hearst. The *Fort Scott Tribune* in Kansas said: "If some of those rich American citizens who are building $100,000 staircases in their private homes, like the vulgarians they are, had much of any sense of any kind, they would take that money and construct with it a first class big gun and present it to the government."[127]

Hearst Wades into the War—Literally

In fact, the insatiable Hearst turned up as a cog in the war machine itself. He loaned his yacht, the *Buccaneer*, to the government for the war and was named an honorary ensign in the navy. Hearst chartered the British steamer *Sylvia* and a number of tugboats and brought twenty reporters, artists, and photographers with him to the battle area. He even sent back reports himself on the battles as he "dodged bullets," getting close to the action. He reported that a shrapnel ball had passed through one of the cans of beef on a pack mule. Creelman suffered a shattered shoulder from a bullet. After the naval battle of Santiago Bay, Hearst and his journalists aboard the *Sylvia* spotted twenty-nine shivering Spanish sailors about a wrecked Spanish ship, the *Vizcaya*, which the *Journal* artists had drawn many times. "Hearst pulled off his pants and shoes and leaped into the surf," says Winkler. "Brandishing a huge revolver, he shepherded the quite willing prisoners into his boat."[128]

Hearst was a participant in the crusade, a knight of the round table, a harbinger of power. He said after the *Maine* blew up, in an editorial beneath a waving flag, "The policy of the *Journal* is aggressive Americanism."[129] The fourth branch of government—the *Journal* and other members of that institution—had its war.

When it was all over he wrote a litany to the power of the fourth estate:

> The force of the newspaper is the greatest force in civilization.
> Under republican government, newspapers form and express public opinion.
> They suggest and control legislation.
> They declare wars.
> They punish criminals, especially the powerful. They reward with approving publicity the good deeds of citizens everywhere.
> The newspapers control the nation because they represent the people.[130]

Media as Voices of Reform

"A SAD WHITE CITY" OF TROLLEY CAR DEAD

The stark eerie picture of a graveyard crowded with tombstones spanned the full-page width, eight columns, of the *New York Journal* on a cold December day in 1895. The cutline said, "If All the 134 People Killed by the Trolley Cars in Brooklyn Were Buried in One Graveyard It Would Look Like This." The headline of the four-column story had a grim poetic touch: "A Sad, White City of the Slain . . . How the Graves of Brooklyn's Trolley Victims Would Look in Serried Array . . . They Would Cover Two Acres and Room Would Be Needed for More . . . Lordly Monuments and Humble Headstones Stand in Grim but Silent Eloquence Side by Side . . . What Schieren Thinks About It . . . The Mournful Trolley Death Roll Is Given Here, While the Picture Tells the Bloody Story More Forcefully Than Words Could." The story tells of the oldest graves and of the new ones. Case histories tell how the unguarded wheels of the trolleys snatch into their bladelike wheels the unwary from crowded streets, many if not most of them children. "Newest of all are the graves of last week's two victims," the article says.

> One of them, a little boy, was killed on Monday; the other, a strong man, on Tuesday. The sportive inconsistency of the trolley was illustrated finely in these two killings. The little boy was mangled so horribly that his distracted mother could hardly recognize him, yet he lived long enough to be taken to a hospital. The strong man was hardly disfigured at all, yet death came to him as quick as a lightning flash.[131]

The names of all 134 victims in three years, their ages, and their dates of death were listed. The crassness of the mayor of Brooklyn, Charles Schieren, was demonstrated in a letter from the mayor to the *Journal*, printed along with an image of Schieren: "To the Journal: There is much to be said on both sides. I believe that in many cases the people who have been injured are themselves largely to blame. Many people are very careless in crossing in front of the cars." The *Journal*'s cutline to the letter: "One Hundred and Thirty-four People Have Been 'Very Careless,' According to Mayor Schieren."[132]

Hearst had conducted the same crusade in the *San Francisco Examiner* earlier. Hearst enlisted the celebrated cartoonist Thomas Nast, who happened to be in San Francisco at the time, to illustrate the article. But it was unfamiliar territory for the artist, and the result was not very impressive. Yet Hearst out of kindness praised it but dropped subtle hints on how it might be redone. At a staff dinner with Nast present, Hearst said, "The cars have been maiming and killing a good many children, Mr. Nast. Sometimes I look at those cars and see not a gripman but a skeleton at the control. The skeleton, it seems to me, leers at the little children at play as they run thoughtlessly across the path of the approaching Juggernaut." Nast was elated with the inspiration and insisted on redoing the drawing. "Death, the Gripman," with its skeleton conductor and trolley spread across half of the *Examiner*'s front page, became one of Nast's masterpieces.[133]

Hearst regularly attacked municipal corruption. Hardly a day went by without a hard-hitting editorial on self-serving politicians ripping off the populace. The editorials were on mundane topics such as "The Spring Valley Grab," the Spring Valley Water Company attempting to monopolize the water supply of Alameda County, California.[134] Hearst urged that electric wires be put underground, and he fought the building of a new post office on unstable swamp land. (It was built but caved in during the 1906 San Francisco earthquake.) The inadequacy of a proposed new city charter,[135] inhuman treatment at the House of Correction, the extent of gambling houses, heavy-handedness and corruption in the Police and Fire Alarm Telegraph office ("The Gong Scandal"),[136] opium drug rings, and the abuses of the Southern Pacific Railroad monopoly were all topics he undertook in his first year at the *Examiner*.

"Annie Laurie" Exposes Hospital Abuses

Participatory investigative journalism was to be a trademark of Hearst, as it was of Pulitzer, who used Nellie Bly in various roles. Bly's counterpart for Hearst was Winifred Sweet Black ("Annie Laurie"), who started with his *Examiner* in San Francisco and followed him to the *New York Journal*. For one story she pretended to faint on a San Francisco street to see what kind of treatment she would get from ambulance drivers and the hospital. She was handled "like a sack of grain" by the drivers. At the hospital a "nasty mixture of mustard water" was forced down her throat, and one doctor, noting her resistance, suggested she be given "a good thrashing."[137] Her story sparked an inspection and the firing of various hospital staff members.

Annie Laurie also pretended to be a worker to get inside a cotton mill and worked in a cannery as a member of the Salvation Army. She dressed up like a boy to get through police lines at Galveston, Texas, in 1900 after a tidal wave had killed 7,000. Working for Hearst's International News Service, Annie Laurie also gained fame as one of the so-called "sob sisters," a quartet of women who covered murder trials and other events with a perceived extra dose of emotion and sensitivity. Others numbered in the foursome were Greeley's granddaughter Nixola Greeley-Smith for the *New York World* and Ada Paterson and Dorothy Dix (Elizabeth Meriwether Gilmer) for the *New York Journal*.[138]

Fisherman Overboard

Some of the participatory investigative stories for Hearst were literally cliff-hangers. One story involved a fisherman clinging onto a rock near the Golden Gate Bridge after his boat was wrecked. The Coast Guard decided the water was too rough to try a rescue and decided to let the man wait until morning. The *Examiner* had other ideas. Hearst engaged a tug and sent a staffer, the athletic H. R. Haxton, to jump in the turbulent water and take a line to the stranded fisherman. The *Examiner* sketches hailed Haxton as a hero. Editorial columns criticized the Coast Guard, which eventually set up a new Coast Guard station.[139]

Later Haxton took a ferry operated by the "villainous" Southern Pacific. With him was a reporter and an artist. Haxton proceeded to fall overboard and screamed for help, as did his associates. A stopwatch was used by the Hearst men to time how long it took for Haxton to be rescued. It took three minutes, forty seconds. In an editorial the *Examiner* criticized the ferry's crew for their slow response. This episode resulted in the initiation of new lifesaving procedures.[140]

In New York at the *Journal* Hearst carried on his crusades against municipal corruption. A front-page article in October 1895 reprinted canceled checks sent from George Greene, Jr., chief engineer of the Dock Department, as a payoff to Tammany Hall Democratic machine boss Richard Croker.[141]

Hearst got involved in municipal corruption stories legally. When the corrupt board of aldermen nonchalantly set out to give a new gas franchise in Brooklyn to special insiders, Hearst went to court. In the role of a citizen and taxpayer, he managed to get an injunction that charged fraud. The *Journal* reported the "$10,000,000 Steal." Within three days the franchise request was withdrawn. Hearst trumpeted on page 1: "While Others Talk the *Journal* Acts."[142]

Media as Voices of Freedom

BARRED BY THE BRITISH

At the outset in his first year as chief of the *Examiner*, Hearst found that his aggressive coverage of local events invited several libel suits, one for publishing a controversial but "truthful" account of a stockholder meeting that disagreed with another version by a participant,[143] and the other for publishing a forged letter that maligned the name of the alleged signer.[144] Hearst won both cases and regarded the victories as blows for the freedom of the press.

Hearst himself sued newspapers and magazines on more than one occasion during his career. In 1907 he sued the *Chicago Tribune* and then the *New York Times* for $500,000 "on the basis of what President [Theodore] Roosevelt was said to have told a *Times* reporter concerning Hearst's relations with California railroad magnates." He sued *Collier's* magazine for $500,000 for Will Irwin's charges in a June 3, 1911, article that said the *Journal* was selling favorable theater reviews under Arthur Brisbane's name for $1,000 each and that a cartoonist and theater columnist were also for hire. None of the cases came to trial.[145]

Hearst could not be "bluffed, bossed or bribed," says Winkler. "Even when his voice was a minority of one, he made that voice heard." An example, says Winkler, was Hearst's lonely crusade to keep the United States out of World War I, a stance which irked the French and British. "The situation was further strained when Hearst succeeded in breaking through the strangulating ring of Allied censorship and bringing his readers some suppressed facts of the war," says Winkler. Hearst communicated with his European reporters through a secret code. In 1914 the British were shocked when he published a picture of the sinking British cruiser *Audacious* with a report that it was torpedoed off the Irish coast by the Germans, a fact that the British had censored.

The British authorities threatened to bar Hearst's reporters from using the mail or cable from England unless Hearst gave assurance he would use only communiqués as they were censored by the British. Hearst told them to "go to hell." The incensed British government followed through with its threat, the French also joining the British. Canadians prohibited Hearst papers from coming into Canada. Hearst worried about access to the paper mills in Canada, but stood his ground.[146] Banned but undaunted, he had to rely on Associated Press writers and special celebrity British writers, such as Rudyard Kipling and George Bernard Shaw.

Media as Definers and Keepers of Values (and Biases)
AMERICANISM WAS HIS RELIGION

William Randolph Hearst had his religion, and he had his RELIGION. Religion, lowercase, meant for him a nominal association with the Episcopal Church. (Pulitzer was also affiliated nominally with the Episcopal Church and contributed to it, and like Hearst his funeral was held in an Episcopal church.) As for RELIGION, Damon Runyon, short-story writer (*Guys and Dolls*, etc.) and long-time sportswriter for Hearst's *New York American* (formerly the *Morning Journal*) and columnist for Hearst's syndicate, King Features, cited Hearst's real religion:

> I remember hearing, long ago, a couple of Mr. Hearst's editors in the office of the *New York American* discussing an editorial that had just come in from him. One of them said: "This Americanism seems to be the Chief's phobia." "Phobia?" said the other editor, who had been around there quite a spell. "That's no phobia—that's his religion."

And in Hearst's old age (seventy-six at the time of Runyon's writing), Runyon observed, "Americanism remains a religion with Mr. Hearst."[147]

Distinctly Anti-British

Hearst's "religion" is further defined by what he was against. First, he was against England. The beginning of Hearst's "monumental anti-British bias," says Lundberg, can be traced back to an archaeological expedition by the University of California in Peru financed by Hearst's mother. The trip ended with cheap purchases of copper mines in the area of old Inca and Spanish gold and silver mines. Peru, which Lundberg notes was under the domination of British bankers, put every hurdle possible in the way of the new venture, all the time trying to get a piece of the action in the new Hearst acquisitions. Meanwhile the British wanted the new Isthmus of Panama canal to be an undefended, unmilitarized waterway like the Suez Canal. Hearst suspected there was some nefarious reason why the British wanted the canal unfortified. When the McKinley administration supported the British view and a treaty made the canal an international undefended waterway, Hearst railed against McKinley. Following a vigorous campaign against the treaty by Hearst papers, the Senate rejected the treaty.[148]

Many factors besides an implied British colonialism and English involvement in his business interests contributed to the anti-British tenets of Hearst's religion. Memories of his reporters' communiqués from Britain banned at the start of World War I cut deeply. He also had battled banker J. P. Morgan over his banking policies; among Morgan's involvements was the handling of loans for Britain, a role that allegedly made Morgan a considerable sum.[149] The Mills and Reid families, who owned the *New York Tribune* that attacked Hearst, had ties through marriage with important British personalities. Whitelaw Reid, who edited the *Tribune* after Greeley's death, himself served as ambassador to Britain, 1905–1912.

Always Pro-German

Hearst, of course, had been pro-German since his youth. He even published an edition of the *Examiner* in German when the kaiser died. The *Journal*, when he bought it, had a German edition, *Das Morgen Journal*. It later became the *Deutsches Journal*, which was suppressed by an order of the Department of Justice in 1917. Lundberg noted that owning a German paper gained considerable German-American business for Hearst, including important brewery ads. "These German Americans, of course, did what they could to stimulate anti-British bias in Hearst."[150]

In later life Hearst interviewed Adolf Hitler and contracted to provide news-service news to the German government. Rodney Carlisle noted: "These contacts, as well as the Hearst editorial policy of printing columns by Nazi propagandists and by Mussolini (as well as by British and French public figures) helped supply his critics with 'evidence' of a personal conversion to Naziism."[151] Yet Carlisle adds: "Hearst condemned the domestic practices of Naziism, but he believed that German demands for boundary revision were legitimate. While he was not pro-Nazi, he accepted more German positions and propaganda than did some other editors and publishers."[152]

Hearst's son, William Randolph Hearst, Jr., who accompanied his father to Berlin but did not see Hitler, said his father's purpose in meeting Hitler was to respond to the request of moviemaker Louis B. Mayer to "intercede with Hitler for Germany's Jews, who were already suffering under the Führer" and to "get a scoop for the Hearst papers."[153]

Hearst apparently had different views of the Japanese. The British link with the Japanese possibly irked Hearst. Lundberg suggests, "When England . . . concluded its alliance with Japan, it was more grist for the Hearst mill, for Hearst had a Pacific Coast capitalist's bias against the Japanese."[154]

American-born Hearst often expressed his sense of superiority at being a pure American. In his Sunday edition of the *Journal* after the destruction of the *Maine*, he wrote under an emblem of the waving American flag about his pure Americanism

---

Citizen Hearst Becomes "Citizen Kane"

One of the most famous movies in American history, Orson Welles' *Citizen Kane*, recalls Hearst and his empire. Yet the 1941 film is really not a literal retelling of the powerful and glamorous life of William Randolph Hearst. There are major differences between the real life and the film. Nevertheless, there was enough similarity in spirit and innuendo to make friends of Hearst try to shut it down, but they failed.

The *New York Times* summarized the movie:

As the picture opens, Charles Kane lies dying in the fabulous castle he has built—the castle called Xanadu, in which he has surrounded himself with vast treasures. And as death closes his eyes his heavy lips murmur one word, "Rosebud." Suddenly the death scene is broken: the screen becomes alive with a staccato March-of-Time-like news feature recounting the career of the dead man—how, as a poor boy, he came into great wealth, how he became a newspaper publisher as a young man, how he aspired to political office, was defeated because of a personal scandal, devoted himself to material acquisition and finally died.

But the editor of the news feature is not satisfied; he wants to know the secret of Kane's strange nature and especially what he meant by "Rosebud." So a reporter is dispatched to find out, and the remainder of the picture is devoted to an absorbing visualization of Kane's phenomenal career as told by his boyhood guardian, two of his closest newspaper associates and his mistress. Each is agreed on one thing—that Kane was a titanic egomaniac. It is also clearly revealed that the man was in some way consumed by his own terrifying selfishness. But just exactly what it is that eats upon him, why it is there and, for that matter, whether Kane is really a villain, a social parasite, is never clearly revealed. And the final, poignant identification of "Rosebud" sheds little more than a vague, sentimental light upon his character. At the end Kubla Kane is still an enigma—a very confusing one.[155]

Welles is bombastic as Kane, a different personality than the squeaky shy Hearst. In the movie Kane and his wife are divorced (not so with Hearst and his wife, Millicent); Kane marries the young blond singer (Hearst and Marion Davies never married); and Hearst was never a poor boy with a prized sled labeled "Rosebud."

Hearst never saw the movie and told his son, William Randolph Hearst, Jr., that he never made any attempts to stop the film. The younger Hearst never saw the movie either "out of principle and deference to the old man," but through the lawyers and accounts of others he felt as if he had "viewed every frame." He offered his critique of the film in his autobiography:

My basic problem with *Citizen Kane* was that its portrait of my father was untruthful and unfair. Kane was depicted as a harsh, loud, imperious braggart. Unquestionably, my father was not that. Pop was also portrayed as a man without conviction. Even his bitterest newspaper competitors would never claim that.

Kane's closest friend ended their long relationship by calling him a "swine," a characterization that may say more about the Welles and Mankiewicz movie-writing than about my father.

Kane was disappointed in the world and built his own. Pop never kept San Simeon to himself. He shared it with thousands of guests who were made fully welcome. In the end, the castle and gardens were given to the state of California and they are now enjoyed by millions of Americans.

Kane strikes his wife. I am certain that my father never imagined such a contemptible act.

Kane's girlfriend had no singing talent. Marion Davies became a popular Hollywood actress with good credits. However, [Herman] Mankiewicz is said to have told friends that the singing failure made for a better plot. That was the one aspect of the film, relayed to the old man, that apparently caused him real pain.

Kane went into rages: smashing his round snow glass as a child, throwing suitcases as an adult. Neither was true of my father.

The portrayal of Kane as my father was completely out of character, as his family, friends, and colleagues would testify. Pop was a soft-spoken man who seldom showed emotion—and certainly never rage.[156]

Citizen Kane opened to rave reviews. Bosley Crowther of the *New York Times*, noting "some disconcerting lapses and strange ambiguities," declared " 'Citizen Kane' is far and away the most surprising and cinematically exciting motion picture to be seen here in many a moon. As a matter of fact, it comes close to being the most sensational film ever made in Hollywood."[157]

Childe Orson in the *New Yorker* was critical of some of the techniques that came to be known as film noir, but praised its message. "Sometimes I thought there was too much shadow, that the film seemed to be performed in the dark. Mr. Welles likes a gloom." But he noted: "Mr. Kane does not come out of all this a melodrama villain. I think it is a triumph of the film, and proof of its solid value and of the sense of its director and all concerned, that a human touch is not lost. Sympathy for the preposterous Mr. Kane survives. Indeed, there is something about him which seems admirable."[158]

philosophy, possibly aimed at foreign-born Joseph Pulitzer and Paris resident James Gordon Bennett, Jr., of the *New York Herald*.

He disliked "undesirables," particularly foreign-born anarchists (the "pestilent brood," he called the Chicago Haymarket "anarchists"),[159] socialists (he gloated at the failure of *John Swinton's Paper*, a socialist labor organ, back in 1887),[160] and Communists.

The Communists charged Hearst with (1) fascism, consorting with fascist-leaning individuals such as the Reverend Father Charles Coughlin of Michigan and Huey Long of Louisiana; (2) being anti-labor despite his pretentions otherwise (using scabs in his California mines and nonunion labor at San Simeon, promoting an "insidious campaign against the Chinese in California"); (3) "glorification of Hitler . . . the Nazi butcher"; (4) founding a youth auxiliary, the Junior Birdmen of

Hearst's "home" at San Simeon, California. (International News Photo)

America, purportedly to teach aviation to youth, but "in reality . . . a fascist youth organization, highly surcharged with the teachings of nationalism and race hatred"; (5) fakery, setting up a contest for youths racing around the world, but allegedly rigged to favor youths in Hearst's big-circulation areas—Chicago, San Francisco, New York; and (6) oppressive capitalism—"Every capitalist newspaper in America is working with Hearst," said Communist apologist James Casey. He recommended shrilly, "Boycott the Hearst press! Support the Communist Party in its fight against fascism."[161]

LIMITS OF CREATIVITY

In terms of professional values and ethics, Hearst was a relativist within the shadow of his twin idols: circulation and power for his newspapers (and for himself). He placed high values on the "scoop." "Get it First" was a Hearst motto (later amended by the editor of the Hearst wire service, INS, Moses Koenigsberg, to "Get it first, but first get it right").[162] Another of his commandments was to think and be creative.

Creativity is a positive value in most editors' minds, but most are also aware of the downside when it is abused. Faked realism still exists today, just as it did when Hearst photographers went to the morgue, put a bow tie on a corpse, photographed it, then painted in the eyes as if opened, and the dead person came "alive" for a portrait in the newspaper. Touching up pictures to improve contrast and for simplification is legitimate, many would agree, but outright distortion—changing the message and image of the picture—is a part of the legacy of the creativity of Hearst and others that still pops up in media. Consider the faked Mideast picture (using models) on the cover of a national newsmagazine or *TV Guide*'s cover on which Oprah Winfrey's face was placed on the body of Ann-Margret. In 1994 *Newsday* used some fakery to show Nancy Kerrigan and Tonya Harding skating side by side on its front cover.

Docudramas and Doctored Pictures Today

There has been a debate concerning television docudramas that do not distinguish between what is real and what is fiction; also phony re-creations that pass as fact, such as depicting a car model as fire-prone by purposely causing a fiery explosion for the benefit of the camera.

And consider book jackets. Curiously, William Randolph Hearst, Jr.'s 1991 book about himself, a highly respected journalist (a winner of the Pulitzer Prize in foreign reporting), and his father, appears to have a modified picture on the cover. The original picture showed the elder Hearst aboard a ship with his arms around two of his sons, WRH, Jr., and John. But John has been painted out of the picture on the book jacket. A false arm has been put on the senior Hearst to make it look as if he is waving. The phony modern book jacket (for which the publishers are probably to blame instead of WRH, Jr.) has taken the two Hearsts from the ship photo and placed them on the back of a train, behind a "20th Century Limited" banner, as if the elder Hearst and junior are on a whistle-stop campaign.

Wherever the debate goes on concerning creativity, improvisation, and even distortion, the name of Hearst can be invoked. The questionable side of his creativity legacy continues, but he was not—and is not—alone.

Media as Businesses

CAPITALIZING ON POPULISM

A complex formula of strategies and circumstances accounts for Hearst's success. Despite his enemies and personal setbacks, Hearst had a way of making everything in which he was involved work for him. Even in politics some believe he was less of a sincere candidate and more of an entrepreneur, knowing that whether he won or lost, the exposure as a candidate—with competing newspapers covering his speeches and activities—was just plain publicity, good or bad. People remembered the name, and the name meant Hearst and his newspapers.

Although William Jennings Bryan captured the presidential nomination of both the Democratic and the populist parties in 1896, Bryan was not getting good press. But Hearst discovered that "the *Journal* could have no greater sensation in New York than by supporting Bryan," says Lundberg. Other newspapers had been presenting Bryan as "a revolutionist, an anarchist, a corrupter of the young, a crack-pot, a fool, an idiot, a nihilist, a four-flusher, a confidence man and a menace to home, religion and public morals." Then the *Journal* "solemnly announced that it was its patriotic duty to support Bryan, the opponent of that arch-friend of the trusts, William McKinley. The effect was tremendous."[163]

Lundberg notes that the day after the 1896 election the *Journal* peaked at 995,000 copies, not only the largest circulation of any paper but also a record. It had taken Hearst only a year to increase the *Journal* tenfold. He had gained a sizable following in rural areas that lacked pro-Bryan newspapers. Cleverly he had prepared out-of-town editions, predated them by three days, and sent them into rural areas. "The *Journal* had, by default, become the standard-bearer of the oldest political party in the nation."[164]

Circulation Wars with Pulitzer

Hearst's gains were reflected in Pulitzer's losses. The average circulation for the *World* from 1896 to 1897 skidded from 312,000 to 289,000. At first glance it would appear that Hearst's wealth was a factor (he had spent millions of dollars from his mother on the *Journal*). But observers such as Roy Everett Littlefield III note that Pulitzer himself was a millionaire and had more access to cash. "A close examination of the *Journal* and the *World* reveals that Hearst surpassed Pulitzer for reasons beyond his securing the best talent by wages," says Littlefield.[165] He cites the reduction of the price of the paper to a penny and an increase in advertising, bolstered by high circulation.

Hearst hired more writers and editors for special departments. While the *World* gave attention to boxing and baseball and hired the first editor of a sports department, H. G. Cockmore, the *Journal* created a department with top sports experts as writers and kept readers informed with statistics and ratings, as well as presenting a generous dose of sports features.[166]

While Pulitzer, an immigrant himself, appealed to older foreign-born readers and expressed a dislike for some groups, such as the Italians, Hearst, at least in his earlier editorial days, was more inclusive (except for his West Coast bias against Oriental immigrants) and held out a welcome hand to young European immigrants. In days gone by, Day at the *Sun* had appealed to readers by using humor and being concise; Bennett and Pulitzer had reached for a middle-class and a wider common-man audience; Greeley had marched ahead with his editorials that maintained a socialist agenda; and Raymond at the *Times* had held sway with proper moral tone and straight news. Hearst's approach proved the most universal among the traditions, closing the generation gaps and class gaps, appealing to rural and urban, as he made relevant the language of sensationalism.

In Hearst Style, *Defender* Debuts

Other newspapers, even new ethnic journals, sought to emulate the Hearst enterprise. The successful *Chicago Defender*, launched in 1905 primarily for a black audience, apparently drew inspiration from Hearst despite its strong social and civil rights agenda. The paper's founder, Robert Abbott, "was running a business and was very serious about it," said Jane Rhodes of Indiana University. Abbott, who

Robert Abbott: Founder of Chicago Defender.

began his paper in the dining room of a Chicago rooming house, was influenced by Chicago yellow journalism, said Rhodes.[167]

Abbott, like Hearst, developed significant special beats. In 1910 Abbott hired J. Hockley Smith to create theater, sports, and society sections. Abbott, who was fond of children, added the Bud Billiken page, which included puzzles, stories, and cartoons for children. From the beginning Hearst had his "For the Young Folks" column in the *Examiner*; this included children's poems and a vertical series of drawings, some of them reprints, such as "Baby's and Kitty's Nice Time—A Pretty Little Tale in Six Spirited Illustrations," from *Paris Monde Illustré*, showing a baby in a tub trying to give a kitten a bath.[168] His *Journal* was the first newspaper to print a whole section of full-color comics.

Role of Department Store Ads

The emergence of the department store, with its inclusion of many stores into one, marked a new way of shopping. "The urban infrastructure (such as street improvements, street cars or railway systems and delivery systems), in place by 1880 or so, expanded the market area beyond a shopper's immediate neighborhood," Gerald Baldasty points out. This "allowed for the concentration of a myriad of goods in one store relatively distant from the consumer's home."[169] The big store away from home depended on newspaper advertising. Hearst lost some of this major advertising over his support of Bryan, but advertisers soon returned. The departments in the paper often were compatible with store departments and provided a special slot for a specialized product. When there was too much news to accommodate all of the ads, as in the case of the Sunday issue after the destruction of the *Maine*, he printed only those that were received first, thus making it seem a privilege to be included in the paper.

Blessed Are the Pure of Heart

Later at the *Journal*, noting that Bennett (Jr.) was doing well in the *Herald* with personal ads, some of them dealing with massage parlors and artist's models available to pose, Hearst cleverly decided to curb Bennett's $200,000 a year profit on personal ads and to make himself look like a moral crusader, particularly in an election year, 1906, when Hearst was running for governor of New York. Bennett had been attacking Hearst's moral and political fitness. Hearst had one of his staffers join the Reverend Charles H. Parkhurst's Society for the Prevention of Vice, and, says Tebbel, the staffer for a year "did espionage work among the fleshpots, visiting lonely ladies, submitting himself to the massages, manicures and Turkish baths offered in the *Herald*." With the "evidence" a grand jury was prevailed upon to indict Bennett for sending obscene material through the mail. Bennett first fled to his yacht. But he did not like the feeling of being "hounded," and he showed up in court and paid fines totaling $25,000. Tebbel intoned, "It was a low blow, an uncalled-for slap at an old man whose newspaper was steadily declining and no longer a threat to Hearst or anyone else."[170]

Media as Political Organs

HE COULD BE FOUND ON BOTH SIDES

William Randolph Hearst did not make his newspapers organs of any political party. He had pleaded with his father, Senator George Hearst, that the *San Francisco Examiner* be edited in such a way that it would not look as if it were a mouthpiece of the Democrats. In time he actually went further in political allegiance and made his newspapers' political philosophy an extension of one Democratic candidate— himself, as he ran for congressman, New York City mayor, New York governor, and the Democratic nomination for president.

Never a captive candidate, he could often be found on both sides of issues; he both wooed and castigated Democratic machine bosses; he could also be accused of socialism, for he favored governmental intervention in transportation services and utilities. Yet he railed much of his life against state socialism and communism.

In his lifetime he favored the following in his editorials and the political planks on which he ran for office: government ownership of railroads, fixed rail fees, teachers' pensions, antimonopoly legislation, a graduated income tax, popular election of U.S. senators (they used to be elected by state legislatures), improved schools, and an "America-first" policy.

Although shy, he could inspire enthusiasm. When his name was put up in nomination for president at the 1904 Democratic convention in St. Louis, with a second by the famous Chicago lawyer Clarence Darrow (later famous for his part in the "monkey" evolution trial in Tennessee and the Chicago Loeb-Leopold murder trial), the delegates exploded with applause. The *New York American* (formerly the *Morning Journal*) made the scene sound like just a little less than the second coming of Christ. "Hearst Is Cheered for 38 Minutes," gushed the *American*. "Convention in Wild Tumult of Applause . . . Cheer for Hearst Came From the Heart, Say Delegates."[171]

Two years earlier, with an eye on running for the top office in the near future, Hearst had made peace with the Tammany Hall Democratic boss, saloon keeper Charles Francis Murphy, and secured the nomination for Congress from the heavily Democratic eleventh district. He won handily (by the largest majority ever received by a candidate for Congress in New York City). He gained a second term two years later, running ahead of his ticket throughout his district.[172]

Quiet Style in Congress

His style was unusual. Perhaps unsure of his high-pitched voice, he did not speak in the House for two years, and only then to rebut some mudslinging on Hearst's name by a Massachusetts representative. Hearst returned the "compliments" by revealing his critic's arrest record. Hearst ran the House floor as he did his newspapers, by controlling a small group of representatives, called the Hearst Brigade. He sat back in silence as they took to the podium with bills he initiated or supported. He tried—but failed—to get through bills calling for prison terms for railroad executives who traded in secret rebates and to have the government buy

Politician Hearst working a crowd. (*Philadelphia Inquirer;* Temple University Libraries Photojournalism Collection)

and run the telegraph lines. He was absent much of the time, but he was usually there for any vote related to his private interests.[173]

Hearst needed the support of William Jennings Bryan to win the Democratic nomination for president in 1904. But Bryan, looking out for his own career interests and distrustful of Hearst, supported rival Judge Alton Brooks Parker, of the New York Court of Appeals, who got the nomination over Hearst.

Almost Mayor of New York

In 1905 Hearst made a bid to be mayor of New York on an independent ticket, the Municipal Ownership League, which Hearst had merged with his own William

Randolph Hearst League. Running without the Tammany machine, Hearst caught the imagination of the city. The Tammany organization emptied ballot boxes into the East River and beat up Hearst workers, but by all accounts he was the true winner. One Hearst poll watcher even had a finger chewed off.[174] Even with the tampering, the vote was close: incumbent George B. McClellan, Jr., 228,397; Hearst, 224,925.

Editor and Publisher used the closeness of the vote to show the power of the press: "Election returns show again the power of the newspapers in directing public opinion. That William R. Hearst received within a few thousand of enough votes to elect him Mayor of New York, indicates the extent to which sentiment can be aroused by papers of wide circulation. Without his three newspapers in New York to expound his ideas, Mr. Hearst would not have got within seeing distance of the goal."[175]

Hearst next aspired to be governor in 1906. He made a kind of peace with Tammany boss Murphy—some regarded it as a corrupt deal. Whatever the case, Hearst won the gubernatorial nomination. As it dawned on the Republicans that Hearst might win, they enlisted their heaviest artillery, the president of the United States, Theodore Roosevelt, who was vice president when President William McKinley was assassinated in 1901.

Blamed for McKinley's Assassination

Critics had tried to put the blame for the fatal shooting on Hearst and his papers. McKinley's assassin, Leon Czolgosz, reportedly had a clipping from the *Journal* in his pocket when he shot McKinley, a fact later disputed. The *Journal*'s editorial policy had been inflammatory against McKinley, portraying him as a pawn of the trusts. Five months before McKinley died of an assassin's bullet, a *Journal* editorial attacking McKinley ended, "If bad institutions and bad men can be got rid of only by killing, then the killing must be done."[176] In the same issue Ambrose Bierce quoted in his column a refrain he had written the previous year, when Kentucky governor-elect William Goebel was assassinated:

> The bullet that pierced Goebel's breast
> Can not be found in all the West;
> Good reason, it is speeding here
> To stretch McKinley on his bier.[177]

In later years William Randolph Hearst, Jr., maintained that Bierce and others at the *Journal* said the senior Hearst never knew of the editorial or column prior to publication. The younger Hearst recalled that his father "learned of the editorial—but not the column—only after the presses had begun to run. The old man ordered the presses halted and the reference to 'killing' eliminated." Yet some of the early edition papers did reach the streets, and "when rival newspapers and other critics saw both the editorial and column, they launched all-out attacks on my father." Hearst, Sr., informed McKinley "that he would drop from his newspapers any future article that McKinley might view as personally offensive. The President sent him a letter of thanks."[178]

Theodore Roosevelt's "Torpedo"

During the gubernatorial election Theodore Roosevelt decided to remind voters of Hearst's "role" or influence in the McKinley assassination. He dispatched Secretary of State Elihu Root to Utica to join Republican candidate Charles Evans Hughes at a political rally at the Majestic Theater. Root spoke directly for the president. The *Tribune* and the *New York Times* had a field day dredging up the old charge against Hearst on behalf of the president. The *Tribune* said: "Root Speaks for President— Vote for Hughes and Good Government, the Appeal from Washington—Hearst Scathingly Arraigned—an Insincere, Self-Seeking Demagogue, Whom Mr. Roosevelt Had Specifically in Mind When Denouncing the Assassin of McKinley— His Election Would Be a Blow to Both Capital and Labor."[179] The *Times* reported: "Roosevelt Calls Hearst Inciter of the Assassin—Through Root He Recalls the Murder of McKinley—Unfit to Be Governor—His Election Would Injure the President's Work—Hearst Men Interrupt."[180]

Root's speech was lengthy, and although it was reprinted in the papers in its entirety, newspapers carried a boxed excerpt at the top of their front pages. Root declared, "President Roosevelt and Mr. Hearst stand as far as the poles asunder." Root recalled Roosevelt's speaking of the assassin of McKinley "as inflamed by the reckless utterances of those who, on the stump and in the public press, appeal to the dark and evil spirits of malice and greed, envy and sullen hatred. . . . This applies alike to the deliberate demagogue, to the exploiter of sensationalism, and to the crude and foolish visionary who, for whatever reason, apologizes for crime or excites aimless discontent." Root added that President Roosevelt "had Mr. Hearst specifically in his mind. And I say, by his authority, that what he thought of Mr. Hearst then he thinks of Mr. Hearst now."[181]

The next day Hearst frantically tried to turn around the Olympus-like onslaught against him. He scheduled thirteen meetings that day, and his voice became so hoarse he could hardly talk. He tried to depict Root as a "servant" of trusts and only incidentally mentioned Roosevelt.[182] Hearst seemed wounded by the thunderbolt.

Barrage of Shots from the *Times*

The *Times'* editorial writer joined in the feeding frenzy and contributed to the dismantling of candidate Hearst. The paper took up the charges against Hearst as the paper saw them and gave its own devastating responses:

> The public inquiry into the fitness of Mr. Hearst to be Governor of this State is about at an end. . . .

He is charged with insincerity. Proof enough. . . .

He has been called a demagogue. He is one. . . .

It is charged that he is unworthy of a public trust. Proved. . . .

Self-interest, not a desire to promote the public welfare, is the mainspring of his ambition. . . .

That he is a radical, a revolutionist, that he is "ambitious, unsteady, unsafe," is the general belief. He proves it in every utterance, he proves it in every issue of his newspapers. . . .

Mr. Hearst is empty. He is a pretender. There is in him neither ideas nor remedial promise, no reform save by smashing the corporations, and with them, a great part of the business structure.[183]

On the Sunday before the election the *Tribune* carried a full-page-width picture of Hughes addressing a crowd in City Hall Park. One front-page story was head-

---

The Lighter Side

When Casey Struck Out

Baseball writers sometimes use the names "Casey" or "Mudville" in their articles as they draw from the famous thirteen-stanza poem "Casey at the Bat." Everyone, it seems, has heard of the poem. But few know who wrote it. In fact, it was some years after orator/actor, bass singer, and comedian De Wolf Hopper had been reciting it from a yellow clipping that the name of the author emerged. The tattered newspaper column had been signed "Phin," which turned out to be the pen name of Ernest Lawrence Thayer, who wrote for Hearst's *San Francisco Examiner*. The poem ran on June 3, 1888. Thayer had been editor of the *Lampoon* when Hearst was at Harvard.

"Casey," by the way, was a name borrowed from a Harvard chum who was not inclined to baseball. Hopper recited the fifty-two-line ballad to audiences more than 10,000 times during his forty-year stage career. (The fifth of Hopper's six wives was the gossip columnist Hedda Hopper, and his only son by Hedda was William Hopper, who played Paul Drake on television's "Perry Mason.")

Several silent movies were made of "Casey"; the first starred Hopper, and a remake starred Wallace Beery. Here is the original version of "Casey at the Bat" as it appeared in the *Examiner*:

Casey at the Bat

The outlook wasn't brilliant for the Mudville
    nine that day;
The score stood four to two with but one inning
    more to play.
And then when Cooney died at first, and
    Barrows did the same,
A sickly silence fell upon the patrons of the
    game.

A straggling few got up to go in deep despair.
    The rest
Clung to that hope which springs eternal in the
    human breast;
They thought if only Casey could but get a
    whack at that—
We'd put up even money now with Casey at the
    bat.

(Continued)

But Flynn preceded Casey, as did also Jimmy
Blake,
And the former was a lulu and the latter was a
cake;
So upon that stricken multitude grim
melancholy sat,
For there seemed but little chance of Casey's
getting to the bat.

But Flynn let drive a single, to the wonderment
of all,
And Blake, the much despis-ed, tore the cover
off the ball;
And when the dust had lifted, and the men saw
what had occurred,
There was Johnnie safe at second and Flynn a-
hugging third.

Then from 5,000 throats and more there rose a
lusty yell;
It rumbled through the valley, it rattled in the
dell;
It knocked upon the mountain and recoiled
upon the flat,
For Casey, mighty Casey, was advancing to the
bat.

There was ease in Casey's manner as he stepped
into his place;
There was pride in Casey's bearing and a smile
on Casey's face.
And when, responding to the cheers, he lightly
doffed his hat,
No stranger in the crowd could doubt 'twas
Casey at the bat.

Ten thousand eyes were on him as he rubbed
his hands with dirt;
Five thousand tongues applauded when he
wiped them on his shirt.
Then while the writhing pitcher ground the ball
into his hip,
Defiance gleamed in Casey's eye, a sneer curled
Casey's lip.

And now the leather-covered sphere came
hurtling through the air,
And Casey stood a-watching it in haughty
grandeur there.

Close by the sturdy batsman the ball unheeded
sped—
"That ain't my style," said Casey. "Strike one,"
the umpire said.

From the benches, black with people, there
went up a muffled roar,
Like the beating of the storm-waves on a stern
and distant shore.
"Kill him! Kill the umpire!" shouted some one
on the stand;
And it's likely they'd have killed him had not
Casey raised his hand.

With a smile of Christian charity great Casey's
visage shone;
He stilled the rising tumult; he bade the game
go on;
He signaled to the pitcher, and once more the
spheroid flew;
But Casey still ignored it, and the umpire said,
"Strike two."

"Fraud!" cried the maddened thousands, and
echo answered fraud;
But one scornful look from Casey and the
audience was awed.
They saw his face grow stern and cold, they saw
his muscles strain,
And they knew that Casey wouldn't let that ball
go by again.

The sneer is gone from Casey's lip, his teeth are
clenched in hate;
He pounds with cruel violence his bat upon the
plate.
And now the pitcher holds the ball, and now he
lets it go,
And now the air is shattered by the force of
Casey's blow.

Oh, somewhere in this favored land the sun is
shining bright;
The band is playing somewhere, and somewhere
hearts are light,
And somewhere men are laughing, and
somewhere children shout;
But there is no joy in Mudville—mighty Casey
has struck out.

lined, "Rout at the Stretch"; another, "Hughes Hailed Victor."[184] And so it was. On the day after the election the *Tribune* trumpeted Hughes' election by a statewide plurality of more than 50,000. Buried in the coverage is a stunning fact: "William R. Hearst carried every borough of the greater city in his race for the Governorship."[185]

Maneuvering FDR's Nomination

Hearst was to encounter another Roosevelt—Franklin D. At the 1932 Democratic convention that nominated FDR, Hearst at first supported isolationist Texas Democrat John Nance Garner, who was speaker of the House. Hearst helped Garner win the California delegation. With Texas's delegates and California's, Garner had eighty-eight delegates for the nomination. When Garner switched his delegates to FDR at a crucial moment, many thought that Hearst had a hand in the move, a thesis some doubt.[186]

Hearst seemed to assume that he would have some say in the new administration. He dispatched a chief aide, Edmond Coblentz, of the *New York American*, to present FDR with a "shopping list" of Hearst's wants. Hearst suggested higher tariffs, a national highway system, flood control projects, and other items in what Carlisle calls an "economic nationalism." He also gave his choices for the cabinet. FDR sent his warm regards and his appreciation to Hearst, then proceeded to choose none of the names on Coblentz's list for the cabinet. Yet when in the early weeks of the new administration FDR began to unveil his comprehensive New Deal government projects, Hearst seemed happy.

The rapport continued for several years until the president signed into law the Revenue Act of 1935. It introduced a 75 percent surtax on incomes over $500,000; previously the surtax had been 59 percent on incomes of $1 million or more. Hearst was the only person in the country with a salary of more than $500,000.[187]

Hearst had a new enemy.

He lived to be eighty-eight (until 1951), long enough to enter the nuclear age and see the forced isolation of nations during the early years of the Cold War.

AN APPRAISAL

Pulitzer's reputation has fared better in history than Hearst's, perhaps because Pulitzer had a more rigorous editorial page and because Pulitzer died before the ascension of modern "isms," such as nationalism, socialism, communism, and isolationism. But both men helped shape the concept of mass communication serving and educating the "crowd," both fostered enterprising—even participatory—reporting, linked political points of view to profits, pioneered in corporate media management, and set political agendas. Hearst's isolationism likely had an effect on prewar reticence and the Cold War after World War II. Both helped determine the occupancy and course of the presidency. They helped set the rules and parameters of competitive journalism, affecting future ethics codes for reportorial and editorial behavior. And true to some earlier precedents overseas and in colonial America, Pulitzer and Hearst showed that newspapers could be responsive to the people, fighting affluent corruption and social ills, while at the same time providing entertainment and distraction for the masses.

QUESTIONS FOR DISCUSSION AND RESEARCH

1. If Joseph Pulitzer and William Randolph Hearst were coeditors of a newspaper, what might it be like?
2. What were Pulitzer's and Hearst's biases? How did they express them and deal with them?
3. Hearst was the greatest sensationalist of all time. Right or wrong? Explain.
4. If you had been Joseph Pulitzer or William Randolph Hearst, would you have done anything differently?
5. Take a copy of your local city or student newspaper. Consider how some of the stories might have been covered differently if they had appeared in Pulitzer's *St. Louis Post-Dispatch* and *New York World* or Hearst's *San Francisco Examiner* or *New York Journal.*
6. "Nellie Bly" and "Annie Laurie" used "participatory journalism" that made them a part of the story. Yet "participatory journalism" can sometimes go too far. Write some guidelines for editors and reporters who want on occasion to become a part of the story.
7. How might "Nellie Bly" and "Annie Laurie" have covered some of the stories that appear this week in your student newspaper?
8. What do you think about publishers running for public office?
9. Take the issues of the day, domestic, national, and foreign. Think of where Pulitzer and Hearst would stand on these issues.
10. Is there any difference between the sensationalism of Pulitzer, Hearst, and James Gordon Bennett? Explain.
11. Joseph Pulitzer pleaded for "accuracy, accuracy, accuracy." This is easier said than done. What are some of the pitfalls in achieving accuracy? What are some things that media can do to strive for accuracy?
12. What were the turning points in Pulitzer's early career? What did he do that prepared him for success?
13. Would Hearst have succeeded if he had not been bankrolled by his parents?
14. In the argument between young Joseph Pulitzer II and the senior Pulitzer over the use of quack and flaky ads, who is right? Why?
15. If Ben Franklin went to work for William Randolph Hearst, what would it be like? Would there be a meeting of the minds in any way? Problems?

ENDNOTES

1. James Feast, "*The Figure of the Crowd in Late Nineteenth-Century America and Its Appearance in Stephen Crane's Writing and Pulitzer's New York World*," Ph.D. dissertation, Department of English, New York University, October 1991, p. 70.
2. Ibid., p. 383.
3. Don C. Seitz, *Joseph Pulitzer: His Life and Letters* (New York: Simon & Schuster, 1924), p. 417.
4. Frank Luther Mott, *American Journalism: A History of Newspapers in the United States Through 250 Years—1690 to 1940* (New York: Macmillan, 1947), pp. 436–439.

5. Andras Csillag, "Joseph Pulitzer's Roots in Europe: A Genealogical History," *American Jewish Archives*, 1987, vol. 39, no. 1, pp. 46–68. *Who's Who in America*, which carried a sketch on Pulitzer until the year he died, 1911, erroneously gave his place of birth as Buda-Pesth, Hungary.

6. W. A. Swanberg, *Pulitzer* (New York: Charles Scribner's Sons, 1967), pp. 6, 7.

7. Seitz, *Joseph Pulitzer*, p. 59.

8. Swanberg, *Pulitzer*, p. 17.

9. Carlos F. Hurd, "Public Services of a Young Reporter-Legislator in the '70s," section commemorating 100th anniversary of birth of Joseph Pulitzer, *St. Louis Post–Dispatch*, April 6, 1947, p. 3.

10. Ibid.

11. *New York Sun*, Oct. 13, 1878.

12. *St. Louis Globe Democrat*, Sept. 5, 1880.

13. *Missouri Republican*, Sept. 22, 1880.

14. Ibid., Sept. 27, 1880.

15. Ibid., Sept. 25, 1880.

16. Ibid., Sept. 25, 1880.

17. *St. Louis Republic*, Oct. 22, 1910.

18. *Post and Dispatch*, Dec. 12, 1878.

19. *St. Louis Evening Post*, Jan. 18, 1878.

20. *Post-Dispatch*, Sept. 30, 1879.

21. Swanberg, *Pulitzer*, p. 77.

22. James Wyman Barrett, *Joseph Pulitzer and His World* (New York: Vanguard Press, 1941), p. 255.

23. Swanberg, *Pulitzer*, p. 11.

24. *New York Times*, Oct. 5, 1909.

25. Barrett, *Pulitzer and His World*, p. 255.

26. *New York Journal*, Nov. 16, 1882.

27. Henry Kellett Chambers, "A Park Row Interlude: Memoir of Albert Pulitzer," *Journalism Quarterly*, vol. 40, no. 4, Autumn 1963, p. 340.

28. Seitz, *Joseph Pulitzer*, p. 59.

29. Joseph Pulitzer Papers, Rare Book and Manuscript Library, Columbia University, Dillon letter to Pulitzer, June 11, 1885.

30. Ibid., Dillon to Pulitzer, July 8, 1885.

31. *Gazette of the United States* (Philadelphia), March 4, 1799. Quoted in Joseph A. Mirando, "The First College Journalism Students: Answering Robert E. Lee's Offer of a Higher Education," paper presented to the Association for Education in Journalism and Mass Communication convention, Washington, D.C., August 1995.

32. Mirando, "The First College Journalism Students."

33. *Proceedings*, National Editorial Association, address by Walter Williams, "The Missouri University School of Journalism—What and Why," at St. Paul, Minn., 1908, p. 127.

34. Joseph Pulitzer Papers, Dillon to Pulitzer, March 27, 1886.

35. Ibid., Gibson to Pulitzer, Dec. 12, 1883.

36. Ibid., Gibson to Pulitzer, Jan. 7, 1885.

37. Swanberg, *Pulitzer*, p. 129.

38. Joseph Pulitzer Papers, Kappner to Pulitzer, Sept. 1, 1885.

39. Swanberg, *Pulitzer*, p. 169.

40. Seitz, *Joseph Pulitzer*, p. 177.

41. *New York Times*, Oct. 5, 1909.

42. Barrett, *Pulitzer and His World*, p. 285.

43. *New York Times*, Oct. 5, 1909.

44. Harvey Saalberg, "The *Westliche Post* of St. Louis: German-Language Daily, 1857–1938," *Journalism Quarterly*, vol. 45, 1968, p. 454.

45. Swanberg, *Pulitzer*, pp. 69, 70.

46. *New York World*, Dec. 27, 1884, quoted in John Stevens, *Sensationalism and the New York Press* (New York: Columbia University Press, 1991), p. 78.

47. *New York World*, April 13, 1884, quoted in Stevens, *Sensationalism*.

48. Joyce Milton, *The Yellow Kids: Foreign Correspondents in the Heyday of Yellow Journalism* (New York: Harper & Row, 1989), p. 41.

49. Hiley H. Ward, book review, Jason Marks, *Around the World in 72 Days: The Race Between Pulitzer's Nellie Bly and Cosmopolitan's Elizabeth Bisland* (New York: Gemittarius Press, 1993), *Editor & Publisher*, June 5, 1993, p. 20.

50. *St. Louis Post-Dispatch*, Oct. 13, 1879.

51. Ibid., Feb. 18, 1881.

52. *New York World*, June 9, 1883.

53. Ibid., June 16, 1883.

54. Ibid., July 4, 1884.

55. Ibid., Aug. 31, 1883.

56. Ibid., Feb. 13, 1884.

57. Barrett, *Pulitzer and His* World, p. 188.

58. *Indianapolis News*, Nov. 2, 1908, quoted in Seitz, *Joseph Pulitzer*, pp. 354, 355.

59. Ibid., pp. 362, 363.

60. *New York World*, Dec. 16, 1908, quoted in Swanberg, *Pulitzer*, p. 422.

61. Swanberg, *Pulitzer*, p. 422, quoting Norman Twaites, *Velvet and Vinegar* (London, 1932), pp. 57, 58.

62. *New York World*, Dec. 16, 1908, quoted in Swanberg, *Pulitzer*, p. 423.

63. *New York World*, Feb. 18, 1909, quoted in Swanberg, *Pulitzer*, p. 426.

64. Swanberg, *Pulitzer*, p. 437.

65. Joseph Pulitzer, "Power of Public Opinion Appraised by Joseph Pulitzer," in the Joseph Pulitzer Anniversary Section, *St. Louis Post-Dispatch*, April 6, 1947, p. 12, originally appearing as "The Power of Public Opinion," in the 1904 edition of *Encyclopedia Americana*, vol. 13.

66. Barrett, *Pulitzer and His* World, p. 83.

67. *New York World*, Oct. 8, 1884.

68. Ibid., Oct. 30, 1884.

69. Pulitzer was possibly fed up with the inundation of letters seeking favors. A James W. Gerard, according to correspondence in the Joseph Pulitzer Papers collection at Columbia University, even wrote: "I hope you have not forgotten your kind promise of last summer, to put me someday on the Supreme Court. There are three vacancies this year" (Jan. 8, 1885).

70. Swanberg, *Pulitzer*, p. 88.

71. Quoted in the *New York World*, May 13, 1883.

72. Ibid., Sept. 30, 1993.

73. David Nasaw, "Dirty-Faced Davids and the Twin Goliaths," *American Heritage*, vol. 36, no. 3, April/May 1985, p. 42.

74. *St. Louis Post-Dispatch*, Sept. 30, 1979.

75. Ibid., Dec. 1, 1879.

76. Daniel W. Pfaff, *Joseph Pulitzer II and the* Post-Dispatch (University Park: Pennsylvania State University Press, 1991), p. 66.

77. Ibid., p. 67.

78. Ibid., p. 118.

79. Ibid.

80. Michael Emery and Edwin Emery, *The Press and America*, 7th ed. (Englewood Cliffs, N.J.: Prentice Hall, 1992), p. 183.

81. John Hohenberg, *The Pulitzer Prizes* (New York: Columbia University Press, 1974).

82. Paulette D. Kilmer, "The Poor Rich and the Rich Poor—How Newspapers Perpetuated Values," a paper presented at a session of the History Division of the Association for Education in Journalism and Mass Communication, Kansas City, August 1993, p. 3.

83. *New York World*, May 13, 1883.

84. Seitz, *Joseph Pulitzer*, p. 415.

85. Frank Luther Mott, *American Journalism* (New York: Macmillan, 1947), p. 448.

86. Ferdinand Lundberg, *Imperial Hearst: A Social Biography* (New York: Equinox Cooperative Press, 1936), p. 53.

87. W. A. Swanberg, *Citizen Hearst: A Biography of William Randolph Hearst* (New York: Charles Scribner's Sons, 1961), p. 81.

88. Lundberg, *Imperial Hearst*, pp. 51, 52.

89. Edwin Emery, "William Randolph Hearst: A Tentative Appraisal," *Journalism Quarterly*, vol. 28, no. 4, Fall 1951, p. 431.

90. Oliver Carlson and Ernest Sutherland Bates, *Hearst: Lord of San Simeon* (New York: Viking, 1936), p. 6.

91. Lundberg, *Imperial Hearst*, p. 20.

92. Ibid.

93. Swanberg, *Citizen Hearst,* p. 33.

94. John K. Winkler, *William Randolph Hearst: A New Appraisal* (New York: Hastings House, 1955), p. 38.

95. John Tebbel, *The Life and Good Times of William Randolph Hearst* (New York: E. P. Dutton, 1952), p. 330.

96. Ibid., p. 68.

97. Winkler, *William Randolph Hearst*, p. 14.

98. I. Orrin Spellman, "Marion Davies: How She Helped Save the Hearst Empire from Bankruptcy," unpublished manuscript. Spellman was a member of the Hearst public relations staff.

99. *San Francisco Examiner*, April 3, 1887.

100. Ibid., July 8, 1887.

101. *New York Journal*, Oct. 13, 1895.

102. Ibid., Nov. 7, 1895.

103. Kenneth S. Kantzer, "The Evangelist of Our Time," *Christianity Today*, Nov. 18, 1988, p. 14.

104. *Examiner*, March 21, 1887.

105. *Journal*, Nov. 10, 1895.

106. *Examiner*, July 4, 1887.

107. Ibid., Nov. 6, 1887.

108. Experienced by the author (H. Ward).

109. *Journal*, Feb. 20, 1898.

110. Ibid., Dec. 11, 1898.

111. The hotel had special memories for Hearst. He had met Sybil Sanderson there before he went to Harvard, and they became engaged. However, her family—her father was a California Supreme Court judge—opposed the two marrying, and the engagement was broken. Sanderson became an international operatic star. Mrs. Fremont Older says the renowned French composer Jules Massenet wrote two of his operas, *Thaïs* and *Manon*, for her. See Mrs. Fremont Older, *William Randolph Hearst: American* (New York: Books for Libraries Press, 1936, 1972), p. 47.

112. *Examiner*, April 3, 1887.

113. *Journal*, Nov. 11, 1895.

114. Swanberg, *Citizen Hearst*, p. 162.

115. Ibid., p. 163.

116. *New York Times*, Nov. 3, 1906.

117. William Quayle Parmenter, *The News Control Explanation of News Making: The Case of William Randolph Hearst, 1920–1946.* Ph.D. dissertation, University of Washington, 1979, p. 43.

118. James Creelman, *On the Great Highway* (Boston: Lothrop, Lee & Shepard, 1901), pp. 177, 178.

119. William Randolph Hearst, Jr., with Jack Casserly, *The Hearsts: Father and Son* (Niwot, Colo.: Roberts Rinehart, 1991), p. 38.

120. "Soldier Boys Write," *Sterling* (Kans.) *Bulletin and Gazette*, May 6, 1898.

121. *New York World*, June 3, 1896.

122. *Fort Scott* (Kans.) *Daily Tribune*, Feb. 23, 1898.

123. "No War With Spain," *Canon City* (Colo.) *Record*, Feb. 24, 1898.

124. "The Gaiety of War," *Gazette*, April 27, 1898.

125. "The Voice of Peace," *Gazette*, Feb. 16, 1898.

126. "One Lesson of War," *Gazette*, May 14, 1898.

127. *Fort Scott Tribune*, May 5, 1898.

128. Winkler, *William Randolph Hearst*, p. 113.

129. *Journal*, Feb. 20, 1898.

130. *Journal*, Sept. 25, 1898.

131. *Journal*, Dec. 15, 1895.

132. Ibid.

133. Winkler, *William Randolph Hearst*, pp. 51, 52.

134. *Examiner*, Nov. 17, 1887.

135. Ibid., Nov. 7, 1887.

136. Ibid., July 3, 1887.

137. Older, *William Randolph Hearst: American,* p. 100.

138. Phyllis Leslie Abramson, *Sob Sister Journalism* (Westport, Conn.: Greenwood Press, 1990), pp. 35, 36.

139. Swanberg, *Citizen Hearst*, p. 56.

140. Ibid.

141. *Journal*, Oct. 31, 1895.

142. Winkler, *William Randolph Hearst*, p. 80.

143. *Examiner*, March 29, 1887.

144. Ibid., Nov. 13, 1887.

145. Mott, *American Journalism*, p. 606; Lundberg, *Imperial Hearst*, pp. 108, 109; Carlson and Bates, *Hearst*, p. 158.

146. Winkler, *William Randolph Hearst*, pp. 12, 13.

147. Damon Runyon, *An Interview with William Randolph Hearst*, pamphlet, circa 1939, in New York Public Library.

148. Lundberg, *Imperial Hearst*, pp. 91–93.

149. Edward T. O'Loughlin, *Hearst and His Enemies*, pamphlet, "Compiled for the Committee of Relatives of American Soldiers, Sailors and Marines of Greater New York," ETO, 1919, New York, p. 15.

150. Lundberg, *Imperial Hearst*, p. 90.

151. Rodney P. Carlisle, "William Randolph Hearst: A Fascist Reputation Reconsidered," *Journalism Quarterly*, vol. 50, no. 1, Spring 1973, p. 221.

152. Ibid., pp. 220, 221.

153. Hearst, Jr., *The Hearsts*, p. 53.
154. Ibid., p. 93.
155. *New York Times*, "The Screen," Bosley Crowther, May 2, 1941.
156. Hearst, Jr., *The Hearsts*, pp. 186–188.
157. *Times*, May 2, 1941.
158. Childe Orson, "The Current Cinema," *New Yorker*, May 3, 1941.
159. *Examiner*, March 13, 1887.
160. Ibid., Aug. 9, 1887.
161. James Casey, *Hearst: Labor's Enemy No. 1*, flyer (Astor, Lenox and Tilden Foundation, 1937), in New York Public Library.
162. Tebbel, *Life and Good Times*, p. 144.
163. Lundberg, *Imperial Hearst*, p. 83.
164. Ibid., p. 85.
165. Roy Everett Littlefield III, *William Randolph Hearst: His Role in American Progressivism* (Lanham, MD: University Press of America, 1980), p. 35.
166. Ibid., p. 36.
167. Jane Rhodes, remarks, panel on African Americans and the Mass Media, Association for Education and Mass Communication, Kansas City, Mo., August 1993.
168. *Examiner*, Aug. 14, 1887.
169. Gerald J. Baldasty, "Business and the American Press," paper presented to the 1990 meeting of the American Journalism Historians Association, Coeur d'Alene, Idaho, p. 5.
170. Tebbel, *Life and Good Times*, p. 132.
171. *New York American*, July 9, 1904.
172. "Hearst Again in Congress—Ran Ahead of His Ticket—Talk of a New Party," *Editor and Publisher* (later *Editor & Publisher*), Nov. 12, 1904.
173. Swanberg, *Citizen Hearst*, pp. 223–227.
174. Ibid., p. 237, citing the *New York Times*, Nov. 8, 1905.
175. "Significance of Elections," *Editor and Publisher*, Nov. 11, 1905.
176. *Journal*, April 10, 1901.
177. Ibid.; originally appearing Feb. 4, 1900.
178. Hearst, Jr., *The Hearsts*, p. 45.
179. *New York Tribune*, Nov. 2, 1906.
180. *New York Times*, Nov. 2, 1906.
181. *Tribune*, Nov. 2, 1906.
182. *Times*, Nov. 3, 1906.
183. *Times*, Nov. 2, 1906.
184. *New York Tribune*, Nov. 4, 1906.
185. Ibid., Nov. 7, 1906.
186. Carlisle, "William Randolph Hearst," p. 127.
187. Ibid.; Carlisle cites Frederick Lewis Allen, *Since Yesterday* (New York: Harper and Brothers, 1939), p. 215.

10

Media and the Idea of Progress

When giving information and dealing with problems, even exposing problems, the media are regarded as a vanguard of progress. The activism of the media owes something to the journalism of the Progressive Era during the first two decades of the twentieth century. In fact, this period was defined as much by the efforts of its crusading, issue-oriented journalists and magazines, as they delved into political and industrial corruption, as by other phenomena. Progressive elements continue into modern society and the media of today.

PROGRESSIVISM VERSUS POPULISM

Some confuse the progressive movement with the end of nineteenth-century populism, and with good reason. Both were people-oriented reform movements, unhappy with the unfair distribution of wealth and angry with the railroads and other giant business enterprises. They shared some political mentors, among them the perennial candidate William Jennings Bryan, whose money policies were rejected but whose eloquent advocacy of popular rule and spirited attacks on the abuses of wealth were remembered.

But progressivism and populism in America differed. The populists, in a Jeffersonian tradition, sought to restore the individual to supremacy by weakening economic centers; progressives tried to accomplish the same things by making government stronger than big business, in the tradition of Alexander Hamilton, using power in the popular interest. Populism looked to the past, seeking to restore agrarian and small business foundations of liberty; progressivism accepted urbanism and large-scale business as inevitable. Progressives added elements of eastern labor movements and the middle class to the western and southern radicalism of the populists. Progressive leaders came from an emerging class of intellectuals, which included journalists, editors, clergy, novelists, sociologists, economists, poets, and historians.

The first generation after the Civil War witnessed the triumph of industry and thought of progress as an advance in the production of wealth. But the next generation, because of the uneven distribution of this wealth, redefined progress as improvement of the welfare of the many, and this became the definition of progress for those calling themselves progressives. They placed human values above material values.

The progressives were less interested in rhetoric than in facts. "Progressives insisted on being concrete," says historian Richard Hofstadter and associates. "Where did the money come from in elections? How much did the construction of the city hall really cost, and how much went as graft to political bosses? And so on."[1] Progressivism had a ready-made role for journalists.

Media as Purveyors of Information/Education

"JUST THE FACTS, MA'AM"

Progressivism affected the way news was handled. Facts became very important in reform-minded stories and in the formula success stories. To espouse reform generalities was not enough; facts were needed as supporting evidence. In the feature vein the same was true. Facts abounded in stories on celebrities—now they were the successful businessmen and women rather than generals and literary figures. What specific things had these people done to facilitate their successful rise in the world? People wanted to know and to participate in the new energy and opportunity. Facts could serve them well.

The turn-of-the-century interest in science and new discoveries influenced all facets of culture. In education, John Dewey's "progressive education movement" emphasized learning by doing rather than by rote. In philosophy, William James and others were espousing pragmatism—that truth is ever changing and that if it works, it is true. In science, empiricism—making determinations on the basis of facts—was the rule. The new mood had its effect on the media. There was a hunger and thirst for facts; mere entertainment was not enough.

Newspapers found themselves more and more in competition with magazines, which could present in great detail all the facts of an investigation, including ample background and an end-of-the-series application of solutions.

Hearst and Pulitzer had blurred the distinction between newspaper and magazine content with their highly illustrated feature spreads and elaborate Sunday feature editions. But the Progressive Era brought with it the challenge of a new kind of magazine emphasis covering the "realism" of the streets and hard facts of a city once left largely to newspapers.

Magazines Lead the Way

More and more newspapers tried to be like magazines. The *New York Sunday World* clamored that its editions made magazines obsolete and that it was "Better Illustrated Than Any Magazine!" while the *Saturday Evening Post* chimed in, "A good magazine is a good newspaper in a dress suit."[2]

As national magazines reached across city, state, and regional boundaries, they could afford to deal substantially with issues without fearing the recriminations that a one-town newspaper might feel from local politicians and businesspersons. As the reigning national magazines, as well as newspapers, presented formulas for success, they were also brooding over the inequities of life—the excesses of the rich and the misfortune and repression of those born to lesser states in life. With their in-depth corralling of information, they were also important in educating a wide sector.

At the forefront of the new exposé, education journalism at the turn of the century (1901) were three of the leading circulation general magazines:[3]

Cosmopolitan.   Founded in 1886 by Paul J. Schlicht, a partner in a printing firm, *Cosmopolitan*, with 350,000 circulation, aspired to be a monthly home magazine but soon took on literary pretensions and featured well-known writers. When the printing firm fell on hard times, *Cosmopolitan* found itself in dire straits. For three months Ulysses S. Grant, Jr., a California lawyer and son of the president with the same name, ran the magazine. But in the nick of time a buyer was found—Joseph Hallock, publisher of the *Christian at Work*.[4] Hallock introduced fiction serials, book reviews, and a discussion feature.

John Brisben Walker, an iron manufacturer, began to take an interest in acquiring *Cosmopolitan*, which was still plodding along with a circulation of only 20,000. In 1889 Walker bought *Cosmopolitan*; this was the same year that he was elected president of the Stanley Automobile Company of America.[5] A former West Pointer, he had served as a military adviser in China. He had also worked on newspapers in Cincinnati, Pittsburgh, and Washington.

Walker improved the quality of fiction, introduced travel articles, and at times engaged in the "yellow" journalism that had become characteristic of Hearst and Pulitzer. Featuring the sufferings of the Cuban peasant, the magazine sought to fan the flames of war with Spain. Walker even ran a four-part series on "A Brief History of Our War With Spain" on the eve of the Spanish-American War, predicting among other things the invasion of North America by the Spanish.

While the magazine fostered some investigative work, it nevertheless, as Tebbel notes, "carried more eulogies of captains of industry and their corporations than any other magazine, at the same time standing alone in calling for government ownership of railroads and trusts. Even Socialists were welcomed to its pages. In brief, it had something for everybody."[6]

Walker sold *Cosmopolitan* to Hearst in 1905. Predictably, "under Hearst the *Cosmopolitan* was more sensational than before," says Mott. "Hearst's idea of a magazine was the Sunday supplement raised to a higher degree of literary performance, but just as readable and attractive."[7] *Cosmopolitan*, still owned by the Hearst corporation, is today primarily a young woman's service magazine.

Munsey's.   Founded in 1889 by Frank A. Munsey, *Munsey's Weekly*, with 590,000 circulation, was a heavily illustrated satirical journal with a section on political and society gossip from Washington. Munsey started in the magazine business with a youth magazine, *Golden Argosy,* in 1882. With hardly any capital, the farm boy from Maine had a long uphill struggle. To save money he wrote his own fiction serials for the magazine. Briefly in 1884 he created and edited a Republican journal, *Munsey's Illustrated Weekly*, to support presidential candidate James G. Blaine. With Blaine's loss to Grover Cleveland, Munsey ended the magazine as quickly as it had begun. In 1888 he converted the *Golden Argosy* into *Argosy* for adults.

Dropping the price of *Munsey's* to a dime proved to be the step that gave his career a boost in 1893. Munsey went on to found *Puritan*, which he merged with *Godey's Lady's Book*, then *All Story*, which he merged with *Argosy* and *Peterson's*. Eventually in 1929, four years after his death, *Munsey's* merged with *Argosy All-Story* to become *All-Story Combined with Munsey's*, with *Argosy* becoming a separate publication. Soon the *Munsey's* name was dropped, and the magazine became *All-Story*.

Munsey, who bought, sold, merged, and founded newspapers wildly, at one time or another owned the *Washington Times; Baltimore American, News*, and *Star; Boston Journal*; and *Philadelphia Times*. In New York he wreaked havoc with thousands of jobs as staffs were shuffled and jobs eliminated. He merged the *New York Press* with the *Sun*, the *Morning Sun* with the *New York Herald*, the *Evening Sun* with the *New York Globe*, and the *New York Mail* with the *New York Telegram*. As we have seen, he bid for the *New York Tribune*, but when the Whitelaw Reid family declined to sell, he sold the *Herald* to the *Tribune*.

He had virtually no interest in in-depth reporting, despite an occasional article that looked like the start of a crusade. "Frank Munsey and his magazine were never a part of the mainstream of 'Progressive,' social reform thought," says Matthew Schneirov. "For Munsey, the whirlpool of real life was primarily the energy of economic expansion and the opportunities it afforded readers as consumers and producers."[8]

McClure's.   Founded in 1893 by Samuel Sidney McClure, a native of Ireland, and John Phillips, his classmate at Knox College, Galesburg, Illinois, *McClure's*, with 360,000 circulation, was meant at first to be an extension of the founders' fiction and feature syndicate. The magazine would use material left over or reprinted from the syndication distribution.

McClure's forte at the start was profiling famous persons, ranging from a section that printed pictures of famous persons at different times in their lives to Ida Tarbell's blockbuster treatment of "Napoleon." Tarbell joined the staff and went out in the field to talk with those who remembered Abraham Lincoln. The series ran in

1898–1899, replete with many pictures of Lincoln. *McClure's* was soon a success in circulation, advertising patronage, and prestige.[9]

McClure, always searching for new writers, paid the upcoming but unknown Jack London a living wage of $125 a month with the charge, "Send us everything you write—we will use what we can, and what we cannot we will endeavor to dispose of to the best possible advantage."[10] McClure hired other future novelists, such as Stephen Crane and Willa Cather, and he hired as editors those who became the foremost investigative writers of the day—Lincoln Steffens and Ray Stannard Baker, in addition to Tarbell.

Squarely in the progressive movement, with its interest on new things, *McClure's* presented articles on exploration, science, wild animals, railroads, and travel, as well as investigations into the corruption in industry and politics at all levels.

McClure and Phillips parted company in 1906 over McClure's grand plans for expansion into a potpourri of projects, including a bank, a housing development, a publishing company, foundations, and an insurance company, all without consulting Phillips. The magazine's circulation gradually declined. McClure sold the magazine to Hearst in 1925, and it ceased publishing in 1930. McClure continued writing on political issues and died at age ninety-two in 1949.

Media as Voices of Reform

RAKING THE "FILTH" OFF THE FLOOR

Muckraking became the term for in-depth, investigative journalism. The term was used to cover a group of enterprising reporters by progressive, reform-minded President Theodore Roosevelt. The president, having battled the trusts (companies holding monopoly control within their industries) and supported the new aggressive journalism, nevertheless found himself irritated by a 1906 article by David Graham Phillips in Hearst's *Cosmopolitan*, "The Treason of the Senate," an exposure of political corruption. Roosevelt felt the reporters were going too far, stirring up too much dirt and muck. Citing John Bunyan's *Pilgrim's Progress*, which tells of a man who could "look no way but downwards with a Muck-rake in his hand" as he continued to rake to himself the filth of the floor,[11] Roosevelt applied the term "muckraker" to the journalists. Roosevelt said in the supposedly off-the-record speech at the newspaper Gridiron Club in Washington:

> In *Pilgrim's Progress* the Man with the Muckrake is set forth as the example of him whose vision is fixed on carnal instead of on spiritual things. Yet he also typifies the man who in this life consistently refuses to see aught that is lofty, and fixes his eyes with solemn intentness only on that which is vile and debasing.[12]

Reports of the speech leaked out, but the president was not offended and repeated the speech on the record as he dedicated the cornerstone of the House of Representatives office building in April 1906. The scenario was perhaps orchestrated for political purposes. Mark Neuzil, of the University of St. Thomas, St. Paul, Minnesota, suggests, "The muckraker speech can be seen in an overall strategy of power and control by the president, particularly in response to his most powerful opponent, Hearst." The effect of the speech, Neuzil says, was to lead Roosevelt to capture "control of the debate over reform and [to strengthen] his position in the Republican Party. At the same time, the president successfully stalled Hearst's presidential ambitions."[13]

Muckraking has these six characteristics, according to Harry Stein: It "exposes a hidden situation, depicts the situation prescriptively, locates an agent of control, indicates preferred action, incites audience response, and maintains authorial autonomy."[14]

A Complex Role

Yet muckraking constituted more than "a literature of exposure," as Edwin E. Slosson, the editor of *The Independent*, put it in March 1906, a month before President Theodore Roosevelt tagged muckraking with its name.[15] But as confused as the muckrakers were about their role, and although "the muckrakers were different things at different times, even within the same article,"[16] says Robert Miraldi, some saw themselves as offering more than just exposé reporting. Charles Edward Russell started a 1908 article on the Trinity Church tenements with a disclaimer: "This is not a muckraking article. It is the story of mystery surrounding the great corporation which administers the temporal affairs of Trinity Church in New York."[17]

Stein suggests that the complex creature, the muckraker, interested in action as well as exposés, bequeathed a tradition that did not evaporate with the end of the Progressive Era but continued into the modern age. He cites the later work of writer-activists such as Ralph Nader, lobbyist for consumer concerns and author of a best-selling book criticizing the auto industry, *Unsafe at Any Speed* (1965), and Rachel Scott, author of *Muscle and Blood* (1974), which told of the extent of workplace diseases and injuries and overall poor working conditions. Stein even includes some modern political pundits who dissect a problem and offer solutions, such as syndicated Washington columnist Jack Anderson.

The Illustrious Muckrakers

Among the prominent muckrakers of the Progressive Era in the first decade–plus of the century were the following:

Jacob Riis (1849–1914). Technically Jacob Riis was a little ahead of the Progressive Era and its muckrakers, playing a kind of John the Baptist role as forerunner of the movement. Born in Denmark, he did not come to America until age twenty-one. He could empathize with the urban poor and the large immigrant populations of New York. He landed a job with a news service, the New York News

Association, and eventually covered the police beat for the *New York Tribune*, then the same beat for the *New York Sun*. Theodore Roosevelt, the reforming police commissioner of New York before becoming governor and president, regarded Riis as "the best American I ever knew" and "closer than a brother."[18] Riis exposed living conditions in the slums, the schemes of landlords, child labor abuses, and industries that contaminated drinking water.

Two things helped Riis get his message out: photographs and a series of bestselling books in which his articles were distilled and printed. It was now possible to take pictures at night with a newly developed flash device. Riis soon mastered the photo technique, nearly blinding himself a number of times because of the pervasive flash created by lighting magnesium powder cartridges in what amounted to a frying pan (thus the term, "flash in the pan"). The pictures made him all the more credible. "Now Riis had tangible proof to back his allegations," says Alexander Alland. "Few listened when he reported that lodgers slept fifteen to a room; his pictures proved it."[19] His books include *How the Other Half Lives*, *The Children of the Poor*, *The Making of an American*, and *The Battle with the Slum*.

Helen Campbell (1839–1918).   Like Riis, Helen Campbell was writing on social ills before the Progressive Era swung into high gear, but nevertheless she likely had an influence on Progressive Era journalism. In 1886–1887 she authored a twenty-one-part series in the *New York Tribune* on "Prisoners of Poverty: Women Wage-Workers and Their Lives," which presented "the sufferings and privations of working women" in poor areas of New York City. A native of Lockport, New York, Campbell was already established as a successful fiction writer, often centering her work on themes set in the slums. In 1879 she had written a six-part nonfiction series, "Studies in the Slums," for *Sunday Afternoon* magazine and a follow-up series of six articles on the same subject for *Lippincott's*. She collected these efforts into a book, *The Problems of the Poor*.[20]

Ida Minerva Tarbell (1857–1944).   Born in a log house in Erie County, Pennsylvania, Ida Tarbell was to challenge the giants of industry in her career. Her father had become an independent oil producer, only to be crushed and run out of business by oil mogul John D. Rockefeller. Early in her life she harbored an urge for revenge on behalf of her father.

Graduating from Allegheny College in Meadville, Pennsylvania, with a major in biology, Tarbell taught Greek, Latin, French, German, and other subjects at Poland (Ohio) Union Seminary. She landed a part-time clerical and footnoting job on a monthly, *The Chautauquan*, a publication of the Chautauqua Movement, which pioneered in adult education and correspondence-school courses. She was soon in charge of the magazine. But restless at thirty-two, she took off for Paris to study at the Sorbonne and to freelance. She did a series on revolutionary French women of the past and a book on French Revolution victim Madame Roland. Tarbell freelanced for *McClure's* magazine, and in 1894 she joined the magazine as an editor.[21]

Ida Tarbell: Exposed Standard Oil.

In the back of her mind she nursed an urge to take on the trusts, namely, Standard Oil, remembering how after the takeover of her father's refinery his partner shot himself, leaving debts for the Tarbell family to assume and leading to the mortgaging of the family home. Once completed, the "History of the Standard Oil Company" ran for nineteen installments in 1902 and 1903. It became a two-volume book in 1904 and was later reissued in one volume.

She tells of the birth of the oil industry, John D. Rockefeller's rise to fame from a job as bookkeeper, his partnership in a produce commission business on the docks of Cleveland, his gamble of large investments in a refinery business, then creation of his own firm and combination of companies. Tarbell chronicles the wheeling and dealing, the conspiracies with the railroads to fix rates, the oil blockades, the legal challenges, the compromises, and the organizing genius of Rockefeller.

Tarbell left *McClure's* in 1906 to join with other writers and editors in launching *American Magazine*. Tarbell wrote exposés for the magazine, one of them a lengthy report on the impact of special interests on the American tariff. When *American Magazine* was sold in 1915 Tarbell took to the lecture circuit and freelance writing.

Tarbell penned twenty-four books, including biographies of two businessmen, Elbert Gray and Owen Young, of whom she approved. Her autobiography, *All in the Day's Work*, published in 1939, five years before her death, took a parting shot at John D. Rockefeller as she described him teaching a Sunday school class she observed in Cleveland in 1905. She details every nuance of his face, with its "thin sharp nose," set teeth and "colorless eyes," and offers a personal judgment: "I was sorry for him. I know no companion as terrible as fear. Mr. Rockefeller . . . was afraid of his own kind."[22]

Lincoln Steffens (1866–1936). Son of a successful Sacramento banker, Steffens studied at the Sorbonne in Paris and three German universities after taking a bachelor's degree from the University of California. He had a successful newspaper career as a reporter in New York at the *Evening Post* and *Commercial Advertiser* before signing on with McClure as managing editor of *McClure's* magazine in 1901.

McClure sent him to meet writers, editors, and leading citizens from a list he had. Steffens first went to Chicago, then to St. Paul, Minnesota, where he interviewed an eccentric lumber tycoon. Acting on a tip, he went on to St. Louis to check on Joseph Folk, a "circuit attorney," the prosecuting officer for the St. Louis district who was making a commotion about bribery schemes in the St. Louis board of aldermen. Folk reported that his world was run by criminals. Steffens' appetite was whetted; he wanted the full story. As a *McClure's* editor he had no intentions of writing the article himself and assigned it to Claude Wetmore, city editor of the *Post-Dispatch*. But Steffens was not entirely satisfied with Wetmore's article: "He had left out some salient facts; he had spared some very conspicuous characters; he had 'gone easy' on the boss, Ed Butler [the boss that Pulitzer dealt with], for example." Steffens filled in some parts. Wetmore "remonstrated; he could not live and work in St. Louis if the article was printed as I had edited it. When I insisted, he compromised. I must sign it with him and take the blame for my insertions. . . . And so I appeared as a muckraker."[23] Both bylines went on the article, which was titled, in deference to New York's famous grafter of the past, "Tweed Days in St. Louis," with the subhead, "Joseph W. Folk's Single-handed Exposure of Corruption, High and Low." It began dramatically, pulling no punches, settling on a prescriptive angle: what one man was doing about it.

Steffens followed with exposé articles on corruption in government in Minneapolis, Pittsburgh, Philadelphia, Chicago, New York, Cleveland, and Cincinnati, as well as focusing on state corruption in New Jersey, Rhode Island, Missouri, Illinois, Ohio, and Wisconsin. A book entitled *The Shame of the Cities* collected the first part of the series; it appeared in 1904 and became a best-seller.

Steffens left *McClure's* in 1906 to become vice president of *American Magazine*, later working for *Everybody's Magazine* and as editor of the *New York Globe*. He had pro-Soviet leanings. When asked about the Soviet Union after he was a part of a diplomatic mission for the United States there, he responded, "I have been over into the future, and it works."[24] His enthusiasm for leftist politics and opposition to the draft in World War I caused him to be blacklisted by many editors. After nearly a decade living in Europe, Steffens eventually settled into the artists' colony at Carmel, California. Bearing the sobriquet of "guru of the left," he took to the lecture circuit. "A pillar of the Stalinist Church in America," socialist Max Eastman said of Steffens in his later years.

David Graham Phillips (1867–1911).   After graduating from the College of New Jersey (Princeton), Phillips, a native of Madison, Indiana, worked for the *Cincinnati Times-Star* and then the *Cincinnati Commercial-Gazette*. After a stint at the *New York Sun*, Phillips went over to Pulitzer's *World* in 1893, first as a correspondent in London; then developing close ties with Pulitzer, he became an editorial writer for the *World*. When his first novel, *The Great God Success*, appeared in 1901, he left to devote full time to freelance writing. In the following ten years he published twenty-three novels and a number of magazine articles.

Like other novelists of the period, Phillips was a realist, depicting corruption in corporations and government. In 1905, a year in which Phillips had already published five novels, William Randolph Hearst's *Cosmopolitan* called on Phillips to develop a series on the Senate, already started by Charles Edward Russell, who did not have time to develop and finish it.

Phillips' venomous views on the Senate were already known through his novels. *The Cost* described how monopolies rigged state legislatures, which at that time chose U.S. senators; *The Social Secretary* told how wealthy persons bought their way into the Senate; and *The Plum Tree* cast aspersions on the Senate itself, describing how a senator manipulated both parties on behalf of a syndicate of rich businessmen. Phillips could be expected to deliver a scathing exposé of the Senate, gloating in the mention of misdeeds and in naming scoundrels, and he did so in his ten-part series, "The Treason of the Senate." Despite criticism from readers, including the president, the articles were effective, and citizens across the country were scrutinizing their elected officials as never before.

Phillips was fatally shot in 1911 in New York at age forty-four by a mentally ill musician who thought that members of his family were maligned in one of Phillips' novels.

Others in the muckraker, Progressive Era tradition were these:

- *Christopher Connolly*, a prosecuting attorney in Butte, Montana (who prosecuted the first man to be hanged by the state of Montana), became a muckraker for *McClure's*, writing on the political wars and business dealings and bribery schemes in politics. His "The Story of Montana" appeared in *McClure's* in September 1906. Also "his stories, which assailed the mining interests, created a nation-wide sensation," his obituary in the *New York Herald Tribune* (Nov. 9, 1933) said.[25]

- *Ray Stannard Baker* wrote for *McClure's* on big banking—(a profile of J. P. Morgan), labor unrest, railroad rate fixing, and the plight of blacks in the South. He was editor of the magazine's syndicated material. In 1906 he moved to *American Magazine,* as did other writers and editors, where he penned his best known series, "Following the Color Line." The series recounting horrors of racism in the South became a popular book. Baker also exposed nefarious practices in religion. His "The Case Against Trinity" in the *American* criticized the ways a New York church gained and misused its wealth, especially its role in owning substandard, disease-ridden tenement houses.

- *Ernest Poole,* upon graduation from Princeton in 1902, moved into the University Settlement House in New York. The house was encouraging writers and would-be writers to move in to help in its role as "a pioneer in social inquiry as a preliminary to reform" and as it sought to generate "a string of investigations of poverty, housing, and unemployment."[26] Poole soon found himself a successful coach in street and rooftop basketball. When the director of the settlement house found himself on a committee of settlement workers to look into child-labor abuses and strategies to lobby for new child-labor laws, he first turned to a former magazine editor to write a report. But when the editor produced a boring pamphlet, the director turned to Poole.

  "For weeks I ranged the crowded quarters of the city," Poole recalled, "talking to wise tough little guys, liking them and making friends by giving them suppers and cigarettes and taking some of them to the big top gallery at the old Academy of Music. . . . By such bribes I got the facts and stories I wanted about their jobs and their lives."[27] He wrote in a report the stories of the boys—some were messengers for opium dens, some had "loathsome" venereal diseases, some spent the nights sleeping on the streets. Poole developed the report into an article and placed it with *McClure's.* He also sold shorter versions to the *New York Post* and *Collier's.*

- *William Hard* studied coroner's records in Chicago and found in one year—1906—that forty-six men had died of industrial accidents in one steel plant alone. His "Making Steel and Killing Men" appeared in *Everybody's Magazine* in November 1907. He called for "public supervision" of steelmaking, not only for humanitarian reasons but also because society had to bear the results of industrial accidents in terms of poverty, demoralization, and vice and crime.[28]

- *Rheta Childe Dorr* articulated the concerns and problems of both working and nonworking women in a 1910 book, *What Eight Million Women Want.* Some of the chapters had appeared earlier as articles in *Hampton's Magazine.* Dorr reported on the rise of women's clubs and women's civic organizations that worked for various causes. She declared: "Women are no longer wholly dependent economically, intellectually, and spiritually on a ruling class of men. They look on life with the eyes of reasoning adults, where once they regarded it as trusting children."[29]

- *Florence Kelley,* a social worker and crusader for the settlement movement that created housing and services in crowded city areas, wrote as a member of the "municipal housekeepers" movement. These women accepted the role of house-keeper and homemaker, but also believed that the home was larger than an individual's home and included the community at large. She wrote for *Survey* magazine and the *International Review*. Her 1905 book *Some Ethical Gains Through Legislation* crusaded for the creation of a federal children's commission.[30]

- *Edwin Markham*, the poet of the muckrakers (one of his famous poems is "The Man with the Hoe"), produced a series called "The Hoe-Man in the Making," describing child labor abuse for *Cosmopolitan*, September 1906. He begins his series:

> Once so the story goes, an old Indian chieftain was shown the ways and wonders of New York. He saw the cathedrals, the skyscrapers, the bleak tenements, the blaring mansions, the crowded circus, the airy span of the Brooklyn Bridge. "What is the most surprising thing you have seen?" asked several comfortable Christian gentlemen of this benighted pagan whose worship was a "bowing down to sticks and stones." The savage shifted his red blanket and answered in three slow words, "Little children working."
>
> It has remained, then, for civilization to give the world an abominable custom which shocks the social ethics of even an unregenerate savage. For the Indian father does not ask his children to work, but leaves them free till the age of maturity, when they are ushered with solemn rites into the obligations of their elders. Some of us are wondering why our savage friends do not send their medicine men as missionaries, to shed upon our Christian darkness the light of barbarism. Child labor is a new thing in human affairs. Ancient history records no such infamy.[31]

- *Charles Edward Russell* worked for a number of newspapers, including the *New York World* (as city editor), *New York Journal* (as managing editor), and Hearst's *American* in Chicago (as publisher). Active in politics, he ran—unsuccessfully—as a candidate of the Socialist Party for governor of New York, for mayor of New York City, and for the Senate. He won a Pulitzer Prize for a biography of orchestra pioneer Theodore Thomas. He wrote prison exposé articles for *Everybody's Magazine*. No muckraking journalism is more gripping than his firsthand account of the abuses in the Georgia prison system that allowed convicts to be leased out to private entrepreneurs. His "A Burglar in the Making," written in 1908, follows a young convicted burglar into the system of horrors.

- *Upton Sinclair*, who did his muckraking through realistic fiction, is best known for *The Jungle*, a book based on his research in the lives of immigrants working in the unsanitary Chicago stockyards. The book first appeared in serial form in the Socialist Party newspaper *Appeal to Reason* before appearing in the form of a novel in 1906. It was one of the ninety novels Sinclair was to write in his long life span of ninety years. An on-again, off-again member of the Socialist Party, he emerged as a Democrat to run for governor of California in 1934 on the platform "End Poverty in California" (EPIC). Fiercely opposed by the *Los Angeles Times* and other media, Sinclair, depicted as a subversive socialist, narrowly missed election. He won the Pulitzer Prize for fiction in 1942 for a book, *Dragon's Teeth*, about the rise of Hitler.

- *Ida Baker Wells-Barnett*, born a slave in 1862 in Mississippi, worked as a schoolteacher before becoming part owner of a newspaper, the *Memphis Free Speech*. When the paper printed her series of articles charging that white competitors were involved in the lynching of three black grocers, a white mob descended on the newspaper and smashed the presses. Threats against her life only made her more adamant. She proceeded to make a crusade against lynching her life's main work.

    Wells-Barnett wrote pamphlets that received a wide distribution, and she was a columnist for the *New York Age* and the *Chicago Inter Ocean*. Her attorney husband, Ferdinand Barnett, owned the *Chicago Conservator*. In 1909 she produced an article on lynching in Illinois for the *Chicago Defender*. She also campaigned for women's right to vote in her writings and lectures. She ran unsuccessfully for the Illinois senate as an independent. Her writings appeared in twenty-five publications, and she launched five books. The last, *Crusade for Justice*, was published posthumously in 1970.

- *Vera Connolly*, among others, kept alive the muckraking tradition even after the Progressive Era had ebbed. Unlike the work of earlier muckrakers who wrote mostly for general magazines, Connolly's investigations appeared in women's magazines, such as *Good Housekeeping, Delineator*, and *Woman's Home Companion*. Connolly, whose work appeared in the 1920s and 1930s, "personified the ideals of the Progressives," says Mary Ellen Waller-Zuckerman. "Like the Progressives, she possessed a strong faith in the essential goodness of people and thought that knowledge would bring about change. Connolly tried to improve society by exposing evil and educating the public, so that citizens could create the country she believed they truly wanted."[32]

    She wrote about the failure of families, juvenile delinquency, and crime. Her articles, usually top-heavy with statistics, often offered solutions to society's problems. She summarized her philosophy:

    > I can't see any value to exposing a public evil unless you have some practical remedy to offer. Nearly always there is a remedy. Often it isn't obvious. To dig it out is sometimes tedious, dull, time-consuming. There's no fire-works to the job. It must be distilled opinions of many persons, many authorities. But if it isn't there, a crusading article is futile, even cruel.[33]

Media as Definers and Keepers of Values (and Biases)
MUCKRAKING'S RELIGIOUS ROOTS

The progressive muckrakers drew on their conservative evangelical bearings to respond to new materialistic forces. In discussing "The Evangelical Origins of the Muckrakers" in *American Journalism*, Bruce Evenson insists, "What chroniclers have paid insufficient attention to is the vital struggle of faith that appears at the center of many of the muckrakers' personal lives and how this warfare became externalized in their writings."[34] He points out how S. S. McClure of the muckraking *McClure's* magazine felt "the Lord had some 'great work' for him to do";[35] muckraker Ida Tarbell, who "received Christ" at age eleven, though cynical kept "a childlike 'conviction of divine goodness at work in the world'";[36] for Lincoln Steffens, "Christianity alone [a radical version of it], he became convinced, provided the only possibility of real reform."[37] Concerning the noted muckraker novelist Upton Sinclair, Evenson says: "Of the criticisms Sinclair suffered in his long career the one he received most gladly was the charge he suffered from a 'Christ complex.' 'The world needs a Jesus,' Sinclair reportedly answered without embarrassment, 'more than it needs anything else.'"[38]

Noting that most of the muckraker journalists came from devout Protestant families, Judson Grenier observes that their writings are full of "Christian moral concepts and Christian symbols. Christian ideals—truth, the Golden Rule, the inherent goodness of man, the power of prayer, optimism—these are the guidestones of individuals whose experience shaped a heightened social awareness." These are consistent with the "faith in the Protestant ethic as a socially-molding force" that was "characteristic of the Progressive years."[39]

Correspondingly, clergy and theologians, often ignored in their pulpits, discovered a new area of influence—an application in service—with the social gospel, so-called because the movement literally took Jesus' directives to minister to the poor and set at liberty those who were afflicted in bondage.[40] Leaders of the social gospel movement ranged from Jane Addams, founder of Hull House in Chicago, who called on "ardent youth of today" to apply traditional Christian values "to bring about juster social conditions,"[41] to Walter Rauschenbusch, a professor of church history at Rochester (New York) Theological Seminary, who espoused "Christian Socialism" in a 1907 book, *Christianity and the Social Crisis*. Historian Richard Hofstadter saw the social gospel movement as "an attempt to restore through secular leadership some of the spiritual influence and authority and social prestige that clergymen had lost through the upheaval in the system of status and the secularization of society."[42] Reform movements and causes—helping to humanize society and spreading the benefits for all—were ways of putting the social gospel into practice.

Progressivism was, like Christianity, goal oriented. History was moving to a judgment day that would also include a new world, a heaven. And the Armageddons—the ultimate battlefields of the future—would be a showdown between good and evil. For progressives a changed society was not a backward look to the better days of the past, which seemed to entrance the populists, but a dialectic movement forward, pitting corporate evil against the humanitarian good. "Ordinarily we say that progress differs from change in that it implies a goal," wrote Arthur Colton, "and that any change is progressive which makes moves toward that goal."[43]

Progressives were convinced that ultimately humanitarian values would triumph over evil. And if society progressed, it would get better, if not achieve perfectibility. Theirs was a linear view of history. Intellectually, the progressives drew from the influence of social Darwinism, applying the evolutionary, progressive concepts of Charles Darwin to the movement of society and its improvement by the survival of the fittest or most enlightened.

The Idea of Progress

The "idea of progress" goes back to biblical times in the Judeo-Christian tradition. The Greeks had their versions of ideal societies, but these were to be established, not evolved. Yet as Robert Nisbet notes, even the Greeks, from their analysis of motion to the formulation of ideas, could not escape some sense of progress. Even Plato, for whom "only the heavenly world of perfect forms is the real world; all else is but appearance," conceded nevertheless that there were "two orders of reality: that of the essentially religious or mystical, the timeless, eternal, and perfect; and that of the material, the social, economic, and political, the order in which we are obliged to live our days. For Plato this order is . . . dynamic, always changing."[44]

But "the idea of progress, according to a widely accepted interpretation," noted Christopher Lasch, "represents a secularized version of the Christian belief in providence. The ancient world, we are told, entertained a cyclical view of history, whereas Christianity gave it a clearly defined direction, from the fall of man to his ultimate redemption."[45]

Progress in biblical terms was somewhat of a contradiction in nature. The faithful were called to improve their lot by dominating the creatures and forces of nature,[46] on the one hand, and practicing love and charity to others, on the other. Although Jesus urged his followers to be "perfect,"[47] nevertheless the total perfection of society, the creation of a utopia, remained for an eschatological event—the second coming of Christ. Although kept alive in the various heresies and sects of the church over the centuries, progress was left to final realization in the afterlife—for the individual, a purgatory (in Roman Catholic theology) to experience before becoming holy, and for society, a newly created city on a heavenly plain, a City of God, as Augustine called it.

It was not until the new faith in the possibilities of the human race in the Renaissance and the intellectual freedom of the seventeenth century that the ideas

---

The Lighter Side

*P*rogressive columnist E. L. Meyer expressed his views on nations who reneged on their loan payments to the United States with a bit of stereotypical humor.

"Token" for a Ride

WASHINGTON—Great Britain and Italy made small "token payments" on the installments of their debts to the United States due Thursday—News Item.

"Mr. Schmackenhoosen," I said, beaming upon my grocer, "I was delighted to receive your memorandum today, calling my attention to the fact that I owe you the trifling sum of $26.34. There was a certain restraint and dignity in your communication, Mr. Schmackenhoosen, which indicate you are a person of uncommon tact, and believe me I shall use all of my power at Washington to have you appointed to the diplomatic corps. I believe the thing for you would be a consular appointment to Bermuda, because as a grocer, Mr. Schmack-enhoosen, you certainly know your onions."

"Vot . . . vot . . ." said the grocer, looking at me slightly pop-eyed.

"Nay, do not overwhelm me with thanks," I protested. "I insist that you would perform meritorious service for our nation. Indeed, you have a lovely ambassadorial waist-line, the perfect 72, though I do believe par is only 68: However, Mr. Schmackenhoosen, you do lack diplomatic training, and that is the reason for my visit to you. I am going to give you practical experience. Now I owe you the sum of $26, and—"

"Und 34 cents," said Mr. Schmackenhoosen grimly.

"Exactly, Now, as you know, it is no longer the fashion to pay debts outright. Oh, dear, no. Such an old-fashioned and uncouth habit. In our time, Mr. Schmackenhoosen, we proceed about such business more delicately, more diplomatically. England owed America 75 millions on an installment yesterday and paid 10 millions as a token; Italy owed us 13 millions and paid one million as a token. You perceive how simple this token business is. I know you will be charmed to learn that I shall settle my account with you on the same delightful basis."

"Now you look here vunce," said Mr. Schmackenhoosen, waving his arms, "I tell you . . ."

"Oh, please, I know exactly what you are going to tell me. You're going to tell how grand it is to run your store along international, diplomatic lines. And I agree with you heartily, Schmackenhoosen. Expansion, that's the thing! We must get away from this narrow provincialism, and move forward to broader horizons. Yes, sir! And this token system is in the vanguard of the New Day, Mr. Schmackenhoosen. What I propose to do is

this. I shall not be old-fashioned and pay my debt to you, but I shall leave with you this friendly little token, which indicates that I am aware of my debt of $26.34 but it doesn't worry me in the least. Here, Mr. Schmack-enhoosen."

With these words I pressed into the honest grocer's palm my token payment, a rare aluminum Schlitz Palm Garden beer-check, good for a nickel in trade in 1910.

Mr. Schmackenhoosen blinked at my token in his hand and swallowed hard. He seemed on the point of thanking me profusely, which always embarrasses me. So I said hastily:

"Say no more, my good friend. I know exactly how you feel. And after you ring up my token, do me the favor of delivering to my home a pound of coffee, a case of beer and a loaf of rye-bread."

Then I skipped rapidly away, having other matters that required my immediate attention.

Some hours later Mr. Schmackenhoosen's delivery boy deposited in my kitchen a tiny package. I opened it with astonishment. It contained a thin shaving of rye-bread, one coffee bean and one cap of a beer-bottle. There was a note in the package, scrawled on a piece of wrapping paper. It read:

"I haf yur order. I am became new-fashion Mr. Meyer und I vud not tink of sending by yur house vun pound coffee, a case bier und a rye-bread. Aber, no! I send heremit yoost some tokens. Ven do ya get me dot dipplemaniac yob? I bet yu I learn dot bizness mighty fast, ja. Sincerely Schmackenhoosen Bros. & Co."

I groaned and tore my hair.

"It appears," I reflected bitterly, "that I have been token for a ride."

Source: The Progressive, vol. 3, no. 82, June 24, 1933.

of progress bloomed. "Science destroyed much of the old cosmology, and at the same time it became, itself, the first major aspect of human life in which men could recognize the progressive principle," says Sidney Pollard.[48] J. B. Bury, writing on the idea of progress right after World War I, sought to salvage the idea from the nihilism resulting from the war by redefining it as a relative term. He noted that "the Idea of Progress had to overcome a psychological obstacle which may be described as the *illusion of finality*." He believed the day would come "when a new idea will usurp its place as the directing idea of humanity." He says that the very doctrine of progress is itself relative and must progress to new terms, "just as Providence, in its day, was an idea of relative value."[49]

Even though the American experience of an optimistic Progressive Era ended with the imposing gloom of World War I and its visible setback in human progress, followed in not too many years by the rise of the Third Reich and the Holocaust, war again, and the tyrannies of fascist and communist dictators, progress—a relative term, as Bury saw it—survived, offering limited hope.[50] With different labels, progress still retained some of the old sociopolitical agenda. From time to time progressive political parties and progressive candidates emerged. Consider the Progressive Party of 1924, a coalition of socialists, labor and radical farm groups nominating Senator Robert La Follette for president; the Progressive Party of 1948, a left-wing third party movement, nominating former vice president Henry Wallace for president; and the Ross Perot–inspired Reform Party of 1996.

And each presidential election has its progressive, dialectical agenda to deal with the complexities of middle-class and urban ills as there are promises of emerging new quasi-utopias. The reform programs, with labels of New Freedom (Woodrow Wilson), the New Deal (Franklin Roosevelt), the Fair Deal (Harry Truman), the New Frontier (John Kennedy), the Great Society (Lyndon Johnson), and the Age of Possibility (Bill Clinton), constitute new canons in the primers of progressivism. Its spirit is kept alive also in the occasional efforts of the media to set the record straight and, adhering to traditional values, to initiate reform by exposure and the presentation of facts.

Media as Fourth Estate: Adversaries of Government

THE MUCKRAKING SCORE CARD

Justin Kaplan, who produced a Pulitzer Prize–winning book on Mark Twain (*Mister Clemens and Mark Twain*) and a definitive biography of Steffens (*Lincoln Steffens: A Biography*), believes the very ascendancy of magazines gave the reform writers special influence. No true national newspaper or television existed. It was up to magazines to be the common medium of communication across the country. *McClure's*, for instance, reached most of the literate people, and "would certainly be read, and eagerly awaited, by anyone in a position of influence."[51]

Thus, with the ability to gain national attention, magazines assumed a measure of authority in the first decade of the twentieth century. This can be seen in their ability to determine the national mood. "Perhaps their major accomplishment was to help bring about a change in public attitude toward the human condition," says Judson A. Grenier. They trumpeted the idea that the ills of society, such as poverty and corrupt practices, were the result of mankind's own doing, and therefore, instead of being inevitable, were treatable and curable. Such a message popularized and propelled the idea that progress was possible.[52]

Acknowledging that "legislative accomplishments are only one measure of the results of muckraking, and the relationship between specific articles and laws is somewhat tenuous," Grenier says, "nevertheless, the record is impressive."[53]

For instance:

- Steffens' series "Shame of the Cities" for *McClure's* resulted in municipal-election and civil-service reform.
- George Kibbe Turner's 1906 article in *McClure's* helped pave the way for the commission plan of city government.
- Ida Tarbell's work on Standard Oil is credited for helping pass the Elkins Act abolishing rebates.
- Ray Stannard Baker's writing on railroads in *McClure's* likely had an influence on passing the 1905 Hepburn Act, which set up the Interstate Commerce Commission and made regulations on railroads stricter.
- Upton Sinclair's *The Jungle* and Charles Edward Russell's articles on the "beef trust" in *Everybody's* likely influenced the Beveridge meat inspection amendment.
- Three writers—Samuel Hopkins Adams in *Collier's*, Edward Bok in the *Ladies' Home Journal*, and Mark Sullivan, writing in both—consolidated public pressure for the Pure Food and Drug Acts of 1907 and 1911.
- Thomas Lawson's "Frenzied Finance" series in *Everybody's* and Burton Hendrick's "Story of Insurance" in *McClure's* led to a New York state probe that ended in insurance reform laws.
- David Graham Phillips' "Treason of the Senate," published in *Cosmopolitan* in 1906, called for direct election of senators. This became law seven years later when the Seventeenth Amendment was passed.
- Burton J. Hendrick's article "Daughters of the Poor" in *McClure's* led to the passing of the 1910 Mann Act (known as the White Slave Traffic Act), aimed at stopping the transportation of women across state lines for immoral purposes.

Further, says Grenier, muckraking most likely significantly encouraged legislation involving child labor, conservation, women's suffrage, lower tariffs, the income tax, judicial reform, and the pursuit of antitrust prosecutions.[54] Even in later days specific works of the muckrakers were remembered. In the 1960s President Lyndon Johnson paid tribute to Upton Sinclair's book *The Jungle* in signing the Wholesome Meat Act.[55] And it is possible to argue that a part of the muckraker investigative tradition stayed alive in the ongoing exposé and investigative reporting of later periods.

Did They Really Succeed?

Yet there are those who downplay the influence of the muckrakers. While crediting the reform muckrakers with creating "a truly national climate of reform," Louis Geiger says the muckrakers were failures at reforming among their prime target, the urban population. He points out most of the legislation of reform in the first decade and the first half of the twentieth century was the result of agrarian or farm-area efforts, and the politicians who led the successful reforms were from farm states. Geiger refers to the Federal Land Bank Act, the Smith-Lever farm extension act, and

Upton Sinclair: His Jungle *resulted in food law changes.*

the Smith-Hughes vocational teaching act as "clearly aimed at redressing grievances of the agrarian interest."[56]

Geiger wants to know where comparable legislation can be found dealing with such subjects as city slums, the blight of poverty and unemployment, prostitution, and isolation of immigrants or racial minorities. "The Negro," he says, "was actually set back further than he already was by the Wilson administration's employment policies, and he got no new legal or constitutional protections. For the immigrant there was a rising threat of nativism and exclusion."[57]

Blaming pressures by business and advertising for bringing an end to the Progressive Era's journalism and insisting that the circulation outlets for the muck-rakers were not all that extensive, Geiger argues that "the times were not yet really right for the synthesis that the muckrakers were attempting. The agrarian side of the nation was still too powerful and opinionated, and the urban side still too fragmented as middle class, ethnic minorities, and the poor to accept wholesale reformism; indeed, even the middle class was unprepared for the urban emphasis offered by the muckrakers."[58]

Media as Vehicles of Sensationalism/Entertainment
WERE THE MUCKRAKERS SENSATIONALISTS?

Did the muckrakers carry sensationalism to new dimensions? Did they leave a legacy for future media of sensationalism as they did of exposé and in-depth reporting?

For a number of reasons the muckrakers do not fit the model of a tabloid brand of journalism that feeds on racy, titillating scandal and the bizarre. (1) The muckrakers wrote very long pieces, even series, in contrast to the extremely short, quickly read pieces of the tabloids. (2) They concentrated on facts, sometimes dull facts that they presented accurately in a fictional format, but they did not confuse fiction with fact. (3) They wrote for magazines that appeared monthly. (4) Their topics were of a broader, deeper scope, often dealing with issues on a systemic basis, rather than offering a quick fix on a subject. (5) They gave a national dimension to the problem at hand. (6) They were interested in reform in law and regulations, whether they explicitly stated this purpose in each article or installment or not. (7) Although they used graphic illustrations, they were more word oriented than the modern tabloids. (8) They embraced ideologies.

Yet the muckrakers were sensationalists. Like the reporting in Pulitzer and Hearst newspapers, their work had the effect of evoking a conversation or "gee whiz" response from the reader, albeit their subjects were of a more lengthy nature. But they proved it was possible to get people talking about abuse in child labor, wronged women in prostitution, prison brutality, cutthroat capitalism, and outrageously corrupt politicians by way of a weekly or monthly treatment in a magazine, just as it was on the front pages of the daily press. The muckrakers' topics were indeed sensational by any standard.

Stories Appealing to the Senses

An approach to "observational reporting" that involves the reader in "the sensory experience," Warren Francke points out, was used by Riis and Russell and others. Francke argues, "If . . . sensory experience is at the heart of sensational reporting, this technique might be considered sensational *per se*, particularly in its application to 'how the other half lives,' i.e., to low life and the dark side. . . . And this side was the more accessible in the early days of organized reporting."[59]

John Durham Peters put it bluntly: "The histories of muckraking and sensationalism are intertwined. The raw truth could be as sensational as the wildest story concocted by the cleverest reporter." The aim of muckraking was to present "the hidden, in both the photographic and pornographic senses of that word. It aimed to bring the social body naked into the public view."[60]

The muckrakers' interest in narrative and fiction techniques also helped make their work sensational. As noted earlier, in the penny press era, and even earlier, articles contained the elements of "story" that go into a sensational account. First, there is "plot," that is, there is a problem to overcome, and this creates conflict—an ingredient of most front-page news and at the core of in-depth, investigative magazine journalism, including the muckraking variety. There are protagonists—the heroes—those who are wronged by the system and who suffer, those on whose behalf some reform is necessary. Pulitzer's *World* wrote about suffering children in the tenements, Hearst about children being killed by trolley cars, Riis about New York slum overcrowding, Edwin Markham about child labor abuse. Such suffering, defenseless heroes gripped the senses and emotions of readers. All this was done through personal stories of heroes and villains, with attention to the finest detail. The muckrakers—like all good sensationalists, as well as many regular journalists—dealt with narrative. They had stories to tell, and they were sensational in subject, in plot, and in the narrative telling.

The Muckraking Novelists

It is no coincidence that muckrakers were foremost storytellers; indeed they were wedded to fiction techniques. Influenced by the trend for realism in the fiction of their times, many were also successful novelists. Samuel Hopkins Adams wrote fifty books, many of them novels;[61] David Graham Phillips, before he was murdered, as noted above, produced twenty-three novels. Former reporters Theodore Dreiser, Stephen Crane, and Jack London had created a legacy of realistic novels.

Nothing short of sensational was Upton Sinclair's novel *The Jungle*, written in the white heat of anger and enlisting at high intensity the emotions of the reader. The book told the story of young lovers from Lithuania who arrived in Chicago almost penniless. The young man, Jurgis, went to work in the Chicago stockyards, and the young couple wed. With them are Jurgis' father, his wife's stepmother, the stepmother's brother, and an orphan cousin. The family is cheated at every turn. The unsanitary conditions at the packing plant are described in detail. Jurgis gets hurt and loses his job. His wife, Ona, and baby die while unattended at childbirth. He is reduced to working as a migrant in the fields and to begging. The cousin, who ends up in prostitution, gives him some money. He finally gets a job in a hotel. The manager is a Socialist. Jurgis goes to a Socialist meeting, and the novel ends with him nourishing a new ray of hope. Sinclair's fiction was true to life even though it was based on a specific ideology. To some extent the muckrakers succeeded in expressing themselves sensationally through fiction while being true to reality.

The language of the muckrakers was also sensational. Caricaturizing senators, Phillips said of two of them, "Our Platts and Burtons have no more moral sense than an ossified man has feeling."[62] Muckraker Poole sensationalized buildings by giving them names like "The Ink Pot," "The Bucket," "The Morgue." In an essay on the need for reform concerning tuberculosis treatment, he described a disease-ridden block in New York as "the lung block," a term he used again in a novel.[63]

Because of a certain sophistication, the muckrakers did not seem to be sensationalists, but in their subject matter and the style they employed, they were.

Media as Businesses

ADVERTISING CONTROL OF NEWS

The Progressive Era saw an encroachment of advertisers on the media. Competition was keen for the new corporate advertising dollar. Inevitably, conflicts between the business and editorial departments emerged. "Advertising became a battleground in which each department could test its respective organizational strength," says Elliot Walton King. Who could control the news, especially news involving an advertiser?[64]

In his series on the American newspaper in *Collier's* in May 1911, Will Irwin lambasted the publisher who was "not an editor with the professional point of view, but a businessman."[65] He said he was discouraged by hearing newspaper publishers at conventions not discussing the state of journalism but rather devoting their time to discussing newspapers as a commodity. He saw the commercialism of the system arising from the fact that a newspaper is not supported by circulation sales but rather by advertisers, a very small segment of the population. Irwin found that for every dollar gained from subscriptions and street sales, the newspaper received, on the average, $3.50 to $4.00 from advertising.

As an example of how this relationship affected newspaper news policies, Irwin turned to Boston. When Boston beer brewers were put on trial for diluting beer, the newspapers ignored the story. Only one paper, the *Traveler*, had the courage to mention the divorce proceedings of a prominent department store family. Irwin concluded that Boston journalism was "decent of speech, cowardly of heart, a prophet when the cause does not touch its own pocket, a dumb thing when it does."[66]

In Philadelphia department stores and other businesses held considerable sway over newspapers. Oswald Garrison Villard, of the *New York Evening Post*, said that when he worked in Philadelphia his newspaper would send him to the large advertisers with the information that "they could have as much space in news columns at any time as they wanted."[67] King tells how the problems persisted in Philadelphia. When a suit was brought against Gimbel's for fire code violations, there was no mention of it in the newspapers until some months later when Gimbel's denial of the charges was printed. In 1917 a strike against the John Wanamaker store, located directly across from Philadelphia's city hall, went unreported.

Brand Names Catch On

Advertising was also taking on national dimensions, and producers and manufacturers were discovering the advantage of marketing their products as "brands," which they found easier to promote. The switch to packaging products under brand labels began with the National Biscuit Company's marketing of the Uneeda Biscuit (cracker). Previously crackers and similar products were sold out of barrels or other containers. The National Biscuit Company individualized its crackers by cutting off the corners and parceling them out in wax-paper-lined cardboard boxes. A multi-faceted, high-powered ad campaign followed. Billboards and streetcar posters carried the one big word "Uneeda"; another ad featured a little boy in a raincoat with his waterproof, airtight box of Uneeda crackers.[68] Million-dollar national advertising campaigns appeared, and with that kind of money came a measure of power.

The role of the advertising agency became more complex and varied. No longer limited to being just "space brokers," buyers of space and placers of ads, agencies offered services from designing ads and preparing art and copy to conducting marketing research.

Trailblazing Ad Agencies

Early agency pioneers included the following:

- *Volney B. Palmer*, a Philadelphia realtor and coal dealer, started offering advertising placement services in 1842. He is possibly the first American advertising agent. By the end of the 1840s he had advertising offices in Baltimore, Boston, and New York, as well as Philadelphia. He specialized in making it easy for advertisers to place their ads in local and out-of-town newspapers and kept a 25 percent commission from the newspapers on all transactions.
- *Francis Wayland Ayer* founded an agency in 1869, using the name of his father in the name, N. W. Ayer & Son; at the time the younger Ayer was only twenty. Originally a "space broker," Ayer developed the "open contract" approach in 1876, whereby he told advertisers what he paid for the space. He would buy the space for the advertiser (keeping a commission) rather than buying the space himself and selling it at inflated prices to advertisers.
- *George P. Powell*, working as a bill collector for the *Boston Post* in 1858, began brokering ads for theater programs in Boston. Opening his own advertising business, he impressed publishers by announcing that he would personally guarantee payment in all transactions. He paid attention to results of advertising, using them to forecast advertising strategies. He published a listing of all U.S. newspapers, *Powell's American Newspaper Directory*, and launched a magazine, *Printer's Ink*, in 1888.[69]
- *James Walter Thompson* began in the advertising agency business as a clerk in New York for the Carlton and Smith agency, which specialized in handling accounts for religious magazines. In 1878 Thompson took over the agency and broadened its services for a more general clientele. Specializing in magazine advertising, he developed the women's magazine market for a new awareness of women as important consumers. He sold the agency in 1916, but the name of J. Walter Thompson remains as one of the more preeminent agencies today.[70]

Albert Lasker: Advertising agency pioneer. (The Bettmann Archive)

- *Albert D. Lasker*, a Texan, as a young man began to work for Chicago's Lord & Thomas agency in 1898 and in six years became its general manager. He built his philosophy around a three-word motto that an acquaintance had given him, defining advertising as "Salesmanship in Print." In other words, advertising had to sell products, not just be content with announcing availability. Although Lasker was not a copywriter, Kingman notes: "he was an outstanding copy editor and was eminently successful in devising powerful ad themes . . . that sold goods in mass volume. His message was not 'come to our store' but, bypassing wholesalers and retailers, he aimed directly at the consumers to build national demand." He pushed for bigger budgets and gave a year's credit to clients, some of them among the largest corporations.[71]

Media as Political Organs
PARTISAN POLITICS ALIVE AND WELL

Although there was an emphasis on the bottom line and anointing of the circulation and advertising departments in their search for the widest market, newspapers did not shed their partisan roles. Even the crusades embarked on by the papers were seen as promoting a political party's interests. Elliot Walton King, observing crusades of Pulitzer, Hearst, and others, says, "In almost every case, the target of the crusade or investigation was of the opposite political persuasion—or allied with a different wing of a political party—than the newspaper."[72]

King asks why the papers were so involved in partisan politics and why editors launched crusades that favored their own party or in some instances ran for office themselves. Even William Allen White was to make an unsuccessful run for governor of Kansas. (And in 1920 the three main candidates for president were all editors: Republican Warren Harding and Democrat James Cox, editors of Ohio newspapers, and Eugene Debs, who had been editor of the Socialist *Appeal to Reason*.) With some 2,600 daily newspapers in 1909, some 1,000 more than in the 1990s,[73] it would be counterproductive to alienate persons of any party. As editor Van Varner of *Guideposts* said in the 1990s, "If you take on a politician, you lose 50 percent at the outset." He does not even use profiles of politicians. "If you use political figures, it colors all you say."[74]

Then why in the Progressive Era, with its circulation wars, were editors political, even partisan? King explains why a logical "evenhanded and politically neutral" approach was not generally followed. Editors still regarded newspapers as a public trust, and speaking up and taking a partisan position in politics is what they thought was expected of them. Second, says King, it was an "easy choice." Politics was good for business. The reader, in the Pulitzer legacy, looked to the newspaper for leadership, whether right or wrong. "Political activity motivated readers to buy newspapers; the more partisan the activity and the more heated the political controversy, the higher circulation figures jumped."[75]

The Progressive Era editors' interest in politics brought them into close relationship with politicians. They had lunch with presidents on down, suggested agendas, and even helped shape future candidates. Henry Watterson of the *Louisville Courier-Journal,* for instance, had a hand in persuading Woodrow Wilson to run on the Democratic ticket in 1912.

La Follette: Progressive Maverick

One prominent politician—an on-again, off-again presidential contender—launched his own reform-minded, muckraking journal. The feisty, superb orator Senator Robert M. La Follette, Sr., in January 1909 sent forth *La Follette's Weekly Magazine* from his home base of Madison, Wisconsin. Senator La Follette (he served in the Senate from 1906 to his death in 1925), former Wisconsin governor (1901–1906), emblazoned on his cover the motto from Jesus: "Ye shall know the truth, and the truth shall make you free" (John 8:32). A hand is shown writing "The Truth" in large letters. "A Remarkable Article 'The Mind of a State' " (Wisconsin) by La Follette's close friend and adviser, muckraker Lincoln Steffens, is promoted on the cover, as well as an article by William Allen White, which is announced for the next issue.

Editorials, articles, and series early in that first year dealt extensively with political corruption and environmental abuse. On politics, La Follette wrote about "wrongful use of money" in a campaign (February 20, 1909), "executive usurpa-

Robert La Follette: Fearless progressive.

tion" of power by President Theodore Roosevelt (January 30), a Senate caucus "composed of a few bosses, a few independents, and many cowards and followers" (January 23), and an article by a congressman denouncing the speaker of the House as "our American Frankenstein" (January 23). On the environment: "Uncle Sam's Vanishing Wealth"—Part 1, "A Significant Picture of America as the Spendthrift Among the Nations—How Our National Resources in Lumber, Coal, Iron, Waterpower, and Land are Being Wasted"; Part 2, "What is Being Done by Patriotic Citizens to Stop the Appalling Waste of our Resources" (February 13, 1909).

La Follette's wife, Belle, launched a column, "Home and Education," which at its outset, says a La Follette biographer, seemed "simple pep talks on behalf of physical education" but which "emerged as the Belle La Follette that people would know in the 1910s and 1920s, the speaker and writer on subjects that were broader than clean politics and votes for women—humane treatment of children, the reclaiming of slums, justice for blacks, protection and fair pay for workers, international conciliation, and disarmament."[76]

In March 1912 in North Dakota, in the first presidential primary ever held, La Follette beat incumbent President William Howard Taft and the new challenger from the Progressive Party, Theodore Roosevelt. La Follette went on to beat Taft in Wisconsin (Roosevelt was not on that primary ticket). La Follette lost in the other primaries and entered the convention with only 36 votes out of a needed 540. His fall from grace that election year is attributed by historians to his testy, ill-tempered late-hour harangue that lasted two and a half hours before a meeting of the Periodical Publishers Association in Philadelphia.

The Courageous Independent

The man who had bombed so badly at the Philadelphia banquet was returned again and again to the U.S. Senate. He stood out as a courageous independent. For example, he made many enemies by strongly opposing U.S. entry into World War I. And despite the silence of the Republicans, Democrats, and the newly organized Progressive Party of 1924 on the Ku Klux Klan, he went on record unqualifiedly opposing the Klan in a letter to E. W. Scripps on August 8, 1924.[77] The letter, says Kenneth MacKay, "accomplished more than the mere clarification of progressive feeling. It smoked out both the Democrats and Republicans who had, with amazing political agility, avoided any direct reference or offense to the Klan up until this time."[78]

La Follette became the nominee of the Progressive Party that year. He polled an impressive 4.8 million votes (Coolidge had 15.7 million, Democrat John Davis, 8.3 million). His tally was the largest popular vote ever won by an independent candidate up to that time.[79] La Follette died in 1925 at age seventy, still senator and still editor of *La Follette's*. He suggested his own epitaph: "I would be remembered as one who in the world's darkest hour kept a clean conscience and stood to the end for the ideals of American democracy."[80]

In 1928 *La Follette's Magazine* was recapitalized as *The Progressive*, a joint venture with the *Capital Times* in Madison. William Evjue of the *Times* was listed as editor. Bob La Follette, Jr., was president of the publishing company, and his brother Philip was secretary. Bob, Jr., had taken his father's Senate seat in 1925 (tragically, Bob, Jr., who later lost his Senate seat to Joseph McCarthy, committed suicide in 1953). Philip became governor of Wisconsin in 1930 and completed three terms as governor.

Media as Voices of Freedom

CENSORING MUCKRAKERS

The question of control over news by business interests does not begin or end with advertisers' efforts to suppress items of which they disapprove or to take advantage of their relationship to the media to insert editorial material favorable to them. Businesses came to exert pressure by buyouts of newspapers. Buyouts by big companies, certainly common today, were very threatening in the early 1900s to a press whose idea of freedom meant independent publishers and editors speaking as they pleased.

The Ultimate Censor

Robert Miraldi, in the chapter "The Muckrakers Are Chased Away" in his book *Muckraking and Objectivity* has a startling subhead that declares, "The Ultimate Censor: Business Buyouts." Journalists worried, as *Editor & Publisher* magazine did, "Shall the Bogey Man Get the Magazine Publisher?"[81] The magazine fretted that some kind of "magazine Trust" could emerge as trusts had in other industries and thereby exert ominous control. The matter became one of concern when *American* magazine—a starship of muckrakers and run by a muckraker—sold out to Crowell Publishing Company, one of whose key officials served as an executive with financier J. P. Morgan and his banking interests.

New Jersey Senator John F. Dryden, who was also president of the Prudential Insurance Company, used his clout to wed news and advertising messages and sought to buy stock in *McClure's*. McClure refused the offer and also rebuffed a bid from Crowell. However, in 1911, *McClure's* was acquired and reorganized by the American Tobacco Company. "The 'bogey man' had gotten *McClure's* magazine,"[82] says Miraldi. Censorship was descending with a heavy hand on the muckraker magazines.

For example, Ray Stannard Baker found his article on textile workers in the *American* hacked up. Miraldi points out, "Sarcastic references to Boston philanthropists were changed to praise for their activities; statements questioning capitalism were deleted as were various critical facts about the mill owner's treatment of workers." Baker complained in a letter to Tarbell, "Does not this raise the question as to who is really editor of the *American* magazine?" He is quoted further as saying that once Crowell's "business men taste blood, they'll pare us down to utter colorness, utter mushiness. Everything must be smooth, sugary, inoffensive."[83] Baker eventually quit in 1915 when his article critical of Henry Ford was killed.

The same was happening at *Collier's*. The owners borrowed money from an industrialist friend, Harry Payne Whitney, but the banking company that managed Whitney's funds had authority over his loans. *Collier's* muckraker Mark Sullivan recalled how bank auditors showed up in the editorial office and started changing copy. He said the bankers demanded, "There must be less muckraking, greater amiability toward business."[84]

Fear of Legal Suits

Businesses used the threat of libel to discourage the reform magazines. McClure began to curb muckraking when he had to pay $55,000 in damages and court costs over an article by Baker on railroad scandals in which Baker charged a Milwaukee businessman with receiving illegal rebates. *Ladies' Home Journal* paid $16,000 to settle a suit over an article on patent medicine abuses.[85] There were countless threats of suits against most of the muckrakers, but in most cases the threats dissolved at the last minute. Nevertheless, the fear of libel had a chilling effect on the newspaper industry, as indeed it does today.

Limited peacetime regulation of the media by the government emerged. If media created monopolies, there could be restriction and control under the Sherman Antitrust Act of 1890. If they were seen as interstate carriers of information, they could come under the jurisdiction of utility regulations and the Interstate Commerce Act of 1887. And if the media enjoyed subsidies from the government, such as the lower second-class rate of postage, the media forfeited exclusive First

Amendment protection, and the government would have some right to intervene in their business, advertising, and circulation matters.

New York Associated Press Restraints

Several new regulation measures came from state supreme courts and Congress. First, the courts clipped the wings of the Associated Press, which had a virtual monopoly on the transmission of intercontinental and international news. The AP, which began in 1848 with close ties with New York newspapers as the Harbor News Association, a few years after the invention of the telegraph, became the New York Associated Press in 1857. A federation of regional Associated Presses developed. The New York AP, remaining dominant, grew more restrictive. The service charged exorbitant rates to its heartland subscribers and forced them to use news they were not interested in, such as shipping notices, while keeping the juiciest items off the wire for their own use.

The Western AP took issue with the New York AP's restrictions on dispersing the news, dropped out of the federation, and in 1892 reorganized as the Associated Press of Illinois. The New York AP folded in 1893. Incorporating in New York in 1900, the AP of Illinois became the Associated Press.

The Newspaper Publicity Act of 1912

The only Progressive Era federal regulation clamped on the press—the Newspaper Publicity Act—came in 1912. The law sought to make the newspaper and magazine industry more open and thus more honest. The measure was aimed generally at those engaging in fraud to perpetuate their image, namely, not disclosing who actually owned or controlled the publication, and also at the practice of giving inflated circulation figures to better attract advertisers. It also hit at the practice of disguising advertising as news. The law, applied to publications using the benefits of the second-class postal rate, said (1) owners of the publication were to be fully identified, (2) accurate circulation figures were to be published, and (3) ads were to be clearly labeled as such and not confused with news items.

Editors, publishers, and press organizations had diverse views of the new law. Those opposed to it thought that "a few populists angry with the press" railroaded through Congress legislation that was counter to the First Amendment rights of publications. "Proponents, on the other hand, asserted that members of Congress knowingly voted for the regulations in order to curb abuses within the industry," says Linda Lawson, "abuses that harmed the credibility of legitimate publishers and advertisers." So it was not a surprise, she added, that "the Newspaper Publicity Act has been praised as a significant reform, condemned as insidious regulation of the press, and dismissed as a toothless nuisance."[86] Critics, objecting mostly to the requirement that the information the government was requiring must be publicized, charged the act was socialistic, ridiculous, and reminiscent of the British Licensing Act of 1662.[87]

But in time the law garnered general support, the good guys with established publications preferring to play by the rules. With circulation figures honestly revealed they could identify fly-by-night operations that had inflated circulation figures; realistic arrangements could be made with the skeptical advertisers who would now pay rates according to actual circulations; quality of newspapers improved with ads clearly sorted out; and any revelations of nefarious control by corporations and others strengthened the hands of the independent and family-owned media.

The complaint that the law was "toothless," however, proved for the most part to be true. The Post Office was not in a position to audit and keep tabs on every publication in the country. As early as 1900 the Association of American Advertisers began to try to verify circulation figures. However, publishers resented the efforts of an all-advertising group. The AAA, reeling under the burden of bearing all the expense itself, became defunct in 1913. In the fall of that year eight groups, with five of the eight board members representing publishers, formed the Bureau of Verified Circulations (BVC). The AAA, however, was revived, this time with publishers involved. Renamed the Advertising Audit Association, the AAA merged with the BVC in 1914 to form the Audit Bureau of Circulations.[88]

FDR's Blue Eagle Restraints

When Franklin Roosevelt's New Deal program in 1933 revived some of the spirit of the Progressive Era cast in the inauguration of federal programs, subtle regulation of the media was introduced and sent a sliver of a shadow over freedom of the press. The controls were defined by codes to which businesses, including newspapers, were to conform. Those who complied could display proudly a symbol of a blue eagle.

The symbol was the brainchild of General Hugh Johnson, whom President Franklin Delano Roosevelt had named to head the National Recovery Administration. The blue eagle symbol, inspired by an ancient Indian figure of a thunderbird, meant to depict the bold move of a desperate nation in the throes of a Depression trying to give wings to recovery.

President Roosevelt went on the air: "In war, in the gloom of night attack, soldiers wear a bright badge on their shoulders to be sure that comrades do not fire on comrades. On that principle, those who cooperate in this program must know each other at a glance."[89]

The program came out of the National Industrial Recovery Act (NIRA), passed by Congress in June 1933. In a way, the act, which was to affect editors and printers along with other businesses as perhaps no other legislation in peacetime had done, emerged as a compromise between businessmen interested in eliminating price wars and unfair competition, on the one hand, and labor spokesmen (such as Senator Hugo Black of Alabama) seeking a thirty-hour week and minimum wage, on the other.

The act allowed businesses to fix prices (thus suspending antitrust laws) and to create production quotas. However, businesses were to accept fair-practice codes that guaranteed better working conditions. The right of collective bargaining for labor was also recognized.

The blue eagle became the symbol of cooperating firms. Those not complying were to be shunned, and there were teeth in the law, too. Robert R. McCormick of the *Chicago Tribune*, archcritic of the New Deal, noted that the National Recovery Administration (NRA), which administered the part of the NIRA that dealt with business and labor relationships (the Public Works Administration [PWA] also was a part of the NIRA), "sent out" orders "with the effect of law . . . so thick and fast" that "business and industry could not keep up with them."

McCormick told of the arrest of two oil company executives, and "in other cases the NRA used extra-judicial methods of coercion, such as confiscation of the Blue Eagle, resulting usually in the closing of factories, the bankruptcy of their owners, and the ruin of their employees." According to McCormick, there were 148,000 complaints made to the NRA in its brief lifetime before the Supreme Court struck down the NRA in 1935.[90]

But at the outset FDR's and General Johnson's cooperation program under the stamp of the blue eagle was hard to resist. Parades were held. The blue eagle emblem appeared in windows and was printed on store goods across the country. Employers and consumers alike signed a pledge of cooperation. "The new emblem became the focus of moral and civil pressure," says Arthur Schlesinger, Jr.[91] A quarter of a million persons marched down Fifth Avenue, in New York's biggest parade to that date, cheered on by a million on the sidelines.

To Illinois editor Paul Goddard, who spoke at the annual meeting of the National Editorial Association in 1933, the new codes were opportunities. "We have been working to have the members charge fair prices," he said. "And it looks as if this is a move in the right direction where the government is trying to stabilize these industries on a fair business basis. They are not going to permit cut-throat competition; they are not going to permit sweatshop operation which has disorganized the business of the country in the past. This is a wonderful opportunity."[92] But the NEA, pressed for funds, was soon complaining that the cost on its part in implementing the codes was bankrupting the organization.[93]

Attempts at regulating the press as a business under the New Deal—although conceived with good intentions—had failed and taken a toll on press organizations. With the "tired bear" of the NRA, as the *New York Times* called it, laid to rest by U.S. Supreme Court fiat in 1935, the NEA and other groups began to get a new breath of life. Another era of progressivism, which came under the New Deal with government controls, was ebbing.

FOCUSING ON PUBLIC RELATIONS

Although the muckraking period of the Progressive Era in the first decade can be credited with stimulating hard-pressed companies—such as railroad lines and Standard Oil—into the need to be public relations conscious, the practice of public relations is as old as the practice of communications. Carolyn Byerly, of Radford University in Virginia, goes back to the "roots of persuasion" and finds the Roman "posted" newspaper, *Acta Diurna*, to be a pioneer effort to influence the public, and she mentions early pamphlets as reflecting the goals of public relations. Certainly, she says, an early example of a successful public relations campaign on a grand scale was the effort of Pope Urban II and his successors in the Middle Ages "to successfully mobilize and maintain a commitment from millions of Europeans to travel and fight distant battles that had little practical daily value for their communities or families."[94] These were the Crusades, and curiously, one still hears the term "public relations crusade."

The Role of the Women's Rights Agenda

Following the Women's Rights Convention in Seneca Falls in 1848, women suffragists developed goals, strategies, and networks to persuade the public of their particular point of view. Women's periodicals—*Lily, Una*, and *Revolution*, for instance—constituted "a key internal public relations tool" by which the women's rights movement could set agendas and work out mutual platforms. The movement used "pseudo-events and other standard, familiar public relations techniques," says Carolyn Byerly, among them suffrage parades, canvassers knocking on doors, and speakers appearing on street corners and in mass meetings. The year before the Nineteenth Amendment enfranchising women was ratified in 1920, the suffrage movement opened its own public relations agency in Washington—owned and operated by women.

Some would trace public relations in the modern era back to the "showmanship" and "puffery" of the great circus showman P. T. Barnum in the nineteenth century. Barnum waxed eloquent promoting exhibits of mermaids, the bearded lady, and weird horses. He regarded his circus as "The Greatest Show on Earth." Today public relations efforts—and advertising—that proffer the partial truth, superlatives, and the dramatic owe something to the master showman Barnum. On the other hand, Marvin Olasky suggests that "the first blunt step toward using the press for public relations purposes was the straightforward, modest bribe." In fact, he says, "payment of fees for favorable newspaper notice—'puffery'—became so common that a Chicago reporter satirized the practice by publishing his rates," charging $2 per line for "setting forth of virtues (actual or alleged) of presidents, general managers or directors. . . . For complimentary notices of the wives and children of railroad officials, we demand $1.50 per line," and so on.[95]

White House Press Relations

Presidential public relations began noticeably with the work of George B. Cortelyou as secretary to President Grover Cleveland and later with President McKinley. In the excited state of the nation leading up to the Spanish-American War, Cortelyou had his hands full. McKinley, trying to keep the country out of war, was receiving 1,000 letters a day, with Cortelyou analyzing the mail each day for the president. Soon Cortelyou was also preparing statements or "releases" summarizing the president's positions on the issues of the day for the newspeople outside his door. Cortelyou accompanied the president on his out-of-town trips, often supervising a carload of

George Cortelyou: Early presidential press agent.

reporters attached to the presidential train. It was not until the presidency of Herbert Hoover (1929–1933) that one person was officially called press secretary. (The first was George Akerson, who, due to in-house political tensions and infighting, remained only a short time.)[96]

When Theodore Roosevelt became president on the death of McKinley in 1901, Cortelyou stayed on to share responsibility for press relations with Roosevelt's own secretary, William Loeb, Jr. (Loeb's son by the same name became a well-known conservative editor of the *Manchester* [New Hampshire] *Union Leader*.) The two had a good working relationship, with Cortelyou carrying the greater responsibility.

In 1903 Roosevelt named Cortelyou the first secretary of commerce and labor. Cortelyou later served as chairman of the Republican National Committee, postmaster general, and secretary of the treasury. In 1909 he became president of the New York Consolidated Gas Company.

President Theodore Roosevelt helped pave the way for modern political public relations. Rodger Streitmatter notes that Roosevelt "expanded the boundaries of presidential news, even using his six children for subjects on a dull day; he chose colorful language that would lend itself to quotes; he recognized the importance of timing; he manipulated reporters, rewarding those he liked, making it difficult for those he did not by limiting their access; and he charmed and flattered the press corps, even dubbing the corps his Newspaper Cabinet."[97]

One important media liaison was Gifford Pinchot, chief of the U.S. Forest Service from 1898 to 1910. He advised Theodore Roosevelt on conservation matters, used news management techniques, prepared suggested news copy in his press bulletins, used special presidential commissions as news sources, and even planned a press cruise on the Mississippi "to alert the public to the need for a national waterways policy."[98]

FDR's Public Relations Finesse

President Franklin Delano Roosevelt (1933–1945) took a leaf on the practice of public relations from his cousin Theodore. Honing presidential press relations to a fine art, Franklin Roosevelt used showmanship, charm, strategy, friendship, surprise gimmicks, and psychology to accomplish his desires for the way news of his administration was to be distributed and understood.

Betty Houchin Winfield, in her study of FDR and the media, regards Roosevelt as the "transitional figure in the evolution of the relationship between the American presidency and the public" in the twentieth century. "Foremost a great communicator," she says, "FDR knew when to speak and when not to. He knew how to use his charm and withdraw it." His standards of dealing with the media and the public became a means by which future presidents compared their press relations.[99]

Among the tenets of Roosevelt's philosophy of dealing with the press—approaches he developed as governor of New York before he became president—were the following, according to Winfield: He made himself available to reporters—as president he held press conferences regularly, alternating times to serve both evening and morning papers; experimented with radio; used humor and kept an upbeat countenance; fed the media human-interest ideas; made a campaign movie as governor, in 1930, a generally unexplored medium for politics; wrote letters to his friends and supporters; hounded the critical press; distributed reprints of favorable articles; made use of new research techniques, political opinion polls; gave autographed pictures and phonograph records to all the delegates at the Democratic convention in 1932; exhibited boldness and "courage" by flying when commercial flying was still new; and was a master of timing, knowing the best time to release news to get the maximum coverage.

As president he planted with reporters questions he wanted answered, but evaded with good humor those he did not want to answer by changing the subject or conspicuously turning aside and good-naturedly ignoring them. He did not hesitate to answer questions he didn't want to answer with disarming statements such as "I haven't the faintest idea." Clowning at times, the president showed up once with a sword, threatening to lop off some heads if the questions weren't right. When someone asked a monetary question he did not want to answer, the president quickly said, "Give me that sword," distracting the press corps and bringing laughter.[100] Perhaps more recent presidents would not have gotten away with such antics. Roosevelt did alienate some members of the press corps by leaking information to favorites. He also had to contend with the publishers, who were 85 percent against him, according to his own reckoning. More likely, 60 percent were against him, as a Democratic National Committee survey showed in 1936.[101]

Photo Realism: FDR's Documentary Photographers

In the 1930s documentary photographs were used as a political and social tool during the Franklin Roosevelt administration. Pictures taken for the historical section of the Farm Security Administration (FSA) reached near avalanche proportions, with nearly a third of a million pictures taken by a staff of six. Under FSA project director Roy Stryker, the photographers, most of whom became some of the best-known names in American photography, sought to document hardship and poverty in rural America, largely to win support for Roosevelt's farm reform measures.

The Migrant Mother

Some of the documentary pictures became classics. Perhaps the best known was Dorothea Lange's 1936 photo of a slim mother

Dorothea Lange's "Migrant Mother." (Library of Congress)

with a troubled face, with chin in her palm and with a shaggy-haired boy huddled on each side, their faces turned from the camera. The photo was taken at a tent camp of destitute pea pickers at Nipomo, California. (When the mother, Florence Thompson, lay dying years later in 1983, at age eighty in Santa Cruz, California, she was still remembered as the "migrant mother" and a "migrant mother hospice" was created by donations to help with her medical expenses.)

Dorothea Lange (1895–1965) grew up not in rural America but in the dense neighborhoods of Hoboken, New Jersey, and the lower east side of New York. At seven she was felled by polio, which left her right leg impaired from the knee down. Children called her "Limpy." The handicap and suffering inspired her photography.

Lange apprenticed with Arnold Genthe, a photographer of the 1906 San Francisco earthquake, in his New York studio. In 1918 she went to San Francisco and opened her own studio. She began going out into the streets and photographing people of misery; she held special shows of her "pictures of people." She met up with economist Paul Taylor, who was looking for a photographer to document the plight of migrant workers. After her work with the FSA, her projects included photographing the evacuation and internment of Japanese-Americans for the War Relocation Authority and working for the Office of War Information, 1943–1945. She was the first woman photographer to have her pictures shown in an exhibit at New York's Museum of Modern Art.

Another famous documentary photographer of the FSA project was Arthur Rothstein, who is remembered most for a "dust bowl" picture of a father and his two little sons running against the wind to their half-dirt-covered house in the heart of a dust storm in Cimarron County, Oklahoma, in 1936. The dust destroyed the camera with which he took the picture.

The Case of the Moving Skull

When Rothstein took a photo of a bleached-white steer's skull on cracked parched ground in the Dakotas, he became the center of a storm of controversy. Critics of Roosevelt's New Deal and its many reform programs felt the FSA photographers, including Rothstein, were just creating propaganda. An editor of the *Fargo* (North Dakota) *Forum* decided that the skull picture was posed—that the skull was a prop that had been moved to the parched ground. The editor waited until Roosevelt showed up in town on a presidential tour before he made the charge. Creating a national sensation, the next day the *New York Tribune* displayed three of the FSA pictures on its front page—two of the pictures seemed to have the same skull but on different backgrounds. The Fargo editor said there hadn't even been a drought that year in the area where the skulls were photographed. Stryker brushed off the controversy. "What the hell," he said, "the point of the picture is that there is a drought. Cattle are dying."[102]

Another FSA photographer, Gordon Parks, documented for the FSA everyday life of people in the slums of Washington. He began his life in Fort Scott, Kansas, the last of fifteen children. When his mother died when he was fifteen, he moved in with a sister and her husband in St. Paul, Minnesota. When her husband threw him out after an argument, Parks supported himself playing piano in a brothel and mopping flophouse floors as he finished high school. He got a job as a busboy at a hotel that featured big bands. He picked out his own tunes on the piano whenever he could. A bandleader liked his tunes and used them, taking Parks on tour with the band.

(Continued)

When the band broke up, Parks got a job with the federal Civilian Conservation Corps (CCC).

Parks acquired a camera, did some fashion shooting, and was urged by the wife of boxer Joe Louis to move to Chicago where he would find sufficient work. He specialized in photographing fashionable ladies and the city's slums, the last winning him a Rosenwald Fellowship, paying him $200 a month. He became the first black photographer to work for *Life* magazine. His subjects became Harlem gang wars, poverty in Brazil, Malcolm X, and European fashions. He also gained fame as a novelist, filmmaker, and composer. He directed the film version of his novel, *The Learning Tree*, becoming the first black to write and direct a Hollywood movie. It was a critical and commercial success, as was another film he directed, *Shaft*, a private-eye thriller. One of his sons, Gordon Parks, Jr., also became a movie director but died in a plane crash in Africa while working on his fourth movie.[103]

Other FSA documentary photographers included Carl Mydans, who became a *Life* photographer; Ben Shahn, who became a well-known artist and a professor at Harvard; Walker Evans, who became an editor at *Fortune*; John Vachon, who went to *Look*; and Russell Lee, who did work for the Arabian-American Oil Company.[104]

In addition to the work of the still photographers for the FSA, Roosevelt made use of a documentary filmmaker, Pare Lorenz. In 1936 he produced *The Plow That Broke the Plains*, about the peril of life in the dust bowl, and in 1938, *The River*, a history of the Mississippi River Basin and the importance of the Tennessee Valley Authority in curbing erosion and flooding.

PR Pioneer Ivy Lee

The first public relations agency was the Publicity Bureau, launched in the fall of 1900 by George Vail, Herbert Small, and Thomas Marvin. With Harvard University among the clients, the firm set about promoting the university's facilities and program. The Publicity Bureau lasted twelve years.

The best known of the Progressive Era corporate public relations practitioners was Ivy Ledbetter Lee. Upon graduation from Princeton he worked for a series of New York newspapers—the *Journal,* the *Times,* and the *World*—usually ending up covering business for the paper. It became clear to him, as a financial writer, that big business and the media in an age of muckraker journalism were in conflict.

Deciding to leave the newspaper business, the young Lee signed on to handle the publicity for Seth Low, who was running for mayor of New York. Low lost, but Lee's work with him led to a publicity job with the Democratic National Committee in the presidential election of 1904. Lee took on independent jobs, such as developing favorable publicity for a group of New York bankers to buy franchises for the right of way of the New York, Port Chester, and Boston Railroad lines.

Lee joined with George Parker, with whom he had worked for the Democratic National Committee, and in late 1904 the firm of Parker & Lee was launched next to the New York Stock Exchange. When one of the firm's clients, the Anthracite Coal Roads and Mines Company, was faced with a strike, Lee was forthright, stating that it was necessary to take the bull by the horns. He said that the firm's aim

Ivy Lee: Public relations trailblazer. (International News Photo)

was not to create veils of secrecy, but rather to supply all the facts available and to aid reporters in verifying the facts. He believed that by presenting the facts up front, understanding could be reached.

In 1906 he was handling public relations for the Pennsylvania Railroad when a train was involved in an accident at Gap, Pennsylvania. Management immediately tried to suppress news of the accident. Lee, however, reversed the approach and personally invited reporters to travel to the accident scene in a private car at the railroad's expense. He provided them with background information and photos. He had been hired to improve relations with the press, and he did.

When John D. Rockefeller enlisted his help during the Colorado coal strikes of 1913 and 1914, Lee advised against using ads to try to get favorable stories in the media. Rather, he got John D. Rockefeller, Jr., to visit the miners' camps and homes and to encourage the development of an employee representation unit to handle grievances and to present ideas for improving working and living conditions. The miners accepted the plan.

The Parker and Lee partnership ended in 1913 when Parker accepted a job as press secretary for the Protestant Episcopal Church. Lee started his own agency, with the Rockefeller family as his chief client. He persuaded Rockefeller to give no exclusives and to play no favorites, treating all reporters equally. But at times, when Lee heard of an exclusive in the works, he would turn around and spoil it by releasing the information to all members of the press. Such meddling made him some enemies in the press.

The elderly Rockefeller senior did not like having a horde of photographers around, and the photographers were complaining they were not getting adequate pictures. Lee compromised by hiring a professional photographer to take pictures and making them available to the press.[105]

Lee's clients feared competition, and therefore he promoted collaboration with the government, even accepting regulation, with which the big businesses could live if they were the only show in town. Olasky says Lee, son of a minister, espoused the social gospel emphasis that a new social order pointing to a heaven on earth could be realized in cooperative efforts.[106]

Understanding Lee's emphasis on collaboration, Olasky thinks, "clears up other mysteries, such as Lee's relations with, and book promoting, the Soviet Union," his *Present-Day Russia*. He saw the two countries evolving toward a middle position of accommodation and urged oil deals with the Soviet Union and loans to the country. Needless to say, Lee was denounced in some quarters, called "Poison Ivy" and accused—by the *Wall Street Journal*—of being on the payroll of the Soviet Union.[107]

Lee's efforts ranged from heading the Red Cross publicity in World War I to supporting strike-breaking policies of his clients. No controversy pursued him more than his work for a leading firm in Nazi Germany. Lee had as a client the chemical-producing American I. G., a holding company of I. G. Farben in Germany. The parent company, worried about anti-German attitudes in the United States as a result of Hitler's purges and persecutions and growing militarism, wanted to improve the image of Germany and Hitler's regime. Lee signed on to represent the parent company for an additional $25,000 a year in 1934. Headlines in the United States denounced Lee. For instance, the *New York Mirror* screamed, "Rockefeller Aide Nazi Mastermind." Lee was called before the House Committee on Un-American Activities in May 1934. He stood fast in maintaining that he never propagandized in the United States for Farben or the German government. He died in November of the same year.

PR Revives the KKK

A dark side of public relations was the work of the Southern Publicity Association of Edward Young Clarke and his associate Elizabeth Tyler. The old Ku Klux Klan was in disarray, but the team of Clarke, who was the son of a former owner of the *Atlanta Constitution*, and Tyler revived the Klan and made it a dreaded and powerful giant. They capitalized on the revival of nativism—fears of blacks, Jews, immigrants, Communists—in the unsteady days after World War I.

Working for a high commission from the Klan under Imperial Wizard William Joseph Simmons, the pair orchestrated appearances in churches, covered cross burnings on top of mountains that could be seen far and wide, and gained favorable publicity in newspapers across the country. Public relations historian Scott Cutlip gives an extended chapter to the rise and then the fall—after financial and sex scandals and exposés by newspapers—of these two public relations practitioners in his history of public relations, *The Unseen Power*.[108]

Public Relations Patriarch

The patriarch of twentieth-century public relations was Edward L. Bernays. Though some (such as Cutlip) wince at the media-bestowed title for Bernays as the "father of public relations," he nevertheless has left important marks on the development of public relations. Bernays first set forth his philosophy in a 1923 book, *Crystallizing Public Relations*, written in collaboration with his wife, Doris E. Fleischman, a former *New York Tribune* editor. In the book he designed the two-way cooperative concept in public relations in contrast to one-way publicity. He created the term "public relations counsel" and talked of "the engineering of consent." Throughout his life he campaigned for licensing of public relations as a profession, a view not shared by some of his colleagues. He died in March 1995 at 103.

THE BEGINNING OF MOVIES

Just two years after Joseph Nicephore Niepce produced the first permanent photograph in 1822, an English physician, Peter Mark Roget, came up with one of the basic theories of the motion picture, "the persistence of vision." Roget's interests ranged from researching the effects of laughing gas to creating the famous word-synonym book named after him, *Roget's Thesaurus* (*thesaurus* is from the Greek and Latin meaning "treasury"). He noticed that when one looked at a picture and then another, for a split second the image of the first picture remained, flowing into the next picture. It was the principle of continuity that underpinned the whole idea of a motion picture, which in reality is a series of still pictures or frames on a strip of celluloid. In silent films, sixteen frames are run per second; for sound movies, twenty-four per second. In each case, with the delayed retention the effect of continuous motion is achieved.

Various devices were created to make use of Roget's theory. There was the Zoetrope, consisting of a revolving drum giving the illusion of clowns, jumping horses, or acrobats, for instance. Another device was the Stroboscope, with the images drawn on a disc. The Praxinoscope made use of a ring of little mirrors with a ring of images opposite the mirrors on the side of a drum. With the turning of the drum, the mirror images flowed together.

How Does a Horse Run?

Perhaps the first motion picture was a chance experiment of Eadweard Muybridge. The English-born photographer was noted for photography in the American west and as the government's official photographer in Alaska in 1868, a year after the purchase of Alaska. He got caught up in a wager that ex-California governor Leland Stanford had with a friend in 1872. Stanford bet $25,000 that a racehorse had all four feet off the ground at some time as it ran. So Stanford hired Muybridge to photograph the race horse Occident to prove one way or another how the horse ran.

The effort was inconclusive, and it was five years before Muybridge got back to the experiment. Meanwhile Muybridge was caught up in a personal drama. He discovered that his wife, young enough to be his daughter, was being escorted about town by the dashing young Harry Larkins. What really angered Muybridge was the discovery of a picture of his infant son Floredo in the possession of the child's nurse with the inscription "Harry" on the back in his wife's handwriting. Muybridge sought out Harry and shot him, wounding him fatally. Muybridge was carted off to

Eadweard Muybridge's series of a horse running. (Courtesy George Eastman House)

jail in shackles. The judge rejected an insanity plea and called for conviction. The jury saw otherwise. Recognizing the right of a wronged husband to defend his honor and that the Bible says, "The man that committeth adultery . . . shall surely be put to death" (Leviticus 20:10), the court acquitted Muybridge. His young wife, Flora, died a few months later of a mysterious ailment at age twenty-four.

In 1878, his earlier work with the race horse in question, Muybridge was again invited by Stanford to photograph a running horse, this time Sallie Gardner. Stanford called in the press to observe the event. Muybridge set up twelve cameras, each connected to a fine black thread across the track. In rapid motion the horse set off the cameras. Indeed, all four feet of the galloping horse were off the ground in the sequence.

In 1880 the San Francisco Art Association sponsored a showing of a horse in motion on a large screen. Although moving cartoons and photographs of a dance, with music, had been slowly projected on a screen one by one before, Muybridge had created the first motion picture.

One of Thomas Edison's assistants, William Kennedy Laurie Dickson, took film strips developed by George Eastman, put sprocket holes on each edge to move the film along in a coordinated fashion, and created the Kinetoscope, cranked and turned by the viewer.

Georges Melies, a French magician, produced more than 500 short subjects, ranging from episodes of jugglers to travel scenes and excerpts of plays. He also presented pantomimed versions of *Cinderella* in 1900, *Bluebeard* and *Red Riding Hood* in 1901, and *A Trip to the Moon* in 1902. Edwin S. Porter, working for Edison, created a narrative motion picture with his *The Life of an American Fireman* in 1903. That same year he produced the first Western, *The Great Train Robbery*.

The Nickelodeons

With the coming of movie projection, the films were shown in vaudeville houses. Eventually converted stores were used. Called nickelodeons, the stores featured a screen, a projector, and chairs. But the nickelodeons "were stuffy, ill-smelling places frequented by the poor and illiterate, and they would not improve until their product was good enough to attract a different audience."[109]

David Wark Griffith, working for the fledging Biograph Studio in New York, "advanced pictures from novelty to art form," says Ella Smith. "He recorded a scene from more than one angle. He took the camera closer to his actors and timed shots for the best effect. He would focus on portions of players, such as their hands—to get ideas across."[110]

Griffith left Biograph in 1913 to head up production at the Mutual Film Corporation. Griffith is best known for his 1915 three-hour epic on the Civil War and Reconstruction, *The Birth of a Nation*. Unfortunately, Griffith, the son of a Confederate Army colonel, perpetuated stereotypes, and in his depiction of the rise of the Ku Klux Klan gave that racist terrorist group a boost in its comeback. He presented "a highly romanticized, sanitized version of the old Klan," says public relations historian Scott Cutlip.[111] "Undoubtedly, the most powerful pictorial appeal of all [for the KKK] was supplied by the continuous showings of *The Birth of a Nation*."[112] Unlike most movies, which have a short distribution time, *The Birth of a Nation* appeared continually in theaters for five years. And as late as 1924, nine years after its release, the film was still being promoted by the Klan. In that year, a Klan-sponsored showing of the film in a Chicago theater broke all records for that theater during the week of showing. Klan members would hand out Klan literature and seek to sign up new members outside theaters showing *The Birth of a Nation*. Arthur Knight observed: "The passions it aroused, the tensions it created lasted beyond the theater. They overflowed into the streets, and race riots and mob action followed in the wake of its presentation in many cities."[113]

"Keystone Kops"

In contrast to Griffith, Mack Sennett, who had worked as an extra for Biograph, created his own studio, the Keystone Film Company in Los Angeles, and set about developing comedies. He particularly liked comical policemen and launched a series of films on the Keystone Kops. His stars in his films included Mabel Normand, who threw the first custard pie in a face in movies; Buster Keaton, who took many a prat-fall; and the greatest of them all, Charlie Chaplin, who satirized the down-and-outer, *The Tramp* (and later, in 1940, a Hitler parody in *The Great Dictator*).

Color was introduced into sequences of *The Phantom of the Opera* in 1925 and throughout Douglas Fairbanks' *The Black Pirate* in 1926. Sound in feature-length movies made its debut with Al Jolson's *The Jazz Singer* in 1927.

QUESTIONS FOR DISCUSSION AND RESEARCH

1. How might a reporter who is labeled a populist be different from a reporter called a progressive?
2. What brought in the Progressive Era?
3. The muckrakers were highly idealistic. Considering their principles and beliefs—some of them religious—suggest ten rules or commandments as a guide for action for muckrakers.
4. Why did magazines prove to be good vehicles for the muckraking journalists?
5. Create a table of contents that would be typical for a muckraker magazine in 1905.
6. Can you differentiate between muckraking and other reporting terms—in-depth reports, investigative reporting, exposés, advocacy, crusades, interpretive journalism, enterprise journalism? Explain.
7. Read an article by a contemporary investigative reporter, and compare it with an article by one of the muckrakers in the first decade of the century.
8. Progressivism has been discussed in connection with the "information" media. Can it be discussed in terms of the "persuasive" media, advertising and public relations?
9. "The work of the Progressive Era muckraker journalists proved successful, bringing results." True or false? Defend your viewpoint.
10. Fact-based muckraking also reflected trends and techniques in fiction. Explain.
11. In what direction did advertising evolve during the Progressive Era?
12. Describe several subtle limited controls enacted over the media in progressive periods.
13. How do you explain the socialistic and nationalistic leanings of many of the muckrakers?
14. Think of ten movies you have seen. Do any of them reflect a "progressive" spirit?
15. Watch a television documentary and note similarities or dissimilarities with journalism of the Progressive Era.

ENDNOTES

1. Richard Hofstadter, William Miller, and Daniel Aaron, *The American Republic*, vol. 2 (Englewood Cliffs, NJ: Prentice-Hall, 2nd ed., 1970), p. 357.
2. Ibid.
3. Matthew Schneirov, "Popular Magazines and the Dreams of a New Social Order, 1893–1914," vol. 2, Ph.D. dissertation, University of Pittsburgh, 1991, p. 25.

4. Frank Luther Mott, *A History of American Magazines, 1895–1905* (Cambridge, Mass.: Harvard University Press, 1957), p. 481.

5. Erwin K. Thomas, "John Brisben Walker," in Sam G. Riley, ed., *American Magazine Journalists, 1850–1900*, vol. 79, in *Dictionary of Literary Biography* series (Detroit: Gale Research, 1989), p. 299.

6. John Tebbel and Ellen Zuckerman, *The Magazine in America, 1741–1990* (New York: Oxford University Press, 1991), p. 77.

7. Mott, *History of American Magazines*, p. 492.

8. Schneirov, "Popular Magazines," vol. 1, p. 224.

9. Mott, *History of American Magazines*, p. 591.

10. Peter Lyon, *Success Story: The Life and Times of S. S. McClure* (Deland, Fla.: Everett/Edwards, 1967), p. ix.

11. The context for the muckraker reference in *The Pilgrim's Progress*: "the Interpreter takes them apart again: and has them first into a Room, where was a man that could look no way but downwards with a Muck-rake in his hand. There stood also one over his head with a Celestial Crown in his Hand, and proffered to give him that Crown for his Muck-rake; but the man did neither look up, nor regard; but raked to himself the Straws, the small Sticks, and Dust of the Floar. . . ."

12. *New York Tribune*, April 15, 1906; reprinted in Arthur and Lila Weinberg, eds., *The Muckrakers* (New York: Simon & Schuster, 1961), p. 58.

13. Mark Neuzil, "Hearst, Roosevelt, and the Muckrake Speech of 1906: A New Perspective," a paper presented at the Asociation for Education in Journalism and Mass Communication convention in Atlanta, August 1994.

14. Harry H. Stein, "American Muckraking of Technology Since 1900," *Journalism Quarterly*, vol. 67, no. 2, Summer 1990, pp. 401, 402.

15. Edwin E. Slosson, "The Literature of Exposure," *The Independent*, vol. 60, 1906, p. 690; see also George W. Alger, "The Literature of Exposure," *Atlantic Monthly*, vol. 96, August 1905, p. 210.

16. Robert Miraldi, *Muckraking and Objectivity; Journalism's Colliding Traditions* (Westport, Conn.: Greenwood Press, 1990), p. 31.

17. Charles Edward Russell, "Trinity: Church of Mystery," *Broadway Magazine*, April 1908, quoted in Neuzil, "Hearst, Roosevelt."

18. Walter M. Brasch, *Forerunners of Revolution: Muckrakers and the American Social Conscience* (Lanham, Md.: University Press of America, 1990), p. 13.

19. Alexander Alland, *Jacob Riis, Photographer and Citizen* (New York: Aperture, 1974), p. 28.

20. Susan Henry, "Reporting 'Deeply and at First Hand': Helen Campbell in the 19th-Century Slums," *Journalism History*, vol. 11, nos. 1–2, Spring/Summer 1984, p. 18.

21. Robert C. Kochersberger, Jr., ed., *More Than a Muckraker: Ida Tarbell's Lifetime in Journalism* (Knoxville: University of Tennessee Press, 1994), pp. 5ff.

22. Ida Tarbell, *All in the Day's Work* (New York: Macmillan, 1939), p. 236.

23. Lincoln Steffens, *The Autobiography of Lincoln Steffens*, vol. 2 (New York: Harcourt, Brace & World, 1958), pp. 372, 373.

24. Ibid., p. 799.

25. Arthur Weinberg and Lila Weinberg, eds., *The Muckrakers* (New York: Simon & Schuster, 1961), pp. 102, 103.

26. James Boylan, "The Rise of Ernest Poole: The Making of a Social Muckraker," presented to the History Division, Association for Education in Journalism and Mass Communication in Kansas City, Mo., Aug. 14, 1993.

27. Ernest Poole, *The Bridge: My Own Story* (New York: Macmillan, 1940), pp. 68, 69, quoted in Boylan, "Rise of Ernest Poole."

28. Ron Marmarelli, "William Hard as Progressive Journalist," *American Journalism*, vol. 3, no. 3, 1986, p. 146.

29. Rheta Childe Dorr, *What Eight Million Women Want* (Boston: Small, Maynard & Co., 1910), pp. 4, 5.

30. Agnes Hooper Gottlieb, "Always an Activist: The Journalism of Reformer Florence Kelley," a paper presented at the Association for Education in Journalism and Mass Communication convention in Washington, August 1995.

31. Edwin Markham, "The Hoe-Man in the Making," *Cosmopolitan*, September 1906, in Weinberg and Weinberg, *The Muckrakers*, p. 361.

32. Mary Ellen Waller-Zuckerman, "Vera Connolly: Progressive Journalist," *Journalism History*, vol. 15, nos. 2–3, Summer/Autumn 1988, p. 81.

33. Undated interview with Alma Kitchell, transcript in Vera Connolly Papers, Rare Book and Manuscript Library, Columbia University, quoted in Waller-Zuckerman, "Vera Connolly," p. 82.

34. Bruce J. Evenson, "The Evangelical Origins of the Muckrakers," *American Journalism*, vol. 6, no. 1, 1989, p. 5.

35. Ibid., p. 8.

36. Ibid., p. 12.

37. Ibid., p. 17.

38. Ibid., p. 21.

39. Judson A. Grenier, "Muckraking and the Muckrakers: An Historical Definition," *Journalism Quarterly*, Autumn 1960, p. 555.

40. Luke 4:18: "The Spirit of the Lord is upon me, because he hath anointed me to preach the gospel to the poor; he hath sent me to heal the broken-hearted, to preach deliverance to the captives, and recovering of sight to the blind, to set at liberty them that are bruised" (KJV).

41. Jane Addams, "The Reaction of Moral Instruction upon Social Reform," *La Follette's Weekly Magazine*, Jan. 30, 1909, p. 7.

42. Richard Hofstadter, *The Age of Reform* (New York: Vintage Books, 1955), p. 152.

43. Arthur Colton, "What Is Progressive?" *The Unpopular Review*, vol. 3, June-July 1915, p. 170.

44. Robert Nisbet, *History of the Idea of Progress* (New York: Basic Books, 1980), p. 27.

45. Christopher Lasch, *The True and Only Heaven: Progress and Its Critics* (New York: Norton, 1991), p. 40

46. Genesis 1:26.

47. Or "complete," Gr. *teleos*—Matthew 5:48.

48. Sidney Pollard, *The Idea of Progress: History and Society* (New York: Basic Books, 1968), p. 107.

49. J. B. Bury, *The Idea of Progress* (New York: Macmillan, 1921), pp. 351, 352.

50. There is even talk of new dimensions of progress, the spiritual side, as anticipated by Pierre Lecomte du Nuoy and Pierre Teilhard de Chardin. William Irwin Thompson, in his books *At the Edge of History* and *Passages About Earth*, sees "a spiraling backward and forward through time" and a movement toward a mystic world (see "Planetary Culture: An Interview with William Irwin Thompson," *Cultural Information Service*, May 1974). C. Owen Paepke in *The Evolution of Progress: The End of Economic Growth and the Beginning of Human Transformation* (New York: Random House, 1992) sees "a new kind of progress" coming about by way of extended life spans and genetic engineering. See also the chapter "The People of the Future" in Hiley Ward, *Religion 2101 A.D.: Who or What Will Be God?* (New York: Doubleday, 1975).

51. John F. Baker, "PW Interviews: Justin Kaplan," *Publishers Weekly*, April 8, 1974, pp. 8, 9.

52. Judson A. Grenier, "Muckrakers Well Educated; Sought Truth, Fame," *Publishers' Auxiliary*, Sept. 25, 1975, p. 26.

53. Ibid.

54. Ibid.

55. Stein, "American Muckraking," p. 402; see also William Parmenter, "*The Jungle* and Its Effects," *Journalism History*, vol. 10, nos. 1–2, Spring/Summer 1981.

56. Louis G. Geiger, "Muckrakers—Then and Now," *Journalism Quarterly*, Autumn 1966, p. 472.

57. Ibid., pp. 472, 473.

58. Ibid., p. 473.

59. Warren Francke, "Sensationalism and the Development of 19th-Century Reporting: The Broom Sweeps Sensory Details," *Journalism History*, vol. 12, nos. 3–4, Winter/Autumn 1985, p. 84.

60. John Durham Peters, "Satan and Savior: Mass Communication in Progressive Thought," *Critical Studies in Mass Communication*, September 1989, p. 259.

61. See discussion of three of his novels—*The Clarion, Common Cause*, and *Success*—in James Stanford Bradshaw, "The Journalist as Pariah: Three Muckraking Newspaper Novels by Samuel Hopkins Adams," *Journalism History*, vol. 10, nos. 1–2, Spring/Summer 1983.

62. David Graham Phillips, *The Treason of the Senate* (Stanford, Calif.: Academic Reprints, n.d.), p. 6.

63. Boylan, "The Rise of Ernest Poole."

64. Elliot Walton King, "Ungagged Partisanship: The Political Values of the Public Press, 1835–1920," Ph.D. dissertation, University of California, San Diego, 1992, pp. 352, 353.

65. Will Irwin, "The American Newspaper: The Advertising Influence," *Collier's*, May 27, 1911, p. 15, quoted in Robert V. Hudson, "Will Irwin's Pioneering Criticism of the Press," *Journalism Quarterly*, vol. 47, p. 268.

66. Ibid.

67. James Melvin Lee, *History of American Journalism* (Boston: Houghton Mifflin, 1923), p. 431.

68. Daniel Pope, *The Making of Modern Advertising* (New York: Basic Books, 1983), pp. 48, 49.

69. Merle Kingman, "Ten Men Who Shaped the Nation's Advertising," in *How It Was in Advertising, 1776–1976*," prepared by editors of *Advertising Age* (Chicago: Crain Books, 1976), p. 23.

70. Pope, *The Making of Modern Advertising*, p. 118.

71. Kingman, "Ten Men Who Shaped Advertising," p. 26.

72. King, "Ungagged Partisanship," p. 408.

73. *Editor & Publisher International Yearbook, 1993*, lists 1,570 daily newspapers in the United States.

74. Hiley Ward, *Magazine and Feature Writing* (Mountain View, Calif.: Mayfield, 1993), p. 263.

75. King, "Ungagged Partisanship," p. 468.

76. Bernard Weisberger, *The La Follettes of Wisconsin* (Madison: University of Wisconsin Press, 1994), p. 94.

77. *New York Times*, Aug. 9, 1924, quoted in Kenneth MacKay, *The Progressive Movement of 1924* (New York: Columbia University Press, 1947), p. 147.

78. MacKay, *The Progressive Movement of 1924*.

79. Carl Burghardt, *Robert M. La Follette, Sr.: The Voice of Conscience* (Westport, Conn.: Greenwood Press, 1992), p. 115.

80. Ibid., p. 116, quoting Belle La Follette and daughter Fola, *Robert M. La Follette*, vol. 2 (1953; reprint, Hafner, 1971), p. 1174.

81. *Editor & Publisher*, Feb. 11, 1911, p. 8, quoted in Robert Miraldi, *Muckraking and Objectivity: Journalism's Colliding Traditions* (Westport, Conn: Greenwood Press, 1990), p. 65. Miraldi says a similar question was asked in February 1911 by other journals—*Independent, Literary Digest*, and *Fourth Estate*.

82. Miraldi, *Muckraking and Objectivity*, p. 66.

83. Ibid.

84. Ibid., quoting Mark Sullivan, *The Education of an American* (New York: Doubleday, Doran & Co., 1938), pp. 286, 287.

85. Ibid., pp. 68, 69.

86. Linda Lawson, *Truth in Publishing: Federal Regulation of the Press's Business Practices, 1880–1920* (Carbondale: Southern Illinois University Press, 1993), p. 65.

87. Ibid., p. 95.

88. Ted Curtis Smythe, "The Advertisers' War to Verify Newspaper Circulation, 1870–1914," *American Journalism*, vol. 3, no. 3, 1986, pp. 177, 178.

89. Arthur M. Schlesinger, Jr., *The Coming of the New Deal* (Boston: Houghton Mifflin, 1959), p. 104.

90. Robert R. McCormick, *The Freedom of the Press* (New York: D. Appleton-Century, 1936; reprint New York: ARNO and New York Times, 1970), pp. 68, 69.

91. Schlesinger, *The Coming of the New Deal*, p. 115.

92. Ibid., p. 18.

93. Will Loomis, "Loomis Puts N.E.A. Cards Face Up; Tells About Debt," *The National Publisher*, July 1936, p. 11.

94. Carolyn M. Byerly, "Toward a Comprehensive History of Public Relations," presented to the Public Relations division of the Association for Education in Journalism and Mass Communication, Kansas City, August 1993.

95. Marvin N. Olasky, "The Development of Corporate Public Relations, 1850–1930," *Journalism Monographs*, no. 102, April 1987, pp. 5, 6.

96. Linda Feinfeld Magyar, "The Evolution of Presidential Press Secretaries," *Media History Digest*, vol. 5, no. 2, Spring 1985.

97. Rodger Streitmatter, "Theodore Roosevelt: Public Relations Pioneer," *American Journalism*, Spring 1990, pp. 99–106.

98. Stephen Ponder, "Federal News Management in the Progressive Era: Gifford Pinchot and the Conservation Crusade," *Journalism History*, vol. 13, no. 2, Summer 1986, p. 45.

99. Betty Houchin Winfield, *FDR and the News Media* (Urbana: University of Illinois Press, 1990), p. 239.

100. Graham J. White, *FDR and the Press* (Chicago: University of Chicago Press, 1979), pp. 10, 11.

101. Winfield, *FDR and the News Media*, p. 73.

102. Werner J. Severin, "Cameras with a Purpose: The Photojournalists of F.S.S.," *Journalism Quarterly*, Spring 1964, pp. 193, 194.

103. Deedee Moore, "Shooting Straight: The Many Worlds of Gordon Parks," *Smithsonian*, April 1989, pp. 66–77.

104. Severin, "Cameras with a Purpose," pp. 197–199.

105. Ray Eldon Hiebert, "Ivy Lee and Rockefeller Press Relations," *Journalism Quarterly*, vol. 43, pp. 329, 330.

106. Olasky, "Development of Public Relations," pp. 27, 28.

107. Ibid., p. 30.

108. Scott M. Cutlip, *The Unseen Power: Public Relations: A History* (Hillsdale, N.J.: Lawrence Erlbaum, 1994).

109. Ella Smith, "Introduction," in Rich Lawton, *A World of Movies: 70 Years of Film History* (New York: Delacorte, 1974), p. 9.

110. Ibid.

111. Cutlip, *The Unseen Power*, p. 375.

112. *Ibid.*, p. 398.

113. Arthur Knight, *The Liveliest Art: A Pamoramic History of the Movies* (New York: New American Library, 1957), p. 35.

11

The Emerging Fast Media: Radio

A society of immigrants and a second generation with new aspirations confronting the old was ready to respond to a stimulus for unity. A gadget was born that would be that catalyst. Farmers and city dwellers in far-flung locations could hear the identical program and message.

With the coming of radio, advertisers, propagandists, even preachers had a new, more extensive "pulpit." Radio allowed politicians to reach faceless millions instantaneously. At all levels there was a craving for the emergence of the next stage, after the telegraph, the phonograph, and the telephone—the miraculous diffusion of sound by wireless radio.

THE ROOTS OF RADIO

As with print media, the roots of radio can be traced back to the ancients. Thales, a Greek philosopher, astronomer, and mathematician who lived from 640 B.C. to 548 B.C., observed friction or static electricity resulting from rubbing amber (a fossil resin) with silk. The Greek word for amber was *elektron*, the root of the word *electricity*. Thales also noticed the attracting power of the lodestone, which he got from a place called Magnesia, from which the word *magnet* comes.

Over the centuries many experimented with static electricity. At the end of the eighteenth century Alessandro Volta in Como, Italy, invented the electric battery, putting electricity into action from a chemical source rather than friction. The *volt*, a unit of electromotive-force-inducing current, is named for him. André-Marie Ampère in France in the early nineteenth century researched electrical currents, creating a magnet out of a spiral conductor fed by a current. He lent his name to the standard unit for measuring the power of an electric current. Georg Simon Ohm, a German physicist, used his name, *ohm*, for designating a unit of electrical resistance.

Practical applications of ongoing electronic experiments started appearing in the nineteenth century. Following Samuel F. B. Morse's inauguration of the electromagnetic telegraph, a transcontinental hookup by Western Union was achieved in 1861. In 1866 a transatlantic cable line linked America and Europe via Newfoundland. By 1876 Alexander Graham Bell had demonstrated that sound and voices could be transmitted by wire. A year later the first telephone line was installed between Boston and Somerville, Massachusetts.

Wireless Between Mountains

The advent of radio had to await the invention of the wireless. But even before the first transmission of voice by telephone, experiments were under way on wireless communication. In 1864 James C. Maxwell in Scotland believed that radio waves existed and could carry communication signals without wires.[1] Heinrich Hertz in Germany proved Maxwell's theory that electromagnetic waves exist in the atmosphere and have frequencies—a number of vibrations or cycles per second.

Mahlon Loomis: First patent for wireless telegraphy.
(Smithsonian Institution)

Although few have heard of him, Mahlon Loomis, who took out the first patent for wireless telegraphy in the United States in 1872, could be regarded as the inventor of radio. In 1866 Loomis had demonstrated sound transmission without wires. He sent up two kites on two different mountain tops in the Blue Ridge Mountains of Virginia. The kites were held up by copper wires attached to galvanometers that could measure the strength of small electric currents. Wireless telegraph signals passed between the two peaks 18 miles apart. Loomis had invented antennas—and demonstrated wireless telegraphy—although traditionally Guglielmo Marconi, of Italy, is regarded as the father of radio. In his *Mahlon Loomis: Inventor of Radio,*

Radio pioneer Guglielmo Marconi (center) with RCA chairperson Owen Young (left) and RCA president E. J. Nally on board the floating lab yacht Elettra *in 1922. (Smithsonian Institution)*

Thomas Appleby[2] maintains that Marconi had examined the Loomis patent in Washington at the time he was seeking his own patent for a wireless system.

In 1895 Marconi transmitted signals between rooftops of post office buildings miles apart in London. A year later he created the Wireless Telegraph and Signal Company, Ltd., which later became Marconi's Wireless Telegraph Company, Ltd. "Always a showman," says Madeleine Jacobs, of the Smithsonian Institution in Washington, Marconi outfitted two American ships to report from offshore to New York newspapers the progress of the yacht race for the America's Cup. In 1901 he achieved international wireless communication, however faint, across the Atlantic between Newfoundland and Cornwall, England.

When the Titanic went down on April 14, 1912, with 1,500 passengers, some survivors gave credit to Marconi's wireless system for saving their lives. But, as Jacobs notes, "the tragedy also brought home the lack of emergency wireless monitoring standards, which were soon put into effect."[3]

Reginald A. Fessenden, playing "O Holy Night" on his violin on Christmas Eve in 1906 and reading the Christmas story from the Gospel of Luke, sent a long-distance voice transmission to ships at sea. A researcher for the U.S Weather Bureau at Brant Rock, Massachusetts, he had earlier demonstrated wireless voice transmission over a short distance using a high-frequency alternator and continuous waves. In his lifetime Fessenden held 500 patents for his inventions.

Lee De Forest in 1906 perfected a tube, called the "audion," that looked like a light and was capable of amplifying a radio signal. A year later he organized the De Forest Radio Telephone Company to serve the New York area. He broadcast mostly music live from the concert halls and even featured Enrico Caruso from the Metropolitan Opera House. One time he broadcast music 500 miles from the top of the Eiffel Tower in Paris.

The First Disc Jockey

Becoming perhaps the first regular broadcaster, Charles David Herrold in San Jose, California, in 1910 put a gigantic antenna on top of a bank building and offered a half-hour news and music program, which became a daily program a year later. Herrold claimed to be the first broadcaster because he had regular programming and targeted an inclusive, broad audience. The Emerys suggest that his wife, Sybil, with her own music programs for young people, may have been the first woman to broadcast her own show. The audience listened to the Herrolds and their programming over several dozen telephone receivers in a store or a "listening room." Perhaps also the first disc jockey, Sybil took call-in requests for songs. Herrold named his operation or station FN, later SJN, and finally KQW in 1921.[4]

Media as Purveyors of Information/Education
FROM SCHOOL KID'S HOBBY TO INTRIGUE

In its early years radio had the effect of an ancient town crier. At first using the Morse code, then voices, "ham" radio operators formed quasi-national networks. News was relayed from one operator to another over distances by young hobbyists in the decade before World War I.

Boy Scouts and Morse Code

Some of the amateur radio operators were Boy Scouts. "Using inexpensive crystals as detectors, oatmeal boxes wound with wire stolen from construction sites as tuning coils, and telephones as headsets," says Susan Smulyan, "the young hobbyists learned from each other, from magazines, from Boy Scout manuals, and from trial and error to build their own equipment." The young designers of receivers and transmitters picked up distant signals and used Morse code to contact one another.[5]

In 1914 amateur radio operators across the country created the American Radio Relay League (ARRL), networking 200 radio clubs and fledgling "stations." Although banned during the war, the ARRL was revived in 1919. Susan Douglas says, "It was the amateurs who demonstrated that, in an increasingly atomized and impersonal society, the nascent broadcast audience was waiting to be brought together."[6]

One of the experimental ham operators was Frank Conrad, an engineer for Westinghouse Electric and Manufacturing Company of Pittsburgh. In 1916 Conrad started broadcasting from his garage a regular music program on station 8XK for Westinghouse. Before 8XK was launched, however, Westinghouse promoted the buying of radio receivers and made them available to many employees. Westinghouse also persuaded the *Pittsburgh Post* and *Pittsburgh Sun* to carry its listings.

The First Station

With sales of the new equipment soaring, Westinghouse decided to install Conrad's transmitter on top of its building. Westinghouse's 8XK was licensed by the secretary of commerce in November 1916 as KDKA, the eighth out of 200 stations licensed before the end of the year. The first had been WBZ in Springfield, Massachusetts. "Transmissions such as Conrad's to many listeners, rather than the prewar use of radio to communicate between two people, changed radio into a potential mass medium," says Smuylan.[7] For that reason, KDKA is usually considered the first actual station on the air.

Yet there are other candidates for "first station," including Herrold's San Jose station, KQW, which provided a schedule in 1912; experimental broadcasts from the University of Wisconsin during World War I; a regular music broadcast on station 2ZK in New York in 1916; and station 8MK broadcast experimentally from the office of William E. Scripps in Detroit in 1916 a few months before KDKA started.[8]

The first station licensed to an African American was 3LF in the District of Columbia in the 1920s. It was operated by Rufus P. Turner, who later invented the world's smallest crystal radio receiving set, built on an ordinary pin.[9]

With a prescient view of the future, David Sarnoff, who as a young wireless operator for Marconi's company in New York had relayed messages of the sinking of the Titanic, in 1915 wrote his superiors at American Marconi a memo that outlined the great potential in the future of radio. He proposed a simple central radio box that could tune in news and entertainment programs from a central transmitter.[10]

News Broadcasts Begin

Offering music and baseball news, the "radio music box" could be used as a prime deliverer of news, Sarnoff said. The potential was there—15 million families—and if only one million bought the box, tremendous profits could be made. The Marconi company, however, brushed the proposal aside. It was five years later when Sarnoff had gone to work for the new Radio Corporation of America (RCA) that his proposal was taken seriously, but even then he was allowed only $2,000 to design the prototype of the radio box. RCA came out with its successful box, Radiola, in 1922, but it was not the first product of its kind; Westinghouse had come out with the first civilian receiver, Aeriola, Jr., in 1921. In 1922 there were thirty radio stations, rising to 732 in 1927; radio "boxes" in that period went from 60,000 to 6.5 million.[11]

The broadcast of news gave the Associated Press concern because the stations were taking copy from the wire bulletins. In 1922 the AP sent its members a message warning them that AP bylaws prohibited the use of its news on the radio. But some stations, responding to the demand, ignored the warning and said they had sources other than the AP.[12] In 1925, however, AP compromised on the problem and said that major news that was not exclusive could be reused by broadcasters who were AP members, provided there were "proper safeguards" and "proper credit" was given.

The American Newspaper Publishers Association (ANPA) expressed a concern over the sponsorship of news. The organization objected to advertising not on the grounds that it was new competition but because it interfered with the entertainment and educational values of broadcasting. The ANPA also objected to the practice of newspapers giving free publicity in the form of radio program listings.[13]

The Potential for Propaganda

There were concerns about the way the new medium would treat news and the potential that it could be used for propaganda. "Broadcasting lends more opportunity for subtle coloring of news by inflection and voice emphasis than is possible in the printed page," said *Editor & Publisher*, "and the possibility is always present that an unscrupulous advertiser and a commentator with weak principles will try to put one over on their audience."[14]

In 1933, the year that Hitler became chancellor of Germany, a weekly editor from Richmond (E. H. Harris) raised a larger concern when he asked: "What can be done to prevent the propaganda of foreign nations from being broadcast across our boundaries. . . . The chief executive or the governing head of one nation, by the use of the radio, can talk directly to the people of another nation, to spread propaganda."[15] This kind of activity did come about, but it worked both ways—for example, consider Axis broadcasts to U.S. troops in World War II, America's employment of the Voice of America radio to influence the Eastern bloc during the Cold War, the use of Radio Martí to subvert Cuba's communist leadership, and in 1994 the U.S. creation of Radio Democracy to influence the people of Haiti.

Media as Businesses

THE QUEST FOR WAYS TO PAY FOR RADIO

A magazine, *Radio Broadcast*, in 1925 conducted a contest on "Who is to pay for broadcasting and how?" Of 800 entries received, the winning one called for a tax on vacuum tubes to be collected by the federal Bureau of Broadcasting.[16] The idea was never taken seriously, however. Others, including Secretary of Commerce Herbert Hoover, proposed that businesses fund stations.

In addition to the sponsoring of early stations by radio-receiver-set producers, other businesses and private citizens got into the act. Radio historian Erik Barnouw points out that stations were started by stores, churches, Bible schools, a stockyard, a marble company, a laundry, and a poultry farm. Several were started as hobbies by men with money.[17] Since some of the programs related to the station owner's products, the stations could be called commercial, but they did not sell advertising time to other manufacturers.[18]

Some city governments sponsored stations; New York City, for instance, had WNYC. Community radio committees also rose up to solicit funds from listeners to pay for radio performers. Advertising was not considered a prime option for financing radio until the rise of the networks. These had a broad enough base to encourage advertising, which brought in the large amounts of money needed to finance the rental of wire lines.

The New "Monster" Attracts Ads

The choice of advertising as a prime means of support for the networks and their programs caused considerable consternation among print editors. "The daily newspaper at first fondled the radio as a plaything," says media historian Alfred McClung Lee.[19] But as Lea M. Nichols, president of the National Editorial Association (now the National Newspaper Association), noted in his presidential message to NEA delegates in San Francisco in 1932, "This one-time pleasing toy became a monster." And the reason, as Nichols, an editor in Bristow, Oklahoma, pointed out, was that "radio grew up and commenced to bid for a slice of the American advertising dollar."[20]

By 1932, however, editors in many parts of the country were looking for ways to beat the radio menace and its threat to "scooping" newspapers in terms of time and "scooping up" dollars that might otherwise have gone to newspapers in those economically troubled years. Their solution was to acquire radio stations. The

Editor & Publisher Year Book for 1932 showed that newspapers owned fifty-one stations, leased two, and were identified in some way with fifty others.

NEA executive H. C. Hotaling, in his annual report to the 1931 convention in Atlanta, indicated how concerned editors were. "There is a growing feeling that there should be some restrictions as to broadcasting," he said. And he referred to an anonymous speaker in a Minnesota editors' meeting who declared, "Failure to regulate radio activities will mean the elimination of the country weekly." And Hotaling added, "This is not the idle statement which some may infer. There are country weeklies in America today, even in small towns, that are fighting for existence because of unrestricted radio competition."[21]

According to *Media Records*, in 1930 the top 107 users of radio time had cut back their advertising in newspapers by 12.5 percent compared to the previous year, while at the same time increasing their use of radio by 63 percent.[22] Lottery ads, considered questionable by newspapers, but used on radio at the beginning of the 1930s, were popular but drew the fire of the NEA and others.[23]

Movies and Television Pose Threat

Then radio advertising dipped, and there was competition from still another new mode of communication, the movie. A study reported by the NEA showed that of the 635 advertisers who bought time on the air between 1929 and 1933, exactly 448, or 70.6 percent, had stopped advertising on the radio in 1934.[24] Soon editors worried less about radio and its threat in advertising; instead they began to turn their attention toward competition from ads in movie theaters in their small towns.[25]

Newspaper publishers became confident that they had won the battle of competition with radio and the latecomer, television. In the 1920s, William Haight in the *Publishers' Auxiliary* recited the limitations of radio and television and the nervous, erratic, jockeying-for-position approach of advertisers as they "scattered" their ads (a philosophy that throws ads the newspaper way, too). Among the limitations were these: "Audiences are badly fragmented into small segments, especially for radio"; "coverage patterns do not coincide with natural trade areas of stores"; "brief messages prove woefully inadequate"; "the fleeting, transitory commercial vanishes quickly from memory"; "special, costly talents are needed for production of effective ads"; "time-lag in getting commercials on the air is inconsistent"; and for radio, in addition, "the inability to picture the product severely restricts radio's usefulness for most stores." And: "Merchants are accustomed to ease and time-saving simplicity with print ads."[26]

The new medium, radio, was never quite sure of its audiences. Broadcasting—spreading information—reached people indiscriminately. Advertisers had to decide whom they wanted to hear the message and how to measure the demographics of listeners. The listening audience was divided in such a way that a privileged segment, the buying audience, was defined. "Clearly, advertisers were not buying time," says Eileen Meehan of the emerging advertising sophistication, "but rather access to an audience. And advertisers did not want to pay for just anybody who happened to tune in; they targeted the consumerist caste, which was but one part of the vast listening public. Thus, toll broadcasting earned its revenues from an invisible commodity, as the consumerist caste became the commodity audience."[27] But the consumer class was seen in segments, such as a ladies' audience or housewives or heads of households (the men), and some groups, such as children, were excluded completely.

Media as Voices of Freedom

WAR FOUGHT IN THE AIR

In 1935 the president of a radio news service, Transradio Press Service, could write passionately of a "war" to secure the freedom of broadcasting. "It has often been said that the next war will be fought in the air," Herbert Moore intoned. "But a battle is in progress in the air at this very moment—the battle between press and radio to determine which shall be first to give important news to the public. . . . The issue is that of freedom of the press of the air."[28]

Independent broadcasters were concerned when the American Newspaper Publishers Association, along with several newspaper syndicates, the wire services, the Columbia Broadcasting System, and the National Broadcasting Company, created the Press-Radio Bureau to provide "limited daily bulletins of state, national and international importance to broadcasters." The bulletins were to be no more than thirty words in length and were to be available at the end of a newspaper day. Obviously these restrictions did not sit well with independent broadcasters.

Since the Press-Radio Bureau could muster only 160 stations out of the 600, there was room for the development of independent news bureaus to serve radio. One such bureau was Moore's Transradio, which by 1936 had 260 subscribers. It provided up to 30,000 words of news daily.[29] And there were cracks in the ranks of the Press-Radio Bureau. Stations bound to the Press-Radio Bureau began developing some of their own news, and the networks were putting on "commentators," all of which helped undermine the Press-Radio Bureau, with its limited offerings. The United Press and International News Service started selling news to radio in 1935. The Press-Radio Bureau expired in 1938. In 1940, AP moved into the radio field.

Presidential Censorship

Government officials, even presidents, have had a direct hand in curbing the free rein of broadcasters. When future president Herbert Hoover, as secretary of commerce regulating radio before the establishment of the Federal Radio Commission in 1927, could not keep flamboyant evangelist Aimee Semple McPherson from straying from her assigned wavelength, he ordered her station shut down. She replied quickly with this telegram:

PLEASE ORDER YOUR MINIONS OF SATAN TO LEAVE MY STATION ALONE. YOU CANNOT
EXPECT THE ALMIGHTY TO ABIDE BY YOUR WAVE LENGTH NONSENSE. STOP. WHEN I
OFFER MY PRAYERS TO HIM I MUST FIT INTO HIS RECEPTION. STOP. OPEN THE STATION
AT ONCE. STOP.[30]

Her station, KFSG ("Kall Four Square Gospel") was allowed to reopen.

The Franklin Delano Roosevelt administration, while skillful in the use of radio, nevertheless directly and indirectly shut down broadcasters critical of the administration. One to suffer FDR's wrath was Boake Carter, who had up to 10 million listeners over eighty-five stations in the late 1930s and was voted the most popular commentator on radio in a poll by *Radio Guide*. Roosevelt directed Secretary of Labor Frances Perkins to find ways to deport Carter, a new citizen, but nothing irregular was found. "The Roosevelt administration was not finished with Carter, however," says Gary Dean Best, "and by the end of August 1938 he was off the airwaves. His attacks on Roosevelt's foreign policy, especially, had apparently by this time created sufficient pressure from the administration and its friends at both his network (CBS) and his sponsor (General Foods) to bring about his banishment."[31]

Similarly, radio priest Charles Coughlin blamed Roosevelt for being forced off the airwaves in 1940. Coughlin first supported Roosevelt and even claimed, at least in one of several interviews with this author, that he helped write FDR's inaugural speech in 1933. But Coughlin, accused of being anti-Semitic and profascist, split with Roosevelt on a number of personal and policy issues and launched a third-party challenge to Roosevelt in 1936. CBS dropped Coughlin's popular Sunday afternoon program, and Coughlin, broadcasting out of Royal Oak, Michigan, organized his own network of fifty-eight stations.

In 1940 Coughlin was ordered by superiors to cease broadcasting. He did not talk about the order for twenty years and said little about it after that. He blamed pressure by Roosevelt on Pope Pius XII. The order came through the local prelate, Edward Cardinal Mooney of Detroit.

Coughlin said in what may have been his last interview before his death in 1979 at age eighty-seven, "The pope never stopped my broadcast." It was "Mr. Roosevelt's use of blackmail on the archbishop of Chicago [Samuel Cardinal Stritch]. It was secret, and I am not going to say any more about it. I was obedient and I showed the priests of America I do as I was told. There is nothing like obedience."[32]

Taming the Jungle of Sound

Then there was the force of federal regulation, reining in "freedom." As early as 1912 it was clear that some regulation would have to be endured by the new industry, with radio operators and "stations" sprouting up across the country. The Radio Act of 1912 gave the secretary of commerce the task of regulating the number of stations and assigning nonconflicting frequencies, but the law lacked sufficient enforcement apparatus. By 1925 the number of stations had risen to 10,000, including 571 commercial stations.[33] The radio box had become a jungle of sound, a confusion of tongues, mixed and overlapping—a veritable Tower of Babel.

In February 1927, President Calvin Coolidge signed into law the Radio Act of 1927, which created the Federal Radio Commission (FRC) with broad powers over radio. The FRC had the authority to issue or reject licenses and to assign frequencies to individual stations and determine their power. The FRC also expected applicants for licenses to demonstrate that they had ample support before a license would be granted. Furthermore, the Radio Act said stations must operate in the "public interest." It started by making all existing licenses expire sixty days after the approval of the act, so as to start with a clean slate. New licenses were to be granted for three years.

Stations therefore had to submit to a measure of government control. One station in particular thumbed its nose at the new regulations and was promptly hauled into court. It was an unlicensed station with its own assigned call letters, W9ZR, St. Louis, operated by George Walter Fellowes. Not only did Fellowes violate the new regulations by broadcasting without a license, but he was also "bootlegging," that is, rebroadcasting material from other stations. The United States v. Fellowes case provided the government with its first chance to demonstrate the power of the new law by shutting down a station operating without a license.[34]

In the three-day trial in May 1930 in a U.S. District Court in St. Louis, Fellowes' attorney tried to show that the power of Fellowes' station was so low as not to constitute a nuisance; however, the prosecution produced witnesses in Missouri and Illinois who testified they heard the station 150 miles away. Sounding a little bit like a participant in the historic Zenger trial, Fellowes' court-appointed attorney asked the jury, "What is to become of personal liberty if the government continues to make regulations like it has for radio broadcasting?"[35] Fellowes was convicted and offered a choice between a year and a day in the federal penitentiary at Leavenworth, Kansas, or deportation to England. He chose deportation.

FCC: Commercialism Wins

Seven years later the Communications Act of 1934 replaced the FRC with the Federal Communications Commission (FCC), with broader responsibilities that included jurisdiction over the telephone and all telecommunications and other electronic media. Today the FCC's responsibility includes distribution of licenses to corporations to sell enhanced wireless voice, video, and data services and a new generation of wireless communication: personal communication services such as cordless telephones, computers, fax machines, and paging devices.[36]

The passage of the Communications Act of 1934 was a victory for the commercialization of radio and later television. An amendment to the proposed act when it was before the Senate in May 1934 would have required the FCC to void all existing radio licenses in ninety days to allow reallocation of the airwaves. Furthermore, the amendment called for allocating at least 25 percent of the radio channels for nonprofit and educational broadcasting. The amendment would have constituted a serious challenge to "the private, oligopolistic and commercially subsidized nature of American broadcasting," says Robert W. McChesney, who noted that the amendment "was opposed with extraordinary vigor by the commercial broadcasting industry."[37]

Behind the doomed measure, the Wagner-Hatfield amendment, was the Very Reverend John B. Harney, superior general of the Missionary Society of St. Paul the Apostle (Paulist Fathers). In 1925 the Paulists had started the first Roman Catholic station in America, WLWL, in New York. "Within two years WLWL was struggling to survive amidst efforts to seize its valuable frequency by commercial broadcasting companies," says McChesney. "In these struggles WLWL found little support from the Federal Radio Commission (FRC), which had been established by the Radio Act of 1927 to bring order to the airwaves. It was these bitter experiences that led Father Harney to the forefront of the battle to reform radio in 1934."[38] Father Harney and his reform movement went down in defeat, leaving the new radio industry to be dominated by commercial interests.

Equal Time: Certifying Crackpots

Stations worried about the implied if not always real threat to news and opinion broadcasting posed by Section 315 of the Communications Act of 1934. That section called for equal time to be provided for those with contrasting views, including candidates. Broadcasters wanted to be assured that the equal-time provisions did not apply to news reports. The controversy came to a head in 1959 when the FCC ordered Chicago stations to give equal time to an offbeat mayoral candidate who dressed up in a red, white, and blue Uncle Sam outfit in his race against the incumbent mayor of Chicago, Richard Daley. Realizing that the FCC policy was in effect giving official sanction to "crackpots," Congress intervened and excluded newscasts, interviews, and political debates from the equal-time policy.

After 1949 stations had to contend with the "fairness doctrine," which maintained that there was a responsibility not just to give equal time to opposing views but to create opportunities for contrasting opinions to be broadcast. In 1949, in amending the 1941 *Mayflower* decision, in which the FCC prohibited the Mayflower Broadcasting Corporation from editorializing, the FCC said that stations, once forbidden to editorialize, could now do so but had to offer time for views of the other side. While broadcasters complained that the doctrine was just one more restraint on their freedom, public interest groups saw the doctrine as an investing of First Amendment rights in the public.

The fairness policy was tested in 1964 when conservative radio preacher Billy James Hargis, in a broadcast over WGGB in Red Lion, Pennsylvania, accused New York writer Fred Cook of being involved in many Communist causes. Cook insisted on free time to reply, but the station declined. The FCC ruled in Cook's favor. The matter went to the U.S. Supreme Court, which backed Cook. The high court said the right of viewers and listeners was more important than the right of broadcasters, with their private agenda and censorship.[39]

In 1972 the U.S. Circuit Court of Appeals, upholding a decision of the FCC, shut down the radio stations of a right-wing minister, the Reverend Carl McIntire. The stations, WXUR and WXUR-FM, of Media, Pennsylvania, were owned by Faith Theological Seminary, whose chairman of the board was McIntire. McIntire had broken away from the United Presbyterian Church and started his own Presbyterian denomination and American Council of Churches in reaction to the liberal National Council of Churches. He used his daily broadcast, "Twentieth Century Reformation Hour," to attack other clergy and groups as modernistic and communist, among other things. McIntire and a small band of followers spent much of their time picketing national and international church meetings, particularly those of the National and World Council of Churches and their agencies. When he bought his two stations in Media over protests of civil rights, labor, Jewish, and church groups, he promised to make time available "on an equal and nondiscriminatory basis to all religious faiths requesting time" and to provide equal opportunities to those with opposing views.[40]

The FCC allowed the sale of the stations, but was soon beset with complaints about the content aired over the stations. The FCC proceeded to deny renewal of licenses when they came up in 1970. The U.S. Circuit Court of Appeals upheld the decision, more so because of the misrepresentation of program plans than on the basis of violation of the fairness doctrine.

McIntire took his broadcast offshore onto a U.S.-registered minesweeper. He opened his program with the words, "Radio Free America, out in the North Atlantic, is on the air." But when a Lakewood, New Jersey, station complained that his signal was interfering with its own, the attorneys for the FCC and the Justice Department obtained a court order to close down McIntire's pirate operation. In the 1990s McIntire was back broadcasting on WTMR-AM in Camden.

Fairness Doctrine Axed

Disillusioned over the controversies over the fairness doctrine and the difficulty in applying it, the FCC in 1981, the first year of the Reagan administration, recommended to Congress that the doctrine be repealed. The FCC followed with a report in 1984 saying that the doctrine ceased to serve the public interest because "the development of the information services marketplace makes unnecessary any governmentally imposed obligation to provide balanced coverage of controversial issues of public importance."[41]

When the Senate and House in 1987 passed a bill with a rider that would have given new life to the fairness doctrine, President Reagan vetoed the bill. Encouraged by the presidential action, the FCC issued a memorandum opinion stating that the fairness doctrine was unconstitutional. In 1989 the FCC's decision to end the fairness doctrine was upheld by the Circuit Court of Appeals for the District of Columbia. A bill before Congress in 1993 to revive the fairness doctrine failed to be acted on.

Media as Political Organs

NO PLACE FOR THE POLITICAL "TWANGER"

Politics has been a part of radio history from the early 1920s, when radio's potential for power and influence was discovered, through to the present day, when presidents and their critics alike take to dueling on the radio.

The first scheduled radio program in America, on November 2, 1920, lasting eighteen hours, reported the election returns, with Warren Harding swamping Democrat James Cox, 16 million to 9 million. A year later, in November 1921, Harding addressed the international community from Europe to Japan to Australia by radio. (Wilson had been heard over the radio earlier.) Harding's successor, the solemn, quiet little man, Calvin Coolidge, found the radio to his liking. "I am very fortunate that I came in with the radio," Coolidge said. "I can't make an engaging, rousing or oratorical speech . . . but I have a good radio voice, and now I can get my message across to [the public] without acquainting them with my lack of oratorical ability."[42] He took his messages to the airwaves on an average of once a month.

Radio began to work for and against potential candidates in the election year of 1924. It took 103 rounds of balloting at the Democratic convention to nominate John W. Davis as the presidential candidate. Davis and the ever-present William Jennings Bryan, both noted for oratorical skills, failed to translate their golden style to radio. Michael Carpini quotes one observer who said: "Mr. Davis . . . has a voice which to the direct auditor has that bell-like quality of his delightful rhetoric. Via radio, however, this muffles and fogs." At the end of the campaign, Davis predicted that radio "will make the long speech impossible or inadvisable. . . . the short speech will be in vogue."[43] Coolidge's inaugural address in 1925 was heard by 15 million, a number greater than the total of all those who had heard past presidents. "Silent Cal" came in fourth in a popularity poll determining the most-liked radio personalities. He even came out ahead of the widely popular entertainer Will Rogers.[44]

Hoover Comfortable with Radio

President Herbert Hoover, who was elected in 1928, was no stranger to radio. President Harding appointed him secretary of commerce in 1921, and he stayed in that post through the Coolidge administration until 1928. As commerce secretary, Hoover called a radio conference in November 1925, the fourth conference in an attempt to resolve the problem of too many stations on the air. He had authority to license stations until the Radio Act of 1927—wrought after intense political maneuvering and ultimate compromise[45]—put that matter into the hands of a commission.

Hoover made good use of radio in the 1928 campaign against Democratic nominee Alfred E. Smith. Radio reached into 30 percent of American homes in 1928. Historian Henry F. Graf says: "Smith proved more appealing in person than on the air. Awkward and unaccommodating before a microphone, he came over as strange—even foreign—to small-town America. Though far less rousing before a crowd, Hoover was more effective on the airwaves."[46] As president, Hoover gave ninety-five addresses over the radio, just nine less than Franklin Roosevelt in his first term.[47]

In 1932 the Republicans for Hoover outdistanced Democrats in use of the airwaves, the Republicans engaging seventy-three hours of air time, the Democrats, forty-three. "Even so," says Carpini, "Hoover was no match for Franklin Delano Roosevelt as a radio orator, the latter having been selected by broadcasting officials as the best political speaker in the nation." Broadcasters liked "FDR's ability to create a feeling of intimacy between himself and his listeners, [and] his adroitness in presenting complicated matters in such simple terms that the man in the street believes he has full mastery of them." But, Carpini adds, "Hoover sounded like 'an old-fashioned phonograph in need of winding.' "[48]

Roosevelt's charm as a radio speaker was the result of various techniques. He spoke slowly, savoring every word as if each were important. He was a phrase-maker, and he spoke with a poetic rhythm, as when he said in his inaugural speech on March 4, 1933, in the midst of the Great Depression, "The only thing we have to fear is fear itself." And when he implored Congress to declare war the day after the Japanese attack on Pearl Harbor, December 7, 1941, he chose his words well when he called the previous day "a date which will live in infamy." His voice brought his personality to his audience, and he always seemed to care about the listener.

FDR's Intimate Chats

Roosevelt began giving an occasional short, chatty talk aimed at the general public from his office in the White House. "You felt he was there talking to you, not to 50 million others, but to you personally," said reporter Richard Strout.[49] CBS started referring to these talks as "fireside chats," picking up on White House aide Stephen Early's comments in a news release, "the President likes to think of the audience as being a few people around his fireside."[50] Laborious preparations went into each of the fireside chats. Usually there were three to ten drafts—once, twenty-two—before he was ready to give the speech.[51] He would rehearse each speech several times.

In 1936, when FDR was running against Kansas governor Alfred M. Landon, the main candidates were made aware of the potential of radio by its use by dissident leaders. In addition to the Reverend Charles E. Coughlin, the Detroit-area thunderer who had 30 million listeners on Sunday afternoon, there were southern Senator Huey Long, religious broadcaster Gerald L. K. Smith, old-age-rights crusader Francis Townsend, and Congressman William Lemke, who headed a third-party front, inspired by Coughlin, the Union Party.

Up against Roosevelt, the prime radio personality, Landon conceded he had to use the medium. The Republicans hired him a voice coach, but there was no audible result. Landon went on boring listeners to the glee of Democrats who tried to get the populace to listen to him because he was such a "flat, dull, twangy-voice" speaker.[52]

President Franklin Roosevelt in a fireside chat. (Smithsonian Institution)

Political parties used radio in other ways. Government agencies, appearing to be doing informational programming, were actually hawking political messages. A program, for instance, of the Agricultural Adjustment Administration amounted to no more that a recitation of the "achievements" of that agency. Republicans aired skits poking fun at the Democrats and their New Deal. These appeared mainly on independent stations, as NBC and CBS had refused to broadcast them.

"Clear channel" stations offered opportunities for the farm lobby to influence politics. The Federal Radio Commission in 1928 earmarked forty of the AM broadcast band's ninety-six frequencies for the exclusive use of one station at night in order to provide coverage to far-flung rural areas. Thirteen clear channel stations formed the Clear Channel Group to work closely with farm issue lobbies, thus corralling the farm vote on special issues.[53]

Eleanor on Radio, Too

The first lady, Eleanor Roosevelt, also entered the political radio action arena. She accepted commercial sponsors, which included a roofing company, a mattress company, a cold cream manufacturer, and the Pan-American Coffee Bureau, which represented eight coffee-exporting nations. "Although she addressed herself primarily to women," say Maurine Beasley and Paul Belgrade, "she sought to widen their interests beyond the confines of the home. Because of her role as first lady, the programs carried an obvious political overtone."[54]

Later presidents, looking back idyllically to the warmth and charm and success of FDR's fireside chats, have continued to give weekly radio chats from the White House. On at least one occasion, President Bill Clinton, who himself conducted a regular weekly Saturday half-hour radio show, used an existing radio call-in program to unleash, as the *New York Times* put it, "an unusually bitter, 23-minute attack on the press, the Rev. Jerry Falwell, conservative radio talk show hosts in general and Rush Limbaugh in particular." Noting that Clinton had won election in part because of his "mastery of talk radio and television," the newspaper said that Clinton, in his call-in to station KMOX in St. Louis, "portrayed the nation's airwaves as being filled with a 'constant, unremitting drumbeat of negativism and cynicism.' "[55]

Media as Fourth Estate: Adversaries of Government
NETWORKS: UNITY WITH POWER

A current example of radio sharing in the power of the fourth estate is "talk radio." In his book on talk radio Peter Laufer cites a cartoon that has a teacher in a civics class asking, "What's the third branch of government?" A bright pupil answers, "Talk radio."[56] Perhaps talk radio has created a separate entity of power, a fifth estate, in a "talkocracy."[57] Talk radio is "a growing power in our society," says Laufer, as it links "lonely misfits and amateur information-distorters."[58]

Radio itself, the one "constant" medium that relates to everybody—the teen, the homemaker, the commuter—"is always there," says Carl Jensen, who heads an ongoing study, Project Censored, at California's Sonoma State University, "whereas magazines, newspapers, television are not necessarily that constant a medium."[59]

Within radio's structures are bastions of power, the broadcasting networks, which indeed rival formal branches of government in the ability to shape culture and which, by the size of their constituencies, can set a political agenda and influence voting and selection processes of government. Growing out of developments in the 1920s that were both cooperative and competitive, the networks offered a scattered listening and viewing audience a unity of messages.

In the early days of radio, it was realized that for this medium to be profitable there would have to be some kind of "national" radio system. It just did not make a lot of sense for newspapers and other companies owning local stations to shoulder the high costs involved in continually creating local programming. It seemed feasible for local stations to rely on centrally prepared programs that could be shared by a number of stations. Networking of stations could provide a wider base with which to appeal to advertisers. There was a homogeneity of population with one language and a common culture and an aroused curiosity to expand on the new "toy." And a networking of stations had predecessors in other sections of society, such as the networking and cooperation of railroads.

But one factor proved to be a main catalyst. A General Electric engineer, E.F.W. Alexanderson, had created a high-frequency alternator in 1914. It could send signals through strong disturbances in the earth's atmosphere that interfered with other voice transmitters. The Alexanderson high-frequency alternator was deemed necessary for a radio corporation to expand.

In 1919 the British Marconi Company offered $5 million for twenty-four Alexanderson alternators, with exclusive rights to use them. Before the deal was consummated, the GE negotiator, GE general counsel Owen D. Young, notified the Navy Department of GE's intention to sell the precious alternators and the rights to use them. The government was not anxious to have an industry such as radio in essence under the control of a foreign company. Acting Secretary of the Navy Franklin D. Roosevelt asked Young to meet with top navy officials. Obliging, Young and naval officials developed "a proposal that would alter the structure of American communications" to present to the GE board.[60] The proposal called for GE to turn down the British Marconi bid and put the alternator under the control of a new company to be created in the United States.

Birth of RCA

The navy said it would put its valuable wireless patents into a patent pool along with patents contributed by GE and American Marconi. The proposal further called for GE to buy out American Marconi and to create a new subsidiary. The GE board, seeing the proposal not only as a patriotic move ending a foreign monopoly but also as an inviting business opportunity, enthusiastically endorsed the proposal. Young named the new subsidiary Radio Corporation of America, and brought aboard two Marconi staffers, Edward J. Nally, president of Marconi's American subsidiary, as first RCA president, and a twenty-eight-year-old David Sarnoff as commercial manager.[61]

To be effective RCA needed access to additional patents. Young and Sarnoff looked first to AT&T, which had rights to De Forest's audion tube. AT&T had enough strength to block others but not a broad enough range of patents to control the industry. AT&T thus joined the RCA consortium, bringing its patents and wired network, and accepting 20.6 percent of RCA stock. Next to join up was Westinghouse, which had the patents of radio pioneer Edwin Armstrong, who, among other things, is regarded as the father of frequency modulation (FM), which adapts the frequency of the radio wave according to the sound being projected and thus achieves a clearer, static-free sound. Then came United Fruit Company, which had done work with wireless as it linked up plantations with banana boats in Latin America; it brought patents on crystal detectors and a loop antenna. Some 2,000 patents covering all facets of broadcasting were now available to the pool.[62]

The Big Three: NBC, CBS, ABC

AT&T in 1926 decided to be free of growing charges of developing a monopoly and to keep its focus on telephones rather than radio. It sold its New York station WEAF to RCA, which joined with GE and Westinghouse to incorporate a separate broadcast entity, the National Broadcasting Company (NBC). The new company would lease telephone lines from AT&T to pick up programs and to connect local stations.

The first program on NBC on November 15, 1926, lasted four hours and was heard on twenty-five stations in twenty-one cities. Listeners heard the New York Symphony, a choral group, a pianist, and the comedy duo of Weber and Fields, from the ballroom of the Waldorf-Astoria Hotel in New York. Folk comedian Will Rogers was heard from a studio in Independence, Kansas, and opera star Mary Garden, singing "Annie Laurie," from Chicago.

NBC was soon operating two networks—a Red network of twenty-five stations served by WEAF (originally with AT&T) in New York and a Blue network of six stations served by WJZ (an RCA outlet), also in New York.

Meanwhile a competing new network, which was to become the Columbia Broadcasting System, was in the incubation stage. Arthur Judson, a concert promoter and manager, had a plan, at first agreeable to Sarnoff, to coordinate the programming of NBC and supply performers for the network. When Sarnoff suddenly changed his mind about using Judson, who managed the Philadelphia Orchestra and the New York Philharmonic, Judson responded that he would start his own network, the United Independent Broadcasters (UIB). Sarnoff burst out laughing, saying that Judson would never find enough money to lease AT&T lines. Judson enlisted the support of the Columbia Phonograph Company, which in 1927 invested $163,000 in the precocious network, partly in reaction to RCA's purchase of the Victor Talking Machine Company.

With an affiliation of sixteen stations, the UIB, now calling its network the Columbia Phonograph Broadcasting System, Inc., had its first broadcast on September 1927. The premiere broadcast was marred by the lack of preparedness by the originating station, WOR, Newark, and by the weather, according to James Roman. The broadcast had to be monitored from a men's room, the only sound-proof space available. Also a thunderstorm during the broadcast added static to the radio signal. Nevertheless, the broadcast featured impressive musical talent and orchestra groups lined up by musical kingpin Judson. The network plodded along, losing money, until it was taken over by the Levy brothers and another partner, Jerome Louchheim, a Philadelphia subway builder.[63]

Gaining control of United Independent Broadcasters (UIB), Louchheim, a friend of cigar merchant Sam Paley (William's father), tried to sell the company to the senior Paley. "Sam, why don't you buy it from me?" Louchheim said to the senior Paley, who owned a cigar firm and had advertised on radio. "You at least have a cigar to advertise and you can make some use out of it." But the senior Paley did not want to risk his money in such a venture. However, the younger Paley had about a million dollars because a block of stock in the cigar company had been put in his name. Like the young Hearst, William Paley "became tremendously excited at the prospect" of acquiring a media outlet, a station, and he was not to be deterred by the shakiness of Judson's network. In the deal with Louchheim, Paley gained control of 50.3 percent of the stock. Recalled Paley, "On September 25, I closed the deal and on the next day, September 26, 1928, was elected president of a patchwork, money-losing little company called United Independent Broadcasters."[64] Paley abolished the broadcasting "arm" as a corporation and changed the name of UIB to the Columbia Broadcasting System, Inc. Paley remained chief executive officer until 1977 and chairman of the board until 1983.

The American Broadcasting Company (ABC) was born in 1943 when the FCC in an antitrust action forced RCA to sell its Blue Network. Buyer of the network renamed ABC was Edward J. Noble, who headed a company that made Life Savers candy.

In 1934 the Mutual Broadcasting System (MBS) was founded when independent stations not linked with the other networks saw the advantage of working mutually with other such stations. In on the ground floor were stations in Chicago, Cincinnati, Detroit, and Newark. The network acquired 19 percent of the nation's stations by 1940, but many of its stations remained linked to the bigger networks and used Mutual programming as filler material.[65] Mutual became involved in various scandals, including accusations of guaranteeing favorable mention to Dominican Republic dictator Rafael Trujillo, and changed ownership six times between 1956 and 1959.[66] MBS passed from ownership by the Amway Corporation to California-based Westwood One in 1985, and two years later Westwood One acquired NBC's radio network.[67]

There has been a proliferation of multiprogram networks. In addition to the big three (ABC, CBS, and NBC), there are National Public Radio (a nonprofit network launched by the Corporation for Public Broadcasting in 1969 and featuring music and news, including the news magazine "All Things Considered" and "Soundprint," a half-hour documentary program), the National Black Network, the United States Radio Network, the USA Radio Network, the Wall Street Journal Radio Network, Reuters Radio, Associated Press Radio, the UPI Radio Network, the Sheridan Broadcasting Network, and, according to *Broadcasting-Cable Yearbook 1989*, 101 regional radio networks.[68]

Media as Definers and Keepers of Values (and Biases)
PRIME VALUE: ENTERTAINMENT

The values that determined the content on radio were—and still are for most media—entertainment values. Jim Bormann, who was a news director for WCCO in Minneapolis and former president of the Radio-Television News Directors Association, made this point as he quoted the philosophy of "one of the leading exponents of the disk jockey operation" in 1955: "We do not believe that our mission in this world is to educate people, because radio is a purely voluntary listening habit—that is, the listener is free to turn the dial or to turn the set off. . . . Programming cannot be based on compulsory listening."[69]

Music was such a mainstay of early radio that, as we have seen, the first commercial radios were referred to as "radio music boxes." When Judith Cary Waller, who had been in advertising work, was called in to launch station WGU for the *Chicago Daily News* in 1922, she turned to music for the first program. She latched onto opera diva Sophie Braslau, who was in town for performances. Braslau had never heard of radio, but agreed to take part in a program. Waller lined up a pianist and violinist to appear with the opera star. A competing Chicago station, Westinghouse's KYW, presented popular music and jazz.[70]

Waller sought to promote "family values." "The *Daily News* took pride in its image as a family newspaper," says Mary E. Williamson. "Waller used newspaper personnel extensively to create radio programs consistent with that image."[71] The women editors at the paper created reports for women; the book review editor of the paper produced broadcast book reviews.

Waller also pioneered in radio sports. In 1925 when a letter from the mother of a handicapped boy asked if her station, now called WMAQ, could broadcast more baseball—no home games had yet been covered play-by-play—she went to "bat" and convinced Chicago Cubs owner William Wrigley, Jr., to allow the station to broadcast Cubs games. The baseball broadcast was the first baseball play-by-play from a home ball field. That same year she also began broadcasting home football games of the University of Chicago and Northwestern University.

Waller is also credited with fostering the careers of Charles Correll and Freeman Gosden, the *Amos 'n' Andy* of radio programming fame. Correll and Gosden, two white men who played two black men who had moved from the South to the North, first appeared as *Sam 'n' Henry* in January 1926 on Chicago's WGN. When Correll and Gosden became involved with a dispute with WGN, they contacted Waller. She succeeded in lining up the comedy duo for WMAQ, but with a name change to *Amos 'n' Andy*.[72]

Racial and Ethnic Stereotyping

Amos 'n' Andy was not the only ethnic stereotyping radio show of those early days of the 1920s. "In the 1920's," says Richard Severo, of the *New York Times*, "the people who wrote scripts for the new medium of radio began to exploit the ethnic and racial diversity that was and is America. They praised it, patronized it, celebrated it and gleefully stereotyped it." He cites as one example *The Goldbergs*, created in 1929 by Gertrude Berg, "whose feelings about Jewish matrons were at least derived from her own background."[73] In 1948, *Life With Luigi*, written and acted by non-Italians, proceeded to stereotype Italians with its "Mamma mia" language. In 1942, *Abie's Irish Rose* debuted, stereotyping Irish Catholics and Jews.

Good humor existed in comedy hours and family shows, underscoring celebrative and family values. On Sunday night young and old could enjoy the Jell-O–sponsored Jack Benny comedy program with sidekicks Don Wilson, Dennis Day, Mary Livingston, and Rochester. Also on that night was the family favorite, Edgar Bergen and his wisecracking wooden dummy, Charlie McCarthy, on the *Chase and*

Some sound devices of radio drama. (Smithsonian Institution)

Sanborn (coffee) *Hour.* On Tuesday was the Bob Hope show, sponsored by Pepsodent toothpaste, with the comedian making memorable a theme song, "Thanks for the Memories."

When "Closet" Meant "Closet"

Another Tuesday family favorite, *Fibber McGee and Molly,* featured a wacky couple played by Jim and Marion Jordan, with running gags such as a closet full of junk that spilled out when it was opened, plus a motley crew of neighbors who visited 79 Wistful Vista, among them the boisterous Gildersleeve and the meek Mr. Wimple.

"*Fibber McGee and Molly* presented a generally positive and nostalgic picture of small-town America," says Arthur Wertheim. He points out that the program's tone was in step with the favorable attitude toward small-town life in American culture during the 1930s. The Great Depression led many persons to take a hard look at the impersonality of urban life. Writers in the 1930s began to focus again on the value of community living. Thornton Wilder's *Our Town* (1938) "stressed the importance of neighborliness and a shared sense of community. *Fibber McGee and Molly* seemed to satisfy a yearning for 'the good old days' at the very time American society was becoming heavily urbanized."[74]

Yet there was concern about the radio programs for children. Parent organizations were worried about the content—violence, frightening scenes—that plagued children's programming back in the 1930s and 1940s, just as parents and special groups today oppose excessive violence and fluff in the Saturday morning television lineup of cartoons. Particularly targeted were the "serials" that ran daily in "the children's hour," 5 to 6 P.M., or just before or after that time. They were distinguished by "cliffhanger" endings, leaving children to stay awake at night worrying about the outcome or envisioning the worst in nightmares.

Little Violent Annie

The first radio serial suspense thriller for children was *Little Orphan Annie*, airing in 1931. The program, aimed at the younger set, followed Annie and other characters from Harold Gray's comic strip—"Daddy" Warbucks, the gigantic Punjab, the sinister Asp, Annie's dog Sandy, and her friend Joe Contasel (played for a while by Mel Torme).[75]

Sponsored by Ovaltine, *Little Orphan Annie* was pretty macabre stuff, as attested to in an article in a 1933 issue of *Scribner's Magazine*:

> Annie, the leading character, is an orphan, and the escapades which comprise the child's day-by-day life approximate a high degree of sadism. She has been kidnapped, chloroformed, rendered unconscious by a deliberate blow on the head, held prisoner several times, pursued over the countryside by the law, imprisoned in barns and hovels and freight cars. She has trailed and captured bank thieves. She has been forced to spend several nights in a deserted shack in the woods to avoid being taken back to a sadistic orphan asylum.[76]

There were many thrillers for the youngster to choose from. Grandparents and great-grandparents who were kids in the 1930s and 1940s likely remember the escapades of *The Adventures of Superman, Buck Rogers in the 25th Century, Captain Midnight, Chandu—the Magician, Don Winslow of the Navy, Flash Gordon, Gene Autry's Melody Ranch, The Green Hornet, Hopalong Cassidy, Jack Armstrong—the All-American Boy, Jungle Jim, The Lone Ranger*, and many more.

Cleansing the "Children's Hour"

While children loved the thriller serials, criticism from parents and educators was unabated. The pressure against the networks over the content of the "children's hour" programming mounted to such an extent that CBS, NBC, and the National Association of Broadcasters in their codes of ethics promised to work toward assuring uplifting content in children's programming.

CBS and NBC got rid of their serials by 1947, while ABC and Mutual still featured nine serials between them, "all with a blood and terror theme, trying to outdo each other."[77]

Some studies and reports showed that the children's hour serials were not really harmful to the child. Some teachers said the programs stirred curiosity and made the children good listeners. The premiums or gifts offered to listeners for sending in boxtops or other endeavors encouraged a wholesome activity for children, according to a report of the Child Study Association. At least the programs and related activities were not neutral. They were contributing something to the formation of the child's value system.

Media as Vehicles of Sensationalism/Entertainment

RADIO'S "BREATHLESS" NEWS

Sensationalism does not always need bizarre headlines, graphic pictures, an overblown layout, or a television screen. Sound can be sensational. In 1994 at the arraignment of football great O. J. Simpson on a double murder charge, a microphone that was placed at the accused's table without permission picked up some sensational dialogue—actually everything in this Hollywood-like murder mystery was sensational. Also in the trial a tape of a 911 call from one of the murder victims, Nicole Brown Simpson, was played. Again, sound was sensational news.

In 1927 radio kept the world informed on the daring flight of Charles Lindbergh across the Atlantic. When he returned, not only did the networks cover a welcoming ceremony at the base of the Washington Monument, but NBC produced a six-and-a-half-hour special on the pilot and the flight.

For six weeks in 1935 radio kept the nation breathless over the sensational trial of Bruno Richard Hauptmann for the kidnapping and murder of the infant son of Charles and Anne Morrow Lindbergh. At the trial in Flemington, New Jersey, a circus atmosphere prevailed. On one Sunday during the trial some 100,000 persons crowded into the little town. Radio reporters were present, but no microphones were allowed in the courtroom, except for the verdict. Hauptmann was sentenced to die in the electric chair.

On the night of the execution, April 3, 1936, thirty reporters were in the death chamber. But the most memorable account was by a reporter who declined to be in the chamber and instead holed up in a nearby hotel waiting for a signal that the execution was complete. Gabriel Heatter had gone on the air expecting to broadcast for only five minutes. But the execution was delayed for fifty-five minutes, with the result that Heatter had to ad-lib the whole time. His commentary expressed his sensitivity:

> I am in a hotel room looking at a certain window . . . as close as I wish to get to a room in which a man is about to die . . . merely waiting for a signal. . . . There will be no reprieve, of that I am certain. . . . [I] wonder what's going on in that room. It wouldn't be a confession . . . no, that silent fellow, lips pressed together, would not confess.[78]

With all that ad-libbing Heatter knew when to stop. In his autobiography he wrote:

> By 50 minutes after eight [the governor] evidently decided Hauptmann would never talk. The signal was given. The most sensational murder trial in history was over. There was nothing else to say after 55 minutes of talk and waiting except: "Ladies and gentlemen, Bruno Hauptmann is dead. Good night."[79]

"Oh, My! It's Terrible!"

Radio was introduced to sensational disasters with the explosion and midair burning of the German dirigible *Hindenburg* on May 6, 1937. A radio announcer from WLS in Chicago was on hand to describe the arrival of the sleek, mammoth aircraft at Lakehurst, New Jersey. Herbert Morrison started out with carefully chosen words telling of the sighting of the great airship. Then, as the world's largest airship burst into flames, Morrison became incoherent as he called to his engineer, Charles Nehlsen: "Get this, Charley! Get this, Charley! It's on fire!"

Morrison's voice became high-pitched:

> It's crashing! Oh, my! Get out of the way, please. And the folks—Oh, it's terrible! This is one of the worst catastrophes in the world. . . . Oh, the humanity! All the passengers! All the people screaming around here. . . . I'm going to step inside

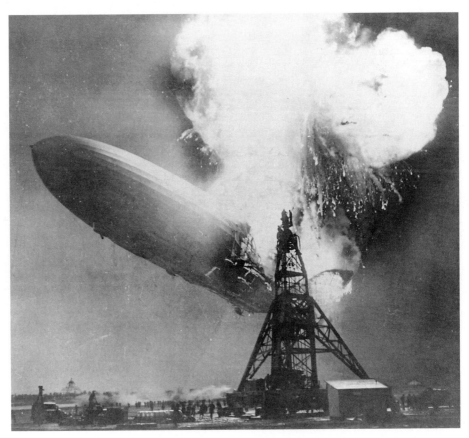

Radio was on hand as the dirigible Hindenburg *plunged in flames to the ground in Lakehurst, New Jersey, in 1937.* (International News Photo)

where I can't see it. I tell you it's terrible. Folks, I must stop for a minute. I've lost my voice. It's the worst thing I've ever witnessed.[80]

After a few seconds, Morrison recovered his composure and continued in a more normal tone.

When Martians Came Visiting

But perhaps the most sensational broadcast of the era was a science fiction hoax that was not merely narrative—a key component in most sensational reports—but was pure fiction. On Halloween eve, 1938, a young Orson Welles and the *Mercury Theatre on the Air* aired a radio drama based on H. G. Wells' novel *The War of the Worlds*. After some minutes of reporting strange happenings and sightings, one of two announcers, with attention to graphic details, solemnly declared:

Ladies and gentlemen, I have a grave announcement to make. Incredible as it may seem, both the observations of science and the evidence of our eyes lead to the

Orson Welles faces press after "invasion" from Mars. (Globe; Temple University Libraries Photojournalism Collection)

inescapable assumption that those strange beings who landed in the Jersey farmlands tonight are the vanguard of an invading army from the planet Mars. The battle which took place tonight at Grovers Mill has ended in one of the most startling defeats ever suffered by an army in modern times.[81]

"Invasion from Mars" carried three disclaimers that it was fiction, but many who heard it over CBS radio in New York and ninety-one of its affiliated stations thought otherwise. As people armed themselves and packed their bags to flee, a mass hysteria gripped the nation. In Newark, New Jersey, ambulances rushed to one neighborhood to protect residents against a gas attack. In one southern community, groups knelt in the streets praying for salvation from the aliens. Stations were flooded with calls. On the night of the broadcast, WCAU in Philadelphia reported 4,000 calls, for instance.

Fiction on Documentaries

The *March of Time* news program, launched by Time, Inc., in 1932, from the outset, used actors rather than real people involved in real events. "Speaking their pieces from scripts one further remove from reality were actors who mimicked persons in the news," says W. A. Swanberg of *March of Time*. Actors usually had at least two roles. William Adams was both President Roosevelt and President von Hindenburg (with a heavy German accent). Ted De Corsia was Herbert Hoover and Mussolini; Westbrook Van Voorhis, Hitler; and Marion Hopkinson, Mrs. Roosevelt, Frances Perkins, and Princess Marina. Each episode was introduced by renditions from a twenty-one-piece orchestra. Sound effects were creative; for instance, a beheading was achieved "by the quick slicing of cantaloupe which then fell into a box of sawdust."[82]

Documentary scholar William Bluem explains if not defends the fiction and drama of *March of Time*. Stations were short of funds, wire and tape recording were not yet developed, he says, and "radio did not have to deal with the visual presence of a person living his own experience as opposed to an actor playing a role. It was not bound by the ultimate authority of the photographic record." Thus actors were used "so long as the recreation of an event could be based upon reality and accepted as real by an audience."[83] However, because of the power of radio demonstrated in the "Invasion from Mars" broadcast, CBS banned the designation of news reporting being applied to any future broadcast using fiction.

With the power of imagination created through the passions and inflections of the voice, radio nurtured the careers of commentators with excitable, emotion-stirring styles. Foremost among the radio broadcasters with the heart-tugging sensational style were Walter Winchell and Paul Harvey.

"Rat-a-Tat" Winchell

Machine-gun-voice Winchell could deliver nearly 250 words a minute in his Sunday night NBC *Walter Winchell's Journal*. Perhaps the most listened-to radio commentator over several decades on radio, Winchell was also a star columnist for

Hearst's King Features Syndicate. A former vaudeville variety showman, he felt he had to hold the audience's attention every second, and he seemed never to pause for breath. Some called him the "thirteenth juror" because of his power in swaying public opinion in the Hauptmann trial. He frequented the Stork Club, a New York nightspot. Here movie actress Grace Kelly gave him the exclusive that she had decided to marry Prince Rainier of Monaco.[84] Winchell opened his broadcasts with, "Good evening, Mr. and Mrs. North America and all the ships at sea. Let's go to press." He would follow with his "predictions of things to come."

Paul Harvey was another fast talker, with a kind of nasal twang, espousing conservative positions with a storytelling technique. When ABC split its radio network into four specialized networks—Contemporary (for young people), Entertainment, FM, and Information networks—in 1968, Paul Harvey was heard on all four networks, making him, according to Bliss, the most-heard newscaster in the United States.[85]

Harvey could usually be found on the "right-wing" side of issues. Considered anti–New York, Harvey drew most of his following from "grassroots" areas. As he whined through his programs, Harvey nearly always gave the impression that he was revealing something unknown and momentous, all a part of a narrative yarn. *Orlando* (Florida) *Sentinel* writer Howard Means said, "Paul Harvey News is a promotion for old values vs. new ones. It is a kind of theater of scantily clad ideas where those values do battle."[86]

"Shock Jock" Stern

Shock jock is the modern term for the sensationalist monologist or small-studio talk-show host or disc jockey. In the 1990s the term was applied to Howard Stern, who broadcast weekdays for Infinity Broadcasting Corporation in New York and over other stations across the country. Shock is what the long-haired Stern in his sunglasses does best. Apparently without a script, with some long pauses sometimes mixed in with his ramblings on people and events, Stern insults far and near. "Over the years, Mr. Stern has enthusiastically pushed the boundaries of permissible conduct on the air waves," reported the *New York Times*. "His routines are spiced with talk about masturbation, the size of sexual organs, and an array of other sexual topics. Mr. Stern has also disparaged virtually every ethnic group in the country."[87] Needless to say, Stern, now a best-selling author and a multimillionaire, has been the object of attention by the watchful FCC. Not only has the content been a problem for the FCC, which has fined Infinity, but the time of airing, after 6 o'clock in the morning when some children might hear the program, has also been an issue.

Two Who Were Murdered

Radio commentators themselves have become the object of sensationalism. Several have been murdered, among them the abrasive Alan Berg of KOA in Denver in 1984 and earlier the popular Gerald E. "Jerry" Buckley of WMBC in Detroit.

Berg had a combative style that some dubbed insult radio. He would insult the intelligence of callers and studio guests, and sometimes the guests would walk out.[88]

Gerald Buckley, murdered Detroit broadcaster.
(AP/Wide World Photos)

Buckley had been campaigning for the recall of the allegedly corrupt Detroit mayor, Charles Bowles. While Buckley was waiting in a hotel lobby to join some friends late on election night (Bowles was recalled), in the early hours of July 23, 1930, three strangers appeared and pumped eleven bullets into him. According to the *New York Times*, the funeral that followed for Buckley (whom some tried to link to illegal bootlegging) saw "the greatest throng that ever gathered in Detroit to attend the funeral of a private citizen. . . . It was estimated that 100,000 persons looked upon the face of Buckley as his body lay in state at the home until after dawn."[89]

Media as Voices of Reform
IN-DEPTH RADIO DOCUMENTARIES

Although radio, as well as the eventual newcomer television, proved to be primarily a news and entertainment vehicle, there were efforts to create programs that supported reform and the betterment of society. Following in the tradition of early documentary filmmaker Robert Flaherty, radio, mixing real happenings with improvised drama using actors, told stories of events and cultures and served as a means of education. The radio documentaries could strongly promote a cause or agency, as they did during World War II, and yet radio documentaries, although limited to sound, could also report in depth and take an investigative approach, seeking change in some aspect of society.

After the war, broadcaster Edward R. Murrow became CBS vice president and director of public affairs, and his talents were put to use in developing in-depth programs. Murrow immediately decided to take a close look at the performance of the press. *CBS Views the News*, a journalism review program, "turned an uncompromising spotlight on the powerful New York City dailies," says Murrow biographer A. M. Sperber. Airing on a Saturday evening, it analyzed objectively the handling of stories by the press, from the tabloids to the *New York Times*. Making publishers bristle, the program, directed by veteran war reporter Don Hollenbeck, "was denounced, red-baited [charged with being leftist or communist], applauded, developing a devoted listenership that included much of New York's working press."[90]

The Lighter Side

A Humorist's Report on Life in the Windy City

Will Rogers—many-faceted humorist in the early days of radio and films and a columnist for 350 newspapers—made a nation laugh. Already a stage personality, he made his first radio appearance in 1922 over two-year-old station KDKA, Pittsburgh, the nation's first commercial station. He made fun of ordinary cowpokes, presidents, especially the bland Calvin Coolidge and Herbert Hoover, and the nation's large cities. He died in an airplane accident with noted aviator Wiley Post in Alaska in 1935. Here are a few glimpses of Will Rogers in Chicago on the *E. R. Squibb & Sons Broadcast*, June 22, 1930:

Will Rogers: Humorist in all media. (Will Rogers Memorial Archives, Claremore, Oklahoma)

Chicago

Well, here we are folks, out in the old city of Chicago. Yes, sir—the great old city of Chicago—broadcasting from a sound-proof studio here. They got this town all wrong. There is no crime or shooting here.

We have got an audience here tonight. We only invited the town's best citizens, just invited the best citizens of the town. We haven't got as big an audience as we thought we would have. We very foolishly barred out the gang leaders and the racketeers, so we are not

(Continued)

full-handed here by any means. We are barricaded here in the Wrigley Building, trying our best to keep from mentioning Beechnut.

Now I will try and describe to you what is going on down on the street here. I am standing right by the window. The Bugs Moran gang are holding down the east side of Michigan Boulevard and the Capones are entrenched on the other side.* It is lucky for us they can't get in here. Yes, they can. Here they come.

That's too bad, too bad. Just drag him right over there, will you? Just get him out of the way here.

This is Graham McNamee,† pinch-hitting for Mr. Rogers. This is McNamee speaking from Station WBBM, describing to you this quiet evening in Chicago. . . . I will give you a little resume of what is going on. A great night. There must be a thousand racketeers. There is not an empty seat—I mean, there is not an empty gun in the place. Boy, what a night this is! This is for the finals. The gang that wins this goes to New York and fights there for the racketeer privilege. Why the coffin rights alone ought to run into a half million dollars here tonight. . . .

Wait a minute—they are shooting up this way. They are shooting here. Here they come—I am hit—tell them—tell them I died—I died announcing.

*George "Bugs" Moran, Chicago mobster, rival of Al Capone.
†Leading master of ceremonies on NBC radio shows of the 1930s.

This is Floyd Gibbons,* pinch-hitting for the late Graham McNamee. When I say Floyd Gibbons talking I mean talking, I don't mean stuttering. It seems great to be back in Chicago and reporting the war here. I have reported wars all over the world, but when I get short of a war to report, I always drop back to Chicago. . . .

I will open the window and let you hear a few of the concluding shots of the battle. This is Floyd Gibbons speaking. Meanwhile, I will turn the microphone back to Mr. Will Rogers who has revived as it is impossible to kill a radio entertainer by shooting him in the head.

Hello, folks. Now, that is just about the idea that most people have of this city of Chicago that we are here in. They really do, you know. And here we are, a nice, little, respectable bunch gathered up here in this Wrigley Building, and the city is as peaceful and quiet. It is so still, it is almost disgusting. I couldn't hardly get anybody to come up here tonight and listen to me talk. Everybody in the city has gone to church, you know. Why, this is just a great, big, overgrown home-loving town, that is all.

*Noted war correspondent and radio commentator.

Source: "Chicago," in Radio Broadcasts of Will Rogers, edited by the Will Rogers Memorial Commission and Oklahoma State University, n.d., pp. 59–61.

Murrow developed a special documentary unit to produce one-hour programs. The first, with Robert Lewis Shayon as writer and producer, was "The Eagle's Brood," which exposed the roots and causes of juvenile delinquency and offered solutions on how to deal with the national problem. Taking six months to produce at the cost of $100,000, the program marked a departure from the largely staged news drama of earlier years.[91] Reviewers called the program "brutally frank," "hard-hitting," and "a piece of tough, clear journalism," and one writer from Newsweek ventured to suggest that CBS had entered the "role of public benefactor."[92]

Other hard-hitting programs followed, among them "A Long Life and a Merry One," dealing with health; "Fear Begins at Forty," problems of aging; and "Among Ourselves," problems of race relations.[93] NBC followed suit and produced in its Living series "Schoolteacher 1947," on public schools; "VD—A Conspiracy of Silence"; and "From Where We Came," the positive side of unions.

The season of in-depth, investigative stories on radio was decidedly chilled by 1950 as a result of the Cold War and the role of the terrorizing House Committee on Un-American Activities. Fearful of writers having become communists or communist sympathizers, the HUAC "commandeered whole batches of radio news scripts," according to Sperber.[94] Bluem found cost a factor in the decline of the radio documentary, which "requires budget, talent, and creative effort, and too few American radio stations have found that they can support this activity."[95] With the arrival of miniaturization and the transistor, radio was seen as a portable entertainment medium, listened to in cars, on the beach, and as background in various rooms in a home or office. Bluem saw television, particularly in its documentary role, as absorbing radio and leaving it a shell or a corpse hardly twitching.[96]

Despite the last rites from Bluem, there has remained an investigative, in-depth documentary side to radio, although the efforts have been largely local and regional. The Investigative Reporters and Editors organization publishes annually or biennially a book of case histories of investigative stories and series, including a section on radio investigative efforts. For instance, Bob Scott and Wendy Black produced a series in 1983 on KOY Radio, Phoenix, that studied and identified the source of trichloroethylene, a volatile solvent and suspected carcinogen that was contaminating several municipal and irrigation water wells east of Phoenix.[97] Harry Beadle in 1984 produced a series for WGST-Radio 92 in Atlanta on a conflict-of-interest situation involving the Atlanta city council president.[98] Jeff Rainford in 1986 did a series for KMOX, St. Louis, identifying twelve "incompetent, unethical or impaired physicians" who had escaped having their licenses revoked by the state Board of Registration for the Healing Arts.[99] These investigations were among those selected for top citations by IRE.

The spirit of investigative reporting and reform, treated in extended documentary fashion, survives on radio—even if its extent is minuscule. Radio, with its music programs, talk shows, and occasional investigative reports, has retreated to being largely a local phenomenon as in an earlier day. It was up to the next newcomer, television, to capture national imaginations and coalesce and mold mass audiences, for better or for worse.

QUESTIONS FOR DISCUSSION AND RESEARCH

1. There are dozens, even hundreds, who contributed to the technology of radio. Report on one little-known radio pioneer. (One hundred of them, for instance, are chronicled in the book *Radio's 100 Men of Science* by Orrin E. Dunlap, Jr.)
2. What are some of the sociological factors that encouraged the development of radio?
3. How did young people help develop radio?
4. Summarize the concerns that publishers and others had about the new technology of radio.
5. What factors worked to keep radio from embracing advertising as a principal mode of support in its early days?

6. Joe Carter, director of the Will Rogers Memorial Museum in Claremore, Oklahoma, says that the tremendously popular performer, radio and film star, and widely syndicated columnist Will Rogers has no match today, that he would be all the comics, commentators, and talk show hosts rolled into one. Do you agree? Who do you think today could aspire to being the number one folk hero, entertainer, and commentator rolled into one?

7. In what ways has the "freedom" of radio been curtailed?

8. What is the "fairness doctrine"? Should it, or should it not, be restored?

9. How effective is the radio as a political instrument today in the age of television? Explain.

10. Should a president who feels maligned by others on radio (and television), as Bill Clinton felt, fight back on radio? Why or why not?

11. What regional or specialized networks serve your town or area? Using the network's resources and interviewing several of its officials, write a short history of that area network.

12. Is sensationalism on the radio different from sensationalism in the print media or television?

13. Among sensational radio broadcasts—the Lindbergh baby kidnapping/murder trial, the Hindenburg disaster, the Orson Welles dramatization of *The War of the Worlds*—which do you regard as the most sensational and why?

14. If your local or university library has a radio section in its archives, listen to one of the once-popular children's radio programs and compare it with current children's educational fare on television. (You could also listen to other famous programs of your choosing and report on them.)

15. Which is the best medium for investigative, documentary, reform-oriented reporting?

ENDNOTES

1. Robert L. Hilliard and Michael C. Keith, *The Broadcast Century: A Biography of American Broadcasting* (Boston: Focal Press, 1992), p. 4.

2. Thomas Appleby, *Mahlon Loomis: Inventor of Radio* (Washington, 1967).

3. Madeleine Jacobs, "Sequel to Marconi's Ship Lab to Sail in '92," *Media History Digest*, vol. 10, no. 1, Spring–Summer 1990, p. 58.

4. Michael Emery and Edwin Emery, *The Press and America: An Interpretive History of the Mass Media*, 7th ed. (Englewood Cliffs, N.J.: Prentice Hall, 1992), p. 269.

5. Susan Smulyan, *Selling Radio: The Commercialization of American Broadcasting, 1920–1934* (Washington D.C.: Smithsonian Institution Press, 1994), p. 13.

6. Susan Douglas, "Amateur Operators and American Broadcasting: Shaping the Future of Radio," in Joseph Corn, ed., *Imagining Tomorrow: History, Technology and the American Future* (Cambridge, Mass.: MIT Press, 1986), p. 53, quoted in Smulyan, *Selling Radio*.

7. Smuylan, *Selling Radio*, p. 14.

8. Hilliard and Keith, *The Broadcast Century*, p. 21.

9. Frank William Johnson, Jr., "African-American Pioneers in Amateur and Commercial Radio," a paper presented to the American Journalism Historians Association, Oct. 3, 1992, at the University of Kansas, Lawrence.

10. Kenneth Bilby, *The General: David Sarnoff and the Rise of the Communications Industry* (New York: Harper & Row, 1986), p. 39.
11. Edward Bliss, Jr., *Now the News: The Story of Broadcast Journalism* (New York: Columbia University Press, 1991), p. 8.
12. Rudolph D. Michael, "History and Criticism of Press-Radio Relationships," *Journalism Quarterly*, vol. 15, no. 2, June 1938, p. 178.
13. Ibid., p. 179.
14. "News on the Air," *Editor & Publisher*, Oct. 2, 1937, p. 28.
15. *National Editorial Association Proceedings*, 1933, p. 10.
16. Smulyan, *Selling Radio*, p. 65.
17. Erik Barnouw, *A Tower in Babel: A History of Broadcasting in the United States* (New York: Oxford University Press, 1966), p. 99.
18. Smulyan, *Selling Radio*, p. 66.
19. Alfred McClung Lee, *The Daily Newspaper in America* (New York: Macmillan, 1947), p. 367.
20. *NEA Proceedings*, 1932, p. 11.
21. Ibid., 1931, p. 29.
22. Edwin Emery, *History of the American Newspaper Publishers Association* (Minneapolis: University of Minnesota Press, 1950), p. 200.
23. *NEA Proceedings*, 1931, p. 87.
24. *N.E.A. Service Letter*, Bulletin No. 81, October 1935, p. 2.
25. Ibid., Bulletin No. 51, February 1933, p. 2.
26. William Haight, "The Competing Media: Weaknesses, Limitations," *Publishers' Auxiliary*, August 24, 1974, p. 12.
27. Eileen R. Meehan, "Heads of Household and Ladies of the House: Gender, Genre, and Broadcast Ratings, 1929–1990," in William S. Solomon and Robert W. McChesney, eds., *Ruthless Criticism* (Minneapolis: University of Minnesota Press, 1993), p. 205.
28. Herbert Moore, "The News War in the Air," *Journalism Quarterly*, vol. 12, no. 1, March 1935, p. 43.
29. Keith Sanders, "The Collapse of the Press-Radio News Bureau," *Journalism Quarterly*, Autumn 1967, p. 550.
30. Herbert Hoover, *Reminiscences* (Unpublished, 1950), p. 11, in Columbia University Oral History Collection, New York, quoted in Barnouw, *A Tower in Babel*, p. 180.
31. Gary Dean Best, *The Critical Press and the New Deal: The Press Versus Presidential Power, 1933–1938* (Westport, Conn.:, Praeger, 1993), pp. 25, 26.
32. Hiley H. Ward, "Coughlin, 30s' Radio Priest, Retains Charisma at 87," Religious News Service, in the *Washington Post*, Aug. 11, 1978.
33. Bliss, *Now the News*, p. 10.
34. Steven P. Phipps, "Unlicensed Broadcasting and the Federal Radio Commission: The 1930 George W. Fellowes Challenge," *Journalism Quarterly*, vol.68, no. 4, Winter 1991, pp. 824, 825.
35. Ibid., p. 826.
36. Edmund L. Andrews, "The Ground Rules for Wireless," *New York Times*, Sept. 29, 1993, p. D5.
37. Robert W. McChesney, "Crusade Against Mammon: Father Harney, WLWL and the Debate Over Radio in the 1930s," *Journalism History*, vol. 14, no. 4, Winter 1987, p. 118.
38. Ibid.
39. "*Red Lion Broadcasting Co.* v. *Federal Communications Commission*," in Donald M. Gillmor and Jerome A. Barron, *Mass Communication Law: Cases and Comment*, 2nd ed. (St. Paul, Minn.: West, 1974), pp. 813–815.
40. William B. Ray, *FCC: The Ups and Downs of Radio-TV Regulation* (Ames: Iowa State University Press, 1990), p. 145.

41. Ibid., p. 107.
42. Michael X. Delli Carpini, "Radio's Political Past," *Media Studies Journal*, special issue on "Radio the Forgotten Medium," Freedom Forum Media Studies Center, New York, vol. 7, no. 3, Summer 1993, p. 23.
43. Ibid., p. 25.
44. Ibid., p. 27.
45. Donald C. Godfrey, "The 1927 Radio Act: People and Poitics," *Journalism History*, vol. 4, no. 3, Autumn 1977.
46. Henry F. Graf, "Election of 1928," in Arthur M. Schlesinger, Jr., ed., *Running for President: The Candidates and Their Images*, vol. 2 (New York: Simon & Schuster, 1994), p. 150.
47. Carpini, "Radio's Political Past," p. 28.
48. Ibid.
49. Richard Lee Strout, "The President and the Press," in Katie Louchheim, ed., *The Making of the New Deal: The Insiders Speak* (Cambridge, Mass.: Harvard University Press, 1983), p. 13, quoted in Betty Houchin Winfield, *FDR and the News Media* (Urbana: University of Illinois Press, 1990), p. 104.
50. Winfield, *FDR and the News Media*, p. 104.
51. Ibid., p. 107.
52. Alan Brinkley, "Election of 1936," in Schlesinger, *Running for President*, vol. 2, p. 184.
53. James C. Foust, "The Farmer and the Radio Man Should Be Friends: Clear Channel Radio Stations and the Farm Lobby, 1941–1968," paper presented to the American Journalism Historians Association, meeting in Tulsa, Oklahoma, September 1995.
54. Maurine Beasley and Paul Belgrade, "Eleanor Roosevelt: First Lady as Radio Pioneer," *Journalism History*, vol. 11, nos. 3–4, Autumn–Winter 1984, p. 42.
55. Douglas Jehl, "Clinton Calls Show to Assail Press, Falwell and Limbaugh," *New York Times*, June 25, 1994, p. 1.
56. Peter Laufer, *Inside Talk Radio: America's Voice or Just Hot Air?* (New York: Birch Lane Press, 1995), p. 11.
57. Ibid., quoting terminology of Washington, D.C., talk show host Ron Aaron, p. 14.
58. Ibid., p. 9.
59. Ibid., p. 154.
60. Kenneth Bilby, *The General: David Sarnoff and the Rise of the Communications Industry* (New York: Harper & Row, 1986), p. 47.
61. Ibid., pp. 49, 50.
62. Ibid., p. 51.
63. James Roman, "Arthur Judson: Shadow Behind CBS," *Media History Digest*, vol. 4, no. 1, Spring 1984, pp. 56–62.
64. William S. Paley, *As It Happened: A Memoir* (Garden City, N.Y.: Doubleday, 1979), p. 37.
65. Christopher H. Sterling and John M. Kittross, *Stay Tuned: A Concise History of American Broadcasting* (Belmont, Calif.: Wadsworth, 1978), p. 157.
66. Ibid., p. 328.
67. Hilliard and Keith, *The Broadcast Century*, p. 255.
68. Bliss, *Now the News*, pp. 468, 469.
69. Jim Bormann, "How Durable Is Radio?" *Journalism Quarterly*, Summer 1957, p. 315.
70. Mary E. Williamson, "Judith Cary Waller: Chicago Broadcasting Pioneer," *Journalism History*, vol. 3, no. 4, Winter 1976–1977, p. 111.
71. Ibid.
72. Ibid., p. 112.
73. Richard Severo, "They Sounded Black on the Radio," in "Books of The Times" column, *New York Times*, Aug. 9, 1991, p. C25.

74. Arthur Frank Wertheim, *Radio Comedy* (New York: Oxford University Press, 1979), p. 230.

75. Marilyn Lawrence Boemer, *The Children's Hour: Radio Programs for Children, 1929–1956* (Metuchen, N.J.: Scarecrow Press, 1989), p. 128.

76. Ibid., pp. 128, 129.

77. Ibid.

78. Irving E. Fang, *Those Radio Commentators!* (Ames: Iowa State University Press, 1977), p. 289, quoted in Bliss, *Now the News*, p. 36.

79. Gabriel Heatter, *There's Good News Tonight* (Garden City, N.Y.: Doubleday, 1960), p. 80, quoted in Bliss, *Now the News*.

80. Bliss, *Now the News*, p. 37.

81. Howard Koch, *The Panic Broadcast* (Boston: Little, Brown, 1970), pp. 57, 58.

82. W. A. Swanberg, *Luce and His Empire* (New York: Charles Scribner's Sons, 1972), p. 86.

83. William Bluem, *Documentary in American Television* (New York: Hastings House, 1965), p. 61.

84. Bliss, *Now the News*, p. 58.

85. Ibid., p. 194.

86. William H. Taft, *Encyclopedia of Twentieth-Century Journalists* (New York: Garland, 1986), "Paul Harvey," pp. 148, 149.

87. Edmund L. Andrews, "F.C.C. Delays Radio Deal by Howard Stern's Employer," *New York Times*, Dec. 31, 1993, p. D2.

88. Andrew H. Malcolm, "Blunt Radio Host in Denver Shot Dead at Curb of Home," *New York Times*, June 20, 1984, p. A14.

89. "Bootlegger Clears Slain Radio Orator . . . Throngs Block Detroit Streets at Funeral of Jerry Buckley, Killed by Gangsters," *New York Times*, July 27, 1930.

90. A. M. Sperber, *Murrow: His Life and Times* (New York: Freundlich Books, 1986), p. 273.

91. Bluem, *Documentary*, p. 68.

92. Sperber, *Murrow*, p. 274.

93. Bluem, *Documentary*, p. 68.

94. Sperber, *Murrow*, p. 275.

95. Bluem, *Documentary*, pp. 71, 72.

96. Ibid., p. 72.

97. Steve Weinberg, ed., *The IRE Book: Summaries of Many Top Investigations from 1983*, published by Investigative Reporters and Editors, Columbia, Mo., 1984, "Contamination Source Pinpointed," p. 14.

98. Jan Colbert and Steve Weinberg, eds., *The IRE Book 2: Summaries of Many Top Investigations from 1984*, IRE, Columbia, Mo., 1985, "City Council's Business Conflicts," p. 15.

99. Stan Abbott and Jan Colbert, eds., *The IRE Book 3: Summaries of Many Top Investigations from 1985 and 1986*, IRE, Columbia, Mo., 1987, "Disciplining Doctors," p. 13.

12

The Small Screen:
Seeing Is Believing

A reader of the science fiction comic *Buck Rogers* in the 1940s could accept the possibility of space travel in the future, but seeing somebody "alive" on a screen across great distances, as the space comic depicted back then, seemed unachievable. Yet had young readers of *Buck Rogers* been following the business and news pages of the daily paper, they would have had a hint that the wonder of television was on the horizon.

EXPERIMENTAL STAGES

Television, in fact, was already here in the 1930s and early 1940s, although it was still very much in an experimental stage. The "picturephone" and television had existed since the 1920s, when pictures—including that of Secretary of Commerce Herbert Hoover, along with the sound of his voice—were sent over the wires. By 1929 the technology seemed complete for the emergence of this new supermedium in homes, ready to replace radios. In that same year Bell Telephone Laboratories demonstrated television transmission in color for the first time.

The First Television Programming

Although the year 1929 was the beginning of the Great Depression and investors became cautious, it was also a time when movies were popular and cheap. Expectations were that television would be even more popular some day than movies. The experimentation went on. In 1930 NBC launched an experimental station at RCA's new Radio City building in New York City. The few thousand viewers in the New York area received postcards announcing programs. The telecasts were

391

Scene from first television drama, "The Queen's Messenger," broadcast in Schenectady, New York, in 1928. (Smithsonian News Service Photo/General Electric Company)

usually very short, partly because of the intense studio lights that made the heat unbearable for performers.

In the Midwest in 1930 the *Chicago Daily News* television station W9XAP featured a music program, *Songs of the Hour*, 6:15 to 6:30 P.M. daily, with blues singer Marcella Lally as host. The paper gave her special attention with a one-column picture, along with an Uptown Cafe musician, on the entertainment and radio news page.[1]

Lally (later Marcella Lally Duke) had been only nineteen when she took advice from her sister, a Golddigger performer on Broadway, to go to a singing audition at radio station WJJD. She had finished two years at a teachers college and was ready to get a job. "My mother didn't mind show business, but she thought it was shaky," she recalled in a 1981 *Chicago Tribune* interview at age 73.[2] "She wanted to make sure I had my teaching degree to fall back on." At the audition, Lally started off on the right note, but soon forgot the words, and ended up singing, "dah, dah, dah, dah." She was asked to come back when she learned the words. She returned and soon was singing on *Musical Matinee*. She worked at several stations before going to work for WIBO, the home of a fledgling enterprise, the Western Television Company.

Thomas Sills, who has specialized in researching Marcella Lally Duke and her pioneer role in the beginning of television broadcasts, says, after "trying to carefully see Marcella's story in the proper perspective, the more I look the more I appreciate her claim as television's first star."[3] And her fame was not just local. Sills provides a clipping from the *New York Sun's* radio section of April 12, 1930, in which a two-column picture of Lally appears under the heading "A Leading Lady of Television" with the cutline "Miss Marcella Lally, who appears nightly over the Western Television." She became a schoolteacher, and after she had retired some still remembered her role in television. The coordinators of the 1982 dedication of the $12 million Dallas Communications Complex invited her as a special guest.[4]

At first television listings appeared with radio listings; the programs were in effect radio programs. A listing might indicate whether a newscaster could also be seen by "audiovision." For example, the typical daily listings for WMAQ explained when the program was synchronized with the visual W9XAP broadcasting. At 12:35 P.M., "there are news flashes. This is a sight and sound of 'audiovision' program which shows an announcer reading the news flashes. This is again followed by a staff cartoonist drawing silent pictures for fifteen minutes."[5]

When CBS launched its experimental television station, W2XAB, in New York in 1931, it was "a gala occasion, the earliest hint of a TV 'spectacular,'" say Irving Settel and William Laas.[6] Kate Smith sang, George Gershwin played the piano, and others well-known on radio performed.

Television was beginning to have something for everybody. The first live coverage of a news event on television was of a fire on Ward's Island, New York City, in 1938, when an NBC crew was filming at a swimming pool across the street and turned to catch the fire. There were variety shows, cartoons, and a Thanksgiving parade for the children, fashion for women, boxing and other sports, feature-length films, and scenes from a Broadway play, Rachel Crothers' *Susan and God*.

The public's appetite for television was whetted at the futuristic World's Fair at Flushing Meadow, New York City, in the spring of 1939. The opening of the fair included a telecast of a speech by President Franklin Roosevelt. The king and queen of England also put in an appearance in a telecast.

Growth After World War II

Just as World War I had slowed the development of commercial radio, World War II—starting in 1939, with U.S. involvement beginning in 1941—came along to slow the development of television. Industry was directing its efforts toward producing guns, tanks, bombers, and fighter planes, not the television industry. But experimentation continued, and four networks—NBC, CBS, ABC, and DuMont—were poised for the day when they would be free to compete in the great expansion of television that was certain to follow the war.

In 1944 Paul G. Hoffman, president of Studebaker Automobile, envisioned the population tapping into the $100 billion saved in war bonds to fuel purchases of television sets and to finance the development of the industry.[7] And as Erik Barnouw points out, not only did consumers have savings to spend, but also manufacturers, switching from weapon production back to consumer goods, were anxious to advertise.[8] There was also a belief that television would be a useful education tool and that it would put entertainment realistically in the living room. But even more important was its symbolic power. Television was a sign of status for middle America.

In the technical war, television won an ongoing battle with FM radio. Both had laid claim to the upper frequencies on the broadcasting bands. The shortage of television frequencies became so acute that the FCC was forced to decide between the development of television or FM radio, the high-quality radio broadcasting pioneered by Edwin H. Armstrong. Armstrong, who at first had the support of RCA, was later to fight RCA over the allocation of television frequencies.

With stations overlapping, with inadequate geographic separation created by earlier FCC rulings, and with a demand for sets that outpaced the supply, the FCC clamped a six-month freeze on new applications for television stations in September 1948. But the freeze lasted until 1952—three and a half years—and had the effect of slowing television growth and giving radio a respite. When at last the decision was handed down, in the form of the *Sixth Report and Order* document of the FCC, it squashed the ambition of FM supporters by relegating the best audio frequencies for television sound transmission, keeping the existing FM frequencies where they were. Devastated, Armstrong in January 1954 hurled himself to his death from a thirteenth-story window.[9]

HOW TELEVISION STARTED

The roots of television can be found in scientific work in European universities in the middle of the nineteenth century. An Italian-born priest working in France, Abbé Caselli, in 1862 introduced "photo-telegraphy," which allowed long-distance transmissions of images by electricity. It was a slow process, transmitting bits of a picture at a time. People could send messages in their own handwriting, but the result was sometimes a garbled mixture of dots and dashes.[10]

English telegraph operator Joseph May in 1873 found that the element selenium could give off small amounts of electricity corresponding to the amount of light reaching it. G. R. Carey in Boston in 1875 revealed that a bank of selenium cells and lamps could assist in breaking up a picture and transmitting its parts over a wire. Selenium is a chemical element in the sulfur group whose electrical conductivity varies with the intensity of light. The process involved an inordinate number of selenium cells.[11]

In 1884 a German engineer, Paul Nipkow, made possible the sending of a picture of a live moving object by means of a scanning disk. The disk was perforated with a a single spiral of holes, each one a little closer to the center. As the disk rotated before the object, light shone through the pinholes. The result was a series of lines projected on a single selenium cell. Nipkow, however, did not succeed in reconstructing the image as a synthesized whole on a screen at the other end.[12]

Mechanical Television

Because of the spinning disk, the approach became known as mechanical television. Three inventors who helped develop this process were Scotsman John L. Baird and Americans Herbert E. Ives and Charles Francis Jenkins. In 1923 Baird and Jenkins transmitted the first silhouette television pictures by wire about the same time. Two years later they transmitted moving silhouettes. Ives, working for the Bell Telephone Laboratories, achieved long-distance wirephoto transmission and helped develop coaxial cable for television.[13]

With the development of the wireless radio and the transmission of the human voice, scientists turned their interest to the prospect of sending visual images by radio waves, with the receiving set reassembling images from electrical impulses. Jenkins created mechanically produced wireless "radio vision" in 1925. He transmitted images of a spinning windmill across the Potomac River to federal officials assembled in Jenkins' downtown Washington laboratory. "For radio vision to work," says John Barrat of the Smithsonian Institution, "the image of a brightly lit object was focused with a camera lens upon a specific area of a rapidly spinning disc. Holes in the disc rotated past the image to be televised. Bursts of light passed through the disc to strike a photosensitive radio tube. The tube converted the light beam into a series of electrical impulses which were then broadcast over radio-wave frequencies."[14] Jenkins' receiver had an identical disk synchronized with the transmitter disk and recreated the lines "from a flickering signal plate in a glowing neon tube." Fifteen still-picture frames flashed out each second to achieve the illusion of motion.

"Mechanical television," however, died about 1934, "mainly because it could broadcast only shadows and silhouettes," explains Nat Pendleton, a historian at the Electricity and Modern Physics Division of the Smithsonian. "Despite expensive and extensive efforts to improve it, picture resolution was bad. In addition, mechanical sets were bulky [and] noisy." Also, "Difficulties arose in maintaining the synchronization of the picture."[15]

The Russian and the Idaho Farm Boy

Meanwhile a Russian immigrant, Vladimir Zworykin, and an Idaho farm boy, Philo T. Farnsworth, both independently experimenting with electron guns and vacuum tubes, paved the way for "electronic television." Earlier work on developing the cathode-ray tube, which contains an electron gun directing a controlled beam of electrons on a screen, was done by Ferdinand Braun of the University of Strasbourg and others. But there were many problems to solve. For instance, there would need to be a camera to break the picture down into its smallest elements and make a

Philo Farnsworth, in his lab with a new type of television cam-era tube in 1938. (AP/Wide World Photos)

sharp distinction between light and shade. Zworykin with his iconoscope and Farnsworth with his image dissector were able to achieve this result.[16]

Zworykin had started his research in Russia under Boris Rosing, who experimented with transmitting images by cathode ray. In 1918 Zworykin decided to pursue his research in the United States, where he eventually found himself up against a farm youth inventor who was accruing patents in related areas.

Few stories of great inventors have the power and inspiration as the story of the Idaho teenager who was to be honored on an American stamp in 1983 as a father of television and inducted into the Inventors' Hall of Fame in Washington, D.C., in 1984. There is almost a sense of hagiography, the story of a saint or anointed one, in the Farnsworth story. Farnsworth was born in 1906 into a devout Mormon family in Beaver, Utah, a town that Mormon leader Brigham Young had commissioned Farnsworth's grandfather to build. Throughout his life Farnsworth referred to his success and insight as an inventor as a result of a kind of "guided tour" from on high.[17] A kind of annunciation preceded his birth, according to his widow. Philo Farnsworth, named after his Mormon-leader grandfather, was the son of his father's second wife, the first wife, Amelia, having died. Before Philo's birth, Amelia came to the father in an apparition and declared that the baby to be born by the second wife, Serena, would be "one of God's special spirits; great care should be taken in his upbringing." The parents regarded the message and apparition as a "sacred experience."[18]

Stories abound of the boy genius, Philo, fixing electrical problems around the Rigby, Idaho, farm where the family moved when he was twelve. The new farm had electricity, and the young Farnsworth created motors from spare parts and installed the motors in farm equipment and his mother's washing machine. He repaired an electric generator when all the adults were at a loss how to fix it.

Elma G. "Pem" Farnsworth, widow of Farnsworth (who died in 1971), asks the following question in her 1990 book about her husband and his experiments: "How could a fourteen-year-old farm boy ever devise something so technically complex as television?" Was it the result of motivation and circumstance or "guidance from a higher intelligence, even God?"[19]

Farnsworth's vision of television came to him in 1920 as he was plowing at the Idaho farm. Studying the rows upon rows of the field, he imagined trapping light in an empty jar and transmitting it, one line at a time, on a magnetically deflected beam of electrons, Farnsworth's brother, Lincoln, recalls.[20] Philo prepared drawings and shared them with his high school science teacher, who was convinced that the teen was onto something.

"The Damned Thing Works!"

Farnsworth worked his way through Brigham Young University and landed private support for his experimentation, opening a lab in San Francisco. On September 7, 1927, he demonstrated the first all-electronic television transmission. It was only a single line, but Farnsworth and his aides knew that, by adding vertical scanning currents and magnetic deflecting coils, they could easily achieve a two-dimensional picture. The team sent a telegram with the news to one of their backers in Los Angeles. It said simply, "THE DAMNED THING WORKS!"[21]

Farnsworth received a moment of fame as movie stars, among them Douglas Fairbanks and Mary Pickford, stopped by to pose for pictures with the new contraption. Vladimir Zworykin showed up on the pretense of working for Westinghouse, where he was employed, but he had actually come on behalf of Sarnoff at RCA, which he later admitted. Hoping to win wider attention and support, Farnsworth showed Zworykin everything. On the way home, Mrs. Farnsworth reports, Zworykin stopped at Westinghouse "long enough to have his former helpers build a copy of the Farnsworth Image Dissector, exactly as Phil and Cliff [her brother] had shown him. Dr. Zworykin took the new tube and reported to RCA."[22]

Eventually Sarnoff showed up at Farnsworth's lab and offered to buy the whole enterprise for $100,000. Farnsworth rejected the offer, and RCA proceeded to develop its own electronic television system, using Zworykin's iconoscope, which was very similar to Farnsworth's image dissector. RCA claimed that Zworykin invented

Vladimir Zworykin, inventor (left), and network founder Allen Du Mont.
(Smithsonian Institution)

the electronic camera tube before Farnsworth and took Farnsworth to court, "possibly hoping to wrangle Phil's patents into their already bulky portfolio."[23]

"The litigation that followed was complex and sensational," says Thomas Ropp. "The turning point came when Farnsworth's attorney claimed Phil had the original idea for the system when he was a high school freshman." RCA's bevy of attorneys regarded this as ridiculous. "The laughter abated, however, when Phil's old science teacher, Justin Tolman, testified. Tolman then proceeded to draw from memory the exact electronic diagram that his young prodigy had left on the blackboard many years before."[24] Farnsworth won the case, but he was discouraged by court costs and the slow pace in the development of everyday television sets for the public. His brother Lincoln later explained, "Television was always right around the corner but that corner was 20 years away."[25] And then the Depression and World War II slowed the pace.

In 1931 Farnsworth went to work for Philco in Philadelphia, where he hired a number of Temple University students and "thought highly of their ability."[26] They worked in intense heat on the top floor of an old battery storage plant in utmost secrecy. However, friction developed with the Philco chain of command. When RCA complained to Philco that Farnsworth's transmissions were interfering with its sig-

Philo Farnsworth was honored in 1983 in a broadcasting inventor series of postage stamps, which also included Edwin Armstrong, developer of FM radio; Charles Steinmetz, who developed the theory of alternating currents; and Nikola Tesla, who patented 100 electronic devices.

nals, RCA told Philco to dump the Farnsworth Company, or else its license to use RCA's radio patents would not be renewed.[27]

Farnsworth's Regrets

Farnsworth experienced a number of personal setbacks: his farmhouse in Maine was destroyed by fire, he suffered a series of breakdowns brought on by exhaustion and substance abuse, a son died, and the majority owners in his company sold out to International Telephone and Telegraph Company (IT&T). Farnsworth went to work for IT&T as president of its television subsidiary. Although IT&T acquired control over Farnsworth's patent portfolio, it never manufactured television sets. "The Farnsworth family today believes Phil's old nemesis RCA made a deal with IT&T to stay out of telephonic communications if IT&T didn't manufacture television."[28] Farnsworth turned his efforts toward finding a way to produce energy by nuclear fusion. He retired to Salt Lake City, where he tried to organize his own company again but lost everything. He lived until 1971, long enough to see the direction of entertainment television. He disliked what he saw, and, says his widow, "As a matter of fact he said he was sorry he had anything to do with it."[29]

Over the Hills with Cable

By the end of the 1940s television was still limited to urban centers and communities within a 50-mile radius of the station. Limitations of distance or topography— hills and mountains could deflect signals—and the 1948 FCC freeze on licensing new television stations largely confined television to urban areas. Yet the demand for television existed in outlying areas. In particular, appliance dealers in the outposts clamored for television reception so they could sell sets.[30] Thus was born community antenna television (CATV), becoming known more popularly as cable television. This involved stringing cables from a central large antenna on a high building or mountain to various receiving sets in the lower environs.

Several persons in Pennsylvania and Oregon, identifying the problem and solving it the same way, created the first television cable systems. Edward Bliss cites the effort of Robert Tarlton, a television salesman in Lansford, Pennsylvania, in 1949. Complaining of poor reception, Tarlton put up a large antenna on a mountain and received telecasts transmitted from Philadelphia, some 60 miles away. He then trailed cable down to the valley community and sold subscriptions to his new cable service.[31]

Mary A. M. Phillips tells the story of John Walson, a power company mainte-nance worker who had an interest in an appliance store in the mountain town of Mahanoy City, Pennsylvania. He stocked television sets but couldn't sell them be-cause of poor reception in the mountainous region. Early in 1948—some dispute the year—he came up with the idea of building an antenna on top of a mountain and stringing surplus heavy-duty twin-lead cable from tree to tree down to his store in town. From there he led wires to homes of colleagues and friends. In a year he had a permanent coaxial cable system in place. He charged $100 for installation, $2 per month for service. A Penn State professor, Patrick Parsons, after interviewing a number of older people in Mahanoy City, decided that a local bar owner, Edward "Peanuts" Trusky, was the first to provide cable service. He installed a television set in his poolroom somewhere between 1947 and 1949 and hitched a line to the home of a friend.[32]

Media as Purveyors of Information/Education
EVOLUTION OF TELEVISION NEWS

Something happened along the way in the history of television news, especially local news. The trivial, the repeated emphasis on raw emotions at crime scenes and fu-nerals, the inconsequential, the subjective, and cuteness all somehow came to dom-inate local television news across the country. The new "you are there" medium with both sound and sight found nevertheless that it had to contend with limitations.

Even as radio news had limits, such as sightlessness, television news had a limi-tation of attention span: news had to be of interest. The listener/viewer could not skip items but was forced to hear them all in sequence. There is, of course, the limi-tation of time; fifteen minutes or a half hour is not much compared to the seemingly endless space offerings of a newspaper. Then, particularly in early years, there was the difficulty of getting reporters, camera operators, and equipment to a news event.

Visual Reality

The limitations encouraged "softness" and insignificance in news features and led to preplanned, predictable news. Barnouw argues that in the early days at least the in-

Television Who's Who of Anchors and News Stars

Besides those mentioned elsewhere, such as Edward R. Murrow and Mike Wallace, a television-history roster of news and news-feature personalities would include the following:

Christine Amanpour. Perhaps the most famous foreign correspondent of the 1990s, Amanpour signed a three-year contract in 1996, worth an estimated $1.5 million a year. She is to file news stories for CNN and special reports for *60 Minutes* on CBS, CNN's competitor—the first such cooperative network arrangement. Born in Iran and a graduate in journalism from the University of Rhode Island, Amanpour has covered nearly all of the 1990s trouble spots, from the Gulf War and Somalia to Haiti and Bosnia.

Ed Bradley. Noted for his role on *60 Minutes*, Bradley, a former sixth-grade math teacher and stringer for CBS, became a war correspondent for CBS in Vietnam. In 1976, on *CBS Sunday Night News*, he became the first black anchorman.

David Brinkley. With Chet Huntley, Brinkley coanchored the *Huntley/Brinkley Report* on NBC from 1956 to 1970. The two were the first coanchors on network television. The more liberal of the two, Brinkley, a former reporter and manager for United Press, was an early critic of the U.S. role in the Vietnam War.

Tom Brokaw. A former White House reporter, Brokaw coanchored *The NBC Nightly News* in 1983 with Roger Mudd, with the hope of imitating the success of *Huntley/Brinkley*. It did not work, and Brokaw became the lone anchor. In 1985, the program was renamed *The NBC Nightly News with Tom Brokaw*.

John Chancellor. When Chet Huntley retired, leaving Brinkley alone, the anchoring at NBC fell to three persons, a kind of trinity—Brinkley, John Chancellor, and Frank McGee. The arrangement did not last. Brinkley moved on to do an evening commentary program, *David Brinkley's Journal*, McGee went to *Today*, and Chancellor became the sole anchor.

Connie Chung. Coanchor of the *CBS Evening News* with Dan Rather and host of a newsmagazine show, *Eye to Eye*, Constance Yu-Hwa Chung began with Metromedia Channel 5 in Washington, D.C. She served as a television news anchor in Los Angeles, worked for NBC news programs, and then anchored CBS evening news programs on Saturday and Sunday. She is married to daytime talk-show host Maurice (Maury) Povich, with whom she plans to coanchor a syndicated news/information program for Dreamworks SK6 Studio beginning in the fall of 1998.

Walter Cronkite. The best known of anchors, Cronkite anchored and served as managing editor of the *CBS Evening News* for nineteen years, 1962 to 1981. In World War II he was a war correspondent for United Press and served as UP's chief correspondent at the Nuremberg war crime trials. From 1946 to 1948 he was UP bureau manager in Moscow.

Sam Donaldson. Known for his keen-eyed, feisty demeanor and questions, Donaldson was Capitol Hill correspondent for ABC News from 1967 to 1977. From 1977 to 1989 he was ABC's White House correspondent, asking presidents hard questions. For instance, he wanted

(Continued)

President Carter to explain his reputation for incompetence. Donaldson became anchor for ABC's *PrimeTime Live* in 1989.

Douglas Edwards. Starting at a local station in Troy, Alabama, in 1932, Edwards moved into broadcast news in Atlanta and Detroit. He served as a foreign correspondent in Europe and the Middle East. In 1948 he was the first CBS newsperson to anchor entire political conventions. In 1948 he anchored CBS's first regular daily fifteen-minute network news program to be scheduled across the network.

Pauline Frederick. A longtime correspondent covering the United Nations, first for ABC, then twenty-one years for NBC, Frederick, after retiring in 1974, was a commentator on foreign affairs for National Public Radio. She first appeared on national television at the political conventions in Philadelphia in 1948. She was the first woman to moderate a televised presidential debate (Gerald Ford versus Jimmy Carter) in 1976. She was also the first woman president of the United Nations Correspondents Association.

Bryant Gumbel. Cohost of NBC's *Today Show* since 1982, Gumbel had been a writer and then editor of *Black Sports* magazine in New York in 1971 and 1972. He was sportscaster and then sports director of KNBC-TV, Burbank, California, from 1972 to 1981.

Chet Huntley. Chester Robert Huntley, coanchor with Brinkley on *The Huntley/Brinkley Report*, began in stations in the states of Washington, Oregon, and California. Ever the businessman (he worked during an artist's union strike for nine days in 1967 while Brinkley refused to appear), he retired in 1970 to run Big Sky,

a $25 million ski resort in his native Montana.

Peter Jennings. Anchor on ABC's *World News Tonight* since 1983, Jennings, son of a Canadian broadcasting executive, worked in Canadian stations and covered Parliament. He coanchored the first nationwide commercial network news show in Canada on CTV. In 1964 he moved to ABC, initially covering civil rights. A producer of documentaries, he was also London anchorman on ABC's *World News Tonight*.

Ted Koppel. Anchor on the ABC News program *Nightline* since 1980, Koppel, who came from England in 1953, joined ABC in 1963. He has been ABC bureau chief in Hong Kong and Miami and has been ABC's chief diplomatic correspondent.

Jane Pauley. Coanchor with Bryant Gumbel on NBC's *Today Show* from 1986 to 1990, Pauley, who is married to *Doonesbury* cartoonist Garry Trudeau, launched her own news magazine show, *Real Life with Jane Pauley* (NBC), in 1990. In 1992 she became cohost of *Dateline NBC*.

Dan Rather. Anchor and for a short time coanchor of the *CBS Evening News* with Connie Chung, Rather had started out working on newspapers, radio stations, and a wire service (UPI) in Houston. He joined a CBS affiliate in Houston as a reporter and became news director. He became a White House correspondent and then worked overseas for the network, in London as bureau chief and in Vietnam. For six years, he was coeditor of *60 Minutes*. He became anchor and managing editor of *CBS Evening News with Dan Rather* in 1981.

Diane Sawyer. Coanchor of ABC's *PrimeTime Live*, Sawyer was enticed away from CBS by ABC with a five-year $7.5 million contract in 1989. At the time she was coeditor of *60 Minutes*. She began her career at a station in Louisville. In President Nixon's White House she was an administrative press officer and was a researcher for Nixon's memoirs, from 1974 to 1978. Joining CBS as a reporter, she became CBS's correspondent at the State Department and then coanchor for *Morning News CBS*.

Eric Sevareid. When he retired in 1977 as national correspondent, Sevareid had been with CBS for thirty-eight years; fourteen of those years he appeared on Walter Cronkite's nightly newscast. Sevareid was a reporter in Minneapolis and reporter and city editor for the Paris edition of the *New York Herald Tribune* before he joined CBS in 1939 as European correspondent. He covered World War II and reported out of Asia, Africa, and Central and South America.

Howard K. Smith. A Rhodes scholar at Oxford University, Smith also studied in Berlin. In 1939 he was a foreign correspondent in London for UP, then Berlin correspondent for CBS in 1941. After covering the war, he became chief correspondent and general manager for CBS's Washington bureau. He left CBS because of a quarrel over his attempt to insert a moral statement at the end of a 1961 civil rights documentary indicating that good people who do nothing are a part of the problem of racism. An early moderator of *Face the Nation* and moderator of political debates, he became a news analyst for ABC in Washington in 1962.

Lawrence Spivak. "A moderator and panelist known for his terrier-like tenacity," the *New York Times* said in the obituary of Spivak. Originator of NBC's issue-oriented program *Meet the Press*, which began on radio in 1945 and television in 1948, Spivak, who retired in 1975, was both moderator and panelist. The show was one of the first to use panels of reporters interviewing national and world leaders. "He had watched his brainchild become a catalyst in enlarging the broadcasting industry's role in news and public affairs," said the *Times* (March 10, 1994). Spivak started his career as business manager of magazines, then as publisher of *American Mercury*.

John Cameron Swayze. In 1948, Swayze was anchoring a ten-minute weekly newscast for NBC beginning in February. In August, CBS had Douglas Edwards on the air for the first quarter-hour newscast across the network. NBC's answer was a fifteen-minute format also, *The Camel News Caravan* (named after the cigarette sponsor), with Swayze. He had a long career in radio in Kansas City. From 1946 to 1947 he was special events director for the western network of NBC in Hollywood.

Barbara Walters. In 1976, Walters broke into the spotlight with a five-year $5 million contract to coanchor *ABC Evening News* with Harry Reasoner. She was also expected to host various interview specials. The mismatch was short-lived, and Walters began dedicating herself to her interview specials, quizzing heads of state and entertainers; in 1979 she began cohosting ABC's news feature program, *20/20*. Reasoner went to CBS to join the *60 Minutes* crew. Walters had earlier cohosted the *Today Show* and served as moderator of a syndicated program, *Not for Women Only*.

troduction of television news was a setback in news coverage. "A favorite pronouncement of the day was that television had added a 'new dimension' to newscasting," he says. "The truth of this concealed a more serious fact: the camera, as arbiter of news value, had introduced a drastic curtailment of the scope of news." He said the idea that a picture was worth a thousand words "meant, in practice, that footage of Atlantic City beauty winners, shot at some expense, was considered more valuable than a thousand words from Eric Sevareid on the mounting tensions of Southeast Asia. Analysis, a staple of radio news in its finest days, was being shunted aside as non-visual."[33]

More serious, Barnouw says, was the dependence on preplanned, staged events, such as press conferences. "Behind every planned event was a planner—and government or business purpose. Television dependence on such events gave the planner considerable leverage on news content."[34] A study of one topic—inflation—on television evening news for 1978–1979 showed that more than 75 percent of network stories dealing with inflation depended on federal government agencies or employees as sources and that only 10 percent of the stories used were from individuals or nongovernment organizations.[35]

Slighting Foreign News

Barnouw found that the advent of television news was a restraint on foreign coverage. A distant crisis in, say, the Near East might be brushed off in a forty-second filmed statement by a government official at a press conference. "Happenings in places away from crews or stringers tended to become non-events. This was true of almost anything in Africa." Following the style of movie newsreels, foreign coverage looked for the pictorial and overplayed "imperial and ecclesiastical panoply."[36]

The new technology of the 1980s and 1990s, while improving delivery capability and sound and picture quality, has put additional physical restraints on television journalists reminiscent of the camera- and equipment-hauling burdens of the early days. Network-television foreign correspondents, reports *TV Guide*, "must now spend far more time in the frantic technical details of delivering the news than in . . . gathering the news," thus diminishing the quality and thoroughness of the coverage. ABC foreign correspondent Charles Glass said: "Out of a 24-hour day, you have perhaps only three hours in the field to gather information. The rest of your time is spent in getting it out—dealing with the crew, making sure the tape is OK, editing, seeing that the satellite works. . . . You're dealing with the communications apparatus, and sacrificing time on the story."[37]

Rituals of Sameness

As with newspapers, the format and content of television news perpetuate certain rituals that make for sameness. Just how similar are news broadcasts? Journalist Frank Greve observed in 1980 that network news on each channel began and ended with the same story. Greve, of the *Philadelphia Inquirer*'s Washington bureau, spending three weeks interviewing top news executives at the networks, marveled that the news operations thought very much alike. He blamed the sameness on many factors, including the rules that "if the competition has it, use it" and "if the *New York Times* or the *Washington Post* reports it, the nightly news should, too." Also, he said, homage is paid to the adages "If it's important but visually dull, tell it. If it's unimportant but visually exciting, show it" and, of course, "Leave the viewers happy."[38]

Television news, though limited in the amount of information and education it can convey, in contrast to the extended space of newspapers and magazines, must concentrate on its central purposes. Like all consumer products, television news seeks to meet certain psychological needs. It gives information that can be talked about, information that others will share. For the television watcher does not get news from a fragmented, isolated source such as a one-community newspaper but instead receives information and entertainment from a far-reaching source—television—that cuts across not only geographic and demographic but also psychological barriers. Television provides the "raw materials for sociability," as Mark R. Levy puts it. Television news can soothe the nerves. "Like situation comedies and detective shows," he says, "the newscasts offer temporary release from the pressing cares of daily existence."[39]

PBS and "Idea" News

But the serious mission of telecast news has not been forgotten, especially on national network news. PBS's experiment in 1976 to launch the *Robert MacNeil Report*, featuring a serious news analyst, the Canadian-born MacNeil, became a success, and the program remained on television with Jim Lehrer as the *MacNeil/Lehrer NewsHour* until MacNeil retired in 1995. "MacNeil and his colleagues decided that they were not about to buy the same old goods at the same old stand," wrote former radio commentator Sander Vanocur in a syndicated column. "They knew they could not compete with the networks in the area of film. They decided to compete in the area of ideas. They decided not to react so much to the news as to anticipate it," with panels of experts interpreting an event.[40] Some of that emphasis rubbed off on the major networks, as CBS, for instance, switched from an ordered shotgun approach to the lead stories of the day to the presentation of lengthy segments on serious subjects such as business, health, and other topics affecting the nation.

Yet television news has had a positive influence on the news industry. As Robert Donovan and Ray Scherer point out, "Certainly, television has forced newspapers to be more honest." They are referring to the use of verbatim quotes in the inclusion of taped words in the telecasts. The print reporter tries not to vary one single word in a quote, since what the person said is verifiable from television.

Effect on Newspapers

As a result of the competition with television, newspapers spend more time providing background for an event and interpreting it, using the greater allotment of space

Robert MacNeil, serious PBS news analyst.

to good advantage. Television meanwhile has developed some lengthier news formats—ranging from magazine news programs such as *60 Minutes* to an all-news 24-hour-a-day network, Ted Turner's CNN (Cable News Network), and C-SPAN (Cable Satellite Public Affairs Network), which keeps the mike and camera tuned unedited to the workings of Congress and other national events, including speeches of the National Press Club and special conferences. A kind of cycle prevails. Print media are influenced by television newscasts that goad them into expanding on topics and providing in the daily paper that which television has difficulty doing in regular newscast formats. And television is influenced by the interpretive emphases and space allotments in newspapers and magazines to develop topically and to expand into larger news formats.

Media as Businesses

THE TREND TOWARD "CHEAP NEWS"

Penn Kimball, professor emeritus of the Columbia University Graduate School of Journalism, laments the redefinition of news that is occurring and sees it as "driven by financial considerations and ratings. News is what networks feel they can afford to cover and what will get on the air as determined by ratings. The wall of separation between the business side and the news side, which had always been under siege, has now been significantly breached."[41]

The emphasis on expanding the profits is causing the networks to go the most economical route. "Cheap news" means not only downsizing in staff but also opting for panel and talk shows and prime-time magazine formulas. New hirings tend to be not traditional news people but "news packagers."

Television news has been affected by trimming in other areas. Cutbacks by government agencies in their communications staffs have meant less ready-made news for the media. And curbs of news operations have been encouraged by politicians, such as President Bill Clinton, cabinet members, and members of Congress, who find ways of taking their messages to the people through speeches and special programs rather than traditional releases. "Washington's TV press corps is caught between a network hierarchy with a weakening commitment to news and government sources anxious to evade their scrutiny," says Kimball. "A headline news service out of Washington that skips over the more complex issues is inadequate in the best of times. When network news resources are curtailed, these shortcomings are magnified."[42]

Disposable Networks

Economic factors and the force of competition, as local news broadcasts expand and cable channels proliferate, suggest that the lineup of networks, like that of political parties, has no guaranteed permanence. Since the FCC ordered NBC to relinquish its Blue network in 1943, thus creating ABC, the network picture has changed. A fourth major network—long before the advent of Fox Broadcasting Company—lasted for eight years, from 1947 to 1955. It was the DuMont network, created by and named after Allen Du Mont, a television manufacturer. There were a variety of reasons for DuMont's collapse. Among them were the strangleholds the other networks already had on communities and the role of Paramount Pictures, which used its stock in DuMont to block growth, as one of its subsidiaries, United Paramount Theaters, sought to merge with ABC.[43]

In recent years Rupert Murdoch's Fox network has begun to take slices off the networks. In 1994 Murdoch invested $500 million in financier Ronald Perelman's New World Communications Group, which owned a number of stations across the United States. In the deal, twelve of New World's stations, including large ones in Detroit, Dallas, and Atlanta, agreed to switch affiliation from ABC, CBS, and NBC to Murdoch's Fox Broadcasting. The deal making could be labeled "Ten Days That Shook the Television World," said *Newsweek*.[44]

The Murdoch coup came on the heels of his successful bid the year before to obtain exclusive rights to broadcast National Football League games. CBS had been broadcasting the games for forty years. Murdoch's bid of $1.6 billion, covering four years, was $400 million above CBS's bid. With the acquisition of stations following the sports deal, it was evident, said *Newsweek*, that "Murdoch was clearly planning an ambush of the networks by using football as a juicy enticement to lure stations to Fox."[45] It all foreboded "the beginning of tumultuous times" in the broadcast industry, observed television critic Jonathan Storm, who was quick to add that the scrambling bore out the fact that "reports of the death of broadcast TV are hopelessly premature."

Televised Sports: Big Business

That television, driven by business perspectives, generates big business was never more obvious than in the sports arena. For example, the televised Super Bowl in football commands the highest costs for advertising, with thirty seconds of broadcast time costing $800,000 back in 1991. Some 118 million people watched the game that year. While the Super Bowl remained free to television viewers, a trend did develop to charge viewers of other sports events, namely top-ranking boxing bouts, broadcast over cable or one-shot pay-per-view. It was a far cry from 1939, when NBC sought and won permission to televise a Brooklyn Dodgers game without paying. But the audience then was a few thousand compared to today's multi-millions.

Sponsors, as they did in the old days of television, still attach their names to television events. Just as there were *The Camel News Caravan, The Kraft Music Hall*, and *Texaco Star Theater* in the 1950s, now there are the Federal Express Orange Bowl and the Mobil Cotton Bowl. And there is power in just the appearance of a corporate name. Since 1971 ads for cigarettes and cigars have been banned on television, but the use of logos is acceptable. Logos can be a gold mine, says Marian Calabro. The Marlboro company image during the 1989 Marlboro Grand Prix could be seen on the screen 49 percent of the time.[46]

Big Events and O. J.

Network news reporting has shown that it can compete with CNN when there is a big news event, an event so important that regular scheduling is scuttled and the unfolding events come forth live. When a preliminary hearing was held in the sensational O. J. Simpson double murder case in 1994, the major networks co-opted almost all their daytime programming to present the hearing. Network ratings soared 20 to 40 percent above regular levels. One day ABC had a 7.5 rating, up nearly 2 percent over ratings on its usual soap operas; CBS had 6.1, up from 5.2; and NBC had 5.4, up from 3.7. CNN had a rating between 4 and 5, up less than 1 percent. The decisions of the three big networks "were relatively easy for two main reasons," concluded Bill Carter in the *New York Times*. The reasons were that "the courtroom coverage wasn't costing them all that much, and there was just too much interest in the story to allow viewers to slip away somewhere else, like CNN." Although the networks ran fewer commercials, they managed to generate "a decent amount of revenue," as one CBS executive put it, while gaining an edge on CNN.[47]

CNN's success with news being broadcast all day began to run into competition in 1994, as other cable channels imitated the CNN around-the-clock news. CNN's ratings dipped by about 25 percent in the first quarter of 1994, and its prime-time audience fell to about 500,000, down from about 693,000.[48] In the mix also was the emergence of regional versions of CNN. For instance, there is New England Cable News (NECN) in Newton, Massachusetts. In service for less than a year, NECN in 1994 won the Associated Press award for best news program in the Boston area, beating out regular network-affiliate programs. The proliferation of regional all-day news channels was expected to expand across the country.[49] In the face of this competition, CNN was trying out new formats, namely adding interview programs, but observers, such as Av Westin, senior vice president for programming at Time Warner, believe it is courting trouble if it loses its all-news identity—and trouble if it remains unmoving against the new competition coopting its format.[50] The business of television has indeed become perplexing.

Media as Vehicles of Sensationalism/Entertainment
TURNING ON TITILLATING TRASH

Just as radio adds a dimension to the definition of sensationalism, because sound can heighten the imagination and emotional involvement, so television with its graphic moving images brings the level of involvement to taking part in "reality." The viewer is present as more than an observer reading newspaper accounts or listening and fantasizing with the aid of sound before a faceless radio box or contraption. Television, presenting literal images down to the last detail, in sharp color definition, even life-size on some screens, brings a new variation to the definition of sensationalism.

On television sensationalism means more than the choice of an exciting or dramatic news subject or the use of narrative techniques or even the emotion building of sound. James Gordon Bennett in the penny press era was sensational because he chose to play up the ax murder of a beautiful young prostitute, Ellen Jewett, and to use storytelling techniques. Sensationalism in radio could be inherent in the event. Remember Morrison's on-the-spot emotional account of the *Hindenburg* disaster, with the frantic tension of his exclamations elevating the level of listener involvement.

For television the event itself—even graphic depiction of war and destruction—does not normally pass as sensationalism. Television sensationalism, egged on by face-to-face competition on a national level with rivals for the same market, makes a conscious effort to titillate with controversy, questionable taste, the lurid, and the prurient. For example, says *Newsweek*:

> It was Halloween week, and the electronic jack-o'-lantern was casting a decidedly weird spell. On NBC, the mini-series "Favorite Son" showed sadomasochistic bondage, near-explicit masturbation and a dog lapping up the blood of a murder victim. On ABC, a made-for-TV movie focused on a psychotic father setting fire

to his sleeping son. On Fox Television's "The Reporters," the big story was about an airline pilot who disposed of his wife by shoving her body through a wood-chipping machine. The talk shows, too, were doing their bit. Morton Downey Jr. hosted a gaggle of strippers while Sally Jessy Raphael chatted with some lesbian marriage partners. Geraldo Rivera? Pretty much a standard week's performance: encounters with former prostitutes and female boxers, topped off with a titillating expose of sexual abuse by doctors.[51]

Newsweek prefers to call the prevailing brand of sensationalism on television "trash TV," while others who are more newspaper oriented use the term "tabloid TV," seeing a parallel to titillating headlines and lurid pictures that invite off-the-street readership. *Newsweek* quotes the Reverend Donald E. Wildmon, conservative executive director of Christian Leaders for Responsible TV, saying, "TV people eat up sensationalism. The only thing that's real to them is in the sewer."[52] And that statement suggests another name, "sewer television."

Of course, there is a history of respectable television talk shows, from the morning *NBC Today* show launched in January 1952 by Dave Garroway and *The Tonight Show* with Steve Allen as the first host in 1950 to the low-key morning talk shows in the 1990s, such as *CBS This Morning* with Harry Smith and Paula Zahn (or NBC's *Today* or ABC's *Good Morning America*), the new "nice" *Rosie O'Donnell Show*, and the nighttime celebrity chitchat of Jay Leno, David Letterman, Arsenio Hall, Conan O'Brien, and Tom Snyder. Nevertheless, "trash television" continued to be a brand of talk show.

Kissing a Pet Pig

In the daytime the Phil Donahue show, which ran for twenty-nine years before it went off the air in 1996, had included "some beefcake bottom-shaking by a bevy of male strippers" and had forced Donahue "to get ratings by putting on a dress or kissing a pet pig that's wearing a tutu and a birthday hat."[53] Such entertainment is mixed in with serious discussions on occasion. Geraldo Rivera featured the outrageous, such as women who have undergone surgery to become men, and develops sensational specials for NBC, such as a 1988 show on devil worship (replete with bloodletting and dismembered corpses), which turned out to be the highest-rated two-hour documentary in the history of network television. Oprah Winfrey's daytime show presented the host as a friend willing to explore anybody's innermost secret. Sally Jessy Raphael, often close to tears after hearing a participant's story, provided a psychologist or other expert on the program to deal with the problem at hand. Maury Povich's original *A Current Affair*, syndicated by 20th Century Fox Television, picked up on sex and crime in the news. For instance, it showed a videotape of young murderer Robert Chambers, Jr., cavorting with young women at a slumber party while free on bail and used a look-alike for the victim, Jennifer Levin, in the Central Park murder; the program also re-enacted the drowning death of NBC correspondent Jessica Savitch in a car in a canal "complete with a ghastly face trapped behind the death car's windshield."[54] Povich, replaced by Maureen O'Boyle, who was with the program from the beginning in 1988, had his own afternoon talk show, which also, critics said, reflected "his love for the sensational."[55]

Latecomers on the daytime television talk-show circuit, including Rolonda Watts, Bertice Berry, and Montel Williams, have varied in seriousness, "but for the most part are derivative of the talk-show masters."[56] And in case the viewer might miss a titillating moment on the daytime talk shows, a composite program, *Talk Soup*, on the entertainment channel *E!*, which also airs Howard Stern's "shock jock" talk show, excerpted the raunchiest segments from all the shows.

Marquette University communications professor Helen Sterk analyzed the television talk shows that were available at her Kenosha, Wisconsin, home and found that most of them (with the exception of the Jerry Springer show) centered on prurient interests and did not tolerate moral judgments. Sterk found that "during any given week viewers may be offered a menu including women who were arrested while naked, transsexual twins, celebrity sisters . . . favorite television commercials, sexual triangles, female pattern baldness and women who harm their children for attention."[57] The conversation is planned to have the greatest shock value and attention-getting value.[58]

"Reality Shock" News

The sensationalism of the talk shows crosses over into news formats. *A Current Affair* bills itself as an "investigative magazine series." *Inside Edition*, produced by Kingworld Features, considers itself a "newsmagazine strip." *Hard Copy*, distributed by Paramount Domestic Television, says it is a "reality-based news series." The ratings on these three programs have become so high that they have often been moved from late afternoon or late night slots to the access time slot, between network news and the beginning of prime-time programming.[59]

The "reality shock" approach, centering on crime, violence and the fear of the unknown, spawned nonfiction programs such as *Rescue 911*, *The People's Court*, *America's Most Wanted*, and *Unsolved Mysteries*. The fascination with unseen powers was seized on by slick televangelists (one of whom, Jim Bakker, went to jail for fraud) and programs dealing with the epiphenomenal, such as Rod Serling's *Twilight Zone* in the 1950s and the more modern offerings, ranging from the macabre *Tales from the Crypt* to *The X Files*, a program on UFO citings and lore.

The overt sensationalism of the television tabloid news magazine programs, the "reality" programs, and the shock talk shows has had an influence on the regular network news shows. "Tabloids are considered a source of sensational stories," says Catherine L. Finn, "yet network news is picking up these stories as well." She mentions the coverage of Gennifer Flowers' 1992 claim of a long-time affair with presidential candidate Bill Clinton and the indictment and trial of William Kennedy Smith on a rape charge, which *Hard Copy* claimed as a scoop. The *New York Times* and other news media "even went beyond the tabloids in what might seem a tabloid-style invasion of privacy," when they gave the name of the alleged victim, Patricia Bowman.[60]

On-Camera Murder

In January 1993, NBC stations showed an on-camera murder; the next day it was picked up by *A Current Affair* and *Hard Copy*, which made it their lead story. The incident involved a distraught man at the grave of his daughter who had committed suicide upon hearing that she was pregnant. When his ex-wife showed up at the grave, the father, blaming the woman for the death, turned a gun on her and killed her. All of this took place in the presence of a news crew from the Spanish-language network Telemundo that had accompanied the man to the site.

The tabloid programs' use of reenactments—which, as we have seen, were sometimes used in early documentary newsreels—found some imitators on television news programs. In 1989, ABC News presented a scene of accused spy Felix Bloch rendezvousing with his Soviet counterpart, a reenactment that was not tagged as such. The most famous reenactment was a 1993 NBC News report on *Dateline NBC* which purported to show that GM trucks tended to blow up on impact in collisions. The program decided to tamper with a GM truck so as to make certain it would explode and burn. NBC offered its apology to GM after the car manufacturer pulled its ads.[61]

The confusion of tabloid news with mainstream traditional approaches is spawned by a similarity of format, says Finn. The tabloids try to resemble a traditional news show by using a similar news desk setup with anchorpersons behind it. Both formats promote the anchors as distinguished journalists; both formats work in fragments, jumping from segment to segment without a coherent context.[62]

The very concept of the now-popular "eyewitness news" format has a built-in sensational aspect. The eyewitness news format was pioneered in the early 1970s by Al Primo of WABC-TV, New York. Researchers discovered that one of the prominent features of this format "was a predilection for stories that dealt with violence." Their study found that WABC, using the personable eyewitness format, spent one-third more time on violence than competing station WCBS and more than twice as much as another station, WNBC. Eventually, "in fact, in the New York market, WNBC and WCBS have shown a tendency to imitate the Eyewitness format's emphasis on violence," the study says. The researchers quote a newscaster from an article in *New York Magazine*: "All of the local news shows seem to be into violence, at least in short bursts . . . because it tends to hold viewers and boost ratings. 'When the execs come down to lecture us,' one CBS producer told us, 'they tell us to do fewer two-minute stories and lots of ten-second ones. And as much sensationalism as possible.'"[63]

Learning from the Movies

Techniques long used in movies can add to the flavor of sensationalism. Repetition on television played an important part in the Rodney King beating that led to trials of Los Angeles police officers. How many times did the average viewer see the video of that incident or the monitoring of O. J. Simpson in his Bronco? And the stop-action, slow-motion instant replay, which ABC president of news Roone Arledge brought to sports coverage, found its way into news programs to help the viewer savor high action and dramatic moments.[64]

Sensationalism gets attention by shocking as it entertains. The soap operas compete by piling scandals on top of scandals. There has been vicious sibling rivalry, careless love, malpractice, artificial insemination, murder, incest, mate swapping, addiction, venereal disease, all "meshing with the old, familiar workings of unhappy families," says *Time*.[65]

The sitcoms—the half-hour family-oriented ensemble farces, usually about a fictional family, that appear in prime time—occasionally make an extraordinary pass at the ratings by summoning unusual attention to a development in the story. Consider, in recent years, Roseanne's kissing another woman, Murphy Brown having a baby out of wedlock and keeping it (then-Vice President Dan Quayle even got involved in this controversy, guaranteeing high ratings), *Three's Company's* coed roommates, Maude (Beatrice Arthur) taking the highly controversial lithium for severe depression in 1976 episodes, a man drowning in a bowl of soup at the dinner table—plus an elderly flasher and pot smoking—in *Mary Hartman! Mary Hartman!*, and *Melrose Place's* HIV relationship. Sitcoms or news programs—the content sometimes seems interchangeable as they bid for attention.

Media as Definers and Keepers of Values (and Biases)
SCANNING A VAST WASTELAND

Almost every month numerous articles and books appear to point their verbal lances at the great panderer to lower tastes (or no taste at all) and purveyor of various societal evils, television. The quality of programming on television has always been criticized. No more scathing and sweeping indictment has been leveled than that of Newton Minow in his first speech as John Kennedy's newly appointed chair of the Federal Communications Commission in 1961. After paying tribute to some good television, namely, selected theater and arts programs and documentaries, in that address before the National Association of Broadcasters, Minow indeed gave a dim view of the vast territory of television:

> When television is bad, nothing is worse. I invite you to sit down in front of your television set when your station goes on the air and stay there without a book, magazine, newspaper, profit-and-loss sheet or rating book to distract you—and keep your eyes glued to that set until the station signs off. I can assure you that you will observe a vast wasteland.
>
> You will see a procession of game shows, violence, audience participation shows, formula comedies about totally unbelievable families, blood and thunder, mayhem, violence, sadism, murder, western badmen, western good men, private eyes, gangsters, more violence and cartoons. And, endlessly, commercials—many screaming, cajoling and offending. And most of all, boredom. True, you will see a few things you will enjoy. But they will be very, very few, And if you think I exaggerate, try it.[66]

Thirty years later, in 1991, Minow again took a look at the landscape of television and asked, "How vast the wasteland now?" Speaking at the Gannett Foundation Media Center in New York, he found the territory even more bleak despite the increased options and choices of programming provided by the proliferation of cable. Minow talks these days of the television viewer having "gone from a vast emptiness to a vast fullness," with all the choices available. But he sees the viewer as not so much sitting in a desert wasteland as lost in it. He quotes from a speech of CBS President Howard Stringer before the Royal Institution in London in 1990: "We see a vast, media-jaded audience that wanders restlessly from one channel to another in search of that endangered species—originality. . . . More choices may not necessarily mean better choices."[67]

Watching 25,000 Murders

To Minow, "the most troubling change over the past thirty years has been the rise in the quantity and quality of violence on television." He said, "In 1961 I worried that my children would not benefit much from television, but in 1991 I worry that my grandchildren will actually be harmed by it." He cited one study that showed that by the time youngsters are 18 they have seen 25,000 murders on television. And "in 1961 they didn't make PG-13 movies, much less NC-17. Now a 6-year-old can watch them on cable."[68]

Furthermore, studies show that violent crimes and murders on television are not the only fare that affects children adversely. Exposure to "realism" in drama has affected the perception of children concerning potential activities. "Specifically," says a study by Dolf Zillmann, Jennings Bryant, and Aletha Huston, "children who had just seen a movie about a drowning reported a lower level of interest in the sport of canoeing than did children who had not seen the drowning." Similarly, children who had just watched a television show about a deadly house fire "were averse to building a fire in a fireplace and much less interested than were those children who had not seen that drama." Such findings "suggest that the effects of exposure to scary media presentations may have broad and enduring implications in the life of a child." Children who are not readers of newspapers and magazines are exposed to the drama and trauma in television news. A study of the effect of television news dominated by the coverage of the Persian Gulf war found a sizable number of parents reporting that their children were upset by television coverage of the war.[69]

Minow cites the failure to use television for education and the failure to use television for children as two reasons for his latter-day conclusion that "the television marketplace has become a severely distorting influence in at least four important public areas," the other two being the failure "to finance public television properly and to use television properly in political campaigns."[70] The head of one children's television watchdog group, Peggy Charren, president of Action for Children's Television, observed, "If television were working, kids would want to go out and clean up the rivers, help the hungry and the homeless, and would know that peace is a good thing and nuclear war is the end of the world."[71]

Congress made an effort to respond to the problem in 1990 by passing the Children's Television Act, which underscores the television industry's responsibility to young children.

Pantheon of Celebrities

Television for all age groups elevates celebrities to its pantheon of gods. From the commercial with the testimony of an acceptable hero image to the authorities and celebrities who are quoted regularly to substantiate a news story, "truth" is confirmed by celebrity and expert testimony. The penny papers of the mid-nineteenth century started writing more about celebrities and began to develop the interview technique, but it has been the role of television to endow the celebrity entertainer and politician alike with degrees of authenticity. "What's so fascinating about TV news is that the guarantor behind its believability—its 'truths' loosely defined—is that of pleasing personalities in particular and entertainment in general," say Ian Mitroff and Warren Bennis.[72]

Some feel television offers a type of religious experience. Quentin Schultze, writing on "Television Drama as a Sacred Text," believes "secular television programming shares with religious worship the necessity of public ritual." As with the mass, he says, "television is structured in prescribed ways so that the worshipers may enter into meaningful communion. Television uses its own liturgies to ensure communal experience."[73] He says the liturgies can be broken into special categories, among them situation comedies, westerns, detective shows, soap operas, and various action formats. As religious ritual, television over the past four decades "has been an American prophet, formulating and reformulating at least three widely believed myths." They are "Good will triumph over evil," "Evil exists only in the hearts of a few evil people," and "Godliness exists in the good and effective actions of individuals." Although he recognizes that these basic statements are commendable, he regards this minimalist religion as not enough. There is little room for transcendence. Schultze says further, "Only on rare occasions and programs has television even hinted at the existence of an omnipotent or omniscient deity. Instead, the tube has traded the mysterious and unexplainable for a more humanly understandable conception of God: virtuous and effective human action," a kind of beneficent or "humanistic pragmatism"—what works for the good of all. "Humankind's ability to ensure its own survival and usher in progress is not delivered from heaven but is the result of the efficacious actions of individual people. These are the saints of prime-time television, solving crimes, reconciling love-lost couples, and clearing up confusion and complication."

Also conspicuously missing from most television dramas are "the cardinal virtues. Television saints accomplish much good, but rarely because of prudence, temperance, or fortitude." Television, he says, "even reduces justice, one of the most significant virtues throughout the history of Western civilization, to the revengeful triumph of good guys over bad guys. In other words, the right conduct of television heroes is rarely set in the context of ethical reasoning or virtuous action."[74]

Media as Fourth Estate: Adversaries of Government

BATTLING TYRANNY AND DEMAGOGUES

Just as Bob Woodward and Carl Bernstein at the *Washington Post* demonstrated the power of print to contribute to the downfall of a president, Richard Nixon, in the Watergate break-in scandal in the 1970s, so television in its early days, many believe, contributed to the downfall of a tyrannical senator, Joseph R. McCarthy of Wisconsin, who held key legislators and a president under his sway. McCarthy's questionable practice of making blanket accusations without giving precise facts showed him to be on unstable ground. Although McCarthy's popularity had begun to wane before Edward R. Murrow and his program *See It Now* on CBS dealt with the issue, Murrow and his straightforward manner came to epitomize the penetrating power television could have on the national affairs agenda. *See It Now*, the first television news magazine, first aired on a Sunday afternoon, November 18, 1951.

Murrow Versus McCarthy

From the first Murrow wanted a sense of reality, and to help achieve it he decided to originate the program in New York's Grand Central Terminal instead of the control room of CBS Studio 41. This tactic helped remove any idea of association with the entertainment fare on television.[75] *See It Now* resembled a newsreel in the *March of Time* movie tradition. Murrow, with virtually total control over the program (he was a member of the CBS board of directors), produced a basically conservative program free of controversy. Murrow was also to become popular in early 1954 as host of *Person to Person*, similar to Robin Leach's more recent *Lives of the Rich and Famous*. Murrow's celebrity-studded *Person to Person* outdrew *See It Now*. But events were getting out of control in the country, and the changing of the climate to one of fear and suspicion would soon involve Murrow and his many friends and would pave the way for the famous documentary on McCarthy on *See It Now*, March 9, 1954.

The climate was right for the rise of McCarthy in the 1950s. World War II was followed by the Cold War, with an almost paranoid fear of the Soviet Union and the new communist giant, the People's Republic of China. Tensions increased in 1948 with the Berlin airlift—a response to a Soviet cutoff of access to Berlin, which sat in the middle of the Soviet sector of occupation. The age of suspicion was exacerbated by the Korean War of 1950–1953, aimed at halting an alleged domino effect of Communism taking over all of Asia, and by fear of the atom bomb. And there was the trial and execution of Julius and Ethel Rosenberg as spies. Harry Truman was beleaguered in the White House in 1950, and Dwight D. Eisenhower, a military man with an expected no-nonsense attitude toward left-leaners, was in the wings.

The times were ready-made for a demagogue such as McCarthy. He could at will call certain individuals "commie" or "fellow traveler" or "Red" and get away with it. Careers were ruined; there were evictions from homes, jail terms, and suicides. Politicians trembled. The influential front-runner for the Republican presidential nomination in 1952, Senator Robert A. Taft of Ohio, backed fellow

Janet and Edward R. Murrow at their farm near Pawling, New York. (Philadelphia Bulletin; Temple University Libraries Photojournalism Collection)

Republican McCarthy. And in order to appease McCarthy, Eisenhower—the man who was to win the nomination and election—deleted praise of his longtime friend and mentor under attack by McCarthy, General George Marshall, a Nobel Prize winner, from a speech, a dark betrayal indeed in dark times.

Radio and television leadership fell into step. A small organization called American Business Consultants, made up of former FBI agents, later renamed AWARE, put out a newsletter, *Counterattack,* which would charge selected persons, the media included, with subversiveness. In a 215-page report in 1950, called *Red Channels,* the organization offered a "Report of Communist Influence in Radio and Television." It pointed a finger at 151 persons. Included were some of the best-known artists and performers, among them composer Aaron Copland, playwright Arthur Miller, and radio–movie man Orson Welles.[76] The networks agreed to "blacklist" all the people on the list, resulting in wholesale firings and the elimination of new applicants for alleged subversive interests or contacts. No proof was required for the charges.

Meanwhile *See It Now*, on its generally noncontroversial course, was not receiving exceptional ratings. Murrow had won a number of awards, but his program did not draw a significant audience. *See It Now* was moved from its Sunday afternoon slot to a 10:30 P.M. Tuesday slot. Some one-third of the CBS affiliates were not broadcasting the program just prior to the March 1954 program on Senator Joseph McCarthy.[77]

The Case of Lieutenant Radulovich

Actually Murrow had begun his attack on McCarthy with the "The Case of Lieutenant Milo Radulovich" on October 20, 1953, followed by "An Argument in Indianapolis," November 24, 1953. He followed the pivotal program on McCarthy in March 1954 with two more, one including McCarthy's reply.

"The Radulovich case symbolized the McCarthy era, for it was a classical case of guilt by association," says Alexander Kendrick.[78] Murrow told the story of a young Air Force Reserve officer who was a senior at the University of Michigan after eight years of active duty in the U.S. Air Force. The military decided the officer was a security risk because of his close relationship to "Communists or Communist sympathizers," which turned out to be his sister and father. The father read radical or "subversive" newspapers, and the sister was alleged to have once walked in a Communist picket line. But all this had nothing to do with the lieutenant's views. The public was about to see a face of a victim of McCarthyism, and it would be someone they would like. Murrow biographer A. M. Sperber says, "Milo Radulovich, filmed at his home in Dexter, Michigan, was articulate, impassioned, with no self-pity, and a good communicator. In TV terms, moreover—youthful, attractive, a family man, white ethnic working his way through college—he was perfect." Radulovich himself said, "If I am being judged on my relatives, are my children going to be asked to denounce *me*?"[79]

The program had its effect on the air force and put a damper on the rampant hysteria gripping the country. The air force called a press conference and said it would drop efforts to blacklist Lieutenant Radulovich.

Murrow anguished over whether to assault McCarthy head-on in a documentary because he did not want to editorialize and lose the sense of objectivity that had characterized his career. But the events were extraordinary, and too many were suffering. Murrow knew that he would soon himself come under attack by the big guns of McCarthy and McCarthy's friend J. Edgar Hoover at the FBI. With military-like savvy, Murrow decided to strike McCarthy first while McCarthy was preoccupied with intimidating a new target, the U.S. Army. By taking on the army itself, McCarthy was making himself vulnerable.

The day—March 9, 1954—arrived with the network slipping the McCarthy exposé into the *See It Now* 10:30 P.M. format without any prior announcement or promotion of its own. (Murrow and Fred Friendly put up $1,500 of their own money for a *New York Times* ad announcing the program but made no mention of CBS, only of the local channel.)[80] Murrow as usual also read the 7:45 P.M. news report as if this was just a regular evening.

Some crank calls were coming in, and security guards staked out the elevators. Ten thirty arrived. "Good evening," Murrow said, following the script and not looking up as cues in the script suggested he do. "Tonight *See It Now* devotes its entire half hour to a report on Senator Joseph R. McCarthy, told mainly in his own words and pictures." They caught McCarthy in contradictions and outrageous statements, such as labeling the Democratic Party as treasonous. They showed a usurpation of power, with McCarthy saying he could call the shots no matter who was president.

"This Is No Time to Keep Silent"

Dramatically at the end Murrow looked right into the camera:

> We will not walk in fear, one of another. We will not be driven by fear into an age of unreason, if we dig deep in our history and our doctrine; and remember that we are not descended from fearful men. Not from men who feared to write, to speak, to associate, and to defend causes that were for the moment unpopular.
>
> This is no time for men who oppose Senator McCarthy's methods to keep silent—or for those who approve. We *can* deny our heritage and our history but we cannot escape responsibility for the result. There is no way for a citizen of a republic to abdicate his responsibility. . . .
>
> The actions of the Junior Senator from Wisconsin have caused alarm and dismay amongst our allies abroad and given considerable comfort to our enemies. And whose fault is that? Not really his. He didn't create this situation of fear, he merely exploited it; and rather successfully.
>
> Cassius was right. "The fault, dear Brutus, is not in our stars, but in ourselves." Good night, and good luck.[81]

Eisenhower eventually snubbed McCarthy by excluding him from invitations to a White House function and described McCarthy as having "set himself above the laws of the land." When McCarthy started accusing his fellow senators of suspicious activity, his star fell. Specifically, McCarthy said that the select committee studying censure charges concerning the senator, led by conservative Utah Republican Arthur Watkins, was the "unwitting handmaiden of the Communist Party." Before the close of 1954 the Senate voted 67 to 22 to censure McCarthy. Disgraced and his mental prowess in question, he died in 1957.

Others besides Murrow and the CBS staff criticized McCarthy, including Democrats—President Harry Truman and Eisenhower's rival in the 1952 election, Adlai Stevenson of Illinois. But Murrow's gallant effort and his *See It Now* made television in a moment of national crisis seem indeed a fourth estate in the government of the nation.

Media as Voices of Freedom
THE FCC SITS BACK

Despite its regulation of the granting and renewal of licenses, the Federal Communications Commission has exerted little influence on controlling and censoring the content of television programs. Television was free to work out its own guidelines, which could prove narrow in response to audience surveys and commercial advertiser pressures. But little effort in specific control came from the FCC.

"Soon after President Ronald Reagan appointed Mark Fowler as chairman of the Federal Communications Commission in 1981," says William R. Ray, who once headed the Complaints and Compliance Division of the Broadcast Bureau of the FCC, "veteran observers of the agency began to have a sense of déjà vu. The wheel had come full turn and they were witnessing the advent of another do-nothing commission as they had during the Eisenhower administration." Yet the Reagan commission was not really doing nothing. "It was busily reinterpreting the Communications Act so as to dismantle much of the structure of broadcast regulation."[82] In fact, the FCC in the Reagan years, Ray says, "became a national disgrace."

Ray cites the nonenforcement of the fairness doctrine, even the designation of it as unconstitutional. And he suggests that the FCC, misinterpreting Supreme Court decisions that applied contemporary community standards and the need for redeeming social value in making determinations about obscenity, "summarily rejected all complaints on that subject." He also indicates that the FCC declined to investigate the overt "fraudulent practices" of television evangelist Jim Bakker "and let him continue to misappropriate contributions of his followers until he was detected in a different type of offense" (a sex scandal).

The FCC has even taken other steps to undermine the basic tenets of broadcast regulation, says Ray, who was given a special achievement citation by his fellow commissioners in 1973. The FCC "has sought to nullify the entire concept that a broadcaster is a public trustee and must serve the public interest in return for being allowed to use one of the limited number of frequencies in the radio spectrum."[83]

The FCC, among other things, Ray notes, had narrowed its definition of "good character," required for a license, to meaning merely that anyone who has not been convicted of a felony, misconduct of a "broadcast related nature," or making misrepresentations to the commission itself could be considered for a license.[84] The FCC also dropped guidelines that required some informational programming for children and limits on commercials during children's programs.

Looking to Voluntary Regulation

Television's own voluntary efforts at supervision, if not censorship, began in the early 1950s when *TV Forecast* magazine helped create the National Television Review Board. It created a code for television, as did the National Association of Broadcasters. The NTRB's Citizen's Television Code said it would deem "objectionable" that which met the following criteria: "immoral, lewd, and suggestive words and actions, as well as indecency in dress"; "a deliberate presentation of vulgar and sordid situations"; "irreverence toward religion or patriotic symbols"; "malicious derision of racial or national groups"; "excessive bloodshed, violence, and cruelty";

or "disloyal or subversive sentiments that might injure the United States." The Television Code of the NAB offered similar sentiments in 1951.[85]

Each network had a censorship department, sometimes employing up to sixty persons. The departments still exist, although staffing has been cut generally in half to thirty. "One of the only reasons the departments still exist at all is that viewers, despite their taste for the lurid, continue to expect greater discretion from network television," says Elizabeth Kolbert in the *New York Times*. But standards are not clear. There are only a few guidelines on sex and language, and they are cast in generalities. The network censors—those in the respective standards and practices departments—see themselves as editors or "facilitators."[86] The voluntary nature of the codes continues, despite criticisms and pressure from groups such as the National PTA, the American Medical Association, and religious groups.

Voluntary censorship has also come into play in matters of national security or sensitive matters such as hostage taking, where coverage might create potential harm to individuals. For instance, heeding a request of NBC News correspondent Richard Valeriani in November 1979, the network decided not to broadcast his discovery that six U.S. embassy officials had escaped being taken hostage by the Iranians and were holed up in the Canadian embassy in Tehran.[87]

Stereotypes Developed

In promoting traditional and consensus values, the voluntary nature of regulation has let various stereotypes thrive. The family and even single-parent sitcoms have created various hard-and-fast images of the role of women as long-suffering although sometimes mean-spirited connivers (*Roseanne*) or, if single, then overly aggressive. The husband is often a soft bit of clay in the hands of the archetypal woman. The children are all cute and bratty, but maneuverable. In advertising sex is exploited and women become objects.[88]

African American and Asian stereotypes still prevail. Also, mass media "have exploited to an excessive degree the stereotype of the Arab," says Jack Shaheen, "in spite of the known detrimental effects of such exploitation." Stereotyping, he says, "is not only a crime against Arabs and Arab nations, but also against the human spirit."[89] Lifestyles of those out of the mainstream, such as homosexuals, continue to be treated humorously by stereotyping.

When a citizens' group led by a United Church of Christ official was waved aside by the FCC as the group tried to speak out against renewing a license for a racist television station in 1964, the group went to court. The UCC Office of Communication, under its director, Everett C. Parker, fought to have the renewal license of WLBT-TV in Jackson, Mississippi, denied.[90] Purporting to speak for the 45 percent of the population of Jackson that was black, Parker used a corps of volunteers to log each hour of the racist broadcasts (the station cut out segments of series that starred blacks, for instance). The U.S. Court of Appeals for the District of Columbia, designated in 1934 to hear appeals from FCC decisions, overturned the FCC verdict and denied renewal of the license. "More significant by far, it established for the first time the right of an average citizen and the public to intervene in licensing proceedings."[91]

With its marketplace philosophy letting economic forces set the agenda and solve problems, the television industry—which, like radio and even print media, depends on advertising to pay the bills—is faithful to a capitalist agenda. Although the extent of the effect of television policies and programming on ideology is complex and not clear, "there is considerable agreement among critical media theorists that television produces and reproduces a dominant ideology,"[92] says Conrad Lodziak. And possibly television and the media in general, with their marketplace mentalities, support freedom in a laissez-faire context.

Media as Voices of Reform
DURABLE DOCUMENTARIES

The documentary became the vehicle within the television industry to give a voice to reform. One of the most dramatic and controversial was a CBS special on migrant workers, "Harvest of Shame," that aired on November 25, 1960, the day after Thanksgiving. It brought to mind muckraker Lincoln Steffens' series of articles, "Shame of the Cities," drawing a part of the title from his series. Edward R. Murrow, as narrator, detailed the daily lives of migrant workers who had no home and were unable to supply adequate food for their families. They were depicted as worse off than slaves. The main interviewer was the soft-spoken David Lowe, who had followed the workers for nine months up and down the east and west coasts. In good muckraker tradition, Lowe described the workers as toiling in the "sweatshops of the soil."

The program was so memorable that ten years later a competing network, NBC, commemorated it with a sequel, "Migrant," and in 1980, another follow-up, "The Migrants."

Genesis of *60 Minutes*

In the 1950s and 1960s it was inevitable that the documentary would evolve with each program usually targeted on one subject, often a political or military topic[93] rather than some domestic abuse that needed correcting. The hour-long format, which gave audiences a chance to escape during commercials, was thought by many to be as tedious as a lecture. That was the feeling of CBS producer Don Hewitt, the originator of CBS's *60 Minutes* and its producer for more than a quarter of a century. In the 1980s, Hewitt reminisced about that show's 1968 inception: "I had by then figured out that what was principally wrong with documentaries was the name 'documentary,'" he said. "No one likes to read documents, so why would they want to watch something called a documentary?" Although critics praised almost any kind of documentary—so named after the nonfiction films of Robert Flaherty and Pare Lorenz—and regarded them as some kind of holy writ, the documentary was "impersonal and often boring to everybody else."[94]

Don Hewitt, sitting on desk (left), executive producer of CBS Evening News with Walter Cronkite, *who is seated with pipe. Hewitt was a developer of* 60 Minutes. *(CBS Archives)*

Hewitt reasoned that television needed to develop different kinds of vehicles, just as print had books, newspapers, and magazines. The documentary seemed to be analogous to a book; the evening news programs, to a newspaper. What television needed, he thought, was a magazine format. "Sometime in 1967 it dawned on me that if we split those public affairs hours into three parts to deal with the viewer's short attention span—not to mention my own—and came up with personal journalism (as Bill Moyers did later on for his documentaries) in which a reporter takes the viewer along with him on the story," Hewitt argued, then "informational programming" would win at the ratings game. Hewitt asked Richard Salant, president of CBS News, "Why don't we try to package sixty minutes of reality as attractively as Hollywood packages sixty minutes of make-believe?"[95] Thus was born perhaps the most successful and the longest-running news-feature-investigative program on television. It held its own on Tuesday night at 10 P.M., but in 1975, when it was switched to 7 P.M. on Sundays, it soared in the ratings.

At First, "Barely Grazing the Skin"

In the early days of the program, some of the coverage was particularly lightweight. For instance, says Bob Woodward, in the first season Mike Wallace "did routine segments on Richard Nixon and Spiro Agnew that barely grazed the skin."[96] In fact, Wallace was so harmonious with Nixon, whom he had covered for CBS in the 1968 election, that Nixon offered Wallace a job as his press secretary, which Wallace declined.

| The Lighter Side |

Television's Interview Twists

Imagine, If You Will

Mike Wallace, at the time Don Hewitt approached him to become one of the reporters on *60 Minutes*, was considering another job— that of press spokesman for President Richard Nixon. Hewitt talked him out of it by declaring that "a press spokesman is a nobody trying to be somebody."

Diane Sawyer, on the other hand, put in eight years with Nixon as a writer and researcher, during and after his presidency. It was a great deal to live down and atone for. When she became the first female reporter on *60 Minutes*, by then the top-rated public affairs program in America, she tried to emulate Mike Wallace in grilling people. In interviewing George Bush, then vice president, Sawyer cited the fact that he had been called a wimp.

"Are you a wimp?" she asked.

On another program, Diane Sawyer visited with John Connally, the former Texas governor, after he had lost his fortune in the oil slump of the early eighties. Talking to him about the fact that even his house and personal possessions had to be auctioned off, Sawyer asked the broke and broken old man how it could have happened.

"Were you stupid?" she prompted helpfully.

Just Wunnerful

What makes a good interviewer is the ability to listen, and the opposite is also true. According to Jack Paar, television interviewers are always desperately trying to think up their next question, and if they become aware that their guest has stopped talking, they would say automatically, "That's wunnerful." Paar recalled in his book, *My Saber Is Bent*, one program during which a patient in an iron lung and an attendant nurse were explaining how the life-saving machine worked, ending with the caveat that if the electricity went off, alas the patient would die.

"That's wunnerful," said the host.

Another of Paar's favorite stories on the subject was Cornelius Vanderbilt, Jr., recounting to a Hollywood interviewer some of his journalistic adventures during World War II.

"I was covering the fighting on the Russian front and one day I was captured by the Russians. I was thrown into an armored car and driven all night to an unknown destination. When I was dragged out of the car I was stunned to see we were at the Kremlin. My captors hauled me into that forbidding bastion, down a long gloomy corridor, and finally hurled me to the floor. Looking up, I saw Stalin glowering down at me!"

At this cliffhanger, Vanderbilt paused for breath and dramatic effect.

"I see," said the interviewer. "Do you have any hobbies?"

Source: Peter Hay, Canned Laughter: The Best Stories from Radio and Television (New York: Oxford University Press, 1992), pp. 102–113.

The program could be almost right-wing at times, particularly in some segments developed by a member of the on-camera team, Morley Safer. Fed information by several conservative organizations, Safer in a segment on mainline (liberal) religion—*The Gospel According to Whom?*—blended shots of collection plates being passed at church with pictures of Moscow's Red Square. "The point, as Morley suggested repeatedly," says Axel Madsen, "was that officials of the National Council of Churches (NCC) might be using Sunday offerings to promote Marxist revolution in the Third World." Madsen noted that indeed church officials had routed some money to a Nicaraguan government literacy campaign, but Safer and producer Marti Galovic neglected to say that the U.S. government had supported the same program with considerable funding. "At least one letter to *60 Minutes* called the broadcast a piece of born-again McCarthyism."[97]

But despite some thinly disguised ideological pieces and pure-entertainment personality interviews—which come with the territory of a magazine format—Mike Wallace and crew developed *60 Minutes'* image as a defender of the citizen and of consumer rights, a vehicle for initiating reform.

Sometimes the *60 Minutes* correspondent went incognito, pretending to be a consumer or some other participant in the story, only to "blow the whistle" at the end of the segment. And the bad guy would eventually go to jail. Such was the case with the odometer-tampering scam aired on December 9, 1990. Steve Kroft pretended to be an investor in the used-car market when he talked with used-car dealer Bill Whitlow, who explained how rollbacks in odometers were done. "Whitlow will buy a trade-in from a used car dealer, roll back the miles and sell it to a different dealer," Kroft said in the lead-in.[98] By the time it was all over Whitlow went to jail.

In other exposés, *60 Minutes* presented documents that showed that the Ford Pinto was a high risk ("Is Your Car Safe?" June 11, 1978); sent three of its crew into a spa at Murrieta Hot Springs, California, whose staff had phony credentials and followed bogus practices, and saw the promoter eventually go to jail on charges of conspiracy and fraud ("R. J. Rudd," November 1, 1978); presented evidence that led to the overturn of a wrongful conviction and release of a man serving a life term ("Lenell Geter's in Jail," December 4, 1983); presented confidential memos from inside a California chemical plant that showed management knew about but did nothing about the plant's chemical waste, which was contaminating wells in the area—the program prodded the state to bring a lawsuit against the company ("The Hooker Memos," December 16, 1979).

Mike Wallace: An Actor

In its pursuit of investigative, reform-minded journalism, *60 Minutes* is noted for a confrontational style, namely, the barbed right-to-the-point questioning of its leader, Mike Wallace. Bob Woodward's tribute to Wallace was not without reason called "Mike Wallace: Grand Inquisitor of *60 Minutes*." Actually Wallace was cast for the part almost like an actor. In fact, in his early checkered career as he looked about for the right direction, he had a leading role as an art dealer in a Broadway comedy, *Reclining Figure*, starring in 100 performances before the play ended.[99] He had hosted radio and television talk and game shows and paid the bills for a considerable time by doing Parliament cigarette commercials.

Wallace, however, always preferred the news operations, and when in 1962 he was devastated by the tragic death of his nineteen-year-old son, Peter, Wallace made a commitment to a news career. The son, between his sophomore and junior years at Yale, had been abroad in Europe that summer and had disappeared in Greece. Not hearing from him, Wallace flew to Greece and, through the consulate, tracked the youth to the village of Camari. A villager remembered a young man of Peter's description setting out for a monastery atop a mountain outside Camari.

Retracing the steps, Wallace found the body of his son, who had fallen from a narrow ledge into a ravine. He had encouraged his son to follow a career in journalism. "And so, in the dark autumn of 1962, Wallace vowed to transform his grief into something positive, to restructure his life in a way that would honor Peter's memory."[100] In 1963 Wallace went to work for CBS radio news, doing an interview series, *Personal Closeup*, and in the summer he was tapped to anchor the *CBS Morning News* and then *60 Minutes*.

Spinoffs of *60 Minutes*

With the success of *60 Minutes* (it made more money than any other show in history), imitations and spinoffs followed. At NBC over the years there were *First Tuesday, Monitor, Chronolog, Weekend, NBC Magazine, Prime Time Saturday, Prime Time Sunday*, and *First Camera*, all failing. ABC failed with *Seven Days* but scored with *20/20* and *PrimeTime Live*. Nonnetwork programs included *Entertainment Tonight, Real People, Hour Magazine, That's Incredible!* and others, plus the tabloid formats mentioned earlier.[101]

PrimeTime Live of ABC News won an Investigative Reporters and Editors award in 1991 for "The Second Battlefield," an undercover investigation reported by Diane Sawyer. The program showed neglect of patients and the incompetence of doctors at a Veterans Administration hospital in Cleveland, Ohio. The program documented the mistreatment of a paralyzed veteran who went three days without food, triggering an investigation ordered by the secretary of veterans affairs.[102]

At NBC, an investigation on *NBC Nightly News with Tom Brokaw* into the lack of standards for mammograms led to an introduction into Congress of a mammogram standards bill. Correspondent Michelle Gillen in a three-part series had uncovered widespread abuse in mammography.[103]

Channels Magazine in 1990 cited NBC's investigative team of Brian Ross and producer Ira Silverman for their work together over fourteen years as they "made life miserable for the bad guys." Their work ranged from exposing a payola scam in the record industry to focusing on the international drug scene.[104]

Network television programs winning Investigative Reporters and Editors awards for 1993 included *Frontline*/WGBH, Boston, for a report on the risks of agricultural pesticides; *5th Estate*, Canadian Broadcasting Corporation, Toronto, for a report on women athletes and sexual harassment; and ABC News' *Day One*, which explored mismanagement and extravagance in charity functions.[105]

Television, despite all its fluff, has demonstrated that there are various levels and outlets for reform-minded journalism.

Media as Political Organs

A HANDY MEDIUM TO CONTROL

Politicians discovered the usefulness of television early. As far back as 1928, in the experimental stages of the medium, General Electric station WYG in Schenectady,

New York, televised New York Governor Alfred Smith's acceptance speech for the Democratic presidential nomination. The Republican convention of 1940 that nominated Wendell Wilkie in Philadelphia was televised on a limited experimental scale. By 1948 politicians had some appreciation for television. Both Republicans and Democrats met in Philadelphia that year. "Why?" ask Hilliard and Keith. "Because Philadelphia was on the coaxial cable linking New York to Washington, D.C., and was also connected by microwave relay to Baltimore. This constituted the largest network audience then available."[106] While both President Harry Truman and Republican challenger Thomas Dewey used television to their advantage, Truman seemed the more savvy. His whistle-stop trek across the country speaking from the back of a train seemed ready-made for the television cameras as he came into their geographical ranges. As it had for advertisers, television had become a practical tool for delivering the messages of the participants in the process of government.

In 1952 Dwight Eisenhower tested the possibilities of televised political commercials. He staged a "town meeting" by recording a series of precisely worded "answers" following cue cards. Then his aides at another time brought in a group of average citizens to ask questions before a camera. Then the prerecorded questions and corresponding answers were matched.[107] Forty television commercials in a series, called "Eisenhower Answers America," followed. The hackneyed ads with Eisenhower talking in almost robotic fashion did not hurt his campaign. Rival candidate Democrat Adlai Stevenson compared the new television approach of packaging a candidate to selling soap and would have little to do with it, declining even to appear in his own television commercials. Eisenhower won, but then again the hero of World War II was so popular he would likely have won without the television spots. Nevertheless the television commercial became a must of campaigns. Today the larger share of a campaign's funding goes into television. And why not? In the 1990s, 92.1 million households own at least one television set—that's 98 percent of U.S. households.[108]

Nixon's "Checkers Speech"

In the 1952 campaign, when General Eisenhower set the tone of mediocrity and artificiality, his running mate, Richard Nixon, tapped the reservoirs of melodrama. While Eisenhower discovered the gimmicks of the short take through questions and answers and all but gave the coup de grâce to the traditional political speech on television, Nixon, beset by charges concerning his handling of campaign financing, used a speech, or rather a fireside chat, to deliver "perhaps the most effective piece of political advertising of our times." It was the "Checkers" speech, named after the Nixon family's dog. Some 9 million sets were turned on—representing half the television households in the country—as Nixon emotionally explained his finances in a theater converted to an NBC studio in Los Angeles, September 23, 1952. Nixon had been besieged by critics after a September 18 front-page story in the pro-Stevenson *New York Post* under the headline "Secret Nixon Fund," with the jump

Television's Greatest Ads

What are the fifty best television ads in the past fifty years? Editors of *Advertising Age,* in a special issue on "50 Years of TV Advertising" in 1995, gave their selections, which are summarized here.

1940s

Gillette. Carton animation, with a jingle, "Look sharp, feel sharp."

Lucky Strike. Dancing cigarettes which end up in a pack with the slogan, L.S.M.F.T.—"Lucky Strike Means Fine Tobacco."

Texaco. A group of men singing, "Men from Texaco . . . who work from Maine to Mexico."

1950s

Alka-Seltzer. A talking, moving tablet.

Anacin. Diagram of a tension headache and relief.

Chevrolet. Dinah Shore singing "See the USA in your Chevrolet."

Timex. Newscaster John Cameron Swayze reports on a watch on a cliff diver as they face arduous waves and smashing against rocks.

1960s

Maxwell House. Percolating coffee with the slogan, "Good to the Last Drop."

Lyndon Johnson. A girl in a presidential campaign ad shown picking a daisy as a countdown for the release of an atom bomb proceeds. (See pages 430–431.)

Marlboro. Cowboys and music from the movie "Magnificent Seven."

Noxzema. A shaving cream ad with Miss Sweden saying "Take it off, take it all off."

Cracker Jack. Actor Jack Gilford intercepts a box of Cracker Jack being passed across the aisle of a train.

Hertz. People coming from the air into a moving convertible as "Hertz puts you in the driver's seat."

Benson & Hedges. Disadvantages of 100-millimeter cigarettes which pop balloons and get stuck in elevator doors.

Alka-Seltzer. Man saying, "Mama Mia, atsa some spicy meatball," and finding relief.

1970s

Budweiser. A beerwagon team of horses strutting.

Volkswagen. A man who drives an economical Volkswagen is favored in the will of a rich uncle.

Coca-Cola. An international group of young people on a hill singing, "I'd Like to Buy the World a Coke."

Lite Beer from Miller. Ex-athletes agreeing, "Everything you ever wanted in a beer—and less."

Xerox. A monk producing copies with a miracle machine.

Life Cereal. Two brothers get a younger brother to sample Life. "Hey, Mikey."

American Express. "Do you know me?"—forgotten celebrities using the card.

American Express. Actor Karl Malden intoning, "Don't leave home without it."

McDonald's. Singing workers, "You deserve a break today."

Dannon. People who live longer eat yogurt.

Southern Airways. Coach class vs. first class illustrated by a crowded transport vs. a Roman orgy.

7Up. Demeaning Coca-Cola and Pepsi's contents, the "uncola nut" is introduced.

Sunsweet. Man disgusted by the appearance of prunes finds them to his liking.

Polaroid. James Garner and Mariette Hartley are affable as they demonstrate the camera.

Chanel. A woman sunning finds a handsome man who has surfaced from the pool at her feet. "Chanel . . . share the fantasy."

1980s

Bartles & Jaymes. Monotonous, ordinary folk on a porch introduce a wine cooler.

Chrysler. CEO Lee Iacocca insisting, "If you can find a better car, buy it."

Wendy's. "Where's the beef?" oldtimer Clara wanted to know, eyeing an inadequate sandwich.

Eastman Kodak. Snapshots of a girl's life up to her wedding.

Eveready. An Energizer bunny powered by batteries is "still going."

Federal Express. A fast talker speaks up for the package deliverer.

Ronald Reagan. Patriotic scenes with the theme, "It's Morning Again in America."

Coca-Cola. Football player Mean Joe Green drinks his Coca-Cola and tosses his jersey to an admiring youngster.

AT&T. A phone call to a mother by a son makes her cry.

Isuzu. An exaggerating car salesman, with correct information also provided.

Nike. Musician Bo Diddley and gridiron hero Bo Jackson strumming guitars, insisting, "Bo knows."

Cheer. A soiled handkerchief is put in a cocktail shaker with water, ice and Cheer and comes out clean.

Apple Macintosh. In this takeoff on Orwell's *1984*, the competitor is the tyrant and enslaver Big Brother.

Pepsi-Cola. Michael Jackson introduces "the choice of a new generation."

Calvin Klein. Brooke Shields models jeans.

California Raisins. Claymation dancing raisins in sunglasses.

1990s

Bud Light. A man talking his way into someone's limousine but making sure it is stocked with the appropriate beer.

Hallmark. A 100-year-old with a card on her birthday.

Levi's for Women. Painted-glass animation features women users of jeans.

Coca-Cola. Computer-animated polar bears with the message "Always."

Source: "The 50 Best: There's no standard in weighing TV commercials, but some really do stand out as pure gold," with introduction by Adrienne Ward Fawcett, *Advertising Age*, Special Collectors Edition—50 Years of TV Advertising, Spring 1995, pp. 36–39.

line "Secret Rich Men's Trust Fund Keeps Nixon in Style Far Beyond His Salary."[109] Other papers joined in with the story, and editorially some called for his resignation from the Republican ticket. Eisenhower, indecisive, tried to appear supportive. Nixon knew he would not only have to go on television but would also have to overwhelm listeners with the show of a lifetime.

Following Eisenhower's advice, Nixon decided to give a full accounting of his finances. Nixon divided his speech into four sections: first, personal background; second, an attack on the Democratic ticket's Stevenson; third, praise for Eisenhower; fourth, a request for letters of support (some 1 million letters and wires of support came in).

In his speech Nixon never gave the names of those who created the secret fund or how the money was spent. (In fact Stevenson had revealed two years earlier that he had his own secret fund but never fully disclosed the sources.) Yet Nixon insisted he was baring his soul. He told what he owed on a house; he owed his parents $3,500 and paid interest on it; he had only $4,000 in life insurance; his wife, Pat, did not have a mink coat. "But she does have a respectable Republican cloth coat. And I always tell her that she'd look good in anything."[110]

Then came Checkers, the cocker spaniel. Nixon, rubbing his face, looking pained, said:

> One other thing I probably should tell you, because if I don't they will probably be saying this about me, too. We did get something, a gift, after the nomination. A man down in Texas heard Pat on the radio mention the fact that our two young-sters would like to have a dog, and believe it or not, the day before we left on this campaign trip we got a message from Union Station in Baltimore, saying they had a package for us. We went down to get it. You know what it was? It was a little cocker spaniel dog, in a crate that he had sent all the way from Texas—black and white, spotted, and our little girl Tricia, the six-year-old, named it Checkers. And you know, the kids, like all kids, loved the dog, and I just want to say this right now, that regardless of what they say about it, we are going to keep it.[111]

Eisenhower, comparing Nixon to a brave soldier because of his performance, kept the dauntless warrior on the ticket, and the Republicans won by a landslide in November 1952.

The "Daisy Ad"

Perhaps the second most famous—and effective—political television commercial was the one aired in 1964 that has become known as the "daisy ad." President Lyndon Johnson, who had succeeded the assassinated John Kennedy a year before, was running for his first full term against the Republican challenger, conservative Senator Barry Goldwater of Arizona. A certain fear of the Soviets and communists in general still held sway in the country, but the dominating fear was the possibility of nuclear war, which could be caused by one trigger-happy finger. America would in-deed need a responsible man in the White House. Liberals and moderates were in fear of putting a conservative—and Goldwater in many people's minds was re-garded as a right-winger—in the White House.

Using a New York recording specialist, Tony Schwartz, the Johnson team came up with an ad built around a countdown. At first they thought of using a count-down in English, then in Russian. Then Schwartz had the "perfect" idea. "You have a little child pulling the petals off a daisy. The camera goes in on the center of the daisy, and that becomes the explosion when it denotates." And that's what they did in the commercial, officially tagged "Peace, Little Girl."

A camera zooms in on a little girl picking petals off a daisy. The little girl is counting: "One, two, three, four, five, seven, six, six, eight, nine, nine—." Then the girl looks up, startled. The camera freezes on the girl, then moves in closeup to her eye until the screen is black. A man's voice, loud as if over a loudspeaker at a test site, comes: "Ten, nine, eight, seven, six, five, four, three, two, one. . . ." An atom bomb is shown and is heard exploding. Then the voice of President Johnson is heard: "These are the stakes—to make a world in which all of God's children can live, or to go into the dark. We must either love each other, or we must die." Then the announcer: "Vote for President Johnson on November 3. The stakes are too high for you to stay home."[112] With a vote almost double that of Goldwater's, 43.1 million to 27.2 million, Johnson won by 486 electoral votes to 52 for Goldwater.

The Impact of Willie Horton

The genre of negative political television commercials, depending on innuendos and half-truths or pure fiction, was perhaps perfected by candidate George Bush when he opposed Michael Dukakis in 1988. Bush seized on the information that an African American named William (Willie) Horton, Jr., a convicted murderer out of prison on a weekend pass in a Massachusetts prisoner furlough program, had raped a woman. Dukakis acted speedily and banned any other convicted murderers from furloughs. Bush decided to make the event cast Dukakis as soft on crime. A Bush commercial followed that showed prisoners leaving jail through a revolving door. A narrator said: "[Dukakis's] revolving-door prison policy gave weekend furloughs to first-degree murderers not eligible for parole. While out, many committed other crimes like kidnapping and rape and many are still at large. Now Michael Dukakis says he wants to do for America what he has done for Massachusetts. Americans can't afford that risk."[113]

A *Washington Post* article by campaign advertising researcher Kathleen Jamieson, of the University of Pennsylvania, concluded, "Never before in a presidential campaign have televised ads sponsored by a major party candidate lied so blatantly as in the campaign of '88." She said the Horton ad invited "the inference—false—that 268 first-degree murderers were furloughed by Dukakis to rape and kidnap. In fact, only one first-degree murderer, Willie Horton, escaped furlough in Massachusetts and committed a violent crime—although others have done so under other furlough programs, including those run by the federal government and by California under the stewardship of Ronald Reagan."[114]

The television political commercial leans to storytelling, if not tattling. A point must be made by invoking an image. Yet "the increasing use of anecdotal support undermines political argument," say Susan Hellweg, Michael Pfau, and Steven Brydon. "Television devalues content in campaign discourse, instead stressing candidate image, a by-product of the importance of the visual emphasis in television communication."[115]

In nearly all phases of television from presenting news to selecting values to participating in the political process, the anecdote becomes the message.

QUESTIONS FOR DISCUSSION AND RESEARCH

1. What are the roots of the origin of television?
2. Why, once the technology was on the horizon, did it take so long for television to become a common household shrine?

3. Have someone watch an evening local television news show and list the subjects and events shown. Then mix up the order on the list. Can you guess the real order in which they actually appeared? You might be surprised. How do you explain the order of importance of subjects and events as they appeared?

4. Write a definition of news and news priority for a newspaper; then do the same for a local television station. Put the definitions side by side. Are there differences? Explain.

5. George Kennan, in his book *Around the Cragged Hill,* suggests, particularly for the homebound, television is "antisocial." For Mark Levy it offers "the raw materials of sociability." In the pursuit of social and society-integrating values, should television be shunned or courted? Explain.

6. What effect do print media now have on television news and vice versa? Where does the cycle end?

7. What is meant by "cheap news"?

8. Compare the formulas for sensationalism as practiced by newspapers, magazines, radio, television, and movies.

9. Some believe television programming is like a religion—its script having the qualities of a sacred text, its repeated emphases the effect of ritual. Can you give examples from programs you watch of the "religiosity" of television?

10. Concerning television values, construct a ten-point code of commandments about what television considers of value. Rank them in order of importance as television managers are likely to regard them.

11. Do television and other media have to report everything controversial a senator or other significant member of government utters, as the media did with Senator McCarthy? How would McCarthy be treated if he made his charges today? What examples of "McCarthyism" can you find on television news and news-magazine programs today?

12. The FCC has not been very effective in regulating television content and in the Reagan years relegated most of its clout to others, such as media organizations. Is this "freedom" working? Explain.

13. How has the investigative documentary survived on television?

14. Research the fixed quiz/game show scandals of the 1950s. Why were these scandals in which answers were fed to favored contestants possible?

15. What latter-day advertising would you add to a list of all-time classics? Why?

ENDNOTES

1. *Chicago Daily News*, Nov. 6, 1930.
2. Marilynn Preston, "Marcella Lally Duke: Television's 'First Star'—But Few Remember," *Chicago Tribune*, Sept. 22, 1981, Section 2.
3. Letter to author, Aug. 5, 1983.
4. Letter from William J. and Jennie V. Bragg, founders, Texas Broadcast Museum, Sept. 28, 1982, to Marcella Lally Duke, a copy provided by Sills.

5. *Chicago Daily News.*

6. Irving Settel and William Laas, *A Pictorial History of Television* (New York: Grosset & Dunlap, 1969), p. 37.

7. J. Fred MacDonald, *One Nation Under Television: The Rise and Decline of Network TV* (New York: Pantheon Books, 1990), p. 35.

8. Erik Barnouw, *Tube of Plenty: The Evolution of American Television*, 2nd ed. (New York: Oxford University Press, 1990), p. 99.

9. Lawrence Lessing, *Man of High Fidelity: Edwin Howard Armstrong* (Philadelphia: Lippincott, 1956), p. 299.

10. W. Rupert Maclaurin, *Invention and Innovation in the Radio Industry* (New York: Macmillan, 1949; reprint, New York: Arno Press and *New York Times*, 1971), p. 192.

11. Christopher H. Sterling and John M. Kittross, *Stay Tuned: A Concise History of American Broadcasting* (Belmont, Calif: Wadsworth, 1978), p. 501.

12. Maclaurin, *Invention and Innovation*, p. 192.

13. Sterling and Kittross, *Stay Tuned*, p. 100.

14. John Barrat, "Once Only a Flicker: TV's 60 Years of Programming," *Media History Digest*, vol. 8, no. 2, Fall–Winter 1988, p. 49.

15. Ibid.

16. Maclaurin, *Invention and Innovation*, p. 194.

17. Elma G. "Pem" Farnsworth, *Distant Vision: Romance and Discovery on an Invisible Frontier* (Salt Lake City: PemberlyKent, 1990), p. 23.

18. Ibid., prologue.

19. Ibid., p. 23.

20. Thomas Ropp, "Philo Farnsworth: Forgotten Father of Television," *Media History Digest*, vol. 5, no. 3, Summer 1985, p. 43.

21. Farnsworth, *Distant Vision*, p. 91.

22. Ibid., p. 130.

23. Ropp, "Philo Farnsworth," p. 49.

24. Ibid.

25. Ibid.

26. Note from Mrs. Farnsworth to author.

27. Farnsworth, *Distant Vision*, p. 145.

28. Ropp, "Philo Farnsworth," p. 57.

29. Ibid., p. 58.

30. Mary Alice Mayer Phillips, *CATV: A History of Community Antenna Television* (Evanston, Ill.: Northwestern University Press, 1972), p. 4.

31. Edward Bliss, Jr., *Now the News: The Story of Broadcast Journalism* (New York: Columbia University Press, 1991), p. 434.

32. Patrick R. Parsons, "Two Tales of a City: John Walson, Sr., Mahanoy City and the 'Founding' of Cable TV," a paper presented to the History Division, Association for Education in Journalism and Mass Communication, meeting in Atlanta, Aug. 10–13, 1994.

33. Barnouw, *Tube of Plenty*, p. 169.

34. Ibid.

35. Tom Bethel, analysis summary of study by the Media Institute, *Television Evening News Covers Inflation, 1978–79* (Washington, D.C.: Media Institute, August 1980).

36. Barnouw, *Tube of Plenty*, p. 170.

37. Joanmarie Kalter, "They're Working Harder, and Enjoying It Less: Foreign Correspondent Burnout," reprinted from the May 9, 1987, issue of *TV Guide*, Triangle Publications, Inc., 1987.

38. Ibid., p. 4H.

39. Mark R. Levy, "The Audience Experience with Television News," *Journalism Monographs*, no. 55, April 1978, pp. 24, 25.

40. Sander Vanocur column, The Washington Post Company, Jan. 7, 1976.

41. Penn Kimball, *Downsizing the News: Network Cutbacks in the Nation's Capital* (Washington, D.C.: Woodrow Wilson Center Press, and Baltimore: Johns Hopkins University Press, 1994), p. 165.

42. Ibid., p. 167.

43. Jon Krampner, "Case of the Fourth Network: Rise and Fall of DuMont Television," *Media History Digest*, vol. 10, no. 2, Fall/Winter, 1990, p. 35.

44. Larry Reibstein and Nancy Hass, "Rupert's Power Play," *Newsweek*, June 6, 1994, p. 46.

45. Ibid., p. 48.

46. Marian Calabro, *Zap!: A Brief History of Television* (New York: Four Winds Press, 1992), p. 97.

47. Bill Carter, "Networks' Simpson Vigil: A Low-Cost Reply to CNN," *New York Times*, July 11, 1994, p. D1.

48. Elizabeth Kolbert, "As Ratings Languish, CNN Faces Identity Crisis," *New York Times*, Aug. 22, 1994, p. D1.

49. Glenn Rifkin, "A News Niche Grows in New England," *New York Times*, p. D11.

50. Kolbert, "As Ratings Languish."

51. Harry F. Waters, et al. "Trash TV," *Newsweek*, Nov. 14, 1988, p. 72.

52. Ibid.

53. Tanya Barrientos, "TV's Talk-Fests," *Philadelphia Inquirer*, April 24, 1994, p. H8.

54. *Newsweek*, sidebar, "The Odd Couple of Sensationalism: Maury Povich and Morton Downey," Nov. 14, 1988, p. 74.

55. Barrientos, "TV's Talk-Fests."

56. Ibid.

57. Diane Huie Balay, "Are Talk Shows Closed to Christian Values?" *National Christian Reporter*, Oct. 15, 1993, p. 1.

58. Wayne Munson, *The Talkshow in Media Culture* (Philadelphia: Temple University Press, 1993).

59. Catherine L. Finn, "*A (Current) Affair to Remember: Tabloid Television News and Its Impact on Network News Organization*," a paper presented to the Radio-Television Journalism Division, Association for Education in Journalism and Mass Communication, meeting in Kansas City, Aug. 14, 1993.

60. Ibid.

61. Bill Carter, "G.M. Suspends Ads on NBC News Despite Apology for Truck Report," *New York Times*, Feb. 11, 1993, p. 1.

62. Ibid.

63. Joseph R. Dominick, Alan Wurtzel, and Guy Lometti, "Television Journalism vs. Show Business: A Content Analysis of Eyewitness News," *Journalism Quarterly*, vol. 52, no. 2, Summer 1975, pp. 216, 217. Quote is from James Brady, "Look Out Walter," *New York Magazine*, Oct. 15, 1973, p. 85.

64. Marc Gunther, *The House That Roone Built: The Inside Story of ABC News* (Boston: Little, Brown, 1994).

65. "Sex and Suffering in the Afternoon," *Time*, Jan. 12, 1976, pp. 46, 47.

66. Newton N. Minow, *How Vast the Wasteland Now?* address at the Gannett Foundation Media Center, Columbia University, New York, May 9, 1991 (New York: Gannett Foundation Media Center, 1991), p. 24.

67. Ibid., pp. 11, 12.

68. Ibid., p. 12.

69. Joanne Cantor, "Confronting Children's Fright Responses to Mass Media," in Dolf Zillman, Bryant Jennings, and Aletha C. Huston, *Media, Children, and the Family*. (Hillsdale, N.J.: Lawrence Erlbaum, 1994), p. 146.

70. Minow, *How Vast the Wasteland Now*, p. 12.

71. John J. O'Connor, "Insidious Elements in Television Cartoons," *New York Times*, Feb. 20, 1990.

72. Ian I. Mitroff and Warren Bennis, *The Unreality Industry: The Deliberate Manufacturing of Falsehood and What It Is Doing to Our Lives* (New York: Oxford University Press, 1989, 1993), p. 15.

73. John P. Ferre, *Channels of Belief: Religion and American Commercial Television* (Ames: Iowa State University, 1990), p. 15.

74. Ibid., p. 26.

75. Jeff Merron, "Murrow on TV: *See It Now, Person to Person*, and the Making of a 'Masscult Personality," *Journalism Monographs*, no. 106, July 1988, p. 4.

76. Robert L. Hilliard and Michael C. Keith, *The Broadcast Century: A Biography of American Broadcasting* (Boston: Focal Press, 1992), p. 125.

77. Merron, "Murrow on TV," p. 6.

78. Alexander Kendrick, *Prime Time: The Life of Edward R. Murrow* (Boston: Little, Brown, 1969), p. 37.

79. A. M. Sperber, *Murrow: His Life and Times* (New York: Freundlich Books, 1986), pp. 416, 417.

80. Kendrick, *Prime Time*, p. 38.

81. Sperber, *Murrow*, pp. 438, 439.

82. William B. Ray, *FCC: The Ups and Downs of Radio-TV Regulation* (Ames: Iowa State University Press, 1990), p. 162.

83. Ibid., pp. 162, 163.

84. Ibid., pp. 163, 164.

85. MacDonald, *One Nation Under Television*, pp. 107, 108.

86. Elizabeth Kolbert, "What's a Network TV Censor to Do?" *New York Times*, May 23, 1993, p. H17.

87. Ron Nesson, "Should TV News Always Tell All?" *TV Guide*, reprint from June 27, 1981, issue, Triangle Publications, Inc.

88. Daniel Riffe, Patricia C. Place, and Charles M. Mayo, "Game Time, Soap Time and Prime Time TV Ads: Treatment of Women in Sunday Football and Rest-of-Week Advertising," *Journalism Quarterly*, vol. 70, no. 2, Summer 1993, p. 437.

89. Jack G. Shaheen, "The Arab Stereotype on Television," *The Link*, published by Americans for Middle East Understanding, New York, April–May 1980, p. 1.

90. Sterling and Kittross, *Stay Tuned*, p. 425.

91. Hiley H. Ward, "Everett Parker: Irascible, Frenetic Champion of the Voiceless," *A.D.*, vol. 12, no. 4, April 1983, p. 23.

92. Conrad Lodziak, *The Power of Television: A Critical Appraisal* (London: Frances Pinter, 1986), p. 32.

93. Michael Curtin, *Redeeming the Wasteland: Television Documentary and Cold War Politics* (New Brunswick, N.J.: Rutgers University Press, 1995).

94. Don Hewitt, *Minute by Minute* (New York: Random House, 1985), p. 27.

95. Ibid., p. 27.

96. Bob Woodward, "Mike Wallace: Grand Inquisitor of *60 Minutes*," *TV Guide*, Nov. 6, 1993, p. 16.

97. Axel Madsen, *60 Minutes: The Power & the Politics of America's Most Popular TV News Show* (New York: Dodd, Mead, 1984), p. 145.

98. Frank Coffey, *60 Minutes: 25 Years of Television's Finest Hour* (Los Angeles: General Publishing Group, 1993), p. 166.

99. Mike Wallace and Gary Paul Gates, *Close Encounters* (New York: William Morrow, 1984), p. 19.

100. Ibid., p. 79.

101. Coffey, *60 Minutes*, p. 193.

102. ABC news release, "ABC News' 'PrimeTime' Live Has Won . . . ," April 1, 1991, Museum of Television & Radio, New York.

103. NBC release, "Report on NBC Nightly News . . . ," Oct. 23, 1990, Museum of Television & Radio.

104. NBC news release, "NBC News' Investigative Team . . . ," Oct. 23, 1990.

105. "IRE Award Winners," *IRE Journal*, vol. 17, no. 3, May–June, 1994, pp. 9, 10.

106. Hilliard and Keith, *Broadcast Century,* p. 118.

107. Craig Allen, *Eisenhower and the Mass Media: Peace, Prosperity, & Prime-Time TV* (Chapel Hill: University of North Carolina Press, 1993), pp. 130, 131.

108. *The World Almanac and Book of Facts* (New York: World Almanac, 1991), p. 318.

109. Edwin Diamond and Stephen Bates, *The Spot: The Rise of Political Advertising on Television* (Cambridge, Mass.: MIT Press, 1984), p. 67.

110. Kathleen Hall Jamieson, *Packaging the Presidency: A History and Criticism of Presidential Campaign Advertising*, 2nd ed. (New York: Oxford University Press, 1984, 1985), pp. 73–75.

111. Diamond and Bates, *The Spot*, p. 72.

112. Ibid., pp. 128, 129.

113. Robert J. Donovan and Ray Scherer, *Unsilent Revolution: Television News and American Public Life* (Cambridge: University of Cambridge Press, 1992), p. 247.

114. Kathleen Hall Jamieson, *Washington Post*, Oct. 30, 1988, p. C1, quoted in Donovan and Scherer, *Unsilent Revolution*, p. 247.

115. Susan A. Hellweg, Michael Pfau, and Steven R. Brydon, *Televised Presidential Debates: Advocacy in Contemporary America* (New York: Praeger, 1992), p. 79.

13

Media and Twentieth-Century Wars and Protest Movements

Although wars and movements to achieve equal rights for all in the United States dominated much of American news in the twentieth century, the media covered them as separate entities. But civil rights leader Martin Luther King, Jr., began to link the two agendas in the last days before his assassination in 1968. The media showed some difficulty in seeing a war waged against an ideology in a peasant nation, on the one hand, and domestic discrimination, on the other, as part of a larger concern. How did the media cover the wars and the rights movements?

DR. KING LINKS VIETNAM WAR AND LACK OF RIGHTS

King dramatically made the rhetorical connection, as he was apt to do in his later days, between war and discrimination in a speech at Grosse Pointe High School in an upscale Detroit suburb in March 1968. After being heckled outside the building, King was introduced by the Episcopal bishop of Michigan, a Grosse Pointer himself, who said he admired King but had questions for him concerning the value of large demonstrations in Washington that paralyzed the city, and concerning King's opposition to the war in Vietnam.

As King began his speech, hecklers rose to holler "traitor" and other epithets. One man, who was dressed in civilian clothes but identified himself as a naval technician, was invited forward by King. Police had the young man remove his coat before he took the podium, where he shouted out his views. After King had returned to the podium, a muffled smoke bomb set off in a rest room caused a further interruption.

King said he wanted the troops back from Vietnam, too. He declared, "The unjust war is tearing up the whole world." Then he proceeded to answer the bishop, the Right Reverend Richard S. Emrich. "I appreciate Bishop Emrich's questions, but the two issues cannot be divided. It is absurd for me to work for integrating schools and not be concerned with a world to integrate. I cannot segregate my moral conscience. The war in Vietnam hurts civil rights more than my stand against the war. There is a time when we must take a position that is not safe or politic or popular."[1]

The ever-solemn King had become the representative voice that linked protests for personal rights in U.S. communities with the ongoing protests of peace activists who sought to end the Vietnam War. By most analyses in the media, King had overextended his concern when he took on the peace quest. Editorialists said he would dilute the civil rights struggle and divert its supporters as he dealt with both the war and discrimination.

The civil rights combatant had joined the ranks of dissidents for peace in a historic speech nearly a year earlier, on April 4, 1967, at Riverside Church near the Columbia University campus in New York. Here King spoke against the war in no uncertain terms. He felt betrayed by President Lyndon Johnson, who was reneging on his commitment to civil rights as he diverted funds to finance the costly war. King knew also that U.S. casualties in Vietnam were disproportionately higher for blacks than whites. And King, an admirer of India's pacifist leader Mohandas Gandhi, was committed intrinsically to the path of peace. King wanted an end to all bombing, a unilateral cease-fire, an agreement that the rebel National Liberation Front would have a role in governing Vietnam in the future, and a date set for withdrawal of all foreign troops.[2]

Assailed by the Press

Opposition to that Riverside Church speech eleven months before the Groose Pointe speech was swift and sweeping. The *New York Times* moaned three days later that the recent speeches and statements of King were aimed at the "fusing of two public problems that are distinct and separate. By driving them together Dr. King has done a disservice to both. The moral issues in Vietnam are less clear-cut than he suggests; the political strategy of uniting the peace movement and the civil-rights movement could very well be disastrous for both causes."[3]

Life magazine, accusing King of overstepping his bounds, tagged the speech "a demogogic slander," as King used his prestige in civil rights to address the war issue.[4] Whitney Young, Jr., director of the National Urban League, and Ralph Bunche, United Nations undersecretary and a director of the National Association for the Advancement of Colored People (NAACP), regarded King as misdirected insofar as King linked the civil rights and peace movements, mixing what these leaders called separate goals.[5]

Although criticism of the war was mounting in 1968, the news magazines—*Newsweek, Time, U.S. News & World Report*—chose to ignore King's views of the war as much as possible. *Time* and *Newsweek* "dismissed crisply" King's outspokenness

Dr. King and Malcolm X meet at the Capitol during a Civil Rights bill debate. (UPI/Urban Archives, Temple University, Philadelphia, Pa.)

on the war, noted Richard Lentz, while *U.S. News & World Report* "ignored King's role in the peace movement."[6] The reasons for the blackout, Lentz suggests, were that "King's words had been most intemperate" and that "King had shared the anti-war cause with black militants, an embarrassment when the magazines were attempting to put as much distance as possible between King and the leading Black Power militant, Stokely Carmichael, of the Student Nonviolent Coordinating Committee (SNCC)."[7] Isolated now even more from the mainstream, King held to his belief that an ideological war and domestic rights abuse had systemic roots.

Freedom and Rights Issues Persist

At the threshold of the century in 1905, President Theodore Roosevelt mediated a peace treaty ending the Russo-Japanese War that saw Japan emerge as a world power. However, concern for the rights of the Manchurians and Chinese was occasioned by Japan's seizure of Manchuria in 1931 and invasion of China in 1937.

World War I erupted on June 28, 1914, amid ethnic tension and conflict, when a young Serbian terrorist, disturbed at the annexation of Herzegovina by Austria, assassinated Archduke Francis Ferdinand, heir to the Austro-Hungarian throne. As the war spread and eventually involved the United States, there was a curbing of the rights of those perceived as favorable to the enemy, German communities and their newspapers and the anti-British, such as the Irish, and their newspapers. World War II, with U.S. involvement in 1941, brought the separation of Japanese-Americans into interment camps, as the media—from films to radio and newspapers—reveled in giving distorted pictures of the enemy.

"It is noteworthy that at at least two points assaults on African-American media paralleled attacks on radical media," says John Nerone, of the University of Illinois. He cites the post–World War I era, when racial violence existed along with the Red scare, and the 1960s, when racial violence was seen as coexisting with "the legal harassment of and extralegal violence against the radical press." It was the same way in the World War II era, he says, when the African-American press "encountered significant official hostility and public suspicion on grounds of disloyalty, much like a range of radical publications."[8]

In all of this, the issue of civil rights for blacks was never far away, for ethnic "outsider" groups were linked in the public mind with radical ideologies.

Media as Definers and Keepers of Values (and Biases)

ELITE GROUPS COMPEL CONFORMITY

When a nation participates in and supports a war, dissent from that national commitment is held accountable to a value system that puts a high priority on absolute conformity. Pacifists, war resistors, and confirmed isolationists, such as progressive Robert M. La Follette and media chief William Randolph Hearst, have often faced public censure. But the primacy in the hierarchy of values exalted not only conformity but also membership in an elite group circumscribed by the austere, no-nonsense tradition of English piety characterized by English Protestantism transmitted by Colonial Puritans (and alive in a host of Protestant denominations) and by eighteenth- and nineteenth-century frontier revivalism inspired by English Methodism.

In World War I, not only those of German origin were suspect and ostracized, but also those who dared to be anti-English. Hearst faced the wrath of the populace and other media over his distaste for the British or anything English. His base of power with his newspaper kingdom protected him from serious punishment. Such was not the case for ethnic minorities who happened to be also anti-English.

The (Bad) Luck of the Irish

Such was the plight of the Irish, who in addition to expressing open hostility to the English—a prime ally of America in the war—dared to preserve their culture and Roman Catholic faith and to cheer for liberation of their homeland. They perceived themselves as Irish-Americans—citizens of a hyphenated variety, much as blacks at a later date cherished a double identity, as African Americans. "Dual loyalty was suspect," says Michael P. Mulcrone. "Hyphenism—other than the Anglo-Saxon variety—was condemned."[9] Unlike mainstream newspapers, Irish-American papers retained a militancy and advocacy in their views. "Irish papers gave voice to immigrant concerns that were ignored by the mainstream press and offered alternative and oppositional interpretations of the news,"[10] says Mulcrone. "Anglophobia" became a dominant message of the Irish-American press.

The entry of the United States into the war on the side of England came coincidentally at the time of peak agitation by the Irish for freedom from Britain in the homeland. Irish freedom demonstrators were attacked by thugs in the streets of New York and Boston. Some Irish organizations and newspapers were intimidated; others continued their cry loud and clear. "The mainstream press, for its part," says Mulcrone, "condemned Irish nationalism as an aberrant, alien force which threatened America's close ties with Great Britain and undermined the American war effort."[11] The mood of contempt for Irish-Americans in the media and at large was helped along by President Woodrow Wilson, who on occasions expressed his displeasure with the Irish. Wilson gave an "antihyphen" speech in 1914 at the unveiling of a monument, and his arguments with Irish activist Jeremiah O'Leary tended to tag the Irish as disloyal.

Mulcrone lays the blame for hostile attitudes toward Irish-Americans in part on successful British propaganda: "Britain maintained a powerful public relations machine in the U.S. The pro-British posture of the mainstream press ensured that British efforts to shape public opinion fell upon fertile ground." Yet more important was the role of the major dailies in the United States. Says Mulcrone: "The most decisive factor in creating a climate which led to the suppression of the Irish-American press was the willingness of large sectors of the mainstream press to give credence to unsubstantiated rumors of German/Irish plots and to equate Irish nationalist aspirations with disloyalty to America." Even the Hearst newspapers, which had no love for the English, took part.[12]

Press Boosts Vigilantism

Some major media apparently embraced vigilantism in their persecution of antiwar "hyphenated Americans, citizens linked to a foreign ancestry or ethnic group." The *New York Times* crusaded editorially for tougher laws to permit summary execution of "unpunished spies." "Although the authorities at Washington have been reticent about spies," said the *Times*, "it is easy to speculate on the reasons why no spy has been shot or hanged in America." It suggested as reasons that the government had yet to catch a spy, the public was not ready for the execution of spies, and capital punishment was illegal unless preceded by a long legal process. "As to the existing laws," continued the *Times*, "there is no doubt they are inadequate. Congress should lose no time in framing legislation to make possible the summary punishment of spies and plotters as a warning that we are determined at last to end the outrages so long perpetrated with impunity by German enemies."[13]

The Lighter Side

Broadcasting Fun Fostered Stereotypes: Abbott and Costello Program

Bud Abbott, the lean, serious one, was the straight man. The other member of the comedy team, chubby Lou Costello, always confused Abbott with his puns and double meanings. Costello could make havoc out of the simplest statement, as he does in the routine "Who's on First," where he uses relative pronouns as the names of players.

Much of their humor was at the expense of "hyphenated" Americans. Here are excerpts from their show that aired on October 29, 1942—during their first year on radio in the midst of World War II. This one is at the expense of Native Americans, who are depicted as primitives, even cannibals.

Abbott and Costello Program for Camel Cigarettes

Music:	*Perfidia intro to:*
Band:	(*Chorus*) C . . . A . . . M . . . E . . L . . . S!
Niles:	CAMELS!—The cigarette that's first in the service presents—(*shout*) *THE ABBOTT AND COSTELLO PROGRAM!*
Music:	*Sweeps up, holds under:*
Niles:	—With the music of Leith Stevens and his orchestra, the songs of Connie Haines and the Camel Five, tonight's guest—Miss Diana Barrymore, and starring—BUD ABBOTT AND LOU COSTELLO.
Music:	*Up to finish*
	(*Applause*)
Costello:	Hey Abbott—HEY ABBOTT!
Abbott:	Costello! Costello, stop that yelling! What's the trouble?
Costello:	LOOK WHAT I GOT, ABBOTT! I just bought a carrier pigeon—I'm going to train him!
Abbott:	You're training a carrier pigeon? WHAT FOR?
Costello:	I want to send a bird to Germany—right in Hitler's face!
Abbott:	Wait a minute, Costello—what's the idea of coming into the studio barefooted!
Costello:	The Government won't let them make shoes any more.
Abbott:	What are you talking about?
Costello:	Didn't the Government say—"EVERYTHING FOR VICTORY AND NOTHING FOR DE-FEET!" . . .
	[Costello reveals plans to put on a play]
Abbott:	Come, come, Costello, tell Diana what the play is all about.
Costello:	Okay—it's the story of Pocahontas and John Smith. Diana, you're Pocahontas and I'm John. As I come walking through the woods, we meet each other—the sun is shining and the birds are singing—
Blanc:	(*As soundman*) Bob-o-link (*Whistles as in opening spot*) Meadow lark (*Whistles*) Bull-finch—

Costello:	QUIET, BOTSFORD! Where was I—oh, yeah—for this part, Diana, you'll have to speak Indian.
Barrymore:	Oh, I speak Indian. I speak several languages—French, Chinese, Turkish, Egyptian—
Costello:	How's your Persian?
Barrymore:	She just had kittens! Ha. Ha. Ha. Isn't that a foul joke?
Costello:	Yeah—and here's the egg to prove it! As I was saying—I meet you in the woods and we fall in love . . . . but your father, the Chief, captures me and tries to cut my head off, but I escape—then he captures me again and tries to chop my head off—
Abbott:	He tries to chop your head off twice?
Costello:	Yeah—it's a double header! Then you come in, Diana, and save me—you throw yourself in my arms and as I stand there with my lips pressed to yours—the curtain comes down!
Barrymore:	Why, Mister Costello—that's wonderful. Why, I'm simply wild about the part!
Costello:	The part where I kiss you?
Barrymore:	No, the part where the curtain comes down!
Abbott:	All right, Costello—get your cast together and let's get on with the play.
Costello:	Okay, Abbott. (*Calls*) EVERYBODY ON STAGE—WE'RE READY TO START THE PLAY . . . and if you all give a good performance, I'll take everybody out for a snort.
Barrymore:	A snort?
Costello:	Yeah—a swallow!!
Blanc:	(*Soundman*) Swallow—(*Whistles*) Blue jay (*Whistles*) magpie (*Whistles*)
Costello:	GET HIM OUTTA HERE! (*Applause*)
Music:	*Intro. for "Keep Smilin'" (Fade)*
Niles:	Here's a swell suggestion from Connie Haines and the Camel Five—she says: "Let's Keep Smilin!" (*Applause*)
Music:	(*Indian music and fade for:*)
Niles:	And now, ladies and gentlemen, this is Ken Niles, about to bring you the treat of the evening—*OUR PLAY*—"JOHN SMITH AND POCAHONTAS," starring DIANA BARRYMORE, BUD ABBOTT, LOU COSTELLO, AND *ME*! Ha ha ha ha. . . . And now to our story—It is a bitter cold winter night—John Smith Costello and Bud Abbott are fighting their way through the forest, searching for food—little knowing that the Indians are on their trail. As they pause to rest, John speaks: CURTAIN!
Costello:	(*Afraid*) Let's not go any further, Abbott—I'm scared! There are a lot of wild beasts in this forest—mountain lions!
Sound:	(*Lion roar*)
Abbott:	Was that a lion?
Costello:	It wasn't somethin' I et! I'M GETTIN' OUTTA HERE! . . .
Abbott:	Listen, we may be close to the Indians. Put your ear to the ground and see what you can hear!

(*Continued*)

Costello:	Okay—oh-oh—oh!
Abbott:	What did you pick up?
Costello:	A gopher, two ants and a worm named Shickelgruber!
Abbott:	What's the matter with you? I thought you were supposed to be a game hunter!
Costello:	I am, Abbott. I'm a *good* hunter. Once I followed a silver fox for three miles!
Abbott:	What happened?
Costello:	I got my face slapped!
Abbott:	I said a *game* hunter!
Costello:	Oh, I thought you said a *dame* hunter!
Abbott:	Shhhh—quiet! There's someone coming through the bushes!
Sound:	*(Rustling in bushes)*
Costello:	Look, Abbott—IT'S A GIRL! AN INDIAN SQUAB!
Barrymore:	Greetings, Palefish!
Costello:	No-no—not fish—FACE!
Barrymore:	Greetings, Fishface! Welcome to the land of Minnie.
Costello:	Ha ha?
Barrymore:	What's so funny?
Costello:	*(Yells)* HOW D'YA LIKE THAT! JUST LIKE A BARRYMORE—WANTS TO STEAL THE PLAY!—Pardon me, folks—I stepped out of character.
Abbott:	Permit us to introduce ourselves. I am Bud Abbott,—
Barrymore:	And I am Pocahontas.
Costello:	And I am John Smith.
Barrymore:	*(Seductively)* John Smith?—I like you—you are nice and plump, John Smith!
Costello:	If you think I'm plump, you should see my sister Kate [singer Kate Smith]!
Abbott:	Tell us, Fair Indian Maiden, are we the first white men you've ever seen?
Barrymore:	No, Wendell Wilkie [presidential candidate] went through here yesterday! . . . I think you had better hide in the woods. If the Indians in my tribe catch palefaces, they roast them alive.
Abbott:	It looks like you're in trouble, Smith. You're a paleface!
Costello:	Well, make me an Indian!
Abbott:	How can *I* make your face red!
Costello:	Tell me a travelling salesman story! . . .
Sound:	*(Whizzing of arrows)* . . .

Source: From the Joe Penner radio-television scripts collection, 1936–1950, Special Collections Department, Temple University.

A news report in the *Times* quoted a congressman urging immediate executions. "When a seditious or traitorous voice is raised here," Congressman Julius Kahn of California, who authored the World War I draft law, told Congress angrily, according to the *Times*, "I hope the hand of the law will reach out and grasp the speaker. I hope that we shall have a few prompt hangings, and the sooner the better. We have got to make an example of a few of these people, and we have got to do it quickly."[14]

Mulcrone suggests that the lynching of pro-Irish Frank Little in August 1917 "was emblematic of the press'[s] willingness to excuse if not sanction mob violence."[15] Little, who stirred up protests against the war and was an organizer for the Industrial Workers of the World, was castrated and hanged from a railroad trestle outside Butte, Montana, by a local mob. Supporting the vigilante action, the *Boston Transcript* noted, "Millions of people who, while sternly reprehending such proceedings as the lynching of members of that antipatriotic society, will nevertheless be glad, in their hearts, that Montana did it in the case of Little."[16] The *Chicago Tribune* said, "The howls of Industrial Workers of the World over the lynching of Little will find no echo in any reasonable heart."[17]

Irish Papers Curbed

Under the postal regulations set in motion in January 1918, six Irish-American papers, as well as magazines, books, and pamphlets that were antiwar, were banned from the mails. Before the end of the year the Irish-American *Freeman's Journal* folded, while another, the *Gaelic-American*, was supported by donations. Yet another, the besieged *Irish World*, gave in and submitted to prepublication censorship of its galley proofs. Virtually every issue of the *Irish World* was censored in this period, Mulcrone says in a later discussion in *Journalism History*.[18] The cult of conformity and consensus, coupled with a pro-English bias against all other hyphenated citizenships, prevailed as dominant values of the World War I era and beyond. Indeed such value ordering continued in society and media expression in later war protest periods. Witness Martin Luther King, Jr.'s joining of his quest for civil rights for blacks with opposition to the Vietnam War against a cacophony of consensus opposition. The biases were prominent intrinsic values.

Media as Voices of Freedom
ESPIONAGE AND SABOTAGE ACTS

The six Irish-American papers banned from the mail as subversive by order of Postmaster General Albert S. Burleson were just a small part of those banned, as restrictions also reined in German-American, socialist, and anarchist publications, even several pacifist journals. Some forty-four publications lost their mailing privileges in the wake of the Espionage Act of 1917, which gave power to the postmaster general to ban from the mails any item he deemed seditious. Another thirty publications challenged by the postmaster general were allowed to continue publication when they consented to publish nothing further about the war.[19]

The Espionage Act was passed on June 15, 1917, to permit the prosecution of isolated individuals who opposed the war or spread dissent and sedition. Already on the books were statutes from the Civil War period that permitted prosecution of conspirators "aiming to resist recruiting and conscription by riots and other forcible means, or seeking by speeches and publications to induce men to evade the draft."[20] But since a person working alone did not fit the definition of conspirator, the government sought legislation that could restrict the rights of personal liberty in a war period.

The act initially designated these three activities as criminal:

(1) Whoever, when the United States is at war, shall willfully make or convey false reports or false statements with intent to interfere with the operation or success of the military or naval forces of the United States or to promote the success of its enemies, (2) and whoever, when the United States is at war, shall willfully cause or attempt to cause insubordination, disloyalty, mutiny, or refusal of duty, in the military or naval forces of the United States, (3) or shall willfully obstruct the recruiting or enlistment service of the United States, to the injury of the service or of the United States, shall be punished by a fine of not more than $10,000 or imprisonment for not more than twenty years, or both.[21]

In May 1918 Congress amended the Espionage Act by adding offenses. Persons could be prosecuted for obstructing the sale of United States bonds; publishing anything causing contempt or scorn of the form of government of the United States or of the Constitution, flag, or military uniform; or promoting the cause of the government's enemies.[22] A provision of the act gave Postmaster General Burleson authority to excise from the mail all publications and other items considered to violate the points of the act.

An additional act was passed on October 6, 1917, the same year as the Espionage Act. The Trading-with-the-Enemy Act set in motion censorship over international and foreign-language media, as it also called for certain economic sanctions against the Germans. While these acts of 1917 solved the Department of Justice's earlier "dilemma" of being unable to stop individuals, they still were not enough for purist superpatriots. The administration wanted stronger powers to rein in the disloyal.

IWW Journal Banned

In the Sabotage Act of April 20, 1918, Congress sought to target the Industrial Workers of the World, a revolutionary labor group founded in 1905 by William (Big Bill) Haywood, secretary of the Western Federation of Miners, assisted by Socialist Eugene Debs and Daniel De Leon. Haywood and the socialists parted in 1908 when Haywoood embraced a philosophy of violent class struggle. When the United States entered World War I on April 6, 1917, the IWW union, popularly dubbed the Wobblies,[23] was quick to denounce the move. The government responded by banning from the mail the official IWW journal, *Solidarity*, and a number of IWW leaders, including Haywood, were indicted and convicted. A terrifying man, the one-eyed, scar-faced giant Haywood was once tried for murder of former governor Frank Steuenberg of Idaho but was acquitted as the result of an able defense by famed lawyer Clarence Darrow. Haywood was convicted in 1918 of obstructing the war effort, but while awaiting a new trial he jumped bail and fled to the Soviet Union, where he remained the rest of his life.

The laws of 1917 and 1918 allowed far more oppressive enforcement than the short-lived Alien and Sedition Laws of 1798–1800, and these twentieth-century laws aimed at curbing wartime dissent remained on the books to be used in later periods of the century. Although the wide-sweeping clauses were repealed in 1921, they were still applicable to clearly labeled antigovernment propaganda sheets. (The Espionage and Sabotage Act, passed in 1954 amid renewed anticommunist hysteria, authorized the death sentence for peacetime spying.) More than 1,500 were arrested on sedition charges, although only ten were arrested on sabotage charges.

The most noted targets of the acts of 1917 and 1918 were Max Eastman and Eugene Debs. Eastman promoted left-wing ideas in *The Masses*, which he edited. The magazine was banned in August 1917 for publishing articles, four antiwar cartoons, and a poem that supported leftist leaders Emma Goldman and Alexander Berkman. *The Masses* was not printed again, but in 1918, Eastman launched the *Liberator*, where he continued to wax eloquent on revolutionary themes. He was indicted under the Espionage Act, but the case was dismissed in 1919. In the 1920s he visited the Soviet Union but was profoundly disappointed at the "totalitarian tyranny" he found. He turned against the Soviet Union and criticized Marxist principles. In later life he lectured widely, made radio appearances, and served as a roving editor for *Reader's Digest* from 1941 to 1969.[24]

The Prison Candidate

Debs is best remembered for conducting a highly effective campaign for president of the United States from prison. In 1920 he garnered 912,302 votes for president as Convict 9653 in the Atlanta Federal Prison in an election that made the suave, hand-grabbing Warren Harding—a Marion, Ohio, editor—president. Debs, editor of the Socialist *Appeal to Reason*, helped found the Socialist Party in Indianapolis in 1901. He began his journalism career as editor of the *Locomotive Fireman's Magazine* in Terre Haute, Indiana, in 1892.

Debs first gained prominence when he covered the trial of Big Bill Haywood, accused in the killing of Idaho Governor Frank Steuenberg. Steuenberg had died when a bomb went off as he opened the gate to the governor's mansion. One man confessed and implicated Haywood. The motive was alleged to be retaliation for Governor Steuenberg's calling out of the militia to break up a strike of Coeur d'Alene miners. With coeditor Julius Wayland, a former real estate speculator and printer who founded the *Appeal* in 1895, Debs prepared a special edition of the *Appeal* for each period of the trial. With 4 million copies sold per issue, the *Appeal* became the paper with the largest circulation in the country in this period. Before Debs came aboard the *Appeal's* circulation was 100,000.

When President Theodore Roosevelt made remarks indicating that he assumed Haywood was guilty, Debs attacked the president by calling him a "servile tool of the Mine and Smelter Trust," and said further: "This coward at the White House outraged decency, first by denouncing untried men as murderers, and second by holding them up to public execration."[25]

Debs went on to fight the arrest of the McNamara brothers in a dynamiting of the *Los Angeles Times* that claimed twenty lives in 1910. (Ironworkers Union executive secretary John J. McNamara received a life sentence, his brother fifteen years,

Eugene Debs' first day at home after release from prison in 1921. (International News Photo)

and both were defended by Clarence Darrow.) Debs alleged in a series of *Appeal* articles that the *Times'* owners themselves, not union anarchists, were guilty.

Debs, who had been singled out for special praise by Soviet patriarch Nikolai Lenin for his "war against capitalists," was arrested on June 30, 1918, on his way to address a Socialist picnic. He was convicted under the Espionage Act and sentenced to ten years. Debs addressed the court in a speech that columnist Heywood Broun called "a miracle" and "one of the most beautiful in the English language."[26] The U.S. Supreme Court upheld the Debs conviction in 1919. Debs was pardoned by President Harding in 1921.

PRESS CONTROL AGENCIES IN THE TWO WORLD WARS

World War I

In April 1917 an incensed America entered the war after three American merchant ships were sunk without warning. Just seven days later, President Wilson sought to control the press. On April 13, 1917, he issued an executive order that set up the Committee on Public Information (CPI). He chose a former editorial writer for the *Denver Post* and former Denver police commissioner George Creel to head the committee.

Creel's tactic proved to be less one of censorship than "service." He chose to inundate the media with government-written news reports, editorials, cartoons, and even advertising copy with patriotic themes. Mott estimates that 6,000 government news releases found their way into most newspapers. "This material was colored with patriotic propaganda; but it was, on the whole, accurate and full of news value."[27] The CPI newspaper, the *Official Bulletin*—the first U.S. government daily paper—reached a circulation of nearly 120,000. The CPI produced news films that appeared weekly in many movie houses. A CPI foreign-language section bombarded foreign-language newspapers with government-prepared releases.

The CPI organized a horde of citizens—75,000 strong—to be volunteer speakers on patriotic and war-support themes. Dubbed the Four-Minute Men, they gave four-minute speeches anywhere they could, from theaters to churches. Carol Oukrop says the force, along with the CPI Speaking Division, "filled the need for the spoken word in mobilizing public opinion—a need filled via radio during World War II, and currently through radio and television."[28]

Although the CPI did not function as a censorship body, Creel made known the restrictions on revealing troop movements called for by a Censorship Board set up by the Trading-with-the-Enemy Act. Creel, a member of that board, sought voluntary compliance with such restrictions, and his plan gained general acceptance. The Associated Press at first balked at Creel's request to delete mention of arrival of American troops, but once the rules for a planned voluntary censorship of such news were better defined, the AP complied.[29]

As in the Civil War, the military exerted censorship in the field. While correspondents were generally free to come and go as they pleased, even to the front lines, they did have to clear their stories with the Military Intelligence Service at the press headquarters of the American Expeditionary Force (AEF), which moved from place to place with maneuvers and as dictated by the outcome of battles.

World War I Journalists

- *Richard Harding Davis.* A veteran reporter of many wars—the Spanish-American War in Cuba, the Boer War in South Africa, the Russo-Japanese War—whose rugged good looks and suave mannerisms made him a model for fashion magazines, Davis joined the Belgian army in World War I in order to secure valid military credentials. Captured three times, he was nearly shot by the Germans as a spy. He reported the war for the *New York Tribune* and several magazines and European papers.
- *Floyd Gibbons.* Suspecting that the ship *Laconia* would be a target for German torpedoes, the adventurous Gibbons took to sea in it anyway. When in 1917 two torpedoes did indeed slam into the British vessel, Gibbons was rewarded with an

exclusive for his *Chicago Tribune*. The next year, while following marines in battle, he was wounded and lost an eye.

- *Peggy Hull*. Working for the *Cleveland Plain Dealer*, Hull was the first woman war correspondent accredited by the War Department. She spent nine months reporting on the Russian revolution and made the first radio broadcast from China in 1924. In 1943, at the age of fifty-three, she donned a military uniform and took off to cover the war in the South Pacific.

- *Mary Roberts Rinehart*. Reporting for the *Saturday Evening Post*, Rinehart reached the front early in the war before other correspondents and reported from within 200 yards of the German lines. She was on the streets of Paris when the Armistice was announced on November 11, 1918. She wrote a tempered account: "The city is on the streets, singing and waving flags. . . . [But] there are no bands, as all of them are at the front, and there are too many women shrouded in black, for whom the victory has come too late."[30] She became famous as a mystery-novel writer and paved the way for this modern genre. She also became interested in spiritualism and would contact her dead husband through mediums.

World War II

In World War II, on December 18, 1941, just eleven days after the attack on Pearl Harbor by the Japanese, President Franklin Roosevelt ordered the creation of the Office of Censorship. He installed Byron Price, a former executive news editor of the Associated Press, as director. Roosevelt had in mind a loose form of censorship that depended on voluntary participation. "Any rigid system of censorship would have encountered enormous opposition not only from the press but also from administration critics," says Richard Steele. "Roosevelt decided instead to rely on journalists to withhold stories they might obtain in spite of government efforts."[31] As an encouragement, the new Office of Censorship would make certain that journalists knew precisely what the government thought should not be released.

Price was no inquisitor-general like Torquemada of the fifteenth-century Spanish Inquisition, bent on oppression of press liberties. "As a career journalist . . . , Byron Price was not at all sympathetic to the notion of limiting the free flow of news," says Frederick Voss in his history of World War II reporting. "In his professional lexicon, 'every act' of press censorship contradicted 'the democratic creed,' and he was more than a little inclined to agree with the AP employee who had declared to him shortly after Pearl Harbor that a censor was undoubtedly 'the lowest form of human existence.'"[32]

Price, however, was realistic enough to realize that some kind of censorship would be needed for a nation in the midst of a global war. He accepted the directorship on the condition, first, that the censorship would be largely voluntary and, second, that he would be responsible directly to the president. He described his version of censorship as the Voice of the Dove.[33]

Price set up the *Code of Wartime Practices for the American Press* and began to distribute his low-key bulletins. He had the public relations skills to plant ideas in the minds of editors. Consider his *Censorship Bulletin No. 3*, January 27, 1942. Marked "not for publication," it was directed "to publishers and editors of all daily newspapers" and offered *suggestions* "for consideration of editors." He made it seem that the suggestions were coming from working journalists, as seen in this example:

> One editor has suggested that newspapers might well consider abandoning articles which idealize the Japanese psychology about suicide. The point is made that by idealizing this psychology we are selling our own people, particularly our soldiers, the idea that the Japs are a tougher customer than anyone else and would be harder to lick because he [sic] does not mind getting killed.[34]

The government did seek to prosecute several papers for violating Price's censorship code. One such paper was the arch-Republican *Chicago Tribune*, which on June 7, 1942, ran on the front page a story headlined "Navy Had Word of Jap Plan to Strike at Sea," that predicted the naval battle at Midway Island. By giving out this information, the government maintained, the paper revealed that the United States had cracked Japan's secret code. The government had been irked earlier, on the eve of the Pearl Harbor attack, when the *Tribune* had revealed U.S. secret plans for defense and deployment of forces in the event of war. The government proceeded to charge the *Tribune* with a violation of the Espionage Act of 1917 and the Censorship Code. Roosevelt asked for a criminal indictment against the newspaper, but the government case floundered when the government failed to identify the secret that was in question.[35]

As in previous wars, the military exercised its own brand of censorship from the beginning: the navy withheld details of the Pearl Harbor attack for fear of giving the Japanese too much useful information. Censorship extended to photographers, as revealed in George Roeder, Jr.'s book *The Censored War: American Visual Experience During World War II*. Roeder presents the contents of a recently opened secret Pentagon file known as the Chamber of Horrors, a collection of war pictures kept from the public. There are, as one might expect, horror pictures of dead and dying soldiers and suggestions of American atrocities. Yet many of the pictures do not deal with battle scenes. For instance, the army censored a 1943 picture of soldiers drinking beer at a party in Egypt and also a picture of black soldiers taking part in an integrated dance contest. Other censored pictures include one of a U.S. general fishing and a Dorothea Lange picture, taken for the War Relocation Authority, that shows a Japanese-American who was wearing a U.S. Navy uniform with decorations from World War I as he checked into a U.S. internment camp.[36]

Unlike George Creel's Committee on Public Information in World War I, Byron Price's Office of Censorship in World War II did not engage directly in publicity efforts and propaganda. Roosevelt preferred to keep the censorship powers and educational/propaganda efforts separate in order to avoid creating one sweeping organization like the one that had muddied the boundaries between free speech and thought control during World War I. On June 13, 1942, Roosevelt set up the Office of War Information (OWI) to coordinate the government's public relations concerning the war. He put a former *New York Times* reporter, novelist, and CBS news radio personality, Elmer Davis, in charge.

During Davis's tenure at OWI until it was dismantled in 1945, he "fought against all suppression of facts, with the result that he sometimes clashed with the military, sometimes winning, sometimes not," says Clifford Montague, who was a feature writer for the OWI.[37] The agency compiled basic news, which staffers referred to as BN; it was broadcast over radio to all parts of the globe twenty-four hours a day. The radio section, regarded as the largest of OWI's divisions, beamed out 2,600 fifteen-minute shows a week. The periodical division published magazines in many languages. *Victory* featured picture spreads like *Life; USA* resembled *Reader's Digest; Voir*, in French, looked like *Collier's* in the United States. OWI even had a magazine, *Amerika*, aimed at acquainting Russians with Americans. Although most of the material was straight news and features, an underlying theme that an Allied victory was certain prevailed.

World War II Journalists

- *Ernie Pyle*. The best known of World War II reporters, Pyle, whom *Time* magazine once put on its cover, began the war years as a freelance columnist chronicling the German air blitz against England, with the *New York World-Telegram* as a subscriber. He covered the invasions in Sicily, Italy, and Normandy, winning the Pulitzer Prize in 1944 for his columns appearing in 400 newspapers. He was killed by a sniper on the island of Ie Shima in the Pacific in April 1945.
- *Sigrid Schultz*. Working in the Berlin office of the *Chicago Tribune*'s German bureau from 1919 and serving as the office's director starting in 1926, Schultz was well-placed and well-known in Germany during the turbulent 1930s when Hitler rose to power. She stayed in Germany after the invasion of Poland in 1939 and reported on the war and the Third Reich from the inside into 1941.
- *Edward Kennedy*. Kennedy, the Associated Press's bureau chief in Europe, covered the war from beginning to end. Kennedy was adept at getting around censors, at times crossing the borders of Spain and Switzerland to file stories free of censorship. Privileged to be present as a part of a small pool of reporters at the formal signing of the surrender of Germany by German generals, he was chagrined at the embargo by military censors that forbade release of the news of the surrender until after a similar ceremony planned with the Soviets. At first Kennedy dutifully withheld release of the story, but convinced at last that the news was being leaked by British and German sources and reasoning that wartime censorship was no longer valid, he released the story and set off jubilant rejoicing in the world's capitals. His action was denounced by fellow reporters.
- *Edward R. Murrow*. The best known of the broadcasters, Murrow covered the war for CBS, from the eve of the war with the takeover of Austria, to the rooftops during air raids on London, to the horrors of the concentration camps revealed at the end of the war. He could condense news succinctly without misrepresentation and spoke with charisma and authority. He headed the U.S. Information Agency from 1961 to 1964.
- *Margaret Bourke-White*. A photographer for *Life* magazine, Bourke-White was the only foreign journalist in the Soviet Union when Hitler's armies began pouring

Ernie Pyle, on vehicle, on Okinawa: Pulitzer–Prize winning correspondent killed by a sniper in 1945. (National Archives)

across the border in June 1941. She was also the first American photographer to be allowed to do a series of portraits of Soviet leader Joseph Stalin. The subjects of her exciting war pictures ranged from sea to air; she shot photos from a torpedoed ship that was sinking with her on it as well as from bombers during air raids.

- *Enoch P. Waters.* Covering the war zones of the South Pacific for three years for the *Chicago Defender*, Waters, one of twenty-seven black journalists in the war, dealt with the daily lives of black soldiers. His reports included exposés of discrimination against blacks in the military. He wrote chatty, personalized articles; in his "Saga of Hill 660," concerning a battle on the island of New Britain, near Australia, he addressed a comfortable American eating breakfast and recounts the bloody, muddy climb of marines up the hill.
- *William Laurence.* A science writer for the *New York Times*, whose wartime insistence on writing about development of atomic power prematurely put him

Margaret Bourke-White took action war photographs for Life *magazine.*
(*Philadelphia Bulletin;* Temple University Libraries Photojournalism
Collection)

under government surveillance, Laurence nevertheless took a leave from the
Times in 1945 to become the official reporter from inside the Manhattan Project,
which was developing the atom bomb. Allowed to visit the secret sites—although he could not write about them immediately—he witnessed the first explosion of an atomic bomb in a New Mexico desert. He later called the occasion
comparable to "the moment of creation." He rode on the plane that dropped
the second atomic bomb on Japan over Nagasaki. His later series on the development of atomic power and the atomic bomb brought him his second
Pulitzer Prize. (His first, shared with four others, was for covering a conference at Harvard.)

- *Ernest Hemingway*. Noted for his short stories and novels, some of them coming out of his days as a reporter for the North American Newspaper Alliance in the Spanish Civil War in the 1930s, Hemingway covered the war in Europe for *Collier's* in 1944. Always wanting to be at the heart of everything, Hemingway could make it sound as if he were in the midst of a battle even though he was on the periphery. He linked up with a band of French Resistance fighters and became a gunrunner for them. It was his influence with the American military brass that enabled him to get arms into France. Savoring a military role, he took part in reconnaissance missions of the Resistance. His actions brought censure from fellow journalists and nearly incurred disaccreditation by the authorities. But he was saved by his celebrity status and influential contacts.

CENSORSHIP AND THE "OTHER" WARS

The Korean War

Americans had come to expect a war once every generation; they experienced a war just before the turn of the century (the Spanish-American War), World War I in the second decade, and World War II in the 1940s. But just five years after the end of World War II, the nation suddenly became embroiled in a faraway war, in Korea. It was not a global war (although American troops fought under the sanction of the United Nations), but it was to prove a costly war. Some 53,000 Americans, including eighteen reporters, lost their lives.

The war began when Communist North Korean forces attacked South Korea on June 25, 1950. After World War II Korea, which had previously been occupied by Japan, was divided at the 38th parallel, with the Soviet forces occupying the north (the Soviets withdrew after they set up a government) and Americans occupying the south.

In the early days of the war, General Douglas MacArthur did not impose field censorship by military commanders, as was the practice in earlier wars. Reporters were free to come and go in the field, and they were often in the thick of it. Consider this report by Homer Bigart for the *New York Tribune* upon his arrival at the front at the beginning of hostilities:

> WITH AMERICAN FORCES IN KOREA, July 10, 1950—American troops in forward positions narrowly escaped another enveloping thrust by North Korean Communists today, and were able to avoid annihilation by great luck in withdrawal. The unit suffered severe casualties and was forced to leave all its heavy equipment behind.
>
> This correspondent was one of three reporters who saw the action, and was the only newsman to get out alive. The others, Ray Richards of International News Service and Corp. Ernie Peeler of *Stars and Stripes*, were killed by enemy fire.
>
> A particularly grisly feature of the action was the shooting in cold blood of seven Americans who were captured by the Communists. The men, four of whom were driving jeeploads of ammunition forward in a last-gasp effort to keep the force supplied, surrendered to the hordes of North Koreans who were overrunning the roads. The Reds dragged them from their jeeps, tied their hands behind them and shot them in the face, ignoring their cries for mercy.[38]

Such on-the-scene reporting, with loaded words like "Communists," "Reds," "hordes," and "grisly," did not make bad propaganda. Perhaps the military had self-serving reasons to want the press corps at the front. Certainly the press was welcome in covering MacArthur's successful landing behind enemy lines at Inchon and the capture of the enemy's capital, Pyongyang—the only communist capital to be liberated by forces of the West. Then suddenly communist China entered the war in November 1950 and drove the U.S. forces onto a 275-mile retreat, the longest in U.S. military history. A marine division fought its way out of a trap at Chosin Reservoir in minus-30-degree weather. MacArthur wanted to extend the air war to China—or withdraw from Korea—but failed to get the support of President Truman. When the press turned critical of MacArthur, MacArthur put in effect a full-scale censorship, which addressed not only the revealing of military information but also the damaging of morale. The censorship code of the Eighth Army in Korea said in part:

> In general, articles may be released for publication to the public, provided (1) they are accurate in statement and in implication, (2) they do not supply military information to the enemy, (3) they will not injure the morale of our forces or our allies, and (4) they will not embarrass the United States, its allies, or neutral countries.[39]

Despite the bravado of the new rules, which threatened court-martials for grave infringement, the relationship of the media and the military was generally symbiotic. Said Mort Rosenblum: "Korea was also reported essentially as us-against-them. Correspondents were assigned jeeps and had free run of the war. Not much was made of censorship rules. Each reporter knew the limits, and most stopped well short of them. It was in Vietnam that the style changed drastically, and that caught a lot of people off guard."[40]

Korean War Journalists

- *Marguerite Higgins*. With experience covering the closing days of World War II for the *New York Herald Tribune*, Higgins was named the *Tribune's* Tokyo bureau chief in 1950. When hostilities started that year she immediately sought out the combat zones. When a field commander denied her access, she appealed to the supreme commander, Douglas MacArthur, who reversed the order, thus paving the way for equal treatment of women war correspondents. Her frontline reports brought her the Pulitzer Prize in 1951 (shared with five male reporters, including Homer Bigart and Keyes Beech).
- *Keyes Beech*. Covering the war from the beginning for the *Chicago Daily News*, Beech won a 1951 Pulitzer Prize (shared with others). He was cited for his graphic description of marines withstanding the onslaught of newly committed Chinese troops at the Changjin Reservoir in subzero weather and the eventual withdrawal from the icy wilderness. "Not in the Marine Corps' long and bloody history has there been anything like it," he wrote. "And if you'll pardon a personal recollection, not at Tarawa or Iwo Jima, where casualties were much greater, did I see men suffer as much."[41]

The Vietnam War

Although Americans did not become involved in a war in Vietnam until the 1960s, the United States had had its hands in Vietnam's affairs since the final days of World War II. At that time agents of the Office of Strategic Services parachuted into Indochina (a large part of which became Vietnam) and gave aid to forces fighting the Japanese. After the surrender of Japan in August 1945, the United States declined to support the French as they sought to reestablish French control of the area. For nine years after World War II the French fought the Communist Vietminh, who were aided by China and the Soviet Union. With the coming of the Korean War in 1950 and the rush to stem the tide of communism sweeping southeast Asia, the Truman administration produced $2 billion in aid for the French. But both Truman and his successor, Dwight Eisenhower, declined to send military aid. In 1954, after a fifty-five-day siege at Dienbienphu, the French surrendered. In the peace negotiations that followed, which involved the major powers as participants, the country was divided into North Vietnam, South Vietnam, and Cambodia. In the north, a communist government was installed, in the south, a "nationalist" government. Ho Chi Minh led the north, and Ngo Dinh Diem, a staunch anticommunist, led the south. Diem refused to take part in any all-Vietnam election, and the standoff began. By 1962 the United States had sent 10,000 military "advisers" and equipment to aid Diem, and some of the "advisers" became involved in military action. The United States was now involved in an undeclared war. Before the U.S. withdrew in 1973, some 8.7 million had served in Vietnam from all branches of the armed services, with 211,324 casualties, including 47,356 battle-related deaths.

Censorship was generally informal and took place in the field with no clear instructions from Washington or the military high commands. An exception to this was military publications, such as *Stars and Stripes* and the Armed Forces Vietnam (radio) Network, which experienced extensive censorship from the U.S. command's Office of Information. President Johnson used all his persuasive powers to encourage restrained coverage and favorable reporting. But he and the military staff knew that, with nearly sixty reporters in Vietnam, many of them foreign journalists, censorship would not work and would backfire politically.

In addition to putting a public relations twist on events—such as deflating casualty figures—as the war heated up and criticism began to mount, the government stopped providing transportation for reporters to the field of action. In one incident four reporters who had chartered their own helicopter died when it crashed. The government also imposed news blackouts on some air strikes. The blackouts were so effective that the government waged a secret bombing campaign against Cambodia for fourteen months in 1969 and 1970.

Physical Censorship.   Much of the censorship, to the extent that it existed, occurred at the scene of the story and was often administered by military police, including South Vietnamese lawmen. Veteran foreign correspondent Peter Arnett, an Australian with the AP at the time, recounts instances of reporters and photographers being roughed up as attempts were made to prevent them from covering an event. Arnett himself, with a gun pointed at his head, was pulled off a news scene by American military police and taken into custody.[42]

This violent kind of "censorship" is described in Arnett's account of journalists trying to cover a self-immolation—a protest suicide by fire—in Saigon:

> A dozen plainclothes security police had pressed their assault against our colleagues, trying to grab [NBC's Grant] Wolfkill's movie camera, the only one at the suicide scene. As he had come to my assistance in an alley months earlier, [David] Halberstam rushed in to assist Wolfkill, plowing through the goons. The cameraman was knocked against a parked car but he was able to pass the camera on to John Sharkey, who then had to contend with a security man jumping on his brawny shoulders. Sharkey passed it on to Halberstam, who tried to make an end run to a nearby hotel, but was knocked down and the camera skittered across the sidewalk. Wolfkill planted a protective foot on the equipment but a plainclothesman kicked it from under him and it flew off the curb into the arms of another policeman, who tucked it under his arm and ran off.
>
> The goons were just beginning to fight. As Sharkey was bending down to help pull Halberstam up from the sidewalk, a policeman smashed a wooden stool on his head, inflicting a wound that took six stitches to close. Wolfkill was clubbed in the back with a pistol butt and looked up to see a policeman waving a gun in his face. It was not the violence he later remembered but the frustration of missing the scoop. "The heartbreaker of having such a sensational event on film and then having it stolen from you."[43]

Photographing the Terror. The unmitigated horror of the war got through to the American public. Negative stories and photographs challenged the purpose of those committed to the war. The My Lai massacre in a Vietnam village, ordered by a trigger-happy Lieutenant William Calley, later tried and convicted of premeditated murder and sentenced to life imprisonment (commuted to twenty years), was detailed by Seymour Hersh of the Dispatch News Service and recorded in heartrending photographs in 1969. A picture by Huynh Cong ("Nick") Ut showing a naked girl and other children fleeing down a smoke-filled road near Trang Bang caught the terror of war in 1972. The point-blank shooting of a young bound prisoner in the head by arrogant Brigadier General Nguyen Ngoc Loan, commander of the South Vietnamese National Police, was captured on film by AP photographer Eddie Adams in 1968. Hersh, Ut, and Adams won Pulitzer Prizes for their efforts.

Perhaps the shock value of the photos was enhanced because the public had grown accustomed to photos appropriate for the living room. Charlotte Niemeyer argues that after the Tet (Buddhist New Year) offensive in the winter of 1968, with massive gains achieved by the enemy Vietcong guerrillas and North Vietnam troops, American war photographs showed fewer battle scenes of action and the dead and more feature material on the soldiers and the South Vietnamese. "The final photographic shift away from life-threatening scenes was apparent after Tet," says Niemeyer. "The public viewed a much more sanitized version of the war."[44] Against a bland backdrop, the photography of a few realists managed to survive editorial and moral censorship.

The Pentagon Papers. Efforts at prior restraint—killing a story before publication—were made in June 1971 when U.S. Attorney General John Mitchell ordered the *New York Times* to cease publishing a series that it had just started on a secret Department of Defense history of the Vietnam War. Mitchell's threat was clear: "Further publication of information of this character will cause irreparable injury to the defense interests of the United States" and is "directly prohibited by the provisions of the Espionage Law." The *Times* proceeded to publish the third installment, insisting that "it is in the interest of the people of this country to be informed." The *Times* played up the attorney general's attempt at censorship on the front page. On June 15 the Department of Justice issued a temporary court order restraining further publication of the series that had become known as the Pentagon Papers. It was the first such order in the history of the nation.

The *Washington Post* proceeded to publish stories based on the papers. The Justice Department sought a restraining order from the federal court in Washington, but Washington Federal District Judge Gerhard Gesell refused the government's request. He cited the Supreme Court's decision in 1931 in *Near* v. *Minnesota*, which denied prior restraint of publication. The case was appealed to the Supreme Court, which ruled six to three on June 30 that the government's attempt to place prior restraint on publication was a violation of the First Amendment. This decision became, as Francis Wilkinson puts it, "a landmark resolution of the conflict between government secrecy and press freedom."[45]

In the 1970s many other major newspapers, in addition to the *Times* and the *Post*, had come to question the war in their editorial policies. For example, the Knight-Ridder newspapers, traditionally moderately conservative and Republican, began to take issue with Nixon and the war.

The ethnic press did not speak with a clear, unified voice. "While the *Afro-American*, the *Courier*, and the *Defender* maintained support for social order during the 1960s, their editorial positions on the Vietnam War did not have a single perspective," says William Leonhirth. "The *Afro-American* opposed the war, the *Defender* supported the war through the Johnson administration, and the *Courier* opposed, supported, and then opposed the war again." Leonhirth suggests that the ambivalence of a part of the black press concerning the war and its complex, unfocused view of the war may in part be a reaction to the white protesters of the war. "The black press in the 1960s also supported middle-class values against which younger members of the white middle class were rebelling," he says. "Perhaps that is why the black press scorned young anti-war protesters who were fleeing the affluence that the newspapers were seeking for their audiences."[46]

The Vietnam War Journalists

- *David Halberstam.* Declining to follow in the steps of a journalistic pack, Halberstam, of the *New York Times*—along with others, such as Neil Sheehan of United Press International and Malcolm Browne of the Associated Press—ventured to offer discouraging reports on the progress of the war, in contrast to official reports that insisted the war was a success. Halberstam and Browne won a 1964 Pulitzer Prize together. Both, along with Sheehan, went on to write books about the realities of the war and its failed efforts.

- *Harrison Salisbury.* A veteran foreign correspondent and editor at the *New York Times* who had won a Pulitzer Prize for a series he wrote as the *Times'* Moscow bureau chief in 1955, Salisbury gained entrance into North Vietnam at the end of 1966 and reported that American bombers were hitting nonmilitary targets and killing civilians. He wrote twenty-nine books and was a frequent target of political conservatives.
- *Dickey Chapelle.* A freelance photographer who had covered the globe, including going ashore with the U.S. Marines at Okinawa in World War II, Chapelle marched through mud and extreme heat with South Vietnamese troops in the early 1960s. In 1965 she died after tripping and activating a land mine.
- *Liz Trotta.* Assigned to Vietnam by NBC, the former *Newsday* reporter covered the jungle fighting and could be seen nightly on *The Huntley-Brinkley Report* and its successor, *NBC Nightly News.* A conservative in politics, she had her share of detractors, among them broadcaster John Chancellor, who called her "Mme. Nhu," a reference to the strong-willed wife of the head of state in South Vietnam. Demoted to local news by NBC, she switched to CBS, where she allegedly encountered sexual harassment and lost her job in a drastic 1985 cutback of staff.

Grenada and Panama

The invasion of the tiny Caribbean island of Grenada by forces of the United States and seven Caribbean nations on October 25, 1983, offered a war so small that the government could exert nearly full control over media coverage. In fact, the Defense Department banned reporters from covering the first two days of fighting on the island, and then for the next two days provided carefully restricted tours of parts of the island for small pools, or selected groups, of reporters. The Pentagon excused the restrictions on the grounds that they guarded military maneuvers and protected the reporters from possible harm.[47] At the same time the incomplete military briefings withheld casualty figures and unfavorable information, such as the accidental bombing of a hospital, and gave out misinformation.

For example, communications lawyer Donna Demac says reports that the lives of American students on the island had been in great danger (one of the reasons for the invasion) were disproven by "independent confirmation that they had been promised by Grenada safe transport home. United States government estimates of the number of Cuban troops on the island were challenged and revised more than once."[48]

A Submissive Public.   Although a groundswell of protest over the shutouts and curbs emerged from the media, the public appeared as if it couldn't care less. Demac suggests that such attitudes were the result of a cumulative effect that reflected reactions to the overaggressiveness of journalists in reporting tragedies and invading private spheres, as well as extensive publicity for libel cases. Yet the main reason, she suggests, might have been the skill of President Ronald Reagan in shifting blame onto the press, as the popular president constantly made the media convenient whipping posts. In any event, the government had broken with the precedent of battlefield access and limited field censorship that had governed previous war reporting. Censorship was centralized and complete. It led an Australian correspondent, broadcasting via satellite to the Pacific Rim, to declare, "We have just seen the end of two hundred years of press freedom in the United States."[49]

When U.S. forces invaded Panama on December 20, 1989, in a move to depose dictator General Manuel Noriega and to "safeguard" American citizens in Panama from perceived threats by Noriega, the government sought to circumscribe journalists by creating military press pools in which selected journalists would cover the action and make the information available to others. *Editor & Publisher* pointed out that press pool reporters were delayed, while aggressive individuals not in the pool had quicker access to the scenes of action.[50]

The Persian Gulf War

"The coalition forces led by the United States won two great victories in the Persian Gulf," Ted Koppel, anchor of ABC News' *Nightline*, told the University of Pennsylvania graduating class in 1991. "The first, over the Iraqi armed forces of Saddam Hussein; the second, over the U.S. media. For much of the time and with few exceptions, the media looked silly, petulant and whiny."[51]

The six-week war beginning on January 16, 1991, to drive Iraqi troops out of Kuwait offered a contradiction. The United Nations–sanctioned force led by the Americans displayed the latest sophisticated war equipment. The new "war toys" included the high tech $4.4 million, nuclear-and-chemical-warfare-protected M–1A1 Abrams tank and the $11.7 million Apache helicopter with a night vision system. In contrast, press relations were anything but modern and enlightened; rather they were a throwback to actions that would befit a feudal warlord.

The government had savored the near-total regulation of the press experienced in Grenada and Panama. Here again, selected press pools would cover the action. Also again, journalists were kept from key sites and allowed passage only on carefully guided tours of the battle zone. There were daily briefings presenting information that the government wanted the public to have.

There were restrictions against the photographing of coffins of dead soldiers returned to Dover (Delaware) Air Force base. Guidelines presented a list of taboos: reporters were not to mention "identification of aircraft origin other than as land- or sea-based," "the methods, unique equipment or tactics of special operations forces," "angles of attack or speeds, but allowing general terms such as 'low' or 'fast,'" and so on.[52] All copy was to be checked by public affairs officers at the scene prior to transmission. Appeals could be made, but then the time lag would effectively kill the story. There were no criminal penalties for airing or publishing forbidden information, but the offender could lose press credentials.

The Media Looked "Silly." The media for the most part—there were some who acted independently—appeared "silly" because they looked like pawns of the Defense Department. "Beyond their informative function, the media were used by the military to help the coalition cause and to confuse the Iraqis," says Richard Jackson Harris. He cited, for example, reporters being taken to the area near the southern Kuwaiti border with Saudi Arabia but not to the area where the real buildup for the ground invasion was occurring. Pools were taken to cover practice maneuvers for an apparent assault on Kuwait's coast, an assault that never came about but rather was used to divert attention from the planned ground thrust from the west. The CIA planted a false story of sixty Iraqi tanks defecting early in the war, with the hope of encouraging actual Iraqi defections."[53]

Those who were handling the press had taken a page from the book on how to run an election from the viewpoint of one candidate. The emphasis of the government was on creating favorable images. Reporters—by design of the government and by acquiescence of many of the editors—looked like public relations personnel. Veteran war correspondent Malcolm W. Browne saw it that way. "In effect," he said, "each pool member is an unpaid employee of the Department of Defense, on whose behalf he or she prepares the news of the war for the outer world."[54]

Most notable among the exceptions—the journalists who thumbed their noses at the pool arrangements and set out on their own—were Bob Simon of CBS and CNN's Peter Arnett. Simon was arrested and held by the Iraqis. Arnett, the only Western journalist to stay behind in Baghdad once hostilities started, had the highest profile. He showed the end result of allied bombing, sometimes the "collateral damage," the effect on civilians. Some fervent patriots in the United States expressed their outrage over this independence in journalism and picketed CNN headquarters in Atlanta.

Reporting on the Corpses.   Perhaps most enterprising of the independents was two-time Pulitzer Prize winner Jon Franklin, who got a job in the Desert Storm mortuary at Dover Air Force Base, off limits to reporters and photographers. He took a three-week course in mortuary science and qualified for a mortuary license before approaching the base for a job. He wrote about the state of the corpses in the *San Francisco Bay Guardian*, which prefaced his article with a warning that the report was "gruesome" but also added: "We believe it is unfair and unconstitutional to sanitize this war. The American people paid for it, and their elected officials made it happen. They should not be deluded about its true costs." Franklin ended his article thus:

> I have seen probably 20 corpses. Some without hands. Some without heads.
> More than half are young African American men.
>   These are the grisly images the U.S. public never saw. And for every American soldier carefully cleaned, rebuilt and delivered home, probably a thousand dead Iraqis melt into the desert sand.[55]

Franklin's observation that "more than half" of the dead were black points up the disproportionate number of blacks in the war. In the Gulf War 30 percent of the U.S. forces were black, while in the total U.S. population 12 percent are black. Reverend Benjamin Chavis, at that time director of the Committee for Racial Justice of the United Church of Christ, writing in *Jet*, blamed the larger percentage of blacks in the Gulf War on the fact that they were literally forced into service by the effect of poverty, unemployment, and restrictions in opportunity.[56] Observers noted also that few blacks showed up on the news talk shows to discuss the war. "What magnified blacks' frustration over what they perceived as an unfair burden of the war on them," said Zhongdang Pan and Gerald Kosicki in a research paper, "was their perceived lack of access to the mainstream news media to express their views. The Rev. Jesse Jackson, for example, was quoted complaining about the almost complete silence of the mainstream media over his visit to Baghdad and what he saw and had to say about the crisis."[57]

Agreement on New Guidelines.   High-level postmortems on media coverage of the war were held by media representatives, and negotiations were conducted with the Pentagon. As a result nine principles of combat coverage were agreed to by media organizations and the Department of Defense. The first two say, "(1) Open and independent reporting will be the principal means of coverage of U.S. military operations," and "(2) Pools are not to serve as the standard means of covering U.S. military operations, but pools may sometimes provide the only feasible means of early access to a military operation."[58] The rules seemed to make independent reporting rather than the pools the norm. (The pools were expanded from thirteen members to twenty-eight in the planned but canceled invasion of Haiti in 1994.[59])

Missing in the post–Gulf War guidelines was an agreement over the issue of prior review of copy by military censors, which resulted in an air of skepticism on the part of the media. Speaking in Washington, Jane E. Kirtley, executive director of the Reporters Committee for Freedom of the Press, said: "Because of the fundamental failure of the two groups to agree on the concept of prior review by the military, they've effectively gutted all the principles. Unless there's agreement about the press's right to access and the press's right to report, nothing's going to happen."[60]

Wall Street Journal Pentagon correspondent John J. Fialka reported that he was "not very hopeful about those rules. They've had rules after Grenada and rules after Panama and now rules after the Gulf. These rules don't change much. If you re-enacted the Gulf today with these rules and didn't change attitudes on both sides, the outcome would be the same."[61]

In the 1990s the military took a public relations approach to the media in the noncombat peace-keeping efforts in Bosnia and Herzegovina. A "Soldier's Guide to Bosnia-Herzegovina," distributed to Army personnel, had a section on "Meeting the Media." It suggested ways to be courteous to the press, and it even advised how to appear on television and to tailor remarks to the limited sound-bite time. At one press conference Maj. Gen. William Nash, NATO commander for the American-controlled sector of Bosnia, sported a T-shirt over his camouflage outfit that said, "Support the media."[62]

Media as Fourth Estate: Adversaries of Government
THE ROLE OF ALTERNATIVE MEDIA

"Dissident journalism is an American tradition," says an alternative movement researcher, Lauren Kessler. "From Tom Paine's revolutionary tracts to today's ideologically and culturally diverse 'other voices,' the alternative media have been an important part of the American political landscape."[63] Alternative media have helped shape American culture and lifestyle, have affected the outcome of elections by siphoning off votes for third parties, and have created an antiwar climate that toppled presidents—in Lyndon Johnson's decision not to run again and in fostering a climate that made Richard Nixon vulnerable.

There have always been publications that are adversaries of government. Laurence Leamer, in his study of the rise of the underground press of the late 1950s, 1960s, and early 1970s, suggests that the dissident tradition goes back to Benjamin Harris and his *Publick Occurrences*, which in 1690 was so critical of the establishment that it was closed down after one issue.[64]

Media Critics and Gadflies

Dissident voices in the twentieth century have included midcentury media critic George Seldes, government gadfly I. F. Stone, and social justice advocate and pacifist Dorothy Day. Seldes, who was active until his death in 1995 at age 104, had been World War I and later European correspondent for the *Chicago Tribune*. Concerned about what he regarded as totalitarian and Fascist elements in the media, Seldes quit the daily newspaper field in the mid-1930s to report on the Spanish Civil War objectively as a freelance writer. For the entire decade of the 1940s he edited *In Fact*, in which he tried to give the "true" facts of international events that were missed or distorted by mainline media. The publication's circulation reached 176,000 at its peak.

Stone was a persistent, fussy man who probed for news ideas and exposés in overlooked but obvious places such as the *Congressional Record* and the ongoing glut of government documents. He followed the "paper trail" that led him to information contradicting official government pronouncements, and his type of journalism was credited with influencing the work of Carl Bernstein and Bob Woodward as they exposed the involvement of President Nixon in the Watergate break-in of Democratic headquarters and the cover-up that followed.

From 1953 to 1971 Stone published *I. F. Stone's Weekly*, in which he exposed the true nature of the unfounded charges of Senator Joseph McCarthy in the 1950s and the flawed policies and inconsistencies of U.S. involvement in Vietnam. Everybody of importance read this paper, from Albert Einstein to the secretary general of the United Nations to actress Marilyn Monroe, who bought subscriptions for every member of Congress.[65] His motto was "Not to get close to power but to speak truth to power." And documentary journalist Studs Terkel paid him perhaps the highest tribute when he said Stone "shone like a beacon light."[66]

Dorothy Day's *Catholic Worker*

Dorothy Day cofounded (with Peter Maurin) the *Catholic Worker* in 1933 and edited and published it for nearly fifty years. She sought to make it a voice of the Catholic Workers movement, which among other things engaged in providing housing and food for the poor. She was keenly interested in making social justice pronouncements and writings of the pope—encyclicals—relevant to workers. The independent publication was consistently pacifist through several American wars, reflecting Day's socialist ways, and Day was jailed several times for taking part in protests. She helped organize various socialist groups, including farm communes. Nancy Roberts, of the University of Minnesota, says, "Dorothy Day's impact reached far beyond the Catholic Left and Catholicism. Through her journalism she challenged several generations of Americans to scrutinize their commitment to social justice and peace."[67] Her biographer, William Miller, adds, "Her legacy was vision—a vision of ending time with its evil nightmares by bringing Christ back on Earth."[68]

Dissent Goes "Underground"

The most remarkable period of dissent in America in the twentieth century peaked in the late 1950s, in the early days of the Cold War and the phobia over communists, and in the 1960s and early 1970s, during the Vietnam War. The dissent movements of this period, noted for their intensity and diversity, were made up primarily of the young, and each group had its own special message, usually embracing cultural concerns or radical politics. The list of papers, many of them short-lived, that existed during this period could possibly go into the thousands. Robert Glessing, who examined the dissenters and their publications in a 1970 book, listed 457 alternative papers.

These papers, most of them tabloid size with extensive though perhaps crude graphics, were made possible by a revolution in printing. The new process saw "hot type," which involved Linotype machines with operators setting cast lines of metal type, replaced by "cold type," a typesetting process that eliminated the need for the expensive and time-consuming hot-metal process. (Today computerized desktop pubishing has made it even easier to launch a newspaper or newsletter with stylized graphics.)

The alternative papers, ranging in content from celebrating a drug subculture and sexual liberation to promoting a political agenda and even espousing independent religious fundamentalism, had one thing in common. All were disenchanted with the prevailing institutions, whatever they might be—government, namely the federal government, with its "Red-baiting" communist scare mentality and penchant for wars, or the embedded discrimination by race or economic class in society, or specialized private-sector institutions such as the churches and synagogues. In particular they opposed the institutional press, which meant virtually every American weekly or daily captained by money-minded capitalist businessmen. A cardinal doctrine of the "alternatives" was that readers of the standard papers were dished up articles based on handouts at press conferences, with nothing or little that was creative for fear that it might rock the status quo.

The dissident papers of the 1950s–1970s are popularly referred to as underground papers, a term that is largely a misnomer. "Underground press" describes the wave of antiestablishment newspapers that at first were drug-culture oriented. Since drugs were illegal, these early papers were tagged the underground press. But as underground paper historian Robert Glessing points out, the name did not fit many of the papers that followed, including the *Movement* in San Francisco, which preferred to be called revolutionary, and the *Los Angeles Free Press*, which preferred to be known as the alternative press.[69]

Sexual content and alleged pornography—prevalent in some papers—perhaps contributed to the underground designation as these papers also came into contact with the law. Roger Lewis tells of law enforcement harassment of certain papers. Perhaps overstating the case, he nevertheless declares: "Pornography busts are a favourite means of intimidation, although those bringing the charges are usually more concerned with the general tenor of the paper than the alleged pornography." He cites *Dallas Notes*, the *Great Speckled Bird*, the *Kaleidoscope*, and *Nola Express* as having had "trouble with trifling obscenity charges." "Sometimes the opposition is less subtle," he says. "The *Kudzu* has been busted, evicted and confiscated, the *Rag* has been bombed, and a number of offices around the country bear bullet-hole marks."[70]

The "underground" tag was cast in stone with the organizing of the Underground Press Syndicate in California in 1967. Member papers agreed to have a free exchange of items and a free paper exchange among members. Eventually relocating to New York, the organization boosted combined readership among member papers to 2 million. The Free Ranger Tribe handled the administration. In 1971 the *Free Ranger Tribe Newsletter* and the *Clearhead*, a paper of the UPS, joined to form the UPS News Service. The organization served 140 American papers and 60 overseas.[71]

The following subsections describe some notable examples of the variety of the underground papers of the 1950s–1970s, a very visible part of the fourth estate, or perhaps it is better called the "fifth estate," as the underground press took issue with the ways and means of the institutionalized fourth estate. In fact, one paper, published in Detroit, was called the *Fifth Estate*.

Village Voice. One of the oldest in the midcentury wave of "underground" papers and certainly the most successful is the *Village Voice*, founded in Greenwich Village in lower middle Manhattan on October 26, 1955. By all counts, the *Voice*, which can go up to 132 pages—not counting entertainment and shopping inserts that may go to 38 pages—in its weekly edition, is more traditional and capitalist than "underground." An issue selected at random in 1994 dedicated 94 pages of 132 to advertising, not counting the insert section, which was largely ads. Yet in its establishment-bashing contents and advocacy of openness in lifestyle, as well as its concentration on the arts and entertainment, the paper has some affinity with the philosophy of the "underground."

In 1996 the *Voice* decided to broaden its base by going to a giveaway plan. It would provide 150,000 copies free each week in its home territory in New York and sell an additional 50,000 copies outside the city. Although believed to be earning $6 million a year, the *Voice*, owned by a pet supply magnate, Leonard Stern, of the Hartz Mountain Corp., had been losing circulation, going from a peak of 142,000 in 1992 to 118,000 in 1995.[72]

The *Voice*'s first publisher, Edwin Fancher, who took the helm at age thirty-one, promised in the first edition that it would be a good neighborhood newspaper, serving lower east side and west side neighborhoods with "thoroughgoing coverage of the special entertainment and other features of this unique neighborhood." Fancher predicted that the entertainment-oriented weekly would gain circulation in uptown Manhattan districts as well. Gradually, however, faced with emerging competition by more radical tabloids, such as the *Realist*, the *Voice* turned its entertainment spotlight also onto off-Broadway productions, foreign and underground films, unconventional art, and such performers as poet Allen Ginsberg and comedian Lenny Bruce.

The *Voice*'s new editor in 1994, Karen Durbin, the first woman to hold the post, promised to make the publication brighter if not lighter in format and content. The front page designs did away with excessive dark ink and "the what's-the-point-anyway mood that Ms. Durbin thought it conveyed," the *New York Times* noted. The new *Voice* editor said further: "There has to, on some level, be a joy in it and not just rage. It has to proceed out of a genuine sort of love for the world and what it could be and what it sometimes is, rather than out of that kind of bitter, you know, hellfire-and-brimstone sense that the world is just a pit inhabited by vipers and toads."[73]

Los Angeles Free Press.   Started in May 1964 in a garage with $15 capital by a thirty-seven-year-old socialist, Arthur Kunkin, in six years the *Freep*, as the paper was known, grew from a four-page giveaway to a forty-eight-page weekly with 95,000 circulation and expenses of $15,000 per issue, according to Glessing. "The *Freep*," says Glessing, "soon gained the reputation of being *against* police brutality and President Johnson's Great Society and *for* acid heads, rock music, and classified mating-game sex advertisements."[74] The *Freep* preferred to bypass the police—in fact, the Los Angeles police declined to issue police cards to the paper; instead, *Freep* reporters would go directly to the accused and print her or his side of the story while ignoring a police version. The *Freep* also engaged in a kind of "space-age muckraking," as Leamer puts it. It theorizes "imaginatively on the basis of commonly available, minutely detailed facts," examples being the development of conspiracy theme articles on the assassinations of John and Robert Kennedy and Martin Luther King, Jr.[75]

Berkeley Barb.   The first issue of the *Barb* appeared in August 1965, with editor Max Scherr borrowing an image from the windmill-tilting Don Quixote by putting a skeletal knight atop a skinny horse, with lance aimed at the campus bell on the University of California campus in Berkeley. In August the paper gained attention for covering troop trains passing through Berkeley with soldiers headed for Vietnam. The *Barb* played up the protests of some of the soldiers, who draped placards out of windows protesting the war, an angle ignored by mainline papers. Abe Peck notes that while "the *Free Press*'s Art Kunkin may have been more active in traditional Left parties . . . the *Barb* was closer to the amalgam of civil rights, antiwar, and New Left activities that collectively were being called 'the Movement.'"[76]

Black Panther. The orientation of a student activist group, the Student Nonviolent Coordinating Committee (SNCC), chaired by Stokely Carmichael, was toward problems of the Third World, especially the oppression of people of color. That orientation, says Milton Viorst, drew SNCC "inevitably to the conclusion that Vietnam was a colonial war, conducted by whites against people of color."[77] SNCC became an all-black organization and its message one of acquisition of black power through more aggressive, militant means. In the wake of the call of the new SNCC chairperson, H. Rap Brown, for a "black revolution," the Black Panther Party was organized at Merritt College, Oakland, California, in June 1966. By April of the next year the *Black Panther* was launched as a vehicle for the party's doctrines, and through its issues—reaching a peak circulation of 85,000—it became a means of support for the party.

Hollywood Free Paper. Although this paper bears a resemblance to the *Los Angeles Free Press*, its readers see the difference immediately. The *Free Paper* is an organ of one of the groups in the "Jesus People" movement that captured the attention of observers in the 1960s and 1970s. Founded in 1969 by a young former nightclub magician, Duane Pederson, the *Paper* sought to be an imitation of the *Los Angeles Free Press*, only with a different message. Funded initially by small gifts from interested evangelical laymen, its first issue featured a dialogue between talk show host Art Linkletter "and his daughter that they recorded just six weeks before she was murdered by those who manufacture and sell drugs."[78] And there was a passage from Scripture set in bold type. From the book of Hebrews, it began, "The man who approaches God must have faith. . . ." The *Paper* also included an abundance of slogans, such as, "Jesus Is Better Than Hash." In an interview Pederson pegged circulation of the paper, which was handed out on corners and at rallies, at 300,000.[79] A book on the Jesus People by Ronald Enroth and others puts the figure at 425,000 with "HFP's simplistic evangelism . . . emulated by a myriad of Jesus People newspapers."[80]

The New "Alternatives"

Other groups and causes in society also spawned alternative, if not underground, papers. As the 1970s began, some seventy-three feminist newsletters and newspapers had been started. In San Diego, there was *Battle Acts*, targeted to working women; in Milwaukee, *St. Joan's*, a quarterly for Roman Catholics; in Washington, *Off Our Backs*. Says Lauren Kessler: "Some were devoted to special groups within the women's movement—blacks, Chicanas, lesbians—others concentrated on literary, philosophic, and political fare. Most covered marches, speeches, legislative action, and court decisions. Many contained journalism that was both personal and angry."[81]

Alternative lifestyle publications emerged. The Gay Liberation Front (GLF) published *Rat*, which attacked capitalist values and "linked gay rights with all the oppressed: the Vietnamese struggle, the third world, the blacks, the workers."[82] The GLF later produced *Come Out!* And others followed: *Gay Power, Gay, Gay Activist* (of the Gay Activist Alliance, GAA), and regional and city gay papers, such as the San Francisco Bay area's *Gay Sunshine*.

A reference book on the independent press, *Alternatives in Print*, published in 1980, a decade after the Glessing estimate, listed 1,400 alternative periodicals, three times the number given by Glessing. "The alternative, or movement, press has changed and grown considerably since the late sixties," says Elliott Shore, who, with others, edited the anthology *Alternative Papers*. Such tabloids as the *Barb* and the *Great Speckled Bird* have either faded out or changed drastically. In their place are papers concerned with more specific issues, such as the *Waste Paper, Science for the People*, and *Union W.A.G.E.* "Today, the number and diversity of independent publications is impossible to estimate."[83]

There is even an attractive digest magazine for the alternative press, the *Utne Reader*. Offering "the best of the alternative press," the magazine, marking its tenth year in 1994, also mixes in, along with articles of the new left and environmental and civil rights movements, articles from such conservative publications as *National Review, American Spectator*, and *American Scholar*, suggesting a kind of ecumenism and mutual acceptance between main-road and off-the-beaten-path alternative journals.

Media as Purveyors of Information/Education

A DRAMATIC "NEW JOURNALISM"

During the turbulent mid-1960s, with growing confusion over America's role in policing the world, namely Southeast Asia, and blacks seeking to address inequities at home, confusion and uncertainty erupted in the media, particularly over the way the media relayed facts and informed readers. The very foundation of objective reporting was challenged by a self-confident, imaginative group of writers who, with the luxury of the longer deadlines of magazines, were able to fully research a story and spin it out at length, garnishing every significant and sometimes not so significant detail to give the recounting of an event the look of fiction, the feel of a novel.

Storytelling Techniques

The New Journalists used dialogue—exchanges between persons—and significant detail that helped the senses create a larger picture. They developed characters with interior personalities, characters who could speak and reveal their thoughts. Above all they created scenes rich with description and detail and mood, and stretched the scenes to cover a large chunk of the overall story. The long piece would then be a series of chunks or sections, developing and moving ahead with an inner force. Gone among these pieces was the traditional formula (which some consider a "hack," rote formula) of the inverted pyramid of facts presented in descending order of importance to answer the Who, What, Where, When, Why, and How of a news story. The emphasis of the new young journalists, encouraged by magazines such as *Esquire, New York, Rolling Stone, Harper's, the New Yorker*, was on "story."

Actually there was nothing new about the New Journalism or its terminology. Other media developments in other times had been called new journalism—for example, when the robust sensational competitive journalism of Pulitzer and Hearst burst on the scene in the last part of the nineteenth century. And fictional, imaginative, and in-depth techniques, had been in vogue in journalism in earlier centuries. From the earliest received texts of Aesop's Fables (sixth century B.C.) and Scripture, there have been accounts of events and of moral action that set the scene and include interior thoughts and dialogue.

Influence of Novelists

Some chroniclers of the New Journalism, such as Edward Gray Applegate, like to credit the modern movement to the English man of letters Daniel Defoe, who in the mid-seventeenth century wrote fact-based novels and political criticism, targeting his writings toward the masses in the convulsive times that saw Charles II after seventeen years in exile restored to the throne in the 1660s.[84]

On the American scene the seeds of the later New Journalism can be found in the writings of Stephen Crane, Lincoln Steffens, Theodore Dreiser, William Faulkner, Ernest Hemingway, and John Steinbeck. The muckraker novelists, such as Upton Sinclair, author of *The Jungle*, could also be named. In fact, a chronicler of the New Journalism, Michael Johnson, makes muckraking one of two classes of New Journalism, the other class embracing those who are "creating a new kind of literature, a journalistic art that is significant immediately as well as historically." Among the works of New Journalism muckrakers he includes Ida Tarbell's *History of the Standard Oil Company*, which in its descriptions assesses the personality of Standard's John D. Rockefeller, and more contemporarily Joe McGinnis's *The Selling of the President* in 1968, appearing in 1969, and James Ridgeway's *The Closed Corporation* (1968), which showed the relationship between universities and the military.[85]

Classifying the New Journalists

In his study of the New Journalists, Applegate placed them in three categories: literary, advocacy, and muckraking.

A pioneer of the New Journalism literary style was John Howard Griffin. For his bestselling book *Black like Me*, Griffin underwent medical treatment to make his skin look black and then posed as a black man in the south in order to expose the pervasive pattern of segregation. Using dialogue between himself and bigoted whites, he revealed his thoughts as if in a novel as he experienced and wrote about each tension-filled encounter.

Truman Capote, in his *In Cold Blood*, created scenes and reported the thoughts of the characters in a true story of crime and punishment in Kansas. Based on known facts, the "nonfiction novel" entered the minds of members of the murdered Clutter family, of Holcomb, Kansas, and their murderers, Eugene Hickock and Perry Smith.

John Sack, another literary New Journalist, was a former UPI reporter and CBS television documentary producer. A former soldier in the Korean War, he wrote about the experiences of M Company in the Vietnam War for *Esquire*, then later turned this material into a book, *M*. He captured graphically the nuances of both the humor and horror of war.

Also in the literary category is Norman Mailer. After graduating from Harvard and serving in the military, Mailer, at age twenty-three, wrote a realistic novel, *The Naked and the Dead*, based on his experience in the army during World War II. A number of books followed on topics ranging from the presidency to boxing to *Why Are We in Vietnam?* He is best remembered perhaps for his 1979 *The Executioner's Song*, a nonfiction novel about executed murderer Gary Gilmore. During intense moments in Gilmore's life, such as the execution by firing squad, Mailer records the details of every second and enters the minds of witnesses.

Hunter S. Thompson, honorably discharged from the military because of non-conformist views, wrote for a number of publications but had difficulties holding a job. He landed at *Rolling Stone*, where he mixed humor with reporting. A thorough political analyst, he mixed fantasy with facts in his *Fear and Loathing on the Campaign Trail*, dealing with the 1972 campaign.

Jimmy Breslin, who worked on New York area newspapers, was a sports columnist who turned to books on sports subjects and humor. His first novel, *The Gang That Couldn't Shoot Straight*, ridiculed the mob in Brooklyn. Even his book on the downfall of Nixon, *How the Good Guys Finally Won: Notes from an Impeachment Summer*, was marked with humor. He wrote Vietnam War short stories in which "description, poetic phrases, and realistic dialogue capture the scene, the characters, the reality of the times."[86]

Tom Wolfe, who worked for the *Washington Post* and *New York Herald Tribune*, wrote in an excessive and metamorphical style. For example, an article in *Esquire* about the practice of customizing cars was titled, "There Goes (Varoom! Varoom!) That Kandy-Kolored (Thphhhhhh!) Tangerine-Flake Streamline Baby (Rahghhh!) Around the Bend (Brummmmmmmmmmmmmmmmmmmmmm). . . ." In 1965 he collected a number of his impressionistic articles into a book, *The Kandy-Kolored Tangerine-Flake Streamline Baby*. In *The Right Stuff* (1982), about the Mercury astronauts—made into a successsful movie—he entered into the minds of the first crew of spacemen and the experimental airplane pilot Chuck Yeager.

Gay Talese, who had been a writer for the *New York Times*, produced an insider's human interest history of the *Times*, *The Kingdom and the Power*. He also wrote *Honor Thy Father*, about a mobster don, and *Thy Neighbor's Wife*, a study of sexuality.

George Plimpton, who had worked for *Sports Illustrated*, engaged in a participatory brand of the New Journalism. He literally became a part of the stories. He boxed a champion, Archie Moore; pitched in baseball games; played tennis and swam against pros; conducted the Cincinnati Symphony Orchestra; and performed as a percussionist with the New York Philharmonic. He worked out in rookie training and played as a quarterback in an exhibition game for the Detroit Lions, giving him grist for a book, *Paper Lion*, in 1966.

In a second category, which Applegate calls advocacy New Journalism, are the writers who strongly espoused an opinion. Here Applegate places Nicholas von Hoffman, a columnist and writer for the *Washington Post* who wrote on politics and social conditions; Michael Harrington, formerly an associate editor of the *Catholic Worker*, who produced a bestseller, *The Other America: Poverty in the United States*, in 1962; and Vivian Gornick, a teacher of English at Hunter College, who wrote for the *Village Voice* from a feminist point of view.

In a third category, muckraking, Applegate places Joseph Goulden, a former *Philadelphia Inquirer* reporter, who wrote an exposé of American Telephone and Telegraph Company's practices in *Monopoly*. He also wrote a new version of the Tonkin Gulf incident in 1964 in which U.S. planes bombed North Vietnam in retaliation for alleged attacks on U.S. vessels in the Gulf of Tonkin. Goulden's book was titled *Truth Is the First Casualty: The Gulf of Tonkin Affair, Illusion and Reality*. Other New Journalism muckrakers in Applegate's list are Philip Stern and Thomas Powers. Stern, a former editor of the *Democratic Digest* for the Democratic National Committee, demonstrated inequities in the American tax structure in his *The Rape of the Taxpaper* (1972). Powers, who had worked for the *Rome Daily American* in Rome, in 1971 wrote *Diana: The Making of a Terrorist*, the story of a radical young woman who died in New York's Greenwich Village, and *The War at Home: Vietnam and the American People, 1964–1968*, a study of attitudes toward the war.

Woodward and Bernstein

Applegate includes in the muckraking category Bob Woodward and Carl Bernstein, whose exposé of President Nixon's involvement in the Watergate break-ins toppled the president. Woodward's and Bernstein's commitment to subjective New Journalism is perhaps best demonstrated in their books. Applegate cites as an example of latter-day New Journalism this excerpt from Woodward and Bernstein's *The Final Days*, when the two writers enter the inner sanctum and the minds of the secretary of state, Henry Kissinger, and the president:

> The President broke down and sobbed.
> Kissinger didn't know what to do. He felt cast in a fatherly role. He talked on, he picked up on the themes he had heard so many times from the President. He remembered lines about enemies, the need to stand up to adversity, to face criticism forthrightly.
> Between sobs, Nixon was plaintive. What had he done to the country and its people? He needed some explanation. How had it come to this? How had a simple burglary, a breaking and entering, done all this?
> Kissinger kept talking, trying to turn the conversation back to all the good things, all the accomplishments. Nixon wouldn't hear of it. He was hysterical. "Henry," he said, "you are not a very orthodox Jew, and I am not an orthodox Quaker, but we need to pray."
> Nixon got down on his knees. Kissinger felt he had no alternative but to kneel down, too. The President prayed out loud, asking for help, rest, peace and love. How could a President and a country be torn apart by such small things?

Kissinger thought he had finished. But the President did not rise. He was weeping. And then, still sobbing, Nixon leaned over and struck his fist on the carpet, crying, "What have I done? What has happened?"

Kissinger touched the President, and then held him, tried to console him, to bring rest and peace to the man who was curled on the carpet like a child. The President of the United States. Kissinger tried again to reassure him, reciting Nixon's accomplishments.

Finally the President struggled to his feet. He sat back down in his chair. The storm had passed. He had another drink.[87]

The genre of New Journalism, although criticized for its reliance on subjective conjectured recreations of situations and conversations and for its pretensions to possess more information than it has, nevertheless inspired much feature and magazine writing. Even religion writers picked up the format. One of the more effective efforts was that of a priest, Walter J. Broderick, in his book *Camilo Torres: A Biography of the Priest-Guerrillero*. The first chapter recounts the last moments of Torres, a disenchanted reform-minded priest who joined up with Colombian rebels. And so does the last chapter. The first tells of the maneuvers of the soldiers looking for the rebels and the final shoot-out from the viewpoint of the soldiers. The last chapter repeats the same scenes, except the reader becomes privileged to enter the minds of the rebels and Torres and share his last thoughts before the cleric is killed by a hail of bullets. The net of the New Journalism's influence had indeed been cast wide.

Media as Vehicles of Sensationalism/Entertainment

A WAR EVENT ITSELF MAY BE SENSATIONAL

Sensationalism in war years has many facets. First, an event itself—such as a big victory or defeat or an assassination—is truly shocking and thus sensational. Second, sensationalism exists because war brings on heightened propaganda efforts, which, Michael Balfour says, "may be defined as inducing people to leap to conclusions without adequate examination of the evidence."[88] Third, sensationalism may be achieved through subtle, even subliminal, means indirectly, as propaganda uses its various techniques and silent languages that are as real as shouted words from a dictator, prime minister, or president.

Consider the sensational happenings of war. When the event that ignited World War I—the assassination of Archduke Francis Ferdinand, heir to the Austro-Hungarian throne, and his wife, the Duchess of Hohenberg—occurred in Sarajevo, Bosnia, on June 28, 1914, there were all the elements of sensationalism: conflict, surprise, and the specter of human tragedy tugging at the emotions. A drop head in a Philadelphia paper said, "Archduke and Morganatic [of lower social rank with no claim to the throne] Consort Die Together; Their Love-Affair Famous," and, "Pair Shot Down in Auto After Bomb Had Failed; Boy, only 18, Is Slayer."[89] To the sound of war and official death were added the recalled romance in high places and the tragic involvement of a teenager—sensational ingredients by any measure.

In the second kind of war sensationalism, in addition to the events themselves, the use of propaganda—information directed, twisted, or created to influence a war enterprise—is a ready form of sensationalism. The half-truth, even the total lie, is employed to create a sensational effect. One classic example of the "sensational lie" propaganda created for news consumption is the extent to which American newspapers played up phony German atrocity stories in World War I. Stories abounded that Germans fed poisoned candy to children and even cut off hands of little children in France so they would not grow up to become soldiers. One of the most outrageous myths was the account of a crucifixion of a Canadian soldier by the Germans.

Subliminal Sensationalism

The third kind of "war" sensationalism, also involving propaganda, was the less obvious, often subliminal, camouflaged persuasion in the media that influenced people, fitting also Balfour's definition of propaganda as "inducing people to leap to conclusions without adequate examination of the evidence." Subliminal sensationalism—the not-so-obvious propaganda sensationalism submerged in the medium—includes these categories.

Fiction.   Fiction may be labeled as such, but it can be fiction with a message. As seen in the sensationalism of the penny press, the element of story determines much of the news value, as attention is paid to characterization, conflict, plot development, and resolution. The Voice of America, the radio arm of the U.S. Information Agency (USIA)—whose aim was to tell the truth, good or bad, but certainly the American version of it—came to use short stories read aloud. Each story had a message, often one of a universal nature. Such was the case of the first Voice of America short story aired on November 7, 1961, for an overseas audience. The melodramatic story of an emaciated, sick soldier, Ed Smith, returning home, presented in broad simple strokes, tugged at the emotions as it presented the futility of war and at the same time exalted the peaceful rural blessings of America.[90]

Music.   Certain moods can be carried by music—the feel of victory, triumph, happiness, and the good life. The Voice of America used "Yankee Doodle" as lighter fare for its theme music, then switched to the more affirming "Columbia, the Gem of the Ocean." Interviews with musicians and other celebrities of the entertainment world were mixed in with more formal words from political leaders. The "swinging" new format, as *Time* put it, created a sensation. Perhaps counterproductively, this approach in the 1960s so impressed the communist nations that they began to pep up their radio programs with more modern music and interviews.[91]

The Power of Silence.   Delaying stories, withholding information, not revealing sources immediately, and accepting censorship without saying so are parts of a silent agenda that can distort news and generate sensationalism as well. When Harrison Salisbury of the *New York Times* went to the enemy capital, Hanoi, North Vietnam, at the beginning of 1967, he reported civilian casualty figures provided by the Hanoi government but waited a few days before revealing his source. He also interviewed the North Vietnam premier without reporting until later that ground rules of censorship were imposed by the official. "By permitting a responsible newspaperman, Harrison Salisbury of the New York Times, to report from Hanoi, the North Vietnam Communists have scored the greatest propaganda coup of the war," said an editorial in the *Toronto Telegram*, quoted in a *Detroit News* editorial. The *News* added, "Just one Salisbury is enough. What a catch for the Hanoi angler and how well baited was that propaganda line."[92]

Culture Bashing.   Bruce Cummings cited an example of a journalist mocking cultures and languages on television for effect. "Sometimes television's stereotyped representation of the 'other,'" he said, "went beyond prejudice and beyond parody, however, really beyond one's capacity for invention." He mentioned *The Today Show*'s Deborah Norville and Bryant Gumbel, who "got into a rollicking repartee over the weird languages those people speak in the Middle East. 'Did you understand a word he said?' Gumbel asked her, after one Colonel Yacoub finished speaking. This reminded him of the time he interviewed someone high up in the Afghan mujahideen ('a big muckety-muck,' Deborah suggested): the guy started talking and Bryant had no idea what language he was speaking. 'Blubbedyblubbedyblubbedy!', Deborah suggested."[93]

Standardizing Symbols.   Amid the acquiescence in creating stereotypes (for example, depicting Germans as beasts) and standardization of biases to further the war effort in World War I, political cartoons offered still another way of sensationalizing through exaggerated propaganda. "Understanding the potential power of the cartoon in propaganda, the U.S. government in an unprecedented (albeit self-serving) patronage of the arts, financed the production of cartoons and other work in support of the war," point out Everette and Melvin Dennis in their study of political cartooning.[94] Noting that American cartoons were a "poor lot," quoting art historian William Murell, they recount how the government sought to regiment cartoonists by creating the Bureau of Cartoons in December 1917. Six months later the Committee on Public Information took over the bureau. The bureau issued bulletins suggesting suitable subjects as approved by the U.S. Food Administration, the Treasury Department, and other agencies. Murrell observed: "Thus a considerable cartoon power was developed, stimulating recruiting, popularizing the draft, saving fuel and food, selling Liberty Bonds, etc. When they were not doing their utmost to graphically urge any and all of the above suggestions, the cartoonists, for the most part, concentrated their efforts on Uncle Sam buckling on armor, or the Kaiser with a bomb, pistol or knout [leather whip]. There were exceptions, of course, but they were difficult to find."[95]

World War II found readers eagerly following comics that contained thinly disguised propaganda for political and patriotic causes. Steve Canyon was in the air force, Buzz Sawyer in the navy. They joined others in pursuing the perfidious enemies, the Japanese and the Germans. Stalwart favorites, such as *Dick Tracy* and *Little Orphan Annie*, promoted America and its causes; yet counterculture ideology later found a popular response in Walt Kelly's *Pogo* and Garry Trudeau's *Doonesbury*.

Media as Businesses

ADVERTISING IN WARTIME

The approach to advertising changed between the wars. Like the rest of the business world, advertising was affected drastically by the Great Depression of 1929. In the years following, advertising sales plummeted from $3.4 billion to about $1 billion a year, and did not recover to the $3 billion level again until 1947. Advertising agencies cut back on personnel or folded. One that weathered the depression successfully was Benton and Bowles, founded by William Benton and Chester Bowles. The agency profitably employed researchers, such as A. C. Nielsen and George Gallup, to discover why buyers preferred one product over another, or rejected both. They found that consumers preferred products that were cheap and also lasting and not the useless and marginal items that many firms were peddling.

The 1930s saw the powers of the Federal Trade Commission extended by the Wheeler-Lee Amendment of 1938, which prohibited false or misleading advertising. Investigations of the FTC turned up such flagrant misrepresentations as the endorsements used by the American Tobacco Company; 50 out of 440 persons who said they smoked only the company's Lucky Strike did not even smoke.

With the shortages of goods in World War II the demand for advertising ebbed. Yet manufacturers sought to keep their names before the public, and many did so by linking their products to the war effort. One maker of nuts and bolts took out full-page ads showing fighter planes and bombers allegedly using its nuts and bolts. An air-conditioning company took credit for sinking enemy ships, since the lens of the periscope in American submarines was finished and polished in a factory cooled by one of its air-conditioning units.

Joining Hands in Advertising

A nonprofit cooperative organization of advertising leaders was formed in 1941 to plan and coordinate national media advertising campaigns in support of the war effort. The Advertising Council, known from 1943 to 1945 as the War Advertising Council, promoted military enlistment, war bond sales, conservation of scarce goods, the planting of gardens, car pools to save gas, even contributing to national security (said one ad that showed a sinking ship, "A Slip of the Lip Will Sink a Ship").

The results during the war years were significant, says Brad Lynch, retired director of corporate communications for N. W. Ayer, Inc., and a director of public relations for the Advertising Council. He points out that 800 million war bonds were sold, 50 million victory gardens were planted, home canning accounted for 40 percent of all canned vegetables consumed, and enlistment in the Women's Army Corps increased 400 percent.

"Some permanent changes resulted" from the wartime work of the council, says Lynch. "Many more women were in the work force to stay. A profligate country had sensed the lasting worth of conservation. Volunteerism—in giving blood, time, money and talents—was an accepted practice everywhere."[96]

In the 1990s the Advertising Council is still going strong. With a paid staff of forty and offices in New York, Washington, and Chicago, the council has an operating budget of $3 million garnered through donations from 400 companies. With a billion and a half dollars of donated advertising space a year, from subway placards to billboards, the council promotes a host of human and social causes, including environmental concerns, job opportunities, religion in American life, and prevention of child abuse.

Media as Voices of Reform

AN AGENDA BEYOND INTEGRATION

From the beginnings of the black press in America, with Samuel Cornish and John Russwurm's *Freedom Journal* in 1827, which attacked slavery and delved into the possibility of colonization in Africa by liberated American slaves, to Frederick Douglass's antislavery *North Star* and the Civil War–era magazine *Douglass Monthly*, to the early twentieth-century crusades of Ida Wells-Barnett against lynching and W. E. B. Du Bois's crusade for equal rights for minorities, including women, in *The Crisis*, to the militant activists of the 1960s, the black media agenda has called for reform and, at times, for economic and cultural revolution.

Reasons for a Black Radicalism

A number of factors moved the agenda from a more general call for equal rights and acquiescence in a framework of integration to the more aggressive stance of black nationalism and black empowerment espoused by divergent new leaders of the 1960s. Contributing to a greater assertiveness and a strengthening of the planks of the agenda were the following:

- A successful black press, including the *Chicago Defender* of founder Robert Abbott and today's John H. Sengstacke; the *Baltimore Afro-American*, founded in 1892 by John H. Murphy and led today by John J. Oliver, Jr.; a news service, the Associated Negro Press[97]; and successful black magazines, namely, John Johnson's *Ebony* and *Jet*.

- The visibility of black celebrities, from writer James Baldwin to various entertainers and sports figures, such as baseball's Jackie Robinson and boxing's three-time heavyweight champion Muhammad Ali, as well as Supreme Court Justice Thurgood Marshall and Edward W. Brooke of Massachusetts, the first black elected to the U.S. Senate by popular vote.
- The breaking of the racial barrier in television, with the first network show hosted by an African American, *The Nat King Cole Show* on NBC, 1956–1957.[98]
- Exposés and investigative reports in the black press, from the early work of Charlotta and Joseph Bass in the *California Eagle*, exposing, for example, discrimination in hospital hiring in 1919 and the hiring of black domestic help under slave conditions in 1930.[99] The African-American press organization, the National Newspaper Publishers Association, has for years given an award for the best investigative and community reporting in the black press.
- Fallout from Franklin Roosevelt's New Deal liberalism that affected some southern editors. Although many still remained faithful to segregation, reform measures were advocated by some, such as editor Harry Mell Ayers of the *Anniston* (Alabama) *Star*, who supported elimination of the poll tax.[100]
- Legal gains, such as the executive order of President Harry Truman to integrate the military in 1948, the Supreme Court ruling that outlawed segregation in public schools in 1954, the Civil Rights Act of 1964, and subsequent laws giving the government the right to send officials into the South to register blacks to vote and another law outlawing discrimination in the renting and sale of housing.
- The growing presence of outside-the-South reporters descending on southern communities to report civil unrest. So many reporters covered the 1956 bus boycott in Montgomery, Alabama, that retired *Montgomery Advertiser* reporter Tom Johnson remembered, "It was causing the atmosphere to suffer oxygen deprivation."[101]
- The concerted efforts, a kind of "holy crusade,"[102] of white northern college students working under experienced black organizers to register black Mississippians in the "Freedom Summer" of 1964.
- The murders of Sunday school children in the bombing of a Birmingham church and civil rights leader Medgar Evers in 1963; civil rights workers Andrew Goodman, James Chaney, and Michael Schwerner in 1964; and Martin Luther King, Jr., in 1968.
- The new civil rights organizations: the Congress of Racial Equality (CORE), the Student Nonviolent Coordinating Committee (SNCC), and King's Southern Leadership Conference.
- The emergence of freedom-movement publications, such as the McComb, Mississippi, *Freedom's Journal*, edited by Barbara JoAnn Lea, the Jackson *Mississippi Freedom Democratic Party Newsletter*, the Jackson *Mississippi Free Press*, and the Vicksburg *Citizens' Appeal*.[103]
- The beginning, although woefully inadequate, of the appointment of minorities to news staffs. For example, the *Washington Post* hired Robert Maynard from the

Robert Maynard: Publisher of Oakland Tribune.

York (Pennsylvania) *Gazette and Daily*. Maynard, whom the *Post's* Ben Bradlee dubbed "the star of stars," went on to become the first black editor and then publisher of a major U.S. newspaper, the *Oakland* (California) *Tribune*.[104]

- Frustration with national leaders, as Lyndon Johnson seemed to forget his civil rights commitments as he pursued the Vietnam War,[105] followed by Richard Nixon's alleged "deal" with southern Dixiecrats to slow attempts at integration,[106] while at a state level Maryland Governor (later Vice President) Spiro Agnew orchestrated a deliberate snub of black leaders.[107]
- The intensity of the rebellion on college campuses, symbolized not only by death on the campus of Kent State University in Ohio, but also by the shooting of demonstrators on the campus of South Carolina State College, Orangeburg, in 1968, in which three were killed and others wounded including Cleveland Sellers, a black power advocate and official of SNCC.[108]
- The rise of charismatic black leaders, namely, Malcolm X and Dr. King.
- Rebellion in the streets, from Newark to Detroit to Watts.
- The development of a militant black party, the Black Panthers, in 1966, which called for armed opposition to white racism and police brutality.[109]

- The report of a presidential commission, headed by Illinois Governor Otto Kerner, which described two racially divided societies in America and a polarization of society enforced by denying rights to blacks.
- The separatist movements of the Black Muslims and black nationalists, which turned from integration and called for black-dominated geographic segments or "nations," thereby raising the ante in discussions of race relations.

The Nation of Islam

Black nationalism took various forms and often had its roots in religious principles and rhetoric. Foremost among the movements were the Black Muslims of the Nation of Islam. In 1930 Wali Farrard of Detroit declared that he had arrived from Mecca with a calling to be a prophet to pronounce judgment on white devils who had enslaved the Black Nation. When he disappeared in 1934, a disciple, Elijah Poole, whom the Prophet had renamed Elijah Muhammad, assumed leadership. Recognizing Allah as the one and only Deity and following a rigid discipline that included abstinence from alcohol and tobacco, the movement preached black separation and the development of black economic and political power. Looking forward to an eventual formation of a black nation, while nevertheless adhering to the law of the land, the movement launched farms and businesses, urging economic independence from whites. The Nation of Islam started its own schools and directed a paramilitary organization, the Fruit of Islam.

One of those inspired by Elijah Muhammad was a young man named Malcolm Little, who was in prison for burglary. Little decided to change his ways, educated himself, and subscribed to the tenets and leadership of the Black Muslims led by Elijah Muhammad. Little, now known as Malcolm X, became the right-hand aide of Elijah and soon one of the group's most prominent orators. Malcolm eventually split with Elijah and founded his own Organization of Afro-American Unity. He called for an economic revolution on behalf of blacks and expanded his vision to include a campaign for human rights at large. He was gunned down while giving a speech in Harlem in 1965. In the 1960s the newspaper *Muhammad Speaks*, with a circulation of 700,000, outdistanced other black newspapers in circulation as it spoke for black separatism and also expressed its opposition to the Vietnam War.

In Detroit a Christian form of black nationalism was developed by the Reverend Albert Cleage, a United Church of Christ pastor who renamed his Central United Church of Christ in midtown Detroit the Shrine of the Black Madonna. He received the support of Betty Shabazz, Malcolm's widow. Cleage linked up with other churches around the nation to develop a Black Christian Nationalist Movement. His blunt and confrontational approach did not sit well with the Detroit newspapers or even with many blacks. Nevertheless, with his newspaper, the *Illustrated News*, and a book, *The Black Messiah*, Cleage was hailed as the "foremost exponent of a black Christology" by *Ebony* and became an inspiration for later exponents of "black" theology. To Cleage, Jesus was black, and the main activity of Cleage's movement was to develop leaders to provide social and economic services for blacks and to establish business cooperatives in black communities. He electrified audiences, as he did at a rally at Detroit's Tiger Stadium for independent presidential candidate Eugene McCarthy in 1968, and he stole the show; Cleage even made an impressive bid to become president of the National Council of Churches. He greatly admired Malcolm X, with whom he appeared on occasion.

Cleage intellectualized the concept of a black nation. Insisting that the concept of black nationhood is determined by whites, who exclude blacks from the rights and benefits of society, he nevertheless detached himself from any back-to-Africa movement or a "geographic separation beyond the separation that already exists in urban ghettos."[110] He saw black power as a transition between "unity" or cooperative work and control of the destiny of blacks. "Nationalism is meaningless unless there is power, structural power."[111]

Facing a Manifesto's Demands

With the mood of militancy in the nation, black leaders could see that seizing the initiative in the business and economic community was a more rewarding route than integration and the mere rhetoric of equal rights. Yet black radicalism went a step further by calling for a goal of "total power," the achievement of goals by an ideology of socialistic principles of redistribution of goods, and a recognition that a violent revolution might occur before the goals could be achieved. Thus a meeting of black leaders at the National Black Economic Development Conference (BEDC) in Detroit, April 26, 1969—a meeting that was closed to the press—adopted a "Black Manifesto" that demanded reparations from churches and synagogues of a half billion dollars for the complicity of white-dominated religious groups involved in the capitalistic racist attitudes of the nation. The money would go for the development of enterprises aimed at improving the economic status of the black community.

A New York black leader, James Forman, showed up at the prestigious Riverside Church and later at a historic Episcopal church in New York during church services to present demands. The media, with their acknowledged middle-class white management, were by and large outraged. The response of the churches was deeply divided, with pronouncements against the manifesto by some, and the eventual funding of black projects through the BEDC by others.

Particularly offensive to critics were statements in the manifesto such as this:

> While we talk of revolution, which will be an armed confrontation and long years
> of sustained gerilla [sic] warfare inside this country, we must also talk of the type
> of world we want to live in. We must commit ourselves to a society where the
> total means of production are taken from the rich people and placed into the
> hands of the state for the welfare of all the people. This is what we mean when
> we say total control. And we mean that black people who have suffered the
> most from exploitation and racism must move to protect their black interest by
> assuming leadership inside of the United States of everything that exists.

And the Black Manifesto criticized the Vietnam War: "Our hearts go out to the Vietnamese for we know what it is to suffer under the domination of racist America."[112]

As the media attempted to deal with the rhetoric, some effort was made to understand how best to interpret the radical manifesto. A column in the *Detroit Free Press*, for example, said there were three ways to read the document: literally, which takes the emotive words and threats at face value; figuratively, which

Another Voice: The Black Cartoonists

A poignant group of commentators and satirists were the cartoonists for black newspapers. Chester Commodore, an internationally known commercial artist, served for fifteen years as chief editorial artist for the *Chicago Defender* before retiring in 1981. His cartoon links international and domestic injustice.

Francis Yancey, editorial cartoonist for the *Baltimore Afro-American* from 1938 through the 1940s, was cartoonist for the *Boston Globe* for twenty-two years. His cartoon questions the civil rights commitment of President Franklin Roosevelt.

Mixed loyalties: Cartoon by Chester Commodore. (Chicago Daily Defender, March 20, 1968)

"He never said a mumbling word"—cartoon by Francis Yancey. (Baltimore Afro-American, Feb. 26, 1938. Reprinted by permission of Afro-American Newspapers Archives and Research Center)

Francis Yancey at drawing board at the Baltimore Afro-American.

takes the manifesto as a kind of charismatic and symbolic document; and realistically, which takes the document at face value without emphasis on special "eyeglasses" by which to read it. The column notes the relationship of all three approaches:

> Realism may not be entirely alien from the literal and figurative approach. Jesus used all three forms of speech. When Jesus said, "Go and buy a donkey" for his ride into Jerusalem, he could be taken literally; when he spoke in parables and riddles, he could be taken figuratively; when he said, "I have come not to bring peace but a sword," he could be taken realistically. . . .
>
> When you read a document realistically, you ask "what does it say," not "what are its most incendiary words. . . ."

And the column goes on to point out that attention could be given to the language of sequence in the manifesto—that events follow and depend on prior events —and to the language of contemporary usage. For example, to criticize capitalism, which has proliferated in many ways, does not make one a Marxist. The pope (Paul VI) "himself has denounced capitalism as a viable way to meet the needs of today's masses."[113]

As for blacks assuming power or a significant place of leadership in the media, some progress was made but it was not significant. "For years [officially since 1978] America's daily newspapers have been in pursuit of an elusive ethnic heterogeneity," Ellis Cose says in *Newsweek*. "In that time, they have raised the percentage of ethnic minorities from under 4 percent to just over 10, but the effort has pleased virtually no one. Minority journalists wonder whether, for all the hoopla, the diversity crusade is largely a farce."[114] News organizations, even with inroads in the hiring of minorities, still reflect white agendas and offer the news of the day as seen through a white perspective. If Sig Gissler, former editor of the *Milwaukee Journal*, is correct, race remains "America's rawest nerve" in the 1990s.[115]

QUESTIONS FOR DISCUSSION AND RESEARCH

1. Why did so many of the media editors and columnists quarrel with Martin Luther King, Jr.'s effort to link the Vietnam War and the struggle for civil rights?

2. Compare the Alien and Sedition Acts of 1798 and the Espionage, the Trading-with-the-Enemy, and the Sabotage Acts of 1917 and 1918. Which group of acts—1798 or 1917–1918—were the most oppressive? Why?

3. In what war of the twentieth century have restrictions against the media covering war zones been the greatest—World War I, World War II, Korean, Vietnam, Panama and Grenada, or Persian Gulf wars? Explain.

4. Should photographs that are gory or controversial ever be censored?

5. Compare the philosophy and work of George Creel's Committee on Public Information of World War I with the philosophy and work of Byron Price's Office of Censorship and Elmer Davis's Office of War Information in World War II.

6. What's the history of the military press pool in wartime? What are the advantages and disadvantages?

7. Make a descriptive directory of "alternative" lifestyle or issue-oriented dissident papers in your area. Proceed in these stages: (a) each student seek to identify as many such papers as possible; (b) then each student select one paper and research its history for a short report; (c) collect student reports on these local and regional papers and make them into a booklet; (d) tape a discussion on how the new and current alternative papers compare to those that have gone before; transcribe the tape and use it as an introduction or postscript for the booklet. (The booklet could be photocopied and distributed to local libraries and even local media for reference.)

8. General assignment reporters in the 1960s could expect to cover protests, demonstrations, even riots. How would you go about reporting such events?

(You might interview a reporter who lived through the 1960s; maybe he or she could be invited to class.)

9. Study one article in your local daily newspaper and rewrite it as a report might be written for an alternative paper.

10. Contrast the New Journalism of the 1960s and 1970s with the New Journalism of Pulitzer and the muckrakers at the end of the last century and the start of the twentieth century. What are the strengths and weaknesses of the New Journalism? Can the techniques of New Journalism be applied in some ways to the writing of a breaking hard-news story? Explain.

11. Each student reads a work of a 1960s–1970s New Journalist and reports. What is unique about that person's style? Can you designate a name or category for that person's writing?

12. In a competitive world, the United States needs to get its message and "sales pitches" out at large. But how? Holly Cowan Shulman asks: "Should propaganda be based on the standards of objective news as developed in the American press, both electronic and print or should different principles govern the broadcasts of the Voice of America? Should there be a propaganda agency at all in time of peace, or should our communications be left in the hands of the private media?"[116] What do you think?

13. As the United States was weighing the option of invading Haiti in 1994, the *New York Times* carried on its front page a story, reminiscent of some stories in the Spanish-American War and World War I, headlined "Orphans of Haiti Disappear, Targets of Murderous Thugs," which began:

> PORT-AU-PRINCE, Haiti—The rusted iron gate of the peeling old orphanage is bound in place with three feet of heavy chain and an ancient padlock, not to keep children in, but to protect them. In Haiti, where gunmen loyal to the military Government have methodically murdered the poorest of the poor, a favorite target is a motherless child.[117]

Do there appear to be elements of propaganda—loaded words, overstatement, patriotic self-righteousness—in this story, or is it objective reporting? Explain.

14. Review the current agenda of Democrats and Republicans, and then study three pages each from *Time, Newsweek,* and *U.S. News & World Report.* Are there any traces of political leanings? Explain.

15. What are some of the factors that helped to develop black radicalism and nationalism? Did the media have a role in encouraging and shaping such movements?

ENDNOTES

1. Hiley H. Ward, *Prophet of the Black Nation* (a biography of Albert Cleage) (New York: Pilgrim Press, 1969), pp. 110–113.

2. Herbert Shapiro, "The Vietnam War and the American Civil Rights Movement," *Journal of Ethnic Studies,* vol. 16, no. 4, Winter 1989, pp. 117ff.

3. "Dr. King's Error," editorial, *New York Times,* April 7, 1969, p. A37.

4. "Dr. King's Disservice," *Life*, April 21, 1967, p. 4.

5. George N. Dionisopoulos et al., "Martin Luther King, the American Dream and Vietnam: A Collision of Rhetorical Trajectories," *Western Journal of Communication*, vol. 56, Spring 1992, p. 103.

6. Richard Lentz, "The Resurrection of the Prophet: Dr. Martin Luther King, Jr., and the News Weeklies," *American Journalism*, vol. 4, no. 2, 1987, p. 61.

7. Ibid. p. 62.

8. John Nerone, *Violence Against the Press: Policing the Public Sphere in U.S. History* (New York: Oxford University Press, 1994), p. 131.

9. Michael P. Mulcrone, "The World War I Censorship of the Irish-American Press," Ph.D. dissertation, University of Washington, 1993, p. 331.

10. Ibid., p. 332.

11. Ibid., p. 335.

12. Ibid., p. 337.

13. "Unpunished Spies," editorial, *New York Times*, Jan. 28, 1918.

14. "Kahn Would Silence Sedition with Rope," *New York Times*, March 25, 1918.

15. Mulcrone, "World War I Censorship," p. 207.

16. Ibid., quoting from "Lynch Law and Treason," *Literary Digest*, Aug. 18, 1917, p. 12.

17. Ibid., Mulcrone, p. 207; *Literary Digest*, pp. 13–14.

18. Mick Mulcrone, "'Those Miserable Little Hounds'—World War I Postal Censorship of the *Irish World*," *Journalism History*, vol. 20, no. 1, Spring 1994, p. 16.

19. Michael Emery and Edwin Emery, *The Press and America*, 7th ed. (Englewood Cliffs, N.J.: Prentice Hall, 1992), p. 256.

20. Zechariah Chafee, Jr., *Free Speech in the United States* (Cambridge, Mass.: Harvard University Press, 1954), p. 37, quoted in Elizabeth Blanks Hindman, "The Evils Congress Has a Right to Prevent?: The Millian Principle and the Espionage Act Cases," a paper presented to the Law Division of the Association for Education in Journalism and Mass Communication, Minneapolis, August 1990.

21. Quoted in Chafee, *Free Speech*, p. 39, and Hindman, "The Evils Congress Has a Right to Prevent?"

22. Chafee, *Free Speech*, pp. 40, 41, and Hindman, "The Evils Congress Has a Right to Prevent?"

23. The word, according to *Webster's New World Dictionary*, is said to come from a Chinese mispronunciation of IWW (Industrial Workers of the World) as "I Wobbly Wobbly."

24. Rutherford Smith, "Eastman, Max Forrester," in Joseph P. McKerns, ed., *Biographical Dictionary of American Journalism* (Westport, Conn.: Greenwood Press, 1989), p. 209.

25. Ibid., p. 20.

26. Ibid., p. 26, quoting Ray Ginger, *Eugene V. Debs: A Biography* (New York: Collier, 1962).

27. Frank Luther Mott, *American Journalism: A History of Newspapers in the United States Through 250 Years* (New York: Macmillan, 1947), p. 626.

28. Carol Oukrop, "The Four Minute Men Became National Network During World War I," *Journalism Quarterly*, vol. 52, no. 4, Winter 1975, p. 632.

29. Mott, *American Journalism*, p. 627.

30. Jan Cohn, *Improbable Fiction: The Life of Mary Roberts Rinehart* (Pittsburgh: University of Pittsburgh Press, 1980), pp. 124, 125. See also Charlotte MacLeod, *Had She But Known: A Biography of Mary Roberts Rinehart* (New York: Mysterious, 1994). Also her autobiography, *My Story*.

31. Richard W. Steele, "News of the 'Good War': World War II News Management," *Journalism Quarterly*, vol. 62, no. 4, Winter 1985, p. 708.

32. Frederick S. Voss, *Reporting the War: Journalistic Coverage of World War II* (Washington, D.C.: Smithsonian Institution Press for the National Portrait Gallery, 1994), p. 22.

33. Ibid., p. 24.

34. Ibid., p. 23.

35. Steele, "News of the 'Good War,'" p. 714.

36. George Roeder, Jr., *The Censored War: American Visual Experience During World War II* (New Haven, Conn.: Yale University Press, 1993).

37. Clifford Montague, "OWI: Winning Wars with Words," *Media History Digest*, vol. 11, no. 2, Fall-Winter 1991, p. 30.

38. Betsy Wade, *Forward Positions: The War Correspondence of Homer Bigart* (Fayetteville: University of Arkansas Press, 1992), p. 127.

39. "Newsmen Subject to Military Control—Text of 8th Army Censorship Rules," *Editor & Publisher*, Jan. 13, 1951, p. 8.

40. Mort Rosenblum, *Who Stole the News?* (New York: John Wiley & Sons, 1993), p. 243.

41. Keyes Beech, "This Was No Retreat," *Chicago Daily News*, Dec. 11, 1950, in Louis L. Snyder and Richard B. Morris, eds., *A Treasury of Great Reporting* (New York: Simon and Schuster, 1962), p. 740.

42. Peter Arnett, *Live from the Battlefield: From Vietnam to Baghdad* (New York: Simon & Schuster, 1994), p. 214.

43. Ibid., p. 118.

44. Charlotte Niemeyer, "Recording the Vietnam War: Photographic Coverage in Newsmagazines from 1964 to 1973," master's abstract, University of Nebraska at Omaha, 1990, in *Journalism Abstracts*, vol. 29, 1991, Association for Education in Journalism and Mass Communication, p. 104.

45. Francis Wilkinson, *Essential Liberty: First Amendment Battles for a Free Press* (New York: Columbia University Graduate School of Journalism, 1992), p. 83. See also David Rudenstine, *The Day the Presses Stopped: A History of the Pentagon Papers Case* (Berkeley: University of California Press, 1996).

46. William J. Leonhirth, "Guns or Butter?: Black Press Editorial Policy Toward the Vietnam War," paper presented to the American Journalism Historians Association, Roanoke, Va., October 1994.

47. *New York Times*, Nov. 8, 1983.

48. Donna Demac, *Keeping America Uninformed: Government Secrecy in the 1980s* (New York: Pilgrim Press, 1984), p. 99.

49. Ed Joyce, *Prime Times, Bad Times*. (New York: Anchor Books, 1988), p. 286.

50. "Press Pool in Panama," *Editor & Publisher*, editorial, Jan. 6, 1990, p. 6.

51. Ted Koppel, "The Second Front: Waging War on the Media in the Persian Gulf," excerpt from Koppel's speech to the University of Pennsylvania class of 1991, *OPC Bulletin*, Overseas Press Club, New York, November 1991, p. 5.

52. *Editor & Publisher*, Jan. 12, 1991.

53. Richard Jackson Harris, *A Cognitive Psychology of Mass Communication*, 2nd ed. (Hillside, N.J.: Lawrence Erlbaum, 1994), p. 151.

54. Malcolm W. Browne, "The Military vs. the Press," *New York Times Magazine*, March 3, 1991, p. 29.

55. Jonathan Franklin, "Inside the Desert Storm Mortuary," *San Francisco Bay Guardian*, March 6, 1991.

56. Benjamin Chavis, "Poverty, Racism 'Drafted' Blacks into Army," *Jet*, Feb. 4, 1991, p. 8, cited in Venise Berry and Kim Karloff, "Perspectives on the Persian Gulf War in Popular Black Magazines," in Susan Jeffords and Lauren Rabinovitz, eds., *Seeing Through the Media: The Persian Gulf War* (New Brunswick, N.J.: Rutgers University Press, 1994), p. 257.

57. Zhongdang Pan, "Explicating Black and White Differences in Opinions About the Gulf

War," research paper presented to the Association for Education in Journalism and Mass Communication, Kansas City, August 1993.

58. "The Nine Principles of Combat Coverage," *Editor & Publisher*, June 6, 1992, p. 73.

59. *Editor & Publisher*, Sept. 24, 1994.

60. Debra Gersh, "New Guidelines for War Coverage in Place," *Editor & Publisher*, June 6, 1992, p. 72.

61. Ibid.

62. Raymond Bonner, "Keeping the Peace in Bosnia, and the Press: In a Switch, the Army Stresses Cooperation," *New York Times*, Jan. 15, 1996, p. D5.

63. Lauren Kessler, "Sixties Survivors: The Persistence of Countercultural Values in the Lives of Underground Journalists," *Journalism History*, vol. 16, no. 1, 2, Spring–Summer 1989, p. 2.

64. Laurence Leamer, *The Paper Revolutionaries: The Rise of the Underground Press* (New York: Simon and Schuster, 1972), p. 15.

65. Peter Osnos, "I. F. Stone, a Journalist's Journalist," *New York Times*, June 20, 1989, p. A23.

66. Robert C. Cottrell, *Izzy: A Biography of I. F. Stone* (New Brunswick, N.J.: Rutgers University Press, 1992), p. 14, quoting radio program transcript, "Modern Times," interview of Studs Terkel by Larry Josephson.

67. Nancy Roberts, "Dorothy Day," in McKerns, *Biographical Dictionary of American Journalism*, p. 174.

68. William D. Miller, *Dorothy Day: A Biography* (New York: Harper & Row, 1982), p. 518.

69. Robert J. Glessing, *The Underground Press in America* (Bloomington: Indiana University Press, 1970), p. 4.

70. Roger Lewis, *Outlaws of America: The Underground Press and Its Context* (Baltimore: Penguin Books, 1972), p. 67.

71. Ibid., pp. 62, 63.

72. Tony Case, "Freebie Fallout," *Editor & Publisher*, March 9, 1996, p. 10.

73. William Glaberson, "In the Out Crowd and Loving It—At Work with Karen Durbin," *New York Times*, Dec. 7, 1994, pp. C1, C8.

74. Glessing, *Underground Press*, p. 18.

75. Leamer, *The Paper Revolutionaries*, p. 29.

76. Abe Peck, *Uncovering the Sixties: The Life and Times of the Underground Press* (New York: Pantheon Books, 1985), p. 31.

77. Milton Viorst, *Fire in the Streets: America in the 1960s* (New York: Touchstone, 1979), pp. 343–381, quoted in Peck, *Uncovering the Sixties*, p. 64.

78. Duane Pederson, *Jesus People* (Pasadena, Calif.: Compass Press, 1971), p. 20.

79. Hiley H. Ward, *The Far-out Saints of the Jesus Communes* (New York: Association, 1972), p. 149.

80. Ronald M. Enroth, Edward E. Ericson, Jr., and C. Breckinridge Peters, *The Jesus People: Old-Time Religion in the Age of Aquarius* (Grand Rapids, Mich.: Eerdmans, 1972), p. 77.

81. Lauren Kessler, *The Dissident Press: Alternative Journalism in American History* (Beverly Hills, Calif.: Sage, 1984), p. 84.

82. Peck, *Uncovering the Sixties*, p. 219.

83. Elliott Shore, Patricia J. Case, and Laura Daly, eds., *Alternative Papers: Selections from the Alternative Press, 1979–1980* (Philadelphia: Temple University Press, 1982), p. 3.

84. Edward Gray Applegate, "A Historical Analysis of New Journalism," D.Ed. dissertation, Oklahoma State University, 1984, p. 15.

85. Michael Johnson, *The New Journalism* (Lawrence: University Press of Kansas, 1971), pp. 87, 88.

86. Applegate, *Historical Analysis*, p. 248.

87. Bob Woodward and Carl Bernstein, *The Final Days* (New York: Simon and Schuster, 1976), p. 423, quoted in Applegate, *Historical Analysis*, p. 287.

88. Michael Balfour, *Propaganda in War, 1939–1945: Organisations, Policies and Publics in Britain and Germany* (London: Routledge & Kegan Paul, 1979), p. 421.

89. *North American*, June 29, 1914.

90. Robert William Pirsein, *The Voice of America: An History of the International Broadcasting Activities of the United States Government, 1940–1962* (New York: Arno Press, 1979), p. 561, appendix 14, "VOA Special English Script #1: The Return of a Soldier," by Hamlin Garland.

91. Thomas C. Sorensen, *The Word War: The Story of American Propaganda* (New York: Harper & Row, 1968), p. 247, citing *Time*, "Swinging Voice," Dec. 9, 1966.

92. "N. Vietnam's Propaganda Coup," *Detroit News*, Jan. 11, 1967.

93. Bruce Cummings, *War and Television* (New York: Verso, 1992), p. 121, citing Margaret Spillane, "M*U*S*H," in *The Nation*, Feb. 25, 1991.

94. E. Everette Dennis and Melvin L. Dennis, "100 Years of Political Cartooning," *Journalism History*, vol. 1, no. 1, Spring 1974, p. 9.

95. Ibid., quoting William Murrell, *A History of American Graphic Humor, 1865–1938*, vol. 2 (New York: Macmillan, 1938), p. 197.

96. Brad Lynch, "Ad Council Marks 50 Years of Crusades," *Media History Digest*, vol. 12, no. 1, Spring–Summer 1992, p. 52.

97. See Lawrence D. Hogan, *A Black National News Service: The Associated Negro Press and Claude Barnett, 1919–1945* (Cranbury, N.J.: Associated University Presses, 1984).

98. Inger L. Stole, "Nat King Cole and the Politics of Race and Broadcasting in the 1950s," University of Wisconsin–Madison, a paper presented at the AEJMC meeting, Kansas City, August 1993.

99. The Basses are discussed in Rodger Streitmatter, "Delilah Beasley: A Black Woman Journalist Who Lifted as She Climbed," *American Journalism*, vol. 11, no. 1, Winter 1994, p. 71.

100. Kevin Stoker, "The New Deal Paradox: A Southern Journalist's Struggle to Create a New South Without Changing the Old One," Ph.D. student research paper, University of Alabama.

101. Ginny Whitehouse, "Only Under the Magnolia: Regionalized Reporting of Racial Tensions in the 1950s," University of Missouri, paper presented to AEJMC meeting, Kansas City, August 1993.

102. See Nicolaus Mills, *Like a Holy Crusade: Mississippi 1964—The Turning of the Civil Rights Movement in America* (Chicago: Ivan R. Dee, 1992).

103. Julius E. Thompson, *The Black Press in Mississippi, 1865–1985* (Gainesville: University Press of Florida, 1993), p. 73.

104. Ben Bradlee, *A Good Life: Newspapering and Other Adventures* (New York: Simon & Schuster, 1995), p. 291.

105. Roy Wilkins, "What Are Johnson's Civil Rights Aims?" *Detroit News*, Jan. 21, 1967.

106. "Nixon Wrecks Guidelines in Payoff to Dixiecrats," *Baltimore Afro-American*, July 12, 1969, p. 1.

107. "Agnew Insults Leaders, Guests Quit Meeting in Bitterness," also editorial, "What It's Really All About, Ted Baby," *Baltimore Afro-American*, April 13, 1968.

108. Mike Davis, "3 Dead, 50 Shot on S.C. Campus," *Baltimore Afro-American*, Feb. 10, 1968, p. 1.

109. See Hugh Pearson, *The Shadow of the Panther: Huey Newton and the Price of Black Power in America* (Reading, Mass.: Addison-Wesley, 1994).

110. "Rev. Cleage Tells You About Negro Separatism," Bee-line question and answer column,

Detroit Free Press, Sept. 1, 1968, p. 15A, quoted in Hiley H. Ward, *Prophet of the Black Nation* (Philadelphia: Pilgrim Press, 1969), p. 25.

111. Ward, *Prophet of the Black Nation*, p. 26.

112. "Black Manifesto: To the White Christian Churches and the Jewish Synagogues in the United States of America and All Other Racist Institutions—Presentation by James Forman, delivered and adopted by the National Black Economic Development Conference in Detroit, Michigan on April 26, 1969," copy released to the press.

113. Hiley H. Ward, "How to Read Manifesto: Literal, Figurative, Realistic?" weekly "Religion Outlook" column, *Detroit Free Press*, June 28, 1969.

114. Ellis Cose, "A City Room of Many Colors," *Newsweek*, Oct. 4, 1993, p. 82.

115. "Race—America's Rawest Nerve," theme of issue, preface, *Media Studies Journal*, vol. 8, no. 3, Summer 1994, p. xiii.

116. Holly Cowan Shulman, *The Voice of America: Propaganda and Democracy, 1941–1945* (Madison: University of Wisconsin Press, 1990), p. 199.

117. Rick Bragg, "Orphans of Haiti Disappear, Targets of Murderous Thugs," *New York Times*, Sept. 9, 1994, p. 1.

14

Magazines, Mergers, and Moguls

Following World War I, a new type of mass circulation magazine—the condensed feature and news magazine—took hold. The most successful of these were *Reader's Digest*, started in 1922, and *Time*, started in 1923 (followed a decade later by *Newsweek*). The times were ripe for media that could present news and articles in summary form, articles written with a narrative style that would keep the commuter awake and serve the middle class on the run. Radio had not yet been developed to its potential, and the quick takes and "sound bites," a form of news presentation later realized in the electronic media, could be manifested in condensed news and literature.

Neither the idea of a newsmagazine nor that of a magazine of condensed or shorter reportage was new. *Pathfinder*, launched thirty years before *Time* and continuing until 1954, rewrote news of interest primarily to rural and small-town readers. Back in 1786, two news magazines appeared several months apart: the *New Haven Gazette* and the *Connecticut Magazine*, then the *Worcester Magazine*. In his history of magazines Theodore Peterson tells of others in the nineteenth century, including *Leslie's* and *Harper's Weekly*, which presented the week's news with pictures and thus were forerunners of the image-roundup publications—*Life* magazine (created by Time, Inc., in 1936), *Look* (1937–1971), and *People* (started in 1974).

The *Literary Digest*, founded in 1890, was close to being a news magazine and also close to being a digest, says Peterson, although he notes that it probably resembled more of a clipping service serving the public.[1] In its heyday before it folded in 1938 the *Literary Digest* reached a circulation of 2 million and was third in advertising revenue among magazines.[2]

Media as Political Organs

AN APPETITE FOR THE AMERICAN WAY

Political ideology was never far behind in the minds of the condensed-format tycoons, Henry R. Luce, cofounder of *Time* and chief of the *Time* empire, and DeWitt Wallace, who with his wife Lila parlayed *Reader's Digest* into the number-one paid-circulation magazine in the United States, with more than 16 million readers in the 1990s.[3] Both Luce and Wallace had strict Presbyterian upbringings, and their outlook reflected a nostalgia for pious values and traditional morality, coupled with an appetite for manifest destiny and a belief in the preeminence of the American way.

The Luce philosophy that "good" America had the moral obligation to dominate the world was recapped in a widely circulated editorial, "The American Century," published in *Life* on February 17, 1941. Luce publicized the editorial in full-page newspaper ads and in mailings to political leaders. He called on Americans to "accept wholeheartedly our duty and our opportunity as the most powerful and vital nation in the world and in consequence to exert upon the world the full impact of our influence, for such purposes as we see fit and by such means as we see fit."[4]

The DeWitt Wallace Condensed Way

Wallace led the readers of his *Reader's Digest* into the valley of righteousness with articles with an excessive anticommunist tone. Wallace wrote articles and placed them in leading publications, then offered shorter versions of them in his magazine. After a piece had appeared in the *Digest*, he often allowed it to be reprinted, all of which gave his views considerable exposure. The editor of the magazine in which the article originally appeared coveted the extended publicity provided by the *Digest* reprints so much that he or she catered to the whims of Wallace. Others, such as Harold Ross of the *New Yorker*, labeled the arrangement dishonest.

John Tebbel and Mary Ellen Zuckerman say, "The system gave the *Digest* power to propagandize its right-wing political views across a broad spectrum of the periodical press." They note that "This criticism grew stronger as the *Digest*'s staff came to include more and more hard-line conservatives. It was clear that the magazine used its columns and those of other periodicals to promote its highly partisan views on everything from sex to communism."[5]

Born in 1889, Wallace was a preacher's son; his Presbyterian minister father was a long-time president of Macalester College in St. Paul, Minnesota. But the younger Wallace was not a churchgoer. Actually the *Digest* he founded was antireligious in spite of its appeal to political reactionaries and fundamentalists.

"In its premiere issue," says John Heidenry in his biography of Wallace, "the magazine struck a racist chord it was to sound in countless subtle variations over subsequent decades." He cites "a crude endorsement of eugenics" in an article reprinted from *Physical Culture* magazine. The author of that article, Albert Wiggam, objected to the shiploads of "ugly women" arriving at Ellis Island. "These women are giving us nearly *three* babies where the beautiful women of old American stocks are giving us *one*." Wiggam seriously suggested adapting the breeding methods of farmers who sought to produce blue-ribbon horses and hogs for competition.[6]

Wallace began his editorial career at the *Farmer* magazine but was fired when he suggested certain innovative ideas. One of these ideas was to condense articles for farmers to read. In 1916 he launched a booklet, *Getting the Most Out of Farming*, and took to the road with a friend to sell the collection of condensations. One night, as he lay awake in a bunkhouse on a Montana sheep ranch, he had the idea of expanding his booklet into a general magazine.

Returning home after World War I, in which he was wounded, Wallace pursued his idea, setting up shop first in New York's Greenwich Village, then in an unheated stable in Pleasantville, New York. His wife, Lila, shared the dream that eventually made them very rich. He died at age ninety-one in 1981, she at ninety-five in 1984.

Though they produced a conservative magazine, the Wallaces apparently were not so conservative in their lifestyle. Wallace once sent a top editor to California so that in his absence Wallace could have an affair with the editor's wife, and Mrs. Wallace dallied with her dance instructor and put him in charge of the construction of the couple's palatial home, High Winds, near Pleasantville so she would have him nearby.[7]

Part of Wallace's *Reader's Digest* formula, Heidenry says, was keeping his operation and success largely a secret so as not to stir the ire of magazines from which he was excerpting but not paying fees. One of the most famous articles was "And Sudden Death," a graphic account of slaughter on the highways in 1935, an article reprinted in nearly every city, with 4 million reprints distributed in four months. Heidenry sums up the three main tenets in the Wallace formula, "graven in stone" and "known to every editor":

> Is it quotable? Is it something the reader will remember, ponder and discuss?
> Is it applicable? Does it come within the framework of most people's interests and conversation? Does it touch the individual's own concerns?
> Is it of lasting interest? Will it still be of interest a year or two from now?[8]

The News Summary Magazine

Time magazine's Henry Luce was born of Presbyterian missionary parents in 1898 in China, where living conditions were primitive and from which the family narrowly ecaped with their lives during the brutal Boxer Rebellion at the turn of the century. Luce spent the first fourteen years of his life with his parents in China and then attended private schools in England and Connecticut.[9] At the Hotchkiss School in Lakeville, Connecticut, he found a firm friend in Briton Hadden. Both enrolled at Yale, where they edited and managed the *Yale Daily News*.

Luce went on to study at Oxford University, then joined Hadden on the staff of the *Baltimore News*. The two raised $86,000 to launch a departmentalized, newssummary magazine, with its own special style of inverted sentences (leading off a quote, for example, with "Said Dr. Jones," instead of putting the attribution inside or at the end of the quote), hyped language, and hyphenated words turning nouns into adjectives—a style that persists today. For example, in an article on actress Winona Ryder, she is described as a "dark, *Walter-Keane-eyed* beauty" who acts in a manner "more subtle than the high-voltage, *I-scream-in-your-face style* favored by most young actors" [italics added].[10] The first issue appeared on March 3, 1923, and featured on its cover eighty-six-year-old Illinois Republican Congressman Joseph Cannon, who was retiring after twenty-three terms.

The two friends took turns as editor and business manager, with Luce taking control upon Hadden's early death at age thirty-one in 1929. Luce eventually launched *Fortune, Life,* and *Sports Illustrated.* His wife was better known than he was. Clare Boothe Luce, once voted in a national poll one of America's most admired women, had been a writer for *Vogue* and an editor of *Vanity Fair.* She was the author of Broadway plays, three of which were made into movies. A two-term Republican congresswoman from Connecticut, she also served as ambassador to Italy and Brazil under Republican President Dwight Eisenhower.

Time *magazine cofounder Henry Luce and wife, Clare Boothe Luce, ambassador to Italy.* (Urban Archives/Temple University, Philadelphia, Pa.)

The Luce commitment to the Republican Party showed in *Time*'s coverage of the parties. After the 1924 election that returned Calvin Coolidge to the White House, *Time* included separate reports on the state of both parties. After praising the Republicans for standing up to the test of the campaign and coming out financially solvent, the magazine turned to the Democrats and gave the party the back of its hand: "Since the Civil War, this Party has ridden to success only four times—twice with Grover Cleveland, twice with Woodrow Wilson. The rest of the time, largely under the tutelage of William Jennings Bryan, its presidential record has been inglorious. Indeed, even when Mr. Bryan has not piloted the donkey himself, he has usually ridden behind the jockey. Numbers of Democrats say his riding has made the donkey lame."[11]

To compete with *Time*, Thomas J. C. Martyn, a former foreign news editor of *Time*, founded *Newsweek*. The magazine originally had a Democratic orientation, with Democrat Averell Harriman, later ambassador to the Soviet Union and governor of New York, as a behind-the-scenes partner of owner Vincent Astor. Its breathless account of the nomination of Wendell Wilkie, a dark-horse businessman, for the Republican presidential nomination in 1940, recorded the wondrous event with disbelief, with some awe reserved for the disarray of the Republicans. The magazine pictured Wilkie as a "neophyte" unparalleled in American politics, created by a mob "packed as high as the steelrafters in Convention Hall" (in Philadelphia) and ridiculed Wilkie as "their gallery god. . . . [T]hey had tired of the bumbling bosses who, in eight long years, had failed to produce an alternative to Franklin D. Roosevelt."[12]

THE FUTURE OF MAGAZINES

Magazines for both the general reader and the specialist come and go. Sometimes the departure is almost like losing a member of the family, as when such giants as the *Saturday Evening Post, Life, Look*, and *Collier's* folded, although some, like *Life* and *Saturday Evening Post*, are reborn as less ambitious monthlies. Although the roster is constantly changing, there remain some 22,000 magazines being published in the United States.

While the magazine world heaved and sighed, with new magazines starting up and others experiencing sudden death, all the time threatened by electronic developments, futurists saw "constants" and predicted the continuation of the slick-paper handheld, page-turning product. Said futurist Roger Selbert: "The constants are the only things you can be sure about in the future. And the magazine format is one of those constants. The electronic word . . . will add to it, it will be another option, it may even displace some percentage of the market, but it's not going to replace the written word."[13]

Old Magazines with New Life

Some very old journals, weathering one difficult time period after another, refused to die—in fact, were revitalized in the 1980s and 1990s. Witness the gains of *Cosmopolitan*, founded in 1886, which ranked twenty-third in the nation, with a 5.4

Television, a survivor, as some great magazines died. Cartoon by Tony Auth of the
Philadelphia Inquirer. (Auth © 1980 The Philadelphia Inquirer. Reprinted with permission of Universal Press Syndicate. All rights reserved.)

percent gain in 1991. In addition, both *Harper's* (founded in 1850) and *Atlantic
Monthly* (founded in 1857) showed profits in 1994 after incurring millions of dollars in
debt over the previous decade, and both were big-time winners in the annual
National Magazine Awards competition in 1994. *Vanity Fair*, in its first life, was published from 1913 to 1936, then revived in 1983, and showed a 25 percent gain in
1991.[14]

Noting the ongoing shortage of paper and its resulting soaring costs, John
Warnock, chair of the board and CEO of Adobe Systems, Inc., maintains that by the
year 2013 the reader (or viewer) will be thinking in terms of "electronic paper." By
this he means that electronic magazines matching the variety and display layouts of
printed magazines will be stored in the computer, and the reader will be able to
print out high-resolution color copies. He foresees that printing out magazines and
magazine sections by computer will offer a considerable cost saving to publishers.
For example, he suggests that 1,000 color catalogs could be delivered at a cost
equivalent to that of delivering one by mail today.[15]

Magazines You Watch

The electronic magazine, in which one pushes buttons and keys instead of turning
pages, began to appear experimentally in the early 1990s. The "first magazine you
watch," *Persona*, debuting in 1990, included features, such as celebrity interviews,

and departments, such as "Video Beat," which offered clips from the latest music videos.[16] *NautilusCD*, "published" on screen by Metatec of Dublin, Ohio, originally for technicians, began to go mainstream with "articles" for a more general audience.[17]

There was a proliferation of low-budget small CD-ROM "magazine" start-ups, among them *Medio, Blender, Go Digital*, and *Trouble & Attitude. Launch*, dealing with music, movies, computer games, and other entertainment topics, debuted in 1995 with an impressive lineup of more than a dozen major ads.

Using AT&T's RightPages technology, some forty journals in an experiment were made available in electronic format to selected departments at the University of California at San Francisco. The pages of the journals were scanned by a New York publisher, Springer-Verlag, a participant in the experiment. The pages were then stored in a database and routed on to UCSF, where the journal database could be searched and selectively printed out. RightPages presents five advantages for publishers, according to RightPages spokesperson Thomas Cannon. "It increases the user's awareness of the materials available, it gives feedback information, it increases copying revenues, it eliminates the 'missing copy' problem and it retains the look and feel of the original publication."[18]

Selective Targeting

Yet the concept of "customization"—meeting the specific interests of the user—is not new. For several decades magazines have been selectively targeting diverse audiences by special inserts. *Newsweek* became the first to customize editorial inserts for demographically determined audiences. *Farm Journal* inserts ads directed at killing the cotton boll weevil for southern states while dealing with the corn borer in issues going to Iowa and other corn-belt states. Some magazines, by dropping an extra section into the subscriber's magazine as it goes through the assembly line, can target certain interests by special ads for that audience.[19] *People* magazine split its run for the first time in 1995 on the murder of Mexican-American singer Selena. Selena appeared on the cover of *People* in the western states, while the magazine's readers in the rest of the country saw the cast of the television show *Friends* on the cover.

As magazines "republish" their editions, making their pages available on-line and customizing them for individual tastes, is a wholly new concept developing? When is a magazine no longer a magazine? Kathleen Endres, of the University of Akron, asks these kinds of questions. "What are the 1990s bringing?" she wonders. "Magavideos or is it videozines? Discazines or Magazettes? MagaROMs or CD-zines? Or, are they just new technology versions of an old favorite—the magazine?" She notes that nowhere in a dictionary definition of "magazine" does it say explicitly that a magazine always has to be in a paper format. She asserts that an electronic magazine has all the ingredients of graphics and variety of articles by different writers and can appear at regular periodic intervals, just as the print-bound product can.[20] In sum, she urges an open-minded attitude toward the ongoing developments. "Video, disc, CD-ROM magazines," she warns, "may be only the first wave of massive technological changes in the offing" in the magazine field.

MERGING: BIGGER, FOR BETTER OR WORSE

Magazines are likely to be a part of a large corporate endeavor, having common "parents" with other modes of communcation, including electronic media, books, telecommunications, and the old-fashioned newspaper. Economic considerations have contributed to the concentration of media power in larger and larger groups and networks. Three factors encourage convergence:

1. *The failure of isolation.* Independent publications, faced with rising costs of newsprint and labor, have found strength in sharing costs through cooperative printing and procurement. Across the board, the lesson—as David Easterly, president of Cox Newspapers, put it in a speech to the Interactive Services Association meeting in Toronto in July 1993—is that "you can't do it all by yourself."[21]

2. *Emergence of a one-world concept.* Marshall McLuhan's one-world community, or "global village," outlined in his books in the 1960s, became a reality some time ago, with instant live transmission from all corners of the globe made possible by new technology, mainly satellites. The further "uniting" of humankind was pushed forward by the disintegration of the political system in the socialist-communist world.

3. *Ascendancy of planetary corporations.* Media critic Ben Bagdikian laments that "a handful of mammoth private organizations have begun to dominate the world's mass media." He predicts that in the near future five to ten "corporate giants" will control most of the major media, from books to videocassettes. "Moreover, each of these planetary corporations," he says, "plans to gather under its control every step in the information process, from creation of 'the product' to all the various means by which modern technology delivers media messages to the public. 'The product' is news, information, ideas, entertainment and popular culture; the public is the whole world."[22]

Global Trends

This global consciousness can be seen in developments in magazine ownership. The French-based Hachette Publications acquired the Diamandis Communications group, which included *Woman's Day* and 105 other magazines in nineteen countries. The German Bauer Group owned *Woman's World* and *First for Women*, distributed largely in the United States.

"It's a wacky world of international publishing," says Russell J. Melvin, vice president for education for the Magazine Publishers Association. He points out that the French *Elle* is everywhere; *Essentials* in England is distributed in Spain and Canada; *Marie Claire* in France is active in England. *Vanity Fair* launched a British edition in 1992. Also in 1992, Lee Eisenberg, former editor in chief of *Esquire*, went to England to create a British version of *Esquire* to compete with *GQ*, which had started a British edition in 1988. And, of course, some U.S.-based magazines long had editions on all continents, namely *Reader's Digest, Time,* and *Newsweek. Reader's*

Digest, the *Journal of Commerce*, and *Business Week* launched Russian editions in the 1990s.[23]

Cross-Media Developments

The development was not just cross-national, but also cross-media. Rupert Murdoch, who launched his media empire originally from Australia, at his peak had 150 media properties on four continents. In the United States these included the Fox Television Network, 20th Century Fox film studio, *TV Guide*, and HarperCollins book publishing company. In Great Britain he controls one-third of the newspapers.

The *Chicago Tribune*, buying into a new national newspaper in England, joined in a venture with the German Kirch Group. Capital Cities/ABC gained close to a majority interest in Telemunchen, a German television production and distribution company, then merged with the Walt Disney Company, creating the largest entertainment

Rupert Murdoch: He controls American magazines, a film studio, a television network, and one-third of the newspapers in Great Britain.

company in the world. The Knight-Ridder newspaper chain acquired Dialog Information Services, which serves eighty-nine nations. Said Marshall Loeb, managing editor of *Fortune*: "Companies have to merge to keep up with Murdoch. A simple publisher has no leverage. There is a move toward global companies. You have to have size to compete in the global [scene]. We've got to be ready for the 21st century."[24]

Blurred Mega-Giants

In publishing, mergers of firms, large and small, continued as they had for twenty years. But the constant succession of mergers seemed to blur, if not eclipse, the identity of renowned firms, as voracious giants got bigger and bigger. Paramount Communications Corporation was already a giant entity when it was acquired, along with Blockbuster Entertainment Corporation, by Viacom, Inc., in 1994. Viacom, a diversified communications company, deals primarily in cable systems, with MTV and Showtime cable channels and other properties (home video distribution, book publishing, a movie studio). Paramount Communications Company, *Publishers Weekly* noted, was already the biggest book publisher in the country, with sales at $1.67 billion a year (for fiscal year ending July 31, 1993), when it merged with Macmillan (which had revenues annually of $300 million). The magazine predicted at the time, "The combined forces of Macmillan and Paramount will indeed create a publishing juggernaut" of great power and force.[25]

Already a part of Paramount book publishing was Simon & Schuster, which in turn had absorbed a major house, Prentice Hall. Included in Macmillan trade book divisions were imprints that had once been separate companies—Free Press, Scribner's, Collier, and Atheneum, as well as eleven children's imprint divisions. Paramount Publishing became the second-largest book publisher in the world, after Bertelsmann A. G. of Germany.

The bidding wars—takeover efforts, hostile or otherwise—continue, and the rooftop over publishing and communcations gets bigger and bigger.

GLOBAL MOGULS OF MODERN MEDIA

At the top of the newly created combinations are executives with immense power. Few, however, qualify as global moguls—far-reaching "conquerors" whose institutions are pervasive and who preside over global enterprises that control vast numbers of diversified media.

John S. Knight. Precursors of the modern mogul are the leaders of newspaper groups or chains. Among them in the United States is the Knight-Ridder Newspapers group of more than thirty newspapers, including leading metropolitan papers, such as the *Detroit Free Press, Miami Herald, Philadelphia Inquirer*, and the late *Chicago Daily News*.

The "Knight" in Knight Newspapers, which merged with Ridder Publications, is John S. Knight, who died at eighty-six in 1981. In 1933 he inherited the *Akron*

Beacon Journal from his father and parlayed it into an empire of influential newspapers. Although Knight was an inveterate gambler who was criticized for printing horse-race results free, Knight's newspapers nevertheless crusaded against gambling and exposed gambling corruption, resulting in the *Miami Herald* winning a Pulitzer Prize for an antigambling series.

A winner himself of the Pulitzer Prize for a courageous editorial in 1968 opposing the Vietnam War and approving dissent on the war, Knight was haunted by repeated personal tragedies. He outlived three wives. His oldest son, John S. Knight, Jr., died in World War II. His youngest son, Frank, died of a brain tumor. Knight's grandson, John S. Knight III, who was being groomed to lead the great newspaper enterprise, was murdered in Philadelphia in 1975. The chain merged with Ridder Publications, headed by Bernard Ridder, Jr., in 1974 to form Knight-Ridder Newspapers, with a circulation of 4 million among twenty-eight newspapers.[26]

Frank E. Gannett.   The largest newspaper chain or group in the twentieth century was launched in 1906 by Frank E. Gannett when he became part owner of the *Elmira* (New York) *Star-Gazette* after stints on *Frank Leslie's Illustrated Weekly* and the *Pittsburgh Index*. He moved on with his colleagues to acquire newspapers in Ithaca, Rochester, and Utica. He bought out his associates in 1924. At the time of his death in 1957, the Gannett group numbered twenty-two newspapers, four radio stations, and three television stations. Today its holdings number about eighty dailies, weeklies in twenty-two states, *USA Today*, and *USA Weekend* magazine.

In 1982 the Gannett Company launched its new daily national newspaper, *USA Today*, on a mission where others, such as the *National Observer*, had failed. With content that read like summarized magazine articles and with a swiftness of delivery and timeliness made possible by satellite transmission of content to regional printing centers, *USA Today* could compete with the late deadline of other papers. One inside page summarized the headline news from all fifty states. Features backgrounded the day's main events and the happenings in entertainment. Mocking the briefness and easy manner of the articles, some critics came to tag the paper as "McPaper," an allusion to the McDonald's fast-food chain.

Al Neuharth.   Pioneering the *USA Today* effort for Gannett was a flamboyant, former Knight-Ridder editor, Al Neuharth. Seven months after the launch, Neuharth unveiled a gigantic *USA Today* banner at a celebration at the Waldorf-Astoria in New York. The banner declared that the target of one million circulation had been reached, and the figure stood at 1,109,587. Critics loudly challenged it. Neuharth secured a nationally acclaimed auditing firm, Price Waterhouse, to check the figures, and the audit "made believers out of everyone," Neuharth recalls in his feisty autobiography. The audited figure was even greater, a miraculous 1,179,834.[27]

Knight-Ridder and Gannett moved toward cooperation in several areas. In 1986 the chains linked two of their main papers—the competitive papers in Detroit, the Knight-Ridder *Free Press* and the Gannett *News*—in the production and business side in order to end a price war that was hurting both papers and to streamline efforts and cut costs by merging operating systems. Joint operating agreements, upheld by the courts, had been around since 1930, and competing newspapers in other major cities, such as San Francisco and Minneapolis, have gone that route.[28]

Then, in an effort to curb the growing presence and competition of regional telephone companies, cable television, and information networks that were reaching millions, eight of the largest newspaper groups, including Gannett and Knight-Ridder, banded together in 1995 to try to link 185 dailies and 20,000 journalists in an electronic news-sharing network on the Internet service known as the World Wide Web.[29] The two chains, plus Advance Publications (Newhouse), Cox Newspapers, Hearst Corporation, the Times Mirror Company, the Tribune Company, and the Washington Post Company, forming together the New Century Network, offered consulting and technical help. They sought to involve local newspapers in developing wider local access to news, features, entertainment information, and talk forums on the Internet. Users would have coordinated shopping opportunities, access to reports, and sound and visual input from specified areas via local media, and advertisers could be enticed to place their messages and images across a wide range. "Each newspaper would be able to create its own 'look' on the Internet and retain its own reporting and editing staffs for local news," said the *New York Times*. "But each would also be able to link with other newspapers, allowing, for example, a reader of the electronic Austin American-Statesman to buy a single copy of the electronic Des Moines Register, if he or she were particularly interested in news developments in Iowa that day, or to buy a subscription to the electronic Houston Chronicle."[30] The electronic developments, with new boundaries of competition, are thus uniting in common efforts even the chains.

One problem with the New Century Network loomed: With widespread sharing of news on the Internet, what will happen to the traditional suppliers, the Associated Press and other wire services? *Editor & Publisher* asked: "What if a tiny Idaho newspaper can offer on-line subscribers access to news generated by 20,000 reporters working for NCN affiliate newspapers? What happens when on-line services that compete with newspapers want to buy news from the Associated Press, which is owned by newspapers?"[31]

Roy Thomson.　A mid-twentieth-century pioneer in global media empire building was Roy Thomson. Born in Canada but based in London, Thomson built a network of holdings, mostly media, on four continents—Europe, North America, Africa, and Australia. In Canada, the International Thomson Organisation, Ltd., newspapers included fifty-two; in the United States, eighty-eight (the largest being the *Repository* in Canton, Ohio); and in the United Kingdom, sixty. The empire included book publishing (eight companies), about 150 journals and magazines (ranging from *Family Circle* in the United States to a host of business, medical, and consumer magazines) and directories. In 1996 the company bought a leading legal publishing firm, West Publishing Co., for $3.43 billion in cash.

A school dropout at age thirteen, Thomson became a janitor and studied a year in a business school. He failed at various jobs, including farming and distributing auto parts. He kicked about until he was almost forty years old, when he stumbled into the newspaper business after being a radio salesman. He invested his meager funds in opening a radio station in North Bay, Ontario, to boost his radio sales. In between running for alderman of North Bay (he won) and for mayor (he lost) he bought two more stations in the area. One was in the newspaper building of the *Daily Press* at Timmins. With only $200 down and promising $6,000 later, Thomson bought the *Daily Press*. With only $2,000 down, he bought a radio station for $21,000 in Quebec, and, with talented staff, within a year the station was worth $100,000. The nonachiever youth, now in midlife, was on his way to becoming a media tycoon.[32]

Thomson, who died in 1976 at age eighty-two, was noted for his quips on money. Among them: "For enough money, I'd work in hell"; "I'll sign anything but a check"; and to Soviet premier Nikita Khrushchev, who asked the media tycoon what use his money was when he couldn't take it with him when he died, Thomson responded, "Then I'm not going."[33]

Robert Maxwell.   Another unlikely candidate to become a media tycoon, or rather, a global media mogul, was another money juggler and charmer, Robert Maxwell. Born in abject poverty in the small village of Aknazlatina, now a part of Czechoslovakia, Maxwell grew up in a two-room, earthen-floor house with six siblings. The children even shared shoes, one wearing a pair in the morning and a sibling wearing the same pair to school in the afternoon. The family and community were devout Orthodox Jews. The young Maxwell (his birth name was Abraham Lajbi but he was registered as Jan Ludvik Hoch) wore a black skullcap day and night and had long ringlets of hair in front of his ears.[34]

At sixteen, at the onset of World War II, Maxwell, lying about his age, joined the Czech army. He switched to a British regiment, changing his name to Leslie du Maurier (after a brand of cigarettes) to hide his real identity from the Germans. Rising to the rank of lieutenant, and changing his name again to Leslie Jones, then to Ian Robert Maxwell, he led his platoon into the thick of battle with the Germans in Europe. For "his magnificent example and offensive spirit," he won the Military Cross; the medal was pinned on him by Field Marshal Bernard Montgomery.

At the war's end in 1945, Maxwell, now captain, was assigned to the Control Commission in the British army in Berlin. He was named press officer for the commission, which replaced the local government. Primarily the young Maxwell, who could speak eight languages, acted as chief censor for the press reports. In 1946 he was named the British representative to the Soviet sector (later in life Maxwell faced critics who charged that he developed a working relationship with the Soviet spy security agency, the KGB).[35]

In 1947 Maxwell joined the Ferdinand Springer publishing firm in West Berlin. Although it had fallen on hard times, the company was still the largest scientific publisher in the world. Maxwell got the company back on its feet, eventually took it over, and gave it the name of Pergamon Press, after a Greek town.

Robert Maxwell: He died mysteriously at sea.

In 1980 he bought a 29 percent stake in the ailing British Printing Corporation (BPC), the biggest printing firm in Europe, and turned it around. Acquisition of the Mirror Group of newspapers in England and Canada, the Macmillan Publishing Company, and *New York Daily News* followed. He served as a member of Parliament in the Labor Party.

Maxwell died under mysterious circumstances in 1991. He disappeared from his yacht at sea in the Atlantic, and his body was found a few days later in the water. Various scenarios prevail: suicide, a heart attack that tumbled him into the water, or murder—being pushed overboard by one of the newly hired crew. His widow vents her suspicions of foul play in her book *A Mind of My Own: My Life with Robert Maxwell.*[36]

At the time of his death Maxwell's empire was crumbling—fast, "like a house of cards," as *Editor & Publisher* put it. Investigators charged that he was involved in a $2 billion fraud scheme involving misappropriated pension funds and loans taken under false pretenses. His holdings were sold off one by one to appease creditors; even his ornate mansion, Headington Hill Hall in England, was sold. His widow complained: "Just before Christmas, the removers took over . . . and emptied my home of its contents of thirty-six years, leaving me with the few pieces of furniture

I had repurchased from the estate or been allowed to keep by the receivers. That night was the saddest of all."[37]

Rupert Murdoch.   Dubbed by *Time* magazine as the man "in the forefront of media moguls seeking global reach,"[38] Australian-born Rupert Murdoch has cut a wide swath in America across all phases of media, leaving his mark on newspapers, magazines, book publishing, radio and television, movies, and the expanding computer world. In addition to Triangle Publications (which includes *TV Guide, Seventeen,* and other magazines), for which he paid $3.1 billion in 1988, HarperCollins book publishing, Fox Broadcasting, and Twentieth Century Fox movie studio, his holdings have included *The Times* of London, *New York Post, Chicago Sun-Times, Boston Herald, Village Voice, New York* magazine, and Delphi, with its on-line services to households.

Admitting that he was planning to develop a global television network, Murdoch paid $525 million in 1993 to acquire Star TV, an Asian satellite television service, whose five satellite channels are capable of reaching two-thirds of the world's population in 38 nations in Asia and the Middle East. He also has half ownership of British Sky Broadcasting, the largest satellite service operation in Europe.

In 1995 Murdoch's News Corporation formed a partnership with MCI Communications. "The deal marks one of the most startling alliances yet in the communications industry," said the *New York Times*, "uniting two companies that have histories of shaking up their respective markets in telephone and television service with a buccaneering approach to competition."[39]

Murdoch can be compared to the media empire builder William Randolph Hearst. Both developed sensationalism to a high decibel level. Both took over fledgling newspapers proffered by their fathers: Hearst, the *San Francisco Examiner*; Murdoch, the *Adelaide* (Australia) *News*. Both were at the beck and call of sensible, strong-willed mothers. Murdoch was only twenty-two when he took the helm as publisher of the *Adelaide News* following the death of his father.

Originally a leftist who kept a bust of Lenin in his room at Oxford and a promoter of investigative reporting at the outset of his media career, Murdoch evolved into a strong rightist in politics. Eschewing politics directly, Murdoch nevertheless appeared to have an occasional hand in politics. In December 1994, following the landside win of Republicans in Congress, HarperCollins, the influential book firm owned by Murdoch's News Corporation, offered House-speaker-designate Newt Gingrich a $4.5 million deal for a book to be written by the yet untried Gingrich. Murdoch professed to see no conflict of interest in the proposed deal; Gingrich eventually backed off, settling only for standard royalties when the book appeared.

Early in his newspaper career Murdoch's formula of sensationalism took shape: violence, horror, and sex. In his tabloids in Australia, horror stories, such as a report on a headless body being found, were regular fare, and a picture of a nude or partly nude female appeared in each issue. The paper was soon on its feet. As Murdoch traversed the world for new media acquisitions, his sensationalist fame preceded him, causing consternation and resignations in his path before he would take over. Yet the "abominable Aussie" could not harbor prurient goings-on or bad taste in his life. He sacked his bright protégé at Fox Studios, Stephen Chao, for hiring a male stripper to make a point about sensationalism at a conference.

Murdoch biographer William Shawcross finds symbolic the relationship of Murdoch to his grandfathers—one a stuffy clergyman, the other a profligate gambler. Rupert is both Rupert the Righteous and Rupert the Wild Card.[40]

Unlike Maxwell, Murdoch, with his somewhat bland and low-key personality, tolerated criticism of himself in the media, whereas Maxwell would likely threaten a detractor with a libel suit.

Si Newhouse, Jr. A low profile, a very low profile, is maintained by media mogul Samuel I. (Si) Newhouse, Jr., one of two sons of the late media empire builder, Sam I. Newhouse, Sr. Si has dominated Advance Publications, the Newhouse corporation, as chair of the board (brother Donald is president). The family fortune is one of the largest in the world—$13 billion—and the media holdings may constitute "the largest journalistic concern in the English language." AJR Advance Publications include one of the nation's largest book publishing groups, Random House (which includes subsidiaries Knopf, Ballantine, Vintage, Fawcett, Pantheon, and Modern Library); leading magazines, such as the *New Yorker, Vanity Fair*, and the Condé Nast group of women's magazines (*Vogue, Glamour, Bride's, House & Garden*, etc.); newspapers (overseen by Donald Newhouse) in twenty-two cities, among them Newark, Cleveland, New Orleans, Springfield, Massachusetts, and Portland, Oregon; a news service, Religious News Service; a Sunday newspaper magazine, *Parade*; and dozens of cable systems as one of the largest cable-television operators in the United States.

S. I. Newhouse, Sr., was the son of poor Russian Jewish immigrants. Growing up in Bayonne, New Jersey, his father's medical problems forced him to drop out of school at age thirteen and work. He took a short business course and got a job as a clerk for a local judge who also owned the failing *Bayonne Times*. Newhouse became general manager of the paper, and it began to show a profit. He earned a law degree in night school, and in 1922 he had enough capital to buy controlling interest in a newspaper, the *Staten Island Advance*. By the time of his death in 1979 at age eighty-four, he owned thirty-one newspapers, plus radio stations and magazines in the United States and overseas. His last several years were "so pathetic that his family did not want anyone to know," says a biographer, Richard Meeker. His mind reverted to that of a child and was captivated by spelling out simple words like *cat* with crayons and chalk.[41]

Yet this business-minded mogul was so successful that he helped shape the newspaper industry. Chain ownership of newspapers went from 5 percent to about 65 percent of all newspapers in S. I. Newhouse, Sr.'s tenure as editor and publisher from 1911 to 1979. "Newhouse did not cause this remarkable consolidation alone," says his biographer, Richard Meeker, writing in 1983, "but he certainly profited from it."[42]

Ted Turner. A mogul of broadcasting, Ted Turner is the founder of the Turner Broadcasting System (TBS) and the Cable News Network (CNN). In a given year (1992, for example) he earns more than ABC, CBS, or NBC. CNN, launched with satellites in 1980, also embraced CNN International and Headline News channels. Constantly trying to buy one of the other networks—all believed to be up for sale, Turner took a surprising different turn in 1995 and began working out a lucrative deal to join Time Warner, Inc. Turner would become vice chair of Time Warner. The merger was approved by the Federal Trade Commission in July 1996 on the condition that the new company would inaugurate a second news channel to compete with its own CNN.

Turner, a world-class yachtsman who won the America's Cup in 1977 and a high percentage of the races he has entered and who has been named Yachtsman of the Year four times, owns the Atlanta Braves baseball team and the Atlanta Hawks basketball team; he also controls the Atlanta Chiefs soccer team.

Robert Edward (Ted) Turner III has had a personal passion for success, inspired by tragedy. His father, owner of a successful billboard advertising business, anguished over the young Ted, who studied classical languages but was kicked out of Brown University for pranks. He despaired of his son's lack of interest in practical matters, namely business. Ted's father, tremendously abusive as well as loving toward his son, killed himself in 1963, fully devastating the twenty-four-year-old Ted. "Is this enough for you, Dad?" the eventually successful Ted Turner said in a college lecture as he looked to the rafters holding a magazine with his own picture.[43]

Turner "spent the better part of his life waiting for an answer to that question, an answer he knows will never come," says biographer Porter Bibb, whose own prize-winning documentary on an early Turner yacht race got the future billionaire interested in broadcasting. Underscoring the success of the man, Bibb, noting that Turner has set ocean racing records that will never be matched, adds, "He has revolutionized the broadcast industry and made Marshall McLuhan's 'global village' real by tying the world together into one live television network. He has even rewritten the very definition of news as something that *is* happening rather than something that *has* happened." Besides being worth $3 billion, "he has also become a one-man diplomatic corps with access, thanks to CNN's enormous influence, almost anywhere."[44] CNN, reaching into countries around the world, in some places heard in the local language, constitutes what is probably the largest news-gathering agency. Turner also owns the prestigious MGM/United Artists movie studio.

Although Bibb faults Turner for some racist remarks in the past and for being charged by his children as being an abusive and irresponsible parent, he gives Turner high marks for probably being "the only honest billionaire in history" and certainly for an active social agenda. "He has turned his business into a bully pulpit of social conscience," says Bibb. "There are no hidden motives in Ted Turner's larger agenda—he is as serious about population control and environmental pollution as Rupert Murdoch may be about tabloid television or Barry Diller about cable shopping."[45]

Turner married film star and former antiwar activist Jane Fonda just before Christmas 1991. There were some similarities in their backgrounds. Fonda also had a parent—her mother—who committed suicide.[46] To some the match seemed to have a social as well as romantic base. Singer Dolly Parton, catching the euphoria of the hour at the wedding reception, raised her champagne glass in a toast: "To the Man of the Year. The Woman of the Hour. The Couple of the Century!"[47]

Katharine Graham.   The status of "media mogul" seems to have been held predominantly by men, as men have dominated politics and other endeavors. Yet one prominent woman publisher, Katharine Graham, chair of the executive committee of the Washington Post Company, which publishes the *Washington Post* and *Newsweek* magazine, perhaps can wear the title of mogul. Books have dealt with the *Post* as an imperial kingdom (Tom Kelly, *The Imperial Post*) and Graham as sitting atop a fiefdom (Deborah Davis, *Katharine the Great*).

Graham came to power by inheritance. Her father, Eugene Meyer, bought the *Post* in 1933. She married a brilliant young man, Philip Graham, who had won hon-

Katharine Graham, president of the Washington Post, *addressing a luncheon of the Advertising Council.*

ors at Harvard. Graham was bent on a political career, until Meyer, who recognized his talents, persuaded him to go into journalism. Charmed by the affable Graham, Meyer installed him as publisher of the *Post*. Graham turned the *Post* into a crusading newspaper, bought *Newsweek* and the *Washington Times-Herald*, and launched the Los Angeles Times–Washington Post News Service.

However, Graham was a manic-depressive. He committed suicide in 1961. The mantle fell to the shy, untried Katharine. With a journalism background that consisted only of some newswriting while in college, she was a quick learner. Backing up her editors, she led the *Post* into courageous decisions and developed a national reputation. The paper, defying a Department of Justice restraining order in 1971, published a series based on the controversial embargoed Pentagon Papers, which detailed the history of U.S. involvement in Vietnam. Three years later the *Post*'s exposé of President Richard Nixon's involvement in the cover-up of the burglary of Democratic offices at the Watergate complex in Washington ended with the president's resignation.

Katharine Graham's star Watergate reporters, Bob Woodward and Carl Bernstein, became the subject of a movie, *All the President's Men*, starring and produced by Robert Redford. In planning the movie, Redford made a call on Graham. Davis reports that she

> had initially been nervous, that morning in March, when Redford came to call on her, but then so had he; in fact he felt himself to be in the presence of a greater legend and a greater human being. Hollywood, as Redford knew, created myth that lived on as American culture. Katharine Graham, a woman of authentic power, could do what he could never do; she created myth that lived on as history, as truth.[48]

QUESTIONS FOR DISCUSSION AND RESEARCH

1. Who is the most powerful media mogul today?
2. What are the pros and cons of "bigness," as mergers and creation of planetary corporations continue?
3. Which one of the media moguls would be the best subject of a movie? Why? What would be the central focus or theme? Who would play the part?
4. What are some of the things that change—and also remain constant—as magazines and other print media enter the age of cyberspace?
5. Think of your favorite magazine. How has it changed in recent months or years, and how might it change in the future?
6. What's the best route to becoming a media mogul if you have no family wealth or special connections?
7. If Henry Luce and DeWitt Wallace were alive and were to enter the communications field, how would they enter it, and what strategies might they use to create a product that would be contemporary?
8. What do you think happened to Robert Maxwell? Are there other possible mysteries among the media moguls? Some of the best investigative reporting begins with asking, "What if . . . ?"

9. Develop a good list of questions to ask one of the moguls today. What would be the most important thing you and readers would want to know? Also develop some follow-up questions.

10. What has been the effect of "condensed" magazines and digests on society? Conversely, how has society affected these summary magazines?

ENDNOTES

1. Theodore Peterson, *Magazines in the Twentieth Century*, 2nd ed. (Urbana: University of Illinois Press, c. 1964, 1972), p. 324, referring to a comment in Calvin Ellsworth Chunn, "*History of News Magazines*," Ph.D. dissertation, University of Misouri, 1950.
2. Ibid., pp. 85, 327.
3. "The 100 Leading Audit Bureau of Circulations Magazines, 1991," provided by Magazine Publishers of America, in Hiley H. Ward, *Magazine and Feature Writing* (Mountain View, Calif.: Mayfield, 1993), p. 16.
4. Quoted in W. A. Swanberg, *Luce and His Empire* (New York: Charles Scribner's Sons, 1972), p. 181.
5. John Tebbel and Mary Ellen Zuckerman, *The Magazine in America* (New York: Oxford University Press, 1991), p. 185.
6. John Heidenry, *Theirs Was the Kingdom: Lila and DeWitt Wallace and the Story of the* Reader's Digest (New York: Norton, 1993), p. 50.
7. Ibid., p. 99.
8. Ibid., pp. 80, 81.
9. Swanberg, *Luce and His Empire*, pp. 29, 30.
10. Richard Corliss, "Take a Bow, Winona," *Time*, Jan. 9, 1995, p. 65.
11. "National Affairs," "Democratic," *Time*, Nov. 17, 1924, p. 2.
12. "Voters' Drafting of Wilkie Like Shot in the Arm to U.S.," *Newsweek*, July 8, 1940, p. 1.
13. Amy Janello and Brennon Jones, *The American Magazine* (New York: Abrams, 1991), p. 224.
14. Magazine Publishers of America, "The 100 Leading Audit Bureau of Circulations Magazines, Second Half of 1991," in Ward, *Magazine and Feature Writing*, pp. 16–18. See also Deirdre Carmody, "A Rebound for Harper's and Atlantic," *New York Times*, April 25, 1994, p. D9.
15. John Warnock, "Electronic Paper," *The Electronic Magazine*, vol. 1, no. 1, May 1993, p. 13.
16. Kathleen L. Endres, "The Future Magazine," *Magazine Forum*, vol. 2, no. 1, Spring 1992, p. 11.
17. L. R. Shannon, "Peripherals: A CD-ROM Magazine Is a Sound Possibility," *New York Times*, April 5, 1994, p. C7.
18. Quoted in "AT&T, Springer, Wiley in Document Delivery Project," *Publishers Weekly*, Oct. 18, 1993, p. 7.
19. Ward, *Magazine and Feature Writing*, p. 23.
20. Endres, "The Future Magazine," p. 12.
21. *Editor & Publisher*, Aug. 14, 1993.
22. Ben H. Bagdikian, "The Lords of the Global Village: Cornering Hearts and Minds," *The Nation*, June 12, 1989.
23. Ward, *Magazine and Feature Writing*, p. 24.
24. Ibid.
25. Jim Milliot, "Paramount Slowly Begins Integration of Macmillan," *Publishers Weekly*, Nov. 29, 1993, p. 18.
26. Charles Whited, *Knight: A Publisher in the Tumultous Century* (New York: E. P. Dutton, 1988). See "Books in Review," Hiley H. Ward, *Editor & Publisher*, Dec. 24, 1988, p. 15.

27. Al Neuharth, *Confessions of an S.O.B.* (New York: Doubleday, 1989), pp. 162, 163.

28. Bryan Gruley, *Paper Losses: A Modern Epic of Greed and Betrayal at America's Two Largest Newspaper Companies* (New York: Grove Press, 1993), p. 19. See "Book Reviews," Hiley H. Ward, *Editor & Publisher*, Dec. 25, 1993, p. 31.

29. George Garneau, "New Alliance Raises Industry Concerns," *Editor & Publisher*, April 29, 1995, p. 9.

30. Peter H. Lewis, "Big Newspapers to Help Locals on Internet," *New York Times*, April 20, 1995, p. D8.

31. Garneau, "New Alliance," p. 9.

32. Susan Goldenberg, *The Thomson Empire* (New York: Beaufort Books, 1984), p. 25.

33. Ibid., pp. 15, 46.

34. Tom Bower, *Maxwell: The Outsider* (New York: Viking, 1992), pp. 6–8.

35. Nick Davies, *Death of a Tycoon: An Insider's Account of the Fall of Robert Maxwell* (New York: St. Martin's Press, 1993), pp. 7, 8.

36. Elisabeth Maxwell, *A Mind of My Own: My Life with Robert Maxwell* (New York: HarperCollins, 1994).

37. Ibid., p. 525.

38. John Greenwald, "Rupert's World," *Time*, Sept. 20, 1993, p. 64. See also Stephen Koepp, "Murdoch in the Mogul's Seat," *Time*, Nov. 11, 1985, p. 66.

39. Edmund L. Andrews and Geraldine Fabrikant, "MCI and Murdoch to Join in Venture for Global Media," *New York Times*, May 11, 1995, p. A1.

40. William Shawcross, *Murdoch* (New York: Simon & Schuster, 1992), pp. 29, 44. See "Book Reviews," Hiley H. Ward, *Editor & Publisher*, Feb. 20, 1993, p. 37.

41. Richard H. Meeker, *Newspaperman: S. I. Newhouse and the Business of News* (New York: Ticknor & Fields, 1983), p. 250.

42. Ibid., p. 253.

43. Porter Bibb, *It Ain't as Easy as It Looks: Ted Turner's Amazing Story* (New York: Crown, 1993), p. viii.

44. Ibid.

45. Ibid., pp. ix, x.

46. Robert Goldberg and Gerald Jay Goldberg, *Citizen Turner: The Wild Rise of an American Tycoon* (New York: Harcourt Brace, 1995), pp. 414, 415.

47. Bibb, *It Ain't as Easy as It Looks*, p. 5.

48. Deborah Davis, *Katharine the Great: Katharine Graham and the Washington Post* (New York: Harcourt Brace Jovanovich, 1979), p. 274.

15

Old Media Meet the New

The history of media has seen episodic changes. The main periods of media history have been determined, first, by the appearance of new products, such as parchment, papyrus, paper and ink, and movable type, then by mechanical and technological developments that resulted in speedier means of communication.

Industrial steam and electrically driven, fast-whirling rotary presses arrived in the nineteenth century. Then the telegraph, the telephone, and the wireless made the transmission of news instantaneous. And, of course, the radio, movies, and television, expanding the world of sound and images of reality into the living room, appeared in the twentieth century.

But the big revolution, comparable to the revolutionary introduction of movable type by Gutenberg, is the bursting forth of computers, with a world of databases, word processors, e-mail, electronic bulletin boards, CD-ROMs, the Internet, Web sites, video digital disks offering participation in manipulating images, and other multimedia components. Hardly an hour in a day goes by without some example of the relationship of the individual to a computer. Twenty-three million adults use home computers each day, and 55 percent of them use computers at work.[1] Marshall McLuhan saw what was happening thirty years ago when he observed, "In our time the sudden shift from the mechanical technology of the wheel to the technology of the electric circuitry represents one of the major shifts of all historical time."[2]

Suddenly there is no separate realm composed just of readers. Society resembles a living organism, with one event immediately affecting others. One experiences the effect of multimedia at once and travels the information superhighways and networks as pulses in a world without apparent boundaries. "Electronic circuitry," McLuhan observed, has a "power of totally involving all people in all other people."[3]

Wooden typewriter built by Peter Metterhofer in 1864. (National Archives)

BIRTH OF THE COMPUTER

The roots of the modern computer reach back to the dawn of history. The word *computer* comes from a concept of "counting"; thus the first attempts at counting, even the first person to notice that there was one animal or one tree in a location, form the genius of computation. Keeping track of things by notches on wood or scratches in stone, putting dots on papyrus as the Egyptians did, or arranging stones in certain orders—even assigning values to the stones, such as one kind of stone standing for "one," or another "ten"—became ways to represent and organize numbers. The word for pebbles in Latin is *calculi*, the origin of *calculation* and *calculus*, a method of calculation by using symbols.

An early manual computer for calculating numbers was a counting board, which the Romans called an *abacus*. Originally a board on which pebbles were placed, the abacus evolved to include beads moved along on string or wire. The placement of numbers on the board could determine their value, thus allowing for a small number of beads.

It was many centuries before the mechanical calculator appeared. The first that worked is attributed to Blaise Pascal, a seventeenth-century mathematician and philosopher. His calculator or computer consisted of a series of eight wheels divided into ten parts, each wheel turned by a stylus or pen. This device could only add and subtract. Another seventeenth-century inventor, German mathematician and philosopher Gottfried Wilhelm Leibnitz, arranged a series of wheels—actually they were rods with teeth cut into them—into a unit that could also multiply and divide.[4]

Charles Dodgson, known by his pen name, Lewis Carroll, the author of *Alice in Wonderland*, created a kind of logic abacus that had a ruled board and counters that could be arranged to solve problems of mathematics and logic.[5]

Father of the Modern Computer

Charles Babbage, an eccentric English mathematician and inventor in the first half of the nineteenth century, is considered the father of the modern computer. He created first a "difference engine" that could solve multiterm, or polynomial, equations. He realized that a machine that could serve a special purpose could be designed to serve a multitude of interests. So he next created the "analytical engine," which could offer a mix of patterns of action. It had the five basic components of any computer: a set of input devices, an arithmetic unit or processor that did the calculating, a control unit which guaranteed that the task ordered would be done, memory storage, and an output mechanism.[6] This analytical engine became the first programmable computer.

Babbage was assisted for a time by a brilliant young woman whom he met at one of his parties (he was forty-two, she was seventeen). Augusta Ada was the daughter of the poet Lord Byron. She is credited by some with helping to design the way the analytical engine was addressed, or programmed. Computer historian Joel Shurkin says she was possibly the first computer programmer.[7] She edited with clarity Babbage's notes for publication, which added to his fame. But his "enchantress of numbers," as he called her, died of cancer at the age of thirty-six, the same age at which her famous father died.

Herman Hollerith, who had worked in the U.S. Census Bureau before becoming a teacher at the Massachusetts Institute of Technology, created a punch-card tabulating machine for the 1890 census. Through holes in the card, information could be sorted to the proper slot.

The Monster ENIAC

In 1946 John Mauchley, J. Presper Eckert, and John Von Neumann created ENIAC (Electronic Numerical Integrator and Computer). Built under contract with the U.S. Army, it was the first all-electronic digital computer (using numbers represented by the digits 0 and 1). A monster in size, it had 17,468 vacuum tubes of sixteen varieties, 1,500 relays, and 6,000 switches. The creature was 100 feet long, 10 feet high, and 3 feet deep, and it weighed 30 tons.[8]

Eckert and Mauchley went on to create a speed demon of a computer for the Census Bureau in March 1951. Dubbed UNIVAC I (Universal Automatic Computer), it "made the tabulator look like an engine from the Middle Ages."[9] Considerably smaller than ENIAC, UNIVAC I (14.5 by 7.5 by 9 feet) could read 7,200 decimal digits per second, which made it the fastest computer up to the time. Enlisted in the 1952

The ENIAC computer had 18,000 vacuum tubes and weighed 30 tons. (National Archives)

election to predict the winner—Dwight Eisenhower and Adlai Stevenson were running—it was brushed off by Walter Cronkite at CBS as "just a sideshow." On election night, however, the computer accurately predicted by 9 P.M., with 7 percent of the vote in, that Eisenhower was the runaway winner over Stevenson, contrary to educated predictions. UNIVAC I, standing by its predictions and proving correct, had vindicated the computer, so much so that UNIVAC practically became synonymous with "computer," much as Xerox became the name for photocopiers.

The consumer could in 1970 buy a handheld calculator that could "run circles" around ENIAC and UNIVAC, as Shurkin notes. "And with that, the computer age really began."[10] Now there are handheld personal digital assistants (PDAs) which, with simple commands, allow a host of activities needed to conduct personal business.

The modern computer is a "thinking" machine; if the right question, properly phrased, is asked, it outstrips human ability and answers with the speed of light. Some scholars even debate whether a kind of "consciousness" can be achieved by computers.[11]

THE SHAPE OF MEDIA IN A NEW AGE

Old media never seem to die. As high technology opens new portals in communication, the former media hold on. Radio did not die. It found new outlets in automobiles and Walkman sets. Movies did not die; instead multiplex theaters in one unit sprouted up at suburban malls and video exploded onto television sets. Indeed movies created for television have become a new form of entertainment.

Newspapers

The entry of newspapers into the electronic age came in the late 1960s and 1970s when the video display terminal (VDT) began to become the principal tool of reporters and editors. The VDT, with a keyboard similar to that of a typewriter, but with a visual display screen instead of paper, offered greater efficiency—fewer errors, greater speed, and increased economic feasibility—as the proverbial Linotype typesetter was eliminated. Reporters were in effect "setting type" from their desks; fewer persons meant fewer mistakes, and fewer hands were cost saving. Two groups in Florida, the *Daytona Beach Journal* and *Cocoa Today*, did the original testing of VDTs in the newsroom; their field tests proved so promising that the new technology developed rapidly.[12]

Death of Videotex.   In the early 1980s newspapers began to try to plug into the future by envisioning the television screen as a means to produce and deliver a newspaper text. Knight-Ridder Newspapers, Times Mirror, and *Time* magazine experimented with pilot videotex formats of the day's news. In "videotex," the news chosen by the viewer appears on demand. The Associated Press lined up leading newspapers in the country for a videotex trial on CompuServe Information Service, "a trial doomed to crash and burn the day it started because it tried to force-feed a print product into electronic news holes," says Michael Conniff, a media futurist and president of *Interactive Sports*. He called all of these initial efforts a "spectacular videotex dance of death."[13]

With all-day television channels offering comprehensive world and national news and specialized channels offering continual sports, legislative, and entertainment coverage, the newspaper itself looked more and more like a bit player in an increasingly larger galaxy. And newspapers, faced with specialization on screen, began to develop new specialized magazine sections. The *Chicago Tribune* inserted a new Spanish-language weekly, *Exito!*, and the *Wall Street Journal* experimented with adding state sections, such as a weekly *Texas Journal*, in Texas. Even in an electronic age, the print version of a newspaper must become more complete, says Joseph Ungaro, retired president of the Detroit Newspaper Agency.[14]

A Newspaper Is More Than Paper.   Yet few would envision the newspaper of the future as just "paper." The *Chicago Tribune*, a pacesetter in new technology, demonstrated a concept that includes many facets. Some of the "stops on the Tribune's superhighway" of information delivery, according to the *American Journalism Review*, are "ChicagoLand Television," the *Tribune*'s twenty-four-hour-a-day regional cable news station; "Chicago Online," which allows customers to use personal computers and modems to call up electronic versions of stories and ads; "Peapod," an electronic food-shopping service; "Picture Network International," a picture research service; and "StarSight Telecast" (in an experimental stage), which allows users to search out programs, and adapt and record them.[15]

Lightweight Flat Panels.   Some observers think the new technologies are already passé. Most media critics, says Roger Fidler, director of the Knight-Ridder Information Design Laboratory in Boulder, Colorado, before it was put on hold in 1996, either play it safe "by incrementally extending known trends and proven technologies and ideas of the past" or leap to "popularized" futuristic technology. He says they fail to see "the emergence of what may be the most significant new media development since the invention of printing, the *flat panel*."[16]

The flat panel made possible the lightweight laptop computers that businesspersons carry and use when traveling. Flat panels, Fidler points out, in combination with microprocessors, memory, and communication links, will constitute a new era of technology. Known also as "digital appliances," most use pens instead of keyboards. It is expected that they will be able to decipher handwriting and respond to voice commands.[17] As they get lighter and lighter, flat panels can indeed lead to a paperless newspaper, some believe, and by making possible a convergence of print, moving pictures, and sound, the devices offer one scenario for the future.

Advertising

Advertising agencies have initiated task forces to deal with the new developments and have formed links with multimedia entrepreneurs and researchers.[18] They have held exploratory conferences on the future, such as a gathering of 100 top ad executives in New York in 1995, presented under the wing of the Coalition for Advertising Supported Information and Entertainment (CASIE), which was formed in cooperation between the Association of National Advertisers and the American Association of Advertising Agencies. The consortium looked for ways to promote advertising in the face of the distractions of interactive television, on-line computer services, and CD-ROMs.

Wired magazine suggested some new rules for successful marketing in the new interactive age. Among them are the following: The product will have to be of a high quality because strategies will be based on repeat purchases and the recommendations of other customers. Long-term, even lifetime, relationships will be forged with customers. There will be attention to "initiating, maintaining, and improving dialogues with individual consumers, abandoning the old-fashioned advertising monologues of mass media."[19]

Personalized Ads and Product Placement.   Ads could be targeted directly to a selected home and tailored to the tastes of the occupant on the basis of accumulated data on each household. A party interested in a particular product—for instance, a new refrigerator—could at the push of a button witness a detailed demonstration. Or a person interested in a cruise could experience being on board ship or testing the inviting water and beaches in more detail, determining the content in virtual reality. As the influence of mass media decreases, along with the emergence of interactive media and one-to-one media encounters, one-to-one marketing becomes necessary to survive in a competitive market and to succeed in an interactive age.[20]

The mixing of entertainment with advertising has taken two other turns: (1) ads provided entertainment to compete with programmed entertainment; and (2) ads became an integral part of the entertainment on the television screen and on the big screen.

The Super Bowl of professional football in 1995 surprised viewers in presenting advertising spots that were more entertaining, by some accounts, than the predictable game between the San Francisco 49ers, who won handily, and the San Diego Chargers. "Was the Super Bowl a super bore? Then you must have watched the game instead of the commercials," said the *New York Times*.[21] Entertaining during the game were such ads as a Pepsi ad with a boy ending up stuffed into a Pepsi bottle; Budweiser beer promoted by a chorus of croaking frogs; the Isuzu Trooper Limited car merged with exotic landscapes; humorous tales of individuals wearing Lee jeans; Rold Gold's "Pretzel Boy" appearing to parachute into the middle of the game and interrupting it; and screen villain Dennis Hopper as a mentally disturbed fan reciting a poem to the ballet of football while standing in front of a giant Nike logo. During the 1996 Olympics ads were sometimes more entertaining than the events.

More and more products were displayed in full view on television programs and in the movies. One even became the centerpiece of a plot. The longest-running sitcom in 1994, *Married . . . With Children*, even carried an entire episode built around a promotion for RC Cola. In the episode, a can of RC Cola appears in the background; the program's hero, Al Bundy, once a football player, is visited by a dream team of gridiron greats—viewers are encouraged to write the name of one of the players on a coupon available in stores selling RC Cola and submit it in a contest. In return for the program's involvement, Bundy got his picture on 100 million RC Cola containers.[22]

In the past it was common for products to be in clear view on the sets of movies; companies paid a range of fees, depending on placement of their product. Says *Wired* magazine, "In the future, we will see a greater fusion of publicity, advertising, and careful product placement in nearly every media outlet."[23]

Books

With the electronic revolution, bookstores in the 1990s began to look more and more like penny arcades of yesteryear, as they became multimedia entertainment and information learning centers. "It's a trend that makes some book purists shudder," said *Publishers Weekly*, "but 'bookstores' that also stock a large selection of various nonbook products—from music CDs to toys and games, from videotapes to software, among other items—are the model store of the future."[24]

Bookless Bookstores? There's even a "bookless" bookstore in Houston. Billed as "the bookstore of the future," Booktronics offers only audio books and CD-ROMs. The store carries 8,000 audio and 1,200 CD-ROM "cultural, education and information titles."[25]

In nearly every issue now *Publishers Weekly* lists and describes new audio books. No wonder. In 1994 audio books were a billion-dollar-a-year industry. In that year 55,000 audio titles were available from 1,400 publishers, according to the 1994 edition of *Words on Cassette*.

The availability of books on-line permitted more extensive browsing by potential customers before they ordered a printout of the book, which stores made available at the same price as hard copies. HarperCollins planned to have all its forthcoming titles also available on-line, with its own Online Bookstore, and Time Warner Electronic Publishing "published" a novel by Douglas Cooper by serializing it on the Internet's World Wide Web, without even preparing a print edition.[26]

In fact, the printing of books themselves is about to be further controlled by the new technology, as digital printing presses and computer-to-plate (CTP) production systems become available. No longer will there be large inventories of unsold books or copies to be returned to publishers by bookstores. The customer in fact orders the book unpublished over the computer, and a copy is produced on point of order.

Quick Books on Demand. Benny Landa, developer of an electronic printer, the E-Print 1000, told *Publishers Weekly*:

> Today you print and then distribute. Tomorrow, you'll distribute and then print. Instead of having one press on the East Coast and one on the West Coast, each producing a half-million copies, you'll have presses in 200 cities, each producing 5000 copies. You produce only the quantities you need, just in time, instead of carrying them in your inventory.[27]

Radio and Television

Shedding its image of offering up mostly local programs, radio began distributing syndicated programs via satellites. Among the players were United Stations, which acquired the RKO Radio Network's sports and news broadcasts; Transstar Radio Network, with its twenty-four-hour-a-day mostly packaged programming; and Westwood One, which bought the Mutual Broadcasting System in 1985 and NBC Radio Networks in 1987. Included in the Westwood camp were shows of popular personalities, such as Mutual's talk-show host Larry King and NBC's sex counselor Ruth Westheimer.[28] Syndicated disc jockeys appealed to younger audiences.

Television networks had generally overlooked younger adult audiences, while cable MTV gained success by targeting young people. The networks began to take stock. In 1992 the *New York Times* could headline a television column with "3 Networks Frantically Seek Fountain of Youth and Profits . . . Only CBS truly believes in viewers over 50."[29] Fox had already shown success with the younger market, becoming the number one network for eighteen- to thirty-four-year-olds. Both

ABC and NBC formulated policies to search out the young, namely, by adding sit-coms aimed at generating young viewers. With the realization that baby boomers were getting older, CBS stuck with the middle and older generations until 1995, when the *Times* headlined a report on January 10 with "With Ratings Slipping, CBS Reaches for Youth." As CBS profits sank 68 percent in the first quarter of 1995, the network desperately began to court a younger audience by lining up new youth-oriented sitcom series and movies.

With competition made keener by the entry of many more players and new technology and delivery methods, networks found themselves at each other's throats. It was "mud-wrestling,"[30] the *Philadelphia Inquirer* said at the beginning of the 1994 football season of the Fox Broadcasting Company's blitz of football tele-casting. Fox, owned by Rupert Murdoch's Australian-based News Corporation, tackled the lucrative Sunday afternoon football contract of the National Football League away from CBS, which had held exclusive rights to the games since 1956. CBS was even outmaneuvered by NBC for rights to telecast the American Football Conference games.

More Networks.   New networks emerged from the drawing board. In addition to four national entertainment networks—ABC, CBS, NBC, and the newcomer Fox added in 1986—two newcomers were added at the beginning of 1995. United Paramount Network (UPN)—offering initially *Star Trek: Voyager, Marker, The Watcher, Platypus Man*, and *Pig Sty*—was parented by the Paramount Television Group, owned by Viacom, and BHC Communications, a subsidiary of Chris-Craft Industries. Paramount's programming was targeted to young men, while the other networks appeared to program for women.[31] The Warner Brothers offspring, Warner Brothers Network (WB Network), put in its initial lineup four sitcoms—*The Wayans Brothers, Unhappily Ever After, Muscle*, and *The Parent 'Hood*.[32] Warner Brothers offered a new approach to the financial relationship between network and affiliates. ABC, CBS, and NBC paid compensation fees to local stations to carry their programs. Fox, on the other hand, did not pay compensation. Warner Brothers, however, turned the whole process around and required the stations to pay the network 25 percent of profits realized by the station's relationship with the network.[33]

Channels for Everybody.   Cable continued to be a major player with its regional and specialized channels—Ted Turner's all-news Cable News Network (CNN) and for a while the Satellite News Channel, co-owned by Group W Cable and ABC, as well as entertainment channels (E!), travel channels, all-weather channels, movie channels (HBO, Showtime, and Disney channels), music (MTV), sports (ESPN), in-teractive shopping channels (such as QVC Network and Home Shopping Network), and other shopping channels (many of them specializing in jewelry, sports prod-ucts, fashion clothes, health, exercise, dieting, and success formulas).

Some fifty-seven cable channels were expected to proliferate to about 500 channels. A convention on the future of cable programming in New Orleans in June

1994 found 100 cable channels and would-be cable channels presenting existing and proposed programs for consideration of placement on channels, funding, and subscribers. They ranged from a Singles Network featuring video classified ads and an Adam & Eve Channel offering adult home-shopping services to a Gospel Network, a music-video jukebox running viewer requests, World History Network, Popcorn Channel (the only one featuring full-length movie trailers on television), and the electronic game Sega Channel.

On the horizon to compete with cable was RCA's Digital Satellite System (DSS), with a mere 18-inch-dish antenna. With appeal to rural areas out of reach of cable—some 12 million American households—it also offered higher-quality reception in picture and sound and promised more offerings, particularly in movies, than cable. It's like "a TV Guide run amok," said *Time*.[34] One service, a "Video Store of the Sky," will offer what will seem an unlimited number of movies, and will enable viewers to access a particular film at different times, perhaps every half hour on various channels. The viewer can select the movie and the starting time with the remote control. "And you don't even have to drive to the video store," said one RCA spokesperson.[35]

Telephone Lines Available. Telephone companies entered competition with cable television, as the telephone companies offered their expansive lines for the transmission of television and interactive fare. The president of CBS, Howard Stringer, left in 1995 to become chair of a new media consortium of three large telephone companies: Bell Atlantic, Nynex, and Pacific Telesis. The new group plans to bring regular and interactive television channels as well as a wide selection of movies into the home. Looking toward development in interactive shopping services, portable phones, and television programming and videos by wireless, MCI Communications joined ranks with British Telecom, a former partner of AT&T, and bought substantial stock in Nextel Communications, a car radio specialist. Motorola, AT&T, Bell South, and Time Warner also entered the competition to develop portable phones, pagers, and beepers to become significant extensions of the electronic network.[36]

In the works since 1970, with the $500 million investment of a Japanese consortium, high-definition television (HDTV) research received a boost in 1993 when the U.S. government allowed three top rivals in HDTV research to join forces to engage in its development. The three groups, which had survived the demands of a testing process for two years, were General Instrument Corporation, the Massachusetts Institute of Technology, and a consortium of Philips Electronics of the Netherlands, Thomson Consumer Electronics of France, NBC, and the David Sarnoff Research Center of Princeton, New Jersey.[37] HDTV, which purports to offer more clarity of pictures and sharpness of sound, is digital, transmitting signals in computer code of ones and zeroes as compared to the traditional, lower-quality transmission by electronic waves. According to a 1992 ruling of the FCC, television stations will be allowed a second channel for HDTV, but must begin transmitting HDTV signals within five years of the adoption of a standard by the FCC.

As interactive computers and television converge and the press of buttons allows a viewer to participate in game shows or switch to different camera angles in

Technicians link pioneer Telstar satellite for international live communication to third stage of Delta rocket. (Courtesy of AT&T Archives)

sports, in virtual reality and HDTV clarity, or to retrieve data, will the term "television" evolve? John Tierney asks in the *New York Times*: "What will the new content do to what is now being called P.O.T.? Content nowadays means movies, music, video games, photographs, books, articles, stock tables, or any digital multimedia combination thereof. P.O.T is plain old television, of which some people are already speaking in the past tense."[38]

Steady Plain Old Television. Yet if the history of new media meeting old holds true to form, a trace of POT will still be there, even amplified. Two former television executives, chairman and senior vice president of the CBS Broadcast

Group, respectively, Gene Jankowski and David Fuchs, believe the networks will be around very much in the way they are today. First, they say, the major networks offer convenience. With network programming, there are no telephone bills, no monthly cable bill, no dish needed, no fee for direct satellite transmission. "The signal, the service, and the audience are already there, a known commodity with a record of half a century of community acceptance."

A second reason for viewing the continuation of the networks with optimism and the emergence of some 500 workable channels with skepticism is the money factor. "Given the fact that the audience is at any given point finite," they say, "and that it is difficult to see how the present seven-hour television day can be significantly enlarged, the endless addition of channels can only lead to an endless subdivision of viewing, in which more and more offerings fight over fewer and fewer users" affecting the advertising dollar. "Here it is not the technology but the economics that become decisive."[39]

REGULATION AND THE NEW MEDIA TECHNOLOGY

The emerging new media and media systems have further complicated attempts at regulation. The Federal Communications Commission, monitor of the airwaves, has been faced with new, somewhat unclear dimensions of broadcasting and telecasting that had hardly been dreamed of in its earlier days.

The role of the FCC over the years since its inception under the 1934 Communications Act has been complex. It assigned frequencies to curb confusion on the airwaves, decided the morals of radio and television with regard to the use of language, fought racism by withholding licenses, protected children from excessive exposure to advertising by fining station violators,[40] and guaranteed equal access, first establishing a fairness doctrine to allow opposing view responses, then annulling the doctrine in 1987. Congress has vowed to revive the doctrine, but did not hasten to do so, partly perhaps because of veto threats by Presidents Ronald Reagan and George Bush and opposition from conservatives. The 1987 decision, however, kept a group of rules that did require "reasonable balance" in certain circumstances. The FCC had taken its action as a result of a 1985 federal appeals court ruling which said the fairness doctrine was not a law but a discretionary rule. In 1993 a second appeals court upheld the first appeals court decision.[41]

The FCC Faces a New World

Regulation of the media was never simple as the FCC sought to balance First Amendment guarantees of free speech and the potential excesses of the marketplace. Now with a potpourri of content from audience participatory programs to the movie videos on television and an interactive technology that embraces satellites and the gargantuan telephone industry, and the appearance on television and computer screens of material from the unregulated world of newspapers and magazines, the world as the FCC used to know it is more complex.

The FCC had been active in determining the development of cable, shaping its "economic potential," rather than allowing the industry to be formed by mere technological development, according to John E. Craft and Frances R. Matera, who teach at the Walter Cronkite School of Journalism and Telecommunication at Arizona State University. The first stage, 1948 to 1965, they say, was an incubation stage where local entrepreneurs were putting together the simple mountaintop systems. Then came stage two, 1965 to 1972, a highly regulated time that sorted out who could receive cable or not following a Supreme Court ruling in 1963, *Carter Mountain Transmission Corp.* v. *FCC*, that said "the expansion of cable television service would cause economic injury to competing television stations." Stage three, 1973 to the present, has been characterized by the "reinvention" of cable, a "wired" nation, a broadband concept that saw a diffusion of many cable channels via satellite technology as a boon to education and public service programs.[42]

Congress deregulated rates in 1986, and the nation saw increasing numbers of cable owners investing in new services, which in turn brought in more subscribers. But the unregulated rates soared out of hand, and Congress in 1992 ordered the FCC to intervene and bring rates down. At first the FCC ordered a cutback of 10 percent on rates, then added another 7 percent, for a total of 17 percent. But the cutbacks only made the nation's 11,000 operators more conservative, and development and extension of cable services stagnated. In 1995 the FCC revised the rate tables again to target primarily the worst price-gougers.

In March 1995 the FCC, active again in license allocations, completed the auctioning of 112 radio frequencies, embracing new wireless telephone systems and "personal communication services." PCS, said *Newsweek*, is "a new generation of wireless devices with more flexibility than wired phones, better connections than cellular and, in theory, lower costs than either."[43]

Profitable Sales of Licenses

At one time, radio frequencies were allocated free, but the new mercenary approach of the FCC initially netted $7 billion. The biggest bidder for the wireless opportunity was Sprint Corporation, which is a part of a consortium with three cable television companies (Comcast, Cox Enterprises, and Tele-Communications, Inc.). Sprint spent $2.1 billion for licenses in twenty-nine city and regional areas. Included were licenses to operate in New York, Detroit, Dallas, and San Francisco. Second high bidder was AT&T, at $1.7 billion, securing the Boston, Chicago, Philadelphia, and Washington markets.[44] Bidding in 1996 pushed toward the $7 billion mark.[45]

Planning to sell off nearly 2,000 wireless licenses, the FCC, in an affirmative action move in 1994, voted unanimously to hold back 1,000 of the new licenses for use by small businesses and firms owned by women and minorities, as ordered by Congress a year before. Some expected the auctions, one of the biggest affirmative action projects, to be challenged in the courts. However, the FCC had prevailed when its policy of preference for minority businesses seeking radio and television licenses was challenged in 1990 before the U.S. Supreme Court.[46]

"A New Day Is Dawning"

A milestone in the development of new media came in July 1994 with the FCC decision to allow the Bell Atlantic Corporation to provide interactive television service in 38,000 homes in New Jersey. The action marks the first time that the FCC authorized a telephone company to provide commercial cable television. It seemed likely that this opened the way for nearly two dozen other regional Bell companies to provide similar service to millions. "A new day is dawning," said FCC Commissioner Susan Ness, quoted in the *New York Times*. "No longer will telephone companies simply provide telephone services and cable companies merely provide video programming services. We can and should begin—as we do today—ushering in a new era of choices for consumers." Among strings attached is the requirement that Bell Atlantic offer 384 channels when it begins transmission.[47]

The FCC also reserved space on the airwaves for a new kind of radio service, digital audio radio service (DARS), which makes use of satellites to deliver programs to radios across the nation, bypassing local AM and FM stations. The FCC, however, held up making any decision about DARS until it had dealt with complaints that it would undermine traditional broadcasters and until the FCC had a chance to define the rules.[48]

The Clinton administration, through Commerce Secretary Ronald Brown, offered a ten-year plan in 1995 to have the Pentagon and other government agencies release a large section of the country's airwaves that they control. These frequencies would be made available for commercial use involving new technologies.

Voices were being heard in the 1990s favoring the development of comprehensive and uniform regulatory goals, if not policies, that would take into consideration the regulation of radio and television networks, the cable industry, telecommunications in general, and the ever-imposing telephone companies in particular. However, some media critics, such as Leo Bogart, author of *The Media System: Making and Marketing Commercial Culture*, dismiss any uniform national policy as smacking of thought control. He does suggest that it is useful to "advocate" national goals for mass communication, such as encouraging "a variety of channels for expression" and subsidizing "forms of expression that enrich the national culture and its collective intellectual resources, but that are not necessarily viable in the commercial marketplace."[49]

In February 1996, President Bill Clinton signed into law the Telecommunications Act, the most sweeping communications bill since the Communications Act of 1934. Most of the old rules and regulations evaporated. The new act broke down the walls that confined media and communication companies to defined turf. They can cross lines. For example, cable companies can enter the phone business; local phone companies can enter the long-distance field and vice versa; and the phone companies can enter cable television. After three years to allow for growth of competition, caps on cable rates will be lifted and subjected to an open market. Caps on the number of radio stations and television stations a company could own were lifted, provided that the television stations did not reach more than 35 percent of U.S. households, a limit that was formerly 25 percent. The act also called for criminal penalties for cable pornographers and ordered makers of new television sets to install V-chips, which will enable parents to block out programs they consider inappropriate for their children.

A second act enacted in February 1996 as part of the telecommunications overhaul legislation, the Communications Decency Act, made displaying "indecent" or "patently offensive" words or images on the Internet subject to high fines and prison terms if they are accessible to minors. In the first test of this decency law in 1996 a federal judge stated that the term "indecent" was unconstitutionally vague and temporarily prohibited its enforcement. Later in 1996 a federal panel of three judges concurred.

A NEW ROSTER OF MORAL AND LEGAL CONCERNS

In cyberspace, new issues are being generated that differ from the issues of the categorical media, such as print, radio, and television. Although the world of the computer and digital technology is flexible and unpredictable, nevertheless new flags have been raised that signal some of the forthcoming battles and arenas. For instance, consider the following questions of morality, sociability, and legal matters:

Are the New Media Putting a Straitjacket on Creativity and Serendipity? In former days, the body politic was concerned with youths idling away their precious time, becoming unfocused, if not drifters, as they paid long hours of homage to pool tables, then pinball machines, and more recently computer games. But now the computer entourage offers satisfaction in many areas on demand.

The joys that characterized contact with formerly reigning media will now be limited. Take channel switching with television, for instance. Harry Marsh says in *Creating Tomorrow's Mass Media*, "Channel surfing with a TV remote device, leafing through the Sunday papers, and wandering about a bookstore are pleasant activities that lead us to information we would not otherwise encounter. How can the structured environment of the New Medium provide us with this kind of serendipity? Some new kinds of slothful habits will have to be developed."[50]

Is the New Technology Making America a Nation of Loners? Newhouse syndicated columnist Robert Lewis offers testimony from psychiatrists suggesting that the new technology—from television to the latest computer systems—contributes to loneliness, particularly among the elderly.[51] *The Futurist*, the magazine of the World Future Society, Washington, D.C., had predicted long ago that, with the eventual development of holographic television, images on the screen would replace real-life companions, again particularly among the elderly. With much of the population already "couch potatoes" watching television, as a new generation becomes glued to computer consoles exploring the Internet and other wonders, isolation—with the accompanying effect of loneliness—continues to be a concern. One can argue that an information superhighway traveler and Internet browser makes many new friends, but, of course, the "new friends" do not appear in flesh and blood.

Does Cyberspace Promote the Proliferation of Pornography? A thirty-seven
nation, interreligious delegation to a conference on pornography held in the
Philippines heard presentations that warned of growing proliferation of
pornography, especially child pornography, available on computers. "Many com-
puter-based bulletin boards offer the equivalent of an entire pornographic bookstore on line," said Dean Kaplan, vice president of the Cincinnati-based Religious
Alliance Against Pornography, the conference's sponsor. Eileen Lindner, conference
chairperson and associate general secretary of the National Council of Churches,
called pornography by computer technology "venomous."

"We're not talking here about girlie magazines," Lindner said. "Offensive
though they are to some people, they are mild in comparison to the vile material
now being marketed all over the world. We are talking about the ruthless exploitation of children."[52] The new V-chip locking device on television sets was expected
to help ferret out unsavory programs, although it was immediately faced by challenges from free-speech advocates.

**Will the Media of the Future Have a Greater Free-for-All Aura of
Sensationalism?** Some worry about the influence of the users of modern media.
Jim Willis in his *The Age of Multimedia and Turbonews* notes that the shape of future
media will be determined by consumers, not by publishers and not by technology.[53] Entertainment and prurient values could thus have a greater influence on
news agendas. The chief executive officer of the Associated Press, Louis Boccardi,
warned journalists against being seduced to lower their standards in order to appeal
to the lowest common denominator. The new order of media will, on the one hand,
expect journalists to be more accountable "because so much information will be
publicly available, and news sources will be able to respond quickly online to what
is written about them," he said. But he added that the new order will demand pre-
caution, too, "so we don't allow the seductiveness of technology to change the principles of what we do."[54]

Is There Any Privacy Anymore? "If you don't want it stolen or publicized, don't
put it on the computer" could be a motto for those using computers. *U.S. News &
World Report*, in a special issue, "Is Anything Safe in Cyberspace?—The Growing
Threats to Your Privacy and Property in the Information Age," noted the beliefs of
police officials that the incidence of crimes involving high technology is going to
soar off the charts. Criminal elements, from terrorists to common thieves, can worm
their way into systems and steal information off computers. Almost anyone with a
computer, modem, and telephone can plug into one's deepest secrets—if they are
on the computer—from personal correspondence to one's income status and credit
history. Little things such as a ZIP code or social security number may be all that the
intruder needs to unlock one's full story.[55]

The secrets of corporations are increasingly the target of the cyberspace criminal. In 1995 Kevin Mitnick was arraigned on charges of committing cyberspace burglary. He was accused of using cellular phone circuits to access corporate computer

systems, stealing information including 20,000 credit card numbers. Six years earlier he had been sentenced to a year in prison for getting into MCI telephone computers, with the result of $4 million damage to Digital Equipment Corporation. He was also wanted in California for breaking into the database of the state's Department of Motor Vehicles.[56] General Electric also lost research information to an intruder in 1994.

Cracking down on computer criminals has yet to develop into an exact science. Whose responsibility is it to apprehend a villain living in the Midwest or New York who steals information from a Dallas or Seattle office without ever leaving her or his home? "Where is cyberspace," asked Robert Lucky, corporate vice president of research at Bellcore, a division of Bell Communications Research, at the annual convention of the American Association for the Advancement of Science, meeting in Philadelphia in 1994. "If this thing [cyberspace] floats over everything and nobody owns it and nobody controls it, there are issues of jurisdiction."[57]

Does Cyberspace Invite Big Brother to Take Over?   There are matters of control over corporations and individuals by the new "big brothers" in the media—the conglomerates, the chains, the new super-parent companies. The aim is a new "synergism," an interaction between elements of a conglomerate to maximize the power of the supercompany's message, says media critic Ben Bagdikian. Believing that every global giant media monster seeks to control as many elements of media as possible, Bagdikian suggests, "In their fondest scenario, a magazine owned by the company selects or commissions an article that is suitable for later transformation into a television series on a network owned by the company." That product then evolves into a script for a movie studio "owned by the company, with the movie sound track sung by a vocalist made popular by feature articles in the company-owned magazines and by constant playing of the sound track by company-owned radio stations, after which the songs become popular on a record label owned by the company and so on, with reruns on company cable systems and rentals of its videocassettes all over the world." In such a pattern, creativity and risk-taking in the arts and communications fades. "The greater the dominance of a few firms, the more uniformity in what each of them produces."[58]

Will First Amendment Rights Be Challenged?   The computer networks and services are subject to censorship from several directions. America Online, on its hundreds of forums reaching 2 million persons, bans the use of profanity, ethnic and sexual innuendos, and derogatory statements. In 1995 America Online shut down the computer bulletin board of fans of singer Courtney Love for breaking its rules. A year earlier America Online had pulled the plug on several feminist discussion groups. The *New York Times*, noting that censors have become "a force on the Cyberspace Frontier," also cited the revoking of a student's access to the Internet by the University of Florida after the student used the university's computers to put out an incendiary political message.[59]

A free-speech issue was raised when a University of Michigan student was charged in 1995 with interstate transmission of a threat, punishable by up to five years in prison, if convicted. Jake A. Baker had written on the Internet about torturing, raping, and murdering a classmate, all in his mind. Not everyone saw it as a crime of assaulting or threatening. "What he has done is published a short story . . . the kind that's probably found on the shelves of adult bookstores. The stupidity on his part is that he named a real person." Speaking was Howard Simon, executive director of the Michigan American Civil Liberties Union, as quoted by the Associated Press. Simon saw it as an invasion of privacy, not a matter of more serious charges.[60]

Individual users of computer networks also try to act like censors. The most celebrated case is that of a Norwegian, Arnt Gulbrandsen, a young computer programmer who opposed the efforts of a Phoenix law firm, Canter & Siegel, using the Usenet computer network to advertise its services worldwide. Every time the firm floated one of its ads, Gulbrandsen spiked it by ordering his computer to intercept and destroy the firm's ad. Gulbrandsen was pleased with the general positive response from other users of the network. But the *Times* observed: "Even longtime network users who applaud such a use of what they call a 'cancelbot' acknowledge that the situation raises broad and troubling issues about censorship in cyberspace." But because of the newness of the technology, "no established case law moderates the debate over censorship in such cases, the way it does for publishing, broadcasting and speech."[61]

What Does It Mean to Copyright Something?   Copyrighting—protecting the reuse of one's created work—used to be a straightforward matter. Contracts specified reprint or serialization or international rights, and the publishing industry had some guidelines as to what constituted fair use in quoting excerpts. Movie and television rights were usually retained by the authors, while "audio" rights were negotiable. But now, with the expansion of the electronic media and the possibility of unlimited reuse in many forms, what are the limits of agreements? Book publishers are insisting on retaining some semblance of control of electronic rights, such as control of redistributing the text of a book on an on-line service.

Noting that "a writer's work can now be made available in many forms" and also that publishing technology is changing, two leading writers' organizations, the Authors Guild and the American Society of Journalists and Authors, issued a pioneer statement on electronic publishing rights in 1993. This document suggested that authors try to spell out use on all specific formats. For instance, the publisher would retain "the right to license the publication of non-dramatic electronic versions of the Work" in specified formats, such as Macintosh CD-ROM, CD-I, and on-line databases, and the author retains "the rights to all other electronic technologies and formats," existing or to be developed. The publisher would act as an agent in the reuse and keep a 10 percent fee, with the author getting 90 percent.[62]

Teachers unions want to know what happens to a professor's work once it is videotaped—for instance, in distance learning, which brings the classroom into the home. "What happens after a program has been videotaped," *On Campus* asked. "The professor must have right of first refusal for the material's reuse, for example, and the right to review course content before each subsequent use, in case the material is out of date." And who owns the course? Should the faculty member arrange a work-for-hire agreement (the employer keeping all rights), a joint ownership contract, or keep full ownership of everything?[63]

Early-morning raids and destruction of computer files have been made in the name of protecting copyright. In the early morning hours on a February day in 1995 in Los Angeles, a former minister of the Church of Scientology, who had become an outspoken critic of the group, responded to loud rapping on his door. He found a tribe of lawyers and police with a writ of seizure—a federal judge's permission to search throughout the house and the computer and "seize" or destroy any copyrighted material of the Church of Scientology. In six hours the invaders of Dennis L. Erlich's home erased hundreds of computer files and took a shelf of books and nearly 400 computer discs. Erlich's crime was that as he criticized the Scientologists, he had failed to get permission for quoted material. Reporter Reid Kanaley, assigned to the area by the *Philadelphia Inquirer*, called the incident "one of the most dramatic so far in a complex dispute that is forcing a reexamination of the meaning of copyrights, trade secrets, civil liberty and free speech in the new digital universe."[64]

The cyberspace world not only talks a new language but in time will develop new sets of laws. The world is smaller than when risk-taker Benjamin Harris came out with his first colonial American newspaper in 1690, but the role of the modern media practitioner is still that of an interpolator and pioneer. The history of media, despite its periods and cycles and sameness within generations, seems always to be hovering over new frontiers.

QUESTIONS FOR DISCUSSION AND RESEARCH

1. How would you divide a chronological history of media in America? In order, what would be the main eras or divisions?
2. What have been the most potent forces in shaping the media? Political, cultural developments? Or technological? Explain.
3. What do you call the age or period in which we live? When did it begin? Did media help to define it?
4. Does a history of the computer belong in a history of the media? What else belongs, or does not belong, in a media history?
5. Through what "eyeglasses" or theme or emphasis should the story of American media history be told?
6. What was the most important era in American media history? Explain.
7. Organize a debate, pro and con, about whether there is a future for the printed newspaper or other print media.
8. Who in this book was the "most"? The one you admired the most, the weirdest, the most humorous, the most significant?

9. Each student select a subject—perhaps a person in media history—and, with the help of a librarian, prepare a report on databases and other computer services that would be productive in doing research on the subject, plus information on accessing the computer in areas mentioned.

10. Are ethical dilemmas—trying to decide what is right and wrong in functioning as a reporter or editor—different in the digital age from the days of the colonial printer and editor?

11. What will an ad of the future look like? What will its components be? Will there be any adaptations in delivery?

12. Will the emerging technology have any effect on the public relations practitioner?

13. Should the FCC be phased out? Has it been effective? Assuming some regulation is needed in a competitive, crowded world, how much is needed, what shape should it take, and what should be covered?

14. Which was the most sensationalist era on the part of the media? Why? Is sensationalism constant, or is it a changing concept?

15. Construct a ten-point platform or set of commandments to guide future journalists based on the issues and experiences of personalities in the history of journalism.

ENDNOTES

1. Survey by the Times Mirror Center for The People and The Press, reported by the Associated Press, "Survey Cites Changes," *Doylestown* (Pa.) *Intelligencer*, May 24, 1994, p. A-7.

2. Marshall McLuhan, *Understanding Media: The Extensions of Man* (New York: Mentor Books, 1964), p. iv, quoted in Eugene F. Provenzo, Jr., *Beyond the Gutenberg Galaxy: Microcomputers and the Emergence of Post-Typographic Culture* (New York: Teachers College, Columbia University, 1986), p. 4.

3. Ibid.

4. Joel Shurkin, *Engines of the Mind: A History of the Computer* (New York: Norton, 1984), p. 34.

5. Margaret Harmon, *Stretching Man's Mind: A History of Data Processing* (New York: Mason/Charter, 1975), p. 43.

6. Christopher Evans, *The Micro Millennium* (New York: Viking Press, 1979), p. 25. See also Martin Campbell Kelly and William Aspray, *Computer: A History of the Information Machine* (New York: Basic Books, 1996).

7. Shurkin, *Engines of the Mind*, p. 56.

8. Ibid., p. 166.

9. Ibid., p. 249.

10. Ibid., pp. 310, 311.

11. See Douglas Hofstadter, *Fluid Concepts and Creative Analogies: Computer Models of the Fundamental Mechanisms of Thought* (New York: Basic Books, 1995).

12. Ray Laakaniemi, Bowling Green State University, "The Development of the Video Display Terminal," paper presented at the Southeast Colloquium of the Association for Education in Journalism and Mass Communication at Stone Mountain, GA, March 1992.

13. Michael Conniff, "A Short History of the Future," *Editor & Publisher*, Aug. 27, 1994, p. 3.

14. Bernard Caughey, "Become Indispensable or Die," *Editor & Publisher*, March 19, 1994, p. 12.

15. "Stops on the Tribune's Superhighway," sidebar in Philip Moeller, "The High-Tech Trib," *American Journalism Review*, April 1994, pp. 20, 21.

16. Roger Fidler, "Newspapers in the Electronic Age," in Frederick Williams and John V. Pavlik, eds., *The People's Right to Know: Media, Democracy, and the Information Highway* (Hillsdale, N.J.: Lawrence Erlbaum, 1994), p. 26.

17. Ibid., p. 27.

18. Melanie Wells, "The Interactive Edge—Part I: Desperately Seeking the Superhighway: Agencies Face a Changing and Uncertain Role," in "Interactive Media and Marketing" section, *Advertising Age*, Aug. 14, 1994, p. 14.

19. Michael Schrage et al., "Is Advertising Finally Dead?" *Wired*, February 1994, p. 126.

20. Ibid.

21. Stuart Elliott, "Advertising: Super Bowl Campaigns Break Long Losing Streak," *New York Times*, Jan. 31, 1995, p. D1.

22. Jane M. Von Bergen, "Married . . . with Promos: Cola Bubbles into Sitcom Episode," *Philadelphia Inquirer*, Nov. 12, 1994, p. D1.

23. Schrage, "Is Advertising Finally Dead?" p. 71.

24. John Mutter, "The All-Media 'Bookstore,' " *Publishers Weekly*, July 25, 1994, p. 24.

25. Matt Kopka, "Hear, Now: Houston's Bookless 'Bookstore,' " *Publishers Weekly*, Sept. 26, 1994.

26. Carol Robinson and Calvin Reid, "10,000 Harper Titles Online; Warner Serializes Novel on Net," *Publishers Weekly*, Jan. 16, 1995, p. 308.

27. Quoted in Paul Hilts, "Outlook 95: The Changing Face of Print," *Publishers Weekly*, Jan. 2, 1995, p. 44.

28. Annetta Miller et al., "Radio's New Golden Age," *Time*, Aug. 3, 1987, p. 41.

29. Bill Carter, "Television: 3 Networks Frantically Seek Fountain of Youth and Profits," *New York Times*, Aug. 3, 1992, p. 8D.

30. Paul Farhi, "It's War: Networks vs. Fox," *Philadelphia Inquirer*, Nov. 26, 1994, p. C1.

31. Jefferson Graham, "Paramount's New Network Takes a Male View," *USA Today*, Oct. 6, 1994, p. 3D.

32. Lynn Eber, "Two New Networks Debut," *Associated Press*, in the *Intelligencer*, Doylestown, Pa., Jan. 11, 1995, p. D–10.

33. Bill Carter, "2 Would-Be Networks Get Set for Prime Time," *New York Times*, Jan. 9, 1995.

34. Michael Marriott, et al., "Flight of the Digital Dish," *Time*, Jan. 9, 1995, p. 61.

35. Hans Fantel, "Little Dishes Promise a Feast," *New York Times*, Feb. 27, 1994, p. 20H.

36. Thomas McCarroll, "War of the Wireless," *Time*, Mar. 14, 1994, p. 89.

37. Edmund L. Andrews, "Top Rivals Agree on Unified System for Advanced TV," *New York Times*, May 25, 1993, p. A1.

38. John Tierney, "Tomorrow's TV: Will They Sit by the Set, or Ride a Data Highway?" *New York Times*, June 20, 1993, p. A1.

39. Gene F. Jankowski and David C. Fuchs, *Television Today and Tomorrow: It Won't Be What You Think* (New York: Oxford University Press, 1995), pp. 185, 188.

40. Christopher Stern, "FCC Not Kidding Around with Kids Television Fines," *Broadcasting & Cable*, Mar. 6, 1995, p. 58.

41. Harry A. Jessell, "Antismoking Coalition Seeks Return of Fairness Doctrine: Group Is Hopeful Clinton FCC Will Reconsider 1987 Repeal," *Broadcasting & Cable*, Aug. 22, 1994, p. 34.

42. John E. Craft and Frances R. Matera, "Broadcast News, Cable TV and the Telcos: A Historical Examination of the Rhetorical Forces Affecting the Electronic Distribution of Information to the American Television Public," a paper presented to the American Journalism Historians Association's annual meeting, Salt Lake City, Utah, October, 1993, pp. 17, 18.

43. Marc Levinson, "It's Raining Phones—Tele-deals," *Newsweek*, Nov. 7, 1994, p. 78.

44. Edmund L. Andrews, "Winners of Wireless Auction to Pay $7 Billion," *New York Times*, Mar. 14, 1995, p. D1.
45. Edmund Andrews, "In Auctions of Airwaves, the Sky Seems to Be the Limit," *New York Times*, Feb. 26, 1995, p. D1.
46. Edmund L. Andrews, "F.C.C. Plan for License Diversity," *New York Times*, June 23, 1994, p. D1.
47. Edmund L. Andrews, "F.C.C. Allows Bell Atlantic to Offer Cable TV," *New York Times*, July 7, 1994, p. D1.
48. Edmund L. Andrews, "F.C.C. Backs Digital Satellite Radio," *New York Times*, Jan. 13, 1995, p. D14.
49. Leo Bogart, "Toward a National Media Policy," *Media Studies Journal*, Spring 1992, p. 92.
50. Harry Marsh, *Creating Tomorrow's Mass Media* (Fort Worth, Tex.: Harcourt Brace College Publishers, 1995), pp. 146, 147.
51. Robert Lewis, "Are We a Nation of Loners?" Newhouse News Service, in the Doylestown, Pa., *Intelligencer*, Jan. 10, 1991, p. C-1.
52. Patricia LeFevere, "Child Porn Proliferates on Internet," *National Christian Reporter*, Feb. 10, 1995, p. 2.
53. Jim Willis, *The Age of Multimedia and Turbonews* (Westport, Conn.: Praeger, 1994).
54. Mark Fitzgerald, "AP Chief: Beware of Yellow Journalism in Cyberspace," *Editor & Publisher*, Feb. 11, 1995, p. 31.
55. Vic Sussman, "Policing Cyberspace," *U.S. News & World Report*, Jan. 23, 1995, pp. 56, 57.
56. Shankar Vedantam, "Leaders Puzzle Over Regulating Cyberspace," *Philadelphia Inquirer*, Feb. 19, 1995, p. A3.
57. Ibid.
58. Ben H. Bagdikian, *The Media Monopoly*, 4th ed. (Boston: Beacon Press, 1992), pp. 243, 244.
59. Peter Lewis, "Censors Become a Force on Cyberspace Frontier," *New York Times*, June 29, 1994, p. A1.
60. "Student Jailed; Told Internet Torture Tale," Associated Press, in Doylestown, Pa., *Intelligencer*, p. A–11.
61. Lewis, "Censors Become a Force," p. D5.
62. "Electronic Publishing Rights," a position statement by the Authors Guild and the American Society of Journalists and Authors, issued Oct. 18, 1993.
63. "Special Report: Riding the Technology Learning Curve," *On Campus*, March 1995, p. 6.
64. Reid Kanaley, "Scientology at Odds with Internet Critics," *Philadelphia Inquirer*, April 1, 1995, p. A1.

Index